Lives in Education

Second Edition

Lives in Education

A NARRATIVE OF PEOPLE AND IDEAS

L. GLENN SMITH, *Northern Illinois University*
JOAN K. SMITH, *Loyola University of Chicago*

with

F. Michael Perko, Elizabeth L. Ihle, Dalton B. Curtis, Jr., Norma Salazar
Martha Tevis, Michael V. Belok, Shirley J. Williams, Jack K. Campbell
Gerald L. Gutek, William B. Lauderdale, Carmen A. Cruz, Claudia Strauss
Ann Horton, Kyung Hi Kim, Jeffrey R. Smith

St. Martin's Press • New York

Editor: Naomi Silverman
Managing editor: Patricia Mansfield-Phelan
Project editor: Diana Puglisi
Production supervisor: Alan Fischer
Art director: Sheree Goodman
Text design: Dorothy Bungert
Cover design and graphics: Joseph DePinho, Pinho Graphic Designs

For information, write:
St. Martin's Press, Inc.
175 Fifth Avenue
New York, NY 10010

ISBN: 0-312-04698-7

Acknowledgments

Mary Barnard, *Sappho: A New Translation,* one poem #86. Copyright © 1958 by The Regents of the University of California and The University of California Press. Reprinted by permission of the Regents of the University of California and The University of California Press.

Beram Salvatvala, *Sappho of Lesbos: Her Works Restored—A Metrical English Version of Her Poems with Conjectural Restorations* (London: Charles Skilton, 1968). Reprinted with permission of Charles Skilton.

Sappho: Poems and Fragments, Guy Davenport, trans. Copyright © 1965 by the University of Michigan. Published by the University of Michigan Press. Reprinted with permission of The University of Michigan Press.

Excerpts from *The Dialogues of Plato* translated by Benjamin Jowett (4th ed. 1953) vol. II., by permission of Oxford University Press.

H. I. Marrou, *A History of Education in Antiquity,* George Lambs, trans. (New York: Sheed and Ward, 1956), 33. Reprinted by permission of The University of Wisconsin Press.

Excerpts from *The Story of My Misfortunes.* Reprinted with the permission of The Free Press, a Division of Macmillan, Inc. from *The Story of My Misfortunes* by Peter Abelard, translated by Henry Adams Bellows. Copyright © 1922 by Thomas A. Boyd; 1958 by The Free Press.

Excerpt from *Sor Juana: Or, the Traps of Faith.* Reprinted by permission of the publishers from *Sor Juana: Or, the Traps of Faith* by Octavio Paz, translated by Margaret Sayers Peden, Cambridge, Mass.: The Belknap Press of Harvard University Press, Copyright © 1988 by the President and Fellows of Harvard College.

"Hombres Necios" by Sor Juana, translated by Norma Salazar.

Excerpts from "Education for the Natives of Alaska . . ." . Reproduced, with revisions, from *Journal of the West,* copyright 1967 by Journal of the West, Inc., 1531 Yuma, Manhattan, Kansas 66502 USA, and reprinted with permission.

To all people who have tried—or who are yet to try—to make teaching better.

Preface

Approach

Lives in Education tells the story of Western education through biographies of individuals—some whose lives represent significant contributions to educational theory and practice, and some whose lives exemplify education typical of their time and place in history. These individuals' lives, work, and ideas illustrate the dynamic synergy between theory and practice in education. *Lives in Education* emphasizes Western and American educational developments, and includes extensive treatments of the contributions of women and representatives of other historically underacknowledged groups.

Our decision to use biography to examine educational issues in the context of their evolution evolved naturally from what our experience as educators has shown us: "Biography turns what might otherwise be lists of meaningless historical names into an endless stream of friends—and students learn better from friends than from anyone else."[1]

Educators are not faceless, interchangeable machines. *Individuals* work, plan, try, aspire, confront, succeed, fail, hurt, rejoice. "Biography reveals life to be a series of often difficult choices, but also demonstrates that adversity is only part of life, not its end," observes political scientist Scott Kirkman.[2] Historian Charles F. Mullett comments: "Historical labels, like last week's slogans, serve their term and are replaced by others equally mortal. . . . It is the living individual who captures the imagination. . . . Queen Mary did not burn Protestantism at the stake, she burnt Hugh Latimer. If history becomes anonymous it becomes inevitable, and the individual is cast out with yesterday's refuse."[3]

So, *Lives in Education* is built around biographical themes for a well-grounded reason: tying abstract ideas to biographies of educators gives readers organizing anchors as aids to memory and understanding. Integrating familiar figures and ideas (e.g., Socrates, Luther) with less-well-known theories and people (e.g., Sappho, Melanchthon) provides security in processing new information. Biography is interesting, and therefore easy for readers to assimilate and remember.

Structure and Interpretation

A few words about this book's structure and interpretation are in order. This is not a "great person" approach to history. We've tried to present educators as human beings, not as great men and women beyond the experience of ordinary people. Moreover, "significance" is a learned preference in the same sense that one acquires a taste for broccoli or chocolate cake. We included some people (Socrates and Pestalozzi, for example) because educators regard them as *de rigueur* given the symbolic importance they have gained. We included others (Sappho and Sor Juana, for example) because they have been unjustly ignored. A few (Wherwell and Butzbach, for example) are in the text primarily because their lives are particularly clear prisms—examples through which something important can be understood—although we assume that every figure is in some sense prismatic. Finally, every person included either wrote something that embodies issues in education or did or said things about which other people wrote. Those for whom no record survives must remain invisible. For all we know, the most interesting happenings in the history of education have disappeared without a trace.

Sources

We have used the best sources available, although new work regularly appears. In some instances (for example, in the cases of Sor Juana, Wollstonecraft, Parker, Young, Cary, and Jackson), authors wrote their dissertations on the subject and therefore based their accounts on both archival and published sources. In other cases (all of the classical and medieval figures and modern ones who worked in languages other than English or Spanish), we have used the best translated work we could find.

We hope readers will use the extensive notes in each chapter to learn more and to compare their own interpretations with ours, because what readers bring to their task is as important as the texts that authors provide. Although each reader encounters the same words, meaning will vary according to what each person brings to his or her reading of the text—what each needs and is able to see. Whether you agree with the premises underlying the narrative or with our conclusions, we hope the account empowers, informs, strengthens, and encourages. Educational problems present themselves daily. A reminder of some of what we have already learned may help frame the coming discourse.

Genesis of This Book

This book had its genesis in 1981 when I picked up a *Scientific American* paperback titled *Lives in Science*. It contained biographies of eighteen scientists: "a hero or two, a saint and a rascal, sunny men of action and sour recluses and a selection of eccentrics, prodigies and sages. What brings them together here is that they lived their lives in science."[4]

I wondered what a similar book on "lives in education" would be like. My own list, plus a survey of two dozen colleagues, yielded names ranging from ancient Greece to the present. Initially, Joan Smith and I wrote short biographical sketches that we tried out on our students at Illinois State, where she was teaching, and at Iowa State where I was a faculty member.

Two publishers were interested in the emerging book. Their expert readers commented favorably, but one added, "you just can't talk about Socrates that way!" Another said, "well written, but take the women out and do a separate book on females in education." To avoid these compromises, I approached Dan Griffin, Executive Director of the Iowa State University Research Foundation (ISURF), who generously secured ISURF's sponsorship.

I drafted one-third of the manuscript, Joan Smith nearly a quarter more, and ten colleagues supplied the remainder. With my coauthors' kind indulgence, I reworked all of the text. Each author proofed and approved the result, but the book as it appeared in 1984 reflected my interpretations and beliefs more fully than those of the other authors. This is even more the case with the second edition.

The first edition has been widely used in the United States and Canada, both as a core text and as a supplement at all levels ranging from undergraduate courses to doctoral seminars, in "Introduction to Education," "History of Western/American Education," "Philosophy of Education," "Foundations of Education," "Curriculum Theory," and other courses whose titles are variations on these themes. The Chicago Public Library shelved the first edition in the reference section.

New in the Second Edition

Comments and suggestions from colleagues who adopted the first edition, and from hundreds of their students, shaped the second edition. Most of Chapters 7 and 8 are new, as is all of Chapter 12. Chapter summaries are also new. In addition to providing review help, the summaries can also serve as advance organizers for readers who choose to use them this way. Finally, an Instructor's Manual is available with this edition of the book.

Acknowledgments

Too many people made contributions to this effort to be acknowledged here; however, I am especially grateful to Lucy Townsend of Northern Illinois University, Nancy LaPaglia of Richard J. Daley College, Martha Tevis of the University of Texas Pan American, and Shirley Williams of the University of Hawaii for their suggestions, and to the following St. Martin's Press reviewers whose comments and recommendations have played an important role in our revision of this book: Leo Anglin, Berry College; Geraldine J. Clifford, University of California, Berkeley; Joseph L. DeVitis, State University of New York, Binghamton; Shirley Heck, Discovery School (Mansfield, OH); Fred D. Kierstead, University of Houston, Clear Lake; George W. Noblit, University of North Carolina, Chapel

Hill; and Thomas F. Stovall, Vanderbilt University. Thanks also to Kathleen Keller, former acquisitions editor for St. Martin's Press, and to her successor Naomi Silverman for positive comments and suggestions. Countless times over the past three years, Caryn Rudy interrupted pressing work to input new material, move and reformat existing text, and produce clean copy. Her professional skill and friendship provided vital sustenance.

—Glenn Smith

NOTES

1. Scott Kirkman, "The Importance of Biography," *History Matters* 4 (November 1991): 1.
2. Ibid.
3. Charles F. Mullett, *Biography as History: Men and Movements in Europe since 1500* (New York: Macmillan, 1963), 5.
4. *Lives in Science: A Scientific American Book* (New York: Simon & Schuster, 1957), ix.

Contents

CHAPTER 4

The Humanists   94

CHAPTER 5

The Reformers 123

CHAPTER 8

The Friends of Education 239

CHAPTER 9

The Progressives 273

The Outsiders 312

CHAPTER 10

The Critics   355

CHAPTER 11

CHAPTER 12

The Paradigm Shifters   412

Introduction

Teaching, especially in schools, can be lonely and frustrating. There is comfort in knowing that others before us have struggled as we do. Some were famous; others remained long unheralded. A number compensated for their own troubled childhoods. Several were both forceful and effective. Some achieved powerful results through humility and persistence.

People in Europe and in those places once under European cultural domination, including the Americas, have constructed their world views through extensive reading in Greco-Roman-based liberal arts and humanities. Teacher education in the Americas has been and continues to be strongly influenced by this tradition. Educators who know how to talk about their own *praxis* (practice) in these traditional terms have an advantage over those who must search for other communication bridges.

From the earliest days of teacher training, history has been part of professional formation. Feeling part of a long and honorable calling is an important reason for knowing our educational heritage. It also puts us in touch with long-standing ideas and vocabulary. The differences in how Protagoras, Plato, and Aristotle thought about "reality," for example, are not only interesting but also critical in our contemporary arguments about how people learn and what is possible. Such labels as *pedagogy, liberal arts, humanities, school,* and *education* are vital parts of current speech. Knowing their derivations helps us decode them and use them more perceptively.

Another advantage in presenting educational ideas and practices in historical context is that we have a natural affinity for history. The narration of events is familiar and natural to most of us. We account for personal decisions and behavior by recounting sequences of prior happenings and experiences that we believe influenced whatever we are explaining. For example, we might account for our absence at a social event with the news that an old friend whom we had not seen for years called unexpectedly. We detail something of our past relationship with the friend to account for our decision. While we might not label such an ordinary event "history," this sequential narrative is practical history. As storytellers, we use all the skills of the trained historian. We select from many events a few that fit our beliefs of cause and effect. Then we construct and deliver to our hearers a story that we try to make plausible. We even consciously or automatically choose language and metaphors that we believe suit our audience. In fact, this is our most usual form of explanation.

An additional use for educational history is as a laboratory. Many people have wanted to make teaching more effective and learning less stressful. Toward that end, educators constantly experiment. The records of predecessors help enormously in the search for progress. Many current experiments have been tried before—earlier educators discovered or invented most contemporary "innovations." Indeed, these have been repeatedly lost and rediscovered. It is always positive, for example, when someone finds out that people learn better (1) when they feel respected instead of condemned, or (2) when they have a compelling reason to learn, or (3) when new ideas or skills are connected through comparison and contrast with existing knowledge, or (4) when active learning involving all the senses is used, or (5) when taught in a language they understand rather than one they don't. Quintilian knew these things two thousand years ago. We will rediscover all of them in the next few years. Personal encounter is often more dramatic than reading, but we cannot afford to constantly begin afresh, ignoring what our predecessors have repeatedly demonstrated. There are other reasons for reading educational history, including the fact that it is interesting and fun, but the ones we've cited provide a framework for study.

Focusing on educational issues through the lives of representative educators is a natural choice. Since the 1700s, people have figured prominently in educational literature. Educators are not faceless and interchangeable: *individuals* work, plan, try, aspire, confront, succeed, fail, hurt, and rejoice.

Some of the figures included herein—for example, Socrates, Plato, Aristotle, Augustine, Aquinas, Locke, Dewey—have been firmly entrenched in the educational pantheon for decades. Others are there because they have been inappropriately excluded in the past: Sappho, Christine de Pisan, Sor Juana, Ella Flagg Young, for example, all made substantial intellectual contributions and lived courageously. Others, like Guibert of Nogent, Euphemia of Wherwell, Johannes Butzbach, and Elizabeth and Emily Blackwell, are included not for the originality of their thought but because their lives are prisms through which we may view educational issues in their times. Finally, people like Freire, Foucault, Coppin, and Winnemucca help round out the emerging picture of educational developments in the modern world.

Have we included everyone who matters? Certainly not. This chronicle hardly tells the whole story of educational history. We have ignored far more educators than we've described, partly because of available space; partly because of what is possible. Decisions about historical content always depend upon two overarching factors. The first is that we can only know about a past for which there is some kind of information, and for the overwhelming amount of human experience there is no written or other "material culture" residue. The other major factor is that what "really happened" is rarely obvious. Rather, authors choose which story to investigate. Then they search available evidence on which to build and with which to document their narratives. The resulting record is an outgrowth, as history always is, of contemporary preoccupations.

For the authors of this book, the narrative that follows illustrates several things about teaching and learning. One is that it connects today's educators with a tradition of which they can be proud. Another is that it recounts a number of vital discoveries about education, offering a context for understanding issues. And it provides verbal and conceptual tools for educators, who often need to present their educational advocacy in powerful narrative form.

What readers bring to their task is as important as what the authors have tried to provide. Every reader will have the same words but meanings will vary according to what each reader needs and is able to see. Whether you agree with the premises underlying the narrative or the conclusions we have drawn, we want the account to empower, inform, strengthen, and encourage. Everyone knows there are educational problems yet to be solved. A reminder of some of what we have already learned should help frame the issues yet to be investigated.

The Greeks

Education is an old activity, but teaching is a new profession. Since human beings have been on earth—between two and four million years, some biologists estimate—people have been learning from each other and their environments. On the other hand, *schooling,* a Greek term implying leisured study by elite groups, is a recent phenomenon.

No one knows when the first school came into being. Perhaps it was in one of the ancient cities of Africa, South America, Mexico, India, or China. Western educational historians generally cite the "tablet houses" of Sumeria (now Iraq) as early centers of organized instruction. From about 3,000 B.C., scribes there kept agricultural records on clay tablets and taught apprentices their art of cuneiform writing.[1] At about the same time, people in Egypt refined the pictographic writing of the Sumerians into a more symbolic form. Later, perhaps around 800 to 700 B.C., people in the Greek islands developed a fully phonetic alphabet—that is, a combination of consonants and vowels totaling twenty-four characters. This development expanded literacy beyond a few specialists because students no longer required many years to memorize thousands of special symbols. It also permitted a written rather than strictly oral transmission of knowledge.

Formal schooling began in the Greek area around the time of Homer (1,000–800 B.C.) as chivalric training for warriors. It gradually became more oriented to written information. Some people specialized in sport and the use of military arms, while others concentrated on "bookish" endeavors, but the two kinds of activities were not mutually exclusive. All citizens in a city-state had access to some of both. Slaves, usually a majority of the city-state's population, got appropriate vocational training.

Formal schooling began at age six and lasted to around puberty. At that point boys of the citizen class finished off their formation as citizen-warriors in the company of adult males. Young women learned "role-appropriate" skills from one or more adult women. One of these female mentors is the subject of our first biographical sketch.

Sappho (c. 630–c. 572 B.C.)

Sappho, the earliest Greek educator about whom we have any information, is also a controversial figure in Western civilization. She was head of what we would call a women's finishing school. While Sappho created no pedagogical theories, she is the first woman we know of who defined women in terms of themselves rather than in relationship to men. The structure of her academy was not unusual for its time. Nevertheless, the issues raised by her school—the relationship of pupil and instructor, the place of women in educational history—remain relevant to our current concerns.

We are certain of little about Sappho, and "about that little there is doubt."[2] Even of her poetry we have only fragments. She wrote more than twelve thousand lines, but only a few hundred survived—and those by accident.

In 1073 authorities in Rome and Constantinople publicly burned all known poems of Sappho and her male contemporary, Alcaeus. About a century ago, archeologists discovered fragments of Sappho's poems while excavating some papier-mâché coffins at Oxyrhynchus, Egypt.[3] These fragments are now all her extant poems. Even weakened by translation, these few make us wish for more. For example:

> Experience shows us
> Wealth unchaperoned
> by Virtue is never
> an innocuous neighbor.[4]

Sappho was born in the town of Eresus on Lesbos, a prosperous Aeolian island colony a few miles off the coast of present-day Turkey. The island's name inspired the word *lesbian,* and Sappho's poetry and the legends about her life have given the word its meaning: homosexual love between women. We must understand the ancient Greeks in their own terms, though. Aristocratic Greeks regarded the open expression of eroticism as normal, and they did not assume that these feelings needed to be heterosexual.

Sappho was probably from an aristocratic family; her father may have been a wine merchant. Lesbos was famous for its wines. As Alcaeus celebrated the island's chief product:

> Let us drink deeply;
> in summer to cool our thirst,

in autumn to put a bright color upon death,
in winter to warm our blood,
in spring to celebrate nature's
resurrection.[5]

When Sappho was young, she moved with her family to Mytilene, the chief city of the island. She had three brothers, the eldest of whom married an Egyptian. Sappho strenuously opposed the marriage, apparently because she thought the woman intended to take her brother's money. Sappho married once, probably an arranged marriage. We do not know at what age, but aristocratic women customarily married at about twenty. The legend is that her husband was a wealthy merchant from the island of Andros. She had at least one child, a daughter whom she named Cleis (her mother's name).

Sappho spent several years in exile—probably because she opposed a dictator named Pittacus. Representing the interests of merchant and poorer classes, Pittacus banished several aristocrats, including Sappho, after an unsuccessful revolt. Her banishment suggests that she may have been politically active.

Before and after her exile, Sappho spent most of her time in Mytilene. While there she taught several young women useful and decorative arts, including how to dance, sing, and play instruments. Whether this was a *thiasos* (girls' school) or a tutorial situation is not clear. One historian has concluded that it was a formal school:

> In Lesbos and probably at other places in Greece there were several such boarding schools, in which the young girls of well-to-do families lived together under the supervision of well-educated, experienced women. They spent their days performing cult rituals in the service of the love-goddess, Aphrodite. . . . They also received instruction in singing, dancing and poetry, learned the rules of social etiquette, good taste, knowledge and sensitivity in the arts of love, practiced an instrument, bound garlands of flowers and did handwork.[6]

Sappho loved some of her pupils, and her feelings about them formed the basis for some of her poems. The following lines give some idea of Sappho's style. She wrote them to a former pupil who had left because of a marriage her parents had arranged:

> Ah, in my mind he shares the high gods' fortune,
> And is their equal, who may come beside you,
> And sit with you, and to your voice so lovely
> 　　Attend and listen!
> And he may hear your laughter, love-awaking,
> Which makes my heart beat swiftly in my bosom.
> But when I see you, Brachea, O my voice
> 　　Fails me and falters!
> And my tongue stumbles even when I glimpse you;
> Through all my flesh the fire goes swiftly running;

> My eyes see nothing, and my ears hear only
>   My own pulse beating!
> O then the sweat streams down me and I tremble,
> In all my body. Pale as the grass I grow!
> And death itself, my strength and powers fading,
>   Seems to approach me.
> So like a poor man I must be contented
> *To worship from afar your golden beauty,*
> *To hear you laugh and speak of all your loving*
> *Only to others.*[7]

We know nothing about when or how Sappho died. A legend dating from several centuries after her time held that she jumped off a cliff. According to the story—which must have appealed to male vanity—she did this because a handsome young sailor rejected her. There is no evidence for either of these traditions, and her poetry suggests she disapproved of suicide:

> To die is evil,
> The Gods think so,
> Else they would die.[8]

We have no contemporary description of Sappho, though tradition holds that she was a small woman. An unflattering story that she was an ugly dwarf circulated well after her lifetime, but there is no evidence to support it. She obviously appealed to one of her male colleagues, who made advances to her in writing: "Violet-crowned, pure, sweet-smiling Sappho, I want to say something to you, but shame prevents me." Her reply? "If your wishes were fair and noble, and your tongue designed not to utter what is base, shame would not cloud your eyes, but you would speak your just desires."[9]

There has long been a tendency to regard Sappho's relationship with her pupils as an aberration rather than as typical of the classical Greek approach to aristocratic education. Neither Sappho's behavior nor her poetry seems to have raised an eyebrow among her peers. According to social historian K. T. Dover, "Greek culture differed from ours in its readiness to recognize the alternation of homosexual and heterosexual preferences in the same individual." The culture also differed from ours in "its implicit denial that such alternation or coexistence created peculiar problems for the individual or society." The Greeks gave a "sympathetic response to the open expression of homosexual desire in words and behavior," and showed a decided "taste for the uninhibited treatment of homosexual subjects in literature and the visual arts."[10]

Sappho's life is important in several ways. For the first time "we hear the voice of a woman speaking about her sex."[11] It also illustrates the underlying elements of a debate over teacher–learner relationships that continues to the present. The sexual aspect of Greek life should not distract us from the central issue. Put simply, can professional teachers—

those who teach for money—be effective? Or should teaching happen only when a strong personal bond exists between teacher and learner? This is the question that Socrates made famous. Before turning to his life, a brief description of ancient Greek educational life is in order. This is the matter of love, sexuality, and education in the Greek context.

GREEK EDUCATION

Through Sappho's poetry, we have had a glimpse of education for girls in the sixth century B.C. After Sappho's time, women's education became more home-centered. In all of the Greek city-states, aristocratic boys received a chivalric education. This formally started at the age of six or seven and continued to about puberty or a little beyond. They went to a *palaestra* (an open-air school). This name originally designated a place for only gymnastic activities. By the fifth century, grammar and music teachers routinely offered instruction at the palaestra. The curriculum was music, gymnastics, reading, writing, and poetry, especially Homer's *Iliad* and *Odyssey*. These epic poems were written in praise of *areté* (honor resulting from a personally heroic deed). The aim of education was to produce well-rounded, courageous, warrior/citizens. While a boy was young, his father assigned a *paidagōgos* (family slave) to accompany him to and from school and to protect him from harm.

In the century after Sappho lived, some city-states became wealthy enough to build large gymnasiums. These were social centers of male society. Around the covered walkways, older men conducted the teenage boys' advanced education, consisting of military tactics, athletic skill, social etiquette, and philosophy.

Mature men watched the young adult males, formed attachments, and courted those whom they found most appealing. Much of the attraction was based on physical beauty. "It must be emphasized that the Greeks did not call a person 'beautiful' by virtue of that person's morals, intelligence, ability, or temperament," writes Dover. The Greeks measured beauty "solely by virtue of shape, color, texture, and movement."[12] The most admired relationships emphasized love, affection, deep friendship, and devotion more than sexuality. Given the close link between Greek ideas of beauty and their open acceptance of sexuality, publicly acknowledged love attachments between older and younger men were common. This approval did not extend to relationships with boys who had not yet become adults (*pederasty*). The transition from boy to man was not precise but generally happened between the ages of fifteen and nineteen. One of the paidagōgos' tasks was to protect a boy from unwelcome approaches at too early an age.

Thus, in aristocratic Greek society, teaching beyond the rudiments in the palaestra was ideally an extension of a strong personal relationship. Any adult male citizen might aspire to become the mentor/teacher (and eventually, lover) of a beautiful teenage boy. He would not do this for money, for to do so would prostitute an esteemed relationship. (Prostitution was legal and existed in several grades, but prostitutes were usually foreigners, not citizens.) To be caught acting as a prostitute or pimp would call the good standing of a citizen into question.

These attitudes and practices grew out of a two-class society in which citizens had most of the rights and slaves did the work. As cities grew, there emerged what we would now call a middle class whose members were free people who owned little or no land. They found themselves at odds with the aristocrats over power and respectability. By the fourth century B.C., many people in this group disapproved of homosexuality, perhaps because it seemed too aristocratic.

THE GOLDEN AGE

When Sappho died in the sixth century, there were no large Greek cities. Some people were quite well off; most wealth was still based in land. Sparta, with its well-developed army, large slave base, and conservative society, was a powerful city-state. Several others grew rapidly in the next few decades, notably Syracuse, Corinth, and Athens. Improvements in naval skills brought expanded trade and wealth.

The Athenians were particularly well placed to profit from these developments. They had an excellent harbor and a fleet of technologically advanced ships, and they developed effective naval tactics. In 480 B.C. the Greeks defeated Persia in a decisive military engagement. The Athenian navy's prominence in this victory gave Athens a psychological and trade boost, launching that city on what later historians would call a "golden age."

Increasing wealth brought several consequences. One was that while the number of aristocrats stayed about the same, the number of artisans and merchants steadily increased. As this middle group below the aristocracy and above the slaves grew and made money in the expanding economy, they pressed for citizenship and full access to the schools, gymnasiums, political life, and legal machinery. Many aristocrats feared and resisted this competitive push from people whom they considered their inferiors. Everywhere except in Sparta, however, they reluctantly conceded much of what the rising group of "free men" wanted. These changes happened in an atmosphere characterized by threats, intrigue, plots, trials, assassinations, occasional battles, and frequent exiles.

Another result of increasing wealth and growing aspirations was a demand for education. Teachers of grammar (reading and writing), music (including poetry), and gymnastics (with military tactics) offered the same kind of teaching for the sons (and perhaps daughters) of the middle class as the aristocracy had long enjoyed. For those who wished to pursue what we might call higher studies (geometry, astronomy, political science, rhetoric, philosophy), there grew up a class of professional teachers called *sophists*.

THE SOPHISTS

Homeric Greece had been rich in gods. The pleasure or anger of one or more of these deities was supposed to account for practically every occurrence from birth to death. If a needed rain fell, farmers said that Zeus had taken pity on them after a previous drought, which had been caused by the ill will of some other god. Every family had its own gods, each city enjoyed a special protector (Athena for Athens, for example), and every special activity or phenomenon of nature engaged the interest of some divine being. Each person had his or her own temple, cult, legends, and rituals which were bound up with every aspect of life. By the fifth century, however, some people were growing skeptical about the religious traditions. Psychologist Julian Jaynes refers to this as the development of consciousness. The emerging awareness that traditional religious explanations did not fit well with experiences is an example of what some contemporary analysts call a "paradigm shift."[13] The sophists, being the advanced thinkers in society, gave expression to this growing skepticism.

Protagoras (c. 490–c. 420 B.C.)

The increased demand for education provided a market for people able to teach the most desired skills. Protagoras, the first person known to have declared himself publicly as a professional teacher, was born in Abdera, an Ionian colony on the coast of Thrace. He was not from a wealthy family and began his adult life as a humble porter. A questionable source has it that Protagoras was educated by Democritus (famous for atomic theory and materialism) after the latter happened to see a device that the young porter had invented for carrying loads. Presumably, Democritus was so favorably impressed with Protagoras's intelligence and disposition that he offered to educate him. The same source holds that Protagoras served as Democritus's secretary for a time; he certainly might have repaid his master with this service while furthering his own learning.

Having gotten an education through hard work and good fortune, Protagoras began a teaching career in the country towns around Abdera. He lived on whatever small fees his pupils' parents were willing or could afford to pay. He was kind to people, and they liked him. He became good at teaching, and his reputation spread.

Protagoras's Philosophy

Protagoras is most famous for asserting that accurate knowledge of being or existence is not attainable by humans. Avoiding speculation about the cosmos, he concentrated on human beings, their knowledge, and society. "Concerning the Gods, I am not able to know to a certainty whether they exist or whether they do not," he said. "Man is the measure of all things—of those that are, that they are, and of those that are not, that they are not."[14] Philosophers and historians have debated whether Protagoras meant that each person's experiences and perceptions are the ultimate measure of reality or whether it is collective human experience that determines this. Disagreement continues over which, if either, of these two ways of viewing reality is better. *Pragmatists* prefer the collective interpretation; *existentialists* prefer the individual one.

Whatever Protagoras's meaning, he thought human beings capable of learning enough about their world to solve their problems, and he believed that everyone could gain excellence. He argued that all citizens, if properly taught, have enough virtue and intelligence to participate in government. "We benefit, I believe, from one another's fair dealing and good character, which is why everyone is eager to teach the next man and tell him what is right and lawful," he said. "Even the wickedest man who has been brought up in a society governed by laws is a just man . . . if you were to compare him with men without education, or courts, or laws, or any coercion at all to force them to be good."[15]

A Practical Course of Study

When questioned about what curriculum he offered, Protagoras replied: "What I teach is the proper management of one's own affairs, how best to run one's own household, and the management of public affairs of the city both by word and action."[16] These were useful skills. The ability to think clearly, speak persuasively, manage one's personal life satisfactorily, and enter prudently into public discourse was a solid basis for success. To do all this within a context of moral integrity and good citizenship certainly would be of benefit. Beyond improving the civic life of the *polis* (community or society), these skills had extraordinary practical value for individuals. In Greek society mass juries ultimately decided all legal questions. Since each citizen was his own prosecutor or defender, the ability to reason clearly and speak persuasively could have profound importance for a person's property, life, or liberty. The practical value of these skills was clear to the Greeks, and Protagoras's successful practice of teaching the elements of an effective speech to people who wanted to learn to be good orators set the pattern for much Greek education and became the central preoccupation of advanced learning in the Roman Empire.

Protagoras understood the value of his instruction and charged accordingly. To the suggestion that his fees were exorbitant, he announced that any pupil who felt the tuition unreasonable could state at a sacred shrine what he thought fair and pay that amount. There is no extant account of any student taking the master up on his bargain.

Some of Protagoras's critics disliked his claim that humans can never have exact knowledge. Others, including Socrates, disagreed with his democratic leanings. Opponents feared his analytic and verbal skills, referring to him as a "slippery arguer in disputatious contests fully skilled."[17]

Protagoras in Athens

After traveling extensively and establishing a large reputation, Protagoras in 433 arrived in Athens, by then the most exciting city in the Greek world. He moved in the highest circles. Pericles, Athens' head of state, befriended him, and many people sought to meet him. After he gave a public lecture, however, conservative elements in the city tried to have him banished. They based their official objections on his comments about the gods, but it was his approving remarks about democratic government that activated their deepest fears. Not content with banning him from the city, the Athenians also voted to burn all copies of his books. "Calling them in by the public crier, and compelling all who possessed them to surrender them," they burned them in the marketplace.[18]

There is no record of what happened to Protagoras after he left Athens. One tradition has him living to ninety. Another asserts that he died in a shipwreck while on his way to Sicily. However he met his end, he left a philosophic legacy that would become popular in nineteenth-century America. As we shall see in Chapter 9, people like Francis Wayland Parker, John Dewey, Margaret Haley, and Ella Flagg Young agreed with his assumptions about democratic government, the educability of all people, and the dignity of teaching as a vocation. Many people now agree about the inexact nature of human knowledge and the desirability of solving individual and social problems on the basis of experience rather than absolutes.

Socrates (c. 470–399 B.C.)

One of Protagoras's most fundamental critics was a younger contemporary named Socrates, who became a much more widely recognized figure. That more people agreed with the main tenets of Socrates' philosophy than with those of Protagoras's, at least until about a century ago, may be a contributing factor. Socrates' life has been so dramatically presented by his pupil and friend Plato that his name has become for many people a symbol of all that is best, most humane, and right in teaching and personal integrity.

Socrates as Hero

With Socrates as with Sappho, a brief caution is in order. Historical people must be understood in the context of their own times. The persistent tendency to read immediate preoccupations back into the past—historians call this *presentism*—is nowhere clearer than in the way people have treated Socrates. The "Socratic method," invented by Protagoras or someone even earlier, has been widely heralded as a good model to follow in teaching. Moreover, Socrates' life has become for many the personification of virtue. The idea that Socrates had love affairs with boys is so unappealing to us that even twentieth-century authors have felt compelled to explain away the evidence. A. E. Taylor, for example, in an otherwise excellent book, glosses over the homosexual episodes in Socrates' life, concluding that these are merely jokes. However, the truth of the matter is simple—they did happen and aristocratic Greeks of Socrates' time thought them normal.[19]

Early Life

Socrates was born in Athens around 470 B.C. His father was an artisan, a stonecutter and sculptor, and his mother a midwife. Later Socrates would joke that he himself was an intellectual midwife who helped bring other people's ideas into the world. There is no mention of his having any brothers or sisters. We know nothing about his childhood. He may have learned his father's trade, but it is not clear that he ever practiced it. Other facts demonstrate his desire to climb to a higher rung on the social ladder in boisterous, growing Athens. His family probably started and supported this ambition. He studied with and may have become the lover of Archelaus, a teacher noted for his sophistic skills and interest in natural science. And he married the granddaughter of a famous Athenian general.

When Protagoras visited Athens, Socrates was in his middle thirties. He had a reputation as a teacher, but was not as widely known as the visitor from Abdera. Apparently the whole city was abuzz with the news of the famous teacher's presence, and Socrates wanted to meet him. To do so, he went with a wealthy young aristocrat—probably one of his own pupils—who wanted to study with Protagoras. This experience gave Socrates the opportunity to engage his competitor in a discussion/debate. Our only account of this meeting comes from Plato, born several years after the event, who probably got his information from Socrates. Plato portrayed the outcome as a draw.

Socrates and his pupil called at the house where Protagoras was staying and found him walking in the colonnade. On either side of him were young men from prominent local families and a number of foreigners (that is, non-Athenians). "Protagoras collects them from every city he passes through, charming them with his voice like Orpheus, and they follow the sound of his voice quite spellbound," said Socrates. "I was absolutely delighted by this procession to see how careful they were that nobody ever got in Protagoras' way, but whenever he and his companions turned round, those followers of his turned smartly outwards in formation to left and right, wheeled round and so every time formed up in perfect order behind him."[20]

Socrates had already begun developing a local reputation as a logician when he met Protagoras. In the next few years, his fame increased.

(His marriage to an aristocrat probably helped.) He was part of Pericles' social circle, he dressed well, and he had money to invest. Whether he made this money from fees, through marriage, or by some other way is not apparent. In later life, Socrates took a second, younger wife out of a sense of patriotic duty because there were too few Athenian men to go around. He lived with both women, and had children by them, but his true love interest was boys. When he was older, Socrates was a severe critic of the sophists' practice of taking pay for teaching. It is not clear whether he felt that way when he was in his thirties.

The only account of Socrates written while he was alive is in Aristophanes' play, *The Clouds*. First produced in 423, it caricatures the Athenian philosopher as a naturalistically inclined sophist who would teach paying students how to make weak arguments seem strong so that they could avoid paying their debts. It is difficult to know how much of the play was exaggerated for comic effect, but it was probably based partly in fact. As a young man, Socrates had flirted with the naturalistic opinions of his teacher Archelaus, but along the way he exchanged these ideas for more traditional beliefs. By the end of his life, and perhaps earlier, he was a strong elitist.

None of this suggests that Socrates was dishonest, unintelligent, or lazy. He was surely not the first and certainly not the last person to alter his views as his social, political, and psychological circumstances changed. He reacted to his experiences and to the atmosphere in which he lived. He earned a record of valor in the Peloponnesian Wars. Because these conflicts had an important part in his eventual death, a brief explanation is in order.

Athens at War

Beginning about 435 and lasting for more than thirty years were a series of armed engagements among various city-states. Sparta, Corinth, and other members of the Spartan League feared the power of Athens, which had been growing since the defeat of the Persians. A series of battles took place, interspersed with years of noncombat. In the early phase, Pericles' strategy was to have all Athenians come into the walled city while the navy raided Spartan territory. Living conditions in the embattled city were not sanitary. Plague broke out, killing many people, including Pericles.

Socrates fought bravely. In 424, he was in battle alongside his lover and pupil, a handsome young man named Alcibiades. Socrates gave up his own claim to a prize for valor in favor of his friend.

Athens was unable to win decisively, partly because of internal dissension over policy. One group, known as "democrats," wanted to prosecute the war aggressively. Among other things, they were attracted to the possibility of making money by capturing slaves and territory. A faction of extreme aristocrats grew increasingly disaffected with the war because they had little to gain from victory and had a greater sense of identity with the Spartan aristocrats than with their democratic competitors at home. Between the two groups were moderates trying to reconcile the two camps. As the war dragged on, the members of both radical groups became increasingly suspicious of one another.

Socrates was linked with the aristocrats in several ways. Alcibiades went over to the Spartan side after bungling a campaign as general for the Athenians. The aristocrats did not particularly mind, but the democrats were outraged, and they had Alcibiades assassinated. Socrates' love affair with him had been common knowledge. In 406 ten aristocratic generals were indicted for allowing many Athenian sailors to drown in a storm with no rescue attempt. Socrates found a legal dodge to block the intended mass trial.

Not long after this, the Spartans caught the Athenian navy off-guard and demolished it. Without supplies from the sea, the city was soon forced to surrender to the Spartan army that had it under siege. The Spartans killed fifteen hundred democrats and created a new government under the control of thirty of the most extreme aristocrats.

Seizing a chance to rid themselves of political opponents and make a tidy profit by confiscating their property, the so-called Thirty Tyrants instituted a reign of terror. Within four months they executed many democrats, moderates, and even moderate aristocrats. Almost everyone else in the city was up in arms against them. The leader of the notorious Thirty was Critias, an aristocrat who had begun his young adulthood as a democrat, but had changed his views under Socrates' tutelage. In fact, Socrates had a number of close friends among the Thirty, though he refused to obey some of their directives.

Socrates' Views

Socrates had taught a generation of young Athenians the ideals, metaphysics (views of ultimate reality), and values that were friendly to aristocracy. These values were "profoundly anti-democratic, striking at the very theoretical roots on which the democratic way of life (even in a slave-owning democracy) was founded."[21] The basic tenet of Socrates' teaching was that knowledge comes not through the senses, as Protagoras had claimed, but through logic and contemplation. He agreed with the Pythagoreans, who taught that (1) ideas and not physical things were the basis of ultimate reality, (2) mathematics was the avenue to truth, and (3) the virtuous few should rule the many, who were incapable of knowing much about mathematics or virtue. The Pythagorean theorem was their symbol of justice. In a right-angled triangle, $a^2 + b^2 = c^2$ without regard to the length of a or b. It followed that talent, virtue, insight, and power could be distributed in vastly different proportions to different parts of society but the society would still be "just" or in geometric balance. It was a theory that fit nicely with aristocracy.

Socrates "was very ingenious at deriving arguments from existing circumstances," and embodied some of his teaching in stories or allegories. Plato related one of these with Socrates speaking (in the first person) to Plato's brother Glaucon:

And now, I said, let me show in a figure how far our nature is enlightened or unenlightened:—Behold! human beings living in an underground den, which has a mouth open toward the light and reaching all along the den; here they have been from their childhood, and have their legs and necks chained so that they cannot move, and can only see before them, being prevented by the chains from turning round their heads. Above and behind them a fire is blazing at a distance, and between the fire and the prisoners there is a raised way; and you will see, if you look, a low wall built along the way, like a screen which marionette players have in front of them, over which they show the puppets.

I see.

And do you see, I said, men passing along the wall carrying all sorts of vessels, and statues and figures of animals made of wood and stone and various materials, which appear over the wall? Some of them are talking, others silent.

You have shown me a strange image, and they are like strange prisoners.

Like ourselves, I replied; and they see only their own shadows, or the shadows of one another, which the fire throws on the opposite wall of the cave?

True he said; how could they see anything but the shadows if they were never allowed to move their heads?

And of the objects which are being carried in like manner they would only see the shadows?

Yes, he said.

And if they were able to converse with one another, would they not suppose that they were naming what was actually before them?

Very true.

And suppose further that the prison had an echo which came from the other side, would they not be sure to fancy when one of the passers-by spoke that the voice which they heard came from the passing shadow?

No question, he replied.

To them, I said, the truth would be literally nothing but the shadows of the images.

That is certain.

And now look again, and see what will naturally follow if the prisoners are released and disabused of their error. At first, when any of them is liberated and compelled suddenly to stand up and turn his neck round and walk and look towards the light, he will suffer sharp pains; the glare will distress him, and he will be unable to see the realities of which in his former state he had seen the shadows; and then conceive some one saying to him, that what he saw before was an illusion, but that now, when he is approaching nearer to being and his eye is turned towards more real existence, he has a clearer vision—what will be his reply? And you may further imagine that his instructor is pointing to the objects as they pass and requiring him to name them—will he not be perplexed? Will he not fancy that the shadows which he formerly saw are truer than the objects which are now shown to him?

Far truer.

And if he is compelled to look straight at the light, will he not have a pain in his eyes which will make him turn away to take refuge in the objects of vision which he can see, and which he will conceive to be in reality clearer than the things which are now being shown to him?

True, he said.

And suppose once more, that he is reluctantly dragged up a steep and rugged ascent, and held fast until he is forced into the presence of the sun himself, is he not likely to be pained and irritated? When he approaches the light his eyes will be dazzled, and he will not be able to see anything at all of what are now called realities.

Not all in a moment, he said.

He will require to grow accustomed to the sight of the upper world. And first he will see the shadows best, next the reflections of men and other objects in the water, and then the objects themselves; then he will gaze upon the light of the moon and the stars and the spangled heaven; and he will see the sky and the stars by night better than the sun or the light of the sun by day?

Certainly.

Last of all he will be able to see the sun, and not mere reflections of him in the water, but he will see him in his own proper place, and not in another; and he will contemplate him as he is. . . . And when he remembered his old habitation, and the wisdom of the den and his fellow-prisoners, do you suppose that he would felicitate himself on the change, and pity them?

Certainly, he would.

. . . Imagine once more, I said, such an one coming suddenly out of the sun to be replaced in his old situation; would he not be certain to have his eyes full of darkness?

To be sure, he said.

And if there were a contest, and he had to compete in measuring the shadows with the prisoners who had never moved out of the den, while his sight was still weak, and before his eyes had become steady (and the time which would be needed to acquire this new habit of sight might be very considerable), would he not be ridiculous? Men would say of him that he went up and down he came without his eyes; . . . and if any one tried to loose another and lead him up to the light, let them only catch the offender, and they would put him to death.[22]

Socrates' Death

With the Spartans preoccupied by internal politics (slave revolts were a constant worry for them), the exiled democrats soon staged a successful though shaky comeback in Athens. The leader of the returned democrats was Anytus, a moderate whose property had been confiscated when he went into exile and whose son had stayed behind to study with Socrates. (The son became a drunkard.) Although Anytus did not try to recover his property and did not attempt to punish the remaining members of the aristocracy, he did blame Socrates for his son's alcoholism, and he wanted satisfaction.

Anytus and two others brought a charge of impiety against Socrates. They alleged that he believed not in the normal gods but in "demoniacal beings," and that he had corrupted youth with these beliefs. (A charge of impiety was the same kind of catch-all for Athenians as income tax evasion or misuse of the mail is to contemporary Americans.) Aristophanes' picture of Socrates as a cynical word merchant was widely known. Socrates dressed carelessly, and he enjoyed all-night dinner parties, at which he had the reputation for being able to drink everyone else under the table. Combined with the general knowledge that Socrates was stringently antidemocratic, it is not surprising that many on the jury must have been unsure just what to make of the old man whom his peers had wanted to decorate for bravery twenty years earlier.

Socrates denied the charges, but a narrow majority of the five-hundred-man jury found him guilty. The court gave him the opportunity of suggesting a suitable penalty. His friends begged him to name a stiff fine that they would pay for him. Instead, he specified a token amount. When a ripple of disapproval ran through the jury, Socrates clinched the matter by stating that even the smallest sum was too much, and the city should give him a life pension. That did it. The Greeks despised *hubris* (unwarranted pride), and the jury voted the death penalty.

Socrates could have avoided this sentence. Friends arranged his escape by bribes and begged him to go away with them to some pleasant spot. Many people on the jury would have preferred seeing the matter end with exile. Socrates, however, refused to go and spent his last days calmly discoursing with friends. One of his wives brought his youngest child and was crying over the injustice of the sentence. He dismissed them with the comment, "Would you rather I were dying justly?" A young blond friend named Phaedo got lots of hugs and affection. "Tomorrow, Phaedo, I suppose that these fair locks of yours will be severed [cut in mourning]," he said while fondling his friend's head and hair.[23]

On the appointed day, Socrates calmly drank hemlock and died. One of his aristocratic young students, profoundly affected by Socrates' final years and dramatic death, immortalized him—"the man we hold best, wisest, most upright of his age"—in a series of accounts that have become classics of Western literature.[24] The young man's name was Plato.

Plato (428–347 B.C.)

Both sides of Plato's family were among the oldest, most aristocratic families of Athens. His mother's cousin was Critias, leader of the Thirty Tyrants, and another of the Thirty was her uncle. This was Charmides, a general killed in 403 in a battle between aristocrats and democrats. Plato's father traced his ancestry back to Poseidon, god of the sea. Conservative politics seemed almost in the family's genes. When Plato was born in 428, his family named him Aristocles (best, most renowned).[25] He later got the nickname Plato because of his robust, broad-shouldered build.

Plato had two brothers, Glaucon and Ademantus, and one sister, Petone. His sister's son, Speusippus, was later affiliated with Plato in his educational work. Plato's father seems to have died when Plato was still young. His mother married her uncle, a man named Pyrilampes who had been implicated in a political murder when he was young. He was acquitted of the charge and seems to have spent the time after marrying his niece in the politically inoffensive pastime of breeding peacocks. There is no information about how he treated Plato or how they got along or, for that matter, what Plato thought about his mother, father, or childhood.

About all that we know about Plato's youth is that he received the kind of education in grammar, music, gymnastics, and poetry that were appropriate for a lad in his circumstances. He mastered grammar, shown by his later power as a writer, and he probably also did well in the other aspects of his schooling. After Plato's time an unproven story circulated that he had wrestled in the Isthmian games. His physical appearance must have been regarded as quite adequate, yet there is no indication that people gave him much attention for his looks.

Effects of Socrates' Death

Plato thought he was headed for a career in Athenian politics, as his whole family was probably preoccupied with the political conflicts of the time. However, his voice was thin and unimpressive, and he didn't seem motivated to a military career. The energetic program of political terror pursued by his cousin Critias repelled Plato, but he never disavowed the theory behind it. What he found really engaging was Socrates and his *dialectical* (arguing various sides of issues) teaching.

When Socrates came to trial, Plato was present. An account written much after the time claims that Plato, apologizing for his youth, stood to speak for Socrates and was shouted down. It certainly could have happened. On the day that Socrates drank the hemlock, Plato was too ill to be present.

After Socrates' death several of his close associates, including Plato, thought going abroad a safer course of action than staying in Athens. A group of them traveled to Megara, where they stayed with some Pythagoreans. Plato went eventually to Cyrene, where he visited a noted mathematician named Theodorus. From there he traveled to southern Italy and Sicily and finally to Egypt. He especially admired the Egyptian priests and their profound sense of ancient culture.

While Plato was in Sicily, he went to Syracuse, where he met Dion, son-in-law of the city's ruler, Dionysius I. Plato and Dion became lovers and lifelong friends. Dionysius I was the strong-handed leader of democratic factions in Syracuse. He understood well and completely disapproved of the implications of Plato's Socratic/Pythagorean messages to Dion. Dionysius had Plato arrested and sold into slavery. Friends ransomed the young aristocrat, and he returned to Athens.

Plato's Academy

Back in his hometown after more than a decade of travel, Plato bought land and a building near a gymnasium and grove of trees (we would probably call it a public park) not far outside of town. The park carried the name of an early hero, Academus, who had been turned into a minor god. Plato's building fronted on the grove of trees, so he and his associates could also use the buildings of the gymnasium. The Academy was the oldest of three state-sponsored gymnasiums in Athens. The other two were the Lyceum, established by Pericles and patronized by the wealthiest citizenry, and the Cynosarges, which foreigners patronized.[26]

Just how Plato's Academy functioned is not completely clear. Later commentators have referred to it as a school and as the first university. These concepts are misleading. The establishment combined the functions of a social club with strong religious underpinnings, a political interest group, and a modern unaffiliated research institute or "think tank." There were no fees, but people needed to be wealthy enough to support themselves in good style or they would be out of place. Young men of about sixteen could join the Academy's fraternity.

Plato's group observed religious rituals, and held frequent *symposia*—dinner parties at which the participants entertained each other with poems, songs, stories, conversation, and generous portions of wine. Some members gave public lectures. There may have been sequenced, formal courses, but this is doubtful. Plato himself seems to have rarely given either public or private lectures. Perhaps he was not comfortable as a teacher. He may have been reluctant to expose his ideas to public scrutiny, having seen a democratic jury hold Socrates accountable for public declarations. Plato described himself as "first among equals" in the establishment. There were no examinations, no graduation, and no certification, but the members shared their work with each other.

Outside of Athens, Plato entered indirectly into political activity. At the request of his close friend Dion, he made two more trips to Syracuse. When Dionysius I died, Dion had Plato tutor young Dionysius II into correct thinking and away from democratic ideas. Dion's opponents, however, convinced the youth to throw the pair out. Dion lived lavishly in exile on an estate near the Academy. An attempt by Plato late in his life to reconcile Dion and Dionysius met with no success, and Plato barely escaped with his hide after some Pythagorean friends interceded on his behalf. Several members of the academic fraternity wrote constitutions and laws for various areas, but Plato and his group avoided mingling in Athenian political life.

For the most part, Plato appears to have lived in quiet comfort with his friends. He had money, probably from his family, and he left two farms and a fair amount of gold and silver to his brother Ademantus when he died. (It is interesting to contrast the communistic ideal that Plato set forth in *The Republic* with the reality of his own inherited wealth. In the idealized Republic, aristocrats could own no property.) Plato indulged poetically and otherwise in the physical pleasures. He is said to have had several male lovers (many of Plato's poetic efforts show a strong preoccupation with the theme of love between man and boy) and at least one mistress. He never married. Some of what Plato wrote sounds as though he opposed slavery; however, he had five slaves of his own. Four of these he willed to Ademantus; the fifth, Diana, he set free in his will.

Idealism

Throughout his life, Plato remained committed to the main tenets of Pythagoreanism. We credit him with developing a "theory of ideas"; however, much of the theory was already explicit or implicit in the doctrines of Pythagoras and his followers. This theory asserted that for every sensible "thing" which we can perceive, there exists an underlying "idea" or universal organizing principle. For example, it is not enough to recognize beautiful statues, buildings, or people. Beauty itself is the organizing universal. Moreover, there is a dichotomy (split) between the world of sensation and the ideal (idea) world. The learner's task is to discover organizing principles or ideas. Plato believed that we do this by thinking, and partly by remembering, the lessons learned in earlier lives by our transmigrating souls. Plato (and the Pythagoreans) believed that mathematics and mystical numerology are the keys for unlocking the secrets of the ideal world.

The arresting feature of Plato's theory is that what is most "real" is changeless. As in the allegory of the cave, the senses give us information that is a shadow or distorted reflection of what is real and true. We can form opinions through our experience of the sensible world, but we never have accurate information. Truth can be ascertained only by our minds (or souls) through contemplation, and only a few of us are capable of knowing this truth. Here Plato's disillusionment with democracy shows strongly.

In *The Republic,* Plato has Socrates proposing a utopian educational system that strongly resembled Spartan practice. All children were to belong to the state. They would be products of group marriages, and a committee would examine them at birth for defects. Children who failed this inspection were to be killed by exposure. Those who survived this scrutiny were to be reared in public nurseries. All would receive traditional gymnastic, grammar, music, and patriotic instruction to age eighteen.

After military training and ten years of active duty, a small number of the best would spend five years of further contemplation and study getting to know rationality and the good. Then a few of the best of these, now thirty-five years old, would spend fifteen years apprenticed to good rulers who knew how to balance wisdom and power. At fifty these few best could become philosopher-kings. All this fit well with Plato's view that the soul must order and control irrational and chaotic impulses within the individual, and philosopher-kings must order and control the chaotic and irrational individuals in society.

Education of Women

Plato argued in *The Republic,* and again at the end of his life in *The Laws,* that women should receive exactly the same education as men, including military training. This view may have had no more relationship to Plato's real life than his theories of slavery and property, but the tradition is that among the Academy circle were two women— Lastheneia of Mantinea and Axiothea of Philus—"who used even to wear man's clothes," says one ancient source.[27]

Plato may have been an early feminist, or perhaps he was simply reaffirming old Spartan ways. (At one time, Spartan women could exercise *gymnos* [naked] in public just as men could.) His views and practices did not have much impact on the lives of ordinary women in his time. Plato's views on women were less negative than those of most of his male contemporaries, who believed that women were inferior to men in all important respects. Greek men rarely wrote about women as intelligent, so Plato's ideas look progressive on this score. He did explain that one main reason for teaching women was that if they were not educated, they did much more harm than did men. This argument, in various forms, would pass as an enlightened justification for women's education for more than two thousand years.

Plato's Conservatism

Educational philosophers have often seen Plato as a genius delivering a system of thought, rather than as a person who typified a great deal of the best and worst of his time and place. To read Plato for his literary and historical value is instructive. His educational and political ideas are elitist and conservative by today's standards.

We have already illustrated Plato's espousal of the political views of his family and class. He ignored experimental science, favoring traditional religious and political ideas. He propounded others' theories, but in an original way. He shared the beliefs of many other members of his social class on politics, economics, social theory, education, sexuality, and infanticide (the practice of examining infants for "defects" and, if any were found, "exposing" the children until they died. It was widely practiced and was one approach to family planning).

Plato put most of his ideas into written dialogues that his followers preserved. These dialogues are so engagingly written that we still enjoy reading them whether we agree with their profoundly elitist implications or not. If the Nobel Prize had existed in the fourth century B.C., the committee might have given Plato an award for literature, but not for political theory.

In his old age, Plato restated some of his earlier ideas, added a few more, and cast them all in a spirit of intolerance and rigidity. He wanted a totalitarian state with censorship of everything, and believed in a state religion with taboos on all forms of sexuality except between people married to each other, and then only for producing children. Death was the penalty for not accepting the preferred religion. In addition, he thought the body was evil and the soul pure.

Plato was sometimes afraid of his anger. For example, a historian writing five centuries later said that on two occasions Plato was in such a "passion" that he wanted to beat a slave. He feared doing it himself, apparently because he might kill or damage the property.[28] A psychoanalyst looking at the Academy's founder might wonder where all his hostility came from. But this is a preoccupation of our time, not of his.

Plato lived to be about eighty-one, and legend has it that he died contentedly at a wedding reception. Friends buried him at the Academy and put up several commemorative inscriptions. One reportedly read:

> Here, first of all men for pure justice famed,
> And moral virtue, Aristocles lies;
> And if there e'er has lived one truly wise,
> This man was wiser still; too great for envy.[29]

At least this epitaph indicates how his associates thought he wanted to be remembered.

One of his younger colleagues built an altar to him. This was Aristotle, a dedicated member of the Academic group, who would continue some of the ideas and traditions learned in Plato's circle and develop others of which the dedicated Platonists would not approve. The Academy itself lasted almost nine hundred years. Both it and Plato's writings became important parts of Western intellectual and educational traditions.

Aristotle (384–322 B.C.)

One of Plato's brightest pupils was Aristotle. He came to the Academy in his seventeenth year from a northern Greek city-state, Stagira. He remained in this Academic brotherhood for the next twenty years, first as pupil and then as teacher.[30] We do not have a complete picture of the relationship between Plato and Aristotle, but historians believe that they shared a mutual friendship and respect. Plato referred to Aristotle as the *nous* (mind) or "intellect of the school," while Aristotle paid tribute to his master years later when he said that Plato "clearly revealed, by his own life and by the methods of his words [that] to be happy is to be good."[31] Even though Aristotle was to become much more scientific and empirical than Plato, he was reluctant to criticize Plato's theory of ideas because of his affection for the Academy's founder. Only truth was more valuable to Aristotle than his love for his Academic colleagues.[32]

Aristotle's Background

Aristotle probably gained his scientific inclinations from his father. The latter was a court physician to a Macedonian king, and it was customary for medical men to train their sons in their profession at an early age. The training included dissection and surgical observations.[33] This may explain why Aristotle eventually incorporated empirical observations into his Platonic views of universal truth.

Orphaned as a teenager, the young Aristotle inherited a substantial sum, including his mother's property in yet another northern city, Chalcis. Shortly after the death of his parents, he traveled from Stagira to Athens, leaving behind a brother, Arimriestus, and sister, Arisneste. Why he went to Athens to study under the sixty-one-year-old Academy head is not clear. Probably it was a natural step for one interested in learning, because Plato and Athens were famous for philosophy.

A Foreigner in Athens

For the next forty-five years (from age seventeen to sixty-two) he pursued what he later called "ultimate happiness" in the form of a contemplative life, even though such a life-style brought him a good deal of hardship and loneliness. While studying in Athens, his biggest problems stemmed from not being an Athenian citizen. He was a *metic* (resident alien) with connections to a region (Macedonia) that aroused intense hostility in certain political circles. These feelings were the result of a collapsing Greek confederacy and a rising Macedonian dictatorship.

His first meeting with this hostility probably came during 347 when, shortly before Plato's death, one of the Greek cities was destroyed. Along with Xenocrates, another Academic, Aristotle probably traveled to the court of the Greek-born Hermias, Aristotle's former pupil and lover at the Academy, who had risen to the status of dictator in upper Asia Minor.

Here, Aristotle spent about three years studying with a small Platonic group. During his stay, he began classifying some of his biological observations. It was also here that he married Hermias' niece and adopted daughter, Phythias. Political turmoil soon forced the group's departure. Hermias was eventually assassinated by the Persians. This loss no doubt left its mark on Aristotle, who wrote a poem eulogizing Hermias.[34]

They next retreated to Sappho's city of Mytilene on the island of Lesbos, where Theophrastus, Aristotle's good friend and fellow Academic, lived. Along with his host, Aristotle spent the next years studying marine life and natural history. It was during this period his daughter Pythias was born. Then the account gets fuzzy. We know that Aristotle also had a son, Nicomachus. Some sources say that after the death of his wife, he took up with her freed slave, Herpyllis, and that she was his son's mother. Other historians doubt that Nicomachus was illegitimate, because Aristotle's will did not treat him as such.[35]

Life as a Teacher

We next find Aristotle (c. 342) back in Mieza at the Macedonian court, where his father had been a physician. Philip of Macedon called Aristotle there to tutor Alexander, his flamboyant thirteen-year-old son, who was destined to become Alexander the Great. Having studied politics and government under Platonic tutelage, Aristotle was eager to take on the education and training of this future ruler. Tradition has it that the philosopher prepared a special edition of Homer for the future king and taught him politics and rhetoric.

Aristotle induced his pupil to rebuild Stagira, which had been destroyed in battle. While his father was away in battle, Alexander served as regent director and launched a building program. He also commanded Aristotle to draw up a constitution and set of laws for the master's old hometown. This caused citizens of Stagira to eulogize Aristotle as "the lawgiver" after his death.

In 334, when Alexander acceded to power, Aristotle returned to a more accepting Athens. Athenian aristocracy was pro-Macedonian, but the populist factions continued to resent the long-arm dictatorial rule of Alexander. The resentment remained mostly buried for the next ten years, although Aristotle felt the sting of many negative remarks. He endured attacks on his physical appearance (they exaggerated his thin legs, balding head, and vocal lisp) and his overindulgence in the sensual pleasures. He seems to have managed to ignore these slanders and to have enmeshed himself in the pursuit of scientifically acquired wisdom.

The Lyceum

Aristotle began teaching with Theophrastus in one of the prominent Athenian gymnasiums, the Lyceum, around 334. Located just outside the city wall, the Lyceum was known for its beautiful orchard groves and *peripatos* (covered walkways). Like the Academy, the school operated as an intimate brotherhood devoted to the pursuit of truth. Aristotle did not charge fees, although he accepted gifts, especially from Alexander. Unlike the Academy, the school had no building, because as a foreigner Aristotle could not own property. He conducted his school in the public peripatos of the gym, a situation which led to his school being called the "Peripatetic School."

Another difference between the Academy and the Lyceum lay in teaching styles. Plato distrusted the written word and lecturing. This feeling was probably reinforced for Plato when, on the occasion of his only public lecture, everyone but Aristotle got up and left. (Aristotle later explained that when Plato announced his title "On the Good," people assumed that they would hear a practical, pleasure-oriented lecture and not an analysis of the transcendental soul.) Aristotle valued both lectures and the written word. Regarding the former, he thought that masters had to be sure to let their audiences know what to expect before embarking on the *diatribe* (discourse). As for written work, the Lyceum became known for its voluminous library.

In the morning, Aristotle lectured to his fellow scholars, who copied the lectures. He used charts, tables, and diagrams when helpful. In the afternoon he would deliver a more popular lecture to the public at large. Dialectics (the dialogues favored by Protagoras, Socrates, and Plato) was not a method that he approved. Aristotle encouraged his band of scholars to pursue all forms of knowledge that interested them. Hence, their work included such activities as collecting the records of Athenian dramatic performances, compiling a list of victors in the Olympic Games, recording various state constitutions, and classifying zoological and botanical data. In the Lyceum, biology—not mathematics—had the place of honor.[36]

Aristotle's Views

While some of Aristotle's scientific observations led to useful knowledge, others did not. He observed, for example, that women had fewer teeth than men. Today, we would say that his sample was not representative of the population, but the findings reinforced his belief that the female was an undeveloped male without potential for full development. Aristotle thought that the female sex was an inferior form of humankind—maimed males—but a "necessary anomaly." He accepted their inferior status in society, as he accepted slavery as a part of natural law.

If all women were emotionally and physiologically inferior, certain men were intellectually and morally inferior. Thus, slavery was the most appropriate and productive state for such men. He also suspected that the heart was the seat of the senses (and the mind or soul) and was convinced that it was the center of all emotion. He thought the brain's function was to cool the blood.[37]

About the moral and social natures of humans, Aristotle may have been more accurate. He thought that people were essentially social animals, living best in a polis. The supreme good, he concluded, was happiness, but he knew that people disagreed over what constituted happiness. For the masses who had little rational control over their emotions, happiness centered in sensual pleasures and material wealth. Aristotle assumed that a certain level of wealth and self-sufficiency was necessary to happiness, but was not the ultimate good. For more superior people, happiness was honor; but, Aristotle argued, neither honor nor a life of political power could lead to happiness. Such prizes were not in the control of their recipients. Their bestowers could take them away, leaving the individual unhappy. Hence, a life that enhanced people's uniqueness (their rationality) was for Aristotle the ultimate good. Most people, however, were not morally and intellectually trained for such a virtuous life, so he concluded that few would or could pursue it. (Aristotle was acknowledging the importance of environmental factors.)

Ideally, *paideia* (education) should cultivate those right habits that would, in turn, develop moral and rational virtues (for example, train children to exercise their rational will over baser and lustier appetites). This ethical and intellectual training or character development of correct habits Aristotle thought could best be achieved by daily practice (for moral virtue) and a liberal education (for intellectual virtue).

For the peripatetic philosopher, a liberal education was one that enhanced and developed the intellect—the essence of humanity. No specific list of subjects would guarantee a liberal education, but it would typically come through such studies as logic, rhetoric, math, music, and the sciences. Aristotle did not believe that practical training for some particular function was liberating, for this was how people trained slaves and animals. Vocational subjects were not liberating because they treated humans as a means to some other end. Learning geared to some goal other than intellectual development, such as producing wealth or gaining fame, was servile and illiberal.

By taking a person's nature and the effect of environment into account, all varieties of people—from the servile to the wealthy and morally/intellectually virtuous—could live cooperatively and productively. For proper social functioning, education should be in the hands of the city-state. Members of a large middle class should govern the city-state because they were the least likely to suffer from the extremes of poverty or wealth. Temperance and moderation were watchwords for this social scientist.

Aristotle differed from his mentor Plato in another, monumental way:

he trusted his natural observations. He also placed the essence of human-ness within human beings instead of in a transcendental soul. And he heralded human differences brought about through the interaction of nature and nurture. Aristotle placed all other essences in their physical/biological containers or bodies. One could carefully study these elements and, through generalizations about them, understand the world. How-ever, Aristotle did not exclude logical deductions based on unobservable intuitions. These he called his "first principles" or "self-evident truths." So his science became a refined Platonic idealism, "employing both induc-tion from experience and deduction from universal self-evident truths."[38] Aristotle was a master logician in deductive, syllogistic reasoning.

Last Days

Alexander the Great died in 323, and the old anti-Macedonian senti-ment lashed out once again at Aristotle. The Athenians formally ac-cused the peripatetic teacher of impiety, his poem to Hermias being grounds for the charge. Recalling the fate of Socrates, Aristotle said, "I will not let Athenians offend twice against philosophy."[39] He withdrew to his mother's estate in Chalcis, leaving the Lyceum school in the hands of Theophrastus.

Aristotle lived at Chalcis only a few months, for he was already suffer-ing from a stomach disorder. From his lonely exile, he wrote to a friend, "The more I am by myself, and alone, the fonder I have become of myths."[40] He died a few months later. His will specified that his remains be removed to Stagira near to those of his wife, as she had requested. Sources conflict as to what actually happened. Stagira seems to have claimed to have had his ashes in an urn.

The Lyceum continued to flourish under Theophrastus, who served as head master from 322 to 286. Then, in the hands of other, less-equipped peripatetics, it started a gradual decline as a learning center. Beyond 86 B.C. it ceased to be an instrument of Greek (or Roman) education.[41]

Despite the Lyceum's demise, Aristotle's influence remained. He did not really found biology, constitutional history, or social science, but he did more for them than perhaps any other ancient. Obviously, he and his colleagues produced some conclusions based on bad reason-ing, yet his work in ethics and politics is unrivaled in fame and influ-ence. One writer has called him "the first of Schoolmen" and "the master of those who know."[42] Seven centuries later he was still influ-ential among Neoplatonists, and in the thirteenth century he was at the center of the intellectual debate that accompanied the rise of mod-ern science (Chapter 4).

In the second century before Christ, the Romans conquered the Greeks. They left the various philosophical schools in operation—there were quite a number of them in several Greek cities by then—because they felt culturally inferior to the Greeks and wanted to study in the famous centers of learning. The Romans did, however, assume control over the selection of the head masters of the schools. One exception to this rule took place in the second century A.D. when Trajan's widow, Plotina, convinced her adopted son, Hadrian, to grant a perpetual exemption to the Epicureans. The school of Epicurus, which stressed temperance as a means of maximizing pleasure and minimizing pain, could always be headed by a Greek. Heads of all the other philosophical schools had to be Roman citizens.[43]

SUMMARY

The ancient Greeks are educationally significant for several reasons. They took the Middle Eastern idea of disciplined study, which the Sumerians invented, and the African notion of liberating study, which the Egyptians developed, and put them into conceptual language that Europeans, Americans, and many other national groups still use. *School* is a Greek word, and *liberal education* a Greek concept. *Pedagogy* has Greek roots, and *gymnasium, lyceum,* and *academy* are all labels we have borrowed from the Greeks. *Idealism, realism, pragmatism, existentialism*—four philosophies of long-standing significance—all trace their origins to Greek thinkers, especially Socrates (Plato), Protagoras, and Aristotle. *Ontology* (what's real), *epistemology* (how we know), and *axiology* (what's important or valuable) are Greek subdivisions of philosophy that we still use.

The idea of striving for integrated intellectual, physical, and moral personal excellence is certainly reinforced by the Greek tradition. The belief that there are culturally essential, or *core* (basic), studies dates to the Greeks. Even the debate over the most desirable relationship between teacher and student has conceptual origins in how the Greeks wrestled with the controversy.

Did everything of educational importance start with the Greeks? No. There was as much distance between the beginning of formal instruction (c. 3000 B.C.) and the Golden Age of Athens as there is from Sappho to the twenty-first century.

Is the Greek tradition wholly positive? Not by any means. Europeans (and Americans) justified slavery by looking to the Greeks. They also have often extended a Greek tradition by denigrating women. Rich, well born, and politically fortunate Americans and Europeans have cited Socrates, Plato, and Aristotle to explain their discrimination against less fortunate citizens.

It is not our agreement with the Greeks that leads us to study them. Because they debated and wrote about educational issues in philosophic terms, it has been helpful to compare our own thoughts and experiences with theirs. This has been a well-established tradition in the education of educators for the last two centuries. The tradition continues to have value, although study of educational thought and experience in other parts of the world can give students a broader perspective.

NOTES

1. Christopher J. Lucas, "The Scribal Tablet-House in Ancient Mesopotamia," *History of Education Quarterly* 19 (Fall 1979): 305–32.

2. David M. Robinson, *Sappho and Her Influence* (New York: Cooper Square, 1963), 14.

3. J. P. Mahaffy, *A History of Classical Greek Literature*, 2 vols. (London: Macmillan, 1908), 1: 202; Arthur [Edward Pearse Brome] Weigall, *Sappho of Lesbos: Her Life and Times* (New York: Frederick A. Stokes, 1932), 321.

4. Mary Barnard, trans., *Sappho: A New Translation* (Berkeley: University of California Press, 1958), 86.

5. John Addington Symonds, *Studies of the Greek Poets*, 3rd ed. (London: A. and C. Black, 1920), 196.

6. Verna Zinserling, *Women in Greece and Rome,* trans. L. A. Jones (New York: Abner Schram, 1973), 8. Spelling Americanized.

7. Beram Salvatvala, *Sappho of Lesbos: Her Works Restored: A Metrical English Version of Her Poems with Conjectural Restorations* (London: Charles Skilton, 1968), 24. Italicized lines are conjectural.

8. Guy Davenport, trans., *Sappho: Poems and Fragments* (Ann Arbor: University of Michigan Press, 1965), 151.

9. Symonds, *Studies of the Greek Poets,* 196.

10. K. T. Dover, *Greek Homosexuality,* (London: Duckworth, 1978), 1; It was not the gender of one's love object but the strength of attraction that counted most; Thomas Africa details the elaborate code involved in "Homosexuals in Greek History," *Journal of Psychohistory* 9 (Spring 1982): 401–20.

11. "She stands upon a lonely peak in the ancient world, but by the fifth century successors had appeared in Boeotia." Zinserling, *Women in Greece and Rome,* 8.

12. Dover, *Greek Homosexuality,* 16.

13. Julian Jaynes, *The Origin of Consciousness in the Breakdown of the Bicameral Mind* (New York: Houghton Mifflin, 1976); Thomas S. Kuhn, *The Structure of Scientific Revolutions,* rev. ed. (Chicago: University of Chicago Press, 1970).

14. Diogenes Laertius, *The Lives and Opinions of Eminent Philosophers,* trans. C. Duke Younge (London: Henry G. Bohn, 1853), 397–98. Cf. R. D. Hicks's translation (London: William Heinemann, 1925), 2: 463–69.

15. Plato, *Protagoras* (Taylor's translation), 327.

16. Plato, *Protagoras,* 319.

17. Diogenes, *The Lives and Opinions of Eminent Philosophers,* 398.

18. Diogenes, *The Lives and Opinions of Eminent Philosophers,* 398.

19. A. E. Taylor, *Socrates: The Man and His Thought* (New York: Doubleday Anchor Books, [1933] 1953). For a recent example of the pedestal view of Socrates, see Henry J. Perkinson, *Since Socrates: Studies in the History of Western Educational Thought* (New York: Longman, 1980).

20. Plato, *Protagoras,* 315.

21. Alban Dewes Winspear and Tom Silverberg, *Who Was Socrates?* 2nd ed. (New York: Russell and Russell, 1960), 71.

22. Plato, *The Republic* (Jowett's translation), 514–17; the quotation preceding the extract from *The Republic* is from Diogenes, *The Lives and Opinions of Eminent Philosophers,* 68.

23. Plato, *Phaedo* (Jowett's translation), 89.

24. Taylor, *Socrates: The Man and His Thought,* 128.

25. Some sources give 429 B.C. and some 427 B.C. as the date of his birth, but we follow Winspear, *The Genesis of Plato's Thought,* 2nd ed. (New York: S. A. Russell, 1956), 161, who argues persuasively for 428 B.C. Unless otherwise noted, biographical information in this sketch is from this source.

26. Mehdi Khan Nakosteen, *The History and Philosophy of Education* (New York: Ronald Press, 1965), 80.

27. Diogenes, *The Lives and Opinions of Eminent Philosophers,* 129.

28. Diogenes, *The Lives and Opinions of Eminent Philosophers,* 127.

29. Diogenes, *The Lives and Opinions of Eminent Philosophers,* 128.

30. Ingemar Düring, *Aristotle in the Ancient Biographical Tradition* (Göteburg: Göteburg University, 1957), 249–50.

31. Robert Maynard Hutchins, ed., "Biographical Note—Aristotle," in *Great Books of the Western World* (Chicago: Encyclopaedia Britannica, 1952), 8: v.

32. John Patrick Lynch, *Aristotle's School: A Study of a Greek Educational Institution* (Berkeley and Los Angeles: University of California Press, 1972), 87.

33. David Ross, "The Development of Aristotle's Thought," in *Aristotle and Plato in the Mid-Fourth Century,* ed. I. Düring and G. E. L. Owen (Göteburg: Elanders Boktryck eri Aktiebolag, 1960), 1–17.

34. H. I. Marrou, *A History of Education in Antiquity,* trans. George Lamb (New York: Sheed and Ward, 1956), 33; Düring rejects the homosexual relationship.

35. Düring, *Aristotle in the Ancient Biographical Tradition,* 263–65.

36. Lynch, *Aristotle's School,* 87–88, 91.

37. Stephen R. L. Clark, *Aristotle's Man: Speculations upon Aristotelian Anthropology* (Oxford: Clarendon Press, 1975), 29, 71ff.

38. Meyer Reinhold, *A Simplified Approach to Plato and Aristotle* (Great Neck, New York: Barron's Educational Series, 1967), 57.

39. Ross, "The Development of Aristotle's Thought," 7; Hutchins, *Great Books of the Western World,* 8: vi.

40. Ross, "The Development of Aristotle's Thought," 7; Hutchins, *Great Books of the Western World,* 8: vi.

41. Lynch, *Aristotle's School,* 140, 207.

42. Walter Pater, *Plato and Platonism: A Series of Lectures* (London: Macmillan, 1910), 141.

43. Naphtali Lewis and Meyer Reinhold, eds., *Roman Civilization* (New York: Columbia University Press, 1955), 2: 296–97.

The Romans

If Greek culture is notable for its intellectual and ethical sophistication, then Roman civilization is best characterized by its intense patriotism. While some historians find the provincial zeal of the Romans refreshing after the degeneracy of the Greeks, others describe the Romans as morally rigid, rural barbarians—slaves to the state—compared to the emancipated, enfranchised Greeks.[1]

For our purposes, we will drop in on Roman society about the time of Sappho (sixth century B.C.). We find a small, religious, landed aristocracy who worked the land themselves. The Latin language reveals just how agrarian the society was. Deriving their alphabet from the Etruscans, an Asian people who tried to rule and urbanize the Roman tribes, the Romans took many words from the soil. For example, *laetus* (joy) described well-manured ground; *felix* (happiness) referred to fertile soil; *sincerus* (truthfulness or sincerity) was pure honey without beeswax; and *frux* (fruitfulness) was profit. The grand Roman villas had their origins in rudimentary farmhouses: The kitchen gardens behind the old one-room houses were partially enclosed to include a dining room and separate *peristyle* (kitchen). The one-room hut became the den, office, and library. After enclosure, the farmyard became a receiving *atrium* (living room), and a *vestibule* (hallway) leading to the atrium completed the arrangement.

LEARNING IN THE EARLY REPUBLIC

A child born into one of the aristocratic clans learned the importance of the family unit as the backbone of society. The *pater* (father) held sovereign authority in all family matters. The mother, a well-respected family member, was responsible for educating her children in the rudiments of learning and the life-style befitting a Roman aristocrat. Daughters stayed home to learn domestic skills. Sons emulated their fathers. From about seven to sixteen, a boy left the care of his mother and came under the tutelage of his father.

By following his father around, the young aristocrat saw all sides of the life ahead of him. At sixteen his home *educatio* (instruction) came to an end. The son put on the *toga virilis* (adult cloak) and became a citizen. However, his education was not finished—ahead lay a year of preparation for public life and at least ten years of military service.

Nothing was so important to Roman citizens as military and public service under divine guidance of their gods. For Romans, these three elements were inseparable. Each *pater* was also the priest in his family, and many later Roman villas contained sacrificial altars. The pater's code for living was a mixture of old tribal customs and priestly commands.

Several *collegia* (associations) of priests, each under the direction of a *pontifex maximus* (high priest), conducted public worship. The aristocracy chose priests from their own group for a term of service. The most influential of the colleges was that of the *augures,* who interpreted the will of the gods by watching birds in flight. These colleges would later perform other duties, such as keeping historical annals and recording laws—tasks which Christian monasteries took up later.

ROMAN SOCIAL STRUCTURE

The legacy of public/military life for the Romans was an outgrowth of earlier tribal customs that were an integral part of the social structure. At the top of the ladder was the landed gentry, originally consisting of about three hundred paters, or clan heads. Most of these upper-class paters had clients—freemen who were dependent upon the paters' patronage for land and protection and who in turn helped the pater, served under him in war, and voted as the pater suggested. These powerful family heads comprised the Senate (the governing body) and furnished the generals of Roman society. Its *curia* (chambers) were in the Forum (town center or marketplace). Next came a group of wealthy bankers and businessmen called *conscripti* or *equites,* the former term denoting their obligation for military service and the latter their military horsemanship. Then came other businessmen, artisans, traders, and farmers—the peasants or plebeians—who were foot soldiers. All these were freemen. The lowest class was the slaves.[2]

As the conscripti grew in wealth and military power, they demanded a voice in the Senate. Their discontent spread to the plebeian classes who finally (494 B.C.) refused to fight or work for Rome until they got some of the conquered lands and more voice in governing the Republic. Longstanding abuse of the plebes eventually contributed to the fall of the Republic. However, their earlier revolts produced rewards: the conscripti gained admission to the Senate, and the senators wrote down the secret tribal and religious codes into a usable set of laws called the Twelve Tables (450 B.C.).

Down to the second century B.C., young Roman citizens memorized these laws. Although the Senate and later emperors would modify, elaborate, and redefine them, these laws remained the basic core of Rome's famous jurisprudence for the next nine hundred years. The Twelve Tables were in the Forum for all to view, and the hodgepodge of tribal ritual and priestly command was transformed from divine law into civil law. This separation of religion and state took a final step when, in 280 B.C., a man named Corincanius began teaching the Roman laws. Soon after, lawyers became more dominant than priests in Roman life.

GREEK INFLUENCE

One other major element in third- and second-century Roman education stemmed from Rome's becoming Hellenized (strongly influenced by the Greeks). As early as the fourth century B.C., Greek ways were as close as Naples, Salerno, Pompeii, Tarentum, and Herculaneum—all in the southern part of the Italian peninsula. As the Romans began conquering the Mediterranean (300–100 B.C.), they found Greek culture and language everywhere. The Romans gradually began to adapt Greek culture to their own life-styles.

The Romans readily absorbed Greek literature. The poet Andronicus of Tarentum taught and wrote in both Greek and Latin, and he translated Homer into Latin, producing the first Latin literary piece. The Romans liked the Greek schools of philosophy, especially those that enhanced a civil course of life. Aristotelian logic and rhetoric became indispensable to the Roman senator-turned-lawyer. These studies allowed him to argue a case more effectively. In fact, such Romans came to be called *orators, pleaders,* or *advocates.* The ethical branches of Greek philosophy even fit the old Roman morality. Orators were admonished to study ethics in order to be good, moral men. In fact, *philosophy* meant logic under the Republic and a prescriptive or normative ethics under the early Empire.[3] At this point rhetoric, logic, and philosophy completed their evolution toward preeminence in Roman education. Young Romans studied the other Greek subjects to a lesser degree. Music (which included poetry) was somewhat important because it lent grace and rhythm to oration. Some Romans liked singing and dancing, others thought these studies either immoral or frivolous. Astronomy was useful to the Roman military because it helped armies locate themselves in war. Arithmetic helped in business, and geometry aided the surveyor and architect, two important professions in Rome. Rome also adopted Greek as its cultured language, and the educated citizenry was bilingual. In fact, Latin had no written literature until after the third century B.C.

Thus, we have the seven subjects that became known to the Romans and their descendants as the liberal arts (*artes liberales*): literature (grammar), rhetoric, logic (philosophy); and less important, astronomy, music, geometry, and arithmetic. Romans called the first three the *trivium* and the other four the *quadrivium*. Physical education was used in so far as it aided hygiene, but most Romans did not care for nude exercise. They preferred elaborate public bathhouses to gymnasiums as their places for recreation.

Bilingual Education

Rome now had all of the necessary ingredients for a Graeco-Roman education. From the second century B.C. on, the Romans had three levels of schooling—all bilingual. The first level was the *ludus* (primary school). As the Republic declined and the Empire rose, more and more aristocratic boys (and some girls) of age seven or so went to a *ludus magister* (primary school master), where they learned the alphabet, then reading and writing together, and finally counting. The ludus was usually in a shop in the town forum. The following is an account taken from a schoolboy's book (200–210 A.D.):

When day breaks I wake up, call the slave, and get him to open the window—which he does at once. I sit up, sit on the edge of the bed, and ask for my shoes and stockings because it is cold. [Otherwise, he would have put on his sandals without bothering about stockings.]

As soon as I have put my shoes on I take a towel—I have been brought a clean one. Water is brought me in a jug so that I can wash. I pour some of it over my hands and face and into my mouth; I rub my teeth and gums; I spit out, blow my nose and wipe it, as any well brought-up child should.

I take off my nightshirt and put on a tunic and girdle; I perfume my head and comb my hair; I put a scarf round my neck; I get into my white cloak. I leave my room with my pedagogue [*paedagogus* in Latin] and nurse and go and say good morning to my father and mother. I say good morning to them both and kiss them.

I go and find my inkstand and exercise book and give them to the slave. Then everything is ready, and, followed by my pedagogue, I set off through the portico that leads to the school.

[He may buy a pastry and eat it on the way.]

My schoolfellows come and meet me; I say hello to them and they say hello back. I come to the staircase. I go up the stairs quietly, as I should. In the hall I take off my cloak, run through my hair with my comb, and go in, saying, "Good morning, master." The master embraces me and returns my greeting. The slave hands me my writing-boards, my ink-stand and my ruler.

"Good morning, everybody. Let me have my place [seat, stool]. Squeeze up a bit." "Come here." "This is my place!" "I got it first!" I sit down and get to work.

I have finished my lesson. I ask the master to let me go home for lunch; he lets me go; I say goodbye to him, and he returns my farewell. I go home and change. I have white bread, olives, cheese, dry figs and nuts; I drink some fresh water. Having finished my lunch, I go off to school again. I find the master reading; he says to us, "Now to work again!"

I do my copying. When I have finished, I show it to the master, who corrects it and copies it out properly. . . . "I can't copy: copy it out for me, you can do it so well." I rub it out; the wax is hard, it should be soft.

"Do the up-strokes and the down-strokes properly! Put a drop of water in your ink! You see, it is all right now." "Let me see your pen, your knife for sharpening the reed pen." "Let me see it! How have you done it? It's not bad. . . . " Or he may easily say: "You deserve to be whipped! All right, I'll let you off this time. . . . "

I must go and have a bath. Yes, it's time. I go off; I get myself some towels and I follow my servant. I run and catch up with the others who are going to the baths and I say to them one and all, "How are you? Have a good bath! Have a good supper!"[4]

As the excerpt shows, the family slave accompanied the boy to the ludus; if the boy was lucky, he could learn Greek from his paedagogus. If the boy missed a lesson or gave a wrong answer, the master flogged his hand with a cane, and whipping as an incentive to learn was the norm. "The youth has a back and attends when he is beaten," said an ancient Egyptian proverb. "The ears of the young are placed on the back." This was the dominant attitude throughout most of the world until rather recently.

Around the age of twelve, the boy went on to a school of the *grammaticus* (grammar teacher). Here he learned Latin grammar, first from Andronicus's translation of Homer and later from the Latin poetry of Virgil: *The Aeneid, King Midas, Pyramus and Thisbe* (from which Shakespeare later borrowed the story of Romeo and Juliet); and he would read from the works of Horace and Ovid. He also studied the Greek classics, learning Greek here if he had not already done so in the ludus or from his slave.

Some people, particularly the wealthy, did not send their children to either the ludus or the grammar school. The cost of attending the ludus was low—the equivalent of half a bushel of wheat per month. This meant that the ludus magister did not have a high status; also most masters wanted as many boys as they could get so their incomes would improve. Grammar masters charged about four times the ludus rate. Those who could afford it often preferred to employ tutors rather than send their children to a public school. This distinction between public and private education—that is, group schooling versus individual tutorial instruction—remained intact in the United States until the mid-nineteenth century.

At age sixteen, boys from the most aristocratic families traditionally spent a year in the company of a distinguished man—in some cases their own fathers—learning the duties, manners, and attitudes of senators. This apprenticeship for public life was called *tirocinium fori*.[5]

The final level of education was that of the *rhetor,* who taught the skills of oratory. Only those boys destined for public prominence went to him, for his instruction normally led to law and the bar (pleading, oratory). Such was the life of Marcus Tullius Cicero.

Cicero (106–43 B.C.)

The Roman historian Plutarch tells us a legend that Cicero, the orator's last name, meant "twisted vine" (*cicer*) and stood for an ugly wart on an ancestor's nose. What is probably closer to the truth is that Cicero's ancestors raised the common crop of chick-peas—also *cicer.* Cicero says in his *Laws* that he came from a modest villa in the mountain town of Arpinum between Rome and Naples.

Traditional Education

Cicero's father was probably from the *equites* class and rich enough to afford a Greek poet as his son's tutor. In any case, we know that Marcus learned both Greek and Latin. At the age of sixteen, he prepared for *tirocinium fori* under Q. Mucius Scaevola, one of the noted lawyers of the time. Marcus went everywhere with him and extended his tirocinium beyond the traditional year to study law. He seems to have feigned a weak constitution, thus avoiding his military duties.

Scaevola died about 88 B.C., and Cicero began practicing law. In the first case to bring him fame, he successfully pleaded against a client of the most powerful man in the Senate, the dictator Sulla. Feeling the need to learn more, and perhaps fearing Sulla's revenge as well, Cicero traveled to Greece (80–76 B.C.) to study philosophy and rhetoric. From Athens he went to Rhodes, where there was a famous lecturer on rhetoric, Apollonius, and another on philosophy, Poseidonius. At Rhodes he perfected the flowery, eloquent style of oratory for which he became famous.

Political Career

The year 72 B.C. found Cicero back in Rome and married to Terentia. Her handsome dowry gave him the finances necessary to enter politics. By 70 B.C. he was accepting another politically explosive case as pleader for the Sicilian town of Syracuse, which had charged a wealthy senator named Verres with bribery, extortion, and unjust tax assessments. Again Cicero won, and Verres fled into exile. This victory, and the courage he showed, won enough support for him to run successfully for *consul* (chief magistrate—two were elected each year) of the Senate. He won the election in 63 B.C., when the Republic was waning and Rome was in its seventieth year of civil war.

The prime cause for this turmoil was the aristocracy's exploitation of the plebes. Members of this class had been unhappy since before the writing of the Twelve Tables in 450 B.C., and they were now angry enough to attempt to overthrow the Republic. The *populares* (plebeian) cause was the liberal one in that it called for more equal distribution of conquered lands and more rights for the peasants. The conservative *optimates* (patricians and conscripti) clung desperately to the Republican Senate by giving dictatorial powers to strong consuls (for example, Sulla had a ten-year term).

No doubt Cicero's courage appealed to the conservatives when they elected him consul. The discontent and resentment against him and the optimates were deep-seated enough, however, for him to lose the following year. Cicero thought he had done a remarkable job, saying: "My own applause has the greatest weight with me." His written works reveal his preoccupation with wealth, his incredible vanity, and his claims of modesty: "If ever a man was stranger to vainglory it is myself."[6]

On the other hand, we see the pride Cicero had in his children through the care he took to provide exceptional tutors for his two sons and in the mania that swept him when his beloved daughter Tullia died. His patience with the chronically ill and grouchy Terentia wore out in his final years. He divorced her for a younger woman named Publilia, but this marriage lasted only a few weeks.[7]

Educational Ideas

Cicero wrote his most important educational treatise, *On Oratory (de Oratore),* around 55 B.C., after his return from a two-year exile imposed while the populares were in power. In this dialogue he appealed to younger generations to aim at a broader education than just the narrow pursuit of rhetoric so common in his day. Thus, he was advising that students get what we would call higher education, and not only the familial *educatio.* (He advised parents to teach Latin thoroughly before embarking on Greek.)[8] In the schools of rhetoric and philosophy, Cicero said, a Roman citizen should receive a broader instruction, one that would produce wisdom, patriotism, courage, Aristotelian temperance, moral goodness, and oratorical eloquence. Studies should include law and rhetoric, philosophy, psychology, politics, ethics, military and naval science, medicine, geography, astronomy, and history. With regard to the latter Cicero wrote: "To be ignorant of what happened before you were born, is to live the life of a child forever."[9] Hence, the orator was to Cicero what the philosopher-king was to Plato. The Romans, however, did not heed Cicero's advice, and education remained largely oratorical.

Last Days

By 44 B.C. Cicero's political and personal lives were coming to a tragic end. On the Ides of March, assassins stabbed to death the newly appointed dictator, aristocrat-turned-populist Julius Caesar. He was a victim of a well-organized plot which included his friend and probably illegitimate son Brutus. Caesar's friends suspected Cicero of participating in the plot (though he was later vindicated), and offered a reward for his assassination.

Cicero's servants persuaded him to leave one of his villas for a safer place. Before his litter was out of the garden, however, soldiers overtook him. According to Plutarch, Cicero "commanded his servants to let down the litter; and stroking his chin, as he used to do, with his left hand, he looked steadfastly upon his murderers, his person covered with dust, his beard and hair untrimmed, and his face worn with his troubles." Most bystanders looked away as he calmly exposed his neck to his decapitators.

His head and his right (writing) hand were displayed in the Forum, where his eloquent voice had so often been heard.[10] Story has it that the wife of one of his enemies disliked him so much that upon passing the rostra where his head was hung, she vehemently stuck his inanimate tongue with her hatpin.[11]

Quintilian (A.D. 35–95)

Cicero's influence on education lived long after his death. From the thirteenth to the sixteenth centuries, it was the basis for the Renaissance ideal of education. Any study of the humanities (study of what is "human") owes its existence in some measure to Cicero.

However, it did not take Rome twelve hundred years to rediscover Cicero. A century after his death, a Spanish-born Roman named Marcus Fabius Quintilianus was already popularizing Ciceronian scholarship. We know little of Quintilian's early life. He was born in Calagurris in northern Spain to the son of a *rhetor* called to Rome. It was in Rome that Quintilian received his education under some of the city's best grammarians and rhetors.

By this time, Rome had settled into dictatorial rule, but not easily. Octavius Augustus Caesar, Julius Caesar's nephew, had restored harmony to the wartorn populace. In A.D. 14 he was succeeded by his weak stepson Tiberius (14–37). Quintilian probably witnessed the despotic rule of Caligula (37–41) and the weak reign of Claudius (41–54). Toward the end of Claudius's rule, Quintilian returned to Spain as a rhetoric teacher and advocate. He became a client of the Spanish governor Galba, and upon the death of the infamous Nero (54–68), the Senate called the governor back to Rome to reign. By then Galba was old and stingy, and so many factions resented him that the soldiers beheaded, "be-armed," and "be-lipped" him a few months later.

Galba likely called Quintilian to Rome to teach. It was not, however, until Vespasian ascended to the throne (69–79) that Quintilian was imperially financed in his profession. Vespasian reduced tax burdens for teachers and endowed the first chair (professorship) in rhetoric in the

Empire. It was to this first salaried chair of rhetoric that Quintilian came. In the next ten years, others were financed by the Empire, but the Roman or upper chair was the first.

Sometime during the rule of Domitian (81–96), and probably around 88, Quintilian left the chair to become tutor to Domitian's two grandsons. He also started writing his famous *Instituto Oratoria (Institutes of Oratory)* as a prescription for his own sons. Then tragedy struck. Both of his sons and his wife died, leaving him to outlive all of the people who meant the most to him.

Educational Theory

The *Institutes of Oratory* is in the tradition of Cicero's *On Oratory,* for which Quintilian had great respect. Like his predecessor, Quintilian believed in a well-rounded study centered on oratory. Good literature took the place of Cicero's history as the medium from which to embark. Unlike Cicero, Quintilian felt that children should learn Greek early. They would learn Latin in any case, but they needed special instruction for Greek.

Quintilian's description of the ideal teacher was both sensible and modern-sounding:

> Let him therefore adopt a parental attitude to his pupils, and regard himself as the representative of those who have committed their children to his charge. Let him be free from vice himself and refuse to tolerate it in others. Let him be strict but not austere, genial but not too familiar; for austerity will make him unpopular, while familiarity breeds contempt. Let his discourse continually turn on what is good and honorable; the more he admonishes, the less he will have to punish. He must control his temper without however shutting his eyes to faults requiring correction: his instruction must be free from affectation, his industry great, his demands on his class continuous, but not extravagant. He must be ready to answer questions and to put them unasked to those who sit silent. In praising the recitations of his pupils he must be neither grudging nor overgenerous: the former quality will give them a distaste for work, while the latter will produce a complacent self-satisfaction. In correcting faults he must avoid sarcasm and above all abuse: for teachers whose rebukes seem to imply positive dislike discourage industry.[12]

For Quintilian, the student must become a good person through his studies—excellent in knowledge, speech, and character. And talent was essential, for without natural gifts, technical rules were useless.

Quintilian was ahead of his time regarding childhood education. He warned that children must not learn to hate those studies that they are too young to love, so he felt teachers should use rewards along with amusement and play. Flogging "is a disgraceful form of punishment fit only for slaves," he said, and should be abolished. It leads to fear which restrains some and unmans others. There is no substitute, admonished the orator, for "knowing" the child and understanding his uniqueness. All children, moreover, deserve equal attention, and class sizes should be small enough to allow for this. Finally, Quintilian thought that schools were better than tutors because they promoted competition, a natural part of society.[13]

Quintilian died (c. 96) during the reign of Trajan, a period of relative tranquillity in Roman society. In stressing humane practices, individuality, and play, he was advocating practices that would take sixteen hundred years for Western society to accept. His concept of the proper *content* of education was influential in the Middle Ages and in the Renaissance. Cassiodorus (discussed later in this chapter), da Feltre, and Erasmus (both in Chapter 4) all read him with approval.

Changing Conditions

By the time Quintilian died, the succession to the emperor's throne was a major problem for the Empire. The Praetorian Guard, a special army unit created by Octavius, was dictating who would be emperor. Originally intended as a bodyguard for the emperor, before long there were nine "cohorts" of these guards, with 600 men in each. From being the protectors of the emperors, the Guard became their powerful masters. Candidates for the emperor's chair had to give a sizable bribe to each of the 5,400 guards before they could be selected. The office almost always went to the highest bidder who, in turn, levied enough taxes to get back the money spent in being elected.

If the Praetorians became dissatisfied with an emperor's performance, they usually assassinated him, giving rise to a new round of bribes. Needless to say, this was not a particularly effective way of getting competent executives. This and other problems led to a gradual decline in the government's vitality, helping the Empire along toward its ultimate fall. As the Empire started to come apart, another force was emerging that would eventually replace the authority of the Roman legions. This was Christianity, a movement that began only a few years after the Empire did.

The empire's problems and the emergence of Christianity were evident during the reign of Nero, born in 37. Nero's mother, Agrippina, put him on the throne when he was seventeen by feeding poison mushrooms to Claudius, her third husband and Nero's adopted father. Mother and son gave a generous donation to the Praetorians and ruled together for a time. However, when Agrippina opposed Nero's wishes to divorce his wife Octavia to marry someone else, Nero, who had learned his mother's tactics well, had guards kill his mother. He was twenty-two at the time. His second wife, Poppaea, convinced him to have Octavia killed. Three years later, Poppaea died in an advanced stage of pregnancy. According to stories, Nero kicked her in the stomach when she scolded him for coming home late from the races. Nero then saw a young boy who looked like Poppaea, had him castrated, and married him in a public ceremony. Nero "used him in every way like a woman." Someone remarked that it was too bad Nero's father hadn't had the same kind of wife.[14]

THE CHRISTIAN TRANSFORMATION

In the summer of 64, a fire burned for nine days and destroyed two-thirds of Rome, killing thousands and leaving hundreds of thousands homeless. Nero had wanted to rebuild Rome and rename it Neropolis, and so rumor spread that he had caused the fire to be set. There was never any proof of this, but to take the heat off himself, Nero decided to blame the Christians, a group that most Romans disapproved of but tolerated. Tacitus, who disliked the Christians, put it this way:

To scotch the rumor, Nero substituted as culprits, and punished with the utmost refinements of cruelty, a class of men . . . whom the crowd styled Christians. . . . First, then, the confessed members of the sect were arrested; next, on their disclosures, vast numbers were convicted, not so much on the count of arson as for hatred of the human race. And derision accompanied their end: they were covered with wild beasts' skins and torn to death by dogs; or they were fastened on crosses and when daylight failed were burned to serve as lamps by night.[15]

Four years later, the Praetorian Guard forced Nero to kill himself. This was not the end of persecution for the Christians, however. Savage treatment had at first slowed the spread of the new faith, but soon, as Tacitus noted, people began to pity the Christians. And more than pity, the striking faith of some condemned Christians gave the public the impression that there must be something to beliefs for which some died so readily. Around 108, the bishop of Antioch, a man named Ignatus, was on his way to Rome to be executed because he would not give up the faith. He wrote letters to friends begging them not to interfere:

I am dying willingly for God's sake. . . . Entice the wild beasts that they may become my tomb, and leave no trace of my body, that when I fall asleep I be not burdensome to any. . . . I long for the beasts that are prepared for me. . . . Let there come upon me fire, and cross, and struggles with wild beasts, cutting, and tearing asunder, rackings of bones, mangling of limbs, crushing of my whole body, cruel tortures of the devil, may I but attain to Jesus Christ.[16]

The example of martyred Christians gave a rigorous, almost revolutionary, stamina to the movement. A century after Ignatus, a young man named Origen (Origenes Adamantius) saw his father beheaded for being a

Christian. He became so ascetic that he finally castrated himself to improve his faith. His extensive writings became quite influential in the movement. By 300 Rome contained an estimated 100,000 Christians, and the movement was spreading rapidly in other parts of the Empire. In 313 Emperor Constantine legalized Christianity and began to promote the religion. (He waited until he was dying to accept baptism.) In 330 he moved the seat of the empire to Constantinople (modern Istanbul, Turkey), which accelerated the decay of political power in Rome. This made the office of bishop of Rome increasingly important. It would be several generations before the Christian church became supreme, but the process was well underway.

Aristocratic families began abandoning the old Roman religion for the new one. Families that had once contested for the emperorship now vied for the bishop's *cathedra* (see) in Rome. By 400 there were magnificent churches. One surprised visitor discovered that the bishop of Rome lived like a prince and acted as if he were an emperor. An increasingly elegant Christian society emerged, featuring aristocratic prelates to whom power and influence flowed as wealthy followers turned to them for guidance.

Roman jurisdiction broke down in the fifth century in almost every area of the western Empire. The office of bishop became the chief administrative, judicial, and even military unit. The same education and training that had prepared one for the office of *prefect* (governor) was a useful background for bishops. The church gradually assimilated Roman educational provisions. As the Empire's military and governmental effectiveness faded in the West, the Roman church took on the job of passing on the language, legal code, educational approach, and organizational structures.

At the heart of the new religion was a potential increase in consciousness, for it stressed not merely legal rituals and proper overt conduct, but also correct thinking and self-analysis. What one *thought* was as important as what one *did*. To achieve salvation a person had to try to be free of both sinful thoughts and base actions, and the approach to perfection called for a rigorous program of self-awareness and control. Perhaps all would fall short, many would give up, but the thread would remain part of the tradition. The Christians did not invent the ideal of perfection, but they combined it with a powerful faith and added the notion that anyone—free or slave, poor or rich, woman or man—could achieve it.

A short time after Constantine declared Christianity the favored religion, serious disunity in the faith became apparent. By the end of the fourth century, eighty different groups claimed to have the one true way. The Roman members of the church exerted particular authority because of the city's prominence. Increasingly, important government officials were becoming Christians; churches grew in size and wealth. At the same time, differences of interpretation—reflecting in many cases competition for leadership—came forcefully into view.

In the early days of the Christian movement, the chief emphasis had been on accepting the teachings attributed to Jesus and on the second coming of Christ. Many converts expected the return of the Messiah in a matter of days, weeks, or at most a few years. When this momentous event failed to occur, believers projected it into the indefinite future. Thus, the immediate problems of organizing, governing, and explaining the new faith became more important.

Many groups claimed to have the only true way. Their differences were not merely abstract. Advocates of conflicting persuasions not only argued with each other, but sometimes resorted to violence to try to get their candidates named to significant offices. Moreover, people from various provinces of the Empire tended to espouse their own regions' interpretations; thus, nationalistic (anti-Roman) sentiments were part of the disputes. By 300 it was not unusual to find Christian factions agreeing more with some non-Christian groups than they did with each other. This situation is illustrated in the remarkable careers of Hypatia of Alexandria and Augustine of Hippo.

Hypatia (c. 360–415)

Hypatia was a well-educated woman, although this was not unusual. Many Roman women were cultured and educated, and quite a few were politically powerful. Unlike respectable Greek women, they did not expect to stay out of public view. Women were not completely accepted in public life, for Roman society was by no means free of a sexual double standard. Hypatia was unique in holding a public chair of philosophy in Alexandria, one of the prominent cities of the empire. So far as our incomplete records show, she was the only woman to have such a post.

Family and Education

We do not know exactly when or where Hypatia was born or anything about her mother. Her father was Theon, the last recorded director of the Museum at Alexandria. The city, founded by Aristotle's pupil Alexander the Great, was nearly seven hundred years old by Hypatia's time. It was one of the leading cities of the empire, with an estimated population of 800,000. It was famous for astronomy, having been the home of Ptolemy, and for medicine, as Galen had practiced there. The Museum was known all over the Roman world as a center of study.

We have no description of Hypatia's education, but because of her father's position she had access to lectures from the leading mathematicians, astronomers, and philosophers of her day. The most influential philosopher in Alexandria during the preceding century was a Greek-educated Egyptian named Plotinus, who lived like a Christian saint, ate no meat, avoided all sexual relations (he did not condemn sex for others), and taught a version of Platonic idealism. He was a friendly contemporary of the Christian ascetic Origen.

Hypatia's Work and Views

Hypatia knew the work of Plato, Aristotle, Plotinus, Origen, and others, and she was part of the Neoplatonic movement. She coauthored with Theon a commentary on Ptolemy's *Syntaxius,* an influential book that rejected Aristarchus's theory that the earth revolves around the sun.[17] Hypatia wrote other works on astronomy and mathematics, but none have survived.

As holder of the chair of philosophy at the Museum, Hypatia "profited so much in profound learning that she excelled all philosophers of that time," according to a Christian historian named Socrates. She lectured on Plato, Plotinus, and "the precepts and doctrines of all sorts of philosophers" to "as many as came to hear her." She also took pleasure in explaining difficult philosophical points to interested listeners anywhere she found them, including in the streets of Alexandria. People "flocked unto her lessons from every country." They credited her with "courage of mind." She "present[ed] herself before princes and magistrates. Neither was she abashed to come into the open face of the assembly." All men, added Socrates, admired her and held her in reverence "for the singular modesty of her mind."[18]

Perhaps Socrates overstated the case. Not *all* men liked Hypatia, although many did regard her highly. Some of her pupils fell in love with her. In true Platonic form, however, she reminded them that they were only in love with a physical appearance and not the true essence or soul. There is no record that she married. Probably she agreed with Plotinus in thinking that marriage would hinder her quest for philosophic perfection, a preoccupation of the Neo-Platonists. She did maintain friendships and correspondence with both Christian and non-Christian colleagues.

Caught between Factions

One of Hypatia's friends was Orestes, prefect of Alexandria. Orestes was not a Christian, and he did not approve of efforts by Cyril, bishop of the Christian church there, to run all Jews, a large minority in the city, out of Alexandria. Angered that Orestes would not support this action, some monks stoned him. When Orestes recovered he had the leader of this group arrested and executed.

Some of the Christians circulated the rumor that Hypatia was to blame—it was she, they claimed, who stopped Orestes from coming over to their side. One day in March 415 a group of frenzied monks, under the lead of one of Bishop Cyril's minor staff members, followed Hypatia. They stopped her carriage, dragged her into a nearby church, ripped off her clothes, and "rent the flesh of her body with sharp shells until the breath departed out of her body."[19] Then they ripped her body apart and burned the remains. Cyril was powerful enough to stop Orestes from having them punished for the act, illustrating the emerging power of the bishops in major cities as imperial power declined. It also illustrates the extent to which some clerics were willing to use the "ways of the world"—assassination, intrigue, power politics—to get what they wanted.

Augustine (354–430)

Like Hypatia, Augustine was an African. He was born at about the same time as Hypatia, and lived through the same turbulent conditions. He and Hypatia never knew each other, and their lives took different courses. Whereas Hypatia was killed by Christians in their struggle for power, Augustine became a major force for the Roman Church in its battle to subdue not only nonbelievers but also competing factions within the Christian community.

Education for Mobility

Augustine was born on the outskirts of the Roman Empire in Thagaste, Africa (now Souk Ahras, Algeria). His father, Patricius, was a citizen who had some education but little money. Augustine's parents understood, as did many other African families in similar circumstances, how valuable an education could be, for without good schooling the African citizen would have to stay in his small town and scrape out a meager living. If he could secure a rhetorical education, however, much was possible: money, perhaps a lucky marriage into more money and influence, and possibly a climb through the civil service into respectability.

Patricius and Monica struggled to educate their son. Patricius worked hard to pay his son's tuition. Augustine had to come home from school for one year because there was not enough money. Finally, a wealthy landowner became Augustine's patron and paid for his education.[20]

At first, school was not pleasant for Augustine. Like other children, he liked to play, but he had to spend his time memorizing spelling, grammar, vocabulary, and arithmetic. Augustine hated Greek and arithmetic and did not learn them well. Since the standard remedy for any school failure, despite Quintilian's admonitions, was a good beating, Augustine got his share of these. (He would later remark on the injustice of adults beating children for playing while the adults defined their own playing as "business.") He developed an excellent memory and a love for Latin literature.[21]

Augustine started rhetorical education at Madaura, a larger town some miles away, but a money shortage again brought him home. At seventeen, he was off to Carthage to further his education. It was an exciting time. He discovered the theater, liking especially sad love stories that made him cry, and entered fully into the social aspects of student life.

Augustine particularly enjoyed the pleasures of female company, which his mother Monica had so often warned him against. However, his fling did not last long. Patricius died about a year after Augustine got to Carthage. Monica, who had put up with some indiscretions from her husband, seems not to have grieved over his death. She redoubled her efforts to get her son to follow Christian teachings and to do well socially.

Under his mother's pressure, Augustine gave up his playboy ways, took a concubine, and began to settle down. Taking a mistress was a form of second-class marriage, tacitly sanctioned when the woman was from a lower social background than the man. Augustine said later that he loved his spouse, but he never mentioned her by name in any of his writings. A son named Adeodatus resulted from this respectable arrangement. Augustine did not welcome the new responsibility at the time, but later he decided that having a child was a good thing and that he loved his son.

At nineteen, still in Carthage, Augustine underwent what he described as a profound religious conversion. He was already a Christian of sorts, having grown up under Monica's influence and having been baptized as a boy, consenting during an illness. This second conversion, however, was something different. It happened when Augustine read Cicero's *The Hortensius,* which said that the highest good was to seek wisdom. Augustine found himself "with an unbelievable fire in my heart, desiring the deathless qualities of Wisdom," and thought this was the way to approach God. He turned to the Bible to find wisdom, but came away with many questions; for example, how to account for injustice, death, cruelty, and sin if God was all knowing and all powerful? Why does a believer pray earnestly to God for help in doing right, and then do wrong anyway?

The Wisdom of Mani

Augustine found his answers in the teachings of a brotherhood of missionaries who called themselves Manichees or Manichaeans, followers of a third-century mystic named Mani. They had elaborate secret rituals and prayers and gorgeous parchment scrolls of Mani's teachings. An "elect" group of men and women pale with fasting taught a dual nature of reality, one of God and one of the devil. God was not all powerful—part of the time He prevails, part of the time the devil does. Humans have both natures: if someone intends well but sins anyhow, the devil has momentarily gotten the better of God, and it is not really the person's fault. This comforting philosophy had an obvious appeal; however, the Roman church bishops in Africa regarded its adherents as dangerous subversives.

Shortly after his conversion to Manichaeanism, Augustine moved back to his hometown to teach grammar and literature. Monica was appalled to learn that her twenty-one-year-old son was a Manichaean and locked him out of her house. Despite this, Augustine soon converted many others to his point of view. However, when a close friend died within a year of his return, Augustine, tired of his mother's nagging, his pupils' rusticity, and his town's isolation, left again for Carthage to continue teaching there.

Continuing the Search

For the next few years, Augustine lived in Carthage. Although he had some difficulties with his wealthy pupils, he did make money and made friends in the governing group. He could see himself becoming a landed gentleman, yet he was not happy. He had tired of Mani's theories but had not overtly rejected them, and Monica was pressing him to return to Thagaste. Some of his associates encouraged him to go to Rome, where they promised introductions to influential people. In 382 he decided to try his luck there.

When Monica heard of his plan, she put strong pressure on him to return to Thagaste or to take her to Rome with him. He didn't like either choice and lied to her in order to slip away. As the wind caught the sail of his ship, he could see Monica, who had figured out his deception, standing on the shore weeping bitterly. When in Rome Augustine fell dangerously ill, and he associated the illness with guilt over leaving his mother behind.

The year Augustine spent in Rome was not especially comfortable, but it was profitable. He met important people and gained appointment to the Chair of Rhetoric in Milan, an imperial resort town. Emperors spent so much time there that Milan had become a second capital, so this was an important post. Monica soon showed up to join him.

The Milan experience was a turning point. Milan's bishop, Ambrose, was already celebrated as a courageous and eloquent figure in the emerging Church. Monica pursued Ambrose, promoting her son to him. She also arranged a marriage for Augustine into a socially superior family, but before the family would agree to the betrothal, Augustine had to rid himself of his common law wife of fifteen years. Although Augustine hesitated, she was soon on her way to an African monastery; Adeodatus stayed with him. The projected marriage had a two-year delay—presumably because the future bride was too young. While waiting, Augustine took up with another woman.[22]

The wedding never happened; whether Augustine or his prospective in-laws called it off is not clear. Instead, Augustine, who had been toying with the idea of a public conversion to the Roman Church under Ambrose, saw a vision and had another profound conversion experience. Ambrose baptized him, and Augustine gave up his pursuit of wealth and fame.

From Rhetorician to Bishop

Not long after Augustine's conversion, Monica died. Augustine decided to return to Africa. By 388 he was back in Thagaste, after side trips to Rome and Carthage. Soon after, both his best friend and his son died. Two years later, Augustine traveled to Hippo on the coast not far from Thagaste and established a monastery there. The local bishop, recognizing a good opportunity, engineered Augustine's election by the congregation as his assistant and likely successor in 395–396. He soon succeeded to the bishop's seat.

Augustine proved as good as his Hippo sponsor hoped he'd be. He was a powerful speaker and writer, and his classical education stood him in good stead in the battle of the Roman Church against competing groups. He publicly debated the most reputable Manichaean advocate and defeated him so soundly the man would not show his face in town again. He tried to do the same with the Donatist group, but they would not take the bait. (The Donatists were a rival Christian sect that did not recognize the Roman bishops. They had their own bishops, and sometimes fought battles with the Roman Christians.)

Augustine spent the rest of his life as bishop of Hippo. He settled disputes and tended to the many religious, legal, personal, and community needs of his district. By the time he died in 430, the Roman Church had defeated its rivals in Africa; however, the Empire had virtually come to an end.

In 429–430 invading tribes called Vandals (hence, our term "vandalism") laid siege to North Africa. Some of the bishops resisted and were killed. Most of the people accommodated the invaders. Augustine lived long enough to watch Roman society collapse in his part of the world. In the summer of 430, he took a fever and died.

Augustine remained a powerful influence because his many writings survived. He became one of the "fathers" of the Western (Roman) Church. His autobiographical *Confessions* are a major source on education, culture, and life in his time. They served as a model for some later people, among them Guibert of Nogent and Peter Abelard (Chapter 3).

The world of Augustine was one of changing conditions. First one and then another non-Latinized group conquered territory that had been part of the Empire. In the fifth century, England fell to the Angles, Saxons, and Jutes, Spain and North Africa fell to the Vandals, and Gaul was taken by the Franks. At the time, most people with a classical education viewed the breakup of Roman political authority as a calamity for civilization. Many Christians, like Augustine, had their faith rooted so strongly in a Roman context that they could hardly imagine any other possibility. For people like Augustine, Christianity outside of Roman civilization did not seem possible.

In the turbulent period following Augustine's death, Roman aristocrats struggled to retain the cultured features of civilization as they had known it. This was not easy. In 455, the Vandals brutally sacked Rome, and in 476 Odoacer became the first non-Roman to occupy the imperial throne of the Western Empire. Much later a historian named Gibbon would cite this as the "fall" of the empire. Aqueducts and other public facilities could no longer be maintained, and diseases and plagues hit the population of Rome, reducing it from more than a million to fewer than 250,000.

THE MEDIEVAL TRANSITION

Metaphor and analogy are essentials of language, but sometimes wrong impressions result. Historians began using the term *medieval* (middle) to describe the period from about 500 to 1200 because they thought of it as an interlude between the "brilliant" cultures of Greece and Rome and the "rebirth" or renaissance of interest in them during the thirteenth to sixteenth centuries. The negative connotations of images such as "dark ages," "a cloud of ignorance descending on Europe;" and "the lamp of learning growing dim" have left the impression that nothing of educational importance occurred during these "Middle Ages."[23]

This mistaken notion is reinforced by the seeming remoteness of medieval life from our own, and by the episodic violence and what seems from our perspective widespread superstition that was common to the time. The intensely religious orientation of so many people, in contrast to the secularism of today, makes our medieval predecessors seem more different from us than they actually were. Medieval people did not invent superstition, violence, or supernatural explanations for everyday events; they inherited them. "Jesus was born into a world pervaded by the supernatural," writes Roland Bainton. "Belief in demons, exorcism, and magic was virtually universal."[24]

Guilt, fear, shame, and threats of damnation were significant controlling elements in medieval society. Some religious leaders stressed the terrors of hell because they thought nothing could move people like "the terrific." The medieval period witnessed a fusion of Christian values with many Greek and Roman educational and cultural practices. From this long evolution came much of the educational structure of the contemporary world. Guilt, fear, shame, and superstition are not unknown in contemporary society.

MAINTAINING ROMAN TRADITIONS

Despite political and economic changes, some Roman families were able to maintain life pretty much as usual, including educating their children in classical Greek and Roman traditions. To do this, they made whatever kind of peace with the new ruling groups they thought manageable. Sometimes they were successful; sometimes not. The transition shows plainly in the lives and careers of the sons of two wealthy families: Boethius and Cassiodorus. Both boys had classical educations, both rose to high rank under the Gothic (German) emperor Theodoric, and both influenced education and thought for a thousand years. Their ends were quite different, though.

Boethius (c. 480–c. 524)

Anicius Manlius Severinus Boethius was born into an aristocratic Roman family about 480. Boethius's father was a high government official who provided his son with a solid liberal arts education before sending him to Athens for years of further study. This experience gave the young Roman a love of the classics, and he translated a number of Greek texts into Latin. As a member of a family that was "one of the richest and most illustrious in the Empire and long distinguished by public service," Boethius entered political life at age thirty. He said that he left his study for public office only because of Plato's belief that philosophers should be leaders. He would find need for the comforts of philosophy before he was finished with politics.[25]

For thirteen years, Boethius was one of Theodoric's trusted officials, rising to the position of master of offices (roughly equivalent to prime minister) and becoming noted for his generosity and eloquence. There was a gulf between the Goths and the Romans, however, which the latter's feelings of superiority did little to narrow. The Goths were Christians, but they were also Aryans (they denied the Trinity). Roman Christians believed in the Trinity, and Boethius had defended this interpretation.

Then, in 523, Justin, emperor of the Eastern Empire, issued an edict against Aryanism. Theodoric suspected that his Roman officials were waiting for an opportunity to depose him and that Justin's new law would be their excuse. Boethius and one other official were charged with treason. Though we can't be sure now, the charges were likely false.

Theodoric may have doubted Boethius's guilt, and he kept Boethius in prison for a year before having him executed. During that time, Boethius wrote his most famous book, *On the Consolation of Philosophy*. The only true happiness lies in union with God, he wrote. Theodoric soon dispatched Boethius to join his creator. "A cord was twisted around his forehead until his eyeballs sprang from their sockets, and then, in the midst of his torture, he was clubbed to death."[26]

Cassiodorus (c. 483–c. 575)

Cassiodorus fared better—either he was luckier than Boethius or more careful not to offend the king—or perhaps a little of both. Flavius Magnus Aurelius Cassiodorus was from Calabria. He too came from a wealthy family and received an excellent classical education. He served Theodoric as Boethius had done, but without being suspected in the alleged conspiracy. His *History of the Goths,* which aimed to show skeptical Romans that the invaders also had noble ancestors and a record of great deeds, may have helped his cause.

When Theodoric lost power, Cassiodorus retired to his family estate in Calabria. There he founded a monastery whose monks specialized in copying religious and secular texts. Cassiodorus set aside a special room called a *scriptorium* for this purpose. He supervised translations and copy work, setting a high standard for both.

Although Cassiodorus did not become a monk himself, he influenced the scholarly part of monastic development. He agreed with Boethius that the seven liberal arts (grammar, rhetoric, logic [dialectic], arithmetic, music, geometry, and astronomy) were the elements of a good education whether one intended a secular or religious vocation. He died on his estate at the age of ninety-two. As a cultured Roman Christian, he epitomized for many the best of both worlds.[27]

Influence of Boethius and Cassiodorus

Of the two, Boethius perhaps had a more specific impact on the history of thought. His translation of Aristotle's *Organon* (logical treatises) and Porphyry's *Introduction to the Categories of Aristotle* were the leading logic texts for the next seven centuries. These kept alive the ideas that would become the basis for the dispute over "universals" and "particulars"—or realism and nominalism—that would flower in Paris and elsewhere. (See Chapter 3.) His writings on the syllogism inspired several centuries of scholarly struggle for greater rationality and more logical expression of thought. His writing made the field of philosophy more systematic than it might otherwise have been in his time, and his books on theology and music were read for centuries.

Both Cassiodorus and Boethius typified the kind of liberal education that Aristotle had advocated and that Roman wealth had made possible. Pursued as an ideal for a thousand years before they lived, it would remain the ultimate standard for many centuries after their time. It was most accessible to aristocrats, because it required leisure. As Augustine's life had shown, a "liberal" education was useful in both church and state, and could transport anyone lucky enough to get one into aristocratic company. Although the Roman Empire was dead, Greek and Roman cultural ideas flourished in Christian schools fastened securely on Roman underpinnings.

SUMMARY

The Romans shaped conversation about education in several ways that are still relevant. Quintilian's insights about the value of play, the use of tangible rewards for achievement, the damaging results of flogging, and the need for sensitive teachers would be "rediscovered" many times before they became standard beliefs among educators. The word *education* comes from the Latin *educatio,* which implies far more than mere instruction. It refers to a child's growth and development as a human being in a nurturing environment. In our own day, several educational theorists correctly remind us that *education* is a more encompassing label than *schooling,* a Greek conception referring to direct instruction of those whose family standing permitted them the extensive leisure required for specialized study.

Also interesting is that the Romans thought of education as practical. The Romans were less preoccupied than the Greeks with the distinction between liberal and practical studies. Indeed, Augustine's life illustrates how practical a Roman education could be. Oratory itself, whose techniques the Romans studied in Greek schools, was the symbol of Roman education because it was a practical road to leadership.

Another element of much interest to contemporary educators is how the Romans used bilingual education. Although there were differences of opinion about which language should be studied first, there was little disagreement over the value of knowing both Greek and Latin. It made available a broad range of literature in two languages and allowed students to refine their knowledge of their native language (Latin) by comparing its structure to Greek.

Finally, although Roman society was clearly patriarchal, the education of women was apparently more generally advanced among Romans than it had been in Greek society. Coeducation at the elementary level was extensive. Women led more public lives than their Greek sisters, and substantial numbers of Roman women received advanced education. There was no semblance of equality in the society, but the Romans extended substantially the definition of what constituted an appropriate sphere for women.

The legal code which the Romans developed formed the basis for canon (church) law, which in turn furnished the underpinnings of common law in England and the United States. Virtually every aspect of American society today is defined in an ongoing way by the courts. This includes education, about which there have been hundreds of court decisions—and about which there will be many more.

Finally, the emergence of Romanized Christianity shaped the language, structure, function, and content of Western education for many centuries. Even in the United States—characterized as it is by extensive cultural diversity and with an official stance of religious neutrality in state-sponsored schools—many of the roots of today's secular education are to be found in over fifteen hundred years of Christian pedagogical development. Indeed, the Romans changed the meaning of the Greek word for *slave* (*paidagōgos*) so that it came to mean "teacher."

We shall see in the next chapter how Romanized Christianity became the avenue for educational conservation and innovation. The monasteries, cathedrals, and religious infrastructure of Europe supplied for well over a thousand years much of what we call formal education.

NOTES

1. H. I. Marrou, *A History of Education in Antiquity,* trans. George Lamb (New York: Sheed and Ward, 1956), 229.

2. Titus Livius, *The History of Rome,* trans. Canon Roberts, 6 vols. (New York: E. P. Dutton, 1912–1924).

3. Aubrey Gwynn, *Roman Education from Cicero to Quintilian* (New York: Russell and Russell, 1964).

4. Marrou, *A History of Education in Antiquity,* 268–69.

5. Marrou, *A History of Education in Antiquity,* 266–67, 274–75, 284–85. See also Arthur D. Kahn, *The Education of Julius Caesar: A Biography, A Reconstruction* (New York: Shocken Books, 1986), 3–27.

6. Plutarch, *The Lives of the Noble Grecians and Romans,* in *The Great Books of the Western World,* ed. Robert Maynard Hutchins, 53 vols. (Chicago: Encyclopaedia Britannica, 1952), 14: 704; Tranquillus Suetonius, "The Deified Julius," in *Suetonius,* trans. J. C. Rolfe, *Loeb Classical Library* (New York: G. P. Putnam's Sons, 1930), 73.

7. Gwynn, *Roman Education from Cicero to Quintilian,* 80; Elizabeth Rawson, *Cicero; A Portrait* (London: Allen Lane, 1975), 224–25, 228.

8. William Barclay, *Train Up a Child: Educational Ideas in the Ancient World* (Philadelphia: Westminster Press, 1959).

9. Gwynn, *Roman Education from Cicero to Quintilian,* 105.

10. Plutarch, *The Lives of the Noble Grecians and Romans,* 723.

11. Albert E. Warsley, *501 Tidbits of Roman Antiquity* (Elizabeth, New Jersey: Auxilian Latinium, 1953), 476.

12. Marcus Fabius Quintilianus, *The Instituto Oratoria,* trans. H. E. Butler (London: William Heinemann, 1921), bk. 2, ii, 5–7.

13. Timothy Reagan, "The *Instituto Oratoria:* Quintilian's Contribution to Educational Theory and Practice," *Vitae Scholasticae* 2 (Fall 1983): 405–17.

14. Ernest Cary, trans., *Dios Roman History,* in *Loeb Classical Library* (London: William Heinemann, 1925), 8: bk. 62, 27.

15. Tacitus, *The Annals,* trans. John Jackson (London: William Heinemann, [1937] 1962), 4: bk. 15, xliv.

16. Kirsopp Lake, trans., "Ignatus to the Romans," in *The Apostolic Fathers,* (London: William Heinemann, [1912] 1965), 1: iv, v.

17. Arab scholars regarded Ptolemy's work so well that they called it *Almegiste* ("the greatest"). Medieval Europe corrupted this into *Almagest.* The book and its views dominated European astronomy until Copernicus, Galileo, and Newton replaced it.

18. Socrates, *The Ancient Ecclesiastical Histories of the First Six Hundred Years after Christ. . . ,* trans. Meridith Hanmer, 3d ed. (London: Richard Field, 1607), bk. 7, xv. Spelling modernized.

19. Socrates, *The Ancient Ecclesiastical Histories,* xv.

20. Jacques Chabannes, *Saint Augustine,* trans. Julie Kernan (Garden City, New York: Doubleday, 1962); John J. O'Meara, *The Young Augustine: An Intro-*

duction to the Confessions of St. Augustine (London: Longman, [1954] 1980); Warren Thomas Smith, *Augustine: His Life and Thought* (Atlanta: John Knox Press, 1980).

21. John K. Ryan, trans., *The Confessions of St. Augustine* (Garden City, New York: Image Books, 1960), 55. Much biographical material in the sketch is from books 1–6.

22. Roland H. Bainton, *The Horizon History of Christianity* (New York: American Heritage Publishing, 1964), 131.

23. "A new theory of history [which] . . . no longer describe[s] 'the middle ages' by a name which implies a barbaric interlude . . . will enable 'medievalists' to produce a truer picture of their period," says Toby Burrows in "Unmaking the 'Middle Ages,' " *Journal of Medieval History* 7 (1981): 127–34.

24. Bainton, *The Horizon History of Christianity*, 37.

25. Helen M. Barrett, *Boethius: Some Aspects of His Times and Work* (Cambridge: Cambridge University Press, 1940), 33.

26. Charles Henry Costner, *The Indicum Quinquevirale* (Cambridge, Massachusetts: Medieval Academy of America, 1935), 62.

27. James J. O'Donnell, *Cassiodorus* (Berkeley and Los Angeles: University of California Press, 1979).

The Monastics

Boethius and Cassiodorus represent something of a bridge between the Roman world and that of medieval Europe. As Roman political and economic structures broke down, a new organizational force appeared that was destined to have major educational significance. This was the monastic establishment, whose houses dotted the European landscape.

BEGINNINGS OF MONASTERIES

Monasteries existed by the early fifth century. Augustine sent his common-law wife to a monastery and founded one himself in Hippo. Hypatia was killed by a group of Coptic monks from around Alexandria.

The beginning of monastic life in the West is traditionally dated with unusual precision. Despite the early existence of religious communities around the time of Christ, the first famous person identified as a Christian hermit was an Egyptian named Anthony. In 271, when he was a little more than twenty, he heard the following words of Jesus read: "If you will be perfect go, sell all you have, and give to the poor, and come follow me." A wealthy man, Anthony gave away his property, except for enough to support a younger sister. Then he sent her to live in a community of religious women—an indication that such Christian nunneries already existed. He had been a loner as a child. After his conversion, he withdrew to the desert where he undertook a solitary life of prayer, self-assessment, manual labor, and contemplation. He lived to a grand old age—well over one hundred—and became famous. As people increasingly sought his advice and assistance, he retired further from civilization.[1]

By the early fourth century, many people were retreating into the Egyptian desert. Inspiration from examples like Anthony was one reason. The fact that authorities did not usually pursue accused criminals into the wastelands no doubt added some converts. Monks were also exempt from taxes, military service, and some forms of required labor. The climate, which permitted year-round existence on a sparse diet in caves on uninhabited land, was an additional factor encouraging solitary life in Egypt. But the main impetus came from civil unrest resulting from the Roman legions' inability to keep invading tribes from the African frontier and from a growing reform sentiment within some parts of the Christian community.

It was at about this time (313) that Constantine declared Christianity the empire's favored religion. While no one was forced to convert, many aristocratic and middle class citizens saw advantages in adopting the emperor's faith. Churches grew in size and wealth. At the same time, differences of interpretation reflecting regional disputes and leadership competition came forcefully into view. As one religious historian put it, conflict brought about "the swift transformation of the Christian church from a persecuted and fervent sect into a ruling and rapidly increasing body, favored and directed by the emperor, membership of which was a material advantage." The resulting relaxation of standards and diminished emphasis on austerity caused the Christian church to become what, in the words of historian David Knowles, it remains:

a large body in which a few are exceptionally observant and devout, while many are sincere believers without any pretension to fervor, and a sizable number, perhaps even a majority, are either on their way to losing the faith, or retain it in spite of a life which neither obeys in all respects the commands of Christ nor shares in the devotional and sacramental life of the church with regularity. Under such conditions there has always occurred a revolt of some or many against what seems to them prevailing laxity.[2]

Each revolt has inevitably contained a strong educational element.

SYSTEMATIZING A MOVEMENT

At the onset, monasticism consisted of individualistic hermits like Anthony. Some ascetics began to associate regularly for spiritual assistance, and soon they were forming groups. A man named Pachomius (286–346) is credited with originating a "rule," or set of written procedures, for monastic life. An Egyptian who converted to Christianity as a young man and tried life as a hermit for a time, he became convinced that living with others made Christian perfection more attainable. He was a superb administrator, with a less ascetic approach to life than some of his contemporary desert dwellers. He forbade meat and wine, but allowed cheese and fish. Pachomius ultimately governed several thousand monks, and his rule formed part of the basis for the procedures that European monastic houses would follow.

Pachomius retained for himself and his monks vows not to engage in sexual activity or acquire personal wealth, and added the obligation of obedience. Giving up one's personal will to the best interests of the group as specified by one's superior became part of spiritual growth. As governor general, Pachomius organized his followers according to economic skills into "houses" of about fifteen to thirty people (bakers in one, tailors in another, and so on). Pachomius's monks floated excess produce down the Nile to Alexandria and sold it, thus providing money for the group's needs and for charity.

A number of seekers after Christian perfection found Pachomius's rule not stringent enough and continued their individual pursuit of salvation. Some chained themselves to rocks. Others boxed themselves into the ground from the waist down. A few followed the example of a Syrian named Symeon, who spent more than three decades on top of a thirty-foot column near Antioch, with bare essentials of life being sent up on a rope. People sometimes came from long distances to seek advice or to invoke the blessings and prayers of such obviously tough-willed saints.

In Italy and Western Europe, this olympic asceticism did not win many converts. A moderate form of group monasticism did catch on, however, and by the time the Germans took over the Western Empire there were thousands of monks scattered about much of Italy, Spain, and France, and they would soon establish themselves in England and Ireland. Most of these groups were small at first, but by the sixth century some were growing larger. They followed whatever regulations their founders preferred and their members accepted. Some, like the one started by Cassiodorus, stressed copy work; many were largely agrarian. All were preoccupied with prayer and contemplation.

Benedict (480–c. 543)

In 480, one of monasticism's most famous leaders was born. This was Benedict of Norcia, author of the most celebrated and widely used set of European monastic regulations. Despite Benedict's later fame, not much is known about his life. He was from a distinguished family in central Italy and was educated in Rome. At a site near an artificial lake where Nero had once had a villa, he tried life as a hermit. He had great difficulty overcoming his sexual fantasies—at least according to Gregory I, who lived just after Benedict's time. The "wicked spirit," wrote Gregory, would not let him forget a woman, the memory of whom "so mightily inflamed . . . the soul of God's servant . . . that, almost overcome with pleasure, he was of a mind to forsake the wilderness." The cure was in a nearby brier patch: "He cast [off] his apparel, and threw himself into the midst of them, and there wallowed so long that when he rose up all his flesh was pitifully torn."[3]

Monte Cassino and the Rule

Finding solitary life difficult, Benedict decided to found a monastery. He was familiar with Cassiodorus's establishment and two or three other noted centers. After several faltering attempts in which his fellow monks found his requirements too severe—to the point that some attempted to poison him, according to one story—Benedict succeeded. He took a group of followers to Monte Cassino, a fortified hill on the Appian Way (military road from Rome to Italy's southern coast).

Monte Cassino has been seriously damaged or destroyed on several occasions, but it was restored each time and remains a symbolically important establishment. Of most significance for the development of education, however, was Benedict's set of regulations. Based on several earlier documents, including that of Pachomius, it laid down a moderate approach to government that ultimately came to be followed by most European monastic establishments.

Benedict's rule assumed poverty, chastity, and obedience. It laid out a system of government based upon the Roman family. The head was called an *abbot* (father). Vacant abbacies were to be filled after consultation with members of the order. Although there were provisions for removing an incompetent abbot, once installed this official was practically immune from impeachment. The abbot was to rule his children (the monks) with love and understanding. Members could not eat red meat unless they were ill. They could have fish, cheese, fowl, wine, and vegetables in season. If a monk broke these or other rules, the abbot could prescribe punishment, including flogging or ultimately dismissal from the order. The spirit of monasticism suggested restraint in the consumption of food and wine, but the abbot was to recognize differences resulting from physical labor, personal need, and climate.

Benedict thought it essential that monks be literate, partly because he was impressed with the copy work of Cassiodorus's group. People needed to be able to read scripture. Hence, if *novices* (new members of the house) were not already educated, they would receive basic reading and writing instruction from the master of novices.

Monastic education went beyond internal instruction for novitiates, as nearly all Benedictine houses also maintained external schools for children who did not intend to join the order. Sometimes a monk or nun from the monastery taught in these schools; in other cases, the house paid a salary to an outsider. Either way, monastic establishments provided instruction in Latin (and sometimes Greek) grammar, rhetoric, logic, and religion to youth. Female houses, of which there came in time to be many, provided this schooling for girls. Originally, most monasteries were in rural areas.

Benedict died at Monte Cassino some time after 546. He had a sister named Scholastica who lived as a nun. Tradition holds that she was an *abbess* (head of a female monastic order), but this is not certain. Women's monastic houses followed Benedict's rule in many instances.

Between the sixth and ninth centuries, monasteries were started in many parts of Europe. Even though most of them were small at first, they often grew to be the most important economic and educational units in their localities. Towns developed around many of the thriving monastic houses.

"HAPPY CHRISTIAN FACTORIES"

The following description of St. Gall (or St. Gallen) in the mountains of Switzerland, while a bit romanticized by the nineteenth-century abbess who wrote it, reminds us of how influential monasteries became. Irish travelers in the sixth century founded St. Gall, and by 800 it was a primary center of learning:

It lay in the midst of a savage Helvetian wilderness, an oasis of piety and civilization. Looking down from the craggy mountains, the passes of which open upon the southern extremity of the lake of Constance, the traveler would have stood amazed at the sudden apparition of that vast range of stately buildings which almost filled up the valley at his feet. Churches and cloisters, the offices of a great abbey, buildings set apart for students and guests, workshops of every description, the forge, the bakehouse, and the mills, for there were ten of them, all in such active operation that they every year required ten new millstones; and then the house occupied by the vast numbers of artisans and workmen attached to the monastery; gardens too, and vineyards creeping up the mountain slopes, and beyond them fields of waving corn, and sheep speckling the green meadows, and far away boats busily plying on the lake and carrying goods and passengers—what a world it was of life and activity; yet how unlike the activity of a town! It was, in fact, not a town but a house—a family presided over by a father. . . . Descend into the valley, and visit all these nurseries of useful toil, see the crowds of rude peasants transformed into intelligent artisans, and you will carry away the impression that the monks of St. Gall had found out the secret of creating a world of happy Christian factories. . . . Visit their scriptorium, their library, and their school, or the workshop where monk Tutillo is putting the finishing touch to his wonderful copper images, and his fine altar frontals of gold and jewels, and you will think yourself in some intellectual and artistic academy.[4]

Tutillo was one of several noted teachers associated with St. Gall. He was powerfully built, had a fine voice, could preach eloquently in Latin or Greek, and was noted for humility. He was especially famous for carving, painting, musical composition, and singing. He knew mathematics and constructed an astrolabe for astronomical work. "Undistracted by desire for visible success and fear of failure, the monk was able to concentrate all his energies upon the task at hand. . . . Refusing to be the slave of the material universe, he became its master."[5]

Life in Monasteries

Monastic life was not easy. Schedules varied by region and by time of year, but the usual hour for rising was from 2:00 to 4:00 A.M. Reading, meditation, singing/chanting, prayer, and religious ceremony occupied about eight hours in the day, as did various forms of work. These were interspersed with each other. Meals, rest, conversation, and sleep took up the remaining eight hours. Bedtime was around dark, as indeed it was for most other people in a time when candles furnished the only artificial light. Work areas and sleeping quarters were often not well heated. In northern climates, monks sometimes suffered frostbite while copying texts.

On the psychological side, the monastic ideal demanded introspection and self-awareness. It was not enough to refrain from making angry or jealous remarks; monks had to learn how not to think them. It was not sufficient to abstain from sexual activity, for (in modern psychological terms) simply repressing or ignoring feelings would not do. It was essential for the monks to be fully aware and to try to come to grips with how they felt.

Although monastic life was difficult, it offered some tangible advantages. Bringing narcissism (preoccupation with self) under control was personally liberating and socially useful. It made possible an educated and cultured existence lived in a context of service to others and encouraged faith in God and taught a set of values that transcended the often violent and sordid conditions of medieval life. This was as true for women as for men. If anyone escaped the ravages of military action—a frequently recurring situation—monastics did. Food was usually adequate, living conditions were simple but as healthful as the society permitted, and often aesthetically pleasing. Sexual abstinence provided a break from a succession of pregnancies and child-rearing responsibilities that typified family life.

Monastic Contributions

Monasteries had many functions, and in the long run "became a politically potent, intellectually vibrant, and artistically rich force which transformed Western Civilization."[6] They were politically significant because they were economically powerful. Monks consigned to the order the wealth their labor created, so monasteries gradually bought tracts of land, built mills and barns, purchased breeding animals, and constructed churches—activities that furnished jobs for many skilled artisans. They also reclaimed mountain, swamp, or forest land that would otherwise have been unproductive. They furnished schooling to boys and girls and took in orphaned children. They possessed the most reliable medical knowledge then extant, and had people experienced in its application. They preserved and improved engineering skills, especially in architecture and surveying, and they provided the only important source of agricultural experimentation in Europe for many centuries.

Far from being merely static repositories of ancient knowledge, monastic houses furnished the conditions for the creation of new information. For example, until the medieval period there was no effective way of writing down how a song should be rendered. Learning songs and chants was a matter of hearing someone else sing them and then memorizing the patterns. In the eleventh century, however, a monk named Guy of Arezzo invented musical notation: "After seeking for a long time for some easy and precise system, Guy one day recognized in the chant to which the hymn of St. John the Baptist was ordinarily sung an ascending diatonic scale in which the first syllable of each line occupied one note." He made his pupils "familiar with the diatonic succession of the syllables, *ut, re, mi, fa, sol, la.* Next he arranged the notes on lines and intervals, and thus produced the musical staff with its proper clefs."[7] Guy himself observed, "after I began to teach this technique to boys, there were some who could sing new melodies easily in three days, which result could not have been obtained by other means in less than many weeks."[8] Criticism of Guy's new method was so severe that he left the monastery, but in 1024 he traveled to Rome where Pope John XIX "warmly received both him and his newly invented garmut."[9] "If there was a single greatest revolution in the history of Western music, this was undoubtedly it," write music historians Piero Weiss and Richard Tarkuskin. "Innovation was now infinitely facilitated."[10]

Monasteries provided accommodations for travelers, who made contributions according to their means in return for this valuable service. Therefore, monasteries needed entertainers—actors, jugglers, clowns, singers, dancers, and others—to provide hospitality to visitors, many of whom were important people. Hence, the monastic house hired a variety of local and regional talent, thus supporting the performing arts.

Monasteries also rehabilitated some criminals. About 986, for example, a woman named Elfrida was directed to establish a monastic house at Wherwell in England. She spent six years there—until she died—reflecting on whether it had been a good idea to murder her husband and son-in-law.

Monastic houses also provided a retirement setting for people who preferred to live their final days in contemplation. Christine de Pisan, for example, spent the last fifteen years of her life at the aristocratic Abbey of Poissy (Chapter 4). Houses could even be a substitute for divorce for people who had finished rearing their families. Peter Abelard's parents, about whom you will read in this chapter, apparently took this route.

THE CAROLINGIAN RENAISSANCE

The northern and western European medieval world was largely rural. Population centers rarely had more than a few thousand people, although towns grew in size and number beginning in about the ninth century. A major factor in the growth of city life and the spread of Christianity to northern Europe was the stability brought about by the political/military success of a Germanic dynasty—the Carolingian—from about 600 to 800. The first member of the Carolingian family to become prominent was Pepin I (the Elder), a nobleman whom the Merovingian King Clothaire II named his "mayor of the palace" or business manager.

Because most of the kings in the Merovingian family neglected administration in favor of palace intrigues and sexual exploits, the Carolingian mayors of the palace gradually gained control of the army, courts, and finances. One of these, Charles Martel (the Hammer), illegitimate grandson of Pope Zacharias, sent the last Merovingian king, Childeric III, to a monastery. In 754 Pope Stephen II declared Pepin III *rex Dei gratia* (king by the grace of God). Pepin gave the papacy a large "donation" of land and set the stage for Christianity to become the official religion of the German part of Europe. When Pepin III died in 768, his two sons, Carloman and Charlemagne, succeeded.

Most of the territory which had once been the Roman Empire was Christian by the seventh century, as was Ireland. But some non-Latinized, northern Germanic and Scandinavian tribes continued to raid British and continental areas. After the mid-seventh century, Arabic converts to Mohammed's Islam rapidly conquered the territory from Jerusalem around the North African rim of the Mediterranean to southern Spain. However, Charles Martel stopped the Moslem advance into Europe in 732 at the battle of Tours in France. Charles Martel and Pepin the Short encouraged Christian missionaries in the German area, but it was Charles who made Christianity the official religion of all the territory that he controlled.

Charlemagne (742–814)

Charlemagne (Charles the Great) was called Karl by his youthful peers. His place of birth is not recorded, but he no doubt had a traditional aristocratic (military) education. He spent more time hunting than reading books. At six feet four inches, he was taller than most of his contemporaries. Energetic, intelligent, honest, and fair-minded, he was an effective king when at twenty-six he began to share power with his brother. The two of them might have been in civil war if Carloman had not died of natural causes three years later.

Some historians have claimed that Charlemagne could not write, based on a story told by Eginhard, his secretary and biographer, that "he tried to write and constantly carried little tablets about with him, that in his leisure moments he might accustom his hand to the drawing of letters, but he succeeded badly, having applied himself to the art too late." But this probably refers to his attempt to learn calligraphy (decorative manuscript writing). He obviously could write: a copy of the gospels, corrected in his hand, has been preserved.[11] Princes often signed documents with an X even though most knew how to write. Aristocrats did not need to write with careful legibility, because they could dictate to secretaries who specialized in writing clearly.

Charlemagne was frequently involved in military actions during the four decades of his rule. He made himself king of Lombardy (northern Italy) early in his reign and reconfirmed the Donation of Pepin to the papacy. Most of his military engagements were successful, and he soon controlled the territory that would later become France, Belgium, Holland, the Netherlands, Germany, Switzerland, Austria, northern Italy, Yugoslavia, western Hungary, and Czechoslovakia. Charlemagne could be ruthless: he gave defeated Saxons a choice of baptism or death, and when they waited too long to decide, had 4,500 of them executed.

On Christmas day in 800, Charlemagne, wearing the robes and sandals of a Roman patrician, knelt in prayer before the altar in St. Peter's Basilica in Rome. Pope Leo III suddenly produced a jeweled crown, and, placing it on Charles' head, proclaimed him Emperor and Augustus.

The empire united Europe as it had not been since the height of the Roman Empire and as it would not be again until Napoleon.[12] But this accomplishment in itself is not as interesting to the student of education as is the so-called Carolingian renaissance, which reached its peak under Charlemagne. His father and grandfather had welcomed monastic establishments and renowned scholars; King Charles cultivated intellectual developments in his realm at least as energetically as he fought battles. His chief lieutenant in this campaign to civilize and Romanize Europe was an Englishman named Alcuin.

Alcuin (735–804)

Born in Northumbria about seven years before Charlemagne, Alcuin was christened Ealh-wine. He was from a good family, and received a classical education at the cathedral school of York near his birthplace. (Cathedral schools were much like external monastic schools.) Archbishop Egbert of York kept Alcuin on as a teacher. About 770 Alcuin became a deacon (a rank in the lay clergy just below that of priest, carrying a salary but not requiring all of the responsibilities of a priest). Eight years later he became head of the cathedral school. He extolled the virtues of monastic life, but never became a monk himself.

Alcuin and Charlemagne met at Parma, Italy, in 781 while Alcuin was on a continental trip to secure books for his school. Charlemagne had already imported several noted scholars, partly by offers of generous pay and partly by his own enthusiasm for each master's skills. He convinced Alcuin to take charge of the palace school at the capital in Aachen (Aix-la-Chapelle). The fact that Danes were burning monasteries in northwest England and that Charlemagne guaranteed a high salary made the offer particularly attractive.

The Carolingian renaissance required the efforts of many people and involved five elements: (1) encouraging monasteries and cathedrals to educate children of serfs as well as those of free parents, (2) correcting existing religious books and making accurate copies of Greek and Roman texts, (3) improving Germanic people's knowledge of Latin and Greek grammar and Romanizing their pronunciation—people in southern Europe thought German accents barbaric and unsophisticated ("the barbarous harshness of their cracked throats when . . . they endeavored to emit a gentle psalmody," said John the Deacon, "out of a certain natural hoarseness sent forth grating sounds like that of carts on a high road"),[13] (4) giving the vernacular (German) language and literature a more systematic written form, and (5) standardizing and reforming religious doctrine and practice by suppressing heretical movements. The curricular framework in which all this was cast was basically the seven liberal arts as advocated two centuries earlier by Boethius.

The first element found expression in letters from Charlemagne to all bishops and abbots in 787 and 789, although it is not clear how completely class distinctions were ignored in education. Copying religious texts was widespread, and included the careful decoration of manuscripts with miniature drawings for which the Carolingian renaissance has become noted. In the matter of pronunciation, Roman cantors gave instruction for singing and Alcuin instituted accent and punctuation marks "as might enable even the unlearned to read without any gross error."[14] German language and literature especially interested Charlemagne. He wrote down popular folk songs and started a German grammar that was finished after his death. Both Alcuin and Charlemagne wrote against religious doctrines that they considered heretical, and Charlemagne did his best to uphold orthodoxy.

Charlemagne was a lively, practical man with a zest for life. He had eight legitimate and ten illegitimate children by four wives and five mistresses. He loved his family, preferring that his daughters stay home and have affairs rather than marry and leave. Charlemagne entertained himself at meals by listening to someone reading aloud Augustine's *City of God*—not through excessive piety, but because he was busy and intellectually voracious. Alcuin, too, enjoyed some sensual pleasures. He sustained his work with "large goblets of Greek wine," and steaming dishes of savory food.[15]

After fourteen years at Aachen, Alcuin accepted Charlemagne's offer to become head of the Abbey of St. Martin of Tours. This was a noted and wealthy establishment controlling some twenty thousand serfs. The fact that Alcuin, who had never been a monk, could become abbot of such a monastery illustrates the complex interrelationship between social origins and leadership positions in church and state. It was not unusual for people of humble birth to join monasteries or hold minor lay clerical offices. Indeed, the church offered considerable avenues for social mobility to the bright, hard-working, and lucky. But abbots, abbesses, and lay clergy of the rank of bishop or higher were usually of aristocratic birth. Given the power and wealth involved in these offices, ambitious families usually wanted as much control as they could get over the most prestigious abbacies and bishoprics.

Alcuin died eight years after going to Tours, after having made the monastery one of the most noted centers of learning of the time. Charlemagne lived ten years longer. His descendants ruled whatever they could hold together of his empire for 173 years. None was as effective as he had been, but many of the educational provisions remained.

THE MEDIEVAL MIND

By the eleventh century, most of Europe was at least nominally Christian, and the monastic idea was widely admired if not universally practiced. People mixed folk beliefs and local superstitions with Christian doctrines; many hoped that they would go to heaven, but feared it would be hell instead. Theologians taught and believed that "many are called but few are chosen"; consequently, most humans would be resting down under in the lower part of the earth, a location later affirmed by Thomas Aquinas. Infants were no exception. St. Augustine had concluded that infants who died before they were baptized went to hell due to their vicarious connection with original sin. Later the doctrine was changed to an eternity in limbo for the unbaptized infant, and a life in purgatory (popular by 1070) for sinners who had not been fully redeemed.

Some people reported detailed dreams and visions of hell. For example, in the twelfth century, Monk Tundale vividly described a constantly agonizing and screaming Satan, bound to a burning gridiron by red hot chains. This devil seized the damned and crushed them like grapes with his teeth, swallowing them down his burning throat. Assistant demons helped devour sinners by beating them to a pulp, boiling them, or slicing them up with saws.

To medieval Christians, the devil was real and could, with the help of his demons, be found prowling around everywhere. Common opinion had it that Satan was a great admirer of women, often using their smiles and wiles to lure innocent men. Some lonely women even helped out the belief. For example, one Frenchwoman admitted that she frequently slept with Satan and through his efforts had given birth to a monster with a wolf's head and

serpent's tail. Demonology included a less serious side as well. People saw
some demons as light-hearted mischief-makers—tearing clothes, producing holes in garments, spoiling food, or throwing up dirt on people who were
walking.

Charlemagne and Alcuin—as did many other well-educated people—
discouraged superstition and regarded as heretical strong emphasis on
images, icons, and relics. Nevertheless, by the eleventh century some
churches and monasteries were participating in a craze for locating saints'
remnants, supported by popular enthusiasm. A church that could boast of
having such relics could ensure itself of a large congregation and a prosperous future. For instance, St. Peter's Basilica claimed to have the bodies of
Peter and Paul. Another church said it had pieces of the real cross of Jesus,
along with his cradle. Still another had the original stone tablets used for
the Ten Commandments. Yet another claimed to have the head of John the
Baptist enshrined in a silver cup.

Some relics were authentic, but the craze grew to ridiculous proportions. Three different churches claimed to have the corpse of Mary Magda-
lene, and five churches in France said they held the one true relic of
Christ's circumcision. Bodies of saints were exhumed and dismembered so
several churches or abbeys might house their remains and become more
famous and powerful. By the thirteenth century, church officials stopped
the most excessive of these practices.

Guilt and terror are brutal feelings for the human psyche, and some
medieval people had bouts with insanity. One historian concludes that "the
flight of thousands of men and women from the world, the flesh and the
Devil into monasteries . . . suggests not so much their cowardice as the
extreme disorder, insecurity, and violence of medieval life."[16] In the remainder of this chapter, we will see some of the basic strengths and fundamental problems of medieval life.

Guibert of Nogent (c. 1064–c. 1128)

By studying Guibert, we can get insight into the medieval personality. Guibert wrote his life story in three short books, using Augustine's
Confessions as a model: his early years, his life as a monk, and his years
as an abbot. His self-analysis reveals an unusual level of consciousness
for the twelfth century—so much so that the French historian LeFranc
has called him "practically a modern man."[17]

Guibert was so preoccupied with introspection that he failed to include standard autobiographical information, such as his place and
date of birth and parental lineage. It is likely, however, that he came
from minor nobility (vassals) in the village of Clermont about thirty-
five miles north of Paris. His parents were betrothed to each other
while they were young teenagers, and had difficulty consummating

their marriage due to what they considered to be a hex placed by a jealous old woman.

Guibert's mother had learned to be "terrified of sin, not from experience, but from the dread of some sort of blow from on high, and . . . this dread had possessed her mind with the terror of sudden death."[18] The inexperienced husband was not able to break this spell of fear until he had conceived a child with another woman. In the meantime, neighbors tried to seduce the bride, but to no avail. Guibert may have been his parents' third child; at any rate he was their last. The labor was so long and difficult that, according to the pious author, his father dedicated the life of his unborn child to God. Though premature and unusually small, Guibert was finally born and his mother lived. However, the boy was made to feel that he had almost caused his mother's death.

Guibert's father died, probably in battle, when his son was eight months old, and Guibert's mother hired nurses to care for his physical needs while she molded his character. He saw himself as his mother's favorite child while a brother "earned his punishment in hell."[19] He thought of his mother as beautiful, proud, kind, intelligent, pure, virtuous, chaste, and strong-willed. He also remembered her as self-centered, cruel, and hard.

Guibert was destined for the life of a cleric, so when he was four or five his mother hired a tutor for him. This tutor seems to have been a surrogate father who played the part with a "harsh love." Longer on anger than knowledge, he often subjected Guibert to brutal beatings for not knowing the things he as tutor could not teach. As Guibert recalls, from the ages of six to twelve he never played, had no friends, and never left the company of his tutor or had a holiday. "In everything," he wrote, "I had to show self-control in word, look, and deed."[20]

After one particularly severe beating from the tutor, Guibert's mother removed his shirt and saw the welts and bruises. Intensely distressed, she gave him the chance to renounce the life of a cleric for knighthood, but he refused. During this period he developed a repressive guilt over all bodily habits. The brutal beatings influenced Guibert's later writings, for he would go out of his way to tell stories pertaining to loss of bodily and sensual control.

When Guibert was about twelve or thirteen, his mother withdrew into a nearby monastery at St. Germer. Getting caught up in a similar elation, the tutor also entered a monastic order. Without a tutor, Guibert had no sense of direction and felt totally rejected, and he became "rowdy." Upon hearing of the boy's debauchery, his mother paid the abbot at St. Germer to take him in. This done, Guibert settled into a life of an oblate (one who lived in a monastery but took no irrevocable vows until he or she was mature enough to make a choice for or against a cloistered life). Shortly after, however, he decided to enter the novitiate against his mother's wishes.

Guibert remained at the abbey under his mother's watchful eye for the next twenty-five years. During this period he wrote of his bouts with insanity: the vivid nightmares he experienced, awakening to see the devil standing over him; his screaming fits over these hallucinations, which ended only when someone would come in and keep him from going crazy; his confessions to his mother of the difficulty he was having in repressing evil (sex-related) thoughts.

In 1103–1104, fearing that he was amounting to nothing, various family members tried unsuccessfully to buy Guibert an abbacy (such bribery was known as simony). At about the same time, members of the new abbey of Nogent heard of his good works and offered him the position of abbot. He accepted and, for the first time in his life, left the control of his mother (who died two years later).

Besides his personal memoirs, Guibert wrote accounts of the first crusade and the bourgeois rebellions in twelfth-century France. From our standpoint, his memoirs are more illuminating than his histories because they reveal an often tormented personality suffering from guilt over his inability to control sensual fantasies.

A NEW KIND OF MASTER

Neither monastic nor cathedral schools made the clear distinction the Romans had made between the kind of instruction given in the ludus and the grammar school—what we differentiate as elementary and secondary. In aristocratic families, mothers often taught their offspring the alphabet and how to read before sending them to school. At school, children expanded their vocabularies through glossaries, which could be either vernacular/Latin or Greek/Latin. They typically learned to read in a psalter (a collection of psalms). They also practiced religious chants, finger computation, and writing skills. Nearly all schools also taught spelling, grammar, poetry, and prose writing. Dialectics (logic), rhetoric, arithmetic, geometry, and astronomy (mixed with astrology) were offered too, but not all teachers were competent in these subjects. After the ninth century, music also became much more specialized.[21]

The example of Guibert's tutor offers some insight into teaching methods, though it is difficult to know how typical he was. Certainly masters resorted to the rod to get their pupils to penetrate the "thickets of the grammatical wilderness." One of Alcuin's contemporaries counseled teachers, probably with no more effect than Quintilian had six centuries earlier: "act with moderation and do not birch them, or they will return to their beastliness after correction. A master who, in his anger, reprimands a child beyond measure should be pacified and corrected. Strong-arm methods may render a child naughtier than ever."[22]

The general atmosphere encouraged docility. Students did not challenge the teacher's knowledge or interpretation: "Be on guard against giving credence to your own discoveries rather than to the examples of your master," was the advice of one monk. "The more one defends his own curiosity, the more he finds himself in error."[23]

The monastic ideal stressed teaching as a Christian duty rather than as a means to gain money or notoriety. The lure of fame and fortune, however, was too much for some people to resist, and the example of men like Gerbert of Aurillac must have spurred the imagination of the ambitious. Born to a poor family in south central France at the end of the ninth century, he attended a local monastic school. Later, he became a noted teacher of music, mathematics, and logic. Scholars flocked to him from France, Italy, Germany, and Britain. Ultimately he became archbishop of Ravenna and indeed closed his remarkable career as Pope Sylvester II.[24] Every poor lad in France must have been heartened by Gerbert's success. Certainly the life of Peter Abelard illustrates the emergence of ambitious professional teachers—a prerequisite for the development of universities.

Peter Abelard (1079–1142)

Most of what we know about Peter Abelard's life and his love affair with the attractive and intelligent Heloise (or Eloise) comes from Abelard himself. In 1132 he wrote a long essay/letter entitled *The Story of My Misfortunes*. Addressed to "a friend," the essay is really an autobiography. Characterized by a rather bitter, egotistical, arrogant tone, it gives an account of his turbulent life to that point. According to the Danish historian Leif Grane, there is evidence to corroborate much of what Abelard claimed in the essay. And, if we remember that the preceding decade of his life had been sheer misery from any standpoint and that his letter had been only intended for the eyes of a friend who could comfort him in his despair, we can perhaps forgive some of his egotism.[25]

Early Life

Abelard said that he became interested in pursuing an academic life as a young teenager. His family lived in Brittany (northwest France) and was of such a social stature that, being the eldest of several boys, he was to inherit his father's estate and become a knight. Instead, he gave up the chivalric life at about age fifteen and headed for Paris, where there were several masters known for their intellectual talents.

One of his first teachers was Roscelin, a notorious dialectician in the eyes of some church authorities, whom he met on the way to Paris. Upon leaving Roscelin, Abelard apparently stopped in other towns. His journey to Paris, which was about 150 miles from his home, took him nearly six years. Upon his arrival around 1100, he went to Notre Dame Cathedral, where William of Champeaux, master of the school and archdeacon of the cathedral, had a reputation as an outstanding dialectician.

No sooner had William noticed his new pupil's keen mind than he fell victim to it. It was customary for young scholars to show deference—almost reverence—to their masters as scholars who were older and had studied longer than themselves. But Abelard pursued his love for logic so passionately that he had no time for such rituals. He soon demonstrated his intellectual prowess by successfully refuting some of William's statements. In defeating the teacher, however, he also crushed the disciples, consequently incurring their wrath. "Out of this," says Abelard, "sprang the beginning of my misfortunes, which have followed me even to the present day [1132]; the more widely my fame was spread abroad, the more bitter was the envy that kindled against me."[26]

The brash young Abelard gained a following and decided to open his own school. As archdeacon, William prevented him from doing so in Paris, so Abelard moved to Melun, a town close to the city.

Beginning a Teaching Career

To Abelard, the archdeacon's behavior was the result of envy, but there may have been more to it than that. A custom reinforced by canon law encouraged masters to receive permissions (licenses) to teach. These came from bishops, but in larger towns the bishops often delegated this authority to their chancellor or *scholasticus*. Sometimes this official licensed masters to handle the various arts, reserving theology for himself. In theory anyone who taught in the diocese, whether at the cathedral or in a rented room, needed the chancellor's approval.[27] It was not uncommon for these "permissions" to be purchased from the official, hence giving him power and profit.

It had also become the unwritten custom, and an essential piece of scholarly etiquette, for established masters to receive new teachers into the fold through a ceremony known as *inception*. This only occurred after an adequate period of study and an initial lecture given under the watchful eye of the master. The headstrong Abelard followed neither of these rituals when he opened his school, but for the time being it did not matter. Shortly after he began his teaching, Abelard "was smitten with a grievous illness, brought upon me by my immediate zeal for study." He returned home to Brittany to convalesce. As it turned out, he was there for several years.

By the time Abelard returned to Paris in 1108, William had left Notre Dame for the Abbey of St. Victor and the life of a monk. He continued giving public lectures, but in rhetoric, not dialectics. Abelard tells us, "To him did I return, for I was eager to learn more of rhetoric from his lips; and in the course of our many arguments on various matters, I compelled him by most potent reasoning first to alter his former opinion on the subject of universals and finally abandon it altogether."

We may well suspect Abelard's reason for returning to harangue his former master. Probably the thought of another victory and more fame had something to do with his motives. In any event, William abandoned lecturing as a career and Abelard's fame increased. In fact, William's replacement at Notre Dame gave up his position to Abelard and voluntarily became his student. Abelard's victory was short-lived, though, as William successfully plotted the removal of this new teacher and replaced him with a professor who did not feel compelled to turn over the teaching to Abelard.[28] According to Abelard, William

> could not long, in truth, bear the anguish of what he felt to be his wrongs, and shrewdly he attacked me that he might drive me forth. And because there was nought in my conduct whereby he could come at me openly, he tried to steal away the school by launching the vilest calumnies against him who had yielded his post to me, and by putting in his place a certain rival of mine. So then I returned to Melun, and set up my school there as before; and the more openly his envy pursued me, the greater was the authority it conferred upon me.

Not long after, William took his monastic brotherhood away from the city to live a more perfect ascetic life. This signaled Abelard's return, and he quickly set about to ruin his new rival's school at Notre Dame. Upon hearing this, William returned to St. Victor to help defend his protege, but to no avail. In fact, says Abelard, "After our master returned . . . [the new master] lost nearly all of his followers and thus was compelled to give up the direction of the school."

Further Study

Abelard was probably ready to reap the fruits of victory when a family incident called him home. All of the children were now grown, so Abelard's parents had decided to dissolve their home and enter monastic life. His father had already done so, and his mother wished to say farewell to her eldest son before following. Abelard traveled to Brittany to visit his mother. Then, instead of returning to Paris, he left for Bec in Laon to study the higher subject of theology with Anselm, Bec's famous abbot and theologian. Abelard tells us that his decision was affected by the news that William—who had been Anselm's student—had become bishop of Chalôns. The Danish historian Leif Grane thinks that Abelard's mother may have argued that the study of theology under a famous master like Anselm would take her son to a bishop's chair.

Anselm was a good speaker but not a particularly adept logician. Therefore, it is not surprising that Abelard found him boring and easy to conquer. According to Abelard, Anselm's lectures consisted of superficial interpretations of the Bible—in other words, empty rhetoric based on faulty assumptions. "When he kindled a fire," says our author, "he filled his room with smoke, but did not light it up."[29]

Abelard quit attending Anselm's lectures, which riled Anselm's disciples, who sarcastically asked Abelard if he thought he could interpret the Holy Writ. He said he could, and invited the challengers to his lecture on Ezekiel the following day. Ezekiel was considered to be the most difficult of all books in the Bible, and even Anselm's followers thought he needed more time, but Abelard replied, "It was not my custom to advance through practice but through talent."[30] He was so entertaining that the students asked for more. Once again he was collecting pupils. Anselm, supported by two devout followers, Alberic of Rheims and Lotulf of Novara, forbade Abelard to give any more lectures, so Abelard left Laon and returned to Paris. A dejected Anselm died shortly thereafter.

Alberic and Lotulf preferred charges against Abelard for delivering these lectures, not because he had no license but because he had begun teaching "without a master." Apparently, the theology lectures were viewed as his inception into the guild of masters, an act which presupposed his own master's approval.[31] This breach of etiquette did not hinder Abelard's appointment as *magister scholarum* (head master) at Notre Dame, the position he had long desired. Such an appointment brought him security, because it meant that he became an irregular canon subject to church authority. An irregular canon was a member of the brotherhood, but took no vows and wore no clerical garb with its respective hair style or tonsure. Such rights were reserved for the regular clergy.

For the next couple of years, Notre Dame gathered an unprecedented number of scholars who came to study under the renowned Abelard. During this period, the area around Notre Dame became known as the Latin quarter because all of the students spoke and studied in Latin. Abelard had no effective rivals, a condition that was probably boring for him, so he turned his attentions elsewhere.

Heloise [Eloise] (c. 1100–1164)

Looking back on his life, Abelard admitted that all this fame and fortune had left him arrogant, and he searched for a new conquest. Such a challenge he found in the niece of one of his canonical brothers, Fulbert. Here is how Abelard told it:

Now there dwelt in that same city of Paris a certain young girl named Heloise. . . . Her uncle's love for her was equaled only by his desire that she should have the best education which he could possibly procure for her. Of no mean beauty, she stood out above all by reason of her abundant knowledge of letters. Now this virtue is rare among women, and for that very reason it doubly graced the maiden, and made her the most worthy of renown in the entire kingdom. It was this young girl whom I, after carefully considering all those qualities which are wont to attract lovers, determined to unite with myself in the bonds of love, and indeed the thing seemed to me very easy to be done. So distinguished was my name, and I possessed such advantages of youth and comeliness, that no matter what woman I might favor with my love, I dreaded rejection of none. . . .

Thus, utterly aflame with my passion for this maiden, I sought to discover means whereby I might have daily and familiar speech with her, thereby the more easily to win her consent. For this purpose I persuaded the girl's uncle, with the aid of some of his friends, to take me into his household—for he dwelt hard by my school—in return for the payment of a small sum. My pretext for this was that the care of my own household was a serious handicap to my studies, and likewise burdened me with an expense far greater than I could afford. Now, he was a man keen in avarice, and likewise he was most desirous for his niece that her study of letters should ever go forward, so, for these two reasons, I easily won his consent to the fulfillment of my wish, for he was fairly agape for my money, and at the same time believed that his niece would vastly benefit by my teaching. More even than this, by his own earnest entreaties he fell in with my desires beyond anything I had dared to hope, opening the way for my love; for he entrusted her wholly to my guidance, begging me to give her instruction whensoever I might be free from the duties of my school, no matter whether by day or by night, and to punish her sternly if ever I should find her negligent of her tasks. In all this the man's simplicity was nothing short of astounding to me; I should not have been more smitten with wonder if he had entrusted a tender lamb to the care of a ravenous wolf. . . . There were, however, two things which particularly served to allay any foul suspicion: his own love for his niece, and my former reputation for continence.

Why should I say more? We were united first in the dwelling that sheltered our love, and then in the hearts that burned with it. Under the pretext of study we spent our hours in the happiness of love. . . . What followed? No degree in love's progress was left untried by our passion, and if love itself could imagine any wonder as yet unknown, we discovered it. And our inexperience of such delights made us all the more ardent in our pursuit of them, so that our thirst for one another was still unquenched.

In measure as this passionate rapture absorbed me more and more, I devoted ever less time to philosophy and to the work of the school. Indeed it became loathsome to me to go to the school or to linger there; the labor, moreover, was very burdensome, since my nights were vigils of love and my days of study. My lecturing became utterly careless and lukewarm; I did nothing because of inspiration, but everything merely as a matter of habit. I had become nothing more than a reciter of my former discoveries, and though I still wrote poems, they dealt with love, not with the secrets of philosophy. Of these songs you yourself

well know how some have become widely known and have been sung
in many lands, chiefly, methinks by those who delighted in the things
of this world. As for the sorrow, the groans, the lamentations of my
students when they perceived the preoccupation, nay, rather the chaos,
of my mind, it is hard even to imagine them.

But finally Fulbert discovered the lovers:

Oh, how great was the uncle's grief when he learned the truth, and
how bitter was the sorrow of the lovers when we were forced to part!
With what shame was I overwhelmed, with what contrition smitten
because of the blow which had fallen on her I loved, and what a tem-
pest of misery burst over her by reason of my disgrace! Each grieved
most . . . for the other. Each sought to allay, not his own sufferings, but
those of the one he loved. The very sundering of our bodies served but
to link our souls closer together; the plentitude of the love which was
denied to us inflamed us more than ever. Once the first wildness of
shame had passed, it left us more shameless than before, and as shame
died within us the cause of it seemed to us ever more desirable. . . .
Accordingly, on a night when her uncle was absent, we carried out the
plan we had determined on, and I stole her secretly away from her
uncle's house, sending her without delay to my own country. She remained there with my sister until she gave birth to a son, whom she
named Astrolabe. Meanwhile her uncle, after his return, was almost
mad with grief; only one who had then seen him could rightly guess
the burning agony of his sorrow and the bitterness of his shame. What
steps to take against me, or what snares to set for me, he did not know.
If he should kill me or do me some bodily hurt, he feared greatly lest
his dear-loved niece should be made to suffer for it among my kinsfolk.
He had no power to seize me and imprison me somewhere against my
will, though I make no doubt he would have done so quickly enough
had he been able or dared, for I had taken measures to guard against
any such attempt.
    At length, however, in pity for his boundless grief, and bitterly
blaming myself for the suffering which my love had brought upon him
through the baseness of the deception I had practiced, I went to him to
entreat his forgiveness, promising to make any amends that he himself might decree. I pointed out that what had happened could not
seem incredible to any one who had ever felt the power of love, or who
remembered how, from the very beginning of the human race, women
had cast down even the noblest men to utter ruin. And in order to
make amends even beyond his extremest hope, I offered to marry her
whom I had seduced, provided only the thing could be kept secret, so
that I might suffer no loss of reputation thereby. To this he gladly
assented, pledging his own faith and that of his kindred, and sealing
with kisses the pact which I had sought of him—and all this that he
might the more easily betray me.

Abelard then left for his sister's house to bring Heloise back in order to marry her. But, according to Abelard, his mistress wanted no part of marriage. First of all, she said that she did not believe that her uncle would be appeased; and second, that it would bring disgrace upon Abelard in his clerical career. She quoted passages from the Bible which scorned marriage. She reminded him of the warnings against marriage given by various church fathers. And finally, she offered Cicero who said that he "could not devote himself to a wife and to philosophy at the same time." Her arguments were to no avail; Abelard could not be swayed. Tearfully she consented, but only on the condition that the marriage be kept a secret among her uncle and a few close relatives.

Marriage

After the marriage, Heloise returned to her uncle's house, and Abelard resumed teaching as if nothing had transpired. Doubtless his students were still singing his love songs, for Heloise tells us that "all streets, every house, echoed with my name."[32] But all of this was just too much disgrace for Fulbert, who told everyone that his niece was married to Abelard. His tattling only added to his indignity, however, because Heloise vehemently denied her uncle's assertions. Fulbert was furious. Abelard continues the story:

> Her uncle visited her repeatedly with punishments. No sooner had I learned this than I sent her to a convent of nuns at Argenteuil, not far from Paris, where she herself had been brought up and educated as a young girl. I had them make ready for her all the garments of a nun, suitable for the life of a convent excepting only the veil, and these I bade her put on.
>
> When her uncle and his kinsmen heard of this, they were convinced that now I had completely played them false and had rid myself forever of Heloise by forcing her to become a nun. Violently incensed, they laid a plot against me, and one night, while I, all unsuspecting, was asleep in a secret room in my lodgings, they broke in with the help of one of my servants, whom they had bribed. There they had vengeance on me with a most cruel and most shameful punishment, such as astounded the whole world, for they cut off those parts of my body with which I had done that which was the cause of their sorrow. This done, straightway they fled, but two of them were captured, and suffered the loss of their eyes and the genital organs. One of these two was the aforesaid servant, who, even while he was still in my service, had been led by his avarice to betray me.

Abelard was convinced that his physical disablement was deserved punishment for his sins. Feeling disgraced, he sought refuge in the monastery of St. Denis in Paris. He also told Heloise to take the vows of the Argenteuil sisterhood. The young bride grieved much at this situation, feeling that if she had just remained his mistress, none of this would have been necessary. She was not attracted to convent life and weep-ingly took her vows only because Abelard commanded her to do so.

The situation was a tragedy of errors, but consistent with the time. First, for a *magister scholarum* to be married would have been un-usual, but having a mistress was common practice. Moreover, while having a mistress would not help his ambitions to become a bishop, it would not be an automatic bar to high clerical office. Heloise's desire to remain his mistress was motivated by the same wish to keep the mar-riage secret. On the other hand, Elizabeth Hamilton says that Abelard controlled his possessive love for Heloise by marrying her and, after his physical disability, committing her to a nunnery so that she could never remarry. Heloise freely and shamelessly admitted that she would have done whatever Abelard asked, since she regarded him as more her master than God.

Leif Grane views their situation differently. He thinks that Abelard was caught between two passions—his love of teaching and his love for Heloise. Yet he made Heloise "so much the central figure of his life that apparently without hesitation he discarded everything he had won in the world of learning."[33] Also, while Heloise's love seemed much more altruistic and selfless than Abelard's, she did not need to fear losing him to someone else (after his incapacity) as he did her.

Abelard as Monk

At St. Denis, Abelard felt no hesitation in judging his companions against the highest standards. With his own sexual passions unexpect-edly removed, he commenced to devote his life to God. Unfortunately, he saw decadence and impiety among his monastic brothers, who cared little for his sermonizing. They did, however, like the attention his stu-dents brought. They pestered him to resume his lecturing, and St. Denis complied by providing rooms and quarters for his disciples.

During this time, Abelard completed a book on theology, but it was condemned by officials at the behest of Alberic and Lotulf. Abelard was forced to burn the only copy of his book, a fate which he said hurt him more than his previous physical wounds. He was also imprisoned briefly. Upon his return to St. Denis (c. 1122), he asked if he could take leave of the abbey so long as he never took other monastic vows. Eventually, permission was granted.

Tired of people and conflict, Abelard decided to seek solace in nature. He erected a small reed-and-straw chapel on a piece of ground presented to him by the nearby bishop about 100 miles southeast of Paris. Abelard called it the Paraclete (Comforter). Again, it did not take long for his students to catch up with him, and soon his chapel was surrounded by huts. Abelard found himself teaching and writing again. From 1124 to 1126 the students cultivated fields and built a large complex of build-ings. Their devotion gave Abelard renewed vigor, but it supplied his enemies with the desire to defeat him once and for all. He said that he lived in constant fear of being dragged up before some council and branded a heretic.

Abelard as Abbot

A desire to escape his enemies led Abelard to accept the offer to be the abbot of St. Gildas in Brittany. His ambition for high office probably entered into the decision as well. But this was tantamount to going from one danger to the next. Abelard wrote:

> The land was barbarous and its speech was unknown to me; as for the monks, their vile and untamable way of life was notorious almost everywhere. The people of the region, too, were uncivilized and lawless. Thus, like one who in terror of the sword that threatens him dashes headlong over a precipice, and to shun one death for a moment rushes to another, I knowingly sought this new danger in order to escape from the former one. I held it for certain that if I should try to force them to live according to the principles they had themselves professed, I should not survive. And yet, if I did not do this to the utmost of my ability, I saw that my damnation was assured. Moreover, a certain lord who was exceedingly powerful in that region had some time previously brought the abbey under his control, taking advantage of the state of disorder within the monastery to seize all the lands adjacent thereto for his own use, and he ground down the monks with taxes heavier than those which were extorted from the Jews themselves.
>
> The monks pressed me to supply them with their daily necessities, but they held no property in common which I might administer in their behalf, and each one, with such resources as he possessed, supported himself and his concubines, as well as his sons and daughters. They took delight in harassing me on this matter, and they stole and carried off whatsoever they could lay their hands on. . . . Since the entire region was equally savage, lawless and disorganized, there was not a single man to whom I could turn for aid, for the habits of all alike were foreign to me. Outside the monastery the lord and his henchmen ceaselessly hounded me, and within its walls the brethren were forever plotting against me. . . .
>
> Oh, how often have they tried to kill me with poison, even as the monks sought to slay St. Benedict! . . . When I had safeguarded myself to the best of my ability, so far as my food and drink were concerned, . . . they sought to destroy me in the very ceremony of the altar by putting poison in the chalice. One day, when I had gone to Nantes to visit the count, who was then sick, and while I was sojourning awhile in the house of one of my brothers in the flesh, they arranged to poison me, with the connivance of one of my attendants, believing that I would take no precautions to escape such a plot. But divine providence so ordered matters that I had no desire for the food which was set before me; one of the monks whom I had brought with me ate thereof,

not knowing that which had been done, and straightway fell dead. As for the attendant who had dared to undertake this crime, he fled in terror alike of his own conscience and of the clear evidence of his guilt.

After this, as their wickedness was manifest to every one, I began openly in every way I could to avoid the danger with which their plots threatened me, even to the extent of leaving the abbey and dwelling with a few others apart in little cells. If the monks knew beforehand that I was going anywhere on a journey, they bribed bandits to waylay me on the road and kill me. And while I was struggling in the midst of these dangers, it chanced one day that the hand of the Lord smote me a heavy blow, for I fell from my horse, breaking a bone in my neck, the injury causing me greater pain and weakness than my former wound.

Heloise as Abbess

In the meantime, Heloise, who had become abbess at Argenteuil, was threatened with eviction for herself and her sisters. The abbot at St. Denis found that he could lay claim to the convent, so he requested that the nuns leave. Upon hearing of their plight, Abelard offered the Paraclete to the sisters. They eagerly accepted and asked for his assistance.

For a brief time, Abelard preached to and helped the nuns. He even envisioned ending his life there near his wife, serving the sisters as their spiritual advisor and preacher. But all too soon the rumors concerning his earlier love affair with Heloise started up again. Unable to quiet these suspicions, he returned to his unruly monastery at St. Gildas. It was during this return that he wrote his autobiographical essay/letter. He said that he hoped death would soon end his misery.

We know from Heloise's correspondence that his letter eventually found its way to her, and it may in fact have been intended for her. She then resumed communication with him, lamenting that after thirteen years she had not changed her feelings at all and that her life was still devoted to and dependent upon Abelard: "For you are the only one capable of bringing me sorrow and joy, or of rendering me consolation."[34]

Heloise called herself a hypocrite because her religious vows had meant little to her. Instead of lamenting their affair, she confessed that she could only sigh at what she had lost. Finally she begged Abelard to at least respond to her letter and provide his Paraclete with guidance. He did respond, saying that life was undoubtedly harder for her now because she was not free of her passion as he was. But he admonished her to see him as a brother more than a lover. In this way they could renew their love in Christ who had "shown them His mercy." They continued to correspond. Heloise asked him to complete a set of rules for her sisters to follow and to compose some new poems, because many of the ones she had by other authors were impossible to put to music. These requests renewed Abelard's energies, and he involved himself totally in their fulfillment.

Abelard's Last Days

In 1141, Abelard's circumstances took another turn for the worse, as he was again condemned for his theological works. One of his enemies, a conservative monk named Bernard of Clairvaux, had launched a vendetta against Abelard. Being close to the pope, Bernard was quite successful in his attack. Convinced of his innocence, Abelard set out for Rome to redeem himself. Fortunately for Abelard, Peter the Venerable, abbot of Cluny, intervened on his behalf, and Abelard could have had no better or more powerful ally. Cluny was the largest and wealthiest monastery in Europe, and its abbot at that time enjoyed power equal to that of the pope. Consequently, Abelard was vindicated and allowed to spend his last years in the reverent peace and quiet of Cluny's main establishment.

Abelard died while studying. His last notes revealed that he was not a broken man, considering himself to be "the greatest master of his time whose legitimate reputation neither envy nor persecution has been able to assail." Peter the Venerable wrote to Heloise after Abelard's death and arranged to have his body removed to her convent in order to fulfill Abelard's request.

Peter the Venerable's letter reveals a different side of Abelard. "I remember having seen no person to compare with him in humility, both as to habit and behavior," he wrote from Cluny. "And although, because I wished it, he occupied a high rank among the great host of our brothers, one would be forced, upon seeing his miserable clothing, to believe him the most inferior of all."[35] The abbot continued by telling how Abelard was content with the least possible of all things; he spent his time reading and praying, and only spoke when he was asked to preach to the brothers or to instruct them in their reading.

Heloise died twenty years later and at her request was buried with Abelard. We don't know if she ever found peace and comfort. In Peter the Venerable's letter to Heloise, he commented that he had long heard her praises sung as abbess, so perhaps she did find the inner peace and piety that Abelard wanted for her.

Abelard's reputation and writing lingered on through his students and theirs. He influenced the intellectual climate that led to the birth of universities and a different approach to the study of theology.

Euphemia of Wherwell (before 1200–1257)

Although there were women's monasteries at least as early as the fifth century, no comprehensive history of female religious orders exists. We have enough isolated accounts to know that they were widespread and numerous. In fact, as one historian notes, "their numbers and the variety of their rules and occupations have exceeded those of all the monks and orders of men put together."[36] These monasteries provided the only systematic academic instruction available to women, other than tutors, for over a thousand years.

Women's monastic houses had internal and external schools. They also furnished opportunities for women to become agriculturists, business managers, teachers, physicians, scholars, and administrators. The career of Euphemia, abbess of the monastery of Wherwell near the south central coast of England, serves as an example of monastic education for women.

We know little of Euphemia's life before she became abbess of Wherwell in 1226. She was a member of the convent and may have been a friend of the preceding abbess, a woman named Maud who had been in charge for forty years. The abbey owned five villages and other property. Euphemia effectively administered the monastery for thirty-one years; under her care, the number of the "Lord's handmaidens" increased from forty to eighty.

Euphemia oversaw numerous repairs and additions to the physical plant, including a large infirmary away from the main buildings. Under the infirmary's dormitory, she had constructed "a watercourse through which a stream flowed with sufficient force to carry off all refuse that corrupt the air." She also had a chapel built for the infirmary, along with a large enclosed garden. She tore down and rebuilt the presbytery of the church and replaced the bell tower over the dormitory when the old one fell down. She moved and enlarged the barnyard area because the "amount of animal refuse was a cause of offense to both the feet and nostrils of those who had occasion to pass through." She also built a wall around the court area and "round it she made gardens and vineyards and shrubberies in places that were formerly useless and which now became both serviceable and pleasant."

Euphemia also rebuilt manor houses and farmhouses in two of the five villages and increased the mill capacity of the monastery. As her biographer said of her, she "so conducted herself with regard to exterior business affairs, that she seemed to have the spirit of a man rather a woman."[37] The lessons of practical administration acquired by thousands of abbesses in the medieval period cannot have been lost on the cumulative experience of women's education.

FROM MONASTERY TO UNIVERSITY

In the dynamic period from the tenth century to the Black Death (1348–1349), much of the organizational structure of the modern world began to emerge. The growth of cities either produced or acted as a catalyst for several changes: (1) a growing bourgeoisie vying with older power groups for access to political privilege and education; (2) the revival of guilds to represent the interests of merchants and artisans; (3) the emergence of monastic orders serving the urban poor rather than the rural, agricultural wealthy; (4) an increasing need for knowledge of law to settle conflicts; (5) the application of logic to religious tradition as a way of reconciling inherited traditions with changing conditions; and (6) a renewed interest in Greek and Roman traditions as tools for legitimizing a variety of interests.

By the eleventh century, western Europe was quite different from the way it had been when Benedict started his monastery at Monte Cassino. Villages dotted the landscape, and some were developing into cities. Before 1100 it would have been unusual to find more than three thousand people in any town north of the Alps, but by 1200 Paris had grown to one hundred thousand people. The villages of Douai, Lille, Ypres, Ghent, and Bruges had each increased to fifty thousand souls. Forests were cleared, swamps were drained, and prairie was cultivated. What had been a barbarian, tribal frontier was now populated by folk who were at least partially Romanized and nominally Christian. The success of the monks had laid the foundation for the next stage of European development.

The area north and west of the Alps was a frontier yielding slowly to the civilizing force of the monastic establishments. Villages developed along rivers, well-traveled roads, and especially near monasteries and castles. As these villages grew, shops became larger, trade increased, and merchants prospered. Some cities began to issue money and other negotiable instruments to make transactions easier.

In most cases, villages were under the jurisdiction of either a monastery or a local noble on whose land they were located. Sometimes both a noble and an abbot or abbess claimed authority. These authority figures arbitrated legal matters, such as privileges and disputed rents. Bishops and archbishops tended to locate their headquarters in the more important cities, thus introducing another claim to authority and source of conflict. Political and military power traditionally rested on land ownership and was, therefore, ultimately rural. However, the growth of urban centers and the money economy offered an increasingly significant counterbalance to this tradition. From the tenth to thirteenth centuries, many towns and cities tried to become independent of the nobles and the Church.

One of the most successful devices for gaining autonomy came in the form of charters or other grants of privilege from nobles or Church officials who needed money. Merchants lent the money in return for assurances of independence. In other cases, citizens resorted to armed revolt, sometimes successful, sometimes not. Guibert of Nogent left an account of what happened at Laon when the bishop tried to suppress the newly formed "commune" (citizens' organization) in 1115:

On the fifth day of Easter week . . . there arose a disorderly noise throughout the city, men shouting "Commune!" . . . Citizens now entered the bishop's court with swords, battle-axes, bows, hatchets, clubs, and spears. . . . The nobles rallied from all sides to the bishop. . . . He hid himself in a cask . . . and piteously implored them, promising that he would cease to be their bishop, would give them unlimited riches, and would leave the country. And as they with hardened hearts jeered at him, one named Bernard, lifting his battle-ax, brutally dashed out the brains of that sacred, though sinner's, head.[38]

The villagers burned the cathedral and went on a rampage of several days before a royal army crushed their revolt.

In their struggles for independence and political power, the city-dwellers found Roman legal and organizational patterns useful. Of particular value was the guild, an ancient Roman form of corporate association with a recognized history of legitimacy. Guilds went by various names: *collegia, scholae, sodalitates, artes, universitae.* The leading merchants were the first to form guilds, but crafts practitioners quickly followed suit. Bankers, notaries, clothiers, wool merchants, physicians and druggists, silk dealers, furriers, tanners, innkeepers, armorers, and others formed themselves into collegia (the classical Roman term for religious associations). The primary intent of these organizations was to gain a monopoly on the trade with which they dealt. They provided many other services: life insurance, schools for youth, burial. In the long run, political enfranchisement came through guild membership, and even the nobility found it necessary to be nominal members in order to participate in town politics.

In their recruitment and admission procedures, most guilds favored the children of existing members, who joined through an apprenticeship that culminated in an examination. Only those who satisfied existing masters of their skill, and who had saved enough money, could be admitted to mastership. This process gave each guild a great deal of power. People who had not reached the final level could work only as laborers for other masters.

Until about the eleventh century, practitioners of the teacher's art had not associated with each other in any sort of legal corporation. In the twelfth century, however, this issue became a matter of lively contest. The growth of cities and of mercantile and craft guilds encouraged liberal arts masters to form their own collegia. Paris, Oxford, and Bologna led the way.

Parisian Developments

The rapid growth of Paris, its central location, and the reputations of people like William of Champeaux attracted young men from all over western Europe. Abelard was a good example of this, and his notoriety helped increase the flow of students.

The whole enterprise was informal and somewhat chaotic. Hundreds, eventually thousands, of teenagers—fourteen or fifteen was the average age—flocked to the booming city, where many of them did not speak the native language. Latin was the medium of study and would do for most shopkeepers, but food and lodging were expensive and the possibilities for losing one's money and innocence were everywhere at hand. Wealthy families sent servants to aid their sons; a number of religious orders bought or built monastic houses to protect their young student members. Boys who did not belong to either of these groups had to get along as best they could. Girls rarely attended.

In general, landlords and merchants had the upper hand. Students had to have food, housing, and supplies, and the guide for setting prices tended to be whatever the traffic would bear. Students were not helpless, however, because most sizable towns wanted both the renown and the profit that came from being centers of study. So the possibility that students would leave en masse for another location acted as a partial counterbalance to the merchants' greed.

An incident precipitated by a Paris tavern riot in 1200 illustrates these circumstances. Some German students were having a drink when the servant of one of them—the bishop-elect of Liège—got into a dispute with the bartender/owner, who struck the servant. The students then beat up the innkeeper and left. He called the provost (superintendent of police) of Paris, who led an assault by armed citizens on a German student hostel. Several students were killed, including the bishop-elect.

An appeal to King Philip II for redress brought quick results, apparently because he feared the students might otherwise leave Paris. The citizens who had attacked the students were sentenced to life in prison. The provost broke his neck trying to escape from jail, but some of the townsmen got away. Their houses were burned. Finally, the king granted a charter to the students and their masters that: (1) guaranteed ecclesiastical rather than civil trial for any scholastics arrested for any cause; (2) required citizens to volunteer information against anyone they saw mistreating a student; and (3) mandated that upon taking office future provosts should appear at an assembly of scholars in a Paris church and swear to respect and protect scholastic privileges.

Student concerns were only one part of a complex picture. Another important factor was the rapidly increasing number of masters of arts who were competing with each other for pupils. Many of the young men who crowded into Paris preferred to stay upon completing their studies. For most, teaching was a natural way to earn a living. This led to an oversupply of masters, forcing down income and threatening established teachers. Common sense suggested two remedies. One was to slow down the rate at which new masters were being created. The other was to increase the supply of students by ensuring that no one could pursue the "higher" faculties of theology, law, or medicine without first spending several years studying the arts under an approved master. Both of these solutions could best be carried out if masters incorporated themselves into guilds.

The Corporation. The process of masters forming a corporation (*universitas*) happened in stages, starting in the closing decades of the twelfth century. By 1230 guilds of masters were firmly established at Paris, Oxford, Bologna, and other cities.

In Paris, the recently formed masters' corporation tried to limit the number of new masters by having the chancellor of the cathedral issue licenses only to those people whom they as a group approved. In 1210 they brought a suit in papal court against the chancellor to this effect. Pope Innocent III sided with the masters. But the chancellor, in keeping with a long tradition of granting licenses to any applicant not guilty of heresy, paid no attention. Perhaps encouraged by the fees and gifts he received from each successful applicant, he saw no need to change custom.

This dispute dragged on for several years. Finally, in 1229 the masters were able to take advantage of an unrelated grievance. Some students had "found sweet and good wine" in a suburban tavern, but when the bill arrived they said it was too high. Words led to blows. The bartender called in neighbors who helped him beat up the students and throw them out. They returned with reinforcements the next day, thrashed the innkeeper, and set his taps running. He called on the provost, who brought an armed band of mercenary bodyguards—"the savage police of a savage city," as one historian refers to them. They killed several students. The masters called a cessation and demanded reparations for the students. They also said they would not return until the chancellor started consulting them before licensing people.[39]

The strike lasted two years. It ended with a papal court limiting the powers of both bishop and chancellor in favor of the masters' universitas. This included recognition of the legality of cessation as a means of redressing grievances—an important concession in the guild's long-range attempts to gain a monopoly over all teaching.

Mendicant Competition. When the masters returned to Paris in 1231, they discovered that some people had not stopped teaching. Masters at several monasteries, especially of the recently formed Dominicans and Franciscans, were not concerned about fees. These groups had formed partly in protest to the Benedictine establishments like Cluny, which they viewed as too aristocratic and worldly. Dedicated to serving the poor and preaching the gospel, the mendicant (wandering) friars had early begun to acquire corporate property around the study centers like Paris and Oxford. They discouraged young members of their orders from studying with most masters, thinking them too worldly. Moreover, the friar doctors (from *docere*, to teach) were willing to offer theological instruction to people without regard to whether they had studied with or been approved by members of the masters' universitas.

Given these conditions, it is not surprising that the secular masters' guild regarded the "black friar" teachers as strikebreakers and scabs. Ultimately, after several decades and numerous legal suits and strikes in Paris, the masters' corporation was able to compel the friar doctors to join the guild and honor the group's rules. Oxford, Bologna, and other study centers witnessed similar conflicts with the same results.

Tensions between university masters and independent teachers continued in some cities for centuries. But a revolutionary change had occurred, as a four-thousand-year tradition gradually ended. From Sumeria in 3000 B.C. to the formation of masters' corporations, education had generally taken place in a free market atmosphere. Anyone could teach who had pupils, and students could leave one master or school for another or study any subjects in any order according to their preferences. But as masters in the great study centers of Europe gained control over licensing—today we call this graduation—the length, order, and level or mastery required in the curriculum were slowly standardized. In the nineteenth century, this kind of control was assumed by national governments and extended to pre-university levels. This control became so strong that by the 1960s some critics of educational arrangements were arguing for a return to the laissez-faire approach of earlier times.[40]

Thomas Aquinas (c. 1225–1274)

The most famous of the friar doctors to study or teach in Paris was a gentle monk named Thomas Aquinas. He was born about 1225 to a noble Italian clan in the family castle of Rocca Secca near Naples. In that era, parents frequently dedicated the youngest son to the Church. So when Thomas was only five, his parents took him to the Benedictine monks at Monte Cassino where he was to be an oblate.

Because of the position of the family, Thomas's parents hoped that their son would become abbot of Monte Cassino, an important political and religious post. The Benedictine order was especially favorable to this aristocratic family because it was a respected, well-established order that was devoted to scholarly, literary, and artistic pursuits.

Aquinas the Student

Thomas's education at the abbey was primarily religious, but also included reading, writing, mathematics, grammar, harmony, and Latin. There is no evidence that he was dissatisfied with his life or training. He probably would have remained there and taken his final vows as a Benedictine monk if times had remained peaceful. The abbey, however, was "a frontier fortress" between the Papal States and Frederick II's Kingdom of Sicily, which included Naples, the abbey, and Aquinas's birthplace. A succession of popes feared Frederick's ambitions—specifically that he would isolate and encircle the Papal States. In 1239, about nine years after Thomas entered the abbey, Frederick was excommunicated for the second and last time by a distrustful pope, thus beginning a long period of strife. Monte Cassino was affected immediately because of its strategic location, and Frederick's troops occupied the abbey and expelled most of the monks.[41]

After returning home for a visit, Thomas enrolled at the *studium* in Naples to study liberal arts and the natural philosophy of Aristotle, the latter being forbidden in some places because of controversies concerning the interpretation of Aristotle's thought. Naples had only recently been established as a study center by Frederick, who was eager for its success. The course of study, therefore, was more varied than at studia influenced more directly by Church officials.

The method of instruction was *Scholasticism,* the kind of dialectical reasoning typical of Abelard's study and teaching. Thomas was probably assigned to one master who was responsible for his student's moral and intellectual development. In pursuing his studies, he read texts, engaged in disputations, and participated in refutations of the master's lectures. Thomas was an avid reader and a serious scholar. However, his handwriting was illegible and never improved in later life. The result was that many of his writings were referred to as *littera inintelligibilis* and could "only be read by palaeographers who have made a special study of them."[42] He was tall, overweight, absentminded, and quiet—characteristics that made him seem dull and plodding to those who did not look beneath the surface.

A well-known story illustrates the difference between Aquinas as he appeared and as he really was. After completing his studies at Naples, he went to Paris and studied with Albert the Great, a respected theologian. He was so quiet during Albert's lectures that the other students nicknamed him "the Dumb Ox." A fellow student, taking pity on him, offered to help him review the lecture, and Aquinas accepted with humble thanks. During the review he so astonished his tutor with his brilliance that the tutor asked Aquinas to tutor him in the future. Eventually Albert learned of his silent, retiring student's talents and brought forth Aquinas's abilities in class by assigning him a difficult question. When Aquinas's turn came to answer his question, he evoked this response from his famous teacher: "We call this man the Dumb Ox but he will eventually bellow so loudly in his teaching that he will resound throughout the whole world!"[43]

Aquinas's attitude about study was summarized in a letter to a young friar:

> Since you have asked me, my very dear John in Christ, how you should apply yourself in order to gain something from the treasure-house of knowledge. . . . Make up your mind to start on small streams rather than to plunge into the sea; for one should progress from easier matters to those that are more difficult. . . . Be slow to speak and slow to take the speaker's stand. Embrace purity of mind; do not neglect prayer; cherish your cell most of the time, if you wish to be admitted to the vintage-room [of knowledge]. Be friendly to all men; do not be curious about the private activities of other people; do not try to be overfamiliar with anyone, for too much familiarity breeds contempt and provides an opportunity for neglecting one's studies.
>
> Do not get interested in any way in worldly talk or deeds. Avoid idle

talk on all matters; do not fail to imitate the example of holy and good men; do not be concerned about what speaker you are listening to; instead, when something good is said, commit it to memory. Be sure that you understand whatever you read. Make certain that you know the difficulties and store up whatever you can in the treasure-house of the mind; keep as busy as a person who seeks to fill a vessel.

Do not seek higher positions. Follow in the footsteps of Blessed Dominic who brought forth and increased the buds, the flowers and the fruits that were useful and wonderful in the vineyard of the Lord of Hosts, as long as he lived.

If you follow these words of advice, you will be able to attain your every desire.[44]

Aquinas the Dominican

While Aquinas was pursuing his studies at Naples, he became acquainted with members of the Order of St. Dominic and decided to become a Dominican rather than a Benedictine monk. This decision greatly distressed his aristocratic family, for the Benedictines were respectable and the Dominicans were a new order that criticized the Benedictines and devoted themselves to preaching among the poor and earning their living by begging. Aquinas's family considered the group and its practices beneath his social station. In later years Aquinas wrote, "On this decision [to enter the religious life], blood relatives are not friendly. . . . So, in such a case, the advice of relatives is especially to be avoided."[45]

His family so strongly opposed his decision that his brothers kidnaped him when he was on a journey with several fellow monks. They brought him to a family castle where he was detained for about a year while his family tried to persuade him to change his mind. His brothers resorted to methods other than verbal persuasion: One evening they sent an attractive young woman to his room to seduce him. Upon seeing her, Aquinas snatched a burning stick from the fire and chased her from the room, whereupon he fell into a deep sleep and dreamed that his loins were bound tightly with a girdle of virginity. He is reported to have never felt lust after that, and he remained a virgin all his life.

" 'From that time onwards,' says his earliest biographer, 'it was his custom always to avoid the sight and company of women—except in the case of necessity or utility—as a man avoids snakes!' "[46] Naturally, he found Aristotle's view of females congenial. His opinion of women can be seen in the *Summa Theologica,* his best-known work. When he discussed the question of whether outward pain is greater than interior sorrow, he quoted Ecclesiastes 25:17: "The sadness of the heart is every wound, and the wickedness of a woman surpasses all other wickedness, as the text implies, so sadness of the heart surpasses every outward wound."[47]

The Dominicans recognized Aquinas's exceptional intellect and sent him to Paris to study and teach, and to earn a master of theology license (an eight-year program). During this time he began his very considerable writings on theology. At the age of thirty-four, Aquinas left Paris and spent ten years in Italy preaching, teaching, and writing. Then he returned to Paris to occupy one of the Dominican chairs of theology, where he continued to produce works of extraordinary length and quality.

Aquinas has been said to have perfected Scholasticism. He is also credited with applying Aristotelian logic to Christian theology. He justified both faith and reason, long considered incompatible: "Since revelation is a 'fact'—true philosophy and theology can never be in opposition when they deal with the same questions," he wrote, "and revealed truths, incomprehensible to the intellect, must be accepted on faith. The finite reason can never comprehend the infinite, but it can prove the validity of the preambles of faith and show that faith is not unreasonable."[48]

Last Years

In 1272 Aquinas was named Regent of Studies for the Dominicans at Naples, where he taught and continued to write until December 6, 1273. "While saying mass that morning a great change came over him, and afterwards he ceased to write or dictate. Urged by his companions to complete the *Summa,* he replied: 'I can do no more; such things have been revealed to me that all I have written seems as straw, and I now await the end of my life.' "[49]

Early in 1274 Aquinas, who was in poor health, set out for a general council of the Church to be held in Lyons. On the way he injured his head on a tree branch and stopped to rest at the Cistercian monastery in Fossanova. There he weakened and died. The Cistercian monks refused to give up the body, and later they "seem to have boiled the flesh off the corpse, so that they could keep the bones 'in a small place.' " In 1369, forty-six years after the canonization of St. Thomas Aquinas, Pope Urban V directed that his remains be returned to the Order of St. Dominic. Today "the relics of Friar Thomas are still preserved in the parish church of St. Sernin."[50]

Aquinas was the quintessential medieval monk. His work, which was not widely appreciated in his day, has modern significance. As we shall note in Chapters 11 and 12, twentieth-century thinkers (Jacques Maritain, for example) still draw inspiration from it.

SUMMARY

Although monasticism may sound strange, distant, and educationally unimportant to contemporary Americans, it represents one of the formative forces in the development of Western education. Monasteries were not only the major avenue for transmitting Greek and Roman cultural ideas and practices, they also provided the conditions for the discovery of new knowledge. Such basic matters as accents in language and the system of musical notation were invented in monasteries.

Far from being a period of "darkness," the medieval period (from about 500 to 1500) was a time of educational and intellectual ferment. Charlemagne's effort to spread education without regard to students' social background is still a goal of most governments and is certainly a centerpiece of American educational effort. Aquinas's reconciliation of faith with scientific investigation remains not only a brilliant solution to a serious problem but also a practical source of rapprochement for two major and contradictory intellectual thrusts in the Western world.

Not the least of the medieval period's contributions to education was the university. Such terms as *chancellor, dean, college, faculty,* and *university* are Roman labels that traveled a long way toward acquiring their modern meanings under the monastics. The medieval university was more than an extension of classical studies and Roman labels; it was a new structure. For good or ill the central educational symbol of modern society, the university—including the central concept of licensing and professionalizing knowledge—had its birth in monastic Europe. The Renaissance and Reformation, discussed in the next two chapters, elaborated and further developed what medieval Europeans had saved and invented.

NOTES

1. David Knowles, *Christian Monasticism* (New York: McGraw-Hill, 1969), 12.

2. Knowles, *Christian Monasticism,* 13. Spelling Americanized.

3. Quoted in Bertrand Russell, *A History of Western Philosophy and Its Connection with Political and Social Circumstances from the Earliest Times to the Present Day* (New York: Simon and Schuster, 1956), 379.

4. Augusta Theodosia Drane, *Christian Schools and Scholars—Or Sketches of Education from the Christian Era to the Council of Trent,* ed. Walter Gumbley (London: Burns, Oates, and Washbourne, 1924), 168–69.

5. Anthony C. Meisel and M. L. del Mastro, trans., *The Rule of St. Benedict* (Garden City, NY: Doubleday, 1975), 10.

6. Meisel and del Mastro, *The Rule of St. Benedict,* 9.

7. Drane, *Christian Schools and Scholars,* 292.

8. Piero Weiss and Richard Tarkuskin, eds., *Music in the Western World: A History in Documents* (New York: Schirmer Books, 1984), 53.

9. Drane, *Christian Schools and Scholars,* 292.

10. Weiss and Tarkuskin, *Music in the Western World,* 54.

11. Drane, *Christian Schools and Scholars,* 124; Pierre Riché, *Daily Life in the World of Charlemagne,* trans. JoAnn McNamara (Philadelphia: University of Pennsylvania Press, 1978), 225.

12. The eastern half of Charlemagne's empire was proclaimed the Holy Roman Empire in 962, and this grandiose title supposedly represented a culmination of Charlemagne's efforts.

13. Drane, *Christian Schools and Scholars,* 119, 123.

14. Drane, *Christian Schools and Scholars,* 119, 123.

15. Drane, *Christian Schools and Scholars,* 120.

16. Will Durant, *The Age of Faith* (New York: Simon and Schuster, 1950), 732.

17. Cited in John F. Benton, ed., *Self and Society in Medieval France: The Memoirs of Abbot Guibert of Nogent (1064?–c. 1125)* (New York: Harper Torchbooks, 1970).

18. Benton, *Self and Society,* 13, 64.

19. Benton, *Self and Society,* 12, 95.

20. Benton, *Self and Society,* 15, 46.

21. Riché, *Daily Life in the World of Charlemagne,* 225.

22. Riché, *Daily Life in the World of Charlemagne,* 213.

23. Pierre Riché, *Education and Culture in the Barbarian West: Sixth through Eighth Centuries,* 3rd ed., trans. John J. Contreni (Columbia: University of South Carolina Press, 1976), 475.

24. Drane, *Christian Schools and Scholars,* 282–89.

25. Cf. Drane, *Christian Schools and Scholars,* 347, 352; Elizabeth Hamilton, *Heloise* (Garden City, New York: Doubleday, 1967); Gabriel Compayré, *Abelard and the Origins and Early History of Universities* (New York: AMS Press, [1893] 1969), 3–23; and Leif Grane, *Peter Abelard: Philosophy and Christianity in the Middle Ages,* trans. Frederick and Christine Crowley (London: Allen and Unwin, 1970).

26. All quotations (with spelling Americanized), except otherwise noted, are from Abelard, *The Story of My Misfortunes: The Autobiography of Peter Abelard,* trans. Henry Adams Bellows (Glencoe, Illinois: Free Press, [1922] 1958); cf. J. T. Muckle, trans., *The Story of Abelard's Adversities: A Translation with Notes of the Historia Calamitatum* (Toronto: Pontifical Institute of Medieval Studies, 1964).

27. Hastings Rashdall, *The Universities of Europe in the Middle Ages,* ed. F. M. Powicke and A. B. Emden, 3 vols. (Oxford: Clarendon Press, 1936), 1: 279–81.

28. Grane, *Peter Abelard,* 40.

29. Muckle, *The Story of Abelard's Adversities,* 21.

30. Muckle, *The Story of Abelard's Adversities,* 23.

31. Rashdall, *The Universities of Europe,* 1: 284.

32. Grane, *Peter Abelard,* 51.

33. Cf. Hamilton, *Heloise,* and Grane, *Peter Abelard,* 63.

34. Grane, *Peter Abelard,* 66.

35. Grane, *Peter Abelard,* 153.

36. Knowles, *Christian Monasticism,* 8.

37. *The Victoria History of the Counties of England, Hampshire, and the Isle of Wright* (Folkestone and London: University of London Institute of Historical Research, [1903] 1973), 2: 132–33.

38. Guibert of Nogent, *The Autobiography of Guibert, Abbot of Nogent,* trans. C. C. Swinton Bland (London: George Routledge and Sons, 1925), bk. 3, chap. 8.

39. Rashdall, *The Universities of Europe,* 1: 292–401.

40. Iván D. Illich, *Deschooling Society* (New York: Harper and Row, 1971); John Caldwell Holt, *Freedom and Beyond* (New York: E. P. Dutton, 1972).

41. Anthony Kenny, *Aquinas* (New York: Hill and Wang, 1980), 1.

42. Vernon J. Bourke, *Aquinas' Search for Wisdom* (Milwaukee: Bruce, 1965), 9.

43. Bourke, *Aquinas' Search for Wisdom,* 43–44.

44. Bourke, *Aquinas' Search for Wisdom,* 17–18.

45. Bourke, *Aquinas' Search for Wisdom,* 25.

46. Kenny, *Aquinas,* 2.

47. Robert Maynard Hutchins, ed., *Great Books of the Western World,* 53 vols. (Chicago: Encyclopaedia Britannica, 1952), 19:778.

48. James Mulhern, *A History of Education* (New York: Ronald Press, 1959), 241.

49. Hutchins, *Great Books of the Western World,* 19: vi.

50. James A. Weisheipl, *Friar Thomas D'Aquino: His Life, Thought, and Work* (New York: Doubleday, 1974), 331.

The Humanists

Life in thirteenth-century Europe was varied and exciting. Monasticism had reached its high point, transforming the sparsely settled regions into productive farms and towns. But as the economies of several regions boomed and towns like Paris grew large, many people found the monastic approach to life and learning insufficient.

In Chapter 3 we noted the beginnings of universities. As these institutions developed, the scholastic approaches to learning (linguistic analysis based on syllogistic logic) ceased to appeal to a wide audience. What emerged was something that has been variously labeled "the new learning," "humanism," and the "Renaissance." Although these are potentially misleading terms, we will use them because they offer a convenient way of referring to certain aspects of this period. Central to the discussion are language and political developments associated with the growth of nationalism.

THE RENAISSANCE

Historians see the Renaissance in varying ways. Some narrow it to the short period from 1350 to 1500, while others extend it from 1300 to 1700. For our purposes, the Renaissance runs from about 1300 to 1600. Those who follow a strict definition of *humanism* include the literary, theological, and political writings of the period. But for us, humanism includes the intellectual activity concerned with classical texts *and* with their application to daily life.[1]

If we look at the politics of the early part of the Renaissance period, we see that in much of Europe, the nations that we know today (for example,

England and France) were starting to coalesce. During the thirteenth and fourteenth centuries, most of these were at war. England and France fought over the French throne from 1337 to 1415 in what is called the Hundred Years' War. Under the German Hapsburgs, the Holy Roman Empire extended its power into what is now Austria, the Czech Republic, and Slovakia in a series of bloody battles with local kings. Add to these wars the beginnings of religious conflict as well as the Black Death (1348–1349), and we have a picture of Europe in turmoil.

It is easy to see why the Renaissance began in Italy, for Italy was an island of relative peace in this sea of trouble. A fairly stable monarchy ruled the southern part of the peninsula, and the pope governed much of the central region. Northern Italy, the cradle of the Renaissance, was composed of a number of independent cities as well as a kind of miniature kingdom under the domination of the city-state of Milan. Although the Milanese Visconti family gradually took over many of these independent cities between 1350 and 1400, there was still relative peace. Led by the cities of Venice and especially Florence, northern Italy concentrated its resources on business, literature, and the arts.

The results were intellectually exciting. As cities became more important and business flourished, a new merchant class grew up, anxious to demonstrate its importance and sophistication. Like the robber barons of nineteenth-century America who plundered the land's resources and then contributed their fortunes to art museums and opera houses, these fourteenth-century businessmen commissioned artists to produce statues and paintings and hired tutors to instruct their children and themselves. Thus, scholars were able to support their writing by teaching for a living, and in a few cases, they were paid simply to think and write. The flourishing economy encouraged such artistic and intellectual pursuits.

Intellectuals shifted away from the scholasticism of the Middle Ages. In the early fourteenth century, the Florentine author Petrarch urged people to ignore Aristotle and read Cicero. Now, dialectics and theology were less important than the writings of classical Greek and Roman authors. It was to these ancient writers that Renaissance thinkers turned to discover both the style in which people ought to write and speak and the eternal truths that ought to govern society.[2]

In order to use the wisdom of these ancient writers, Italian authors carefully studied ancient texts. This created problems. Books were still copied by hand, so there were few of them around. And since many of the classical works had been written over a thousand years before, the odds were small that copies would have survived at all, much less in one piece. Many Greek and Latin works had been lost, either because all the copies had been destroyed or because they sat undiscovered on the back shelves of monastery libraries. Parts of some works survived, and there were a number of whole works which had been copied with so many mistakes that they were nearly useless. Another major problem was that few people in western Europe could read classical Greek. While scholars knew about

Homer and other classical Greek authors and, in a few cases, even had copies of their works, only a handful of monks were able to read them in the original language.

Renaissance scholars worked hard to solve these problems. They edited many inaccurate texts and attempted to reconstruct entire works from the remaining fragments. Library searches sometimes yielded copies of works that people thought no longer existed. For example, in 1418 Quintilian's works were discovered in the library of St. Gall. Books were copied and recopied, so that a number of scholars and wealthy people were able to amass extensive libraries.

The problem of learning Greek was solved, in part, by historical events in the East. During the early Renaissance, the Greek city of Constantinople came under increasing pressure from the Ottoman Turks, who had taken over much of Asia Minor. People, including scholars and teachers, began to flee to western Europe. They taught the Italian humanists and their pupils to read Greek and opened up a whole new world of literature in the process. Typical was Manuel Chrysoloras (c. 1355–1415), who introduced the study of Greek classics at the University of Florence.

THE HUMANITIES

The Medicis, a powerful Florentine family that flourished from 1389 to 1534, encouraged original literature and new art, such as that of Leonardo da Vinci and Michelangelo. They also sponsored activity designed to find and preserve copies of Greek and Roman masterpieces. In 1445 the family borrowed a Greek name, *academy,* for an institute it founded in Florence. The purpose of this academy was to further the study of art and literature, including history. The Medicis coined the term *humanities* to represent this kind of study.

The Renaissance focused on understanding the human condition by studying history and on expressing this understanding in an elegant style, like that of Cicero. Major emphasis was placed on writing—not just in Latin but also in the vernacular. In the hands of various religious reformers, this was the beginning of mass elementary instruction in English, German, Italian, and other European languages.

The first of what would come to be called the "new learning" was not religious. It began with the poetry of people like Dante Alighieri (1265–1321) and his fellow Florentine, Francesco Petrarch (1304–1374) and was furthered by the work of Parisian-born Giovanni Boccaccio (1313–1375), who wrote poetry and stories like *The Decameron* and lectured on Dante's work at the University of Florence. Boccaccio's literary activity had early counterparts in England. Walter Map (1103–1175), an Oxford archdeacon, wrote in English of England's heritage, including the first full written account of King Arthur and his sixth-century knights. Geoffrey Chaucer

(1340–1400) wrote *The Canterbury Tales,* patterned after Boccaccio's *Decameron.*

All of these efforts helped to stir the intellectual excitement that became the Renaissance. Western Europe was exposed to long-forgotten classical literature. Scholarship was no longer unconcerned with the events of daily life; rather, the humanists used the writings of orators such as Cicero and the histories of Herodotus and Xenophon to inspire the ancient virtues of personal integrity and civic responsibility.

The Renaissance thus served as a bridge. On one side lay medieval education with its emphasis on scholastic philosophy and theology. On the other was modern schooling, which would stress vernacular languages and natural science. It is in the context of this shift in Western society, with its accompanying anxiety, that we view the accomplishments of Vittorino da Feltre.

Vittorino da Feltre (c. 1378–1446)

Given Vittorino's stature as a Renaissance humanist, it is somewhat strange that we know little about him. Like many other teachers, he was devoted to his work and wrote little himself; perhaps he was so impressed with Roman and Greek literature that he felt unable to match their excellence. At any rate, before his death he destroyed the only writing he had done, some poems composed in his youth. What we know comes from the accounts of others, which are uniform in their praise.

Early Life and Education

Vittorino was born at Feltre, in the eastern Alps, in 1378 or 1379, the son of a minor official. The first record we have of him is when he entered the University of Padua in 1396, the same year that the University of Florence hired Manuel Chrysoloras as the first professor of Greek in the West.[3] Padua, like Florence, was very much under the influence of the "new learning," with its emphasis on the classics. Petrarch had given his library to the university, providing it with many new texts. A great number of the students were from nearby Venice, which was a contact point between Greece and western Europe.

Vittorino's education began with members of the arts faculty, with whom he studied Latin grammar and literature, philosophy and rhetoric, and canon (church) law, which was a fairly typical course of study for the time. Padua's curriculum was still medieval. The only unusual feature was the study of canon law, suggesting that Vittorino was considering a career in the church.

Like many talented but poor students, Vittorino paid for his schooling by teaching younger boys. Although we are not sure exactly when he completed his studies, he definitely finished by 1411. He received his *Laurea* (doctor's degree), but never wore the academic robes and ring to which he was entitled. Such an action was typical of the quiet and simple life-style which he would maintain until his death.[4]

Even after completing his degree, Vittorino remained around the university for almost twenty years, teaching and studying. He became interested in mathematics, which at that time was not usually a part of the curriculum. To satisfy his curiosity, he contracted with a private teacher to give lessons to his children in return for mathematics classes for himself. By the end of his stay at Padua, he was teaching both Latin grammar and mathematics as a private tutor.

A major influence on Vittorino during this period was Gasparino Barzizza, who came to the university as a teacher in 1407. Barzizza was devoted to the study of the Roman author Cicero, whom he believed to be a model of literary style, personal virtue, and citizenship. Vittorino was one of Barzizza's students, and it is probably from him that he picked up his conviction that classical literature could be reconciled with a Christian life.

Another important influence on Vittorino was Guarino da Verona, a fellow student at Padua who was also to become a famous teacher. In 1415, Vittorino left Padua for Venice and spent eighteen months studying Greek with Guarino, who had established a school there. Guarino was one of the few people in Western Europe who could speak and write Greek, having been a student of Manuel Chrysoloras.[5]

Vittorino as Teacher

Armed with this new knowledge, Vittorino returned to Padua to begin his own school. Because schools were individual operations and there was no compulsory education, each teacher had to attract his own students, and Vittorino seems to have had no problem doing so. He had extensive knowledge of Latin and was skilled in mathematics, and he was sought after as a teacher of Greek. Thus, Vittorino had no shortage of paying customers, and was able to take poor children along with the wealthy. In effect, he set up his own scholarship program, using the high fees charged to wealthy youngsters to subsidize the education of the poor. This concern with providing schooling for any talented boy was not unique to Vittorino, but it was one of his lifelong activities.

In 1422, Barzizza resigned his professorship at the University of Padua to take up another one at Milan, and Vittorino, age forty-four, moved into Barzizza's old position. Something seems to have gone wrong, for Vittorino resigned his new position the same year and left Padua. This brief interval was his only brush with university teaching.

In 1423, da Feltre began a school at Venice for the children of wealthy merchants. The situation was close to ideal. Because of Venice's ties with Greece, he had the opportunity to purchase some scarce Greek books. He was near his old friend Guarino and other scholars, and his reputation guaranteed him all the students he could handle. However, he had no sooner gotten settled than he packed up his belongings and moved again.

He had received an offer he couldn't refuse. Marquis Gianfrancesco Gonzaga of Mantua was looking for a prominent teacher for his household. Because his title was not solid, he wanted to compensate by proving to everyone that he was sophisticated and intelligent (not to mention wealthy) enough to hire a well-known teacher and thinker. He had first approached Guarino, who refused. Vittorino, too, declined the offer, but Gonzaga wouldn't take no for an answer. He asked Vittorino to set his own salary, and told him he could use his time as he saw fit. While accepting this offer would end any possibility of a career in the Church, the opportunity was too good to pass up. In 1423 Vittorino moved to Mantua, where he was to spend the rest of his life.

At the court of the marquis, Vittorino was responsible for the education of five children. In addition, he accepted students from other prominent Mantuan families, as well as the children of some of his own friends (for example, those of Guarino), and as many as seventy poor students. The marquis was true to his promise of support, even providing for the school an elaborate villa that da Feltre christened "La Giocosa" (the pleasant house). This property gave Vittorino a perfect setting. He believed that the environment for a school should be pleasant and that there should be room for the pupils to engage in physical activity.

Several years earlier, Vittorino had been influenced by the writings of Petrarch on education, as well as by a recently discovered manuscript by Quintilian on teaching. At Mantua, he set about putting the ideals of these authors into practice. In the Middle Ages, Latin had been studied primarily as a tool for further work in philosophy and theology with little attention to style. Greek had been studied by only a few monks. Vittorino set about reversing this. Beginning with basic grammar, he went on to Roman and Greek literature. Textbooks of the period were difficult for students to understand, with the hardest material frequently presented first and with no explanation.[6] Vittorino went through the texts line by line, talking about literary style, explaining difficult terms, and lecturing on themes and characters.

Vittorino's school placed great emphasis on memory training and public speaking. He required students to speak Latin and to learn to write it. In order to learn Greek and improve their Latin, they would take a passage from a Greek author and translate it into Latin, using the style of a Roman writer. While Greek was less emphasized than Latin, the major Greek poets and historians were studied. The goal was to make the students as fluent in Latin as they were in Italian, and to teach them enough Greek to read the classics. All of these efforts aimed at producing the Renaissance ideal—individuals who would live lives of personal honesty and civic responsibility. Vittorino believed that both virtues could be learned from the study of the classics.

Vittorino never married; his students were his family. In the class-room, he spent extra time with those who needed help or were especially talented. Outside of school, he listened to their problems and helped them smooth over difficulties with their parents, and in warm weather he took them on field trips. Since the students lived with him, he knew them well and they, in turn, regarded him as a sort of extra parent.

Vittorino was deeply convinced that education was not simply a mat-ter of intellectual activity. The same austerity that caused him to buy rough wool clothing and to wear sandals even in the winter made him insist that even his wealthiest pupils live simply. Unlike Guarino, he believed that physical activity was an important part of education, and encouraged students to play games and engage in athletic competition. Along with this, he communicated his own deep religious faith, and made religion a part of the normal classroom study. He took the students to mass several times a week and required that they follow his example of confessing their sins to a priest at least once a month. By involving himself in the extracurricular life of the students, Vittorino hoped to show them that education helped establish moral values as well as com-municated knowledge.

Vittorino's own life exemplified his conviction that classical learning should lead to personal morality and public service. He found time to take part in the life of the city, continually helping the poor with finan-cial gifts and educating many of their sons free of charge. He often gave anonymous gifts to churches and clergy. While he was well paid by the marquis, he spent almost everything on his students, the poor, and the Church. At his death, his entire estate consisted of a small piece of land, his books, and his clothing.

Vittorino's health, which had never been good, broke down in 1444. The following year, he had continual attacks of fever. On February 2, 1446, he died at Mantua, and he had a simple funeral, as specified in his will.

Contributions

How should we evaluate Vittorino da Feltre's contributions to West-ern education? Intellectually, he was highly competent but not outstand-ing. His mastery of Greek was never great, and he left no writings. Unlike some other humanists, he wielded little direct political power. Because his activities were confined to Padua, Venice, and Mantua, he had only a small circle of friends. While we have six hundred of Guarino's letters to friends, only six of Vittorino's have survived.

Vittorino is remembered because of his unique ability to translate the values of an era into a specific educational program. His school was steeped in the Renaissance pursuit of virtue and love of learning. His own life proved that the ideal could be achieved. Destined never to achieve intellectual greatness, he was the teacher of humanists (such as Lorenzo Valla) who would shape their age. One scholar put it this way: "Vittorino's school at Mantua . . . lasted from 1423 to his death in 1446, and its extraordinary qualities—the social mixture of princes and poor men, the humanity with which the humanities were inculcated, the psychological finesse and moral fervor of the master—have made it the most famous school of all times."[7] While this appraisal is somewhat exaggerated, the survival of Vittorino's ideas in the writings of students and friends is the best possible testimony to the effect he had on the lives of those around him and, through them, on the development of Western civilization.

WOMEN AND THE NEW LEARNING

Historians have generally portrayed the Renaissance as a movement that embodied an enlightened attitude toward education for women. It is true that some famous humanists (Erasmus, for example) advocated education for women, but most males did not favor sexual equality in any sphere, including schooling. However, a number of female humanists took issue with this attitude, and in the fourteenth century, a public debate began over the place of women in society. This was the beginning of a series of controversies that are not yet entirely resolved.

Christine de Pisan (c. 1364–after 1429)

Christine de Pisan was born in Venice in late 1363 or early 1364. Her father, Tommaso di Benvenuto da Pizzano, was a well-paid official of the city of Venice. He was from Pizzano, a village near Bologna. He studied at Bologna and was elected to a position as lecturer there in 1342. His specialties were medicine and astronomy, including astrology. His wife was the daughter of a friend and was probably a number of years younger than he. Christine was their first child.[8]

Tommaso was ambitious. He was buying property around Bologna with his Venetian salary when the king of France, Charles V, invited him to visit Paris. Charles was the most famous ruler in Europe, and Paris was the most celebrated city. Charles was interested in astrology, and Tommaso was noted for his knowledge of the field. It was a good opportunity for Tommaso, and he took it. The family stayed in Bologna while Tommaso tried out his new situation, and four years later they joined him in Paris, where he had become one of the king's close advisors.

Life in Paris was good for Christine and her two younger brothers. The family lived comfortably on Tommaso's royal salary. Christine had nice clothes and, although she was not of the aristocracy, some of her friends were from the most powerful families in France. Her education was typical of what liberal humanists approved for aristocratic and wealthy middle class girls at the time: manners, morals, etiquette, reading, and writing.

Christine overheard many conversations between her father and his intellectual friends, but paid little attention to them, and while she was around the king and other significant political figures, she did not think much about politics. She behaved herself and developed the skills and attitudes that a good girl should. Although not thinking of herself as beautiful—she did say that she had a pleasant and sound body—she attracted a lot of male attention as a young teenager, and her mother and father arranged a marriage for her in 1379 when she was fifteen. Marriage at this age was normal for her time; in fact, fifteen may have been considered old, for the general attitude was that women bloom early, mature fast, and fade quickly. Thus, parents commonly arranged marriages for twelve- to fifteen-year-old girls and men did not usually marry until their mid-twenties or later.

Marriage

Christine's father had numerous offers for his daughter's hand, some from wealthy and aristocratic men. He rejected these in favor of Etienne of Castel, a student/scholar of twenty-four from a well-established but not rich family in Picardy, whom Christine had known all her life. She thought him "beautiful both in face and in body" and he seems to have returned her high regard. They were a happy couple. The king helped by giving Etienne a good position as secretary and notary.

One year after Christine and Etienne married, the king died. His successor, Charles VI, was a twelve-year-old whose advisors did not like Christine's father. He quickly lost his position and became a sick, helpless old man. Etienne did well, however, soon becoming a well-paid councilor to the king. Although Christine's family, including her two younger brothers, depended on Etienne for support, this seems to have been no strain financially. She and Etienne bought a large house and had seven servants.

In 1381 Christine had a daughter. Later came a son, who apparently did not live. Then in 1385 she had another boy whom she named Jean. She said the births were difficult and painful, but she seems to have loved her children and to have been a good mother. Her father died, and her mother (whom she regarded as a kind and good person) moved in with her family, as did her two younger brothers. It was a busy life and Christine was happy.

In 1389 Etienne died suddenly. He had gone with the king on some routine business to Beauvais, about forty miles north of Paris and had become ill. There was no doctor, and before anyone could figure out what was wrong, he died. "I was so confused with grief that I became a recluse, dull, sad, alone and weary," she later wrote about her reaction to the unexpected news. She hoped she would die herself, and it would be many years before she stopped thinking almost constantly of her misfortune. The pressing demands of her young children as well as the need to support her mother and two younger brothers, soon forced Christine to act in their behalf.

A Widow's Education

The behavior expected of any young widow was that she mourn briefly and then remarry. This was particularly true for someone like Christine, who was attractive and well situated socially and financially. She was accustomed to a life-style that required money, and now she had little, for her husband's salary stopped immediately upon his death. He had bought some property that he intended to go to her, but it was tied up in the courts. Despite these problems, she refused to marry again.

Christine hired lawyers to help her get the back salary and property that were her husband's. Believing the lawyers dishonest, she fired them and went to court herself to try to resolve the matters. The justices delayed, played tricks, and shifted her case to other courts. For a woman to represent herself in court was so unusual that when she went out in public, men whistled and made sexually explicit remarks. She pawned her furniture, borrowed money, and continued the fight. After seven years she got the back salary; after seven more, she won part of the property that should have gone to her in the first place. "Leeches of fortune" was what she called the officials involved in this long dispute.

To understand what Christine went through, we must review the treatment of women up to that time. The Christian movement had accorded some status and importance to women, and the women's monasteries offered an alternative to the dependence of marriage, but most of the Church fathers were suspicious of sexuality and regarded women as Satan's agents to tempt men. Moreover, power rested on military strength, and this was a male enterprise; with rare exceptions, women were excluded from practical military knowledge. Both civil and canon law gave husbands almost complete power over their wives. Civil law excluded women's testimony in court because of their "frailty," and imposed only half the fine for a crime against a woman as for the same offense against a man.

Aquinas's justification of Aristotle did some useful things for human thought, but it did not advance equality between the sexes. Following Aristotle, Aquinas argued that nature always wants to produce a male, and woman, therefore, is something defective. Aquinas also believed that women are weak in body, mind, and will. They need men for everything; men need women only to have children. Women should regard men as their natural masters and be happy to submit to their discipline. Children should love their fathers more than their mothers. Not all men agreed with Aquinas, but his attitude was popular.[9]

In her grief and frustration, Christine wrote a *ballade* (poem) to vent her feelings. Friends said she should write more, and she did. These were mostly love poems written in French. To help pass the time and to increase her knowledge of the world, the young widow began to read. She started with history, and read several Roman and a number of medieval authors. Finally she came to the standard item of French courtly education: the *Roman de la Rose,* a poem of twenty-one thousand lines written about a century earlier. The chief author was Jean de Meun, a French cultural hero. He had woven into his allegorical poem current beliefs and knowledge on every subject under the sun.

The "Women's Quarrel"

One of de Meun's topics was the nature of woman. According to him, she was selfish and disloyal. She couldn't keep secrets, deceived men viciously, and was an easy victim of flattery. Men suffered continuously from woman's nature, a fact known since ancient times.

De Meun's poem made little sense to Christine. She did not think his description fit her or many of the women she knew. She had spent years trying to get justice from the courts, putting up with taunts, pressure, and deceit. As one historian put it, "This may be the first recorded instance of a woman's feminist consciousness being raised by her life experiences."[10]

Christine wrote a reply, criticizing de Meun for devoting so much space to techniques for seducing virgins. (It shouldn't take much planning anyway, she said, if women were as simpleminded as de Meun thought.) She also turned on its head the common religious argument against women, favored by Aquinas, de Meun, and others, that since God had made man first and had then made woman from a small part of man, woman was to man about as significant as one small rib is to the whole organism. Christine pointed out that, since God created woman not out of ordinary clay but from the body of man, "the most noble of earthly things," woman could be superior to man.[11] Finally, she indicted de Meun for his contention that marriage was an unnatural state since people were not monogamous by nature and would violate their vows. Christine pointed out that this attitude was clearly against Christian doctrine.

No one had ever criticized the greatest poet of France, and now he was being attacked by a woman! Many people thought this preposterous. One of the king's secretaries, a man named Gontier Col, tried to silence Christine through intimidation and insults. Col wrote that Christine had not likely thought of the criticisms herself, and that she was probably being used by others. This was the only way he could account for the fact that a woman had written anything against that "true catholic, solemn master, doctor in theology and excellent philosopher who knew all that the human understanding can know."[12] But Christine would not be bluffed, and defended her position effectively and courteously. She won some powerful supporters, notably Jean Gerson, chancellor of the University of Paris.

This *querelle des femmes,* as it came to be called, certainly did not end in Christine's time, but her work was an important beginning of the public debate about women's rights. Part of the controversy involved the extent to which women should be educated and what the curriculum should be. Most humanist educational theorists approved of educating aristocratic women, but cautioned that material that might excite women sexually should be censored. The argument that women were too frail to stand up to schooling or that they would suffer nervous breakdowns if they studied "difficult" subjects like mathematics did not come up until after Christine's time.

Her own experiences and observations convinced Christine that women could learn as well as men if they were taught the same things. She believed that learning was the "greatest of all riches" and that it would be good for all children to know "what a splendid thing it is to have a liking for knowledge, and how wretched it is to be ignorant!"[13] When a man expressed his disapproval of Christine's desire to learn by saying, "It does not become a woman to be learned, as few of them are," Christine replied quickly, "It less becomes a man to be ignorant, as so many of them are."

In one of her later works, she posed the question of why so many male writers expressed poor opinions of woman's nature. She had one of her characters give two possible explanations: (1) that it all began with Eve, and men have not gotten over their grudge; and (2) that men secretly realize but don't want to acknowledge that women are superior to them, both in capacity and in "nobility of natures."

Christine de Pisan was not anti-male. Apparently, she held both her father and her husband in the highest esteem, and she also respected and liked a number of other men. She was a strong advocate of marriage, and felt that hers had been good even if it had been too short. As one of her biographers summed it up, she had simply come to think that "women must have their own definite place in the scheme of things, not a place in opposition to the world of men, but of equal importance to theirs. . . ." Five hundred years later, women (and some men) would advocate the same idea, and it would still meet with opposition.

Professional Author

Christine earned a living as a writer for about fifteen years starting around 1400. She was one of the first to do this (the printing press did not yet exist and there were no royalties for authors). Her fame as a poet spread, and more and more people wanted copies of her work. She made these as requested, even having some of them illustrated, and presented them with an appropriate dedication. The new owner almost always supplied a gift of money in return.

Christine did not confine herself to poetry. In 1404 Philip, Duke of Burgundy, asked her to write a history of the reign of Charles V, who was his brother. She was glad to comply because she had respected the king. She read the official chronicles, interviewed people who had been around Charles, wrote her own recollections and the stories her father had told her, and then organized her account around her perception of the kind of person he was. Thus, she developed many of the techniques used by later historians and biographers. Her account contained information that would have otherwise been lost. Male historians used it heavily, but often did not cite it. Christine also produced what are now called self-help books. She wrote, among many other things, a book of practical advice to women on how to get along in the world and solve their problems.

Christine became an astute political observer and predicted civil war would occur if reforms were not made in France. She was right and she also predicted that England would take the opportunity provided by French unrest to try to seize land in France. Although she was no democrat, Christine believed the common people had grievances that should be corrected, and she wrote letters appealing to those in power to help change things.

As she saw war coming, Christine read everything available on all aspects of fighting and chivalry. Then she wrote a long manuscript on military tactics: when to fight and when not to, how to supply troops, what to do about morale, how to treat civilians, a complete treatment of heraldry, and many other related topics. She may have written this book for her son, Jean, for whom she had secured a knightly education in two aristocratic households. She did not mention him, and we do not know what happened to him. It is possible that he was killed in the fighting, which began in 1410.

Celebrating Female Leadership

In 1418, Christine went to the Abbey of Poissy just a few miles northwest of Paris, near Argenteuil where Heloise had been. Her daughter had chosen, at about the age of fifteen, to join the abbey. Christine did not wish this for her daughter, but she did not forbid it. She and her daughter had remained on good terms, and the daughter repeatedly urged her mother to give up all the struggle and come to the monastery. For ten years, Christine wrote nothing. Then, in 1429, she penned one last poem to commemorate the actions of another famous woman— Jeanne d'Arc.

By the late 1420s, England was winning the war against France, and the English occupied Paris. The French king, Charles VII, had never been crowned. A sixteen-year-old girl named Jeanne, who lived in the eastern French town of Domremy, heard voices and had visions of religious figures telling her to save France and take the king to Rheims to be crowned. Her father, a prosperous farmer named Jacques d'Arc, swore he would drown her before he would let her go, but she got a horse and rode 450 miles in eleven days to reach the king. Charles VII accompanied her to Rheims and was crowned.

Her greatest moment occurred at Orléans, which had been under siege by the English for some time. By her presence and her leadership of troops in battle, Jeanne inspired the French army to victory over the English, and raised the siege of the city.

Christine de Pisan was delighted at the news of Jeanne's triumph. She wrote in celebration of the event, "What an honor for the feminine sex, which it seems that God loves!" Nothing else was heard from her. "The year of her death is not known," says one biographer, "but one cannot help hoping that she died soon after that swansong, and did not live long enough to hear of the terrible end . . . of the maid who had crowned her long belief in women and defeated the enemies of the country she loved so well."[14]

The "terrible end" for Jeanne d'Arc came in 1431. Not long after Christine's poem was written, Jeanne was captured by French forces not loyal to the king. Charles, who owed her a great deal, did nothing to help, and the English got her through a large bribe. Under English supervision she was put on trial for heresy. She was told to disavow the voices she heard, but she would not. Having paid heavily for her, the English king wasn't about to let her go. He had her burned at the stake. Choking on the smoke, she said the voice of God had not led her astray. France had a hero who proved Christine's belief that women could do anything men could.

Despite Jeanne d'Arc's courage and Christine de Pisan's forceful style, women's progress toward equality was slow. Toward the end of the fifteenth century, some of Christine's work was among the first material to be published by Caxton on his printing press. Most of it, however, remained unpublished, and soon after her time, her work was practically unknown in Europe. It is only now being resurrected.

RELIGIOUS REFORM AND THE NEW LEARNING

By the late fifteenth century, the "new learning" was spreading to many important centers of learning in northern Europe. The next three biographies illustrate this fact and also show how humanism became linked with religious reform.

Johannes Butzbach (1478–1526)

Johannes ("Hans") Butzbach was born in Miltenberg, in what is now Germany. When he was less than a year old, he went to live with his father's sister because his mother was pregnant. (The notion that a married woman should enjoy any right over her own body, including the right to refuse sexual intercourse with her husband, was foreign to both law and practice. Thus, it was usual for women to be pregnant again soon after giving birth.[15]) Farming children out to relatives was common practice. Hans was probably lucky, because his aunt was childless and, according to his later recollection, cared for him "most lovingly and tenderly."[16]

At six years of age, Hans's aunt sent him to school. However, it was not a good school, and he disliked the experience and soon encountered another custom that had not changed in the thousand years since Augustine's day: "When I did not want to go," he wrote, "she saw to it that I was driven by sharp switches."

When Hans was about ten, his foster mother died. At this turn of events, he returned to his original home and renewed his efforts to play hooky. "My mother took me by the collar and dragged me to school," he wrote. The master gave his assistant permission to "beat him severely as he deserves." Two decades later, Hans described what happened in the following words:

> Wrathfully the heirling . . . stripped my clothes from me and bound me to a post; and then the harsh man exerted all his strength to beat me without mercy. My mother . . . heard me screaming and wailing so terribly that she turned quickly, came to the door, and . . . shouted at him to stop. But he, as though deaf to her cries . . . struck all the harder; meanwhile the whole school had to sing a song. When he stopped attacking me so savagely, my mother forcefully opened the door, and rushed in. But when she saw me bound to a post and so horribly cut up by the heavy blows and covered with blood, she fell swooning to the floor.

When Hans's mother revived, she "attacked the schoolmaster with harsh imprecations" and swore that her son would not return to school.[17]

Wandering Scholar

Hans then undertook a different educational venture: "While this was happening to me, our neighbor's son, a grown student, returned from a foreign school. He ingratiated himself with my father and requested that I be put to study with him." The young man assured Hans's father, Conrad, that "elsewhere, with him, I would, in a short time, make greater progress in learning than I would here in years." Conrad agreed to send him away with this "scholar." The parents bought their son clothes, books, and supplies; and they gave their young neighbor money and the promise of more if it was needed. In return the neighbor promised to take good care of their son and to send word often of his well-being and progress. Conrad made the sign of the cross over a jug of wine and each person in the family, and the neighbor drank a solemn toast to seal the bargain. Then, accompanied by sobbing goodbyes from both parents, the neighbor and his young charge set off for nearby Nürnberg.

It had long been customary for scholars as young as thirteen or fourteen to wander from place to place in search of noted teachers. (Abelard took several years to reach Paris because he stopped to study with people along the way.) It was also commonly agreed that wandering students, being by definition novice churchmen, could beg for their food if they were in need.

In the German-speaking area, the wandering scholars came to be called *bacchants*. The precise history of the term is not clear: it may have been derived from the term *vagantes* (wanderers) or from Bacchus, the god of wine. Many of the wandering bacchants seemed to have a preference for alcoholic beverages, and as a group they were not generally noted for high morals or good manners. But by Butzbach's time, the practice was well established, and his father had himself been such a wanderer. Perhaps that was why he cried so much when Hans left—he knew the hardships that awaited.

Hans embarked on his new life anticipating high adventure; by the end of the first day he got a good indication of how things would go. Many of the bacchants had younger boys as pupils, who were called "abc-shooters"—"abc" because the pupils were supposedly learning their abc's; "shooter" from *Schutzen,* which can mean protector or defender. Shooters were expected to beg for their bacchants. The bacchant stopped at an inn a few miles from Miltenberg and threw a party with some of the money the Butzbachs had given him. Hans went to bed with no supper. Succeeding days were worse. The farther away from Miltenberg the pair wandered, the more cavalier the bacchant became. After two months the money ran out and Hans had to "beg in villages that were so filthy and muddy, that I often waded in mire to my ankles, sometimes even to my calves; and at times, like one walking in dough, I could move neither forward nor backward." He hated this, but if he resisted, the bacchant beat him "with his fists and staff." This, too, was customary. "Sometimes I was attacked so viciously by watchdogs that, I believe, if the owners had not come to my assistance, I should have been torn to pieces."

Ultimately the pair ended up in Kaden, Bohemia. The rector there gave them a student lodging, but after a time they moved 250 miles southeast to Eger (in present Hungary) because they feared an outbreak of plague. There bacchant and shooter got positions as tutors in well-to-do families, but the "scholar" beat Hans severely when Hans refused to beg for two other bacchants. The family offered their young tutor protection, but he ran away out of fear of the bacchant. He worked briefly in an inn, from which he was more or less kidnaped by a Bohemian aristocrat.

Hans spent the next few years in and around Prague working for several different noblemen, and was generally treated well. He learned to ride and swim. He liked the food, but later his feelings of German nationalism and his monastic training led him to write of "the barbarous speech of the super-barbarous Bohemians."

At about eighteen, Butzbach made his way back home. His father had died; his mother was remarried and pregnant. His stepfather apprenticed him to a tailor. The two years he spent there, Butzbach remembered with regret: long hours, hard work, "harsh words from my master and the household, and sometimes hard blows, cold and heat, hunger and thirst in the extreme; what I had to suffer in these and many other kinds of distress, could hardly be written in a large book."

Humanism at Deventer

With his apprenticeship ended, Butzbach found a position as tailor to the monastery of St. John the Baptist in the mountains of Rheingau. His experiences as a lay brother and his recollections of his father's desire that he become a priest turned his thoughts to a religious vocation, but most monasteries would not take adults unless they had a needed skill or were already educated.

Butzbach's mother gave him money so he could return to school. He went to Deventer in the Netherlands, a school founded in 1380 by the Brotherhood of the Common Life. This school, and some others run by the Brotherhood, had become famous for teaching humanism or the "new learning." Many monasteries, partly in response to the criticisms of reformers, recruited heavily in these schools. To successfully complete the course at Deventer meant automatic offers from desirable establishments.

Butzbach's first attempt to get an education failed, for he had little money and was academically unprepared. He was much older than most of his classmates, and his sense of inadequacy and the resulting discomfort were large. So he quit. But a little later, his mother obtained more money for him at considerable cost to herself. Butzbach's stepfather gave him five florins. "He knew also that my mother had a treasured florin which she had received from Hillig [Butzbach's father], with which he had betrothed himself to her. With all authority, he demanded it for me." Butzbach's mother tried to slip him a different coin, and "a terrible quarrel arose between them, which ended in my mother being severely beaten and having her hair torn." Butzbach dropped his luggage and money, "and with my bothers and sisters, offered resistance to my stepfather in order to protect mother. I succeeded in dragging her from under his feet." The stepfather later apologized, saying the fight was due only to his great interest in seeing his stepson get an education.

Butzbach returned to school, and this time did better. Although he almost quit several times, in two years, he moved from the eighth class (eleventh was lowest) to the third. He suffered a variety of stress-related ailments: boils, fevers, scabs all over his body, swollen limbs, and ulcers. When he heard a representative of the monastery of Laach (near Koblenz, Germany) make a recruitment speech when he was twenty-two, Butzbach decided to join. He and one other Deventer student made the trek to Koblenz, but only Butzbach took the final vows. He later became master of novices, and at twenty-nine he was chosen the house's prior, an office he filled until his death thirteen years later. He seems also to have been ordained a priest, thus fulfilling his parent's chief ambition for him.

In Retrospect

Butzbach was a sensitive person who felt keenly the wrongs and injuries that he experienced. He was neither exceptionally intelligent nor singularly courageous. He did not invent any pedagogical theory, and he did not comment perceptively on his educational background. Yet he coped successfully with his life experiences. His account contains a pervasive mood of subdued self-pity, but he described himself as having achieved a measure of calm victory over his turbulent feelings.

Butzbach's account supplies details of educational life in the fifteenth and sixteenth centuries. Like Guibert of Nogent five centuries earlier, Butzbach saw nearly everything in terms of God's will, the tug between good and evil, and the supernatural forces described in the teachings of the Church. His schooling at Deventer was superior in its time, producing men like Desiderius Erasmus and others who favored reform. But although Butzbach's monastery was part of the internal Church reform movement, his own thinking remained conventional. For instance, Butzbach recommended that his younger half-brother undergo the ordeal as a shooter, seeing no way to break the cycle in which both he and his father had been trapped.

Desiderius Erasmus (c. 1466–1536)

Desiderius Erasmus's birth appeared inauspicious. He attended Deventer in the same century as Butzbach, and later he came to be known as the "prince of humanists."

Later in his life, Erasmus intentionally obscured details of his birth. He was born the illegitimate son of a priest and a physician's daughter. Poverty and a weak constitution led him to be sensitive all his life. His early education was with the Brothers of the Common Life, and at about age thirteen he was orphaned. Erasmus maintained that his guardian pressured him into entering an Augustinian monastery at eighteen. He was ordained a priest at twenty-two, left the monastery, and came under the patronage of the Bishop of Cambray, who gave him financial aid and permission to study at the Sorbonne.

As an adult, Erasmus classified himself as a citizen of the world, with Holland his homeland and Latin his tongue. He traveled from country to country and enjoyed many friendships. Invited to England, he was a confidant of Thomas More, John Colet, and other English humanists.

His connection with them was so close that he was considered by some to be an English humanist. He lived for a time in each of the major countries of Europe, but made only one trip to Rome.[18]

Erasmus as Author

A prolific writer all his life, Erasmus produced literary works from schoolbooks to theological treatises. His major work, *In Praise of Folly,* satirized the excesses of society. His *Enchiridion,* or *Handbook of the Christian Soldier,* has been called "the book that made the Reformation" because in it Erasmus spoke out against the abuses in the Church and the need for reform.[19] He also translated the New Testament from Greek into Latin, although the work was replete with errors and was condemned at the Council of Trent. His criticism of Luther in *On the Discussion of Free Will* was the first public attack on the teachings of that reformer.

Erasmus is known as one of the great writers of Renaissance humanism. He believed in the reform of the Church and directed his efforts to that end until his death. His stature in Church history has been questioned by some because he was a moderate unwilling to leave the Church, but in the present ecumenical age, his reputation is once more being restored.

Some have questioned whether he was primarily a Christian or a scholar, but Erasmus considered himself first and foremost a Christian. He made no distinction between scholar and Christian, believing that ignorance was the enemy of Christ. His first rule (promulgated in the *Enchiridion*) was "to understand as clearly as possible [about Christ] and about the Holy Scriptures handed down by His spirit, . . . not to entertain belief only by lip service—coldly, listlessly, hesitantly, as most Christians do—but let it permeate your whole being, let it be deeply and immovably fixed until there is not even an iota contained in Scripture that does not pertain to your spiritual well-being."[20] His second rule for the Christian soldier was "to enter upon the way of spiritual health, not slowly or timorously, but resolutely, wholeheartedly, with a confident— if I may use the expression—pugnacious spirit, ready to expend either your goods or your life for Christ."[21]

As a Christian moralist, Erasmus reconciled the study of the ancient philosophers with a Christian outlook by stressing the lessons one could learn by reading them as history:

> They err, therefore, who affirm that virtue is won by handling affairs and by contact with life, without aid from the teaching of philosophy. . . . A long and manifold experience is, beyond doubt, of great profit, but only to such as by the wisdom of learning have acquired an intelligent and informed judgment. Besides, philosophy teaches us more in one year than our own individual experience can teach us in

thirty, and its teaching carries none of the risks which the method of learning by experience of necessity brings with it.[22]

By *philosophy,* Erasmus meant theory, knowledge, and social and historical lessons learned from the past.

Erasmus was a pacifist. He did not think the world could be Christian unless it was a peaceful, well-ordered place, and he opposed rulers and rich people who promoted war, the former for territorial gain and the latter for money. He objected to rulers who exposed young men "to so many dangers, and often in a single hour . . . make so many and many an orphan, widow, and childless old man."[23]

Educational Views

For Erasmus, the aim of education was social as opposed to strictly individual. He addressed a nobleman with the fact that "your children are begotten not to yourself alone, but to your country: not to your country alone, but to God."[24] He stressed faith and good works more than dogma, for the good deeds of individuals would result in a well-ordered social structure. This ideal society could be accomplished only through a liberal education.

According to Erasmus, the best education was a return to the ancient Greeks and Romans. To those who would condemn the study of classics, Erasmus argued that (1) it was through these cultures that Christianity was first spread; (2) this study was needed by anyone who wanted to search out the truths of religion and scripture; and (3) their study was approved by early fathers of the Church, including Basil, Jerome, and Augustine.

Erasmus referred to public schools in several of his writings. By this he meant what the Greeks and Romans had—a school in public rather than tutors at home, and he stressed that noblemen and statesmen had a philanthropic obligation to help poor but deserving students. Along with Thomas More (whose practice of educating his daughters Erasmus greatly admired), he wanted women to be educated in a carefully censored curriculum.

Erasmus told parents that learning begins at birth. He pleaded for early learning of Latin, saying, "It is as instinctive with children to imitate as it is easy for them to remember." He did not think that the study of Latin would appeal to children, but counted on teachers to inspire the young. He thought teachers should be sensitive to the talents of individuals so that each child would be able to pursue the right course of study for his or her particular bent. Disapproving of harsh discipline, Erasmus recommended instead that the unmotivated be "turned out to the plow or the pack saddle." Erasmus favored reaching the young with games. He cited an instance in which the letters of the alphabet were made into cookies to be eaten as they were learned. He urged parents to find good teachers for their children.

Texts

Erasmus's schoolbooks were widely used during the sixteenth and seventeenth centuries. Along with William Lily, Thomas Linacre, John Colet, and Cardinal Woolsey, he developed *Lily's Grammar,* which Henry VIII proclaimed England's authorized Latin grammar in 1540. This grammar was used in English schools for several hundred years.[25]

Many of Erasmus's schoolbooks were put together for other purposes and were later adapted for the use of schools. *The Colloquies,* printed originally without his knowledge in 1518 as the *Familiarium colloquiorum formulae,* had a long and checkered career. The first edition was a collection of single sentences, conversations, questions and answers, useful to a beginning Latin student.

As the original *Colloquies* began to gain wide acceptance, Erasmus began revising and expanding many of the formulae into longer pieces. The result was "a book of unusual variety: debates on moral and religious questions; lively arguments on war, government, and other social problems; advice on how to train husbands, wives and children; discourses on innkeepers, beggars, pets, horse thieves, methods of study—all this and much more."[26] Adults read the book for pleasure and information.

Erasmus introduced boys to the elements of oratory in *De Utraque Verboram ac Rerum Copia (On Copia of Words and Ideas),* printed in 1500. A sixteenth-century student defined *copia* as the "faculty of varying the same expression or thought in many ways by means of different forms of speech and a variety of figures and arguments."[27] Students of that period spent much time trying to express Latin texts and sentences in different ways. For this purpose, Erasmus's book and others were of great use. "Attaining good style . . . is a matter of no little moment," said Erasmus. "What clothing is to our body, diction is to the expression of our thoughts."[28] The *Copia* went through 235 printings by 1600.

One of Erasmus's techniques was to present a proverb followed by extensive comment. One example is *Festina lenta* ("make haste slowly"), on which Erasmus commented that it has within it a riddle since it has contradictory terms. How can one make haste slowly? The answer is that sometimes it is better to proceed slowly in deciding on a course of action, but once a decision has been made to move quickly. He pointed out that this proverb was a favorite of two great Roman emperors: Octavius Augustus and Titus Vespasianus.[29] A great number of proverbs or expressions discussed by Erasmus are still part of common speech. Some examples:

A necessary evil.
There's many a slip twixt the cup and the lip.
Leave no stone unturned.
Let the cobbler stick to his last.
Dog in the manger.
A rare bird.

One swallow doesn't make a summer.
I'll sleep on it.
Up to the ears.

The success of Erasmus's work was phenomenal. *Adagia* was translated into English, French, Italian, German, Dutch, and other languages. The work went through 120 editions before 1570, and it is still used. The *Copia* was one of the "best-sellers" of its time. The *Colloquies* was one of the most widely used textbooks in the sixteenth and seventeenth centuries, and it gained notoriety when the University of Paris banned its use, it was condemned by the Council of Trent in 1564, and Charles V invoked the death penalty for its use in schools. (The book made strange allies—Luther joined Charles V in condemning it.) Yet only the Bible outsold it up to 1550.[30]

Niccolò Machiavelli (1469–1527)

Erasmus and many reformers did not separate humanism from religion, but we must be careful not to confuse *humanism* with *humaneness*. Some Renaissance people were the very essence of charity and, like Erasmus, thought kindness inseparable from learning and living. The central thrust of humanism, however, was the study of humans through the classics. It did not necessarily imply a particular assumption about morality, as the works of Machiavelli reveal.

Niccolò Machiavelli was never a teacher like Vittorino da Feltre, nor was he directly involved in educational policy formation. He had a good education but was not a scholar like Erasmus. However, Machiavelli had a profound indirect influence on the development of education in the West. In order to understand that influence, it is first necessary to see what political and social events shaped his thought.

Florentine Politics

Florence, where Machiavelli lived, was the political and military capital of northwestern Italy and a major European commercial city. Italy at that time was a collection of independent cities. Some of these had been republics for a long time (Florence had been so since at least 1000), and the more powerful of them ruled a good deal of territory. Florence controlled the city of Pisa and other areas.

The greatest ruler in the Medici family, which ruled Florence during most of the fifteenth century, was Lorenzo de' Medici (1449–1492), called the Magnificent. Lorenzo was a great patron of the arts and a shrewd politician, and under his leadership the city prospered, though at the price of personal freedom.

Niccolò was born in 1469, during the height of the Medici rule, to an upper middle class family. His father, Bernardo, was a lawyer and book collector. During Niccolò's youth, Lorenzo de' Medici took over the Florentine government. Gradually, politics, once an honorable profession, became less respectable. In 1478, the city revolted against the Medici, an uprising which failed because the city's hired soldiers were ineffective.[31] But Piero de' Medici, who succeeded his father Lorenzo, was incompetent, and in 1494, he and his supporters were forced into exile. Florence once again took on a republican form of government with a system of elected officials, most of whom held office for short periods of time (maximum two years) because the people feared the threat to their liberty posed by officials who were entrenched in power. Since someone was always being elected to office, the city was constantly abuzz with political activity. In observing all of this, Niccolò learned lessons he would later formulate into political theories. He concluded that the success or failure of a city depended heavily on the ability of its prince.

Diplomatic Career

Machiavelli entered the Florentine civil service in 1498 as second chancellor, or as a secretary in the state government. His first diplomatic mission, in 1500, sent him to France. During this period, Italian politics had become even more complicated because although Italy was fragmented, large states across the Alps were beginning to form into modern nations. Spain had been united under Ferdinand and Isabella, Germany was being drawn together by the Holy Roman Emperor, and France was coalescing into a single nation. These possessed more power than the isolated Italian cities, and all of them had their eyes on Italian territories.

In 1499, the French seized Milan and claimed Naples. Venice and the pope cooperated. The Spanish moved in to counter the French presence, and ended up getting a piece of Naples. Florence, like the other city-states, had to pay "protection" to friends and enemies alike. Frequently, it was hard to tell exactly which were which.

As a result of these invasions, Florence, which had allied itself with France, lost Pisa, and Machiavelli's mission in 1500 was to get French support for a Florentine effort to retake Pisa. The mission produced no long-term results, but was a personal success for Machiavelli. For the first time, he saw how government and commerce were conducted in another country.

In 1502, two key people came into Machiavelli's life: Piero Soderini and Cesare Borgia. A highly respected but anti-aristocratic citizen, Soderini was elected chief magistrate of Florence for life. Soderini took to Machiavelli and sent him to negotiate with Cesare Borgia, the duke of Valentinois, who was becoming a major political force in Italy.

An illegitimate son of Pope Alexander VI, Borgia was conspiring with his father's help to unite all of Italy. Allied with the French, Borgia proved a formidable leader. Machiavelli's task was to stall the Florentine alliance. In the process, he got a firsthand look at a shrewd, powerful man who seemed on the verge of completing the impossible task of uniting Italy. Borgia's exercise of power, an "iron fist in a kid glove," would become Machiavelli's model for statesmanship in his major work, *The Prince.*

Soon, however, Borgia's luck ran out. In 1503, his father the pope died. Cesare himself was seriously ill. The new pope, Pius III, died after twenty-six days. Elected in his place was Julius II, a lifelong enemy of the Borgias, who had forced him to spend ten years in exile. Until his death in 1513, Julius would wage a relentless crusade to drive the French from Italy, making war on Venice and pressuring Florence in his attempt to build an anti-French alliance. He would eventually ruin Cesare Borgia and bring down the Florentine republic.

In 1503 Machiavelli went to Rome to appeal to the pope for aid against the Venetians, who had just attacked Florence. In 1506 he tried to raise a Florentine militia—a nonmercenary force—a pet project throughout his life, and went on a second mission to the pope. In 1507 he became secretary of the Council of Nine, a new group set up to oversee Florence's military affairs. He also traveled to Germany in 1507 to negotiate a treaty and to spy on Emperor Maximilian's war plans. In the next several years, he traveled extensively on state business. During all this time, his wife and several children remained at home.

Despite the efforts of Machiavelli and his colleagues, there were far too many diplomatic fires to be put out. Florence stubbornly insisted on keeping its alliance with France, despite waning French influence in Italy. Pope Julius II became stronger and stronger, and took vengeance on those Italians who had sided with France. When the French withdrew completely in 1512, the pope reclaimed a number of northern Italian cities and demanded that the Florentines enter the anti-French alliance.

Machiavelli now became as much a soldier as a statesman. Always on the move, he recruited and trained a militia, knowing that an army was Florence's only chance for survival. His efforts, however, came too late. The pope attacked Florence with a professional Spanish army, which crushed the untrained militia.

Loss of Power

The Florentine defeat spelled the end of the republic. The pope, heavily in debt to the Medici, removed Soderini as head of the council, and within a few months the Medici resumed control. Like most of the Florentine diplomats, Machiavelli hoped to keep his job under the new administration. He regarded himself as a servant of the state rather than of any particular individual, but the Medici did not agree, for he was identified too closely with the old regime. Machiavelli was virtually the only major civil servant dismissed by the new government.

Things went from bad to worse for Machiavelli. He had to pay a large fine and could not leave Florentine territory for a year. Then he was implicated in a plot to overthrow the new government and was arrested, imprisoned, and tortured. Only with the election of Pope Leo X in 1513 (ironically, a Medici) was there a general amnesty that freed Machiavelli from prison.

Paradoxically, what appeared to be an unrelieved disaster in Machiavelli's life freed him from the day-to-day tasks of diplomacy and gave him time to think and write. One scholar has compared his life during this period to a meadow beginning to bloom after a long winter. Machiavelli began to reflect on his experiences and the political situation of Florence.[32]

Writing Career

The first important writings to come out of this reflection were the *Discourses,* essays on the themes of the Roman historian Livy. Machiavelli's goal was to study the qualities of an ideal republic. In the humanistic tradition, Machiavelli used Livy's writings as a springboard to propose some of his own political ideas. Good laws, he argued, were absolutely necessary for a free society, as was a balance of interest groups (especially to avoid the kind of tension between nobility and other people that had created so many problems in cities like Florence).[33] Moreover, he continued to insist that the voice of the people had to be taken seriously. Laws had to support the customs of the society, and political decisions reflect the specific times.

In the midst of these reflections on the nature of republics, Machiavelli made an abrupt shift to a study of the qualities of an absolute ruler. This work, *The Prince,* was written in 1513 and is the most famous of his books. Many handbooks for rulers already existed, and this style of writing, called the "mirror of princes," sought to challenge leaders to greatness by laying before them the virtues of classical rulers like Augustus Caesar. Humanists used such classical models as patterns for contemporary life.

Machiavelli combined information from Latin authors with his own experience to illustrate his themes, one of which was the unreliability of hired armies. Machiavelli recognized that mercenary troops have no loyalty to the state, but only to the highest bidder, and cannot be relied upon in a tough fight. (This was the belief that got him started building an army of conscripts when he was in Florence's government.) The quality which Machiavelli thought most desirable in a ruler, and which he spoke of again and again, was *virtù* (personal force or charisma). A successful prince, according to Machiavelli, ought to be feared but not hated, and should think constantly in strategic terms. Other qualities are virtues or vices depending on whether they help or hinder the political functioning of the state. Because all citizens' well-being depends upon the state functioning well, Machiavelli thought that usual considerations of personal morality do not apply to heads of state. Ends always justify means.

For Machiavelli, the other important forces in life were *fortuna* (fortune) and *necessità* (necessity). The latter can be used by the shrewd ruler to create opportunities, provided that he has *virtù*. *Fortuna* can also be counterbalanced, but only by swift thought and decisive action. In what was perhaps his most famous image, Machiavelli compared fortune to a woman who must be held and beaten in order to be controlled. Patriotism was important to Machiavelli, and he closed *The Prince* with an impassioned plea for a strong ruler to unite Italy and heal the wounds caused by its invaders (the northern Europeans).[34]

In 1520 the small republic of Ragusa offered Machiavelli a diplomatic post. He refused because it would have meant leaving Florence to serve foreigners. Finally, in 1521, the Medici gave him a small commission to negotiate with a group of Franciscans and asked him to recruit a famous preacher for Florence while he was about it. Although this was hardly the sort of thing he had been used to, Machiavelli jumped at the chance to ingratiate himself with the Medici.

More Political Turmoil

Just as things had begun to improve, however, the wheel of fortune turned again. In 1521, the Medici Pope Leo X died and was replaced by a stiff and pious Flemish cardinal, Adrian VI. Cardinal de' Medici, who had hoped to be elected, returned to Florence and took up the reins of government. In June 1522, there was a move to assassinate the Cardinal, and Machiavelli's friends were again among the plotters. In the same year, Machiavelli's brother Totto, a good and pious priest, died. Again Machiavelli returned to the country to think and write.

In 1523, Pope Adrian died, and this time, Cardinal de' Medici was elected. The new pope, who took the name Clement VII, allied himself with the Germans when his French allies were defeated. The emperor agreed to support the Medici rule in Florence. Machiavelli went to Rome to present Clement with a copy of his Florentine *Histories,* dedicated to him. In return, the pope gave him a minor commission, the first of several which were to come in the next few years. It seemed that Machiavelli's career was back on track.

Fortune once again intervened. The pope's enemies (there were many) challenged his rule. Machiavelli found himself once again preparing Florence for war while trying to arrange a peace. In May, however, Rome fell to an army of Spanish and German mercenaries who pillaged the city. They forced the pope to take refuge in the fortress of Castel San'Angelo and pay a ransom for his release. Italy was now firmly under the control of foreigners. Florence ordered the young Medici ruler to leave the city.

Machiavelli had again supported the wrong people, this time the Medici. Another diplomat was promoted in his place, and Machiavelli, who had first suffered because he had served a republican government, was passed over by another republican government. He died shortly afterward, on June 21, 1527.

Significance

Machiavelli was a man of action. As a diplomat, he practiced the deception he had advocated in *The Prince*. He virtually abandoned his wife and five children (the first of whom, at least, was a complete disappointment to him) in favor of a life-style that included a series of affairs and at least one mistress.[35] It is not entirely clear what he believed in, for in spite of his insistence that all ethics depend on the situation, he seemed attached to the medieval Christian attitude that to seek after monetary gain is evil. And as the English essayist Macaulay pointed out, Machiavelli must be seen in the light of his times. The complicated politics of Renaissance Italy encouraged a devious approach to life.[36]

Machiavelli stood at the doorway of the modern era, and might well be considered the first political scientist, seeking to provide a reasoned explanation for human activity in the political sphere. As a result, he insisted that politics have its own set of rules apart from those that govern other institutions. Brutal as this sounds, Machiavelli described what he saw without the hypocrisy that is frequently a part of political rhetoric.[37]

The emphasis Machiavelli placed on experience also marks him as a modern person. Classical examples abound in his works, but his own experience was the most important source. His firsthand experience of the danger of indecisive rulers in Florence resulted in his glorification of decisive action. He used the classics and built on them rather than worshiping them. Because of that, he was a humanist—though hardly a humane one.

SUMMARY

The Renaissance is important because it refocused educational orientation, away from an exclusively religious purpose to greater emphasis on the human condition. Experience, enlightened by selected Greek and Roman authors such as Cicero, informed the concerns of Renaissance men and women. There was as much emphasis on the creation of new art and literature—which reflected classical style—as on studying the past.

One of the most important dimensions of the "new learning" was the development of vernacular languages (such as English, Spanish, German, Italian, and French) and of extensive literatures in them. This meant that formal schooling became again, as it had been under the Romans, bilingual or multilingual. Every educated European learned Latin (and possibly Greek and Hebrew) and his or her own tongue. Greek labels, such as *gymnasium, academy,* and *lyceum,* came to be applied to centers of classical study.

The Renaissance is also important because it spawned the women's movement in education. It was not because humanists like Erasmus advocated restricted education of women that we identify a new impetus for women's education. Rather, it was the courageous and literate challenge of Christine de Pisan for gender equality in education and life that marked the Renaissance as a time of change in the history of education for women.

Finally, it is important to remember that the humanities included study of all aspects of human beings: beautiful and ugly, triumphant and pathetic, generous and mean. Although humanists like Vittorino da Feltre embodied humane gentleness, the hard-headed realism of Niccolò Machiavelli was also part of the humanist tradition. The Reformation would keep the classical and vernacular thrusts of the Renaissance while reclaiming the earlier religious purpose of education.

NOTES

1. Cf. Denys Hays, *The Italian Renaissance in Its Historical Background* (Cambridge: Cambridge University Press, 1961), 1; Hans Baron, *The Crisis of the Early Italian Renaissance: Civic Humanism and Republican Liberty in the Age of Classicism and Tyranny* (Princeton: Princeton University Press, 1966), xxvii–xxviii.

2. R. R. Bolgar, *The Classical Heritage and Its Beneficiaries* (Cambridge: Cambridge University Press, 1963), 255.

3. William H. Woodward, *Vittorino da Feltre and Other Humanist Educators: Essays and Versions* (Cambridge: Cambridge University Press, 1921), 2.

4. James Bowen, *A History of Western Education,* 3 vols. (New York: St. Martin's Press, 1975), 2: 225.

5. Woodward, *Vittorino da Feltre,* 16–17.

6. The information on Renaissance classroom practice comes from an unpublished paper by Anthony Grafton of Princeton University, "How the Humanists Learned Greek: A Study in Classroom Practice," presented at the Newberry Library Renaissance Conference, April 23, 1982.

7. Hays, *The Italian Renaissance,* 154.

8. Enid McLeod, *The Order of the Rose: The Life and Ideas of Christine de Pizan* (London: Chatto & Windus, 1976). All biographical details are from this source.

9. For an expanded discussion, see L. Glenn Smith, "From Plato to Jung: Centuries of Inequalities," *Educational Horizons* 60 (Fall 1981): 4–10.

10. Phyllis Stock, *Better than Rubies: A History of Women's Education* (New York: G. P. Putnam's Sons, 1978), 42.

11. McLeod, *The Order of the Rose,* 48.

12. McLeod, *The Order of the Rose,* 66.

13. McLeod, *The Order of the Rose,* 70.

14. McLeod, *The Order of the Rose,* 160.

15. See Clive Wood and Beryl Suitters, *The Fight for Acceptance: A History of Contraception* (Aylesbury, UK: Medical and Technical Publishing, 1970).

16. All information on Butzbach in this biographical sketch is from Johannes Butzbach, *The Autobiography of Johannes Butzbach, A Wandering Scholar of the Fifteenth Century,* trans. Robert Frances Seybolt and Paul Monroe (Ann Arbor: Edwards Brothers, 1933).

17. Whipping was accepted as necessary for controlling children, but the severity and relish with which this man administered his thrashings caused many people in Miltenberg to hate him. To get him out of the school, the town council made him a bailiff in charge of prisoners.

18. George Faludy, *Erasmus* (New York: Stein and Day, 1970), 3, 109.

19. Faludy, *Erasmus,* 91.

20. Raymond Himeluck, trans., *The Enchiridion of Erasmus* (Bloomington: Indiana University Press, 1963), 85.

21. Himeluck, *The Enchiridion,* 87. He went on to lay down twenty more rules and an epilogue for many of the vices.

22. Woodward, *Desiderius Erasmus Concerning the Aim and Method of Education,* in *Classics in Education,* vol. 19 (New York: Bureau of Publications, Teachers College, Columbia University, [1904] 1964), 36–37, 191.

23. Robert Ulich, ed., *Three Thousand Years of Educational Wisdom* (Cambridge, Massachusetts: Harvard University Press, 1961), 257.

24. Woodward, *Desiderius Erasmus,* 48–49, 187, 193–215.

25. T. W. Baldwin, *Small Latine and Lesse Greeke* (Urbana: University of Illinois Press, 1944): 96–97.

26. Craig R. Thompson, trans., *The Colloquies of Erasmus* (Chicago: University of Chicago Press, 1965), xxxvi.

27. Donald B. King and H. David Rix, trans., *On Copia of Words and Ideas* (Milwaukee: Marquette University Press, 1963), 9.

28. King and Rix, *On Copia of Words and Ideas,* bk. 1, chap. 16.

29. Margaret Mann Phillips, *The "Adages" of Erasmus—A Study with Translations* (Cambridge: Cambridge University Press, 1964), 171–89.

30. Will Durant, *The Reformation* (New York: Simon and Schuster, 1957), 283.

31. Felix Guibert, *Machiavelli and Guicciardini* (Princeton: Princeton University Press, 1965), 20.

32. Ridolfi, *The Life of Niccolò Machiavelli* (London: Routledge and Kegan Paul, 1963), 146.

33. Federico Chabod, *Machiavelli and the Renaissance* (London: Bowes and Bowes, 1958), 42–47.

34. Niccolò Machiavelli, *The Prince* (New York: W. W. Norton, 1977), 114.

35. Ridolfi, *The Life of Niccolò Machiavelli,* 74–75, 207.

36. Cf. Thomas Babington Macaulay, "Machiavelli," in *English Essays,* in *The Harvard Classics,* vol. 27 (New York: P. F. Collier and Son, 1910): 381–421.

37. John Freddero, "That Notorious Little Book," *The Stanford Magazine* 10 (Summer 1982): 15.

The Reformers

From Abelard's day to the late 1400s, more than seventy-five universities started. By 1490, seventy of these were still functioning.[1] The Roman Catholic Church had passed its highwater mark and was in many respects in a slow decline. There were still many pious believers, but every level of the church had dark corners needing reform. The papacy had always had its highs and lows. There were more downs than ups in the fourteenth and fifteenth centuries. Discipline was lax in many monasteries. The functions of priests were often performed by vicars (substitutes) who had to charge fees for baptism, marriages, and other church functions because the titular priest kept most of the salary for himself. That the church had become for some an avenue to privilege and a way of avoiding grinding toil was evident even in Abelard's time. Special canon courts in which professional churchpeople were tried for civil offenses gave them a decided edge over the rest of the population. The only crime usually punishable by death for a member of the religious establishment was heresy. Murder or lesser crimes by a cleric against a non-Church person usually provoked only a fine.

The taxes paid by peasants, merchants, and small farmers helped support the relatively luxurious lives of professional churchpeople. Many ordinary folks resented the mockery of students and other clerics who had the protection of canon law but felt little need to observe the Church's obligations. When economic and social resentment combined with feelings of thwarted nationalism, the stage was set for what historians call the Reformation.

John Wycliffe (1320–1384)

There had been recurring efforts to reform abuses since the early days of the Christian movement. In late-fourteenth-century England, an Oxford lecturer voiced almost all the criticisms that Luther, Calvin, Zwingli, and others would level at the political/religious establishment more than a century later. This was John Wycliffe, the mouthpiece of a strong anticlerical group in the English court.[2]

Background

John was from Hipswell, Yorkshire, in north England, near the village of Wycliffe. He became a lecturer in theology at Oxford after having studied there, and spent 1360 as Master of Balliol College. After being ordained as a priest, he received several *benefices* (salaries) from the pope. These were from parish churches (with vicars acting in his stead), while John continued to teach at Oxford. He wrote on many subjects; some of his writings pleased anticlerical and anti-Roman elements in the government.

Annually, England paid a large "tribute" to the pope. But in 1366, the English king, Edward III, refused to pay and assigned Wycliffe to write a justification.[3] He complied, arguing that charity begins at home and that England needed the money more than did Rome. In any case, he said, the pope was entitled to any money only as an act of charity—a free offering. When a leading member of the anticlerical party, John of Gaunt, proposed confiscating some of the church's property, Wycliffe preached several sermons justifying the idea, even suggesting that the English church become independent of Rome. Most people were not willing to go that far, but the idea of confiscating Church property was attractive, especially to Edward III. With it, he could maintain fifteen earls, fifteen hundred knights, sixty-two hundred squires, and have quite a lot of cash left over for himself.[4] The king rewarded Wycliffe with the rectory of Lutterworth for his service.[5]

Ideas

Wycliffe anticipated almost every major argument of the later Reformation. He said that "good works" did not save people, for their destinies were predetermined. Only God could provide salvation through His grace. Good works might indicate that one was among the elect, but they did not affect the outcome. He also said that Christians answer directly to God and need no priests or intermediaries. He thought that no priest or church should have any property. Ideally, believers should own everything in common. (Despite this position, he said the "powers that be" are also ordained of God, and he apparently did not give up his own income.) He attacked church professionals for favoring the rich while not caring for the poor. He called them "robbers," "ravishing wolves," "gluttons," "devils," and "apes."[6]

Various Church officials made efforts to silence Wycliffe, but because papal leadership was not strong in England and Wycliffe had a good deal of popular as well as aristocratic support, these efforts were not successful. In 1381, however, a revolt shook England, and one of the leaders, a preacher named John Ball, quoted Wycliffe to justify the insurrection. Although Wycliffe denied favoring armed rebellion against authority, the king had him barred from Oxford anyway. He retired to Lutterworth where he organized a band of Lollards (poor preaching priests) who expounded his ideas. He and two others translated the Bible into English. He believed everyone should be taught to read it.

Wycliffe's ideas traveled quickly through the university circuit to other countries. In his last years he was embroiled in controversy. Some Church authorities called him heretical, and Pope Gregory XI condemned some of his ideas. However, he wasn't silenced. Thirty-one years after his death, his ideas became so influential in the thinking of reformers that the Council of Constance, as part of an attempt to silence one of his advocates, had his bones removed from Lutterworth and thrown into a nearby creek.

Jan Hus (1369–1415)

The Council of Constance also condemned the rector of the University of Prague to be burned at the stake for advocating ideas similar to Wycliffe's. This rector was Jan of Husinetz, the most popular preacher in Prague at the time.

The University of Prague was less than fifty years old. It was divided between Bohemian (mostly Czech) and German students and masters. The Germans outnumbered and outvoted their Czech colleagues. Hus, selected as rector in 1402, was a strong adherent of Wycliffe's ideas and the recognized leader of the Bohemian reformist party. Almost every issue split along national lines. The Bohemians wanted church reform; the Germans championed the papacy. Hus and his party believed in (naive) realism; the Germans advocated nominalism (Chapter 3).

To complicate the picture, there was a struggle over the papacy. The Czech king, Wenceslaus IV, was trying to stay neutral because he was barely hanging on to his throne. The Bohemians supported Wenceslaus; the Germans did not. When Wenceslaus altered the voting balance in the university to give the Czechs more clout, the Germans called a cessation and left town.[7] This disruption was in 1409. Two years later, Hus was hiding out from the archbishop, who pursued him hotly for preaching heresies.

In 1414 a general council met at Constance to resolve rival claims to the papacy. It seemed a good time to iron out some of the other difficulties in the Church, including Hus's opposition. Emperor Sigismund (King of Hungary and Holy Roman Emperor) promised a safe-conduct for Hus to attend the council. The council, alarmed at Hus's teachings, had him imprisoned, and after a trial in which Hus was not allowed to defend his opinions, he was condemned. Sigismund and others urged the reformist professor to renounce the beliefs that offended the council, but he refused. Thus, in July 1415—one thousand years after the mob killed Hypatia—Hus walked under guard to the stake. Rejecting one final chance to retract, Hus said he hoped to be with Wycliffe in heaven; however, if Wycliffe was in hell, he would be glad to join him there.[8] As noon approached, the fire consumed Hus, who died singing hymns. The archbishop of Milan committed his soul to the devil, and Hus's executioners threw his ashes into the Rhine. As a result of Hus's death, a reformist civil war broke out in Bohemia, with almost all Czechs viewing Hus as a martyr. (Five hundred years later they would proclaim the day of Hus's death their chief national holiday.)

Europe's turbulent political climate, fed by movements to reform the Church, continued throughout the fifteenth century. By the 1480s, the Ottoman Turks controlled the Balkans and would soon stand at the gates of Vienna. United resistance to this invasion was hardly possible in a Europe that was more and more politically divided and nationalistic. In Germany, internal problems had encouraged a power shift from the emperor to individual towns and regional princes.

Martin Luther (1483–1546)

It was into this world of conflict and change that Martin Luther, the Reformation's most famous character, was born on November 10, 1483. He was the second son of a prosperous Saxon miner. His world was one in which there was a strong belief in the constant presence of evil spiritual powers, and which tended to view religious observance mechanically (you do something for God, He does something for you).

Youth and Schooling

After early studies at local schools, young Martin went to the University of Erfurt at seventeen, completing his bachelor's degree in 1502 and his master's in 1505. We know little about him during this period. About this time he began to show the tendencies toward depression and religious self-examination that would continue for the rest of his life.

In July 1505, the young master of arts was caught in the open during a thunderstorm. Fearing that he would be killed by lightning, he vowed to enter a religious order if he were spared. Although he wasn't obliged to keep a vow made under fear, he nevertheless entered the monastery of the Augustinian hermits at Erfurt fifteen days later. (The fact that he made his decision so quickly may indicate that he was ready for some kind of life change.) The community that he joined was the most prestigious in town, and was serious about observing monastic rules. For someone who had been plagued with doubts about his salvation, entry into such an order would have been a logical step.

Martin's relationship with his father was a key factor in his development. Hans Luther was a man given to impulse: when Martin entered the monastery Hans immediately disinherited him, only to reinstate him a few weeks later. At the dinner following Luther's first mass, Hans publicly rebuked his son for not having been as obedient as he should have been. While it is oversimplifying to lay the Lutheran Reformation solely at the doorstep of a son's unresolved conflict with a domineering father, Martin's difficulty in dealing with church authority probably had some root in this paternal relationship.[9]

Luther's clerical formation was brief, for he was ordained less than two years after he entered the monastery. After ordination, he continued his study and in 1508 was appointed a lecturer in philosophy at the University of Wittenberg. After several years, he was recalled to Erfurt, where he became involved in the study of theology.

Spiritual Conversion

During these years, Luther's early peace in the monastery gave way to despair. He had become gripped by *Anfechtung,* or a human struggle with temptation involving deep religious conflict.[10] Luther had been exposed to the nominalist theology of William of Occam, which insisted that God could never be known by human reason or pleased by human activity.[11] The young priest, already guilt-ridden, began to despair of his salvation as he could see no possibility of ever pleasing God. Counselors encouraged him to remember that repentance begins with the love of God and pointed out that "God is not angry with you, you are angry with Him."[12] Luther sank deeper into depression.

The period from 1513 to 1518 witnessed Luther's spiritual conversion. He began to realize that, through scripture, individuals can come to faith by God's grace and be made just by Him despite their own sinfulness. The answer to his problem of how to achieve salvation was not through his own actions. He could do nothing to merit salvation by himself. Instead, by receiving the grace of God in faith, he found peace by throwing himself on God's mercy and letting God do the work.

Luther continued his theological education during this crisis, receiving his doctorate in 1512, and went back to Wittenberg to teach. University education during this time was different from today. Instead of offering individual courses, a lecturer would begin a running commentary on some work and continue until the book was finished, however long it took. Then he would take up another book and begin the process again. Starting with the Psalms, Luther lectured on the Bible, continuing on to Paul's letters to the Romans, Galatians, and Hebrews. The fact that Luther chose to comment on Galatians and Romans is significant because these letters of Paul explicitly deal with the question of how people are made just.

Luther's movement away from the Church of Rome was not sudden. Only over time did his theology take shape and his questions about the authority of the pope develop. One of the principal events in this process, which began in 1516, was the controversy over indulgences. Traditionally, the Church taught that even after sins were forgiven in confession, some temporal punishment was needed. The Church could commute this punishment on condition that the penitent perform certain actions or say certain prayers. By Luther's time, these indulgences had become so associated with financial offerings that it appeared people could buy their way out of purgatory.

Break from Rome

In 1510 the pope was in the process of rebuilding St. Peter's Cathedral, and he offered an indulgence to those who confessed their sins and made a financial contribution to the building fund. John Tetzel, a Dominican priest, was given the task of preaching the indulgence in Luther's part of Germany. Tetzel, whom no one ever accused of being subtle, went from town to town preaching and gathering funds, claiming that "when a coin into the coffers rings, a soul from purgatory springs."[13]

Luther was offended by Tetzel's preaching for several reasons. First, Tetzel put the indulgence into a more prominent place than the sacrament of confession, which was a prerequisite for it. Second, half of the money collected went to the German banking family of Fugger to pay for the transportation of the funds to Rome and to repay the family for helping the local bishop buy his office. Less than half of the money Tetzel collected ever went into the building fund.

Luther preached against the indulgences in 1516, arguing that they were opposed to true repentence. A year later indulgences became the central theme of his famous Ninety-Five Theses, which he posted on the door of the castle church at Wittenberg. The action in itself was not particularly radical: the door was used as a kind of bulletin board to post the propositions of a professor who wished to debate an issue. What was radical was that the theses (propositions) circulated in printed form throughout and began to be treated as a manifesto, enlisting the support of other reform-minded individuals.

Opposition to Luther began to mount, but no immediate action was taken against him for political reasons. The Holy Roman Emperor, Maximilian, was dying, and one of the leading candidates for his job was Charles I of Spain. If Charles were elected emperor, much of Europe, including large sections of Italy, would be united under a single strong ruler. The *curia* (papal court) feared that it would be squeezed out of power if this occurred. A key to the imperial election was Frederick of Saxony, one of the electors. He ruled Luther's section of Germany. While an unknown Augustinian priest who had strange ideas inspired no fear in the curia, Frederick did. Papal authorities, therefore, proceeded against Luther cautiously.

Papal representatives tried to get Luther to retract his ideas, but their efforts only caused him to raise ever more serious questions about the Church. What had been a relatively simple questioning of indulgences now extended to the authority of the pope and the value of certain sacraments. Luther had come to believe that "where the word of God is preached and believed, there is the Church," independent of pope or bishop.[14]

In 1519 Charles became emperor, and there was no longer any need for the papal court to humor Frederick. In 1520 Luther was excommunicated, although the decree could not be promulgated in much of Germany because of support for him. The pace of the Reformation began to accelerate. Luther wrote for an ever-widening audience. In 1521, he was declared an outlaw at the Diet of Worms and went into hiding under Frederick's protection at Wartburg Castle. He continued to write, and eventually returned to Wittenberg in triumph. In 1525, he married Katie von Bora, a former nun.

During the later period of his life, Luther tried to temper the ideas of more radical reformers. While Luther had raised questions about the scriptural bases for several of the sacraments, he had never challenged the mass. Now, Zwingli and others proposed doctrines more anti-Roman than Luther's. Luther's criticism of learning that was not biblically oriented was amplified by Carlstadt and others into the contention that all education was anti-religious and dangerous. They concluded that most schooling, and especially university education, ought to be abolished.

On Education

It was against the background of these controversies that Luther's ideas on education began to emerge. For him, education was necessary to Christian life, because a person's eternal salvation depended upon the ability to read and understand Scripture. Thus, Luther provided a strong religious reason for basic literacy. He also saw human life as divided into three interrelated spheres: the family, the state, and the church. Each of these was important; each contributed to salvation. And, Luther argued, all were benefited by an educated population. In a "Letter to the Christian Nobility of the German Nation" (1520), he insisted on this. He also argued for a reform of the arts and theology faculties in all German universities.

Luther's first major educational work, the "Letter to the Mayors and Aldermen of All the Cities of Germany on Behalf of Christian Schools"

(1524), took up these themes in some detail. In it, he argued that schooling had deteriorated as a result of political turmoil. Because some parents neglected instruction out of a lack of piety or their own inability to teach, the welfare of the state demanded that mayor and aldermen support schooling—even to the extent of providing funding. More was demanded, however, than mere literacy training. The study of languages and the liberal arts was necessary. Because Scripture had been tainted by inaccurate translations, any educated man (university education was not usually available to women) needed to know the classical languages—"the scabbard in which the word of God is sheathed."[15] The needs of civil government also demanded liberal education in order to provide competent officials.

Luther expanded the theme of an educated leadership in the "Sermon on the Duty of Sending Children to School" (1530). He argued for schools to furnish ministers for the spiritual sphere of human activity and to provide civil authorities for the political sphere. For parents to provide a son for the ministry was a service to both the spiritual and temporal realms, Luther reasoned, because civil peace was one of the fruits of the ministerial office. He said that the temporal ministry was not as important as the spiritual, yet it was still ordained by God. Without it people would not be able to live together in society. Lawyers and scribes were important because they formulate the laws and help people learn them.

Luther further argued that schoolmasters were especially important, almost as significant as ministers. In fact, said Luther, "If I had to give up preaching and my other duties, there is no office I would rather have than that of school teacher. For I know that next to the ministry, it is the most useful, greatest and best; and I am not sure which of the two is to be preferred."[16] If a country could not provide people for such key roles, he argued, it deserved to perish.

Less idealistically, Luther pointed out that education for the ministry virtually guaranteed employment, because a great number of parishes had no pastor. Similarly, he thought competent civil servants, also in short supply, were likely to be rewarded with wealth, importance, and prestige.

These religious and secular reasons for why the state should support education were among Luther's favorite points. According to him, the state should compel attendance at school so that individuals would be available to fill the spiritual and secular offices, just as the state could draft individuals into the military to ensure national defense.

Luther's involvement in the practical side of education was also extensive. His translation of the Bible into German was one of the great educational achievements of the time. A measure of its success is that between 1522 and 1534, twenty thousand copies of the New Testament were printed. Also of educational value were the more than thirty popular hymns he composed. In an era in which many could not read and more could not write, an efficient way of communicating religious ideas was in hymns, which could be sung and remembered. That some of these have survived to our own day ("A Mighty Fortress Is Our God" is one) testifies to their appeal.

Luther was involved in founding a Latin school at Wittenberg that provided what we would refer to today as elementary, secondary, and higher education for boys as well as a primary school for girls. He also helped sponsor a reform of the University of Wittenberg along evangelical lines, with biblical theology taking primacy over scholastic philosophy.

Significance

It was as a teacher and preacher that Luther made his greatest educational contributions. His role was that of the charismatic leader rather than speculative thinker or organizational administrator. Even before his split with the Church, Luther was a popular lecturer at Wittenberg. University enrollment had declined to fifty in 1525, but rose to seven hundred by 1543 largely because of Luther's lectures. Contemporary accounts paint a portrait of a teacher deeply concerned about the material and spiritual welfare of his students, as well as one good-humored enough to join in their initiation rites and games. After his marriage to Katie von Bora, his house became a center of student activity. Many of the students lived and ate with his family. Concerned with the intellectual and religious development of those he taught, he found them scholarships and occasionally wives as well.

Luther committed the last years of his life to teaching, preaching, and spreading the Reformation. His lecturing continued, as did his constant discussions, many of which have been preserved in *Table Talks* (transcripts of his mealtime conversations). Frequently, he traveled to assist some local community in its reforming effort or to settle disputes. He undertook a winter journey in 1546 to help settle a family dispute between two princes in Mansfield, and on the return trip, he grew increasingly weak and died on February 18 before reaching home.

Luther's contributions to education came mainly from the theological underpinnings he provided for schooling. Luther taught that each person was responsible for his or her salvation, and the means to that end was found in Scripture. Thus, the ability to read Scripture provided a religious basis for schooling. Although Luther had no concept of separation of church and state, his insistence that the state had an obligation to support education helped set the stage for tax-funded instruction and compulsory attendance laws. His disenchantment with speculative scholastic philosophy moved Protestant schooling in the direction of more practical learning. He helped to bring about a change in the religious fabric of Europe and, in the process, helped to recast the direction of European education.

Philipp Melanchthon (1497–1560)

If Martin Luther was the heart of the German Reformation, his younger colleague and friend, Philipp Melanchthon, was its right arm. A brilliant teacher and superb organizer, Melanchthon put many of Luther's reforms into operation.

Philipp Melanchthon came from a relatively prosperous family: his father was a metalworker, probably an armor maker. Philipp, born fourteen years after Martin Luther in 1497, was a child of the Renaissance. After his father's death in 1507, his granduncle, John Reuchlin, one of the most distinguished humanists of the age, guided Philipp's early education. By the youth's fifteenth birthday, he could read and write Latin and Greek and was acquainted with grammar, arithmetic, rhetoric, history, and geography.[17]

At the age of twelve (only slightly younger than usual for the time), Philipp enrolled at the University of Heidelberg. He concentrated on classical languages, and, more gifted than most of his professors, he studied largely on his own. He received his bachelor's degree in 1511 and his master's in 1514. Early in his education, he became convinced like Luther that scholastic philosophy was wrong. Unlike Luther, he laid the blame not on Aristotle's ideas, but on poor translations that distorted the meaning of the text. Accuracy in translation was to become one of the major concerns of Melanchthon's life.

In 1518, Melanchthon went to Wittenberg University as professor of Greek, where he fell under Luther's influence. He had already become convinced of the need to return to a study of the Bible to understand the Christian life. He had begun to raise questions about the Catholic church even before he met Luther, whose presence at the university acted as a catalyst for the development of Melanchthon's theology.

In many ways, Melanchthon fits the stereotype of the eccentric genius. He was thin, walked with a limp, and had a speech impediment. Luther described him as wimpish. He was so completely absorbed in his study that Luther had to convince him that marriage would be more than a perpetual inconvenience to his scholarship. In intellectual matters, however, Melanchthon was neither absentminded nor clumsy. Theologically, he probably exerted a stronger influence on Luther than Luther did on him, and the older man was awed by his intellectual abilities. He possessed many talents which Luther lacked. Whereas Luther's thoughts were frequently unpolished, Melanchthon's were clear and specific. In situations in which Luther's short temper was likely to get the best of him, Melanchthon was contained and reasonable. His role as the official representative of Lutheran Protestantism at every major discussion between Protestants and Catholics from 1529 to 1560 is testimony to his ability to think quickly and speak diplomatically.

Utility of the Classics

Melanchthon disliked the intricacies of scholastic philosophy, but he was a fan of Aristotle and believed that a true understanding of his works would be useful in promoting the Christian faith. Like the Renaissance humanists, he saw a positive value in the study of classical languages. These could open religious books not available in translation. His goal was *Beredsamkeit,* "learned piety," which was the cultivation of all the powers of the human spirit. The use of humanism as an educational tool to promote evangelical principles was one of his convictions.

To Luther's educational thought, motivated by medieval values and Reformation theology, Melanchthon added the humanistic values of eloquence and usefulness. Knowledge was to be judged by its purpose. The value of traditional studies like grammar, rhetoric, and logic was to aid clear thought expression. In addition to these subjects and the study of language, history was important because it encouraged German patriotism and showed how God had worked in human life.

The curriculum Melachthon proposed gave expression to all of these values. Learning was divided into three major areas, each with its particular subjects. The teaching of thinking and reading demanded a knowledge of classical languages (Latin, Greek, and Hebrew) as well as logic and rhetoric. The teaching of natural reality was accomplished through physics, cosmology (the philosophy of the universe), physiology, and psychology (more the philosophy of how we know than the experimental psychology of today). Finally, the study of ethics and politics would help people to grow in the third necessary area, that of practical life.

Melanchthon's educational theory is most clearly seen in the *Visitation Papers* of 1528. Reform-minded professors from Wittenberg had been asked to make a survey of religious and educational life in Saxony. Their reports painted a dismal picture about religious observance and educational opportunity. Melanchthon responded by constructing a plan for improving local educational institutions. In the first part, he detailed the major principles of Christian faith to be taught and carried out. In the second, he proposed a model for schooling. The *Visitation Papers* exhorted people to send their children to school and set down qualifications for teachers. Each school, according to the scheme, was to be divided into three classes. In the first belonged those who were beginning the study of Latin. In the second was added the study of grammar and a bit of religion. Finally, in the most advanced class, grammar, meter (in order to compose poetry), reading, writing, singing, logic, rhetoric, and religion were to be taught. Eventually, Melanchthon added a lower class to serve as a bridge between the ordinary schools, which taught vernacular reading and writing, and the classical school designed to prepare male students for university study. These reforms later served as a model for German school development.

Educational Activities

Melanchthon was a consultant in the foundation or reform of a wide variety of schools. At least fifty-six German cities sought his advice when beginning schools. Throughout his life, he worked to improve the quality of teachers and the support of cities for schooling, continually urging decent salaries to end teacher moonlighting. Like Luther, he considered the role of teachers to be like that of ministers, since they, too, were concerned "with godly things."[18]

His ideas were most clearly put into practice in the universities. His reorganization of the University of Wittenberg resulted in a more humanistic approach to the teaching of philosophy and the hiring of humanists to teach mathematics and medicine. Melanchthon also helped reform the Universities of Rostock and Frankfurt-on-the-Oder. He revised the curricula at Colgne, Tübingen, Leipzig, and Heidelberg, and founded the Universities of Königsberg, Jena, and Marburg. His abilities as an organizer as well as theoretician made him an important figure in the development of a whole network of evangelical schools. Melanchthon also found time to continue his scholarly pursuits. Unhappy with the quality of available texts, he wrote books on rhetoric and logic, ethics, physics, Aristotelian philosophy, and Greek and Latin grammar. Dissatisfied with the available editions of the classical authors, he turned out new ones and wrote summaries to accompany them. He advised Luther in such projects as the translation of the German Bible and the formulation of theological position papers.

Though never formally ordained, Melanchthon took his ministry to students seriously. Like Luther, he was a popular teacher, attracting fifteen hundred listeners to some of his lectures. A fatherly man, he loaned students money on the slightest pretext, counseled them, and helped them find jobs. Perhaps this special interest in the welfare of his pupils was a result of a need to compensate for the disappointingly average abilities of his own children.

Melanchthon's death in 1560, three years after that of his wife and fourteen years after Luther's, marked the end of the first phase of the Reformation. Melanchthon had been unsuccessful in taking on the mantle of leadership after Luther's death, for he did not have the charismatic quality needed to fill Luther's shoes.

Melanchthon had systematized and put into practice what Luther had believed and preached. These efforts had resulted in a strong call for popular education, motivated by gospel values. German schooling, like its counterpart in other European countries, remained divided along class lines, with the ordinary people learning to read and write in German and the privileged few studying the classics and going on to the university. Schooling may have been more extensive than it had been during the Middle Ages, though evidence on this point is scanty.

Vernacular schooling for non-aristocratic girls probably became more widespread, but the Reformation tended to diminish classical schooling opportunities for women. Wherever politics made possible confiscation of Church property—in England, for example—governments tended to seize monastic land and buildings. In the process most external schools suspended operations. Those for males were often refounded, but most of those for females remained closed. The result was a net loss of classical schooling opportunities for women in Protestant areas. Most Protestant (and Catholic) males agreed with Luther's basic conclusion about male and female roles, though they might not have expressed the reasons as curiously as he did: "Men have broad shoulders and narrow hips, and accordingly they possess intelligence," said Luther. "Women have narrow shoulders and broad hips." The conclusion? Women "ought to stay home; the way they were created indicates this, for they have broad hips and a wide fundament to sit upon." They should "keep house and bear and raise children."[19]

If the Reformation did not bring the surge of opportunities for women that historians have thought, it did have far-reaching effects on education. Universities were becoming more broadly oriented toward the humanities rather than being confined to the study of philosophy and theology. The theory had been formulated that schooling was a duty of the state, which shared responsibility for the salvation of souls with the church. The link had also been made between political stability and popular education. These ideas, forged in the furnace of the Reformation, would be carried across the Atlantic by European settlers and find early expression in schooling in the Americas.

Ignatius Loyola (c. 1491–1556)

A major figure in this Catholic Reformation was a Spanish knight, Ignatius of Loyola. Ignatius was born in 1491 to a family of minor nobility. He was baptized Inigo and later changed his name to Ignatius. After the death of his parents—he was about fourteen—he was raised by his older brothers and trained to be an officer. Ignatius became a typical swashbuckling soldier, interested in chivalry, wine, women, and song. We know, for example, that in 1515 court proceedings were instituted against him for an unnamed but extremely serious crime.

The path of advancement for someone like Ignatius usually involved entering the military service of some prominent noble: the more powerful the lord, the greater the likelihood that the soldier would make a name for himself. With this in mind, Ignatius became a junior officer in the service of the Duke of Navarre, a distant relative. The decision was to prove fateful for the direction of his later life.

Under the strong rule of Isabella the Catholic, Spain had prospered. In 1504, however, she had died, leaving a disputed throne. One major candidate for the throne, her son-in-law Philip the Fair of France, died in 1506, leaving Isabella's husband, Ferdinand, as the logical successor. The country remained peaceful until his death in 1516; then, things began to come apart. Ferdinand had designated his principal advisor, Cardinal Cisneros, as temporary ruler after his death. However, Crown Prince Charles had designated his tutor, Adrian of Utrecht, to govern until he took control. The arrival of Charles from Belgium in 1517 to claim his throne settled that problem. Initially successful, Charles left the country to be crowned Holy Roman Emperor, a title to which he had just been elected, and the country rose in revolt. While the revolution was caused largely by Spanish resentment over foreign rule, some nobles used the opportunity provided by the civil unrest to claim independence from their lords and the monarchy. Ignatius was involved in the military campaigns of the Duke of Navarre against the rebels.

With Spain weakened, the French saw an opportunity to bring the disputed territory of Navarre back under their control. A French army laid seige to the regional capital of Pamplona, and among the city's Spanish defenders was Ignatius Loyola. During a fierce battle, Ignatius was struck by a cannonball which slightly wounded one leg and shattered the other. After the leg had been set by French doctors, he was sent home to recover.

Ignatius's recovery was long and painful. The French surgeons had either set the fracture incorrectly or else the leg had been moved on the trip home. As a result, the leg had to be reset. Ignatius saw that the leg was healing in such a way that it would be slightly deformed. Fearing that he wouldn't be able to wear the tight boots then in fashion in Spain, he ordered the doctors to saw off a piece of bone which protruded, along with the flesh around it. After doing this, they put the leg in traction and waited for it to heal. The end result was a long and painful recovery, during which Ignatius nearly died.

Conversion

For someone as active as Ignatius, being forced to lie still in bed was as bad as the pain. To distract himself, he sent servants to search the castle at Loyola for interesting reading material, preferably novels that dealt with military exploits and romance. Unfortunately, the only books that could be found were a life of Christ and a copy of *The Lives of the Saints*. Figuring that any reading material was better than none, Ignatius started through these books. As he read, his view of life began to change. Instead of dreaming about the noble deeds he could do for some lord, he began to think about the great things he could accomplish for God. Romantic as always, he decided to make a pilgrimage to the Holy Land, and then to enter some monastery in which he could give his life to prayer and penance.[20]

After his recovery in 1522, he set out on what was to become a far longer pilgrimage than he had expected. He made an all-night vigil at the shrine of Our Lady of Montserrat, where he left his sword and elegant clothing and departed for the town of Manresa where he would live as a beggar for the rest of the year.[21] In the winter of 1523, he began his pilgrimage to the Holy Land, traveling by way of Venice and Rome. Such a pilgrimage was an involved affair, and almost anything (capture by pirates, shipwreck) could happen on the ocean voyage. For someone like Ignatius, who begged for the money he needed as he went, the trip was a real adventure. Despite numerous difficulties, he arrived in the Holy Land and visited the Christian shrines, returning to Europe in 1524.

Ignatius as a Student

During the pilgrimage, Ignatius decided to become a priest. His early education had given him basic literacy in Spanish but no command of Latin and no formal training in philosophy and theology, so he had no choice but to begin school all over again. At the age of thirty-one, this proud soldier studied basic Latin alongside boys less than half his age in a Barcelona school. Like many older students, he found that learning was difficult. In spite of his age, he made progress and in 1526 went to the University of Alcalá to begin higher studies. He attacked college studies without any definite plan, spending a year and a half attending whatever lectures he wanted to in the hope that this would somehow prepare him to study theology.

During this period, Spaniards were deeply suspicious of any unusual religious movements, fearing they would give Protestantism a foot in the door. The Inquisition, a powerful Church court, examined every person suspected of heresy. Those found guilty could be burned at the stake. Even if innocent, a suspect might spend a long time in prison before being cleared. During his time at Alcalá, Ignatius was investigated by the Inquisition and was ordered to stop preaching and to change his rough style of dress. He transferred to the University of Salamanca in 1528 and was imprisoned for twenty-one days, after which the Inquisition found him innocent and released him. On several other occasions, this staunch defender of Catholicism would come under suspicion for his unusual lifestyle and preaching.

In 1528, Ignatius left Spain for France to become a student at the famous University of Paris. On arriving there, he discovered how little his self-selected university training had prepared him for serious study. Once again, he had to start at the beginning, learning the basics of Latin grammar and literary style with young boys.

The medieval course of studies at Paris was divided according to subject matter. First of all a student began with the Latin and Greek classics and then moved on to philosophy. After this program had culminated in the master of arts or doctor's degree (the latter was a master's degree with a fee added), an ambitious student proceeded to the study of theology, culminating in the doctor of theology degree. There was a clear hierarchy of study: first humanities, then philosophy, and finally theology. Anyone who wanted to be considered really well educated studied this curriculum.

Ignatius began this structured program in 1529, receiving the master's degree in 1533 and the doctorate in 1534. In that same year, he began studying theology with the Dominican priests at the university. His formal study ended in 1535, however, when persistent stomach troubles forced him to quit without receiving the theological doctorate.

While Ignatius was studying, he engaged in a variety of other activities. His greatest gift was not literary, philosophical, or theological, but leadership. In Spain, people had gravitated toward him, and his charismatic personality was also evident at Paris. Beginning with two friends with whom he roomed, Francis Xavier and Peter Faber, he gathered a group of deeply religious young students and faculty. After Ignatius led them individually through a thirty-day period of prayer based on his own religious experiences, several changed the direction of their lives. Ignatius became the leader of this group of highly talented young men.[22]

Gradually, these friends began to believe that God wanted them to work together, but they were not entirely sure of the direction their lives should take. In August 1534, Ignatius and six of his associates made promises of poverty and celibacy, and vowed to go to the Holy Land to convert the Muslims. If they were unable to get to Palestine, they promised that they would go to Rome and ask the pope what they should do. For the next year or so, the companions were separated, with Ignatius first back in Spain recovering his health and later preaching and giving the "Spiritual Exercises" in Venice. In 1537, he sent the others to Rome to ask the pope to allow them all to be ordained. Permission was obtained and Ignatius and his friends became priests in June 1537.

The whole group now went to Rome, where two of them began to teach theology at the pope's request. The political situation in Palestine would not allow them to go there as they had wished, so at the pope's urging they remained in Italy to help revitalize the Church there.

The Jesuits

Initially, the group had been drawn together by their friendship and had become a band of "reformed priests." Now, they decided to ask for recognition as a religious order, with a definite structure and purpose in the Church, and in 1540, the Society of Jesus was formally recognized as a religious order within the Church.

The new order was different from others. Benedictine groups had insisted that members build their activities around permanent monasteries in which they would live throughout their lives. The Franciscans, Dominicans, and other mendicants had allowed their members to be transferred from place to place, but they were still bound by long periods of prayer in which the entire group was expected to participate. Going against this tradition, Ignatius insisted that the members of the Society be mobile, with no institutions which they were obligated to serve on a permanent basis. Less emphasis was placed on prayer in common, and more on private prayer. Ignatius's goal was to have a group of highly trained priests able to go anywhere their services were needed. This organizational vision, which seems rather ordinary today, was radical in those times, and Ignatius frequently found himself battling outsiders who wanted to turn the Society into a more traditional order.

The Society initially saw its mission as evangelical rather than educational. Various Jesuits, as they came to be called, began to preach throughout Italy, while others tried to check the spread of the Protestant Reformation in Germany. Several early Jesuits were theological advisors at the Council of Trent, which met in 1542 to correct Church abuses and attempt to stem the Protestant tide sweeping Europe. Others were active in spreading Christianity to Africa and the Far East, working in India, Morocco, and Ethiopia. The Society itself was growing phenomenally. From its small beginnings with Ignatius and his friends, it had grown to fifteen hundred members by 1554.[23] Such rapid growth necessitated formal training for the new members. While Ignatius and his friends had all received excellent educations at Paris, many of the new recruits were not well educated. Because Ignatius believed strongly in the need for educated priests, he sent candidates for the order to Paris and other universities for training of the sort he and his companions had received. The first Jesuit connection with schools was in these residences for Jesuit students at universities such as Paris, Louvain in Belgium, Padua in Italy, and Alcalá in Spain.

From these residences, it was a short step to founding separate Jesuit colleges to train recruits in humanities, philosophy, and theology. The College of Gandia in Spain, founded in 1545, was such an institution. Eventually, some of these colleges started to accept non-Jesuit students, too, beginning the Jesuit tradition of secular education.

In 1548 the first Jesuit school designed specifically for lay students was founded at Messina in Italy.[24] After this, a variety of other Jesuit institutions developed, including the German College at Rome, founded in 1552 for non-Jesuit priesthood students, and a boarding school at Vienna in 1553. By the time Ignatius died in 1556, he had approved the foundation of thirty-nine colleges or universities (the latter offered advanced degrees), thirty-three of which had already opened.[25] The Jesuits were especially effective because the pope granted Ignatius power to confer all university degrees and to delegate that authority. This rapid creation of colleges and universities forced the older universities to adopt new methods and curricula to compete.

During the last years of his life, Ignatius took a direct hand in supervising a variety of other religious activities. Besides the colleges and universities, Jesuits were involved in activities as different as preaching and founding homes for reformed prostitutes. During this time, Ignatius's health was getting worse. The old stomach troubles had returned and became severe. After a painful illness, he died on July 31, 1556.

Educational Significance

Ignatius's importance to the history of Western education lies in his organizational genius. He had begun his education too late in life to be a great scholar, but his native shrewdness had made him a sharp observer of how universities were run, and he put the knowledge to good use in founding the Society's colleges.

For him, all education, no matter the subject, had a religious purpose: it was undertaken to aid in knowing and loving God.[26] For members of his order, study was a preparation for helping others; for lay students, it was a way of discovering God's working in the world. Like many Renaissance educators, Ignatius believed that God lay at the basis of all serious study. At the same time, he saw education as involving more than the individual and God. Its goal was to make each person a more useful member of the church, citizen of the state, and participant in the local community. Education was not aimed simply at personal conversion: it was to bring about the transformation of the whole society. Study in a Catholic college or university should inspire the student with love of Church and country, along with concern for others.[27] Only if a person used all the resources available, Ignatius believed, could God be given His greatest glory and human needs be best served.

This philosophy of education resulted in a practical approach to the curriculum. Whatever was viewed by the community as important subject matter could be brought into the Jesuit schools, as long as it was directed toward love of God and service of others. Subjects like law and medicine were not to be taught as religion courses, but rather were to be taught in such a way that Ignatius's twin goals might be achieved. Ignatius took the best educational elements of his day, organized them from a Catholic perspective, and taught them in a way that fit the needs of the particular time and place.

This is not to say that the Jesuit curriculum depended solely on what was fashionable, for Ignatius had a definite hierarchy of values. Because religion was so important to him, the study of theology was supreme. After this ranked the study of philosophy and of arts and sciences, since these "dispose the intellectual powers for theology and are useful for the perfect understanding and use of it."[28] The study of Latin and Greek classics was also emphasized for two major reasons. First, as Melanchthon had pointed out, the classics help students learn the languages necessary to study Scripture and the early Christian writers. Second, because the study of the classics was an important ingredient in education of this time, it would enable Jesuit graduates to compete with students trained in other universities. In one of his letters, Ignatius commended: "For ourselves, theology would do well enough with less of Cicero and Demosthenes. But as St. Paul became all things to all men in order to save them, so the Society [of Jesus] in its desire to give spiritual assistance seizes upon the spoils of Egypt to turn their use to God's honor and glory."[29] He stressed that while all education is important, that which relates most directly to God is most valuable.

Teacher Education

Loyola required all Jesuit teachers to send him weekly accounts of their classes, a practice that underscored the importance of improving teaching to the members of the Society (later, the reports were sent to other superiors). What made the Jesuit approach to education ultimately so potent was the systematizing that took place during the four decades following Loyola's death. The third General Superior of the Society, Father Francis Borgia, took office in 1565. He directed every Provincial in charge of a group of Jesuits to establish formal teacher training, and by the 1580s this aspect of Jesuit teacher education was further formalized. Each prospective teacher was to be "taken in hand by someone of greater experience" for two months or more. They were to have supervised practice in the methods of reading, teaching, correcting, writing, and managing a class. Teachers who do not know how to do these things well, said a Jesuit source, "are forced to learn them afterwards at the expense of their scholars; and then they will acquire proficiency only when they have already lost in reputation; and perchance they will never unlearn a bad habit." The need for training was further justified in 1586:

> Sometimes a bad habit is neither very serious nor incorrigible, if taken at the beginning; but, if the habit is not corrected then, it comes to pass that a man, who otherwise would have been most useful, becomes well-nigh useless. There is no describing how much amiss Preceptors take it, if they are corrected, when they have already adopted a fixed method of teaching; and what continual disagreement ensues on that score with the Prefects of Studies.[30]

Observational visits from an experienced supervisor at least every fortnight became a regular part of each teacher's life. In 1584, General Superior Claudius Aquaviva named a commission of six experienced educators to codify Jesuit educational practices. They met in Rome for nine months, and studied the educational process. They prepared a preliminary document which Aquaviva circulated to experienced Jesuit educators in every province. (The earlier work of the Brethren of the Common Life was influential.) After extensive discussion and suggestions, a revised draft was issued in 1586. Five years later, a new version came out after much discussion, containing extensive pedagogical commentary justifying each part of the plan. The final *Ratio atque Institutio Studiorum Societatis Jesu* was issued in 1599.[31]

In addition to the systematically organized curriculum, the Jesuit approach to education included the following elements: (1) short, well-organized presentations containing a small number of key concepts followed by breaks allowing exercise and movement; (2) carefully varied repetition of each key concept; (3) equal treatment of everyone, with no separation or special arrangements for nobility; (4) supervised physical education and games; (5) peer teaching of certain parts of lessons to reward pupils' good work; (6) frequent disputations (debates) with appropriate rewards for excellent performance (a precursor to the present moot court in law schools); (7) limited self-government with a variety of offices filled by students; (8) regular holidays interspersed with carefully planned instructional days; (9) readily available books and supplies; (10) student drama as an aid to learning; (11) specific talks with boys who needed correction rather than general admonitions to everyone; (12) extensive supervision by teachers who were setting good examples (and sparing use of corporal punishment under carefully specified conditions); (13) pupils graded by age and readiness; and (14) keeping younger pupils with the same thoroughly prepared teachers for two or more years.[32]

This was the most extensive, deliberate, unified, and self-correcting approach to teacher training that had ever been attempted. The results were dramatic. In 1607, an estimated eight to ten thousand youth were attending Jesuit schools in Poland, and one source notes that "between 1606 and 1620 it is estimated that the Polish Protestants lost two-thirds of their churches."[33]

Even their most ardent opponents acknowledged the Jesuits' instructional skills. Many Protestant reformers engaged in savage polemical attacks against Roman Catholics; often, concrete political and military attacks were made as well. The same Protestants agreed with specific Jesuit pedagogical reforms on the practical grounds that only by adopting Jesuit teaching practices could Protestants hope to compete.

John Amos Comenius (1592–1670)

Protestants turned their attention to questions of educational method, curriculum, and organization partly out of fear that if they did not improve their own schools the Jesuits would attract their children.[34] The career of John Comenius, one of the notable figures in the history of education, is a product of the religious wars associated with the Reformation. Like Erasmus, he is sometimes referred to as a citizen of the world—in his case because he spent so little of his life on his native soil. He was born Jan Kominsky on March 28, 1592 in Moravia (in today's Czech Republic) near the Hungarian border. Later he Latinized his name to Comenius.

Details of Comenius's early life are sketchy. He was the youngest of five children and the only boy. His parents were moderately well off peasants who, like most of their neighbors, were members of the Unity of Brethren, a Protestant group in the Hus tradition. John's father, Martin, was a prominent man in the church in Uhersky Brod, a sizable town near John's birthplace. In 1604, however, both parents and the two youngest sisters died, and the orphaned boy spent a short, unhappy time with an aunt. By age sixteen he was in a grammar school maintained by the Brethren in the town of Prerov.[35]

Of Comenius's early education we know little. Leaders of his denomination shared Luther's and Melanchthon's general views on the importance of teaching, and every church provided a school. Comenius had attended this kind of schooling since childhood and probably had learned Latin grammar before he arrived at Prerov. In any case, he studied it there. He boarded in the home of Bishop John Lánecký, the school's rector. Lánecký treated Comenius almost as a son, calling him favorably to the attention of a nobleman who was sympathetic to the Brethren's cause. This man sponsored John's attendance at the Calvinist Gymnasium of Herborn (near Marburg in central Germany).

Comenius finished the course of study at Herborn in about two years and then traveled a hundred miles south to spend a year at the University of Heidelberg, a noted center of Protestant reformist theology. (Melanchthon had helped design the curriculum.) In 1614, the twenty-two-year-old Comenius left Heidelberg, perhaps because he had run out of money. He walked more than two hundred miles to Prague and then to Prerov, where he began teaching at his alma mater. Two years later, he was ordained a priest of the Unity of Brethren. About the same time, he married a young woman of good family with a sizable dowry.

Shortly after his marriage, Comenius accepted a pastorate. The rest of his life would primarily be devoted to serving his church—first as priest, then as secretary, and finally as the chief bishop. His educational activities were integral to but not the main preoccupation of his existence. The basic thrust of Comenius's work was theological and political, but his most lasting contribution was pedagogical.

War against Darkness

It is impossible to understand Comenius without reference to the chaotic religious, military, and political developments of Europe during this time. Coterminous with most of Comenius's adult life, the Thirty Years' War was a series of battles from 1618 to 1648 involving Sweden, Denmark, France, Spain, and several German states. There were a number of causes and ramifications—dynastic, territorial, economic, nationalistic—but religious differences provided the package in which it was all wrapped. Thus, a year without war was rare in seventeenth-century Europe, and sometimes entire towns were eradicated in devastating battles.

Comenius is usually depicted as an ecumenical man of peace. This was true to a point: He deplored war and frequently called for unity, but he meant Protestant unity. Like many zealous people, Comenius believed firmly that the road to amity lay in convincing those who differed from him of their fundamental errors. He was a full-blown partisan in the wars—not as a soldier but as a propagandist and political organizer. He was a man of his time and culture, a war-torn Europe in which many people understood reality in almost exclusively reformist Christian language and metaphor. The concept of separation of church and state was no more thinkable for him than for Ignatius. His personal raison d'être was so inextricably in counterpoint to Roman Catholic and Jesuit ubiquity that he cannot be understood apart from his response to what he both admired and described as "forces of darkness."

In 1622, four years after the Thirty Years' War started, Comenius's wife and two infant sons were victims of a pestilence. Two years later the young priest married Dorothy Cyrill, daughter of a Unity of Brethren bishop, and soon the Moravian Brethren moved to Leszno, Poland, a Unity stronghold. Besides living in Poland, Comenius spent time in Sweden, England, Hungary, and Holland, and he never returned to his homeland.

Comenius lived another forty-three years after leaving Moravia. He outlived his second wife and married a third, Jane Gajus, who also died before he did. During this time, Comenius wrote more than two hundred books and pamphlets in an effort to bring about the defeat of his foes. His political judgment was colored by statements from mystics who told Comenius what he wanted to hear, that the second coming of Christ was imminent and that it would initiate a thousand-year reign of peace. To help speed this event, in 1651 Comenius asked Prince Sigismund of Hungary to wage a holy war against the Hapsburgs and the papacy.

When Comenius died at seventy-eight, his memory was failing, almost all of his friends and colleagues were dead, most of his books had been burned, his flock was scattered, and his church was in disarray. His reputation as theologian and political leader had been tarnished by his trust in discredited mystical prophecies and wrong bets on which armies would triumph. Despite this pessimistic finish, he lived his last years in relative physical comfort in Amsterdam.

Comenius as Educator

Comenius began teaching Latin when he was twenty-two. For the next two decades, he spent part of his time as schoolmaster. Educational improvement was in the air, as reformers in both Protestant and Catholic countries were experimenting with and expanding curriculum, making learning easier and more pleasant, and extending schooling opportunities. The Jesuits discouraged corporal punishment, advocated play and physical education, and encouraged teachers to take a personal interest in each pupil.[36] In 1615 an Irish Jesuit named William Bataeus, teaching at Salamanca, published a Latin/Spanish text (in parallel columns) titled *Gateway to Languages,* which was quickly and widely translated. In 1631 at Leszno, Comenius published a Latin text patterned after Bataeus's work, *Gateway to Languages Unlocked.* This book quickly caught on because Protestants were eager to compete with the Jesuits, whose educational successes they viewed with combined admiration and fear.

With his pedagogical reputation established in northern Europe, Comenius received offers from English and continental Puritans. During 1641–1642 he was in England, but outbreak of civil war there caused him to leave. After some traveling and negotiating, he eventually settled in Elbing, a town on the coast of Prussia. He selected the location at the suggestion of Axel Oxenstierna, chancellor of Sweden, with whom he had signed a contract to revamp Swedish textbooks. He spent the better part of six years in this task, while devoting his first attention to a futile effort at uniting Protestants.

In 1648 Comenius returned to Leszno, the town that he thought of as his home. There he buried his second wife, married his third, and became senior bishop of the Bohemian branch of the Unity of Brethren. From 1650 to 1655 he worked on school reform in various Hungarian towns in which the Unity movement was strong. Then he returned to Leszno, where he publicly supported the Swedish Protestant king, Charles X, in a war against the Catholic Polish king, John Casimir. The Swedes lost the war—at least they failed to win it—and in the process Polish troops destroyed Leszno. Comenius went to Amsterdam, where he spent the remaining fourteen years of his life.

Reputation

From his death in 1670 to 1842, neither Comenius's name nor his work was well known. However, since then, Comenius has been depicted in German, English, American, and some French histories of education as the founder of modern, secular, government-controlled, tax-supported, mass school systems. This depiction started with the work of Karl von Raumer in 1842, who wrote one of the first biographically oriented accounts of educational development.[37] In the twentieth century, Americans called Comenius "the pioneer of modern educational science."[38] UNESCO made him a "patron saint"; Soviet, Polish, East German, and other eastern European writers have depicted him as a reformer and a Czech hero. But this depiction of Comenius as a modern person out of step with his own times is misleading. He is interesting to students of education precisely because he is so typical of seventeenth-century Protestants. What he advocated was being discussed by a number of reformers. A few examples will illustrate: first, in reference to teaching methods and learning theory; second, in the matter of school structure and administration.

Teaching Methods

We have already seen in Butzbach's youthful experiences that pupils often suffered from poor instruction. By Comenius's day, many people were criticizing these practices, and Comenius joined their number. Schools he called "slaughterhouses of the mind," saying that he wanted "to free the school and young people from very difficult labyrinths."[39] He thought this could be done by having pupils study *things* before *words,* by waiting until children were ready to study, by carefully organizing material and experiences in "natural" order, by encouraging much practice, and by stimulating interest through examples and classroom dramatization. "Tempt the student to plunge willingly into work," he said. This meant having teachers who were thoughtful, patient, well-trained— much after the Jesuit pattern. When Comenius encountered Hungarian opposition to his suggestions, he explained himself as follows:

> My whole method aims at changing the school drudgery into play and enjoyment. That [fact] nobody here wishes to understand. The youth, including the well-born, are treated altogether as if they were slaves; the teachers rest their esteem upon stern faces, rough words, and even in beating, and wish to be feared rather than loved. How many times have I pointed out—privately and publicly—that this is not the proper way, but always in vain! I have also advised from the very beginning that some theatrical plays be introduced, for I have learned from experience that there is no more effective means for the expulsion of mental flabbiness and the arousing of alertness. But I was told that such playthings (as the producing of comedies in schools) should be left to the Jesuits; that I had been called for serious work. I used to reply: "But these playthings lead to serious goals; the Jesuits are truly the sons of the world, ingenious in their affairs, while we are truly the sons of light, unforeseeing in our affairs. They entice to themselves the most gifted heads of the whole world by their pleasant method, and make them fit, by the exercise of that kind, for their life tasks; while we remain backward with ours." The I added: "If we had not introduced into our schools in Poland that kind of exercise, all would have been at a standstill; with it we succeed not only that our people do not send their sons to the Jesuits, but that some come to us from theirs.[40]

Comenius thought, as did many others at the time, that ideas come rather directly from sense perceptions. Hence, he believed that a pleasant physical environment was important and that pictures were desirable in classrooms. Indeed, Comenius was among the first people to use pictures as an integral part of a language text.

Structure of Schools

Comenius agreed with Luther, Melanchthon, and other Christian reformers that everyone needed to be able to read the vernacular, that writing and computation skills were desirable, and that knowledge of classical languages and literature should be more widely diffused among the male population. Comenius thought women as intelligent as men, but believed that their primary household role made classical studies less essential.

The need for universal literacy meant that every village should have a vernacular teacher and that all larger towns should have classical schools. Comenius preferred classes graded by age, with one teacher in charge of each class. He thought a skilled teacher should have no difficulty with eighty or more pupils in a room, and classes of this size were usual in Europe and the American colonies. He believed that children could help teach each other. Teachers should be reasonably compensated, perhaps on a par with the lesser clergy. Comenius thought a basic salary could be guaranteed from the town treasury or through some other source, but saw nothing wrong in charging fees to those parents or guardians who could afford them. He hoped wealthy citizens would consider it a duty to contribute money to pay tuition for poor children.

Comenius believed that civil and ecclesiastical authorities should cooperate to make schooling available and to supervise its quality. The contemporary American or French concept of separating church and state was unthinkable to him—the notion that schools should be without religious orientation would have been as blasphemous to him and his Protestant confreres as to their Catholic competitors. The purpose of education was for Comenius "that every single individual shall rise out of darkness and barbarism."[41] A Christian school was essential for this.

It is difficult to assess Comenius's educational significance. He was part of a network of Protestant reformers that included John Drury, Samuel Hartlib, John Milton, and George Snell in England; Joachim Junge, and Wolfgang Ratke in Germany; Axel Oxenstierna in Sweden; and Comenius's teacher and friend Johann Heinrich Alstead. They in turn shared many of the ideas advocated a little earlier by Francis Bacon (1561–1626) in England and earlier still by Peter Ramus (1515–1572) in France and Erasmus in Holland.[42] This network extended into the American colonies. Comenius was reportedly offered the presidency of Harvard in the 1650s, but turned it down.[43] The Unity of Brethren were active missionaries in North Carolina and Pennsylvania, and the general attitudes of Comenius and his circle were shared by colonial leaders in New England from the 1630s to the 1670s.

SUMMARY

Reformation leaders made education the central focus of their programs for change. Wycliffe, Hus, Luther, Melanchthon, Loyola, Comenius, and other Reformation figures saw education as essential for salvation. They assumed schools were the structural mechanism through which instruction should be given.

Historians have tended to see the Catholic and Protestant reformations of the sixteenth and seventeenth centuries as having quite different impacts on the development of education. The Catholic Reformation, typified by Ignatius Loyola, is often depicted as a powerful force of conservatism in pedagogy. In contrast, Protestant reformers, of whom Comenius is the most frequently and positively cited educational example, are seen as part of the early development of progressive methods and state (secular) systems of instruction. Actually, Loyola and Comenius were remarkable for their similarities, not their differences. Their *Weltanschauungen* (world views) were practically the same, notwithstanding the fact that Loyola had been dead for thirty-six years when Comenius was born. Both were devout Christians for whom church and state were fundamentally intertwined, and each combined intense zeal with thorough practicality. Their educational approaches were virtually identical and contained numerous elements of what is currently regarded as "best practice" in teaching. At the same time, neither Catholics nor Protestants favored secularization of instruction. Thus, although the Reformation was politically divisive, it was a positive force in educational development because Protestants and Catholics competed so ferociously to provide attractive and effective schools.

The Reformation did less for women and for equalizing educational opportunity than has sometimes been assumed. The emphasis on vernacular schools for all and classical schools for leaders was the basis for two-track school systems in all European countries. Inexpensive elementary, folk, or petty schools taught basic vernacular literacy and religion to common folk. Elite gymnasia, grammar schools, lycées and academies taught Latin and other university preparatory subjects to boys from families who could afford expensive tuition.

The democratizing influences of the American encounter, as we shall see in Chapters 6 and 7, challenged and ultimately altered this structure. The preeminence of schooling, as opposed to other possible ways of organizing instruction and learning, has remained for many a basic tenet. The centrality of religion is more controversial. The idea that a small elite should have access to more and different schooling than others has not survived as a reputable notion among many, although a few theorists continue to advocate it. Attitudes about this last item derive from basic assumptions about how humans learn, as we shall see in Chapter 6.

NOTES

1. Hastings Rashdall, *The Universities of Europe in the Middle Ages,* ed. F. M. Powicke and A. B. Emden, 3 vols. (Oxford: Clarendon Press, 1936), 3: map facing 558.

2. George M. Trevelyan, *England in the Age of Wycliffe, 1368–1520* (London: Longmans, Green, 1925).

3. James E. T. Rogers, *The Economic Interpretation of History* (New York: G. Putnam's Sons, 1888), 75; R. L. Poole, *Wycliffe and Movements for Reform* (New York: AMS Press, [1889] 1978), 88.

4. James W. Thompson, *Economic and Social History of Europe in the Later Middle Ages, 1300–1530* (New York: Century, 1931), 449.

5. J. R. Tanner, et al., eds., *The Cambridge Medieval History,* 8 vols. (Cambridge: Cambridge University Press, 1932), 7: 486–495.

6. F. D. Matthew, ed., *The English Works of Wyclif, Hitherto Unprinted* (London: Truebner, 1880), 96–104.

7. Mandell Creighton, *History of the Papacy During the Reformation,* 5 vols. (London: 1882), 1: 359.

8. Henry Hart Milman, *History of Latin Christianity,* 8 vols. (New York: Sheldon, 1860), 7: 487.

9. Erik H. Erikson, *Young Man Luther* (New York: W. W. Norton, 1962).

10. Gordon Rupp, *The Righteousness of God* (London: Hodder and Stoughton, 1953), 105ff.

11. Anders Piltz, *The World of Medieval Learning,* trans. David Jones (Totowa, New Jersey: Barnes and Noble Books, 1981), 245ff.

12. Cited in John Todd, *Martin Luther* (Westminster, Maryland: Newman Press, 1964), 36.

13. Todd, *Martin Luther,* 115.

14. *Resolutio Lutheriana super propositione decima tertia de potestate papae* (Leipzig, 1519), cited in Todd, *Luther,* 162.

15. "Letters to the Mayors and Aldermen of All the Cities of Germany on Behalf of Christian Schools," in *Luther on Education,* ed. F. V. N. Painter (Philadelphia: Lutheran Publication Society, 1889), 186.

16. "Sermon on the Duty of Sending Children to School," in Painter, *Luther on Education,* 264.

17. Clyde L. Manschreck, *Melanchthon: The Quiet Reformer* (Nashville: Abingdon Press, 1958), 140.

18. *Corpus Reformatorum* 11: 298ff., cited in Manschreck, *Melanchthon,* 146.

19. Julia O'Faolain and Laura Martenes, eds., *Not in God's Image: Women in History from the Greeks to the Victorians* (New York: Harper and Row, 1973), 196.

20. [Ignatius Loyola], *St. Ignatius' Own Story,* trans. William J. Young (Chicago: Loyola University Press, 1956), 9–11.

21. Cf., Loyola, *St. Ignatius' Own Story,* 17–24, for an account of Ignatius's religious experiences during this time.

22. Paul Dudon, *St. Ignatius of Loyola,* trans. William J. Young (Milwaukee: Bruce, 1949), 148, 204.

23. Cited in George E. Ganss, *Saint Ignatius' Idea of a Jesuit University* (Milwaukee: Marquette University Press, 1954), 24.

24. Allan P. Farrell, *The Jesuit Code of Liberal Education* (Milwaukee: Bruce, 1938), 26.

25. Ganss, *Saint Ignatius' Idea of a Jesuit University,* 24.

26. Cf., for example, Ignatius's letter of June 1, 1551 to Fr. Antonio Brandao, published in Loyola, *St. Ignatius' Own Story,* 99–107.

27. George E. Ganss discusses Ignatius's pragmatic educational philosophy in "Education for Business in the Jesuit University," *Jesuit Educational Quarterly* 23 (January 1961): 137.

28. Loyola, *The Constitutions of the Society of Jesus,* trans. George E. Ganss (St. Louis: Institute of Jesuit Sources, 1970), pt. 4, ch. 6.4, 191; quotation from 12.3, 214.

29. Letter of Ignatius, 1555, cited in Farrell, *The Jesuit Code of Liberal Education,* 136.

30. Thomas Hughes, *Loyola and the Educational System of the Jesuits* (New York: Charles Scribner's Sons, [1892] 1912), 160–61.

31. R. Schwickerath, in *Cyclopedia of Education,* ed. Paul Monroe, 5 vols., s.v. "Jesuits, Educational Work of" (New York: Macmillan, 1911–1913).

32. Hughes, *Loyola,* 255, paraphrases one of the early Jesuit fathers: "Few things are to be taught in each class, but accurately, so that they remain in the minds of the boys; the teacher is to remember that these young intellects are like vases with a narrow orifice, which waste the liquid, if it is poured in copiously, but take it all, if it comes in by drops."

33. John Edward Sadler, *J. A. Comenius and the Concept of Universal Education* (New York: Barnes and Noble [George Allen and Unwin], 1966), 24.

34. L. Glenn Smith, "For the Greater Glory of God: Religious Competition and Educational Improvement, 1565–1650" in *History of Elementary School Teaching and Curriculum,* vol. 1 of the *International Series for the History of Education,* ed. Giovanni Genovesi, et al. (Hanover: Universität Hanover, 1990), 1–7.

35. Unless otherwise indicated, biographical information in this section is from Mathew Spinka, *John Amos Comenius—That Incomparable Moravian* (Chicago: University of Chicago Press, 1943).

36. "Jesuits, Educational Work of," *Cyclopedia of Education.*

37. Karl von Raumer, *Geschichte der Pädagogik vom Wiederaufblühen klassicher Studien bis auf unsere Zeit* (*History of Pedagogy from the Revival of Classical Learning down to Our Time*), 4 vols. (1843–1855).

38. I. L. Kandel and Paul Monroe, "Comenius, John Amos," *Cyclopedia of Education,* 2: 135–41.

39. Kandel and Monroe, *Cyclopedia of Education,* 2: 135–41.

40. Spinka, *John Amos Comenius,* 129–30.

41. Sadler, *J. A. Comenius,* 225.

42. All these mentioned, s.v. *Cyclopedia of Education.*

43. Henry Barnard, ed. and comp., "A History of Harvard College, 1636–1684, Primarily from Eliot's History of Harvard College," *American Journal of Education* 9 (1860): 129–138.

The New Educators

To make time periods more understandable, historians coin phrases that bring certain aspects of an era into sharper focus. This *Zeitgeist* or "spirit of the times" approach includes such labels as "Golden Age of Greece," "Medieval Period," "Renaissance," and "Reformation." Labels for the seventeenth and eighteenth centuries include: "Age of Absolutism," "Age of Enlightenment," "Age of Reason," and "Scientific Revolution" (with its concomitant industrial transformation). Those stressing the monarchical nature of European politics with the common belief in the divine right of kings have favored the image of absolutism. Others have emphasized intellectual developments that replaced a priori deduction with inductive experimentation, a substitution that led to major economic and industrial changes.

THE ENLIGHTENMENT

These two centuries can be understood through the words of German philosopher Immanuel Kant (1724–1804) who, in 1784, defined the term *enlightenment* as "man's emergence from his nonage," meaning not a lack of intelligence but rather a "lack of determination and courage to use that intelligence without another's guidance." He urged, *"Sapere aude!* Dare to know. Have the courage to use your own intelligence!"[1] It is from this perspective that we approach the Enlightenment era.

Politics and Economy

The shift in power from city guilds to regional kingdoms had stifled the growth of commune (self-governing) towns. Local nobility warred over European turf until a victor could claim supreme dominance. The most famous of these monarchies was that of the French Bourbons with its "Sun King," Louis XIV (reigned 1643–1715). Others included the English monarchies beginning with James I (1603–1625) and ending with George III (1760–1820); the German Hapsburgs, commencing under Ferdinand I (1556–1564) and ending (in a Hapsburg-Lorraine union) with Francis II (1792–1835); and the Hohenzollern House, continuing from the time of Frederick I (1415–1440) to the time of William II (1888–1918).

Continual discoveries in the new world brought wealth and trade expansion:

With an unending stock of new data coming in, whether from more careful observation, better instruments, more elaborate analysis, or from penetration of new regions of the earth, the intellectual leaders of Europe faced a tremendous task in merely validating, cataloguing, and ordering their expanding fund of knowledge.[2]

Economic power in the hands of bourgeois businessmen shifted from Italy and southern Europe to northern Europe and finally to England, where the Industrial Revolution was beginning. Mercantilism, with its emphasis on state wealth rather than individual wealth or happiness, was the basis for economic policies until the middle of the eighteenth century when Mirabeau and other French thinkers challenged this notion. They called for laissez-faire policies leading to more economic freedom. Consequently, by the time Adam Smith's *Wealth of Nations* appeared in 1776, the stage had already been set for some of the ideas that were to become embodied in capitalism.

Even with colonial expansion, increased wealth, and growing trade, the quality of life for many Europeans did not improve. Instead, the continued warfare under absolute monarchs increased tax burdens. Mercantile policies left most European states in varying degrees of social and economic distress. At the other end was England, where the seeds for the industrial and intellectual revolutions had taken root. In the soil of monarchical and middle class struggles, Lockian ideas of a propertied citizenry under democratic rule began to sprout.

People and Customs

Europe was steeped in deep and long-standing class distinctions. Many governments discouraged marriages between social classes, and Spain made it illegal. In the upper classes, marriages were arranged so that romantic attachments tended to occur outside the marital union. In eighteenth-century France, the mistress became a courtesan of many talents, including the art of intellectual conversation. These skills reached perfection in the *salonières* who ran the famous French salons.

With economies still basically agrarian, large landed estates promoted primogeniture and entail so that property would not be carved into pieces for the many heirs. Serfdom continued in parts of eastern and central Europe. In other rural areas, peasants owned land or rented a considerable amount of it from nobles, who often allowed them to pass renting privileges on to their sons. Next came peasants owning or renting enough land to barely maintain their families. At the bottom were the farm-servants and hired laborers who could scarcely manage a subsistence level but who continued to grow in numbers. For many peasants, extensive schooling—despite Reformation theory—was often an unrealized dream.

Certain urban areas grew rapidly. By the 1780s London boasted 850,000 inhabitants. Paris claimed 650,000, and Amsterdam and Vienna each had around 200,000. European population as a whole was estimated at 160,000,000.[3]

The late-eighteenth-century growth of cities (with its accompanying rural decline, especially in England and Wales), was a direct result of industrial and technological changes. But merchants were hardly on equal footing with the landed gentry unless they could buy a substantial amount of property. Even on the continent, peasants were soon wandering into the cities in search of work created by industrialization. They formed a growing urban proletariat. In France, however, most people stayed out of the cities, believing that "the nation's true prosperity lay in the treasures of the earth."[4] Here again, education was connected to property and wealth, and universal schooling was generally frowned upon. John Baptist de LaSalle and his Brothers of the Christian Schools had political problems because they started and maintained schools for the poor.

To think of a European consciousness would be stretching a point, and to describe a national consciousness would be stretching it further, even for the educated upper classes. Nevertheless, the term *cosmopolitan* had universal meaning in literate circles; it meant "European." A few voices cried faintly for a unified Europe and mistakenly thought it had arrived with Napoleon (1769–1821). Even before Napoleon—and despite England's intellectual influence and economic power—France managed to stamp its seal on this "enlightened" age. French was the cosmopolitan language of conversation and diplomacy. Paris was the center of culture and art. It would take a disillusioned post-Napoleonic era to produce widespread national self-identification with such identities as Englishman, German, or Spaniard. As for women, any extensive consciousness-raising was still many years away—even though, as we shall see in Chapter 7, the Mexican poet Sor Juana Inés de la Cruz set the stage in the 1680s, and Mary

Wollstonecraft followed a century later with her *Vindication of the Rights of Woman.*

English Intellectual Heritage

English philosophers prepared the canvas for much of the work that was crafted by French philosophers Voltaire, Diderot, and Rousseau, and ultimately expanded upon by others. Therefore, let us briefly note three English writers who influenced Voltaire enough to put the French Enlightenment in motion.

First came Sir Francis Bacon (1561–1626). The younger son of nobility, Bacon spent three years at Cambridge followed by diplomatic service in France and law study at one of England's prestigious Inns of Court. Although he lost in his ambitions for political office, he did successfully practice law. He acquired wealth, property, and a secretary—Thomas Hobbes (1588–1679)—who would carry on his philosophical empiricism. In the last twenty years of his life, he rose from attorney general to become the king's chancellor.

Bacon wrote a great deal. In his *Advancement of Learning,* he proposed a new system of thought—the inductive study of nature through experience and experiment. To embark on such a study, students had to clear their minds of all a priori deductions learned at the syllogistic hand of the Scholastics. Going beyond Scholasticism, Bacon also discarded most ideas based on Plato and Aristotle. He believed that the only trustworthy knowledge came through observing nature. Beyond this, human beings could know nothing. With this new scientific system would come power. By observing and obeying nature, human knowledge and power could meet. Bacon thought that scientific knowledge would transform society and possibly human nature itself.

Second was Sir Isaac Newton (1642–1727). Born of landed but humble country stock, Newton was educated in a local grammar school beginning at age twelve. His teachers thought him idle and inattentive, neglecting important subjects for others that appealed to him. After two years his widowed mother took him out of school to help with farm chores. Fortunately, an uncle recognized the youth's mathematical genius, and made arrangements for him to enter Trinity College, Cambridge. Newton earned his baccalaureate in four years and became a fellow of the college, lecturing and writing throughout the next thirty-five years of his life. He has been credited with systematically describing "the scientific method" in research and developing an approach to calculus that helped him give more convincing expression to some of the astronomical theories of Copernicus, Galileo, Brahe, and Kepler. He contributed to our knowledge of growth, light, and optics. He also maintained a strong interest in astrology.

Third, there was John Locke, who tried to do for psychology what Newton had done for physics.

John Locke (1632–1704)

Historian Merle Curti called John Locke "America's Philosopher."[5] He strongly influenced political theory and epistemology, or the study of how we know. His pedagogical ideas were typical of the governing class of the early American colonies.

Life

John was the eldest son of a country lawyer who tutored him during his early years. At fifteen, he attended Westminster, one of England's great "public schools," but the curriculum bored him. He flirted with royalist political philosophy, but returned to his family orientation of Puritanism. At twenty he enrolled at Christ Church, Oxford. For the next fourteen years, he was student, tutor, and lecturer at Oxford.[6]

Locke studied medicine and experimental science. He was a member of the British Royal Society, the chief scientific body in England. Though his fame did not rest on his own research, his philosophic justification of experimental methods was important. His knowledge of medicine helped his later career. He performed liver surgery on Anthony Ashley Cooper, who shortly thereafter became the first Earl of Shaftesbury. Cooper thought Locke had saved his life and became a patron and friend, opening several doors to employment. Locke also imbibed a practical liberalism from Shaftesbury, which he incorporated into his justification of popular government.

Locke spent several of the middle years of his life in Holland, for Shaftesbury's opposition to Charles II and James II, coupled with Locke's justifications for revolution against them, made England a dangerous place until the late 1680s when Parliament brought William and Mary to power. Locke divided his last years between London and the Essex country estate of Lady Damaris Masham. She was married to a member of Parliament, but in earlier years Locke and Lady Masham had exchanged love letters. Locke never married. He died at Lady Masham's house in the fall of 1704 at the age of seventy-two.

Political Views

In *Two Treatises on Government,* Locke elaborated a theory of constitutional law and popular government. He opposed absolute monarchy, basing his argument on "natural law." Nature's principles caused people to unite into a community:

> Men being, as has been said by nature all free, equal, and independent, no one can be put out of this estate and subjected to the political power of another without his own consent, which is done by agreeing with other men, to join and unite into a community for their comfortable, safe, and peaceable living, one amongst another, in a secure enjoyment of their properties, and in a greater security against any

that are not of it. . . . When any number of men have so consented to
make one community or government, they are thereby presently incorporated, and make one body politic, wherein the majority have a right
to act and conclude the rest.[7]

Here was the heart of constitutional republican theory.

Locke established legislative power as the fundamental law of com-
monwealths. In the final analysis, power remained in the hands of the
people through the legislature, which would take power from the executive if there was any wrongdoing. The power entrusted to legislators
could be taken from them by the electorate if the legislators acted contrary to the people's trust.

Educational Ideas

While Locke was in exile, a friend asked for advice on bringing up his
eight-year-old son. The letters which Locke wrote became *Some Thoughts
Concerning Education,* published in 1693. Locke criticized the schools of
his time for relying on corporal punishment, and in Cicero's tradition, he
recommended tutors instead. According to Locke, schools might make a
boy "better able to bustle and shift" among peers, but "that boldness and
spirit which lads get amongst their play fellows at school . . . has ordinarily such a mixture of rudeness and ill-turned confidence that those
misbecoming and disingenuous ways of shifting in the world must be
unlearnt." Thinking of his own time at Westminster, Locke reminded his
friend of the "mal-pertness, tricking, or violence learnt amongst schoolboys," and concluded that the "faults of a private [that is, tutorial] education [are] infinitely to be preferred to such improvements."[8]

Locke advocated four outcomes: virtue, wisdom, good breeding, and
learning. Virtue's foundation was the result of good religious training, or
as Locke wrote, "a true notion of God." This was best implanted by simple
acts of devotion, such as morning and evening prayer. Wisdom was the
result of natural temper, the use of mind, and experience. Two types of ill-
breeding were extreme bashfulness and "misbecoming negligence and
disrespect in our carriage." One rule would help in avoiding both: "not to
think meanly of ourselves and not to think meanly of others."

Locke looked to fathers as well as tutors to educate young gentlemen:
"And 'tis not the waggeries or cheats practiced amongst schoolboys, 'tis
not their roughness one to another, not their well-laid plots of robbing an
orchard together, that make an able man . . . but the principles of justice, generosity, and sobriety, . . . qualities which I judge schoolboys do
not learn much of one another." Locke advised getting the best possible
tutor, a far better investment than a large estate or toys and other
trifles, for said he " 'tis not good husbandry to make his fortune rich, and
his mind poor."[9]

Tutors had to be honest, he asserted, because children would easily
perceive when they were slighted or deceived. Locke thought that

schools and parents both overemphasized Latin grammar and the memorization of rules; rote learning took the place of thought and understanding. Many children were ill-schooled by devoting too much time to Latin and Greek. He argued for a more natural way of learning Latin with time devoted to the rules of grammar, and thought that children should not be wearied with lectures. Locke also wrote in some detail about the need for a proper balance between freedom and authority—the true secret of education.

Utility was Locke's main criterion for selecting subjects to be learned. He thought that a child should learn Latin and French and also recommended arithmetic, geography, chronology, history, geometry, and astronomy. Later, young gentlemen should learn civil law and graceful English. He also advocated study of the sciences, citing the writings of Robert Boyle and Sir Isaac Newton. Dancing, fencing, and riding were appropriate, but not music or painting. A gentleman should learn husbandry and the skills of a carpenter, joiner, or turner. Locke considered these fit and healthy recreations for a man of study or business. He favored learning a variety of trades and some bookkeeping.

Epistemology

Locke's most influential educational ideas dealt with the theory of knowledge. Plato, Descartes, and others had held that certain principles were inborn truths. An empiricist, Locke disagreed, arguing that innate ideas did not meet certain necessary tests. For example, if ideas were innate, they should be found in everyone, even in infants, savages, and the uneducated.

Locke formulated a *tabula rasa* theory of the mind. It held that a child's mind is initially blank. "All ideas come from sensation or reflection and are recorded in the mind which acts like a blank piece of 'white paper,' that fills up from *experience*," he said. "That is, we either experience external sensible objects, or we witness the internal operations of our minds as we employ our thought processes."[10]

Locke called for religious toleration, but like Comenius, meant mainstream Protestants tolerating each other. He was suspicious of all mysticism, religious visions, and miracles, advocating maximum religious liberty consistent with orderly society. This liberty, however, should not extend to atheists or Roman Catholics who were, in his opinion, too dangerous to be trusted.

Locke appealed to American colonists who wanted to justify greater liberty for themselves but who feared radical change. His emphasis on utility rather than the elitist tradition of the liberal arts fit with the practical needs of the new world's frontier society, while his preoccupation with the education of middle class and aristocratic males was comforting to traditionalists. In stressing that all knowledge was relative and experiential, Locke not only offered a justification for rethinking the basis of curriculum, but "cast doubt on the possibility of achieving universally valid knowledge."[11] Two centuries later "progressive" educators would cite Locke with approval.

Jean-Jacques Rousseau (1712–1778)

These same progressives would also cite Jean-Jacques Rousseau, who was born in France four years after Locke died. Rousseau differed in three ways from Locke, Comenius, the Jesuits, and most other Enlightenment educational theorists: (1) Their search for more effective and pleasant teaching methods grew largely out of competition with various religious groups, whereas Rousseau was secular. (2) Their ideas were cast in religious and philosophic prose, whereas Rousseau's were in novelistic and autobiographical form. (3) They laid the foundations for more humane methods and a more practical curriculum, but did not question the school structures of their time. Rousseau wanted to sweep these structures aside and start afresh with a radically different approach to teaching and learning. For all these reasons, his work has appealed to some reform-minded educators down to the present.

French Huguenots (Protestants) suffered persecution in their Catholic-dominated country. Consequently, many refugees crossed the border into the Swiss cantons of Berne, Zurich, and Geneva. It was to the latter Reformation town that Rousseau's great-great-grandfather, Didier Rousseau, made his way in 1549. His craft was clockmaking. Didier and his sons and grandsons settled into a respectable, quiet life of hard work and some profit. But Jean's father, Isaac, cracked the traditional mold.

Isaac had an incurable wanderlust. Even after he married his childhood sweetheart against her affluent father's wishes, he found himself yearning to see Constantinople. How long he left his wife, Suzanne, and their son, François, is not clear, but Suzanne "conjured him to return" so that advances made to her by other men in the town would stop. "He sacrificed all and did so," Jean-Jacques later said. "I was the unfortunate fruit of this return, being born ten months after, in a very weakly and infirm state. My birth cost my mother her life, and was the first of my misfortunes."[12]

Early Life

Isaac solicited the help of his unmarried sister, Susan, and a nursemaid by the name of Jacqueline. Together the three of them seem to have provided all the tender loving care necessary to the fragile child. If all was not rosy, Rousseau did not seem to have been aware of it, having only happy memories of his childhood. He thought he was the favorite of the family (to the neglect of his older brother who turned out to be the "bad seed"). Isaac would often embrace his youngest son with convulsive sighs and tears as he recalled how much he missed his wife and how much Jean-Jacques reminded him of her.

Rousseau remembered the motherly warmth and attention of his Aunt Susan, whose singing filled his home with sweetness and gaiety. Under his father's care, the young boy was not allowed to play with children his own age, although Isaac made certain that his son learned to read. The manner in which Jean-Jacques acquired this latter skill was unique. Jean-Jacques's mother had left a modest library of romance and adventure. Isaac felt that these would be entertaining books from which his son would develop a love for reading. Father and son found themselves so engrossed in these adventures, however, that they would alternately read to each other all night until the volume was finished. Ashamed of such overindulgence, the father often confided to his son that he was himself more of a child than Jean-Jacques. Rousseau later said that this "dangerous custom" allowed him to acquire too intimate a familiarity with adult passions which he was too young to understand. By the time he was seven, his mother's library had been exhausted, and he got access to his maternal grandmother's collection of Christian, Roman, and Greek histories. "I had conceived nothing—I had felt the whole. This confused succession of emotions . . . added an extravagant, romantic notion of human life, which," he wrote in his *Confessions,* "experience and reflection have never been able wholly to eradicate."[13]

In his adult life, Jean-Jacques Rousseau expected the most ideal treatment and care from his friends, but consistently received less. Such experiences invariably left him outraged or defensive and melancholy.

When young Rousseau was ten, his father fled Geneva. Isaac's volatile temper had gotten him into a minor brawl with a French army captain. The Geneva council sided with the officer, and Isaac chose banishment over imprisonment and asked his brother to look after Jean-Jacques. This brother, Uncle Gabriel Bernard to Jean-Jacques, had a ten-year-old son who was also called Bernard. For tutoring, the two boys boarded for three years with Pastor Lambercier and his unmarried sister, until both were accused of theft. Rousseau said that neither was guilty, but both were punished. They could never again feel the same affection and respect for their teachers-turned-accusers as they had before the incident. Rousseau also learned, under the paddle of Mademoiselle Lambercier, to associate beating with erotic pleasure.

Shortly after this incident, the boys returned briefly to the uncle's house. It was now time for them to enter into some sort of professional training. Being the son of a general, Cousin Bernard was destined for engineering and the life of a well-bred suburbanite. Jean-Jacques, not having much income from his mother's estate, was committed to be an engraver's apprentice.

At fifty-three, Rousseau remembered Mr. Ducammon, master engraver, as a most abhorrent fellow: mean, suspicious, and brutal, with the harshest methods of discipline. Under his stern eye, the young teenager turned from a tender, affectionate boy into a liar, cheat, and petty thief. Jean-Jacques learned to spend his free hours—especially Sundays— away from the city and engulfed in the pleasures of the countryside. Often he would barely make it back before the city's gates closed for the night.

A Wandering Life

One evening in 1728, upon seeing the bridge draw up and the gates begin to close, Rousseau resolved to run away. In so doing, he made the momentous decision of his life—to embark upon a vagabond career that would bring his volatile nature sometimes to the heights of ecstasy and too often to the depths of despair.

He headed toward the Catholic town of Confignon in Savoy, ten miles south of Geneva. Blissfully enjoying the delights of nature, it took young Rousseau several days to reach his destination. Upon arriving, he went to the vicar's house, for Rousseau had heard that the vicar and his family wanted to destroy the Protestant republic of Geneva. Reassured by good wine and the promise of protection, sixteen-year-old Jean-Jacques agreed to place himself in the hands of a Mrs. Warren (Madame de Warens), a recent convert who received a yearly pension to care for such waywards. Her house in Annecy was fifteen miles south of Confignon. Thinking that he had put himself in the hands of some shriveled up old shrew, Jean-Jacques was overwhelmed to find his captor young (around twenty-eight), plumpish (but not offensively so), pretty, and friendly. He did not know whether to romaticize her or matronize her. It took him several years to settle into a comfortable mother–son relationship.

Totally smitten with Warren, Jean-Jacques wished only to stay by her side. She decided, however, that he should journey across the Alps to Turin (in northern Italy) and take instruction in the Catholic religion. Shortly, Isaac and Uncle Gabriel rode into Confignon. Upon hearing from the vicar that the boy had gone to Annecy, the uncle returned home. Isaac went on to Warren's. Here, he learned that his son had left for Turin only the day before. " 'Ah! the unhappy boy!' cried Isaac, with tears running, as they did so readily, from his weak eyes; 'now indeed have I lost him forever!' "14

In his *Confessions,* Rousseau assessed his father's paternal behavior this way:

> My father [and] his friend . . . contented themselves with lament- ing . . . my fate instead of overtaking me, which, (as they were on horseback and I on foot) they might have accomplished. . . . By a simi- lar negligence, my brother was so entirely lost that it was never known what had become of him. . . . [Isaac] was a good father, particu- larly to me, whom he tenderly loved; but he likewise loved his plea- sures, and since we had been separated other connections had weak- ened his paternal affection. He had married again at Nyon, and, though his second wife was too old to expect children, she had rela-

tions. My father was united to another family, surrounded by other objects, and a variety of cares prevented my returning often to his remembrance. He was in the decline of life, and had nothing to support the inconveniences of old age; my mother's property devolved to me and my brother, but during our absence the interest of it was enjoyed by my father. This consideration had no immediate effect on his conduct, nor did it blind his sense of duty; but it had an imperceptible effect, and prevented him making use of the exertion to regain me which he would otherwise have employed; and this I think was the reason that, having traced me as far as Annecy, he stopped short; . . . and likewise explains why, on visiting him several times since my flight, he always received me with great kindness, but never made great efforts to retain me.[15]

Rousseau entered the monastery at Turin on April 12, 1728 and was baptized; eleven days later he was on his own. For the remainder of 1728 and part of 1729, Rousseau worked as a footman (uniformed manager of horses) in two different aristocratic households. He was employed in the first until the lady of the house died. He left the second when he embarrassed himself and the attractive but somewhat arrogant daughter of the family. While waiting tables, Rousseau corrected a wrong French usage by his employer. The girl gazed admiringly upon him, and Rousseau became so nervous under her gaze that when she asked him for water, he spilled it all over her.

He took to the road again, this time with an old friend from Geneva, but soon grew weary of his companion. Longing to see his "Mama Warren," he set out for Annecy. Not knowing what kind of reception to expect, he was pleasantly surprised when she consoled him and said that he was probably too young to be out trying to survive on his own. For the next little while—it is hard to know how long—the seventeen-year-old basked in the attention which his new mother figure gave him. But Warren was acutely aware that he still had no profession, so she sent him off to a seminary to get the rudiments of Latin for the life of a priest. Rousseau hated Latin and was a hopeless failure. Next he tried music, which he dearly loved even though he had no talent for it. Under the tutelage of a friendly but alcoholic music master, Rousseau learned what he could until the man became victim to his habit.

Upon his return to Annecy, he discovered that Mama Warren had gone off to Paris with her lover/business manager, Claude Anet. Rousseau innocently frolicked with a few of the maidens in a nearby villa. Then, after several days of waiting for Warren, who did not return, he decided to accompany Warren's maid to her home in Switzerland. He stopped to see his father, but Isaac could only cry over the lonely life his abandoned son led instead of offering to make a home for him.

Rousseau traveled on to Lausanne, where he set himself up as a music professor, but his training was far from complete. He hardly knew how to read or write music, but that did not deter him. Living off the credit of his kindly landlord, he composed a score that he planned to conduct at a local concert run solely for promising amateurs.

The day for his concert finally arrived, and a nervous Rousseau distributed his score to the musicians and stepped up to the podium. The musicians laughed. When the music began, the audience began to murmur and chuckle. Rousseau, sweating profusely, continued to the agonizing end. Humor was not the reaction he had intended, but the audience was put into such a good mood that some managed to compliment him when it was over. This increased Rousseau's humiliation and despair, and he fell in to a great fit of depression. After trying to teach a few "nasty pupils," who made fun of how little he knew, the neophyte musician gave up his self-imposed professorship and accepted an offer from an acquaintance who was attendant to an officer in Paris.

Rousseau set out for the capital dreaming of a career as a military leader. When he learned that his services were to be those of a valet and not an officer, the proud but dejected Rousseau left for mother Warren's house and the comfort that a long journey through the French countryside could bring. The year was 1731. For the next six years, Rousseau lived with Warren in a somewhat unusual liaison.

What we know of Warren comes from Rousseau's *Confessions*. According to him, Françoise Louise married Mr. Warren when she was only fourteen. He was much older. Shortly afterward, she took her first lover, who taught her that there was nothing wrong with sexual unions so long as couples were discreet. Fancying herself as having a head for business, she chalked up healthy debts for her husband. Then she became a Catholic and negotiated a yearly stipend from the King of Sardinia for the care of future converts. As the close friend of the bishop, she enjoyed social prominence. Rousseau did not say what happened to Mr. Warren.

It was probably in 1734 that Warren turned her sexual attentions to her "little one," as she had called Rousseau on occasion. Rousseau noticed a change in her—she had become withdrawn and quiet. When he asked her why, she engaged him in a walk and explained that a certain older neighbor was about to take advantage of him. To save him from this exploitation, she proposed showing him the ways of love herself. Jean-Jacques felt severely confused. She gave him eight days to come to a decision—a period which he said was one of the longest in his life. Feeling toward her as he did, Rousseau thought that the proposed affair smacked of incest, but he was afraid to reject her. After his consent, she gave herself to the twenty-two-year-old in a cold, impersonal way. With mixed feelings of fear, impatience, dread, and desire, he managed to consummate the relationship.

Rousseau said, to Warren's credit, that he and Anet remained friends through these rather awkward years. Sometime around 1736, however, Anet succumbed to pleurisy and died. This left Rousseau next in line as business manager. It is difficult to tell how well he played this role, for it was during this time that he developed a burning passion to be a writer of Voltaire's caliber, and he had never given up his desire to be a composer. These seemingly unobtainable goals often left him in a state of despair, although he remembered these years with Mama as some of his happiest.

In 1737 his health suffered. He said that he had the vapors, a hypochondriacal ailment. Nevertheless, Warren insisted that he make a trek to the medically famous town of Montpellier in southern France. Upon his return a year later, he found his place occupied by a man several years his junior.

For a time, Rousseau pretended that nothing had changed. After a couple of stays with Warren and a brief tutoring job, however, Rousseau took leave of his dear Mama for good. He headed for Paris, center of the French Enlightenment.

In Paris, Rousseau lived in a sleazy hotel near the Sorbonne. He became friends with twenty-nine-year-old David Diderot, who would become a leading intellectual of the Enlightenment. He met other fashionable young men and women who, having nothing better to do, flirted with the ideas of the Enlightenment philosophers. Several young married women took an interest in Rousseau and secured for him a job as the personal secretary to the French ambassador to Venice. Rousseau eagerly anticipated his new role, but he found Ambassador Montaigu stupid and arrogant. Rousseau's blunder was in not putting up with inferior traits in one of superior social station. Montaigu fired him.

Back in Paris in 1745, Rousseau resumed his residence in the hotel and copied music for a livelihood. The landlord had hired a new seamstress, a twenty-two-year-old named Thérèse Lavasseur. Rousseau began defending the poor woman, who was the brunt of jokes, and the rather pathetic Thérèse came to depend on his friendship. He began living with her and her dominating mother, promising never to leave her or marry her. He said that he tried teaching her, but she lacked the facility for learning. She never read well and could not spell or name the months of the year in order. After twenty years of instruction, she had difficulty telling time. Numbers gave her trouble, especially when it came to counting money, and she also tended to use the exact opposite of the word she meant. Nevertheless, Rousseau thought that she had a pure and innocent heart, devoid of all forms of deviousness, and that she was a superb cook and housekeeper.

To this ignorant companion, who was to live with him for the rest of his life, Rousseau attributed the ability to see the sometimes negative motives of his various friends and associates. When he became involved in heated quarrels with friends, she reinforced his suspicions. In time, Rousseau became the father of Thérèse's five children—all of whom, by his own account, he gave to foundling homes. His motivation in abandoning his children is not clear. He argued that he was not cut out to be a father, and that the children would get a good upbringing in foundling homes. Each child, he said, would learn a trade and lead the uncomplicated life of a peasant rather than struggling with fame in the world of high society. He must have wondered if Thérèse was up to motherhood. She had an affair with Rousseau's friend James Boswell (the biographer of Samuel Johnson) while living with Rousseau. All five children may not have been his.

Rousseau continued to meet and be patronized by the wealthy young women of Paris. One of his mentors was the Marquise d'Epinay. She wanted him to act as her secretary while she wrote a book about her views on education. He had already met the very stiff but "Frenchy-German" military hero Melchior Grimm, who later became part of the French Enlightenment and Epinay's lover.

In 1749 Rousseau learned that the Dijon Academy was sponsoring an essay contest on the topic, "Has the restoration of the arts and sciences corrupted or purified morals?" He contemplated entering and shared his ideas with Diderot, who was in prison for some offensive passages in his *Letters on the Blind*. Diderot encouraged Rousseau, whose essay argued that humans are by nature good and that it is society's institutions that have made them bad. To Rousseau's surprise, he won the contest and became an overnight sensation.

Rousseau's essay developed a theme that he had begun a decade earlier when he tried writing an operetta. It had featured Columbus arriving in America, waving his sword and singing "lose your liberty" to the Indians.[16] European fascination with Native American "liberty" had been piqued by several late-seventeenth-century descriptions of life among the Hurons. These accounts written by Louis Armand de Low d'Arce, Baron de Lahotan, circulated widely in France after 1703. They became the basis for *Arlequin Sauvage,* a popular play about a Native American's visit to Paris and a young Parisian named Violette who falls in love and goes to live with him in American freedom. *Arlequin Sauvage* impressed many people, including the romantic Rousseau. "During this era the thinkers of Europe forged the ideas that became known as the European Enlightenment," writes Jack Weatherford, "and much of its light came from the torch of Indian Liberty that still burned brightly in the brief interregnum between their first contact with the Europeans and their decimation by the Europeans."[17]

Rousseau accepted invitations to fashionable dinner parties, but to be true to his views, he wore a peasant's fur hat and an old purple robe. His upper-class acquaintances knew that he had scant training in either arts or sciences, so, between his silly costume and his lack of formal knowledge, the high-strung, bewildered, famous, and miserable Rousseau became the newest toy for the idle rich. The higher his fame soared, the more frightened, suspicious, reclusive, and volatile he became. His outbursts at being misunderstood began to alienate upper-class friends.

In a society that still prized a strong, masculine reserve, his angry defensiveness was soon labeled as insanity.

The first serious charge of lunacy came over his *grande passion,* the Comtesse d'Houdetot. Rousseau was not attracted to the Marquise d'Epinay, but her sister-in-law, the Comtesse d'Houdetot, set him aflame. At the age of forty-five, he seemed unable to control himself. He wrote romantic letters to her. The countess was friendly but did not share his passion. She was already involved with Saint Lambert, a military hero and figure of the French Enlightenment.

Saint Lambert accused his mistress of sexual involvement with Rousseau. The countess, in tears, pleaded with Rousseau to clear her name. Diderot advised him to tell Saint Lambert that he had the utmost regard and affection for the countess and that nothing unfaithful had occurred. Rousseau did this in a letter, but blamed Lambert for breaking up his friendship with the countess.

Rousseau also decided that the Marquise d'Epinay was responsible for Lambert's finding out about his feelings for Houdetot. He lashed out at Epinay, saying that he was tired of being chained to her. Grimm came to Epinay's rescue and broke with Rousseau, declaring that he never wanted to see him again. Diderot was appalled at Rousseau's outburst and questioned his sanity. The marquise, on the other hand, seemed hurt but contrite. Rousseau tearfully apologized, as did she. She had been planning a trip to a famous doctor in Geneva and asked Rousseau to accompany her. He refused, giving ill health as his reason. Grimm and Diderot saw this as still another betrayal, and his alienation from them was permanent. Later Rousseau confessed that Thérèse had told him that the marquise was going to Geneva to end an unwanted pregnancy. Actually, she was suffering from tuberculosis.

Other members of elite society remained friendly to him. In 1758 the Duke and Dutchess of Luxembourg offered him a house on their estate. Rousseau accepted and moved in with Thérèse. For the next four years he lived here and produced three of his most famous works: *The New Heloise,* a love story based on the romance of Abelard and Heloise that sealed his fame in the hearts of women all over Europe; *Émile,* an idealized treatise on the proper education of a boy; and *The Social Contract,* a political essay that opened with the assertion that humans are born free but everywhere are in chains. It concluded even more strongly than John Locke had done "that rebellion was justified whenever a government failed to satisfy the people it ruled."[18]

Even though *Émile* had passed the Catholic censor in France, another church official found it heretical and called for Rousseau's imprisonment or exile. In *Émile,* Rousseau not only rejected the notion of original sin, but attacked all but the fundamentals of Christianity. Most authors published their books outside of France to avoid the tight censorship codes. *Émile* came out in May 1762. By June the author was banished to

Switzerland and his book was burned in France. Hoping to return to his native Geneva, he was surprised when Geneva took away his citizenship. He ended up in Berne.

Voltaire, an old friend-turned-enemy, decided to take pity on the outcast. In 1758 Voltaire had jealously denounced Rousseau as a monkey and a madman. He enmity may have sprung from Rousseau's success (apparently Voltaire had trouble accepting this) or from the fact that Rousseau had encouraged Geneva not to build a theater because he believed such an institution led to corruption. Voltaire was a playwright living in Geneva at the time. But now in 1762, he offered his home to the fugitive. Unfortunately, Rousseau never responded to the offer. Voltaire vowed revenge for this slight, and issued a scathing and disgraceful pamphlet. Anonymously, he circulated an inaccurate picture of Rousseau's shortcomings as a father, concluding that he exposed all five children on the doorstep of an orphanage. Until his death, Voltaire continued to resent Rousseau's popularity

In 1765 Rousseau started his *Confessions* and decided to accept Scottish philosopher David Hume's offer to bring him to England. On his return to Paris to get his passport, throngs of people greeted him; however, he only wished to be left alone. In England it was the same way. Hume found the wandering philosopher charming and easy to get along with and could hardly imagine quarreling with him. Shortly after Thérèse's arrival, Rousseau requested that he, his dog Sultan, and Thérèse be allowed to live in the country away from the social gatherings that he had learned to detest.

Hume consented, although he did not think that it was a good idea, fearing that Rousseau would get too melancholy with so little to do. Perhaps he was right. At any rate, the English papers got wind of some scandalous gossip about Rousseau, and their tone changed from praise to criticism. At a loss to understand this change, the excitable philosopher accused Hume of treachery or at least disloyalty. Hume was shocked as were the few remaining friends Rousseau had in Paris.

In 1767 Rousseau returned to Paris under a false name. He finished his *Confessions* and started the *Dialogues* and *Reveries*. In 1768 he acted as his own minister and married Thérèse in a mock ceremony. Finally, in 1778, he accepted the hospitality of the Marquis de Giradin at Ermenville. He reached there in spring and was taken with the natural beauty of the setting. He became a frequent companion to the marquis's young son and even played the harpsichord in a makeshift concert. Giradin said that Rousseau was content.

On July 2, 1778, Rousseau rose at his usual hour of 5:00 A.M. and walked to the park. At 7:00 he drank his coffee but complained of feeling weak and cold. Then, agonizing over a severe pain in his head, he fell forward and died. An autopsy showed that the cause of death was a hemorrhage. His former friends—Grimm and others—spread the tale that he had commited suicide. On July 4, 1778, he was buried on the Giradin estate as he had requested.

During the French Revolution the people elevated Rousseau to the level of secular saint. His remains were moved to the Pantheon in Paris and laid near those of Voltaire. The cliquish Paris group continued their derogation of him by asserting that insanity drove him to suicide. His old Enlightenment friends never forgave him for his emotional nature in an age when men were supposed to be tough, stoical, reserved, and heroic. A year after Rousseau's death, Thérèse married the gardener of the Giradin estate.

Educational Views

How shall we rate *Émile?* The book bothered many people, but not reformers with an interest in providing an education for the masses, or "the people," as European aristocrats were fond of saying. The work is divided into five books. The first three deal with the rearing of a boy, Émile, in natural surroundings. The last two place Émile as a young man in society.[19] Rousseau wanted a state-funded system of education. Because instruction was still in clerical hands, he gave Émile an unmarried, secular tutor.

Rousseau thought that removing the child as much as possible from parental control would make nature become the tutor's guide. Émile was given as much freedom to explore his surroundings as safety allowed; there was no swaddling, so the child could move freely. Baby Émile was breast-fed by his mother—not a wet nurse as was the custom—because the mother had a natural love for her son.

Once he developed muscular control, Émile began moral training. Moral education, however, did not come in the form of adult preaching. Rather, the tutor and parents taught by setting a good example. If they were kind, understanding, and not superficial or affected, Émile would be the same way. Punishment was not necessary, said Rousseau, for children learned by suffering the consequences of their actions. Self-love was universal and necessary to preserve humankind. Out of it could grow both compassion and pity for significant others (parents) who had nourished and cared for the soul. These two feelings were a healthy basis for morality, but to distort them into dying for one's honor was unnatural and false.

Émile's intellectual education began after his moral training was well established, sometime around the age of twelve. Émile acquired academic knowledge selectively. He read *Robinson Crusoe* and studied natural science. As practical application of natural subjects would enhance Émile's adequacies, he worked with his hands and learned a skilled trade. Writing, acting, and music were not part of his instruction. All subjects having to do with humans living in society—history, philosophy, religion, politics—had to wait. By fifteen Émile was healthy, alert, agile, and self-sufficient. At eighteen Émile encountered religion and eventually learned about the corruption of society through field trips to the city and study of the humanities.

In his twenties, Émile concerned himself with love and marriage. Up to then, Émile had not experienced sexual passion. But once he did, the tutor had to find him a companion—a suitable female companion. The tutor had already told Émile the truth about sex when the boy had asked about it; part of that truth was that it was best to marry. Together they looked for Sophie, a name they chose together because it "augurs well." (The last book was entitled *Sophie,* Countess d'Houdetot's first name.)

Sophie's education, while also important, was different, as her function was to please Émile. She subjugated herself to him and made herself useful and agreeable. These duties she learned from childhood. She was also gay, musical, and possessed of an alert mind, making her fit company for a thinking Émile. The proper study for women was men: "A woman's education must . . . be planned in relation to man." To please him, "to win his respect and love, to train him in childhood, tend him in manhood, to counsel and console, to make his life pleasant and happy, these are the duties of woman for all time, and this is what she should be taught when young." Sophie's religious faith was up to Émile, and she had already learned to be ashamed of her sexuality so that she was modest. Apparently Rousseau thought that women were not naturally as good as men.

Rousseau had the tutor and Émile search everywhere, including the city, for the ideal mate. They finally discovered fifteen-year-old Sophie in the country. Émile and Sophie entered into a three-year courtship, during which Émile sought the tutor's guidance, before the couple finally married. When Sophie became pregnant, Émile asked the tutor to remain to train their child. Rousseau had already indicated that Émile's tutor must be young; now we know why.

This romantic notion of education is understandable in view of Rousseau's life. Its impact on other educational thinkers was strong. Rousseau would be consulted from Pestalozzi through Dewey—a span of over 150 years. Unfortunately, his prescriptions were not always clear, and each of his followers had difficulties making the doctrines work. For centuries, political theorists, historians, and educators have dealt with the tension between individual freedom and social necessity. It would become a perplexing dilemma for progressive educators as demonstrated by their varied explanations of what Rousseau meant by this enigmatic statement: "No doubt Émile ought to do what he wants to do, but he should do nothing but what you [the tutor] want him to do."

Rousseau's proposals for educating young men were controversial, but his thoughts on women's education caused no stir. They were conventional for the time. Within a few years of his death, however, a young British woman declared war on the long-standing attitudes that confined women to separate and inferior educational, social, and political spheres. She fueled a debate that grew to large proportions by the end of the nineteenth century and that remains a significant area of controversy today. Her name was Mary Wollstonecraft.

Mary Wollstonecraft (1759–1797)

Mary Wollstonecraft established herself in the historical record as an eighteenth-century feminist theorist and as a writer of pedagogic stories.[20] She interpreted the relations between the sexes to explain how women learned to be submissive and how women and men could live equally in relation to each other. Her best known book and the work which gained her international recognition, *Vindication of the Rights of Woman* (1792), contained her analysis of women's subservience. It proposed an egalitarian alternative to the sex-based inequities she observed in British society. Her writings (between 1786 and 1797) were set against the background of revolution in France and working-class agitation in England.

Born on April 27, 1759 near London, Mary had one older and two younger brothers plus two younger sisters. Her father inherited enough money for the family to have lived comfortably, but he overspent on his own pleasures and managed badly. The family had to move often, and the daughters had to work if they did not marry.

Wollstonecraft tried most of the occupations available to middle class, literate, single young women—and found them denigrating. She left home in 1778 at the age of nineteen, and for the next two years was a companion for a wealthy elderly woman at the health resort of Bath. In 1783, Wollstonecraft, her friend Fanny Blood, and one of her sisters opened a day school at Newington Green in north London. Another of her sisters eventually joined the three women. Various personal and financial difficulties, as well as Blood's unexpected death in 1785, led Wollstonecraft to close the school in 1786. During the next year she worked as a governess for an aristocratic family in Ireland.

Between the closing of the school and Wollstonecraft's move to Ireland, she wrote her first pedagogic book, *Thoughts on the Education of Daughters*. It was published in 1786 by Joseph Johnson, a London bookseller and printer sympathetic to English radicals. She again turned to writing after her unhappy and short-lived employment as governess, and by 1788 decided to carve out a literary career for herself. In that year, Wollstonecraft moved to London from Ireland with Johnson's help, and he provided her with regular work as a reviewer for his new magazine, the *Analytical Review*. Through her association with Johnson, Wollstonecraft joined company with London's leading political radicals. These included Thomas Paine, Thomas Christie, William Godwin, and the artists William Blake and Henry Fuseli. In 1790 she publicly became one of them when she wrote *Vindication of the Rights of Men*. This was an angry response to Edmund Burke's conservative *Reflections on the Revolution in France,* and was one of the first challenges to Burke's writing. Two years later, she wrote *Vindication of the Rights of Woman.*

Power of Education

Wollstonecraft's ideas about women's rights were grounded in her understanding of the functions of education in school and in the home. At the root of her explanation for women's subjugation lay the premise that pedagogy served to empower or disenfranchise particular social groups. Wollstonecraft categorized people by sex first, then by class. She focused her analysis on middle class women, the group to which she belonged.

Wollstonecraft argued that through their education, men learned to think rationally, which she believed to be vital for doing everything from running government to disciplining a child. This asset was intentionally missing from women's education. Wollstonecraft claimed that the omission of training in reason supported women's servitude. She believed that female education in eighteenth-century Britain denied women both their reason and their liberty, rights to which they were entitled. The power to think rationally would lead to the liberty of women.

In 1792 Wollstonecraft wanted a rational education for women because it would produce independent women and it would lead to a society in which men and women were equals. By 1796, when she began the novel *Maria, Or the Wrongs of Woman,* the second of these goals did not seem viable to her, and she no longer wrote about equality of the sexes. *Maria* dramatized the impossibility of Wollstonecraft's earlier dream, and concluded that rational education should teach women to live on their own without male companionship. Independent women should live either with other women or alone. In both the *Vindication* and *Maria,* Wollstonecraft explored how different education of the sexes produced subservient women and dominating men.

Wollstonecraft worked against the backdrop of the "reform" movement in girls' education that aimed at ennobling female domesticity. The reformers, who included Maria Edgeworth, Thomas Day, and Dr. Erasmus Darwin, hoped to produce women who could benefit the progress of British society. They wanted to provide a practical education to improve girls as wives and mothers. Domestic work was the way women could best contribute to the growth of British culture. The reformers objected to instructing girls in only the "accomplishments": drawing, dancing, sewing, playing a musical instrument, and learning a modern foreign language.

At the heart of this movement lay the ideal of the middle class woman: that she not earn a living but be economically dependent; that she not while away her leisure time on self-indulgent activity, but use her extra hours to improve herself and her family; that she manage her household skillfully and raise her children competently; and above all, that she know her place as subservient to her husband. This ideal reflected broader changes in women's relationship to production and to the socialization of children. Middle class British women's contributions to family wages diminished over the course of the eighteenth century. Consequently, their symbolic significance as wives changed from partner to object of wealth and from childbearer to childrearer.[21]

As children gained recognition and importance, their well-being became associated with motherly care. "Motherhood" developed as a socially desirable position. New occupations for women, that of teacher and writer, developed over the same period. Except in rare cases, however, these vocations did not provide women with the prestige that a husband and child afforded. A stigma was attached both to a woman who worked and to the work itself. If a married woman sought employment because her family needed money, both she and her husband were considered failures.

While Wollstonecraft accepted female domesticity and shared the general belief that formal education could improve a person, she also liked Enlightenment ideas of rationality and the utopian optimism characteristic of English liberalism. These ideas underlaid her vision of an independent woman, most likely married, who could earn her own living respectably if she needed or wanted to do so. She based her pedagogy on the supremacy of reason and affirmed that rational thinking led to rational actions, which could produce republican government. She fully accepted the premise that all people, regardless of property holdings or sex, were endowed with rights that no government could deny. A free nation based on laws established by representative government could exist where individuals would be economically independent and politically equivalent. Education was the means to achieve the new society, and schools were to be the agents of change.

Curing Inequality

Vindication focused primarily on the conditions of oppression suffered by middle class women. Wollstonecraft used the term *oppression* to indicate a lack of choice in all spheres of life: social, economic, political, intellectual, physical. Women, as oppressed individuals, did not have a "civil existence in the state." They were unrepresented citizens similar to the "class of hardworking mechanics" whom despotic governments oppressed. Regardless of their economic status, however, women endured oppression by men.[22] Wealthy women, Wollstonecraft believed, had nothing significant to do with their time and consequently focused their unused minds on their looks and on domestic inanities. She argued that because they could not engage in enterprise useful for the improvement of British society, aristocratic ladies were restricted to a narrow, domestic world of servants, children, guests, and lap dogs.

She recognized that working class women sustained a different kind of subjugation because marriage did not provide economic security as it did—if it worked right—for middle class women. Not only did working class women have to take menial, underpaid jobs, but they were also subject to sexual abuse. Wollstonecraft presented this issue dramatically in *Maria*.

Wollstonecraft proposed a national system of coeducation to produce independent women capable of making rational judgments. An elementary school would house children from all social classes between the ages of five and nine. She advocated dressing girls and boys alike so the instructor and the students themselves would have difficulty distinguishing male and female and rich and poor:

> All [would be] obliged to submit to the same discipline, or leave school. The schoolroom ought to be surrounded by a large piece of ground in which the children might be usefully exercised, for at this age they should not be confined to any sedentary employment for more than an hour at a time. But these relaxations might all be rendered a part of elementary education, for many things improve and amuse the senses, when introduced as a kind of show, to the principles of which dryly laid down, children would turn a deaf ear. For instance, botany, mechanics, and astronomy, reading, writing, arithmetic, natural history, and some simple experiments in these pursuits should never encroach on gymnastic plays in the open air. The elements of religion, history, the history of man, and politics, might also be taught by conversations in the Socratic form.[23]

In an elementary school, no distinctions would be made on the basis of either sex or class. Past the age of nine, however, working class boys and girls would be separated from each other in the afternoons so that they each could learn skills particular to their sex. These children were also to be trained in a different place from the wealthier pupils.

Wollstonecraft suggested training in skills that would enable working class people, especially women, to maintain their economic independence. Her pedagogy attempted to prevent the working classes from suffering the degradation of poverty by providing individuals—again mainly women—with a trade. Wollstonecraft suggested that working and middle class divisions be maintained in schools for older children as well as in society, but that conditions within each sector be improved.

Wealthier boys and girls would continue to be instructed together in a liberal arts education, aimed at preparing for university study and professional careers. By suggesting that girls be provided with this sort of preparatory schooling, Wollstonecraft proposed the radical notion that the ancient professions be open to women.

Wollstonecraft assumed that equality between the sexes would be the inevitable result of coeducation, but she did not insist that it be classless. In other words, women of the different classes would not be equals socially, but they would certainly be equal to men of their own station.

Neither man nor woman would control the other. Each would be free to govern his or her own life. Women would no longer be male playthings or objects of admiration and lust; rather, they would be colleagues or companions of men. In this society of equals, women would be rational mothers within marriages based on companionship.

Disillusionment

Vindication expressed a utopian wish for a future where neither sex dominated the other. By 1796, when Wollstonecraft began to write *Maria, Or the Wrongs of Woman,* her optimism had waned. This was partly because of her own romantic experiences between 1792 and 1796. She had been attracted to the painter Henry Fuseli in an emotionally ambiguous way, desiring to live with him and his wife but apparently not wishing to become his lover. To her surprise, he rejected her and retreated from their friendship by canceling a trip to Paris that the Fuselis and Wollstonecraft had planned together to witness the events of the French Revolution. Wollstonecraft went to Paris, and there began an ill-fated liaison with Gilbert Imlay, an American businessman.

She and Imlay lived together for almost a year starting in 1793. During this time, she took the name Imlay, ostensibly because Americans were safer in Paris than were British citizens. In May 1794, she gave birth to a daughter whom she named Fanny Imlay in memory of Fanny Blood. That year was the steadiest period of their relationship. Then Imlay saw her infrequently for brief intervals, always promising to return for good. The intensity of her feelings made their periods of separation unendurable for her. At one point, she tried suicide. When she learned that he was involved with an actress, she made a second attempt by jumping into the Thames.

Wollstonecraft's need to be economically independent enabled her to get back on her feet and to start writing again. At about this time, she entered into the most comfortable and satisfying attachment of her life, a relationship with the philosopher William Godwin. Their intellectual attraction soon broadened into marriage.[24]

Their marriage is generally described as a happy one, although Wollstonecraft could not bring herself to believe it would last. She was unable to trust Godwin's love. The intensity of her need for emotional certainty and her inability to trust someone's love probably stemmed from her marginal position in her original family. Her unhappily married parents denied her their attention and affection and in turn Wollstonecraft became possessive in her attachments—including her female friendships—and suspicious of love shown to her. Yet she was emotionally dependent on the loved one for self-definition. Throughout her life, Wollstonecraft dealt with this tension from her twin needs for dependence and independence. This conflict formed the contours of her life and gave direction to her ideas. Her polemical and pedagogical writing developed around the issue of independence, while her autobiographical fic-

tion illustrated the impediments to that end. Although *Vindication* has
enjoyed the greater renown, Wollstonecraft's gloomy *Maria,* offers a
closer look at her personal struggle for independence. As a writer, Wollstonecraft turned to the novel almost as a vehicle for self-analysis. Although *Maria* revealed Wollstonecraft's emotional past, it also contained
new attitudes about the purposes of female independence.

The story of *Maria* revolved around the plight of two women: Maria
Venables, a middle class woman who had been imprisoned in an insane
asylum by her husband; and Jemima, her impoverished female guard.
Mutual biographical recountings of these two women to each other
served as the literary device through which Wollstonecraft portrayed
the primary result of male domination of women.[25] Not only were the
minds and opportunities of Maria and Jemima restricted, but men
threatened their very existence. By acquiring rational education, both
women understood their oppression, fought against it, and survived.

Jemima's mother, a maid, had been seduced by a fellow servant with
promises of marriage. The woman became pregnant; the man turned
away. The father virtually disowned his daughter, Jemima, and sent her
to serve with another family. The master of her new household raped her
and forced her to submit to him thereafter.

His wife eventually caught the pair, blamed Jemima for seducing her
master, and turned her out of the house with no money. In order to
survive, Jemima resorted to prostitution. She eventually met a wealthy
old man who took her as his mistress; his sexual demands disgusted her.
Upon his sudden death, his family put her out on the street penniless.
Several other episodes occurred before Jemima wound up in the work-
house. All of them revealed the degradation that a poor and "ruined"
woman met.

Jemima related her story to her prisoner Maria, who wholeheartedly
concurred with Jemima's insights. Maria had also been victimized by
male greed and self-indulgence, and her story included the details of her
husband's deceptions. He pretended to love her but only wanted her rich
uncle's money. Maria had expected to find companionship based on mutual respect; instead, marriage had meant the end of her happiness and
the legal transfer of her inherited money to her spouse. She could alter
her situation in one of three ways: by choosing to live apart from her
husband if he agreed, by committing suicide, or by killing him. Divorce
action initiated by a woman could succeed only if the husband constantly and severely beat his wife. George Venables did not hurt Maria
physically, although he tortured her psychologically. Maria escaped
from his house, only to be recaptured and incarcerated in a madhouse.
His wife's running away indicated her dementia, because sane women
remained with their husbands.

In the asylum, Maria fell in love with a male prisoner who promised
to care for her always. They planned a successful escape together with
Jemima. After their escape, Maria and Jemima formed a domestic part-

nership. Jemima agreed to live with Maria only if she could be Maria's housekeeper. Both women acknowledged social class boundaries but saw each other as women first who could provide sanctuary for each other's broken lives. Maria gave birth to a girl and in keeping with Wollstonecraft's expectations of fathers, Maria's lover left. Maria and Jemima eventually turned their backs on oppressive male society to live a reasonably free existence with each other.

In *Maria,* as in *Vindication,* children continued to be part of women's sphere. Wollstonecraft retained her earlier view that a middle class woman should be a mother, although the importance of motherhood did not seem to apply as directly to working class women. Wollstonecraft pictured Jemima in maternal activity as Maria's caretaker in the asylum and later as her servant caring for Maria's child, but Jemima herself never became a mother. Wollstonecraft accepted the procreative link between the sexes, but tried to eliminate the responsibilities and burdens of being a wife. By recounting many incidents of male domination, Maria taught her child about the conditions necessary for women to live in freedom.

Wollstonecraft was not able to eliminate all the difficulties of being female from her own life. Not only did her childhood experiences color her adult relationships, but her love affair with Godwin resulted in her pregnancy. Soon after her marriage to William Godwin, she gave birth to her daughter Mary (who kept the habit of writing in the family by authoring *Frankenstein*). However, Wollstonecraft was denied the chance to teach her second child. Complications after delivery (puerperal or childbed fever) brought death to Wollstonecraft at the age of thirty-seven.

Significance

Wollstonecraft has been called the "first feminist philosopher worthy of the name." This is an extravagant claim in view of the work of Christine de Pisan and of Sor Juana Inés de la Cruz (Chapter 7). Wollstonecraft did present the earliest powerful argument in English for extending to both sexes the human rights heralded by the French Revolution and by English liberals. "The *Vindication* was the first effective challenge to the entire system of male supremacy, to the traditional concepts of masculinity and femininity, and the presumption of female inferiority," says Mary Anne Warren. "It created an international sensation, made Wollstonecraft the most infamous woman in Europe, and inspired Horace Walpole to call her a 'hyena in petticoats.' "[26]

In a modern context, her explicit disagreement with Rousseau makes sense. To justify a different education for Sophie, Rousseau postulated that little girls are naturally quieter than boys, having a genetic predisposition toward dolls and dresses instead of active play. "I have, probably, had an opportunity of observing more girls in their infancy than J. J. Rousseau," wrote Wollstonecraft. "I will venture to affirm that a girl whose spirits have not been dampened by inactivity, or innocence tainted by false shame, will always be a romp, and the doll will never excite attention unless confinement allows her no alternatives."[27]

Many people ignored Wollstonecraft's arguments, portraying her as hysterical; however, she developed virtually all of the elements in the continuing debate over male–female relationships. Her contention that independence, rationality, and strength of character were no more male than female characteristics has a contemporary ring. Indeed, one of the major rationalizations for why most contemporary school administrators are men has been that males are more likely than females to possess the "right" psychological characteristics for leadership. This claim is now under serious indictment.[28] Wollstonecraft challenged it nearly two centuries ago.

Victor of Aveyron (c. 1788–1828)

In the year that Wollstonecraft died, peasants in southern France sighted a naked boy running through some woods. Over the next two years, he was seen several more times. During the winter of 1799–1800, gossip circulated that Rousseau's noble savage had been found wandering in the southern French province of Aveyron. However, he was hardly the picture of Émile. Authorities guessed his age at around twelve to fourteen. He was four-and-a-half feet tall and ran on all fours, swaying from side to side. He was dirty and made wild guttural sounds. Paris newspapers dubbed him the "enfant sauvage de l'Aveyron"—the Wild Boy of Aveyron.[29]

He was given to the care of a young physician, Dr. Jean-Marc-Gaspard Itard (1774–1838), who had become interested in the scientific study of retardation and sensory impairment. Itard and others hoped that this "savage" would shed light on the basic issue of the Enlightenment—that is, the nature of human beings. Itard named the boy Victor and eventually brought him to the Institute for Deaf Mutes in Paris. There Itard made provisions for his own housekeeper to care for Victor and embarked on a program designed to develop the boy's social, sensory, emotional, and speech skills.

Itard worked with Victor for four years, keeping a diary of observations made throughout this time. He thought that Victor progressed in all areas except the emotional. Finally the doctor abandoned the work because he felt that he could go no farther with Victor. As the boy passed through adolescence, he seemed to become more violent toward the other children in the hospital. Consequently, he was forced to live with Itard's housekeeper on a permanent basis. He died in 1828 at about age forty.

Itard's work with Victor elevated to a new level the emerging discussion of who could be educated and to what extent. The Jesuits and their

Protestant competitors had already demonstrated that how quickly and how much people learned depended on how they were taught. The speculations of people like Locke and Rousseau suggested that the environment in which people tried to learn was much more important than had been generally thought. The emerging sentiment favoring mass systems of public instruction lent impetus to the discussion. Itard pushed the issue further in two ways: by supposing that even idiots (both a professional and popular term at the time) could learn more than anyone had supposed; and by testing the matter experimentally, rather than by speculation only. Itard was disappointed in not getting Victor to a verbal language phase—the boy remained mute, although he could recognize some words and phrases—but this problem did not mar the significance of the undertaking. Almost everyone thought Itard had failed, but the debates over why he had failed brought to light conflicting assumptions about what produces success or failure in teaching/learning situations. For example: Was Victor a congenital idiot beyond help? Had early emotional isolation made him retarded? Were Itard's methods wrong or inadequate?

In his quest to instruct Victor, Itard developed a large variety of teaching materials. The following list will illustrate:

> a plank painted black on which everyday objects were placed and their outlines chalked; the same objects suspended underneath their designs; letter cutouts to form names; a vertical board displaying a red disk, blue triangle, and black square, and the corresponding cardboard cutouts hung from nails; similar boards with the same forms in one color, or circles of contrasting colors, or kindred geometric forms, or circles or similar hues, or irregular patches of color; a board with twenty-four slots containing two-inch letters printed on cardboard; the corresponding letters in metal; a board with two equal circles, each having six points on the circumference for placing letter cutouts; drum, bells, shovel, drumstick; various sweets, drinks, snuff; a narrow-neck vase containing hot and cold nuts, acorns, stones, a penny and a die, metal letters; a blindfold; goblets, books, nails, a skewer, chalk, various household objects.

Those who visited Victor toward the end of his life felt that he had lost whatever ground he had gained with Itard. Nevertheless, the debate continued. The chains binding the insane, the retarded, and other deviants were gradually broken. (Chaining the insane in asylums had been outlawed in France in the 1790s.) Now new ground was being broken in the education of the retarded and handicapped. Itard was an early pilgrim on this road and his student, Edward Seguin (1812–1880), traveled even farther. Their efforts contributed much to the field of anthropology, to the theories of Montessori (see Chapter 11), and to the birth of special education.

Enlightenment ideas of expanding political liberty, improving the most extreme economic conditions of the poor, and extending schooling opportunities to all youths followed many trails in Europe and America. We have noted a few of these in the thoughts of Locke, Rousseau, and Wollstonecraft. Another significant figure in these developments was a German-speaking Swiss citizen named Johann Pestalozzi. He was particularly important because several of the German states, in the shadow of Napoleon's domination, started tax-funded school systems early in the nineteenth century. They did not want educational ideas from anyone who looked too French, much less the wild-sounding Rousseau. They turned instead to the town of Yverdon in Switzerland, where Pestalozzi was said to be conducting an interesting pedagogical experiment.

Johann Heinrich Pestalozzi (1746–1827)

Although the name Pestalozzi is Italian, the family had been citizens of Zurich for two hundred years when Heinrich was born in 1746. Some members of the family had done well in the years after Heinrich's Protestant forebears had migrated from Chiavenna. By the eighteenth century, however, early deaths and ill fortune had taken a toll.

Heinrich's grandfather was pastor of a poor suburban parish near Zurich. The family's adult males could vote and stand for election to the city council—a carefully restricted citizenship privilege. This fact underscored respectability, but none of the Pestalozzis had run for the council in a long time. Heinrich's father, Johann Baptist Pestalozzi, was a surgeon. This was not the high status position that it is today. Only physicians had university training. Surgeons merely apprenticed and usually lacked the knowledge, equipment, or facilities for operations more complicated than bloodletting. Heinrich's mother, Sussana Holtz, was from the country town of Wadenswil, which was part of the city-state of Zurich. No resident of the area outside of Zurich proper could be a citizen, but her family was on the rise and a number of the men were noted as physicians. Perhaps Sussana married Johann Baptist for the family's respectability.

The Pestalozzis had three children: Johann Baptist, the oldest; Heinrich; and Anna Barbara, the youngest. At thirty-three the senior Johann Baptist died. Sussana did not remarry, but hung on tenaciously to respectability. She "was a shy woman who lived quietly because of her small means and her country origins," as one biographer put it. A young servant named Barbara Schmid (Babeli) seems to have been the glue that held the family together. She stayed with Sussana for over forty years, turning down better offers and marriage to keep her deathbed promise not to leave the family as long as she was needed.[30]

Early Life

The death of his father was traumatic for young Heinrich and his family. Babeli took charge of most aspects of daily life as Sussana suffered paralyzing bouts of grief and depression. Sussana and Babeli tried to compensate for Heinrich's loss of his father by protecting him from the harsher aspects of the world, at the same time punishing him for relatively minor transgressions. He did not play with neighborhood children, who made fun of him with nicknames such as "Queer Harry of Foolstown." Sussana sent her two sons to the most desirable schools in Zurich, but Heinrich could not concentrate on study and spent much of his time daydreaming. He planned on a grand scale, plunged into projects with enthusiasm, and abandoned them when difficulties arose.

As a teenager Heinrich joined the Society of Patriots, a group whose members advocated stoic ethics, Spartan self-discipline, and a variety of reforms based on Rousseau's writings. They aspired to perfection and virtue. Heinrich wrote for their publication, *The Monitor,* and got himself jailed for three days. About this time he read *Émile.* He took it as gospel, though later he would call it an "impractical dream-book." Meanwhile, Heinrich considered himself a Rousseau naturalist. He and the Patriot's informal leader, nicknamed Menalk, discussed their dreams for the future. Heinrich had already tried the ministry under the tutelage of his grandfather, but rejected it (he forgot his sermon and stumbled over the Lord's Prayer). He started to study law, but found the work difficult and uninteresting. Now, he hoped to lead a "natural" life on the land by farming.

Menalk died suddenly, and Heinrich pursued his girlfriend, Anna Schulthess, sister of a fellow Patriot and member of a respected Zurich family. Nanette, as her friends called her, was eight years older than her new suitor. She did not love Heinrich, and her parents objected that the young man had no profession. In reaction to her domineering mother's cautions, however, she consented to a secret engagement.

Life as a Farmer

In preparation for his forthcoming responsibilities as a husband, Heinrich embarked on the adventure of learning to farm. He left for the canton of Berne planning to spend eighteen months on the farm of Johann Rudolf Tschiffeli, a wealthy man who had established a model farm to show the best methods of growing clover, potatoes, and madder (from which a dye was made for the newly emerging cotton industry). Nine months later Pestalozzi was back in Zurich. The Schulthess family was surprised. He reassured them that he understood farming well enough to produce crops on his own land—if only someone would lend him money to buy a farm. He was ready for some of the "great and important undertakings" with which he had promised Nanette their lives would be filled.

Pestalozzi got some money from his family, borrowed more from a Zurich banker, and bought about sixty acres near the village of Birr in the Berne canton. It took fifty separate transactions to put the final package together, because most land was owned in small plots. He rented a house and started plowing. He alienated his neighbors by refusing to honor a centuries-old tradition of allowing people to take shortcuts across his land. He feared they would ruin his crops.

Now that he was established as a farmer, Pestalozzi wrote Anna that they could get married. Her parents had consented to a public announcement of the engagement when Heinrich bought his farm on the understanding that the couple would wait until the farm was making money. Anna wavered between the enthusiasm of her fiance and the cautions of her mother, and finally agreed to marry her confident suitor. Her parents refused their blessings, a dowry, and a church wedding. Anna was thirty-four and sick of her mother's advice, so she went ahead with a quiet wedding. The couple moved into their rented farmhouse to lead the idyllic life described by Rousseau.

To Anna's regret, it quickly became evident that Frau Schulthess had been prophetic. It was one thing to talk of seeking perfection in simple country life. Over a glass of wine in the company of fellow Patriots, the natural life sounded ideal. Reality was much different: a grim old farmhouse, an ill-tempered husband who came home filthy, hateful neighbors, boredom and isolation—that was Anna's life in the country. The couple quarreled. Anna tried to make the best of her unhappy circumstances. Heinrich alternated between self-reproach and defensiveness. Ultimately, he ignored present difficulties by dreaming of grand future schemes.

Three months after their wedding vows, the couple conceived their only child. The boy, whom they named Jean-Jacques (after Rousseau), was born in 1770. Pestalozzi intended to raise the boy "naturally." Pestalozzi was also building a grand new house at the time. Anna's family had relented and had given her a dowry, but within a short time that money was spent. The house went unfinished. They put a roof over the part that was done and let it go at that. After about four years, the bank asked Pestalozzi to repay his loan, but he could not. Again Anna's family supplied enough money to save the house and some of the land. Pestalozzi had ready explanations to account for the failure of his farming business. People cheated him, he said, and Tschiffeli had not taught him the right things. Besides, his neighbors were jealous and spread bad stories about him, which was why the bankers asked him to repay the loan. His plan had been a good one; it was not his fault that it failed.

Parent and Teacher

During the time that the farming venture was reaching crisis conditions, Pestalozzi was busy giving his little son, Jacqueli, a "natural" education. When the boy was less than four years old, his father began what he considered to be Émile-like instruction, and he kept a diary describing what he did. He was intrigued at Jacqueli's delight in discovering that water runs down hill; however, when the little boy did not answer questions correctly, Pestalozzi felt it was a sign that the child was trying to get his own way. The whole matter of the child's will bothered Pestalozzi. In a curious departure from *Émile,* he required Jacqueli to read every day. If he refused—which he often did at first, partly because he could not read— the punishment was solitary confinement. It did not take the boy long to cooperate. On one occasion little Jacqueli had a bout with what Pestalozzi called rheumatic fever. When Jacqueli resisted taking medications, the doctor recommended to Pestalozzi "that, when he was quite well, we should now and then give him harmless but unpleasant drinks and powders, so that, in case of need, he would not mind so much." Pestalozzi "saw the soundness of the idea at once."[31]

Pestalozzi's efforts to instruct his son convinced him that parents should never "teach by words anything which you can teach by actual experience of things as they are. Let him see, and hear, and find out, and fall, and get up again, and make mistakes—never let words take the place of actions. . . . Let him always be busy and active and, most of the time, free. You will find that Nature is a better teacher than man." When Jacqueli's curiosity led him to investigate more things around the house than Pestalozzi wanted him to, a perfect occasion for an object lesson arose. "If, for example, I wish to forbid his annoying practice of touching all sorts of things, I go about it in this way," Pestalozzi wrote in his diary. "I put two bowls on the table, one cold, one extremely hot, and wash my hands in the cold one and place the hot one in such a position that the little one is certain to touch it and so burn his hand. 'People should not touch things which they know nothing about' is my only remark as I soothe the pain of the burn with some oil. A few days later I put some hot eggs in the same place; he immediately takes hold of them and burns himself again. Then I say, 'I don't like you to be always burning yourself; leave things alone till you know something about them; you should have asked what it was that stood on the table and whether you might touch it.' "[32]

After a few months of tutoring Jacqueli, Pestalozzi shifted his interest to a new project. He decided to turn his Neuhof (new farm) into a "poor school." It was common for farmers to take in young apprentices and work them hard for meager pay, which is what Pestalozzi proposed to do. He would teach orphans and poor children how to grow, spin, and weave cotton and how to garden, cook, and sew. He would sell the products of their industry at fairs, and his farm would become profitable. He explained that it was not only good for the children to work long hours but it was also desirable for them to have grim accommodations and sparse food. After all, they were from poor families and would live in poverty. The sooner they grew accustomed to what was in store for them, the happier they would be in their necessary conditions. He was so sure this method would do well that he predicted branch sites of other such schools.

The poor school experiment lasted about four years. Most parents took their childen away after a few months because they thought Pestalozzi was using them to make money for himself. By the end of the time, the farm was not producing enough vegetables even to feed the Pestalozzi family, and the failed enterprise was something of a local disgrace. Anna had a nervous breakdown. Someone (probably Anna's parents) sent a family servant, an eighteen-year-old woman named Lisabeth Naff, to help out. She raised enough garden to feed the family.

Pestalozzi spent his time roaming the countryside. His behavior was erratic and his dress careless. People called him "pestilence" and "scarecrow." A short man with wild, bushy hair, he was so distraught that he did not watch where he was going on his walks, and was often covered with mud from having fallen. A friend had said that even when Heinrich was young, he could not "address anyone or do anything without making an unfavorable impression through his hasty, uncouth, and thoughtless behavior." When he became excited while talking, he tended to unconsciously draw himself closer and closer to his conversant's face while his voice grew louder and more shrill. Neither his personal appearance nor his business acumen improved with age. On one occasion, he managed to borrow some badly needed money to buy provisions for his nearly destitute family, but on his way home gave it to a stranger who told him a hard luck story.

Throughout this period, some people remained friendly to the Pestalozzis. The Countess of Hallwil, a widowed neighbor, befriended Anna. In fact, Anna lived at the countess's castle during much of the time after 1780. She and Heinrich were together infrequently during the remaining thirty-six years of her life.

Literary Career

A Schulthess family friend, the editor Isaac Iselin, gave Pestalozzi an opportunity to write for his journal, *Ephemerides*. With his help, Pestalozzi wrote a series of moralistic stories, entitled *The Evening Hour of a Hermit,* and a short story expanded into a novel called *Leonard and Gertrude*. This latter was an account of a good woman (Gertrude) who kept her family together despite odds and gave moral uplift to a sagging town. The book included touching scenes of Gertrude teaching her children by the hearth. The story did not make much money, but it received some favorable reviews and established Pestalozzi's name as a promising novelist.

Buoyed by success, Pestalozzi turned to writing with characteristic enthusiasm. He entered contests, submitting hymns, moral tales, ideas for novels, political tracts, and philosophical treatises, and dreamed of becoming a playwright. He sent copies of his manuscripts to anyone he thought might help him get an appointment, but none came. He rarely finished any of the projects, and what he did complete was dull, rambling, and repetitive. In general, he reflected the point of view of whatever government was in power, hoping that some of his writing would "prove that I am suited for a government post." Until 1798 none of this worked, and he later admitted in a letter to the Countess of Hallwil that during this period he would have liked to "spit in every man's face."[33]

In 1798 Napoleon's troops invaded the area we know as Switzerland and set up the Helvetian Republic. Pestalozzi wrote favorably about these developments and encouraged people to accept the new government. Since the fighting had left orphaned children, the new government decided to establish a poor school at Stans where a Capuchin monastery had empty buildings. They offered Pestalozzi the job of operating this rescue mission. After two decades of trying to secure a government job, he finally had one. "I am undertaking one of the greatest tasks of our time," he said in leaving for his new assignment.[34]

Return to Teaching

In the beginning, Pestalozzi had charge of about fifty children. Except for a housekeeper, he was alone with the responsibility of organizing the school and developing a plan for teaching the children some vocational skills and how to read and write. According to Pestalozzi, all went well despite hardship. "I am wiping out the disgrace of my life," he wrote to the Countess Hallwil. "The virtue of my youth is being restored." The only account we have is one left by Pestalozzi himself. He accepted more children than his resources could support. Some children acted "willfully." "When children were persistently obstinate and rude severity was necessary, and I had to use corporal punishment," he later wrote. Pestalozzi assured his readers that the children welcomed his ear pulling and blows, but he added, "others misunderstood me." Government inspectors visited the school, but could not understand what Pestalozzi was doing or what he had planned. At the end of five months, they closed the school. Orphans stayed with the Capuchins, other children returned to their homes, and Pestalozzi was out of a job.[35]

After a period of depression, nervous fits, and throwing up blood, Pestalozzi managed to secure a position as assistant in the poorest school in Burgdorf, a small town in the Emme River valley. The school consisted of seventy-three boys and girls from noncitizen families. Its chief aim was to teach the pupils to read and spell. However, his success with the girls is questionable, since he never called on them, an attitude reflected in *Leonard and Gertrude:* "Books should be to a woman like a Sunday gown, and work like her everyday clothes," said Gertrude.[35] After a short time, the parents asked for Pestalozzi's dismissal. He then taught for a few months in a small "dame school."

Details of what happened next are confusing. Most writers have depended on Pestalozzi's explanations, but an account based on diaries of another man who was a central figure in what transpired suggests the following sequence of events.[37]

During the time that Pestalozzi was teaching in the dame school, the Helvetian government in Berne appropriated the castle at Burgdorf for the purpose of establishing an *école normale*—that is, a normal (ordinary) teacher training school. By turning out skilled teachers with correct political views, the government hoped to extend its base of support. J. R. Fisher, a twenty-seven-year-old Berne inspector of schools, accepted the job of organizing the normal school. The plan was to locate children whose parents were too poor to adequately support and educate them. They would be moved to Burgdorf, housed with local families, and educated at the castle. When they reached an appropriate age, they would go out to be village teachers. The other crucial element in this plan was to hire one or more good teachers to be in charge of the children's development.

Fisher found the pupils he needed and their main teacher, Hermann Krüsi, in the eastern Swiss canton of Appenzell. At twenty-five Krüsi already had an excellent reputation based on six years of dedicated work in village schools. He brought twenty-six children across 120 miles of mountains to begin the work. When he arrived he met Pestalozzi, whom Fisher had allowed to occupy a room in the castle. Fisher had also secured for Pestalozzi a position in a boys' school in Burgdorf. (Pestalozzi had felt under so much tension in the dame school that he thought he had suffered a heart attack.) Thus Pestalozzi was teaching in a school for the sons of poor citizens—there was also a school for sons of wealthier citizens—and living in the castle where Krüsi lived and ran a school.

Krüsi's school prospered and local pupils began to attend. Fisher caught typhus and died after a few days. Pestalozzi suggested to the youthful Krüsi that he was about to open a school of his own but that it would perhaps be better if they combined forces. Krüsi agreed and wrote to a friend he had known in Appenzell, inviting him to join the effort. This was J. G. Tobler, a forty-year-old man who had studied theology at Basel, had spent a number of years as a tutor and teacher, and had developed a keen interest in child psychology. The Helvetian government continued its support. It granted the castle rent-free, provided gardening land and a supply of wood for heat, and furnished a subsidy for printing curricular materials. There were salaries for Krüsi and Tobler, which they shared with Pestalozzi and other co-workers who later joined them. One of Tobler's friends soon arrived to help. This was Johannes C. Buss, a twenty-four-year-old bookbinder whose father had been a servant in a famous theological school in Tübingen. Buss had done well in preparatory school and had intended to enter the theological seminary, but a new rule prevented working class boys from attending. He was bitterly disappointed at having to learn a trade and welcomed Krüsi's invitation to teach art and math in the Burgdorf castle.

The relationship between the four men was cordial. Krüsi, Tobler, and Buss were unassuming men from lower class backgrounds. Each was dissatisfied with his own knowledge and teaching performance and wanted to improve. They knew Pestalozzi's general reputation—many people said he was crazy and recounted stories of his erratic behavior— but they were willing to look beyond the surface, for there was something about him that drew them to him. Each felt a little sorry for him, but at the same time they accorded him respect. He was considerably older than the others and, as the author of *Leonard and Gertrude,* had some standing as a literary figure. None of the three could make much sense of what Pestalozzi tried in the classroom: he yelled in a high-pitched voice, made pupils repeat complicated sentences they did not understand, and insisted that all learners do two things at once—for example, shout the sounds of the alphabet while having a drawing lesson. All three shared Pestalozzi's grand dream of a better world if only they could unlock the secret of effective teaching.

The Burgdorf experiment prospered from the first. At the same time that Itard was teaching Victor, Krüsi, Tobler, and Buss were working out new teaching materials: movable letters for reading and spelling, pebbles and beans for arithmetic, drawing exercises as preparation for writing, slates and slate pencils instead of pens and paper. The three of them did most of the teaching as well. Pestalozzi said prayers in the evening, worked up lists of consonant/vowel combinations that the children were to practice orally in order to help them spell and read, and continued his writing projects.

After eighteen months, some officials from Berne inspected the school. They were generally impressed with what they saw. Pestalozzi explained to the visiting delegation that what they saw were his ideas in practice. One of the inspectors, J. S. Ith, wrote a widely circulated report praising the school and describing the approach. Several German-language periodicals reprinted it and credited Pestalozzi with having invented a new method of elementary teaching.

A steady stream of visitors from many parts of Europe came to Burgdorf to see the school. If "Father" Pestalozzi's "assistants," as he now insisted his co-workers refer to him and to themselves, were surprised that what they had thought of cooperatively had been transformed into "Pestalozzi's method," they did not say anything to the outside world. They continued to believe in the value of what they were doing. Krüsi recruited other friends whose skills were invaluable in the school's development. The young "assistants," busy with their work, allowed "Father Pestalozzi" to represent himself to visitors however he wished.

In 1801 Jacques Pestalozzi died at Neuhof. His life had not been happy. After his father's short-lived natural instruction, his mother tried to teach him reading and religion. At twelve he still could not read. Heinrich sent him to Basel to apprentice in a friend's shop. There the lad developed symptoms of falling sickness (epilepsy) and returned without learning a trade. Pestalozzi blamed himself briefly, then decided it was his friend who had ruined his son. Jacques was described as "a grumbler and hard to please," and as dull and irritable. He had convulsions accompanied by delusions. Pestalozzi liked other young men much better than his own son, saying to one "Oh, if only you were only my son! Then I should not be going out of the world so lonely."[38] (Jacques was still alive at the time.) Anna and Heinrich had managed to arrange a marriage for their son in the 1790s to Anna Magdalena Frolich. She was three years older than Jacques and brought a dowry which Heinrich spent. Jacques and Anna ran the Neuhof (and a cotton works on it) until he died. The parents met at their son's graveside—probably the first time they had seen each other since Pestalozzi had left for Stans. After that, Anna went back to the Hallwil castle, and Anna Magdalena returned to Burgdorf with Pestalozzi, where she worked as a housekeeper for several years and finally remarried. (She died in Yverdon at the age of forty-seven from a pestilence brought in by troops camped nearby.)

Back at the Burgdorf castle, Father Pestalozzi managed with Krüsi's help to add several new assistants to his staff. The most notable of these was Johannes Niederer (1779–1843), a young Protestant minister from Appenzell. Among the new staff were also Johannes von Muralt (1780–1850), a young man from Zurich whom the children liked very much, and Joseph Schmid (1787–1850), a fifteen-year-old, strong-willed lad from Austria, who quickly learned how to manipulate Pestalozzi.

In 1804 the Helvetian government fell, and the individual cantons resumed their governmental powers. Napoleon decided that a divided Switzerland might serve his interests better than a united one. There was a backlash against French interference in German-speaking cantons like Berne, and the Berne city council sent an inspection team to reexamine what was now known as Pestalozzi's school. This time the report was not favorable. The Berne officials issued an eviction notice, though they did offer on a yearly basis a house left vacant by a religious order in Munchenbuchsee. All salaries stopped.

Yverdon

One contingent from Burgdorf accompanied Buss and another assistant to an abandoned castle near the town of Yverdon in the new canton of Vaud. This was a French-speaking area and Pestalozzi was identified as a supporter of the earlier French-inspired central government. Pestalozzi and the main group of pupils and assistants went to Buchsee. They soon joined the others at Yverdon, however, because the Buchsee area already had a school on the estate of Phillip Emanuel von Fellenberg (1771–1844). His father had been governor of the area in which the Neuhof was located and had been kind to Pestalozzi. The younger Fellenberg bought the estate (called Hofwyl) in 1799 and had opened two different schools: an expensive one for the sons of aristocrats and an industrial training school for poor boys. The difference between Fellenberg's poor school and the one Pestalozzi had tried at Neuhof was that Fellenberg's worked. The boys learned farming and technical/engineering skills with which they could make a living. (They also had better food than pupils at Pestalozzi's school up the road.) Pestalozzi left for Yverdon.

The institute at Yverdon lasted in some form for twenty years. But the internal workings were never tranquil, and by 1810 the most able assistants began to leave. Pestalozzi's operating procedures made life hard for co-workers. Everyone was up and going by 5:30 A.M. In the early days assistants taught ten hours a day and lived and ate with the boys. Three nights a week after dinner all assistants met to discuss pupil progress, thrash out problems, and make suggestions about "the method." Pestalozzi did not attend these sessions, which gradually changed from cooperative to contentious. As tensions mounted in the group, quarrelsome sessions lasted far into the night. Pestalozzi received individual reports from each assistant afterward.

Everyone was to work for no individual credit, and what anyone wrote or did belonged to Pestalozzi for public credit. Pestalozzi popped into classes at unexpected times to make suggestions. He often awakened at two or three in the morning and started dictating to his secretary (or to one of the assistants), and expected others to accommodate his own irregular schedule by immediately correcting and recopying his scribbled notes. His mood swung between elation and dejection. In his frequent depressions, he exploded with negative remarks to and about others. He would usually apologize later, but a growing residual of hurt and resentment ran through the ranks of assistants.

By 1808 the undercurrent of unrest in the school was strong. At the New Year's Day address, which he always gave and which was a major occasion, Pestalozzi brought in a coffin, complete with skull-and-crossbones decoration, and stood with the death box beside him during the address. He knew he had not done well, he said, but he would shortly be dead and out of the way. After his death he hoped that all would pull together for the common good. He loved all of his assistants like true sons.

Tobler left. In 1810 Johann Elias Mieg, a Heidelberg man who was the school's business manager for four years, left. The institute was soon in grave financial trouble. Mieg returned two years later in response to pleas to help get the establishment back on its feet, but found Pestalozzi so disagreeable that he left again. In 1812 Pestalozzi dictated his "dying thoughts" to Krüsi after accidentally jamming a knitting needle into his ear. He again appealed for unity. He recovered and Anna inherited enough money to rejuvenate the Institute. Pestalozzi was irritated because she held back some of the money for their grandson, Gottlieb. Anna also gave the Neuhof to Gottlieb under terms that made it impossible for Pestalozzi to ever sell it.

A large bone of contention with all of the older staff was that Pestalozzi treated Schmid as his favorite while blaming others for his own failures. Before Schmid arrived, the staff worked hard and sacrificed much, but somehow it was Schmid who got the master's approval. Schmid knew Pestalozzi's needs and fed them. For example, on Pestalozzi's birthday in 1809, Schmid presented a manuscript entitled *The Elements of Form and Number*. Pestalozzi regarded this as a major theoretical breakthrough, and published it under his own name. (It seems to have made no lasting contribution to educational theory.) Niederer especially resented Schmid because he himself had been Pestalozzi's chief ghostwriter up to that time. The competition finally came to a head over a woman for whose attention both were vying. She chose Niederer, and Schmid left in a rage. He started a school of his own in Austria and wrote a scathing attack on Pestalozzi and Yverdon.

Student Life

An English student at Yverdon about 1814 wrote an account of his recollections. He had attended Westminster, one of England's "great public schools," before going to Switzerland. He remembered Pestalozzi as a kindly but eccentric old gentleman. He thought the treatment better than at Westminster (notorious for floggings), but remembered the teaching as boring and the food as sparse. The lessons he described as hour-long rote memory sessions repeated in unison. He remembered the Latin/Greek tutor as competent and kind. Besides learning those two subjects, he said what the pupils mostly got was a "love for natural history and a very unambitious turn of mind." He recalled the classrooms thus:

> . . . a number of detached chambers, each of which issued upon a corridor. They were airy—there was plenty of air at Yverdon—and lofty as became so venerable a building; but they were unswept, unscrubbed, peeled of their paint, and, owing to the little light that could find its way through two very small windows punched out of the fortress walls, presented, save at mid-day, or as the declining sun illumined momentarily the dark recess, as comfortless a set of interiors as you could well see. It required, indeed, all the elasticity of youth to bear many hours' daily incarceration in such black-holes, without participating in the pervading gloom. Such dismal domiciles were only fit resorts for the myopic bat, who would occasionally visit them from the old tower; for the twilight horde of cockroaches, which swarmed along the floor, or the eight eyed spiders who colonized the ceiling. . . . If these apartments looked gloomy in their dilapidations and want of sun, the somber effect was much heightened by the absence of the ordinary tables and chairs, and whatever else is necessary to give a room a habitable appearance.[39]

In 1815, Anna came to Yverdon to live for a little time before she died. She was buried on the grounds, and Pestalozzi took the occasion of her funeral to rally support from his assistants. By this time, however, Schmid was back, for Pestalozzi had decided he could not live without him. The institute was again in serious financial trouble, so Pestalozzi gave Schmid a free hand in running the place. Schmid increased the workload and cut salaries, which was the last straw for the few remaining old hands. Krüsi started his own boys' school in Yverdon in 1816. The following year Niederer quit to join his wife in running a school. (This was not the woman over whom he and Schmid had quarreled. It was Rosette Kasthofer, the owner of a girls' school in Yverdon.) Niederer explained his reasons in a public statement that left Pestalozzi "seized with such a rage, even frenzy, that he was in danger of losing his reason."

With everyone but Schmid gone, the teaching was left to the older boys, who were quite young themselves. Finally, even they rebelled against Schmid. The institute was in such monetary difficulties that Fellenberg offered to help. Pestalozzi agreed to merge what was left of his failing school with the ones at Hofwyl. But when the newspapers carried the story that he needed assistance, he became enraged and tore up the agreements. Schmid raised some money by taking up a subscription for Pestalozzi's "collected writings," but these were slow in appearing and many of the subscribers failed to pay their pledges.[40]

Yverdon's Demise

As financial and other difficulties mounted, Pestalozzi increasingly blamed his early associates. He attacked Krüsi and Niederer, calling them false friends. At about the same time Schmid got Pestalozzi to request a major extension of the rent-free agreement on the castle (so Schmid could continue using the facility long after Pestalozzi died). However, Krüsi and Niederer brought a suit against Schmid that ultimately resulted in his being declared an undesirable alien by the Vaud government. In 1825 Pestalozzi, Schmid, and four pupils left Yverdon for the Neuhof. The other teachers refused to go. "They did not think they owed it to Pestalozzi to sacrifice their careers," as one writer put it.

Pestalozzi tried again to start a poor school at Neuhof, erecting a building with money from an appeal. However, no teachers and few pupils came, and the school did not open. Finally, he decided to devote his time to writing, and renewed his attack on his former associates, especially Niederer and Krüsi. In *The Story of My Life as Head of the Institutes in Burgdorf and Yverdon,* he again accused his former colleagues of treason. Neiderer went to his files and retrieved personal letters, legal documents, and financial accounts to support his indictment of Pestalozzi's motives and personality. He felt that Pestalozzi had betrayed the idea and power of "the method" which he and others had worked hard to build up. Fellenberg also refuted Pestalozzi's claims in articles in the Zurich newspapers. When Pestalozzi read the replies to his comments, he became agitated, contracted a fever, dictated a vindication of Schmid as his true friend and savior, and died. None of his old associates attended the funeral. Schmid spent the rest of his life in Paris, but nothing more was heard from him in education.[41]

Pestalozzi's unhappy life and personal difficulties were major factors in the ultimate demise of the institute at Yverdon. Nevertheless, the educational discoveries of the dedicated band of experimenters became part of the ongoing search for improving mass education. Their major discoveries came at Burgdorf, and many international visitors saw demonstrations of the method in the first few years at Yverdon.

People all over Europe were looking for ways to provide elementary vernacular education for everyone, including the poor. This was particularly true in some of the German states. In 1809 a philosopher named Johann Gottlieb Fichte made a series of addresses following Prussia's defeat by Napoleon. He called for a government-sponsored school system in Prussia and specifically cited Yverdon as a model. Over the next few years, the Prussian government paid for a number of men to spend time in Switzerland studying "Pestalozzi's method." After observing Krüsi and other assistants, they took away various notions of what the method was and of what "object teaching" meant. However there was general agreement on several items: (1) all people, including the poor, could and should learn; (2) learning began at birth and therefore required parental attention; (3) instruction should involve dialogue between teacher and learner and should be centered around objects more than books; (4) drawing, music, and physical activity were essential parts of learning; (5) teachers could improve by discovering how to properly structure their presentations and by finding out how children learned. The latter included the notion of beginning with simple and concrete rather than complex or abstract material and of relating new information to what children already knew.

"Pestalozzianism" and object teaching found their way to several countries, especially Prussia, England, and the United States. There were many routes. Most of the people who had worked at Burgdorf or Yverdon started their own schools in Europe and North America. Many visitors to Yverdon wrote their own accounts of what object teaching meant, so that a growing literature emerged.

Much of this writing found its way to American educationists through Henry Barnard's *American Journal of Education* (see Chapter 7). After 1862 another source for Americans was the normal school at Oswego, New York, where Hermann Krüsi, Jr., after a thorough training by his father, joined others in showing a generation of American teachers what object teaching meant. The English version of Pestalozzianism reached Americans through Robert Owen (see Chapter 8); Owens's son studied at Yverdon. Finally, a major part of the German tradition continued in the kindergarten movement, which began through the work of Friedrich Froebel, who made the trek to Yverdon to learn how to teach better.

Friedrich Froebel (1782–1852)

In his autobiography Froebel tells us, "I was early initiated into the conflict of life amidst painful and narrowing circumstances; and ignorance of child-nature and insufficient education wrought their influence on me."[42] He was referring to the unfortunate circumstances surrounding his birth and early years.

Froebel was born on April 21, 1782 at Oberweissbach in the Thuringian Forest (part of a small principality in the state of Schwartzburg-Rudolstadt, Germany). He was the last of five sons born to a mother who died when he was nine months old. His four brothers were August, who went into business and died young; Christoph, a clergyman in Griesheim who was the father of Julius, Karl, and Theodor; Christian, who was associated with Friedrich after 1820; and Traugott, who studied medicine at Jena, became a doctor, and was appointed burgomaster at Stadt-Ilm. His father, Johann Jacob, was a Lutheran minister belonging to the conservative school of Protestantism. His parish consisted of about five thousand people spread over half a dozen villages.

Family Life

When Friedrich was four years old, his father remarried. Prior to this time his care was entrusted to servants and his four older brothers, to whom he had become devoted. With the arrival of a new mother, the four-year-old turned much of his love to her. He soon felt her rejection, however, when she became pregnant and gave birth to a son.[43] From this point on, Friedrich became introspective and self-analytical. His natural curiosity and energy were labeled as mischievous by his parents; yet he was acutely aware that this assessment was inaccurate. His home environment was as physically confining as it was psychologically constricting, for he was not allowed to wander outside the fences and hedges surrounding his house.

Friedrich had difficulty learning to read from his father, who often lost patience while instructing the youth. Consequently, the boy was sent to school for the rest of his education. However, his father did not send him to the village boys' school, but rather to the one for girls. Froebel later described the school as "exactly suitable for a child such as I was."[44] At some point in all of his youthful experiences, he realized that he was not going to Hell and began to identify with Jesus—discoveries that he later regarded as his introduction into higher spiritual life.

At age ten, Friedrich went to live with a maternal uncle. His life with his uncle was opposite from that with his father. He joined the upper class of the town school and slowly entered into the sports and games of the schoolboys, thereby strengthening his underdeveloped physique.

He returned to his father's house in 1797. After much deliberation, it was decided with his approval that he should become an apprentice to an agriculturist in order to become a forester and learn valuing, geometry, and land surveying. Although his older brothers Christoph and Traugott were studying at the University of Jena, Froebel did not join them because his stepmother was afraid there would be no money left for her own son's university education. His father wanted him to seek a post in the treasury, but that would have meant starting as a personal servant to a higher treasury official—something young Froebel regarded as against his nature.

Education and Early Career

It turned out that the forester was not expert in many of the areas in which he was supposed to instruct the young apprentice, and he blamed the youth for his own shortcomings. In typical fashion, young Froebel withdrew inwardly while teaching himself some geometry. However, the forester wrote a letter of complaint to the father. Friedrich was able to defend himself to his father and his brother Christoph, but not to his stepmother, so once again, he was confined to his father's house.

When his father needed to send money to his brother Traugott, who was studying medicine at Jena, Friedrich was made messenger. The intellectual atmosphere of this university town in 1799 was exhilarating, and with the help of his brother and a small inheritance from his mother, he persuaded his father to let him stay and matriculate. In the one summer and three semesters that he was there, he found he liked geometry best and experimental physics least.

A financial problem arose for Traugott, and Friedrich made him a loan. By the end of Friedrich's first year, the elder boy had not repaid the money, and Friedrich was going into debt. Father Froebel decided that Friedrich had been irresponsible and refused to pay his debts. He later changed his mind when Friedrich agreed to leave Jena and to relinquish his claim to any paternal inheritance. In the meantime, however, Friedrich spent some time in the university prison, where he studied geometry, Latin, art, and Scripture. When he was released he returned home and continued to read voraciously from his father's library until he went to Hildburghausen to study agriculture in 1801. However, son and father remained estranged until 1802 when, prior to the father's death, he forgave Friedrich.

For the next fifteen years, Froebel held various positions: actuary in a forestry department; land surveyor, secretary, and accountant at a large country estate; student of architecture at Frankfurt; teacher; tutor; vistor (twice) to Yverdon; student at the universities of Göttingen and Berlin; and Prussian Volunteer Corps soldier fighting Napoleon. During this time Froebel blossomed into a Christian mystic searching for his own calling and Christlike life on earth.[45]

Finally, in 1816, realizing that instructing the young held a special attraction for him, he opened the Universal German Educational Institution at Griesheim in Rudolstadt. Establishing this school had special family meaning. Froebel's favorite brother, Christoph, had died of typhus while tending wounded soldiers, leaving a wife and three children. Friedrich vowed to become a father to these orphaned children and decided to open a school in Christoph's home in Griesheim. Christoph's widow later bought a farm in Keilhau, and Froebel moved the school there. In September 1818, he married Henrietta Hoffmeister, a friend from Berlin "with a like love of nature and of childhood as my own, and a like high and earnest conception of education." Shortly thereafter, Frau Froebel deeded her farm to her brother-in-law and went to live in Volkstadt.[46]

The Children's Educator

In Keilhau prior to his marriage, Froebel had been joined by his army soulmates Heinrich Langethal and William Middendorff, but the next decade was unsettling. In 1826 he published *The Education of Man,* a full-scale account of his educational theories and principles. By 1828 Middendorff's nephew, Johannes Barop, joined the Keilhau school staff, and together the group planned for a national education institute in Helba. However, they abandoned the plan two years later for lack of support. From 1831 to 1837 Froebel was involved with four other schooling ventures in Wartensee and Willisau (in Lucerne), Burgdorf (in Berne), and Rudolstadt. Finally, in 1837 he settled in Blankenburg and opened the Institute for the Occupations of Little Children.

In this setting Froebel began developing a series of didactic materials which he called *gifts* and *occupations.* The gifts were six sets of concrete geometric shapes that children could manipulate to discover the ideas of nature and the quality of things in the universe. They were arranged in order from simple concepts and operations to more complex. The first gift, "potential," consisted of six soft balls of various colors—the primary ones of red, yellow, and blue, and secondary colors of green, violet, and orange. This gift revealed unity of size, shape, and texture while demonstrating individuality or diversity of color. For Froebel this gift was analogous to the child's soul, which also had potential.

The second gift, "origination," included three wooden geometric forms, all demonstrating either explicitly or implicitly the elements of plane, line, and point: a sphere, a cube (regarded by Froebel as a sphere turned inside out), and a cylinder (the evolution of both spheres and cubes). This evolution related to the soul's free movement as it developed. Gifts three through six, "building gifts," were cubes, divided and subdivided various times and in various ways to expose smaller cubes, oblong blocks, bricks, and triangular prisms. Through these the child learned numbers, geometry, arithmetic, parts of a whole, separation, production, and evolution, and also the genealogy of family and the production of successive generations. Froebel also developed gifts seven and eight, but there is disagreement as to what they were and how they were to be used.[47]

The occupations developed from using the gifts, and put into practice what the child had learned from the gifts. The occupations also utilized materials that could be transformed: paper constructing, cardboard cutting, sand molding, clay modeling, and wood building. There were also the occupations of sewing, weaving, and drawing—all of which involved self-activity, one of the most important principles in the Froebelian method. To round out his program, Froebel included more self-activity— games, plays, singing, and dancing.

Although he was never really known as a philosopher or writer, Froebel did try to popularize his theories and practices through journal articles, lectures, and a book of songs, games, and stories called *Mutter und Kose-lieder (Mother and Nursery Songs)*. In 1840 Froebel and his associates began using the name *kindergarten* (children's garden) for establishments in Blankenburg and Rudolstadt. In 1849, he started another institution in Liebenstein to train teachers, but there were personal as well as professional setbacks. In 1839 his first wife died. He remarried in 1851 against the wishes of his Keilhau associates. They regarded his second wife, Louise Leven—thirty years his junior—as socially inferior.

In 1850 he met Baroness Bertha von Marenholtz-Bülow, who became instrumental in making the kindergarten an international movement. A year after Froebel's first meeting with Bülow, the Prussian government banned all kindergartens, calling them un-Christian. (Froebel was too democratic-sounding for the conservative regime then in power.) After that, Froebel's health started to fail, and he died on June 21, 1852. Eight years later the ban was removed through Bülow's efforts, and Froebel's widow began to train kindergarten teachers again.

It was under Frau Froebel that Bülow's American counterpart to the movement, Elizabeth Palmer Peabody, studied in 1867–1868. In America the first German-speaking kindergarten was opened in 1855 in Watertown, Wisconsin, under Margarethe Schurz, Froebel's student. Peabody opened her first kindergarten with instruction in English in Boston in 1860. Finally, in 1873 Susan Blow financed the first public kindergarten in St. Louis. By the twentieth century, kindergartens were an important element in American education.

SUMMARY

The European Enlightenment assumed human perfectibility through rationality. Six educationally significant themes characterize the movement:

1. *Rationality* and the desirability of addressing all human issues through human intelligence. At least as old as Protagoras, this idea gained popularity as Enlightenment thinkers gave it renewed emphasis.

2. *Scientific naturalism* was closely allied with rationality. Although Benjamin Franklin was an exception, most famous Enlightenment thinkers were not practicing scientists. They did approve of efforts to find natural explanations of human phenomena. Some had visions of "a world subject to laws and regularities which could be grasped and explained by the unaided power of human reason."[48] Others agreed with Locke that human experience was not everywhere the same, and therefore that no single unified reality or truth was possible.

3. *Anticlericalism,* though not necessarily antireligious in its broader sense, was a prominent feature of Enlightenment thinking. Some, like Voltaire in his savage caricature in *Candide,* saw everyday Christianity as an excuse for injustice, pain, unhappiness, and superstition. Others, like Locke, spent little time attacking established churches, but nevertheless wanted to minimize dependence on supernatural powers (miracles) to explain reality and wanted to minimize sectarian conflict.

4. *Human happiness* was the ultimate measure of value. This meant that personal growth and awareness, as in Rousseau's thought, was a legitimate educational goal. The correct standard against which to measure curriculum was not liberalness, as asserted by Aristotle, but usefulness as advocated by Locke.

5. *Experience* was the basis for all learning. This meant that everyone's experience was potentially educative. Young children, as Froebel thought, impaired children, as Seguin and Itard suggested, and women, as Wollstonecraft wrote, could and should be allowed to learn.

6. *Learning effectiveness* could be increased by the use of concrete objects, movement, songs and games, logical sequencing, and by relating new learning experiences to established ideas.

Many of today's educational beliefs and practices are rooted in the Enlightenment, and not all controversies over which Enlightenment philosophers argued have been laid to rest. Ensuring maximum educational opportunity to all individuals and groups is a logical extension of Enlightenment thinking. As a desirable policy, this idea is now widely agreed upon, but not fully implemented. The argument persists between those who believe that reality is for everyone the same (most twentieth-century educational psychologists) and those who believe there are fundamentally important differences in groups' and individuals' experiences in defining their realities (proponents of bilingual education). The place of religion in education and life is still a matter of controversy.

In staying with the European side of educational developments through the middle of the nineteenth century, we have gone far past the discovery and colonization of vast territories. The fifteenth- and sixteenth-century efforts to transplant European cultural, educational, and social beliefs and institutions to Africa, Asia, Australia, and the Americas is a story of far-reaching implications for the present. We shall take up the North American part of this story in succeeding chapters, especially with reference to the geographic area which is now the United States of America.

NOTES

1. Peter Gay, *Age of Enlightenment* (New York: Time-Life Books, 1966), 11. Information for the introduction comes from M. S. Anderson, *Eighteenth Century Europe, 1713–1789* (London: Oxford University Press, 1966); Max Beloff, *The Age of Absolutism,* 1660–1815 (New York: Harper and Row, 1962); Isaiah Berlin, *The Age of Enlightenment* (New York: Mentor Books, 1956); and Frank E. Manuel, *The Age of Reason* (Ithaca: Cornell University Press, 1951).

2. William H. McNeill, *The Rise of the West: A History of the Human Community* (Chicago: University of Chicago Press, 1963), 686.

3. Anderson, *Eighteenth Century Europe,* 59.

4. Anderson, *Eighteenth Century Europe,* 13.

5. Merle Curti, *Probing Our Past* (New York: Harper, 1955), 75.

6. For biographical information, see Richard Ithamar Aaron, *John Locke,* 3rd ed. (Oxford: Clarendon Press, 1971); Maurice William Cranston, *John Locke, A Biography* (New York: Macmillan, 1957); John David Mabbott, *John Locke* (London: Macmillan, 1973); and Kathleen M. Squadrito, *John Locke* (Boston: Twayne, 1979).

7. John Locke, *An Essay: Concerning the True Original Extent and End of Civil Government,* in Robert Maynard Hutchins, ed., *Great Books of the Western World,* 53 vols. (Chicago: Encyclopaedia Britannica, 1952), 35: 46.

8. John Locke, *Some Thoughts Concerning Education* (New York: Oxford University Press, 1947), 253–55.

9. Locke, *Some Thoughts Concerning Education,* 256, 272.

10. John Locke, *An Essay Concerning Human Understanding,* ed. Alexander Campbell Fraser, 2 vols. (New York: Dover, 1959), 2: 46.

11. McNeill, *The Rise of the West,* 686.

12. Jean-Jacques Rousseau, *The Confessions of Jean-Jacques Rousseau, Now for the First Time Translated into English Without Expurgation,* 2 vols. (N.p.: privately printed, [c. 1896]), 1: 3; biographical information also comes from Colwyn Edward Vulliamy, *Rousseau* (London: G. Bles, 1931).

13. Rousseau, *Confessions,* 1: 6, 11.

14. Vuilliamy, *Rousseau,* 19.

15. Rousseau, *Confessions,* 1: 65.

16. William Brandon, *Indians* (New York: American Heritage, 1985), 104.

17. Jack Weatherford, *Indian Givers: How the Indians of the Americas Transformed the World* (New York: Fawcett Columbine, 1988), 124.

18. McNeill, *The Rise of the West,* 687.

19. Jean-Jacques Rousseau, *Émile, Or on Education,* trans. Alan Bloom (New York: Basic Books, 1979).

20. Eleanor Flexner, *Mary Wollstonecraft* (New York: Coward, McCann & Geoghegan, 1972); Ralph Wardle, *Mary Wollstonecraft—A Critical Biography* (Lincoln: University of Nebraska Press, 1951).

21. Juliet Mitchell, *Women's Estate* (New York: Vintage Books, 1975), chap. 5.

22. C. J. Barker-Benfield, "Mary Wollstonecraft: Eighteenth-Century Commonwealth Woman," *Journal of the History of Ideas,* 50 (January-March 1989): 95–115; Mary Wollstonecraft, *Vindication of the Rights of Woman* (New York: W. W. Norton, 1967), 220, 223, 285.

23. Wollstonecraft, *Vindication*, 251.

24. Flexner, *Mary Wollstonecraft*, 181–216; Wardle, *Mary Wollstonecraft*, 185–206, 215–250; C. Keegan Paul, ed., *Letters to Imlay* (New York: Haskell House, 1971).

25. Janet Todd, "Reason and Sensibility in Mary Wollstonecraft's *The Wrongs of Woman*," *Frontiers: A Journal of Women Studies* 5 (Fall 1980): 17–20. This synopsis is based on Mary Wollstonecraft, *Maria, Or the Wrongs of Woman* (New York: W. W. Norton, 1975).

26. Mary Anne Warren, *The Nature of Woman: An Encyclopedia and Guide to the Literature* (Iverness, CA: Edgepress, 1980), 497.

27. Mary Wollstonecraft, *Thoughts on the Education of Daughters* (1786), 81, cited in Warren, *The Nature of Woman*, 497.

28. Linda McPheron and Joan K. Smith, "Women Administrators in Historical Perspective: Toward an Androgynous Theory of Leadership," *Education Horizons* 60 (Fall 1981): 22–25.

29. Harlan Lane, *The Wild Boy of Aveyron* (New York: Bantam Books, 1977).

30. Kate Silber, *Pestalozzi: The Man and His Work* (New York: Schocken Books, 1973), 4. Unless otherwise noted, biographical information is from this source.

31. John Alfred Green, *Life and Work of Pestalozzi* (London: W. B. Clive, 1913), 32.

32. Green, *Life and Work of Pestalozzi*, 41–42.

33. Silber, *Pestalozzi*, 56, 115.

34. Silber, *Pestalozzi*, 112.

35. Silber, *Pestalozzi*, 114; Green, *Life and Work of Pestalozzi*, 77.

36. Karl von Raumer, "The Life and Educational System of Pestalozzi," in *Pestalozzi and His Educational System*, ed., trans., and comp. Henry Barnard (Syracuse: C. W. Bardeen, [1901]), 84–85. Eva Channing, trans., *Pestalozzi's Leonard and Gertrude*, Heath's Pedagogical Library 6 (Boston: D. C. Heath, 1885): 86.

37. Cf. Hermann Krüsi, *Pestalozzi: His Life, Work, and Influence* (Cincinnati: Wilson, Hinkle, 1875), 13–64, 67–100, and von Raumer, "The Life and Educational System of Pestalozzi," 84–86.

38. Silber, *Pestalozzi*, 78.

39. "Pestalozziana," *Blackwood's Magazine* (July 1849), reprinted in the *American Journal of Education* 31 (1881): 35–48.

40. Silber, *Pestalozzi*, 236.

41. Schmid's younger sister, Katarina, had married Gottlieb. They had one son, Karl, who never married, and was a teacher at the Technical University of Zürich.

42. Emilie Michaelis and H. Keatley Moore, trans., *Autobiography of Friedrick Fröbel* (Syracuse: C. W. Bardeen, 1889), 3. Unless otherwise noted, biographical information is from this source.

43. Michaelis and Moore, *Autobiography of Friedrick Fröbel*, 8. His stepbrother, Karl Poppo, was born in 1786 and died March 25, 1824. He was first a teacher, then a publisher.

44. Michaelis and Moore, *Autobiography of Friedrick Fröbel*, 52–60.

45. Michaelis and Moore, *Autobiography of Friedrick Fröbel*, 52–60.

46. Robert B. Downs, *Friedrick Fröbel* (Boston, Twayne, 1978), 28.

47. The gifts are discussed in Downs, *Friedrick Fröbel*, 47–54.

48. McNeill, *The Rise of the West*, 683.

The
CHAPTER SEVEN
Americans

Europeans like Rousseau, Pestalozzi, and Froebel wrote about changing education to make it more flexible, practical, and child-centered—better suited to common people. Their influential ideas circulated widely. Yet another force altered the form and content of teaching more profoundly than any European theorist. This was the conquest of America, a process that radically modified European life, culture, and education. Indeed without America, Locke, Rousseau, and many other European theorists would not have written as they did.

When Froebel died in 1852, the development of new ideas and institutional forms was well advanced owing to Europe's encounter with America: "The career of Western civilization since 1500 appears as a vast explosion, far greater than any comparable phenomenon both in geographic range and in social depth," is how one historian put it. "Incessant and accelerating self-transformation, compounded from a welter of conflicting ideas, institutions, aspirations, and inventions, has characterized modern European history."[1] People brought to America their "whole European culture complex," wrote another: "institutions of economics, religion, and government; . . . ideas, mechanical techniques, tools, clothes, and . . . dependence on those forces of civilization" that held them in their "groove[s] of class and circumstance."

The American environment continuously recreated this complicated culture complex into something else. "The change to new ways and attitudes came because nature would not yield to the old ones." People "had to devise something to which it would finally yield."[2] "Had Europe and America not come together through Columbus or some other connection, the industrial revolution would never have happened," according to anthropologist Jack Weatherford. "The peasants of Europe, Asia, and Africa would have continued tilling their fields while craftsmen produced small quantities of needed goods in their workshops. Life would probably have continued as it had for thousands of years. But," adds Professor Weatherford, "once the two great civilizations of the Old World and the Americas collided, technological progress exploded . . . into the flurry of development that radically altered the traditional way of life of the whole world."[3] European writer and critic Tzvetan Todorov puts it succinctly: "The discovery of America, or of the Americans, is certainly the most astonishing encounter of our history. . . . The conquest of America . . . heralds and establishes our present identity."[4]

Latin Christianity, already a powerful intellectual and cultural force, took on a military dimension by the ninth century with Charlemagne's decapitation of 4500 heathen to encourage the baptism of their remaining peers. By the fourteenth century all of western Europe and most of eastern Europe was officially Christian, and there had been several attempts to capture Jerusalem and other Asian cities. By the fifteenth and sixteenth centuries, when adventurers under Portuguese and Spanish flags discovered America and other territories previously unknown to Europeans, they had no qualms about using force to "propagate His holy name and His Gospel throughout the universe," as Christopher Columbus wrote.[5]

Initial conquests in North America occurred under Spanish auspices. In addition to Mexico, Spaniards founded colonies in what is now Florida, Louisiana, Texas, New Mexico, Arizona, and California. They also explored present-day Oklahoma, Kansas, and Nebraska. The goal was always to effect the "conversion of Souls" and afford the Spaniards "profits and advantages," as Friar Antonio de la Ascension wrote in 1620.[6] European colonizers desperately wanted (and needed) the wealth of the newly discovered territories, and they genuinely believed—indeed, knew beyond any possibility of doubt—that Latin and Christianity were infinitely superior to the languages and beliefs of indigenous Americans.

Of all the wonders of discovery, none was as marvelous as the eighty million native Americans—and millions more sub-Saharan Africans encountered about the same time—of whose existence Europeans had been unaware. Were these new people essentially like Europeans, and only in need of instruction in language and religion so they could be assimilated into the family of civilized people? Or were they one of the incredible variety of new species of life, not quite human and therefore part of the new "horn of plenty" provided by God for European convenience and profit. Missionaries, both Roman Catholic and Protestant, leaned toward the "noble savage to be assimilated" idea; those who focused primarily on improving their own income and living conditions often preferred the "less than human" theory. The two views ran throughout American history, and strong residues of each are recognizable in the present.

Both of these theories had in common an assumption that the cultures of the colonized were inferior. For example, missionaries destroyed all they could find of Aztec written/pictographic records in the early years of the Mexican conquest, aiming to remove indigenous culture so they could replace it with their own. "Language has always been the companion of empire," wrote Spanish grammarian Antonio de Nebrija in 1492.[7]

In the long history of cultural encounter, colonized and colonizer have each brought to the interaction their own sets of values (axiologies), fundamental assumptions about how things must be (ontologies), and what constitutes knowledge (epistemologies). Not only the meaning each person has found in these cultural interactions but the attitudes and actions of all the individuals involved can occur only within the range of what each person's axiology, ontology, and epistemology permits. "Each of us is the other's barbarian; to become such a thing, one need only speak a language of which the other is ignorant: it is merely babble to his ears."[8]

Colonizers concentrated their efforts on "selecting from among the young men and boys such as appear the most docile, talented and capable" some to learn the colonizer's language and religion. "It is a very easy matter, by this method, to teach the children our language, and they, as they grow up, will teach it to their companions and to their children and families," wrote de la Ascension.[9]

A few missionaries thought conversion would be more efficient if they used the language of the colonized. One of these was a Dominican named Diego Durán (1537–1588), a Spaniard who grew up in Mexico after the age of six. Durán lived with the Indians, learning their language, music, beliefs, metaphors, and ceremonies. A devout Christian, he resisted attempts to incorporate indigenous practices into Christian ritual. At the same time, he explained Aztec beliefs to Europeans in cultural terms with which they were familiar. Human sacrifice, for example, was like God telling Abraham to kill Isaac or analogous to God sending His only son to die for the sins of all. Durán drew many parallels to show that the Aztecs were more like the Spaniards than most people believed. He wrote a *History of the Indians of New Spain* (1581) that explained both the Aztec's religion and their history. It was not published until the nineteenth century.[10]

If Durán remained a "divided being: a Christian converted to 'Indianism' who converts the Indians to Christianity," one of his contemporaries went even further in his nonjudgmental attitude toward native culture. This was the Spanish Franciscan Bernardino de Sahagún, who spent his adult life in Mexico. His contemporaries criticized him even more harshly than they did Durán for not condemning and suppressing native culture.

Bernardino de Sahagún (1499–1590)

From Bernardino's native village in north central Spain, a healthy lad could easily walk in a week to the venerable University of Salamanca, some 125 miles away. At an appropriate age, Bernardino made this journey. He had a talent for and interest in learning languages. After studying grammar at Salamanca, he joined the Franciscan order. A biographer who knew him personally wrote that Bernardino was so handsome that members of his order sought to protect him by keeping him from appearing in public. The same source assures us that Bernardino faithfully kept his monastic vows.

At thirty, Friar Bernardino arrived in Mexico City. He began studying Nahuatl, the language of the Aztecs. He was not the first priest to learn this Native American language, but pushed the process one step farther than anyone else. In 1536, the Franciscans started a seminary for catechizing some of the sons of the former Aztec nobility. Sahagún decided to teach the boys Latin—not simply a smattering so they could say the catechism, but fully as if they were European. Many colleagues (non-Franciscans) "laughed heartily and mocked us, considering it as beyond doubt that no one would be able to teach grammar to people who possessed so few aptitudes." Within two or three years, the detractors' laughter turned to concern. Students "were able to penetrate into every subject which concerns grammar, and speaking, understanding and writing Latin, even to the point of composing heroic verses."[11]

By this process, Sahagún turned his students into experts on the Nahuatl language. Because they understood the structure, vocabulary, and usages of both Nahuatl and Latin, these students were able to teach the Spaniards the "properties of the words and of their own ways of speaking, as well as the incongruous things which we say in our sermons or which we put into our teaching."[12] By giving the colonized full access to the deepest secrets of the colonizer's knowledge base, Sahagún went farther than many of the colonizer's were willing to go.[13] The result was immediate criticism: "When the lay brothers and the priests were convinced that the Indians were making progress and were capable of doing still more, they began to . . . raise many objections, . . . saying that since these people were not to . . . [join a monastic order], what good would it do to teach them grammar?" They might get heretical ideas, "and it was also said that by reading the Holy Scriptures they would realize that the ancient patriarchs had several wives at once, even as they themselves were in the custom of having."[14]

Sahagún persisted despite his colleagues' disapproval. He wrote books, verse, and songs, many of which did not survive. Much of the resistance he encountered was passive rather than overt. Superiors sometimes cut off funds, leaving him no copyists. One provincial governor used a trick to get some of Sahagún's writings, and sent them to

Spain. A contemporary speculated bitterly that the manuscripts "no doubt will be made into wrapping papers for grocers."[15] Even in his old age Sahagún had to do much of his own copying. One monumental work did survive, though it was not published until the nineteenth and twentieth centuries. This was the four-volume *Historia general de las cosas de Nueva España* (*A History of Ancient Mexico*). It took Sahagún forty years to complete the study, and it is a monument to his energy, courage, imagination, and resourcefulness.

Because the Spanish had tried to destory everything written in Nahuatl, to gather information for the history Sahagún asked native dignitaries in two Aztec cities to select "several skillful and experienced persons" who could answer questions about Aztec culture and about the conquest. With the help of four of his best Indian students, Sahagún spent nearly three years interviewing these men. Sahagún and his students compared the resulting extensive interview transcripts, written in Nahuatl, with pictographic texts the Indians had hidden from the colonizer's flames, and then spent a great deal of time and energy carefully organizing the material around themes into chapters. Then, his students and informants went through the manuscript and "corrected and added many things." Satisfied that the Nahuatl text was as complete and correct as possible, Sahagún translated it into Spanish. Finally, he asked several Mexicans who had learned European art techniques to illustrate the bilingual text. A present-day French literary critic has called Sahagún's book a "unique monument of human thought," and "the first sketches of a future dialogue, the unformed embryos that herald our present."[16]

Sahagún was a committed Christian missionary. Yet, the methodology he pioneered and used so scrupulously was essentially that of present-day ethnographic researchers. And his evangelizing Christian approach did not blind him to the negative results of eradicating indigenous culture. The Spaniards "made it their task to trample on all customs and on all ways of governing themselves the natives possessed, with the claim to reduce them to living as in Spain," he wrote. "By the mere fact of considering them as idolaters and barbarians, we destroyed all their ancient government." What the Europeans introduced, Sahagún observed, worked less well for Native Americans than had the indigenous practices which had been "in closer relationships with their aspirations and their needs."[17]

A growing body of literature now suggests that as Europeans tried to replace native ways with Greco-Roman Christianity, they also borrowed extensively from indigenous cultures. European colonizers adopted the transportation network that Native Americans had developed. They took over foods, medicines, fibers, and housing techniques, and adapted democratic governing procedures they first saw in America. Euro-Ameripeans, as one scholar has labeled the dominant group after colonization, used classical Greek and Roman concepts to justify slavery.[18] The more populist tradition of [North] American politics had deep roots in the "long house of the Iroquois and the humble caucus of the Algonquins," Jack Weatherford wrote. "The process of learning democracy through the experience of the frontier and Indians continued without regard to the supposed classical models. Even after the founding of the United States, the Indians continued to play a significant role in the evolution of democracy because of their sustained interactions with Americans on the frontier."[19] Indian influence on democratic movements was evident throughout the Americas.

In the clash and juxtaposition of two cultures, Sahagún saw the outlines of an alternative that required neither assimilation nor subjugation. He and his contemporary Diego Durán found strengths and weaknesses in both cultures. Sahagún's commitment to and respect for European and American approaches suggested the possibility of coexistence and even hybridization. In time new cultural forms, possessing elements of both Spanish and ancient Indian ways but distinct from either, would emerge. In the meanwhile many people would live *nepantla*—"in the middle."

Sor Juana Inés de la Cruz (1648–1695)

Sor Juana Inés de la Cruz was born in the Mexican town of Nepantla half a century after Sahagún died. Nun, poet, playwright, feminist, and educator, she died at the age of forty-six, leaving an indelible mark on both literature and the history of thought. She is sometimes called *La Decima Musa*—"the tenth muse."

By the time Juana Ramírez was born on November 12, 1648 in the mountains near Mexico City, an elaborate system of social differentiation had evolved in the Americas. Along with romanticizing the "noble savage," Europeans deeply feared the decivilizing influence of the American wilderness. Anyone born into the New World was tainted.

We know little of Juana's father except that he was from Spain. This made him the social superior of her mother, a Creole—or a person of full Spanish ancestry born in the New World. Creoles, no matter how wealthy or aristocratically descended, rarely tried to go to Spain to live, and this was especially true for women. Most Spaniards in the New World were males. A few high officials brought their wives with them; most left their families in Spain. Spanish men could legally marry Creole women, but rarely did so. Instead, they formed a kind of second-class arrangement (as St. Augustine had done 1,000 years earlier). This was the case with Juana's mother and father.

Children born of such unions could enjoy high status if the father acknowledged and claimed them. For example, Payo Enriquez de Rivera (who would become one of Juana's friends) was illegitimate, but rose to the position of archbishop and viceroy because his father, the count of

Alcala de los Gazules, recognized him and provided him with status and support.[20] However, Juana's father abandoned the family when she was about two; perhaps he was recalled to Spain. Juana, her two older sisters, and their mother went to live in her maternal grandfather's house in Amecameca, thirty miles southwest of Mexico City. He was not poor, and he willingly offered his daughter and granddaughters protection and support.[21]

Juana had an intense desire to learn: "I had not yet reached the age of three when my mother sent my older sister to receive reading instruction in one of the places called Amigas," she recalled in an autobiographical account. "I was impelled by my love and mischief to follow her; and seeing that she [my sister] was given a lesson, I developed a burning desire to learn to read."[22] She demanded a lesson from the teacher, saying that her mother had ordered it. Although the teacher did not believe her, she gave the little girl instruction anyway. Seeing Juana's desire and ability to learn, the teacher kept up the lessons. By the time her mother discovered what was happening, Juana knew enough to continue learning on her own.

After her precocious beginning, by age six Juana was engaged in the study of reading and writing, and "all the other labors and sewing abilities degrading to women," as she later put it.[23] This would soon change. When she was eight, her grandfather died. Her mother, perhaps out of economic necessity, soon agreed to another second-class marriage. The birth of don Diego followed, and Juana's mother (who would have three more children by Diego Ruiz Lozano y Centeno) made arrangements for her youngest daughter to live with an aunt and uncle in Mexico City.[24]

We don't know how Juana felt about the move. She had earlier asked her mother to allow her to dress as a male so she could attend the university in the capital. Mexican historian Josefina Muriel notes that women of this era frequently wanted to dress like men in order to realize what was forbidden to them, pointing out that Spanish literature has many instances of women dressing up as men: "looking for adventure, in defense of their lost honor, or as vengeance due to some kind of abuse."[25] This practice continued into the twentieth century. Mexican artist Frida Kahlo dressed as a male in the 1920s to attend the university. "My inclination to letters was of such power and vehemence," Juana Ramírez recalled decades later, "that neither the reprimands of others—and I have received many—nor my own considerations—and there have been not a few of these—have succeeded in making me abandon this natural impulse which God has implanted in me."[26]

Despite her mother's efforts to have Juana pursue a typically female curriculum, the curious young woman read most of the books in her grandfather's library. At eleven, shortly before she departed for Mexico City to live with her mother's relatives, she briefly enjoyed fame in Amecameca for writing a *loa,* or prologue to a religious play. Her prize was a book.[27]

Juana's move to Mexico City to live with her Aunt Maria Ramírez and Uncle Juan de Mata, even if it may have been initially frightening, represented a childhood dream come true. Her relatives secured a tutor, Martin de Olivas, who introduced her to Latin. (It was customary for women to receive instruction from private tutors because they could not attend the university.)[28] Just twenty lessons gave her a sufficient basis to pursue the language on her own, and as a motivational technique, she cut her hair when she failed to learn her lessons fast enough. Because long hair was a symbol of beauty, her cropped hair was a public embarrassment and a sign (to her) of stupidity.[29] Latin was the language of culture and, along with some Greek, was common among educated women in Old and New Spain. Therefore, Juana with her knowledge of Latin was able to achieve higher education without setting foot in the university.[30]

By age sixteen, Juana was becoming known all over Mexico City as an attractive and intellectually accomplished young woman. She had continued to write religious poetry. At about this time, her aunt and uncle were able to place her in the palace as a member of the vicereine's (viceroy's wife's) court.[31] In the palace, Juana established a lasting friendship with the viceroy and his wife, the Marquesa de Mancera, who became like family, providing her with warmth, friendship and protection.[32]

With the Marquesa's approval, Juana continued expanding her knowledge. The viceroy, amazed at how much she had read, arranged to have her examined by forty learned men from the university. According to Father Calleja, her friend and first biographer who got the story from Viceroy de Mancera himself, Juana's examination was a dazzling success: "In the manner that a royal galleon might fend off the attack of a few canoes, so did Juana extricate herself from the questions, arguments, and objections these many men, each in his specialty, directed to her."[33] He said that she won the respect and admiration of everyone present.[34] As a result of this examination, many people in the capital heard of her erudition, and her knowledge continued to expand by daily contact with the prominent men who visited the palace. They in turn were delighted with her poetry and her attention, and everyone seemed to approve her studies during this time. She was living in harmony with her immediate world.[35]

From sixteen to nineteen Juana seems to have enjoyed life in the court. She knew all the local officials and met visiting dignitaries. She was a frequent guest at the dinner parties given by the viceroy and his wife. She had continuous male attention because of her natural attractiveness and her celebrity status.

It was a sparkling life that could not continue, for as a Creole woman of nineteen, Juana had limited choices. She could marry a Creole, follow her mother's example and consummate an unofficial marriage with a Spaniard, or join a religious order. Some Sorjuanistas have concluded that an unhappy love affair led to a decision for convent life, but there is no evidence for this speculation.[36] Juana herself—by written declaration and by her life—said that what she wanted most was the freedom to dedicate her life to study. "I became a nun because, although I knew that that way of life involved much that was repellent to my nature, . . . nevertheless, given my total disinclination to marriage, it was the least unreasonable and most becoming choice I could make to assure my ardently desired salvation," she said. She went on to explain that she wavered while deciding whether to take up the life of the cloister because of "its incidental, not its central aspects." She amplified this explanation, citing "my wish to live alone, to have no fixed occupation which might curtail my freedom to study, nor the noise of a community to interfere with the tranquil stillness of my books. This made me hesitate a little before making up my mind."[37]

On August 14, 1667 Juana Ramírez entered the Carmelite convent of San José. Novitiates brought no dowry because the rules of this Capuchin ("discalced" or barefoot) nunnery required its members to live "without any comforts or financial security." Conditions were so severe, writes historian Asunción Lavrin, that most initiates became sick "a few days after professing and two-thirds of the community (at least) were constantly in the infirmary."[38]

For fifteen months, Juana recuperated and considered her limited choices. On February 24, 1669 she left San José for the convent of St. Jerome. Instead of the austere solitude of the Carmelites, she had a servant and eventually bought her own cell (apartment). She took the name of Sor (Sister) Juana Inés de la Cruz.[39]

When Sor Juana joined the convent of St. Jerome, Father Antonio Nuñez de Miranda personally took care of all the preparations for the celebration, inviting the most prominent people from the clergy and the nobility. "He assembled the luminarias with his own hands," Oviedo tells us, "because he didn't want the devil to tempt Juana Inés," as she was both attractive and intellectually accomplished. "God could not have sent a greater calamity to this kingdom," than to permit Juana Inés to stay outside of convent walls, Father Nuñez reportedly said.[40] Father Nuñez, a Jesuit with strong ascetic tendencies, was politically well connected and a kind of juror in the Mexican Holy Office (or Inquisition).

Joining a religious community was usually expensive. Elaborate initiation ceremonies were costly and required substantial dowries. Juana had no money of her own and no male family members to provide a dowry. Father Nuñez paid the expenses of the initiation, and a wealthy sponsor furnished the several thousand pesos needed for the dowry. Later, Father Nuñez would say that he arranged the sponsor's gift—a claim that Sor Juana disputed:

> For when . . . [I entered the convent] I had only for a brief time had the good fortune to know Y[our] R[everence], and although I owed you the realization of many desires concerning my state, which I shall always value, . . . in the matter of my dowry, long before I met Y.R., my godfa-

ther, Captain D[on] Pedro Velázquez de la Cadena, had arranged it, and it was in his negotiating this endowment for me and in no other thing that God provided me the solution; so that such an assertion [as you make] is baseless.[41]

The demands of communal life were not excessive in St. Jerome. Each nun had quarters that included a kitchen, sitting room, bath, and sleeping quarters for herself, her servant(s), and one or more girls entrusted to her supervision. Most cells were two-story apartments. St. Jerome also had a number of rooms called locutories, which were visiting parlors where nuns could entertain nonconvent guests. A row of wooden bars separated the nun from her visitors, but extensive conversation was possible. Some convents expected as much as eight hours a day of prayer, singing, and contemplation. Some required all meals in common and insisted that members of the chapter never be alone. This was not true of St. Jerome, and Sor Juana apparently found it possible to spend much of her time in study.

Sor Juana participated fully in the life of the convent. She served three terms as bookkeeper, a position that gave her considerable responsibility for the house's extensive property and investments and required her to interact extensively with people outside the convent. She wrote plays that were performed by some of the girls who were studying in the convent, and maintained a voluminous correspondence and entertained an extensive circle of friends and admirers, including the viceroy, vicereine, and other members of the court, who called often. "Whether arguing the most difficult questions with scholastic rigor, advancing with greatest delicacy her comments on various sermons, or spontaneously composing verses in diverse languages and meters, she astounded us all, and won the acclamation of the most severe critic among the assembled courtiers," wrote a contemporary.[42]

Father Nuñez became Sor Juana's confessor about the time she joined St. Jerome. For several years Juana Inés apparently followed her confessor's advice seeking permission ("which I then held more necessary than that of his Excellency the Archbishop Viceroy, my Prelate") for anything she published. Father Nuñez seems to have fully approved her activities for a time, proofing and correcting at least two carols before they were published.[43] However, at some point Nuñez began offering objections to Sor Juana's activities, which included writing love poetry in the baroque Renaissance style popular at the time.

It is not clear whether he objected prior to 1680, but tension between Nuñez and de la Cruz reached a crisis in 1680. A viceregal inauguration was imminent, and the ceremony was to be an occasion of extensive public celebration. The cabildo (town council) commissioned Sor Juana and Carlos de Sigüenza y Góngora to take charge of the ceremony and write special poetic orations for it. There was no more prestigious commission. It would provide for Sor Juana the opportunity to fully demonstrate her abilities. It also helped her establish a friendship with the new viceroy, Marquis de la Laguna, and his wife, María Luisa Manrique Lara. (María Luisa had already become Sor Juana's friend and protector, encouraged her writing, and from 1689 to 1692 would have two volumes of Sor Juana's work published in Spain.)[44]

Sor Juana accepted the commission. She designed one of the two triumphant arches, and Sigüenza y Góngora conceptualized the other. She chose Neptune as her theme and composed an allegorical poem. But Nuñez opposed *Neptuno Alegórico,* calling it mundane and inappropriate subject material for a nun. In his roles as confessor, self-appointed mentor, and surrogate father, Nuñez began urging the celebrated nun to read and write more around traditional religious themes and less about worldly matters. He accused Sor Juana of rebelling against the "masculine authority of her spiritual guide," and saw it as his duty to redirect Sor Juana's activities toward seclusion in the convent.[45]

Sor Juana rejected Nuñez's arguments and proceeded with the triumphant celebration. Nuñez began to publicly criticize the nun whom he had earlier encouraged to study. Finally, Sor Juana challenged her confessor in a private letter:

> Peace in Christ
>
> For some time now various persons have informed me that I am singled out for censure in the conversations of Y[our] R[everence], in which you denounce my actions with such bitter exaggeration as to suggest a *public scandal,* and other no less shocking epithets. Although my conscience might move me to my own defense, for my good name is not mine alone but is linked with my lineage and with the community in which I live, nevertheless I have chosen to bear my suffering in view of the supreme veneration and filial affection that I have always felt toward Y.R., preferring that all your objections fall upon me rather than have it seem that I had crossed the line of what was proper or that I was lacking in respect in replying to Y.R. . . . Not being unaware of the veneration and high esteem in which Y.R. (and justly so) is held by all, and that they listen to you as if to a divine oracle and appreciate your words as if they were dictated by the Holy Ghost, and that the greater your authority, the more is my good name injured; with all this, I have never wished to yield to the entreaties made to me, . . . that I reply, judging that my silence might be the most delicate way in which the anger of Y.R. would be cooled; until with time I have come to realize that on the contrary it seems that my patience irritates you, and thus I determined to reply to Y.R., without impugning my love, my obligation, and my respect.[46]

Juana Inés reminded her confessor that she initially tried to reject the commission to design "the Arch of the Church."

This is my unpardonable offense, which was preceded by my having been asked three or four times and my having as many refused, until two lay magistrates came who before calling upon me called first upon the Mother Prioress and then upon me, and commanded in the name of His Excellency the Archbishop that I do it because the full chapter had so voted and His Excellency approved.

Now it would be with that Y.R., with all the clarity of your judgment, put yourself in my place and consider what you would have replied in this situation. Would you answer that you could not? That would have been a lie. That you did not wish to? That would have been disobedience. That you did not know how? They did not ask more that I knew. That the vote was badly taken? That would have been impudent audacity, vile and gross ingratitude to those who honored me by believing that an ignorant woman knew how to do what such brilliant minds solicited. So I had no choice but to obey. . . . Well, now, my Father and dear sir, I beg of Y.R. to put aside for a moment your affectionate counsel (which always sways even the most saintly) and tell me, Y.R. (since in your opinion it is a sin to write verses), on which of these occasions was the transgression of having written them so grave?[47]

The fame that came to Sor Juana from the success of her Allegorical Neptune brought jealously as well as praise.

What great punishment would Y.R. wish for me than that resulting from the very applause that confers such pain. Of what envy am I not the target? Of what malice am I not the object? What actions do I take without fear? What word do I speak without misgiving?

Women feel that men surpass them, and that I seem to place myself on a level with men; some wish that I did not know so much; others say that I ought to know more to merit such applause; elderly women do not wish that other women know more than they, young women, that others present a good appearance; so that from all sides comes such a singular martyrdom as I deem none other has ever experienced.[48]

Some sisters were even jealous of her "reasonably good handwriting . . . for no other reason than they said it looked like a man's writing." She had "to deform it purposely, and of this the entire community is witness."

Then why do you find wicked in me what in other women was good? Am I the only one whose salvation would be impeded by books? . . . Why must it be wicked that the time I would otherwise pass in idle chatter before the grille, or in a cell gossiping about everything that happens outside and inside the house, or quarreling with a sister, or scolding a hapless servant, or wandering through all the world in my thoughts, be spent in study?

And all the more as God so inclined me, and I have not seen that it was against His most holy law nor contrary to the obligation of my state; I have this nature; if it is evil, I am the product of it; I was born with it and with it I shall die.

Y.R. wishes that I be coerced into salvation while ignorant, but, beloved Father, may I not be saved if I am learned? Ultimately that is for me the smoothest path. Why for one's salvation must one follow the path of ignorance if it is repugnant to one's nature?

Is not God, who is supreme goodness, also supreme wisdom? Then why would He find ignorance more acceptable than knowledge?

That St. Anthony was saved in his holy ignorance is well and good. St. Augustine chose the other path, and neither of them went astray.

What, then, is the source of your displeasure and of your saying "that had you known I was to write verses you would not have placed me in the convent but arranged my marriage"?

But, most beloved Father (only compelled and with diffidence do I utter what I would prefer not pass my lips), whence your direct authority (excepting what my love gave you and will give you always) to dispose of my person and the free will God granted me? . . .

Am I perchance a heretic? And if I were, could I become saintly solely through coercion? Would it were so, and that saintliness were a thing that could be commanded, for if that were so, I should surely be saintly; but I judge that one is persuaded, not commanded, and if by command, I have had Prelates to so command; but precepts and external coercion that make one circumspect and modest when they are moderate and prudent cause despair when they are too strong; only God's grace and assistance can make a saint.

What then is the cause of such anger? And of the injury to my reputation? Or holding me up as scandalous before everyone? Do I offend Y.R. in some manner? Have I asked you to assist me in my needs? Or have I disturbed you in any other spiritual or worldly matter?

Sor Juana dismissed Father Nuñez as her confessor, asking him to "not think of me, unless it be to commend me to God."[49]

Sor Juana's allegory and arch were successful. She came to be great friends of the new viceroy and his wife, and in the next several years she flourished. But the skirmish with Nuñez was not over. This misogynist would wait for a more opportune moment to assert the Lord's will against a woman who refused to stay in her place.

At about the same time as her letter to Nuñez—and perhaps generated by her conflict with him—Sor Juana wrote a scathing poetic indictment of male domination of women:

> Foolish men, you who blame
> women without cause;
> you, promote the very flaws
> to which you give women fame.

If to hopeless evil you belong;
within them wickedness incite,
why do you wish them to do right
if you encourage them to do wrong?

You fight their resistance with haste,
and then, with such appalled gravity,
You say it was their own levity
that brought them immoral disgrace.

Your boldness wrapped in "pure" white sheet
hides seemingly unaware
in closet as a ghost: beware;
it will frighten you when you meet.

You want, with such foolish presumption,
to find in the search of your way,
Thais as your fiancee,
and Lucretia in possession.

What mood can be so strangely queer,
that one in need of counsel and advice,
soils the very mirror of wisdom; twice
accusing it of being unclear.

With kindness and disdain to sell
you have a similar condition;
complaining if someone treats you with admonition,
jesting, if someone treats you well.

None can ever win your game,
because you accuse the one who is most true
of being ungrateful if she refuses you,
and the one who accepts, of shame.

You always so foolishly behave,
with contradicting rule;
you charge one for being cruel,
and at another for unchastity, you rave.

How should any woman know what to do,
she, whom you pretend to love in kind,
if the one who is prudent offends you blind,
and the one who is unchaste angers you?

Furthermore, between boredom and pain
your love relates; if you commend she
who is pure and not free,
in good time you will complain.

Your loving sorrows blind
allow your wings to soar iron clad,
and after you have made women bad,
you want them to be good and kind.

How can you wrongly call
her in an erroneous passion:

she who falls by imploration,
or she who implores after the fall?

Or who is more to blame and never win
even if they do whatever dismays:
the one that sins for the pay,
or the one that pays for the sin?

Well then, why are you frightful
of your own guilt?
love them the way you have built,
or make them rightful.

Stop soliciting and, in contrast,
accusing with fake concern
the affection of the woman you earn,
by making her purity not last.

Well, with many weapons I revel
knowing what combats men's arrogance,
since in promise and persistence
you unite world, flesh, and devil.[50]

Beginning of a Crisis

In 1688 a series of events began that ultimately brought crisis. Viceroy de la Laguna and María Luisa returned to Spain. Although María Luisa arranged for the publication of a volume of Sor Juana's writing in 1689 and an expanded printing in 1690, the fame and praise this brought Sor Juana also increased the jealousy and irritation felt by critics in Mexico City.

Around November 1690, the bishop of Puebla, Fernández de Santa Cruz, heard Sor Juana explicate a theological treatise. He asked her to write out what she had said and send it to him. She did and he published it under the title *Carta atenagórica,* or *Letter Worthy of Minerva.*[51] A second volume of Sor Juana's work, arranged by María Luisa appeared in April 1692 in Seville, Spain. In the meanwhile, other developments had altered the balance of power in Mexico City.

The Indians and many *castas* (castes) in New Spain lived in difficult conditions. The governing Spaniards tended to keep the lowest-status groups at subsistence levels while the Church, the court, and many lesser officials profited. Religious orders, including the Jesuits, and some Creoles tried to mitigate the most rapacious aspects of colonialism, but large sectors of the population were marginalized. This had resulted in a major revolt in 1624 and some smaller uprisings from time to time. In June 1692 a revolt exploded in Mexico City that was serious enough to frighten the Spanish crown as well as those with a vested interest in the established order in New Spain.

Trouble began in June 1691 with storms and extensive flooding in the capital. There was some loss of life and extensive property damage. Rains continued through July, damaging much of the fall wheat crop.

Vegetables were also in short supply because of the unusual weather patterns. Viceroy Galve tried to alleviate the food shortages, but he did not fully understand the marginal existence of many of his subjects or the depth of their hatred of the *gachupines* (Spaniards). His short-term measures included price controls, requesting supplies from other regions, and asking for prayers.

"There were murmurs against the government among the vast Indian population; these the Viceroy tended to discount. He regarded the natives as children," writes historian Lewis M. Hoskins.[52] When they could not get flour, Spaniards turned to the Indians' maize, which they ordinarily disdained. By May 1692 corn was also in short supply. Indians suspected Galve and others of the ruling class of manipulating price controls for personal gain. Galve and some others thought the Indians were hoarding corn to artificially inflate the price.

From Crisis to Revolt

A rapid series of events led to confrontation. Near the close of the market on June 6, shoppers sensed that the supply of grain was running out. They pressed forward and crushed an infant to death. Word of this incident spread and the next day the crowd was even uglier. One of the attendants at the market struck a woman with a whip when she insisted on service, and she collapsed. A crowd of people marched to the viceroy's palace but could not gain entrance. They settled for Archbishop Aguiar y Seijas, who promised to insist that they get better treatment.[53]

The next day, corn ran short again and a woman was trampled in the melee that followed. Her companions said she was dead, but some Spaniards thought she was faking. The crowd stoned the viceroy's mansion, and the few soldiers present tried to stop the crowd but ended up scrambling to close the gates. Two or three of them were caught outside as the gate slammed shut, and the crowd ripped them to pieces. Within half an hour the crowd of a few hundred people had swelled to an estimated ten thousand. "Down with the viceroy and all who defend them," they shouted. "Down with the Spaniards and the Gachupines who are eating up our corn! Hurrah for the king! Hurrah for pulque! Death to the Spaniards! Down with bad government!"[54]

For the next several hours looting and burning was extensive. About fifty people, mostly Indians, died in the riot, the majority burned to death as the palace and several public buildings were torched.

Viceroy Galve raised a large militia and had a number of people (mostly Indians) shot, hanged, or whipped. The *audiencia* forced Indians into ghettos, required them to wear traditional (rather than Spanish) dress, closed the pulquerias, outlawed public gatherings of more than five Indians, and forbade Indians to carry swords or machetes.[55] (In February, Galve had disqualified from public office anyone who had not formally studied Spanish.)[56]

Ultraconservative archbishop Aguiar y Seijas came out of this disturbance strengthened, while Galve's reputation suffered. The archbishop had met with the crowds, had heard their grievances, and had tried to quiet them before the major riot broke out. As the riot began Aguiar was in the thick of things, armed only with religious objects, trying to calm the rioters and telling them they had a good viceroy. Galve was hiding in a convent waiting for the trouble to subside. When normalcy returned, Galve got most of the blame, not only for allowing the riot to unfold but also for his inappropriate and ineffective response.

Power Shift

Seventeenth-century Mexican society was in dynamic tension. Conflicting interests and attitudes found expression in the court, university, and church and in their respective overlapping and interconnected bureaucracies. "The viceregal court performed a dual civilizing role," wrote Nobel Laureate Octavio Paz. It furnished "the models of aristocratic European culture, and it offered for emulation a way of life different from those of the Church and the university." Within the Church's secular clergy opinions and operating attitudes could be quite divergent. The religious orders—notably the Jesuits, Dominicans, and Franciscans in New Spain—competed with and often opposed each other. The Jesuits had a grand vision of a Catholic world. To achieve it they wanted, in places like Mexico and China, to incorporate indigenous practices and beliefs into Christian worship and to convert the political and social elite who would in turn bring along everyone else. The Dominicans and Franciscans found the Jesuit approach repugnant. They persuaded the pope to denounce this aspect of Jesuit assimilationism, but the papal court also found attractive "the grand plan of the Society" to create a worldwide society "under the sign of Rome."[57]

Much of the debate took place in sermons, a few of which ended up in print. This was the case with Sor Juana's 1690 *Letter Worthy of Minerva*. She was commenting on a sermon preached four decades earlier in Lisbon by a Portuguese Jesuit named Antonio de Vieyra, but apparently not available in Mexico City in Spanish until the 1680s. The letter made her a celebrated participant in the exciting controversies of the time.

Much of the Sorjuanista commentary in both Spanish and English has reported and analyzed the content of the *Carta atenagórica*. The fine points of the theological dispute are less interesting for most late-twentieth-century readers than the politics involved. Paz argues that the importance of Sor Juana's criticizing a sermon by this particular cleric was that it was—for those who cared, and this meant most of the Spanish and Creole elite in Mexico—a veiled but easily recognized slap at Archbishop Aguiar y Seijas. If this speculation is correct, the archbishop and his supporters would have fully understood that it was intended to embarrass him. Knowledgeable people would have instantly recognized that Bishop Fernández de Santa Cruz was sponsoring the publication of the *Carta* by his use of the pseudonym Sor Filotea de la

Cruz, a nun and "student" of Sor Juana. Aguiar's abhorrence of women was widely known, so the masterful critique by one nun and its supposed publication by another would have been a source of special delight for the archbishop's foes.

Fernández de Santa Cruz and Sor Juana had both spent many years in the ebb and flow of courtly politics. They were intelligent, experienced, and realistic. They must have anticipated the debate and controversy that followed publication of the letter critiquing Vieyra's sermon, although they may, as Paz suggests, have underestimated its intensity. What they could not have foreseen in 1690 was the change of power that would occur in 1692.

Interpreting Sor Filotea's Letter

When Sor Juana received her copy of the pamphlet from Puebla containing her own and Sor Filotea's letters, she spent several months constructing a closely argued reply. This is the source of much of our biographical information about Sor Juana and is now regarded as one of her most important works. It expanded upon many of the themes mentioned in her private 1681 letter to Father Nuñez and stands as a forceful justification of her life and of the rightness and value of women's education. Along with a partly autobiographical poem entitled "First Dream," it is a ringing defense of intellectual equality between the sexes.

Santa Cruz did not print the *Response* which his letter invited because by the time it was ready Sor Juana had learned that Aguiar y Seijas would attack her by seizing assets of her convent. Her monastic establishment answered directly to Aguiar. He began laying claim to property that Sor Juana and her sisters had long enjoyed without dispute. There was nothing the bishop of Puebla could do about this because the convent was not in his jurisdiction. Under different circumstances, the viceroy could have been counted on to control Archbishop Aguiar, but by July 1692 he was in no position to help even if he wanted to.[58]

Denouement

By 1693, Aguiar compelled Sor Juana to take Father Nuñez back as her confessor. She gave up most and perhaps all of her books and scientific instruments for sale. Oviedo, a pro-Nuñez contemporary, portrayed this as voluntary, a result of Sor Juana's realizing her spiritual errors. Another contemporary account by her nephew Torres indirectly refutes Oviedo's claim. Paz questions whether she had any kind of change of heart, and Sor Juana herself retracted nothing she had said or written.

In April 1695 many of Sor Juana's sisters in the convent fell ill from plague. After several days of intense care for the sick, Juana herself died from the illness, and was buried in the convent. She was forty-six.

Two volumes of Sor Juana's work were already in print when she died. A third volume, including her *Response to Sor Philothea,* was published in Spain in 1700. Other editions and printings appeared in the first three decades of the eighteenth century, but by 1750 the work of the controversial Mexican nun was hardly known anywhere.

Sor Juana's work lay dormant for a century and a half. Then, in the latter part of the nineteenth century, German scholars began investigating baroque literature. This "opened the way to a revival of interest in Sor Juana," observed Margaret Peden in 1982. "But it is only in the twentieth century, beginning in the twenties, intensifying in the thirties and forties, proliferating in the fifties, and continuing unabated today, that this literary interest became significant."[59] It appears a safe assumption that at least some of Sor Juana's work is about to be recognized as part of the Western literary canon.

Sor Juana is now a recognized literary figure in all of the Americas. It remains to consider what her life and writing mean, especially for education. There are two educational areas in which she is clearly relevant today. One of these involves the education of girls. The other is the education of adults, especially women.

Much of Sor Juana's 1681 letter to Nuñez and her 1691 *Reply* to Fernández de Santa Cruz is about the value and propriety of women's education. There are several facets to this defense. One is a long list of learned women she cited to support her argument. A few of these were figures from mythology, but more than thirty were real people. Several were Christian saints, but Sor Juana carefully pointed out that they were educated *before* sainthood and that their erudition had not interfered with their canonization.

Another striking feature of her defense of the same curriculum for women and men was her skillful use of Jesuit conceptualizations. She explained the study of many secular subjects as a preliminary basis for studying theology—the queen of the sciences. This was patterned after Ignatius Loyola's hierarchy of studies. She listed logic, rhetoric, physics, music, arithmetic, geometry, architecture, history, law, the Church fathers, and astrology (astronomy) as subjects worthy of serious study.

In laying claim for women to all academic subjects pursued by men, Sor Juana took a long step toward full curricular equality for women. Not only would she not concede a separate sphere of studies for women and men, she playfully suggested that men could profit from women's traditional studies. "But, Madam, what is there for us women to know, if not bits of kitchen philosophy? As Lupercio Leonardo said: one can perfectly well philosophize while cooking supper. And I am also saying, when I observe these small details [of everyday life]: If Aristotle had been a cook, he would have written much more."[60]

Sor Juana was well versed in canon law and used this knowledge to claim a wider territory than people like Nuñez and Aguiar wanted to allow. She reminded Nuñez that he had no authority over her that she did not give him. When pressed, she knew how to obey legitimate authority without giving into the intent behind it.

Sor Juana knew the society in which she lived would not tolerate a suggestion that women study in the university along with men. She let this go but pressed at least for private, individual study. "Who has forbidden that to women?" she asked:

> Like men, do they not have a rational soul? Why then shall they not enjoy the privilege of the enlightenment of letters? Is a woman's soul not as receptive to God's grace and glory as a man's? Then why is she not as able to receive learning and knowledge, which are the lesser gifts? What divine revelation, what regulation of the Church, what rule of reason framed for us such a severe law?
>
> Are letters an obstacle or do they, rather, lead to salvation? Was not St. Augustine saved, St. Ambrose, and all the other Holy Doctors? And Y.R., with such learning, do you not plan to be saved?
>
> And if you reply to me that a different order obtains for men, I say: did not St. Catherine study, St. Gertrude, my [spiritual] Mother St. Paula, without harm to her exalted contemplation, and was her pious founding of convents impeded by her knowing even Greek? Or learning Hebrew?[61]

Sor Juana was both a theorist and a practitioner of what is now called adult education. She taught adults by her writing and through her conversations, which was mostly what would now be labeled informal instruction. Because it was informal, her co-learners all participated voluntarily and motivation was not a problem.

In addition to teaching through poems, hymns, plays, essays, and conversations, Sor Juana was herself a lifelong learner and, to use another current term, an autodidact. She described herself as having no choice in either of these. The desire to learn was an unavoidable part of her nature, and when she tried to suppress this propensity to study in her early convent days, "it exploded like gunpowder."[62] As to her approach, she said: "My studies have . . . been so extremely private that I have not even enjoyed the direction of a teacher, but have learned only from myself and my work."[63] When not occupied by her convent obligations, her time was taken by "reading and more reading, study and more study, with no other teacher than books themselves. One can readily imagine how hard it is to study from those lifeless letters, lacking a teacher's live voice and explanations. Still [I] happily put up with all those drawbacks, for the sheer love of learning."[64]

How did this woman who claimed the whole sweep of the arts and sciences of her day direct her own advanced study? At any given time she pursued several subjects simultaneously. She alternated topics that she found difficult with those she particularly enjoyed:

> As I had no material goal in mind, nor any limitation of time constraining me to the study of any one thing to meet degree requirements, almost at once I was studying different things or dropping some to take

up others, although this was not wholly unsystematic since some I called study and others diversion. The latter brought me relaxation from the former. It follows from this that I have studied many things.[65]

Although Sor Juana described herself as so consumed by a desire to learn that she felt compelled to study, she did not characterize the process as easy. Not only was it hard to learn without a teacher; she said it was especially difficult to work "without fellow students with whom to compare notes and try out what had been studied." Combined with these obstacles, she suffered the same interruptions and competing demands for her time and energy as most contemporary adult learners:

I do confess that in this respect my hardship has been beyond description; hence I cannot say what I have with envy heard from others: that learning has not been hard work for them. Lucky they! . . . Many times I gave up and stopped, then started in again from the sheer urge to learn—and not only my own conscience, which was a party to this suffering, but the consciences of those who shared my life. . . . And to think that this unlucky bent of mine has been strong enough to overcome all these things![66]

Her family of religious sisters demanded time and attention in the same way as do families of adult students now.

[D]uring the free time we both had, I would go and comfort them and relax in their company. I realized that at such times I was neglecting my study and so made a vow not to enter a single cell unless obedience or charity required it of me. For, in the absence of a curb as harsh as this love would have broken through a control arising from mere resolve. Knowing my frailty, I would make this vow for a month or a fortnight and then, allowing myself a recess of a day or two, I would renew it. The free day was intended not so much to give me a rest as to prevent their considering me unbending, withdrawn, and unappreciative of the undeserved affection of those dearest sisters.[67]

Sor Juana learned not only from books but also from everything in her environment—"from everything God has created," as she put it:

all of it being my letters, and all this universal chain of being my book. I saw nothing without reflecting on it; I heard nothing without wondering at it—not even the tiniest, most material thing. For as there is no created thing, no matter how lowly, in which one cannot recognize the *me fecit Deus* [God made me], there is none that does not confound the mind once it stops to consider it. Thus, I repeat, I looked and marveled at all of them, so much so that simply from the person with whom I spoke, and from what that person said to me, countless reflections arose in my mind.[68]

Finally, Sor Juana noted that the learning process continued as she rested:

And not only that, . . . even my sleep was not free from this constant
activity of my brain. In fact, it seems to go on during sleep with all the
more freedom and lack of restraint, putting together the separate images it has carried over from waking hours with greater clarity and
tranquility, debating with itself, composing verses, of which I could
draw up a whole catalogue for you, including certain thoughts and
subtleties I have arrived at more easily while asleep than while
awake.[69]

Little wonder that some have called Sor Juana "the tenth muse."

Recovering the Hispanic American past is important for several reasons. First, contemporary people of Hispanic background involved in
teaching and other forms of educational leadership in the United States
may find it helpful to know they are continuing a long, rich tradition.
This is especially important in professional training by "socializing novices in the field. In their first exposure to the field's history, novices
experience their field as one of heroic achievement, see its larger tradition, and enlarge their narrow vision," writes Harold Stubblefield.[70]

Second, inclusion of previously invisible persons and groups is important for self-image enhancement of future practitioners from that ethnic group. More important, current and future professionals who are
not from the historically ignored population need a richer tapestry
against which to understand themselves. To know the past from the
view of the other is to move beyond an "us" and "them" view of the
world.

Third, recognition of a legitimate Hispanic past in formal United
States education and in nonformal and informal learning may be a
precondition for United States educators recognizing the value of including recent work of Latin American colleagues. Translations of Brazilian
Paulo Freire are currently the only works by a Latin American recognizable by United States and Canadian educators. Yet, a valuable and
growing Spanish language education literature exists. Many Latin
American educators know the English language literature of their specialties. Few of their counterparts in the United States know Spanish or
have any inkling that information and ideas of considerable value and
potential interest are close at hand.

Sor Juana's outspoken commentary grew partly out of the restless
energy of the new world, which continued to assert itself in the face of
traditional authority. It is difficult to know the effect of her poem
about oppression of women. In the long run, it must have quickened
the consciousness of many, as it continues to do even now. Meanwhile,
the conditions of life in the New World, while difficult in many ways,
made possible some educational opportunities for women that had not
existed on a wide scale in traditional European society. The need to
find new responses to the demands of America's environment affected
women as much as men. Women's inventive responses were as impor-

tant as those of their male counterparts in evolving new survival and coping techniques.

EARLY SCHOOLING EFFORTS IN NORTHEASTERN AMERICA

Just as Spanish colonizers found their customary techniques, beliefs, and practices challenged by America, so did other European colonizers. From the first, European settlers feared the debilitating effects of the endless frontier. No sooner were their colonies well planted than efforts began to establish schools. The Swedes in Delaware and the Dutch in New Amsterdam imported teachers. By the 1640s officials in Virginia, Massachusetts, and Connecticut feared that colonists were too careless of school arrangements. One result was legislation requiring parents and masters to see that all children could read and had a trade. Larger towns were to have classical schools and smaller ones some kind of vernacular instruction. This was a concrete expression of what Comenius and his confreres were advocating. Some colonial governing authorities added the practice of fining areas that did not comply and sending the money to the closest school.

Two unique aspects of the American colonial situation affected the way schools evolved. The first was an early deviation from classical farming patterns. For many centuries, European farmers had clustered their houses together in villages and traveled out to till their plots, and the original colonial land distribution system was based on this assumption, with each person receiving small strips in several locations rather than one larger one. Colonists quickly rejected this pattern, and began buying, selling, and trading to get all their property together. They built houses directly on their consolidated plots rather than around the village common. Colonial authorities, steeped in European attitudes, tried to discourage this departure from tradition; after a devastating Indian raid, Connecticut officials pointed out that God obviously intended people to live in towns. But neither the original plan, later warnings, nor fear of attack halted the practice.[71] And when settlement patterns changed, assumptions about schooling proved unworkable. When villages ceased to be the characteristic mode of living, schools had to move to the country, too.

The second new element was the environment. Overriding all other concerns was survival. Just as the school's location shifted to accommodate new living patterns, its calendar was altered to fit with agricultural necessity. School was held in the winter so it would not interfere with farming operations, and attendance varied with weather conditions. Children who lived on the far side of a stream, for example, could not get to school during periods of flooding. It was not realistic for teachers to assume that students would arrive at precisely the same time every day or that everybody would be present on a given day.

Thus, European colonizing authorities—British, French, Spanish, Swedish, and Dutch—all intended to retain control of education. By the middle of the sixteenth century, that control was already slipping in Mexico, as we have seen with Sahagún. In the northeastern colonies, and certainly on the frontier beyond them, most local communities were effectively in control of their own schools by 1700.

Schools cropped up as soon as enough families lived within two or three miles of each other. Members of these communities usually constructed one-room buildings out of local materials, and sometimes the same building served as both school and church. Families either taxed themselves (usually in proportion to the amount of land owned or improved) or simply paid tuition. Often a combination of the two methods coexisted. Taxation often provided a base salary and the teacher was free to charge a specified fee per child, including a larger amount from those who had not paid any tax. There was nothing to stop enterprising teachers from getting up schools entirely based on fees subscribed by parents. Teachers usually collected any tuition due either monthly or at the end of term. They had a direct economic incentive for keeping pupils and parents satisfied.

The one-room community school was the dominant form of elementary instruction in America for more than two centuries. As late as 1928, the United States Office of Education noted that 63 percent (153,306) of all the elementary school buildings (244,128) in the country were still of the one-room variety.[72]

In the English-speaking colonies, community schools had a variety of labels—*petty, district* or *subdistrict, country, old field,* and others—but the most unusual label was *common school.* Trustees (usually three, five, or seven) elected by the community the school served made policy and paid the bills. They also hired the teacher. "Rates" (head taxes), tuition, and general monetary policy were open to discussion and vote by all adult heads of household at an annual meeting. These meetings were "invaluable laboratories of democracy," according to historian Wayne Fuller.[73]

Common schools reflected the languages, religions, and general cultural—even political—values of the communities they served. Because each school's geographic area was limited, it was not unusual to find a high degree of agreement among parents on these issues— especially during the early years of a settlement. The next biographical sketch illustrates how completely each community controlled the schooling for its children and how thoughtfully many teachers of one-room schools approached their tasks.

Christopher Dock (1698–1771)

German-speaking people settled in several colonies throughout the seventeenth century. William Penn visited the Rhine Valley in 1671 and 1677. In October 1683, thirteen Mennonite families came from Crefeld to settle in Philadelphia and founded Germantown. Waves of German

immigration followed. By 1727 an estimated 20,000 Germans had settled in Pennsylvania. English authorities grew so alarmed at the flow of
Germans that they required all male ship passengers over age sixteen to
swear a loyalty oath to King George II. By 1755 an estimated 80,000
Germans in Pennsylvania constituted more than one-third of the colony's citizens.[74]

Life

Historians know little of Christopher Dock's background before he
came to Pennsylvania. Most of the limited information we have about
his life is contained in *Schul-Ordnung (School Management)*, his treatise about his teaching methods. There are also immigration records and
letters of friends and acquaintances, including journalist and publisher
Christopher Sauer. Using these sparse records, historians have sur-
mised Christopher Dock's place of origin, his career in Germany, and the
date of his arrival in America.

Dock was born around 1698 in the Rhineland-Palatinate, a state located in western Germany along the Rhine River. He was almost certainly a teacher in this region. No information of his father's occupation
or his family's social status exists.[75] He was a Mennonite, a sect of a
European religious reform movement called *pietism*. Because of their
unorthodox beliefs, pietists suffered persecution from both Roman Catholics and Protestants. Dock came to America to escape persecution and to
teach according to his beliefs without outside interference. Arriving in
1718, Dock bought a farm near Skippack, Pennsylvania. For ten years,
he taught in Skippack and the nearby town of Salford. Then, in 1728,
Dock left teaching to be a full-time farmer. During this period he married and had several daughters. His writing contains no references to his
wife or children, so little is known of his family life. His will left a farm
to his oldest daughter.

In 1738, Dock returned to teaching. He also wrote poems and hymns
and was a calligrapher. He remained a schoolmaster for the rest of his
life. One day in 1771, he entered his schoolhouse alone. When he failed
to come out, someone discovered him dead kneeling at his desk with his
hands folded as if praying.

Pietist Beliefs

Like Dock, most early German immigrants to Pennsylvania were
Mennonite pietists. This new Christian sect rejected traditional views of
organized religion. Pietists "influenced all the churches of the Reformation." Whether in opposition or as a supplement to the doctrinal and
confessional emphasis of the Reformed and Lutheran churches, "they
emphasized 'heartfelt' religion accompanied by self-analysis based on a
personal, emotionally experienced conversion resulting in the application of this experience to daily life."[76]

Mennonites held that religion, as well as education, should be a matter of individual preference without government interference. In the German states however, church and state were allied, with the state assuming—as Luther and Melanchthon had advocated—more and more control over education. The government appointed, supervised, and paid teachers. Mennonite parents felt they had insufficient influence on their children's schooling, and that teachers were often negligent of their duties.

The Mennonites' strong opposition to this state system was a major reason they migrated to America. The community-based common school appealed to them. Thus, in Pennsylvania as in other colonies, people established schools under control of the families of the community. In Skippack, for example, the people built a schoolhouse in 1717 and appointed their own schoolmaster. Attendance was voluntary and most participants paid tuition. Parents expected to contribute to their children's education at home, while the schoolmaster complemented the parents' role. The first master of the new Skippack school was Christopher Dock.

Views on Education

Dock's educational ideas reflected Mennonite beliefs. In 1750, Christopher Sauer, Jr., a close friend and ex-pupil, asked Dock to write a treatise describing his teaching methods so that other teachers could learn from him. Dock hesitated because it might "appear that I wanted to set up for myself or with the world a reputation, testimonial, and ill-smelling honor, which, if it were indeed the case, would earn for me before God and all true Christian hearts no honor at all, but rather mockery and shame." He said such a work, "could be of no benefit to my soul's welfare and salvation. It would only be food for self-love. . . . Many souls have already been overpowered by this robber."[77]

Members of the Mennonite community urged Dock to relent. Despite reservations, his strong sense of duty to his friends and his calling won out. He "considered the spoiled state of youth and the many offenses of this world whereby youth is spoiled and is made to stumble by its elders," and decided to write about the best Christian methods of educating children.[78] The result was *Schul-Ordnung*, which was published after his death.

Dock wrote that education should be aimed at the internal development and spiritual growth of the child under the ultimate guidance of Christ. As did many eighteenth-century masters, Dock used Scripture to teach reading and numbers and to suggest models for good behavior. Rejecting the policy of restricting education to those wealthy enough to pay for it, he wrote: "The poor beggar's child in filth, rags, and lice, if he is otherwise good and willing to be taught, must be as dear to . . . [the schoolmaster] (even if he should not receive a penny for it in his life) as the child of a rich man, from whom he can expect good compensation in this life. Compensation for teaching the poor child follows in the next world."[79]

Dock also rejected corporal punishment, for violence could never contribute to the spiritual welfare of the child: "The slap of the hand, hazel twig, and birch rod are, to be sure, means to prevent an evil outburst, but they are not means for changing the wicked heart," he wrote. "All of us are by nature since the Fall [of Adam and Eve] in such a condition that we are more prone to evil than good, as long as the heart remains unchanged in this condition and is not renewed by the Spirit of God."[80]

For offenses such as swearing, lying, and stealing, Dock asked children to account for why they committed such acts. Often, he said, children did not realize that what they were doing was wrong. He would explain to them, using the Scriptures, the reasons the particular act was evil. If the child understood and promised to never do it again, no punishment followed. For repeated offenses, Dock would seat offenders on a punishment bench and have other pupils (bondsmen) monitor them. The more often they became guilty, he said, "the more bondsmen must be involved to remind them of their promise and admonish them very earnestly to be careful and avoid the punishment."[81] Dock knew—as many teachers since have discovered—that encouragement and peer pressure are more effective motivators than punishment. The pupils must understand for themselves the reasons for proper behavior instead of merely doing certain things because adults tell them to: "The words 'You shall' and 'You must' do not have the same tone as 'I obey with pleasure.' For the latter tone the schoolmaster needs no rod, and it is lovelier to hear and easier to answer for." Proper education must be based upon mutual love and respect. The teacher must sincerely love pupils if they are to return love and respect.[82]

During the last years of Dock's life, a political controversy over language broke out in Pennsylvania. English colonial leaders had long worried about the assimilation of the swelling German population, and in 1753, the British sponsored the formation of a Society for the Propagation of the Knowledge of God Among the Germans. This group founded charity schools for German children in six towns. Bilingual teachers sought to make children more proficient in English as a way of weaning them away from German. Sponsors of the project feared that, if Britain and France were to be at war, the Pennsylvania Germans might side with the French.

Benjamin Franklin and other prominent Pennsylvanians supported the English charity schools. Christopher Sauer, Sr. (and his son, who had studied with Dock), owned a German-language printing press and was a chief organ of opposition. From 1739, they issued a newspaper that was said to have been "universally read" by Germans.[83] Sauer and most other Pennsylvania Germans thought of themselves as loyal Americans and saw no inconsistency in keeping their mother tongue. The charity school movement soon failed, Christopher Sauer, Sr., died, and most Germans learned English. But the controversy over whether all Americans must use English and learn a single body of cultural knowledge is as alive today as in 1750.

As the eighteenth century drew to a close, many American leaders wrestled with two problems. One was how to get more respect for American culture from Europeans. They especially wanted acknowledgment from England that "the muses do not sicken and die" when they cross the Atlantic, as one writer put it. The other problem, actually the reverse of the first, was how to keep frontier influences from corrupting and barbarizing the more civilized East while continuing to adopt and adapt Native American and frontier knowledge into standard practice. The lives of Thomas Jefferson and Noah Webster illustrate these issues.

Noah Webster (1758–1843)

Noah was born on October 16, 1758 in Connecticut. He thought his early education inadequate, but he became a proficient reader and writer, and a master of journalistic style. His father was a staunch Calvinist of modest background and means; his mother claimed to have been descended from William Bradford, Governor of Plymouth. Noah imbibed many of the heady ideas of the Enlightenment, reading Rousseau and others. His religious enthusiasm was not pronounced in his earlier years.

In 1774, he entered Yale College. When he finished, there was no family business to enter, for his father's financial position was at a low point. The only professions open to him were teaching and the ministry. He briefly chose schoolteaching: "The education of youth [is] an employment of more consequence than making laws and preaching the gospel, because it lays the foundation on which both law and gospel rest for success."[84]

Faced with the difficulty of making his own way, his basic attitude was formed by his belief that he had prevailed against great odds. Joel Barlow, a Yale contemporary, expressed their common circumstances in a letter to Webster: "You and I are not the first in the world to have broken loose from college without friends and without fortune to push into public notice. Let us show the world a few more examples of men standing upon their own merit and rising in spite of obstacles."[85]

Webster proposed to do just that and, as his later writings show, he believed others could do the same with a little help. Anyone could rise in the world if only they formed the proper virtues and secured the necessary knowledge. He became increasingly convinced that religion and morality were essential foundations of virtue and of social and political stability. By 1808, he was a firm Calvinist, and he caught the spirit of the times and became an ardent nationalist. Thus was formed the second basic attitude that permeated all of Webster's thinking and writing. He was an American through and through.

Noah Webster was versatile. He was at different times editor, pamphleteer, compiler of schoolbooks, lawyer, politician, and scholar. He labored the longest part of his adult life on *An American Dictionary of the English Language* (1828). This was the culminating work of his plan for the education of American youth begun in 1783 with the publication of his first schoolbook, *A Grammatical Institute of the English Language*. This famous speller was to exercise an enormous influence upon Americans. The original copy had 119 pages, but it gradually evolved into a much longer book, containing fables, woodcuts, lessons on domestic relations, and a moral catechism. Webster intended to call the speller *The American Instructor*, but Ezra Stiles persuaded him to give it the longer, more pretentious title. As the speller evolved in 1788, he changed the title to *The American Spelling Book*. To the public, it was simply the "blue-backed speller."

Standard practice in Europe and America had been to spell vernacular words however they sounded. People who would not have dreamed of spelling a Latin, Greek, or Hebrew word more than one way would routinely spell some English words in two or three ways within the same document. Thus, *civilitie, civiliti,* and *civilitee,* might all be acceptable spellings for *civility*. Webster's dictionary and speller standardized spelling and usage patterns.

More important than Americanizing spelling was the incorporation of a large number of new American words. "Europeans, upon first arriving in America, lacked the words to name what they saw in the new environment," observes anthropologist Jack Weatherford:

> They recognized some of the animals, such as deer, bear, and wolves, and misapplied European names to some creatures, such as buffalo and robins, but even when they exhausted all of these names, America had strange animals, plants, geographical configurations, and weather that needed new words. From the beginning the Europeans had to use Native American words to name animals such as *moose, caribou, raccoon, opossum, chipmunk, barracuda, manatee, cougar, puma, jaguar, terrapin, chigger,* and *skunk.*
>
> They also had to use Indian names for trees and plants such as *hickory, pecan, persimmon, mahogany, mangrove, maypop, mesquite, yucca,* and *saguaro*. Particularly in the area of food plants, the colonists took many of the Indian names, including *maize, hominy, squash, avocado, pemmican, manioc, cassava, papaya, pawpaw, tapioca, succotash,* and *scuppernong.*
>
> Even the topography of the continent appeared strange and alien to the Europeans, and they had to adopt Indian words such as the Choctaw *bayou* and the Taino *savanna,* the latter identifying a grassy plain with few trees, a concept also expressed by the Quechua word *pampas.* In the Canadian tundra, explorers adopted the Cree word *muskeg* to denote the sphagnum bogs of decaying vegetable matter. The upland coastal

swamps usually found in wooded areas of the southern Atlantic Coast became known as *pocosin* from the Delaware word for such areas. The Algonquian word *podunk,* meaning a corner of isolated land or a small neck of land, passed into English as the name of a Massachusetts community, but came to signify any remote locale. . . .

Even the weather of the Americas called for new words. The Europeans immediately recognized that the giant storms that blew up from the Caribbean in the late summer and fall far surpassed in scale and ferocity the simple squalls and rain showers implied in the English word *storm.* They had to use a Carib word, *hurricane,* to name the fierce storms of the Caribbean. Similarly, white settlers applied the Salish word *chinook* to both the moist, warm winds that blew in from the Pacific and the warm, dry winds that blew from the Rocky Mountains onto the northern plains of the United States and Canada. From the Paiute language the settlers took the word *pogonip* to describe the ice fog or clouds of ice crystals common in the western mountains.

The word *blizzard* probably derives from an Indian word, although its origin is now lost. According to the *Oxford English Dictionary,* the first written record of *blizzard* comes from the frontiersman Colonel Davy Crockett in 1834. Since Crockett used it without explanation, as though the reader would already know the word, we may assume that *blizzard* had already attained common usage by that time. . . .[86]

Webster's dictionary and speller naturalized into American English many Native American terms and new American English terms to describe phenomena with which Europeans had previously been unacquainted. "New circumstances . . . call for words, new phrases, and the transfer of old words to new objects," as Thomas Jefferson would observe.[87]

Webster's purposes were clear. He intended to promote American literature and uniformity of speech, patriotism and nationalism, morality and virtue, and religious truth. He also wanted to develop a system of national education. He said *The American Spelling Book* might facilitate the education of youth and enable teachers "to instill into their minds with the first rudiments of language, some just ideas of religion, morals and domestic economy." Webster thought of the speller as a vehicle of self-advancement, and an "engine of nationalism."[88] In fact, all of Webster's schoolbooks aimed to prepare youth for getting ahead. They would teach the young American how to speak and write correctly and how to behave while providing a body of useful knowledge and a basis for morality. Although the speller did not contain morning or evening prayers, it was heavily laden with religious material, and later Webster incorporated a "moral Catechism." The virtuous person would be religious, and the religious person would be virtuous. Religion, he thought, served as the basis of good character.

Webster was optimistic about improving people's morals and manners ("character in action") under the proper conditions. He believed the United States was the ideal place to try this experiment. Here was an opportunity to build a new society, free of previous corruptions. Uniform laws, manners, and language had created national character and cohesion in older societies. The United States needed its own uniformity, and education of young American republicans was of primary importance as the forming of nationality and national character needed to be deliberate and could be only accomplished through a general system of education for all Americans.

Webster thought "diffusing literary and moral improvement among the poorer classes of citizens, in connection with religious instruction, will be no less our pleasure than it is our duty." He saw this as the means of drawing from the obscure retreats of poverty the miserable victims of ignorance and vice, enlightening "their minds and correct[ing] their evil habits," and "raise[ing] them to the ranks of intelligent, industrious, and useful members of society."[89] His was a reassertion of John Brinsley's ideal (1622) of compelling "a barbarous people to civilitie."

Like Locke, one basic criterion by which Webster measured all educational activity was usefulness. For Webster, what determined which parts of European education were applicable to America was usefulness and whether they were conducive to republicanism. Sending boys to Europe for an education (including the "grand tour" of Europe that wealthy families often provided for their sons) or securing teachers from there was a mistake, he argued. Boys educated in Europe during their impressionable years were apt to return as Englishmen, Scotsmen, or Frenchmen. He proposed substituting a tour of the United States as the capstone of an American youth's liberal education.

Webster wanted English as the chief focus of language study. The "dead languages" (Latin and Greek) had once been necessary and were still valuable for scholars and members of the learned professions, but English was now the repository of as much learning as the languages of Europe, and it had many advantages other languages did not possess. What gain would a merchant, mechanic, or farmer derive from an acquaintance with the Greek and Roman tongues? Even if Latin and Greek had value, would the advantages compensate for the loss of valuable time employed in studying them to achieve competence? "Life is short, and every hour should be employed to good purposes," he affirmed. How could parents justify years of studying classical syntax when they could be better spent on English writers of ethics, geography, history, commerce, and government? Webster conceded that Latin was useful for epitaphs, inscriptions on monuments and medals, and writing designed for perpetuity.[90]

Webster approved the study of grammar. He agreed that memorizing definitions, rules, and parts of speech was irksome, but thought that if grammar could be "taught by the help of visible objects, [so that] children [could] perceive that differences of words arise from differences in

things, . . . the study [could become] entertaining as well as improving."
The senses were the "inlets of our knowledge." Abstract definitions
could be repeated without being understood, "but that a table is the
name of an article and hard or square is its property is a distinction
obvious to the senses and consequently within a child's capacity."

Educational Criticisms

Webster advocated an elective system in higher education. Why could
not students, as they were in the "common schools," be advanced from
lower to higher classes as a reward for industry and achievements rather
than moving from one year to the next with their classmates? He advocated specialization instead of a broad education, and did not believe that
a planter should have to study conic sections or a merchant the rules of
Greek: "Life is too short to acquire, and the mind . . . too feeble to contain,
the whole circle of sciences." Even the greatest genius could not master
all subjects. People intending to qualify for a profession, "should attend
closely to those branches of learning which lead to it."[91]

Webster described the arts and sciences that every male should learn.
Everyone should write and speak their native language correctly; and
"the rules of arithmetic are indispensably requisite." A boy's education
should be adjusted according to his intended occupation. The farming
areas should provide the country schools with "some easy system of
practical husbandry." Reading books of this type would store in mind
facts that might not be understood in youth but which later would be
recalled into practice. "This would . . . pave the way for [agricultural]
improvements." Young men destined for the mercantile line, after mastering their own language, might then study a living language or two
that would be useful in their business. They should also study chronology, geography, mathematics, history, laws of commercial nations, business principles, and general principles of government. By sixteen, boys
would complete this practical education. "Such a system of English education is . . . preferable to a university education," Webster concluded.
"Indeed it appears to me that what is now called a *liberal education*
disqualifies a man for business."[92]

Webster worried about what he saw as the lack of good teachers in
academies and common schools. Schools should be staffed with able men
of "unblemished reputations"; it is not clear whether he thought women
might also qualify. He preferred no education to a bad one, for the vices
and habits that children would pick up from incompetent and immoral
schoolmasters were much more difficult to eradicate than "to impress
new ideas." If the pupils had esteem and respect for the master, he would
have authority. This in turn would lessen the likelihood of dependence
upon the rod because pupils would fear the displeasure of the teacher
more than the rod.

Webster also saw as a defect of schools too many books filled with
undue respect for foreign and ancient nations. "Every child in America

should be acquainted with his own country" and "should read books that furnish . . . ideas that will be useful to him in life and practice," wrote Webster. "As soon as he opens his lips, he should rehearse the history of his own country, he should lisp the praise of liberty and of those illustrious heroes and statesmen who have wrought a revolution in her favor." Webster stood ready to write the texts for this purpose.[93]

Webster was also convinced of the importance of education for American women, because they formed the disposition of youth and controlled the manners of the nation. Women should be taught to speak and write English in addition to arithmetic, geography, and literature. He did not feel he could prescribe a course of reading for all women, but he did think that they should be acquainted with the writers on human life and manners. Their education should form their manners, and it should be useful—that is, should fit them for traditional forms of female activity.

Webster had a clear view of what was needed. Together, the American states were by no means a nation. They possessed for the most part a common language, one criterion of a nation, but the number of non-English peoples was substantial. Irish, Scots, French, and others flocked to the United States. There were the old Dutch and German groups, and immigration continued apace: "during the quarter-century from 1790 to 1815, . . . two hundred and fifty thousand came."[94] Webster bent his efforts to forge an American nationality and sense of identity. He wanted to develop a sense of nationality, patriotism, and a prosperous body of individuals and nation. At the same time, he became prosperous and well known through his book sales. And he advanced the idea of a common culture and "standard" English usage through his dictionary. He was optimistic because he thought the forces of enlightened morality were defeating barbaric diversity.

A more famous contemporary of Webster's—a few years older, considerably wealthier, and from aristocratic Virginia stock—would be famous for politics. This was Thomas Jefferson, primary author of the Declaration of Independence and third president of the United States. He wanted to be remembered for his efforts on behalf of education.

Thomas Jefferson (1743–1826)

Thomas Jefferson was born on April 13, 1743 to Peter and Jane Randolph Jefferson in Shadewell, Virginia, almost at the foot of Monticello. The land, which was to become Albemarle County, was one of small, tree-covered mountains, fertile valleys, and clear streams running between shaded riverbanks. The land was part of Thomas's earliest education, land which his father, Peter, surveyed.

Peter Jefferson was a prominent surveyor. His work included assisting Professor Joshua Frey of the College of William and Mary in establishing the boundary between Virginia and North Carolina for the official map of Virginia. The Jefferson frontier hospitality attracted such visitors as Ontassere, a famous Cherokee orator. Native Americans often camped near the Jefferson home on their way to councils in Williamsburg. Thomas Jefferson's early contact with Native Americans formed a lasting sensitivity to their plight against a civilization that was slowly engulfing them.[95]

Thomas's early encounter with Native Americans not only sensitized him to their needs, but he early recognized that Native Americans had much to offer European immigrants. He himself collected ethnographic accounts of Native Americans and encouraged others to do so as well. He asked Charles Thomason, perpetual secretary of the Continental Congress and full member of the Delaware Nation, to prepare extensive material for *Notes on the State of Virginia*. Thomas Jefferson did not go as far as Thomas Paine or Benjamin Franklin in advocating the adoption of Native American ways, but he incorporated such elements as removing incompetent public servants through impeachment rather than assassination and the addition of new territories as full partner states, rather than staying permanent colonies to the original thirteen states.[96]

A supportive home environment prepared a strong foundation for young Thomas. Peter Jefferson, though he had little formal schooling himself, was well read and one of his son's greatest teachers. By the age of five Thomas was enrolled in an English school, and at nine he attended a Latin grammar school under the instruction of Scottish clergyman William Douglas. After the death of his father in 1758, Thomas spent three years at the classical school of Rev. James Maury, an Anglican linguist. He studied Latin, Greek, French, the classics, and the violin. He learned to dance a minuet, and display the character and moral attitudes required for community respect.

In 1760, Jefferson entered the College of William and Mary. Although his educational formation had been that of a gentleman, he had absorbed the spirit of freedom and independence prevalent on the frontier. He thought the college narrow, provincial, sectarian, and preoccupied by excessive loyalty to the crown, the favor of slaveholding planters, and a general fear of progress. Describing William and Mary as a boarding school for boys, he stayed only two years. Despite his disapproval of the school, Jefferson formed many friendships at William and Mary. These included Governor Fauquier, Peyton Randolph, Patrick Henry, John Page (who would later become Governor of Virginia), and Professor William Small, whom Jefferson called a "model by which he measured his aims and conduct."[97] After leaving college, Jefferson devoted five years to the study of law and Anglo Saxon with lawyer George Wythe, mentor of John Marshall, first United States Supreme Court chief justice. At the same time, he began what turned out to be a lifelong interest in collecting a library. (By 1815 it contained 6,487 books and was sold for $23,950 to form the nucleus for the Library of Congress.)

Beginning in 1767, Jefferson spent his time managing his farm and practicing law. On January 1, 1772 he married a widow named Martha Wayles Skelton, and in the summer of 1776 he represented Virginia in the Continental Congress. Although writing the Declaration of Independence is his best-known accomplishment, Jefferson declined to continue in Congress. Instead, he returned to Virginia to propose legislation that shaped the spirit of its constitution.

Jefferson wrote a bill "for the more general diffusion of knowledge." It proposed that each county be divided into "hundreds" or wards about six miles square (roughly the size of New England "townships"). Each ward was responsible for teaching reading, writing, and arithmetic. Citizens not able to pay could send their children to school at community expense for up to three years. After that, everyone was to pay for instruction except a select few from those "whom nature hath endowed with genius and virtue." Every year a "visitor" (official) would select the boy of "best genius" from each school to attend one of twenty grammar schools to be established in the state. These were to be advanced classical schools teaching Greek, Latin, geography, and mathematics. Boys thus selected would have one or two years of tuition-free instruction, after which only "the best genius" of the group would be allowed to finish the college preparatory course. By this means "twenty of the best geniuses will be raked from the rubbish annually, and instructed, at the public expense." At the end of six years instruction, one-half would be discontinued (from among whom the grammar schools would be supplied with future masters) and the other half, chosen for the "superiority of their parts and disposition," would be sent for three years to the College of William and Mary. These ten would then furnish "to the wealthier part of the people convenient schools at which their children may be educated at their own expense." By this meritocratic competition at least of few of "those . . . whom nature hath fitly formed and disposed to become useful instruments for the public," Jefferson wrote, "should be . . . educated at the common expense of all, [rather] than that the happiness of all should be confined to the weak or wicked."[98]

Jefferson failed to get sufficient legislative support to pass the bill, as a majority of his contemporaries trusted their community schools more than did Jefferson. His plan was too classical and too elite for many of his practical-minded fellow Virginians. Bills to create a public library and to change the College of William and Mary to be more like European universities also failed. Although defeated, Jefferson managed to eliminate two professorships of divinity and had them replaced with law, medicine, anatomy, chemistry, and modern languages. Jefferson thought useful facts from Greek, Roman, European, and American history preferable to the Bible for moral training: "History, can apprise students of the past and enable them to judge the future, while availing them of the experience of other times and other nations."[99]

Jefferson was both an apostle of American democracy and a product of his times and education. He favored women's education for conventional roles. Of his own daughters' education he said, "Considering that they would be placed in a country situation, where little aid could be obtained from abroad, I thought it essential to give them a solid education, which might enable them, when become mothers, to educate their own daughters, and even to direct the course for sons, should their fathers be lost, or incapable, or inattentive."[100] His daughter Martha made the education of her children the object of her life, and she and her father put together a catalogue of books for a course of reading.

According to Jefferson, a great obstacle to good education for women was the inordinate passion for novels, and the time lost in that reading which should be instructively employed, which poisons the mind, destroys its tone, and revolts against wholesome reading:

> Reason and fact, plain and unadorned, are rejected. . . . The result is a bloated imagination, sickly judgment, and disgust toward all the real businesses of life. . . . For a like reason, too, much poetry should not be indulged. Some is useful for forming style and taste. Pope, Dryden, Thompson, Shakespeare, and of the French, Moliere, Racine, the Corneilles, may be read with pleasure and improvement.[101]

Jefferson believed the study of French "an indispensible part of education for both sexes." He also advocated dancing, drawing, music, and household management:

> Drawing is thought less of in this country than in Europe. It is an innocent and engaging amusement, often useful, and a qualification not to be neglected in one who is to become a mother and an instructor. Music is invaluable where a person has an ear. Where they have not, it should not be attempted. It furnishes a delightful recreation for the hours of respite from the cares of the day, and lasts us through life. The taste of this country, too, calls for this accomplishment more strongly than for either of the others.
>
> I need say nothing of household economy, in which the mothers of our country are generally skilled, and generally careful to instruct their daughters. We all know its value, and that diligence and dexterity in all its processes are inestimable treasures. The order and economy of a house are as honorable to the mistress as those of a farm to the master, and if either be neglected, ruin follows, and children destitute of the means of living.[102]

At the age of 73 Jefferson, having failed to reform William and Mary as extensively as he thought necessary, undertook a successful campaign to found the University of Virginia. The form and architecture appear to have been his own, and both were strongly European. Many of the faculty were from Europe. Earlier, Jefferson had suggested transferring the University of Geneva to the United States. (George Washington rejected the plan.)

Jefferson bridged the European Enlightenment and grass roots frontier democracy. Given his mother's claim to an elite family and the substantial estate his father left, Jefferson might have settled for a comfortable life as a leisured Virginia gentleman. Instead, he devoted much of his energy to public service. Except for the University of Virginia, most of his specific educational proposals were not enacted. His optimism about the improvability of society through education became part of the shared faith of a group of nineteenth-century reformers who called themselves the "friends of education" (Chapter 8). In common with Protagoras, they thought that even the worst cases could be improved to some extent by a proper education. And they agreed with Jefferson that instruction should be systematized at the state or federal level.

> I look to the diffusion of light and education as the resource most to be relied on. . . . That every man shall be made virtuous, by any process whatever, is, indeed, no more to be expected, than that every tree shall be made to bear fruit and every plant nourishment. The brier and the bramble can never become the vine and olive; but their asperities may be softened by culture, and their properties improved to usefulness in the order and economy of the world. And I do hope that, in the present spirit of extending to the great mass of mankind the blessings of instruction, I see a prospect of great advancement in the happiness of the human race.[103]

Meanwhile in the West, the process of learning democracy through experience and interaction with Native Americans continued without regard to the supposed classical models. Even after the founding of the United States, indigenous people continued to play a significant role in the evolution of democracy because of their sustained interactions with settlers on the frontier. People on the frontier constantly reinvented democracy and channeled it into the eastern establishment of the United States.[104]

SUMMARY

The discovery and colonization of America by Europeans transformed Western society. The cost in human life was high among colonizers and was staggering among enslaved Africans and embattled Native Americans. Europe was enriched. An amazing cornucopia of foods, fibers, and pharmaceuticals poured out. New technologies resulted. Education became more localized, practical, and community-based than it was in Europe.

More subtly—and more importantly—most Americans became in an important sense bi- or tricultural. While that condition inevitably caused some anxiety and conflict, it produced a degree of self-awareness and improvisation not otherwise possible. Bernardino de Sahagún remained a

Spaniard, but he got beyond the limitations of monoculturalism by steeping himself in the Nahuatl language. Sor Juana Inés de la Cruz transcended the limits imposed by European culture because the unique conditions under which she lived allowed it. Christopher Dock demonstrated that one could be just as loyal and valuable a citizen speaking German or speaking English, and that firm, insightful kindness in a teacher always gets better results than anger and punishment—in any language. Noah Webster illustrates both the yearning for cultural unanimity and the optimism made possible by diversity. And finally, Thomas Jefferson reflected great faith in education's possibilities and a residue of elitist suspicion that educational arrangements should not be left to individuals and communities.

Much of our contemporary world is a result of the millions of cultural interactions of the sixteenth, seventeenth, and eighteenth centuries. Our issues of equity, fairness, and justice are rooted in the conflicts of that period. Possible solutions can be informed by our knowledge of them.

NOTES

1. William H. McNeill, *The Rise of the West: A History of the Human Community* (Chicago: University of Chicago Press, 1963), 567.

2. Walter Prescott Webb, *The Great Frontier* (Boston: Houghton Mifflin, 1952), 33.

3. Jack Weatherford, *Indian Givers: How the Indians of the Americas Transformed the World* (New York: Fawcett Columbine, 1988), 57–58.

4. Todorov, *The Conquest of America: The Question of the Other,* trans. Richard Howard (New York: Harper & Row, 1984), 4–5.

5. Cited in Todorov, *The Conquest of America,* 10.

6. Herbert Eugene Bolton, trans., "A Brief Report . . . ," *Spanish Exploration in the Southwest, 1542–1706,* ed. Herbert Eugene Bolton (New York: Barnes and Noble, [1908] 1946), 131.

7. Quoted in Todorov, *The Conquest of America,* 123.

8. Quoted in Todorov, *The Conquest of America,* 190.

9. Antonio de la Ascension, "The Method to be Observed in Subduing and Settling the Realm of the Californias," in Bolton, *Spanish Exploration,* 128.

10. See Todorov, *The Conquest of America,* 217.

11. As cited in Todorov, *The Conquest of America,* 220.

12. Todorov, *The Conquest of America,* 220.

13. Philip G. Altbach and Gail P. Kelly, *Education and Colonialism* (New York: Longman, 1978), 15.

14. Quoted in Todorov, *The Conquest of America, 221;* see also Luis Nicolau D'Olwer, *Fray Bernardino de Sahagún (1499–1590)* (México, D.F.: Bibliógrafos Asociados, S. A., [1949] 1990), 125–132.

15. Todorov, *The Conquest of America,* 221.

16. Todorov, *The Conquest of America,* 240–249.

17. Todorov, *The Conquest of America,* 237–238.

18. Scipio A. J. Colin III, "Voices from Beyond the Veil: Marcus Garvey, the Universal Negro Improvement Association, and the Education of African-Ameripean Adults" (Ed.D. diss., Northern Illinois University, 1987).

19. Weatherford, *Indian Givers,* 146–147.

20. Josefina Muriel, *Cultura femenina novohispana,* (México: Universidad Nacional Autonoma de Mexico, 1982), 143.

21. Anita Arroyo, *Razón y pasion de Sor Juana* (México: Editorial Porrua, 1971), 10.

22. Francisco Monterde, *Sor Juana Inés de la Cruz: Obras completas* (México: Editorial Porrua, 1985), 830.

23. Monterde, *Sor Juana,* 830.

24. Octavio Paz, *Sor Juana Inés de la Cruz, o las trampas de la fe* (México: Fondo de Cultura Economica, 1982, 1988), 126.

25. Muriel, *Cultura,* 144.

26. Sor Juana Inés, *Reply to Sor Philothea,* trans. Alan S. Trueblood (Cambridge, MA: Harvard University Press, 1988), 211.

27. Julio Jimenez Rueda, *Los empenos de una casa* (México: UNAM, 1940, 1964), ix.

28. Arroyo, *Razón,* 19; Muriel, *Cultura,* 144.

29. Monterde, *Sor Juana,* 830.

30. Muriel, *Cultura,* 144.

31. Diego Calleja, *Vida de la madre Juana Inés de la Cruz—religiosa profesa en el covento de San Jeronimo de la cuidad imperial de México;* cited in Muriel, *Cultura,* 144.

32. Paz, *Trampas,* 130.

33. Paz, *Sor Juana Inés de la Cruz or, the Traps of Faith,* trans. Margaret Sayers Peden (Cambridge, MA: Belknap Press of Harvard University Press, 1988), 98.

34. Antonio Alatorre, "Sor Juana y los hombres," *Temas de historia Mexiquense* (México: El Colegio Mexiquense, 1987), 135.

35. Muriel, *Cultura,* 146.

36. Norma Salazar Davis, "Sor Juana Ines de la Cruz, Feminist and Educator," *Journal of the Midwest History of Education Society* 19 (1991): 33–43.

37. Alan S. Trueblood, trans., *A Sor Juana Anthology* (Cambridge, MA: Harvard University Press, 1988), 213. Most historians and biographers who have commented on Juana's struggle with her decision (e.g., Muriel, *Cultura,* 147) assume that she had the ongoing advice of Antonio Nuñez de Miranda, a respected Jesuit several years her senior. He would become her confessor, but not earlier than 1669. At that point Father Nuñez probably joined other "learned persons" in assuring her that religious obligations would not interfere with her studies and that the church approved of nuns pursuing an education.

38. This was in reference to a different house and a century later, but apparently all Carmelite houses had similar characteristics. See Asunción Lavrin, "Values and Meaning of Monastic Life for Nuns in Colonial Mexico," *Catholic Historical Review* 58 (October 1972): 375.

39. Muriel, *Cultura,* 147; Arroyo, *Razón,* 30.

40. Oviedo, *Vida Exemplar,* 133–134.

41. "Letter from Sister Juana Inés de la Cruz written to the R[everend] F[ather] M[aster] Antonio Nuñez of the Society of Jesus," in Paz, *Sor Juana,* 500.

42. Paz, *Sor Juana,* 131.

43. "Letter from Sister Juana Inés," in Paz, *Sor Juana,* 496.

44. Alatorre, *Sor Juana,* 141.

45. Alatorre, *Sor Juana,* 142.

46. "Letter from Sister Juana Inés," in Paz, *Sor Juana,* 495–496.

47. "Letter from Sister Juana Inés," in Paz, *Sor Juana,* 496–497.

48. "Letter from Sister Juana Inés," in Paz, *Sor Juana,* 496–497.

49. "Letter from Sister Juana Inés," in Paz, *Sor Juana,* 499–500, 502.

50. Monterde, *Sor Juana,* 109.

51. Fernández de Santa Cruz wrote her on November 25 saying that he had her *Carta* printed. Presumably he sent one or more copies along with his letter. Letter trans. Norma Salazar with assistance from Katrina Davis Salazar.

52. Lewis M. Hoskins, "Class and Clash in Seventeenth Century Mexico" (Ph.D. diss., University of Michigan, 1945), 160.

53. José Ignacio Rubio Mañe, *El virreinato: Orígenes y jurisdicciones, y dinámica social de los virreyes,* 4 vols. (México: UNAM, 1983), 2: 42–43.

54. Hoskins, "Class and Clash in Seventeenth Century Mexico," 178.

55. Antonio de Robles, *Diario de Sucesos notables, 1665–1703,* ed. Antonio Castro Leal, 3 vols. (México, D.F.: Editorial Porrúa, 1972), 258.

56. Reales cédulas, 23 February 1692, vol. 24, fol. 7–8, Archivo General de la Nación, México, D.F.

57. Paz, *Sor Juana,* 39.

58. The fact that Fernández de Santa Cruz had refused Galve's "request" for grain from Puebla during the crisis in Mexico City probably strengthened Aguiar's hand against Santa Cruz.

59. Margaret Sayers Peden, trans., *A Woman of Genius: The Intellectual Autobiography of Sor Juana Inés de la Cruz* (Salisbury, CT: Lime Rock Press, 1982), 10.

60. Trueblood, *A Sor Juana Anthology,* 226.

61. "Letter from Sister Juana Inés," in Paz, *Sor Juana,* 499.

62. "Letter from Sister Juana Inés," in Paz, *Sor Juana,* 499.

63. "Letter from Sister Juana Inés," in Paz, *Sor Juana,* 499.

64. Trueblood, *A Sor Juana Anthology,* 212.

65. Trueblood, *A Sor Juana Anthology,* 215.

66. Trueblood, *A Sor Juana Anthology,* 217.

67. Trueblood, *A Sor Juana Anthology,* 218.

68. Trueblood, *A Sor Juana Anthology,* 224.

69. Trueblood, *A Sor Juana Anthology,* 226.

70. Harold Stubblefield, "Learning from the Discipline of History," *Adult Education: Evolution and Achievements in a Developing Field of Study,* ed. John M. Peters and Peter Jarvis (San Francisco: Jossey-Bass, 1991), 335.

71. Public Records of the Colony of Connecticut, 1678–1689 (Hartford, CT: F. A. Brown, 1882), 8. For a survey of the history of American education, see John Pulliam, *History of Education in America,* 4th ed. (Columbus, OH: Charles E. Merrill, 1980).

72. U.S. Department of the Interior, *Statistics of State School Systems, 1927–1928,* Bulletin 1930, No. 5 (Washington, D.C.: Government Printing Office, 1930), 30.

73. Wayne Edison Fuller, *The Old Country School: The Story of Rural Education in the Middle West* (Chicago: University of Chicago Press, 1982), 45.

74. Samuel Edwin Weber, *The Charity School Movement in Colonial Pennsylvania* (New York: Arno Press and the New York Times, [1905] 1969), 7–10.

75. Gerald C. Studer, trans., *Christopher Dock: Colonial Schoolmaster* (Scottdale, PA: Herald Press, 1967), 35–45. All biographical information is from this source.

76. Studer, *Christopher Dock,* 19.

77. Christopher Dock, *Schul-Ordnung* in *Christopher Dock: Colonial School-master,* trans. Gerald Studer, 268–269.

78. Dock, *Schul-Ordnung,* 271.

79. Dock, *Schul-Ordnung,* 272.

80. Dock, *Schul-Ordnung,* 282.

81. Dock, *Schul-Ordnung,* 283–284.

82. Dock, *Schul-Ordnung,* 284.

83. William Smith, *A Brief State of the Province of Pennsylvania,* 3rd ed. (London: Printed for G. Griffith, 1756), 28 as cited in Weber, *The Charity School Movement,* 21.

84. Frederick Rudolph, ed., *Essays on Education in the Early Republic* (Cambridge, MA: Harvard University Press, 1965), 59.

85. Harry R. Warfel, *Noah Webster: School Master to America* (New York: Macmillan, 1936), 735–736.

86. Jack Weatherford, *Native Roots: How the Indians Enriched America* (New York: Fawcett Columbine, 1991), 198–199.

87. Robert McCann, William Cran, and Robert MacNeil, *The Story of English* (New York: Viking, 1986), 111.

88. Noah Webster, *The American Spelling Book, Containing the Rudiments of the English Language,* last rev. ed. (Wells River, VT: Ira White, 1843), vi.

89. Warfel, *Noah Webster,* 139.

90. Rudolph, *Essays,* 72–77.

91. Rudolph, *Essays,* 45–46, 51.

92. Rudolph, *Essays,* 48–55.

93. Rudolph, *Essays,* 55–60.

94. Marcus Lee Hansen, *The Atlantic Migration, 1607–1860* (New York: Harper Torchbooks, 1961), 47.

95. Charles Flinn Arrowood, ed., *Thomas Jefferson and Education in a Republic* (New York: McGraw Hill, 1930), 4.

96. Weatherford, *Indian Givers,* 133–145.

97. Arrowood, *Thomas Jefferson,* 7.

98. Arrowood, *Thomas Jefferson,* 81–82.

99. Arrowood, *Thomas Jefferson,* 86–87.

100. Arrowood, *Thomas Jefferson,* 177.

101. Arrowood, *Thomas Jefferson,* 177–180.

102. Arrowood, *Thomas Jefferson,* 177–180.

103. Thomas Jefferson, *Democracy,* ed. Saul K. Padover (New York: D. Appleton-Century, 1939), 141–142.

104. Weatherford, *Indian Givers,* 147.

The Friends of Education

Most European immigrants to America came from regions that were officially Roman Catholic or Protestant, and some came from areas that were in dispute. Even nonbelievers in Europe could not avoid religious taxation and citizenship rights and responsibilities anchored in sectarianism.

As members of different sects emigrated, and as previous immigrants disagreed over doctrinal matters, they realized that in America people could not be forced to acquiesce in beliefs with which they disagreed or stay in a community where they felt oppressed. The right to vote had been tied to orthodoxy in Massachusetts, Connecticut, and Virginia, but on the frontier governance was not often associated with any established church. People quickly learned the value of ignoring differences that were simply personal beliefs. Indeed, apparent indifference to sectarian religion by many frontier residents was one of the worrisome indicators to eastern Americans and to New Englanders recently arrived at the frontier, a sign that established values were in jeopardy.

There were several waves of religious revivalism. The first one, called the *Great Awakening,* ran from 1720 to the 1740s. Persuasive evangelists advocated more feeling, more emotional enthusiasm in religion. (The Pennsylvania pietists discussed in Chapter 7 were part of this.) In concentrated periods of preaching (revivals), many people converted. While the enthusiasm of the moment passed quickly for some, new sects—or new branches of existing religious groups—resulted from the converts. Missionizing revivalists preached regularly in America. Several sects sponsored these, notably the Methodists (dissenting Anglicans) who sent "circuit riders" throughout the frontier supporting themselves by preaching.

Revivals came to be frequent activities in many parts of the country, especially in summer. In remote areas, they furnished an important social outlet. People came from miles around, camped out, heard sermons every day, met new people (young singles used this as an opportunity for courting), and argued about theological, political, philosophical, and economic ideas.[1]

From about 1800 to 1830, revivals became so numerous that some historians have referred to the phenomenon as the "second great awakening." From this period, and originating on the frontier in western New York, came such new denominations as the Church of Jesus Christ of Latter Day Saints (Mormons), the Disciples of Christ, and several "spiritualist" groups.[2] Each of these groups later splintered while older denominations, such as Methodists, Baptists, and Presbyterians, also fragmented into multiple subgroups. In addition, New England Congregationalist missionaries, with Calvinist zeal, became interested in spreading Christian doctrine to Africa and the Pacific.

All this religious activity had a profound impact on the way education developed in two closely related ways. First, the progressive splintering of Protestant sects provided a forum and a practical means of self-determination for people who might otherwise have been educationally disenfranchised. People tend to group themselves socially according to status, income or property, and shared values or beliefs. Hierarchies of power and influence tend to develop within their social organizations. Every time even a small number of people within an established sect began to feel excluded or estranged from the leadership there was an opportunity to convince like-minded folk to break away and form a new group. Those who spearheaded the revolt became instant leaders, influential in setting the new sect's rules.

Second, one of the early actions of most new groups was to open schools, especially academies or colleges. A Greek word resurrected in the Renaissance, *academy* was the term religious dissenters in Scotland and England used when they started their own institutes for sons who were barred from Oxford and Cambridge. As some of these dissenters (including clergy) immigrated to America, they became teachers and brought the academic concept with them.[3] Typically the curriculum included the classical grammar education plus practical subjects—accounting, surveying, navigation—and modern languages, algebra, science, philosophy, and religion. While a major reason for founding academies was theological, the net effect was to broaden educational opportunity. Any time parents felt their children were not readily accepted, they could leave an established sect to start another where their children would feel welcome.

The new groups generated on the American frontier, such as Methodists and southern Baptists, stressed local (congregational) governance over hierarchical control. Eventually, local governance found its ultimate expression in the Disciples of Christ and their later breakout groups, the Churches of Christ, who had no organization or officials beyond the congregational level. In religion, it was the organizational equivalent of the common or district school that recognized no authority beyond that of the local trustees. "This democratic revolution in theology wrenched the queen of sciences from the learned speculations of Harvard, Yale, and Princeton men and encouraged the blacksmith, cooper, and tiller of the soil not only to experience salvation but also to explain the process," writes religious historian Nathan O. Hatch. "Its genius was to allow common people to feel, for a fleeting moment at least, that they were beholden to no one and masters of their own fate."[4]

SOCIETY AND SCHOOLS IN THE NEW REPUBLIC

The war American colonists fought for independence from Great Britain from 1776 to 1783 appeared to have little immediate impact on education. Independence, however, brought increased use of schools as a means of social development and control, because the peace treaty brought the new country land as far west as the Mississippi River. The Continental Congress had these vast western territories surveyed into square townships six miles on each side with thirty-six sections of 640 acres each. Each territory could become a state, equal with the original thirteen, as soon as its population reached fifty thousand.

Citizens who arrived before the Revolutionary War, and who ran the risks involved in breaking with England, felt their investment should be protected from the stream of people pouring in from Europe.[5] While many of the earlier arrivers in the original thirteen colonies shared this feeling, those in Massachusetts, Connecticut, and Virginia had a special sense of concern because of the cultural and political prominence those colonies had long enjoyed. They wanted the western territories to be part of the new country, both for future expansion and as a buffer against Spanish and French interests: "We have need of the Floridas and must have them," wrote sixth-generation Bostonian John Proctor in 1818.[6] But Proctor and other New Englanders feared social, moral, and cultural deterioration as settlement pushed beyond the mountain ridges that ran from western New York to northern Georgia. The next day, after writing, "and what we must have, we will have," Proctor noted the "more than savage barbarity of [Andrew] Jackson" in Florida, calling it "lawless insolence."[7] (Jackson had hanged two British citizens in Florida for stirring up Seminole resistance against encroaching settlers.) New Englanders did not want to be outvoted by western interests.

As a safeguard against the possibility that emerging western settlements might pay insufficient attention to education, the Continental Congress decreed in its 1787 land ordinance that the sixteenth section in each township in the Northwest Territory was to be dedicated to education. Whenever those sections of land were leased, rented, or sold, the proceeds were to be set aside for education. Easterners insisted on a provision that no more than six new states could be created from the territory so that the new states would not be able to outvote the original thirteen in the Senate.[8]

Three general forces combined to focus attention on education in the new republic: One was this fear of well-established Americans that the wilderness would corrupt advancing waves of settlers. A second was the Reformation conviction that every individual was responsible for acquiring his or her own version of salvation and religious virtue. Indeed, not only was each person responsible for his or her education, people whose family and economic backgrounds had previously made schooling inaccessible expanded this line of thought to mean that people had a right to seek as much education as they wanted. The third was the growing faith, rooted in the European Enlightenment, that human society and conditions could be improved by extending education. Benjamin Franklin, George Washington, and numerous other leaders of opinion in the late eighteenth and early nineteenth centuries authored "educational plans" for either whole states or the nation.[9]

SECTIONALISM AND CONTROL

The first half of the nineteenth century witnessed dramatic physical expansion. In 1800 most settlement was still concentrated in the East, and much of the territory that would be part of the country by 1850 still belonged to France or Spain. As the country expanded, so did educational development. By 1860 hundreds of colleges and thousands of academies had been founded, most by religious sects. In fact, 80 percent of the colleges and an even higher proportion of the academies no longer exist today. Yet, while they lasted—anywhere from a few months to several decades and longer—they provided a vast array of educational services to a wide variety of constituents.

This flurry of educational activity did not put everyone at ease. Almost every college or academy was "public" in the long-standing sense of the word and most communities had common schools. Many New Englanders thought of themselves as cultural leaders. Some even worried that New York City was surpassing Boston in population and commercial importance. At the same time, English and Continental commentators denigrated American culture as being primitive, and this bothered people who craved European acknowledgment of American legitimacy.[10] It was freewheeling, uncouth "westerners" from emerging areas like Kentucky and Tennessee who caused Europeans to think of Americans as barbaric—or so at least many New Englanders thought. "You once said to us," a teacher wrote back to Connecticut, "you thought we might find at the West, as you did at the South, an astonishing stupidity and indolence, and I think I have seen something of it."[11] The election of Andrew Jackson in 1828 was especially galling to many northeasterners.

In practice, many easterners combined fear of the frontier with feelings of religious intensity. From 1846 to 1856, nearly six hundred women left New England under the auspices of the National Board of Popular Education to teach school and win converts to mainline Protestantism. They were evangelists of culture and of a proper New England attitude.[12] So much of this activity was Protestant that the phenomenon has come to seem synonymous with Protestantism, but Roman Catholic missionizing embodied many of the same values.[13]

POLITICIZING EDUCATION

From the American Revolution to the Civil War, two broad patterns of thought emerged about education. Both favored schooling, seeing it as a means of improvement. One group viewed education as a personal, family, or local responsibility with some social obligation for those too poor to pay for it. The other, stressing the need for planning and control, was energized by the three forces mentioned above and generally emphasized social (township, state, national) systems over individual (family, local) choices.[14]

Down to about 1830 the lines between the groups were fuzzy and few people fell cleanly into one or the other. As the Civil War approached, there was increasing polarization. Those who favored social control (or *state action* as it would come to be known in legal terms) identified more and more consciously with each other and began to refer to themselves by labels such as "the friends of education." By implication, anyone who was not a friend of education was a foe, favoring ignorance and vice over enlightenment and virtue. So the conversation was becoming framed in a political context.

Friends of education were found in every state and territory, but they seemed to be concentrated in New England. Three men are now identified more than others as the early leaders: James G. Carter and Horace Mann were from Massachusetts; Henry Barnard hailed from Connecticut but also worked in Rhode Island and other states. Carter began his work in the 1820s, Mann and Barnard in the 1830s. All three—and a substantial number of men and women who shared their views—worked for state legislation to bring order to what they saw as chaotic, undisciplined, and wrong-headed individualized approaches to schooling.[15]

Horace Mann (1796–1859)

Horace was the fourth of five children born to Thomas and Rebecca Mann. The three boys and two girls in that family were the third generation brought up on the farm near Franklin, Massachusetts. The Mann homestead was self-sufficient: crops, livestock, and human labor provided food, clothing, and shelter. Unceasing attention to chores and the daily grind wore on Horace. Though a strong work ethic remained a lasting value, he wanted some vocation other than farming. The Mann household stressed both formal and informal learning of youngsters, and the rudiments of literacy and morality were made available to Horace both in the home and in a common one-room school. His older sister Rebecca heard his lessons—even when "winter school" was not in session.[16]

The Reverend Nathaniel Emmons attended to the religious affairs in Franklin. Emmons was well educated, steeped in and totally committed to the tenets of his faith, and thoroughly persuasive about the need to fear God. He pictured God as a force of awful and eternal retribution, ever-vigilant to punish wrongdoing. As a young man, Horace wrestled against such a view in search of a benevolent diety. At age sixteen Steven, Horace's older brother by two years, missed a church service to go fishing and drowned. For Emmons this was a most infamous offense against the Almighty and the event underscored the wisdom of an abiding fear for righteous punishment. The tragedy, overwhelming for Horace, solidified a sense of fatalism and a dark dimension to his character.

Steven's drowning came a year after the death of Thomas Mann. Horace's help was needed on the farm, but he had decided to pursue a profession.

The Years in Preparation

At eighteen Horace began preparation to meet the entrance requirements of Brown University in nearby Providence, Rhode Island. He dedicated his first year of work to self-directed study. Then, he hired a classicist for the study of Latin and Greek and a minister noted for success in teaching mathematics. Mann passed the oral examination conducted by a three-man board and entered as a sophomore.

His dedication to college work and his involvement in extracurricular activities and important debating societies brought him recognition from faculty and peers. In 1819, Brown awarded Mann the bachelor of arts degree and named him valedictorian.

Mann settled near Franklin to work as an apprentice in a law firm. Less than a year later, he accepted an offer to become a tutor at Brown, but thought his pupils lazy and impolite. After only two years, he left Brown to enroll in Tapping Reeve's law school in Litchfield, Connecticut.

Skillful in moot court presentations, Mann earned his colleagues' respect at the customary informal debates of law. Better still, the intellectual excitement and friendly atmosphere seemed to take the edge off his somber compulsiveness, and he enjoyed parties and social gatherings.

When he completed law school, Mann practiced in Dedham, Massachusetts. The legal field was saturated with lawyers of every stripe, and the community at large held them in no great esteem. Once again, an enormous capacity for work, a need to succeed, and a trust in virtue set Mann above the crowd.

Dedham, an expanding commercial center, provided the perfect environment for Mann's professional ambition. Speeches at important and well-attended public celebrations brought Mann popularity and initiated important private business contacts. His legal practice expanded beyond individual litigation into the complex and profitable arena of corporate law. He invested wisely, became a respected member of the business community, and maintained a rigorous schedule of correspondence with fellow lawyers and friends across the state. He worked actively for the Republican party. After five years in Dedham, Mann won election to the Massachusetts General Court.

Legislative Years

Mann spent a decade in elective office. They were years of political triumph and personal tragedy. His colleagues quickly understood that Mann would not knowingly violate his lofty moral standards. He was trustworthy, prepared, and an able speaker. He worked hard on committee assignments that put him in a leadership role. He fought hard for many causes, ranging from religious freedom to railroad expansion, temperance to the proper care of the insane. He was most eloquent and tenacious when championing moral causes that affected society's disenfranchised—for example, those committed as insane to jails and poorhouses.

Those labeled as insane were discarded to the most wretched of primitive jails and poorhouses, where they were left, poorly nourished, to suffer the extremes of the natural elements and to live in their own filth. Mann launched a statewide survey to document the exact treatment and support given to the cause of the insane. He made visitations to see firsthand the conditions of their care and studied the relevant literature in search of more enlightened treatment procedures. He presented before the General Court the first case promoting state assistance for the insane—an impassioned plea for his bill to finance a hospital for their care, and chaired a governor's commission to carry out the mandates of that legislation. He personally directed the efforts of that commission to establish the first state hospital for the insane in Massachusetts, breaking new ground in everything from architecture to operational procedures. His effort was momentous, revealing much about his personality.

While Mann was taking charge of his political life, his personal life seemed at the mercy of capricious forces. He fell in love with Charlotte Messer, third daughter of Asa Messer, the president of Brown University, who had chaired the committee that examined and accepted Mann as a student and had later hired him as a tutor. Though thirteen years younger than Mann, she willingly accepted his proposal of courtship. All correspondence and visits met Mann's rigorous requirements of good taste. At the height of his bliss, Charlotte lost energy and developed a persistent cough and sallow complexion. Mann knew the signs well, for his father too had died of consumption.

Mann and Messer were married on September 29, 1830. They settled in Dedham, but Charlotte spent most of her time in Providence under the care of her parents. Mann was keeping a vigil at her bedside when she died on August 1, 1832, at the age of twenty-three.

Charlotte's death devastated Mann and the tragedy festered inside him. As he lived out his mourning, he became morose and reclusive, his hair turned white, and his dress became drab and sloppy. His interests took an antimaterialistic bent, and he showed unusual ambivalence on matters of religious conviction. Withdrawing from politics, he became openly disillusioned with his former colleagues in the statehouse. Yet there remained a persistent and lurking attachment to humanitarian causes and occasional acknowledgments that such causes could spark active interest and personal involvement.

Friends refused to accept his decline into a pathetic figure. Their efforts to stir him to action were aided by signs of blatant self-interest by elected officials, mob violence in the streets, and indifference toward the disenfranchised by the moneyed class. Convinced that such social malignancies were primarily an outgrowth of Jacksonianism and the "spoils system," the Whigs mounted an especially energetic political campaign for state offices in Massachusetts. Mann finally allowed his name to be entered on the Whig slate for state senator. The Whig victory was sweeping, and Mann took office in January 1835. After one year, Mann was elected president of the senate and was reelected on the first ballot in his second year. He looked like future gubernatorial material, but the fiery disposition toward political causes had been blunted by his personal tragedy.

The legislature passed a statute that created a board of education to act in an advisory capacity to the state government. Several of Mann's friends, who had been selected to serve on the board, thought that a humanitarian cause might revitalize his activist tendencies, and suggested that he consider the secretaryship of the board of education. Mann at first feared he would be relinquishing tremendous political power to accept a post which granted no formal powers and for a social cause that was not part of his experiences. Finally, he accepted. According to biographer Jonathan Messerli, "he now hoped to superimpose a new altruistic purpose. Taking the classical stance of a martyr and envisioning himself clad in an armor of 'truth and duty,' which shielded him against the slings and arrows of his adversaries, he stood ready to face the imminent challenge."[17]

The Years as Educator

Mann read the available literature about the education of young people and garnered information on the status of Massachusetts education. He began by contacting powerful friends who set up "conventions" across the state, and Mann applied his oratorical skill to promote his cause. On these trips Mann inspected schools and requested the advice of public officials and parents. He constantly mailed out circulars requesting information about textbooks, buildings, and financial support. He sought and often gained pledges to improve local schools.

By January 1838, when he was ready to submit his first report to the board, Mann had traveled more than five hundred miles on horseback and collected and organized an impressive fund of information about the status of education in Massachusetts. Given Mann's presuppositions, which he projected into intense idealism, it is not surprising that what he saw was total disorder and blatant inadequacies: defective school buildings, unprepared teachers, confused and erratic local taxation policies, insufficient funds, scanty materials and books, and deficient supervision. Mann and other friends of education used their assessment of educational inadequacy as a basis for advocating centralized systems of schools instead of the community-controlled common schools that had been typical for more than a century. Their interpretation became the official view of most United States educators.

There were two important elements in this process, which transpired from the late 1820s to 1855. The first involved the elaboration of a particular form of organization and control. The second consisted of the reshaping of definitions to support the new organization.

Organization and Control

From his new position as official spokesperson for education, Mann led other friends of education in arguing for several interrelated items:

(1) All common or *elementary schools* were to be tuition free, with support to come from local and state taxes.

(2) All schools in each township were to be under the direct control of a superintendent.

(3) All curricular offerings and teaching materials were to be standardized and put under the control of the superintendent instead of parents and individual teachers.

(4) All pupils were to be grouped by age into "graded schools," meaning that the rapid promotion and peer teaching of the one-room school had to go.

(5) All teachers were to be licensed by the superintendent or by the state after training in normal schools or institutes so that unlicensed teachers could not be hired by the trustees.

(6) All parents were to be compelled to send their children for a minimum number of days for each of a specified number of years, with fines and possible jail terms for those who did not comply.

To build public sentiment in favor of this organization and approach, Mann wrote newspaper articles, gave speeches, and lobbied legislators with information claiming that those areas which adopted the township organization had superior schools to those choosing to leave educational decisions at the individual, family, and community level. Other friends of education took up this theme and searched for evidence to support their belief that more state action was needed to beat back the forces of ignorance.

Reshaping Definitions

In a subtle but largely unconscious development, Mann and the friends of education began in the 1840s and 1850s to redefine several long-standing terms. *Common school* had long been understood to mean any school offering elementary instruction, regardless of funding or religious sponsorship, and was a label with strong positive connotations in America. Mann and others gradually came to use the label to refer only to schools that were part of the township organizational scheme. The friends of education began referring to common schools that charged tuition as *private schools,* and common schools that were primarily supported by tax funds but were not part of a township organization were referred to as *country* or *district* schools. In cities, they gave the label *charity* to schools charging little or no tuition and not part of a township organization. Often they included an adjective such as *poor* or *inadequate* or *miserable* when mentioning country, district, or charity schools. ("The term 'countrified' was an epithet of reproach," remembered a Connecticut resident of the period around 1800.)[18]

Mann coalesced support for his version of common schools through his annual reports, his hundreds of speeches, and the *Common School Journal* (which he founded and edited) because he crafted arguments that appealed to a variety of important constituencies. To businessmen insecure about violence and vandalism plaguing the cities, Mann sold the common school as a means of building character and promoting protection of property. The benefit to the rich was further linked to a hope for the poor in that education would prevent poverty and diminish animosity due to social distinctions. Mann calmed fears that these schools might be "Godless institutions," insisting that a common school system would recognize religious obligations. To reassure those frightened by the prospect of doctrines alien to their own being taught, Mann promoted nonsectarian (Protestant) education, in which teachers would advance those common principles of the various sectarian creeds and read, without comment, from the King James Bible. And finally, to that constituency committed to and concerned about the furtherance of a democratic state, Mann held that the school would instill democratic ideals and training in self-government.

He spoke and wrote about curriculum development, teacher qualifications, motivation, discipline, methods of teaching reading, and—with phrenology receiving his unequivocal endorsement—learning theory. He established teacher institutes and argued for circulating libraries within school districts and for local–state partnerships in support of public education. He fought for uniform, politically acceptable textbooks and for improved school buildings.

One accomplishment of Mann's was such a source of pride to him that it deserves special mention. In 1838, philanthropist Edmund Dwight drew him aside at a social gathering and guaranteed $10,000 to improve teaching in Massachusetts, with the condition that the state legislature match the amount. With the Dwight incentive, Mann successfully fashioned a legislative package that not only provided for state assistance but also required local financial support for the establishment of normal schools. The first tax-funded normal school opened in Lexington, Massachusetts in July 1839. By the mid-1840s, several such institutions were thriving in Massachusetts, with one-year programs capped by three weeks of practice teaching.

Final Campaigns

In the early spring of 1843, to the amazement of acquaintances, Mann abruptly proposed marriage to a close friend, Mary T. Peabody, who had for years been secretly in love with him. They spent their honeymoon on a tour to study foreign social institutions, especially the Prussian schools. The observations of these schools recorded by him and Peabody formed the content of his *Seventh Annual Report.*

In 1848 Mann resigned his secretaryship to accept the seat in the U.S. House of Representatives vacated by the death of John Quincy Adams, and there distinguished himself as an adamant critic of slavery. His unbending opposition to the Compromise of 1850 (with its provision for a fugitive slave law that compelled the government to protect the work of slavehunters) jeopardized his political future. His vehement attacks on the compromise angered many Whigs, and under the leadership of Daniel Webster, they wrested from Mann the 1850 nomination for the Eighth Congressional District seat. He ran as a Free Soiler and came away the victor by a margin of forty-one votes.

In 1852, Mann was selected the first president of Antioch College in Yellow Springs, Ohio. That Antioch should prosper was crucial because it sought to give expression on America's frontier to what Mann considered immensely worthy causes: nonsectarianism and coeducation. Though frail, Mann drove himself on behalf of his new moral campaign. Struggling under what he regarded as primitive conditions, he and Mary were able to make the college operational but were not able to overcome the mismanagement of the trustees. Ironically, Antioch went bankrupt and was made fiscally sound in April 1859, as the school was auctioned off to wealthy eastern friends of the Manns. Their commitment was that Antioch as well as Mann's educational principles were to be preserved. Exhausted by the workload and pressures at Antioch, Mann could not stave off a bout with typhoid, and he was dead by early August.

Radical Republican Assimilation

From 1830 to 1860, there was no predominant political party associated with the friends of education. Some were Whigs, some Democrats. By 1860 many of them were Republicans, though some were Douglas

Democrats and a few were Constitutional Unionists and Breckenridge Democrats. Many, perhaps a majority, were Congregationalists or Presbyterians, and a significant number were Masons.

Until the Civil War was nearly over, the friends of education played down their political affiliations, at least when talking about educational issues. When the war ended, members of Congress struggled with how to reconstruct the Union, including on what terms to readmit the seceded states. Two perplexing questions swirled about their efforts: Why had the Great Rebellion happened? How could a recurrence be prevented? Several members of Congress who were friends of education offered a simple explanation: The North had free, common, public schools; the South did not. Skeptics countered by pointing out that most of the Confederate leadership was well educated. Advocates of the common school explanation conceded this point, but added that the leaders of the Confederacy were evil men. The mass of southerners were good but ignorant folk who did not know slavery was wrong or that seceding from the Union was illegal.

This highly questionable explanation was clearly false if common school was understood in its traditional sense. It was much more credible using the friends of education definition because most southern states did not have statewide systems. (North Carolina was an exception ignored by advocates of the cause of common schools, newly defined.) Despite its flaws, the explanation appealed to enough members of the Reconstruction Congress to make one of the prerequisites for reentry into the Union a provision for common schools in each seceded state's constitution.

Connecticut-born educational publicist Henry Barnard had authored legislation in Rhode Island and Connecticut similar to the Massachusetts bill that created Mann's position and served also as each of those state's first full-time education official. ("You are my guide, my hope, my friend, my fellow laborer and fellow-sufferer in 'the cause,'" Barnard wrote to Mann in 1843).[19] Barnard celebrated the cause and publicized the lives of many friends of education in the *American Journal of Education,* which he founded and edited from 1855 to 1880. Barnard and other partisans of the time referred to their movement as "the common school revival." Largely due to Barnard's publicity in the *Journal,* Mann came to be known as the "father of the common school"—a title that misled later commentators into believing that there were relatively few common schools prior to his work.[20]

The thirty-one volumes of the *Journal* stand as a lasting tribute to Barnard's educational commitment and contributed immensely to educational developments in the United States. Through its pages readers were given firsthand knowledge of the latest designs in school architecture, plus educational history and reports of European experiments. Yverdon and Pestalozzi were everyday terms to American educators because of Barnard's journal. There was also a fascinating experiment in New Harmony, Indiana that Barnard reported. This latter-day Pestalozzian utopia was the vision of Englishman Robert Owen, who attempted to create heaven on earth through his dream of a new commonwealth.

Robert Owen (1771–1858)

English capitalist turned utopian socialist, Robert Owen headed a transatlantic movement that attracted converts in Europe and America. In developing an educational theory combining many strands, Owen saw education as a total process of character formation and argued that "man's character was made for him and not by him." For him education would create a new society based on the equality of persons inhabiting a community of common property. Dedicated to creating a new society through character formation, Owen advocated infant education as the first step in the process. His educational plan called for conditioning children in the correct dispositions and fitting men and women to live in communal society.

Early Life

Robert Owen was born in 1771 in Newtown, Montgomeryshire, in north Wales.[21] He remembered himself as a precocious child who mastered his lessons quickly. He judged himself to be popular with peers and adults and agile in games and dancing. This self-confidence gave him an optimistic but sometimes unrealistic appraisal of his own powers.

In 1781, ten-year-old Robert left Newtown to seek his fortune in industrial Manchester where, from 1781 to 1789, he worked as shop boy and assistant in a drapery shop. At twenty, Owen established his own cotton-spinning plant and gained sufficient prominence in Manchester's business community to be named a member of the Literary and Philosophical Society and the board of health.

In 1799 Owen (and some partners) purchased David Dale's cotton mills in New Lanark, Scotland. Owen married Dale's daughter, Ann Caroline, and located in New Lanark, where he planned to create a model factory community that would earn a profit and yet be a humane place for its workers. A typical early-nineteenth-century English factory town, cotton mills dominated New Lanark's bleak landscape. Entire families and a large number of ill-clad and undernourished orphans worked the mills. Six-, seven-, and eight-year-old children worked from six in the morning until seven at night. The ever-optimistic Owen catalogued the problems to be solved at New Lanark: distrust, disorder, theft, drunkenness, personal quarrels, and religious contention. "Any general character, from the best to the worst, from the most ignorant to the most enlightened, may be given to any community, even to the world at large, by the application of proper means; which means are to a great extent at the command and under the control of those who have influence in the affairs of men."[22]

Owen curtailed the sale of gin and worked to reduce alcoholism in New Lanark. He improved the homes, streets, and sanitary conditions in the town. Fuel and clothing were sold by the company stores at profitable but reasonable prices.

He stopped employing young children in the mill. He preferred twelve as an entry age, but yielded to parents who wanted their children to begin work at ten. Owen also established an educational institute for children between five and ten at no expense to their parents.

Education at New Lanark

Owen, who thought character was formed by environmental forces, denied that human beings were responsible for their behavior. Artificial rewards and punishments stimulated antagonism and egotistical competition, fixed children's existing character, and worked against changing their internal dispositions. Owen thought educationally valuable rewards and punishments resulted from experiencing the natural consequences of actions. He wanted children to recognize that their actions had social consequences.[23]

Owen's basic instructional method involved simple, direct conversations about objects, although these lessons were but one part of a varied and often inconsistent curriculum. Like Rousseau, Owen felt that reading began too early with materials that were not easily understood by children, and he advocated that children should not read anything that they could not understand and explain in their own words. Owen believed that little volumes of voyage and travel illustrated by plates, pictures, and maps were most appropriate to children's interests. He also advised that lessons not last more than thirty-five minutes. He thought writing should begin as soon as children could copy a text, and approved of dictation in which the child copied the teacher's words. Short sentences illustrating history or geography were most suitable for teaching writing. To teach arithmetic, Owen recommended using Pestalozzian principles by which learners began with concrete objects, counted them, added them, and subtracted them. Only after relating quantity to objects were students to proceed to more abstract computations. Owen integrated instruction in natural history, geography, and ancient and modern history because they could be taught by extemporaneous lectures to classes of forty children.

Always antagonistic to organized religion, Owen contended that people's inherently good characteristics needed only a correct environment to come to perfection. Although he wanted moral education based on his view of human nature and social science, Owen reluctantly compromised with New Lanark parents who wanted the catechism taught to their children. He also sought to cultivate the aesthetic side of children's nature. All children above age five were taught singing by ear and by notes. Owen believed that dancing was a pleasant, healthful, natural, and social exercise that improved carriage and deportment.

Owen's Social Theory

As his fame spread, Owen turned to lecturing and writing, believing that he was creating a "New Moral World." In 1813, his *A New View of Society* proclaimed a new form of education conducive to social change. Owen accepted increased economic growth and productivity as beneficial. A modernizer who believed that much of early industrialism's hardships were unnecessary, he argued that abundance for all could be achieved without human suffering. He felt that it was the working classes who had paid for industrial growth with their suffering. For him, this price was too high, as well as unnecessary. Owen regarded the cooperative community as the ideal environment for shaping the moral inhabitants who would dwell in the new social order.

Because humans were not responsible for forming their own character and behavior, class hatred was irrational and irrelevant to achieving the new society.[24] Owen's rejection of class conflict led Karl Marx and Friedrich Engels to condemn him as a utopian socialist deluding the working classes and detouring them from their true revolutionary role. Engels in *Socialism, Utopian and Scientific,* commended Owen for his social analysis but condemned his failure to understand the significance of class antagonisms.

Assuming that a properly controlled environment would produce the desired personality type, Owen became a thoroughgoing social engineer. His educational theory assumed that human character is made by life in society. Recognizing the formative role of enculturation, human character resulted from the basic experiences that persons had as members of a social group, living within a particular societal mode. The reconstruction of society would lead to a fundamental reshaping of human character. By living in a properly constituted community and by being educated in the laws of society, the citizens of the new social order would end the chaos of the old, irrational, disintegrative society. Owen believed that European institutions, resting on long-standing and deeply embedded traditions, were more difficult to reconstruct than those of the United States, which were newer, more flexible, and more amenable to reorganization. Hence, he came to the United States in the middle 1820s to embark on the New Harmony communitarian experiment.

Owen in America

From 1824 to 1828, Owen sought to implement his social and educational theories in New Harmony, a small Indiana town that he had purchased from the Rappites, a sect of German Pietists. His invitation to any and all who would be communitarians brought an unusual assortment of scholars, scientists, zealots, opportunists, farmers, and eccentrics to the southern Indiana town. Some of the Harmonists were well-known (William Maclure, Thomas Say, Gerard Troost, and Joseph Neef); others had no particular claim to fame.

Owen planned a community of equality at New Harmony with which the inhabitants commonly owned the town's property. He planned to develop comprehensive educational institutions, ranging from nursery schools to adult education lectures: "The world will thus be governed through education alone since all other governments will then become useless and unnecessary. To train and educate the rising generation will at all times be the first object of society, to which every other will be subordinate."[25]

New Harmony Experiment

A key provision in Owen's New Harmony plan was the abolition of private property, the source of human and social evils. Common property and common education, the "great equalizers," would erode class conflict and contention. On May 1, 1825, the "Preliminary Society of New Harmony" organized "to improve the character and conditions of its own members, and to prepare them to become associates in independent communities, having common property."[26] Ten months later, on February 5, 1826, Robert Owen proclaimed the "Community of Equality." Members of the community

> shall be considered as one family, and no one shall be held in higher or lower estimation on account of occupation. There shall be similar food, clothing, and education, as near as can be furnished, for all according to their ages; and, as soon as practicable, all shall live in similar houses, and in all respects be accommodated alike. Every member shall render his or her best services for the good of the whole, according to the rules and regulations that may be hereafter adopted by the community. It shall always remain a primary object of the community to give the best physical, moral, and intellectual education to all its members.[27]

Owen's plan for a new American social order did not succeed. The inhabitants of New Harmony endlessly debated constitutions, quarreled over property division, and disputed social and educational theories. With the community in disintegration, Owen and his chief associate, William Maclure, quarreled, took each other to court, and then divided what remained of the community of unity. In 1828, Owen left New Harmony and returned to his native England where he continued to work for communitarianism, the improvement of working conditions, and the creation of universal education until his death in 1858.

Owen, Mann, Barnard, Webster—indeed most theorists who considered themselves part of the reforming tradition—advocated tax-funded schools for all. They thought individuals would be improved both morally and intellectually and that society would benefit. But who should decide the curriculum? Traditionally the answer had been that parents and the local community chose. With more and more Roman Catholic immigrants arriving, the friends of education, most of whom were descended from Puritanism, began to doubt the wisdom of continuing this tradition. The conflict shows clearly in the life and activities of John Hughes.

John Hughes (1797–1864)

Bishop John Hughes of New York was neither teacher, educational theorist, nor school administrator. In spite of this, he was a key figure in the development of Catholic schooling in America. Ironically, he was also partly responsible for the development of American public education along secular lines.

Early Life and Career

Hughes was born in northern Ireland in 1797, the third son of a poor farmer. Life was especially difficult for the Irish during this period. Much of Ireland's land was owned by absentee landlords and farmed by local tenants. The Irish were a conquered people, unable to govern themselves or practice their Catholic religion freely. Hughes later reminisced about being told as a boy that "for five days I was on a social and civil equality with the most favored subjects of the British Empire. These five days would be the interval between my birth and my baptism."[28] As soon as he formally became a Catholic, he sacrificed most of his civil rights. In the long run these early experiences of religious persecution would motivate his crusade for Catholic rights in the United States.

Due to these problems, John's father went to America with his second son Patrick and in the following year sent for John. The boy arrived in Baltimore and went to work as a gardener at Emmitsburg, Maryland, the location of the most famous American Catholic seminary of the period, Mount St. Mary's. Hughes tried several times to gain admission, but the rector, the Reverend John Dubois, felt that the school was already too crowded and that Hughes, at twenty-one, was too old to be a successful student. It seems that Hughes simply rubbed Dubois the wrong way.[29]

Hughes, however, was already showing the stubborn streak that would make him a difficult opponent in future years. He refused to give up his dream of becoming a priest and eventually gained admission to the seminary through the intervention of Elizabeth Bayley Seton, an Episcopalian widow who had converted to Catholicism and was the founder of a community of nuns. (Seton would later become the first American-born saint.) At twenty-three, Hughes finally gained admission to the seminary.

For the most part Hughes was a loner, separated by age and personality from his classmates. As a prefect (student disciplinarian), he had a reputation for being stern and humorless. Students delighted in playing pranks on him, and faculty members thought him proud and stubborn. His only source of support was the Reverend Simon Brute, the seminary's saintly religious counselor who would one day also be a bishop (as would Dubois).

Hughes was ordained in 1826 and almost immediately became involved in a religious controversy that established his style of action. The unsettled character of the Catholic church in America in the early nineteenth century meant that it attracted more than a few undesirable clergy from overseas. European bishops or religious superiors who were having problems with a priest would occasionally give him the choice of going to America or leaving the priesthood. Others came because they couldn't get along with their parishes and hoped to make a new start in another country. The result was an American church in which bishops had little actual authority.

Previous to Hughes's ordination there had been a conflict for some years in Philadelphia between the bishop and laypeople over whether the bishop had the right to appoint parish priests. Through newspapers Hughes exchanged letters with Protestant clergy over this issue. Here as in later fights, Hughes's style was anything but restrained, meeting attack with counterattack instead of taking a more diplomatic approach. Nevertheless, he began to establish a reputation as a champion of Catholic rights.

Along with these flashier activities, Hughes worked hard at the traditional aspects of his priestly ministry. He was a concerned pastor for his people, and worked to provide for their religious needs. Besides supporting his own congregants, he helped to raise money for several communities of sisters and was instrumental in the founding of a Catholic orphanage in Philadelphia. Hughes gained respect from Catholics and Protestants alike by remaining in the city during a cholera epidemic in 1833 to minister to the needs of his flock. Initially an uninspiring preacher (he memorized one sermon and used it on every occasion), he improved his style to the degree that he was soon traveling as far as New York to be a guest speaker for special occasions. This oratorical ability was put to the test in 1833 in a series of public debates with a Presbyterian minister named John Breckenridge. Over the course of a hot summer the two hurled charges and countercharges at each other over the comparative merits of Catholicism and Protestantism. Hughes's arguments were theologically thin at times, but he never seemed to lack insults to hurl at his opponent. Blunt and aggressive, he was emerging from an uncertain seminary career as a confident and forthright spokesperson for American Catholics.

Given his leadership ability and increasing visibility it was inevitable that Hughes would become a candidate for bishop. In 1833 he was considered along with John Baptist Purcell—the new president of Mount St. Mary's—for the post of bishop of Cincinnati, but a mix-up prevented Hughes from receiving the post. An American bishop who was consulted by the Rome officials responsible for appointing bishops recommended that Hughes be sent to Cincinnati rather than Purcell, since Hughes was a self-made man who would understand life in a frontier town better than the more-cultured Purcell. However, the Roman official who made the appointment thought that Purcell was the self-made man, and appointed him instead.[30]

In spite of this confusion and the bluntness which made many Catholic leaders nervous about him, Hughes soon became a bishop. Dubois had become bishop of New York in 1826, but now aged, it was obvious that he needed assistance. In 1837, Hughes was appointed coadjutor bishop of New York, meaning that he was a kind of co-bishop, rather than merely an assistant. Dubois had a series of strokes shortly thereafter, and Hughes took over the diocese in 1839. While it was logical under the circumstances for Rome to give Hughes full power, a clash with Dubois came immediately. The older bishop bitterly resented being forced to hand over control and withdrew into himself. Never a fan of Hughes's, the older man would refer to him only by his formal title until the end of his life.

The Schooling Controversy

In 1839, Hughes went abroad to raise money and recruit personnel for his diocese. During his absence a controversy erupted that would provide the platform from which he would make a distinctive contribution to American educational history. In order to understand the conflict, however, we must first have some sense of what life and schooling were like for Catholic immigrants in nineteenth-century America. During the colonial period American society had generally been anti-Catholic. Then, during the Revolutionary War prominent American Catholics like Charles Carroll, a signer of the Declaration of Independence, had made Catholicism more acceptable. Most of these early Catholics were from Maryland and tended to be wealthy and well-educated with the same English manners and customs as their Protestant neighbors.

The great influx of European Catholic immigrants in the early nineteenth century was different from these earlier Anglo-American Catholics. Largely German or Irish, they had few of the manners and little of the education of the Maryland gentlefolk. Their different way of speaking English (or inability to speak it), obvious poverty, and cultural differences encouraged the hostility of native-born European Americans. Their presence also drove down wages, because desperate immigrants were often willing to work for lower wages than were others. This encouraged even more resentment.

The Catholic faith of the immigrants became one more thing the native citizens held against them. While American Protestants had at least tolerated the Maryland Catholics, the continuing arrival of these newcomers caused many Protestants to fear that America was being taken over by Catholics, whom they had been taught to regard as agents of the devil. Throughout this era Protestant magazines expressed this fear, and that a future Catholic takeover of America would see the pope move to the United States and take up residence in the Midwest.

These fears were a serious part of the outlook of many nineteenth-century Americans In 1825, 11 percent of New York's population was Irish; by 1845, this had increased to 35 percent. In fact, by 1855, more than half of the city's residents were foreign-born and more than half of the foreign-born were Irish.[31]

These great immigrations brought an ever-increasing number of children, either foreign-born or with immigrant parents, to cities like New York. In New York, in the first years of the nineteenth century, much of the schooling for those unable to pay was in the hands of an organization called the New York Free School Society. Founded in 1805 by wealthy Protestants, the Society sought to provide free or low-cost education for those unable to afford the city's other schools. Like other educational ventures, including those supported by church groups, this free-school society was given a share of state tax money to accomplish its purpose. At this time separation of church and state was not yet an issue, and *public* did not mean antireligious.

The first controversy over the use of tax money for religious schools in New York came in 1824. In that year it was discovered that a local Baptist church was using school money from the state of New York to build a church. In the furor that resulted, the state legislature gave the city council the right to distribute and supervise the use of state school funds in New York City. As a result, denominational schools were cut off from state funding.

While all of this was going on, the New York Free School Society, which was now called the New York Public School Society, had become the major sponsor of schooling in the city. In addition to receiving the lion's share of the state school money, the Public School Society was also given a special real estate tax by the legislature. By 1840 the society was in control of nearly one thousand schools in New York City.

Although free schools in New York were no longer under denominational control, their tone was still highly religious. A sort of general Protestantism permeated the atmosphere and curriculum of the schools. The King James (Protestant) version of the Bible was used as a textbook, and students were taught to regard Protestantism as the highest form of religious belief. Many of America's school leaders agreed with Horace Mann that Protestantism was *the* American religion and should be taught as part of the American school curriculum.

The curricula of public schools of the era were frequently anti-Catholic. History books stressed how Catholic monarchs in Europe had burned Protestant reformers at the stake and insisted that Catholicism was really superstition rather than Christian religion. Not surprisingly, such bias discouraged Catholic attendance at public schools. Of twelve thousand Catholic children in the city in the late 1830s, only a few were in the common schools. Since there were only a few Catholic schools in the city (eight in 1839), most Catholic children simply didn't go to school.

By the time Hughes arrived on the scene, New York Catholics were angry about having to pay taxes for schools their children weren't able to attend. In 1834, Bishop Dubois had tried to have Catholic teachers hired in a school district in which most of the pupils were Irish, as well as to have Protestant religious principles removed. The Public School Society rejected his request, arguing that Catholics were asking for privileges granted to no other religious groups.

Catholics then began to seek political support for their position. In New York's governor William Seward they found an ally. Seward, who would later become Lincoln's Secretary of State, believed strongly in the inalienable rights of people as expressed in the Declaration of Independence and in the Judeo-Christian idea of the unity of humankind. More practically he saw the possibility of improving his political position by gaining the support of New York's Irish Catholics. Thus, he encouraged Roman Catholics in 1840 to petition the city council for a share of state funds in order to support their own schools. This petition was rejected by the council, which argued that giving state money to the Catholics would amount to public support of a religious denomination.

At this point, Hughes returned from Europe and took direct charge of the Catholic efforts. Under him the fight broadened from one for public funds into a demand for tolerance of religious differences and respect for immigrant rights. Catholics rallied to Hughes, not only to gain school support, but also to express their frustrations at social and economic discrimination. In a series of debates with Hughes, the anti-Catholic sentiments of Public School Society officials swiftly surfaced. It was probably lucky for Hughes that they did, since only the anti-Catholic rhetoric of society leaders prevented his own superficial treatment of the school issue from becoming apparent.[32]

An attempt to reach a funding compromise was unsuccessful and in 1841 the city's aldermen voted again to deny the Catholic petition. Catholics took the battle to the state legislature. In April 1841 New York Secretary of State John Spencer—who was also the state superintendent of schools—presented a plan to the legislature that threatened the domination of the Public School Society. According to this plan the religious tone of the local schools would be determined by the religion of the majority of residents in a school district. Effectively, this would give Catholics control of their own schools.

The debate now centered on which of two views of public schooling would become law. The one advocated by the Catholics was that the majority should be able to determine the shape of the local schools. The other advocated by almost everyone else was that there should be some kind of public control, but some limits should be placed on a community's power to force its views on all children. The Public School Society, now on the defensive, opposed any attempt to make the public schools in Irish neighborhoods more Catholic in tone.

While all of this was happening, New York was preparing for state elections. This caused Hughes to shift his attack to the political sector, demanding that local candidates take a stand on state aid to Catholic schools. The results of the 1841 elections showed that although Catholics were not an absolute majority, they held the political balance of power. While those candidates who had only Catholic support lost, the regular Democrats who failed to receive Catholic endorsement were also defeated. The Catholic vote had become a decisive factor in the local political equation.

In 1842 the matter of restructuring New York's public schools came before the legislature again. Funding of Catholic schools seemed to have faded somewhat as an issue; instead, the new bill provided for the local election of public school commissioners, an action calculated to break the power of the Public School Society. The society's efforts to stop the legislation were unsuccessful, and in November the Assembly passed the new school law and the Senate followed suit in April (by a one-vote majority). The bill was signed into law by Seward three days before the spring New York City elections. In the resulting election riots, the Catholic bishop's house was nearly burned with the elderly Dubois still inside, but the domination of the Public School Society was ended for good. While the Bible was still used in the city's schools, within a year Jewish citizens who had sat quietly through the earlier controversies would protest the schools' Christian orientation, and other groups would later file test cases causing the eventual removal of religion. As one commentator has pointed out, the result was that "for the first time in its history, New York City would have a school system that was directly controlled by the people and entirely financed from the public treasury."[33]

While this legislative solution represented an end for Seward, it was only a midpoint for Hughes. The bishop saw the victory in terms of the evils it ended rather than the benefits it conferred. As time went on, Hughes began to attack as godless the very schools from which he had helped to remove Protestant religious influence. Having helped to provide immigrants with the means of controlling their own children's education, New York's bishop proceeded to turn his back on the public schools.

After the "school war" of 1840–1842, Hughes concentrated more of his efforts on developing a network of parochial schools to replace public ones. By 1854 there were 10,061 pupils studying in New York's twenty-eight parochial schools and in 1862 the number had increased to 15,000. In the process of crusading for Catholic rights, John Hughes had also become a leader among the American Catholic bishops in promoting a separate network of schools to meet the particular needs of immigrant Catholics.[34]

In building New York's Catholic schools, Hughes relied on his usual style of leadership, demanding absolute control. Typically blunt and aggressive, he quarrelled with at least one community of sisters over his right to direct their activities and fought with the Jesuits, who staffed Fordham University, over the ownership of part of the school's property. While Hughes was always a superb organizer, his lack of diplomacy seemed at times to create as many enemies inside his church as outside.

Hughes began to emerge as a national figure during this period. In 1847 he preached to the U.S. House of Representatives and in 1860 was voted by the heavily Protestant senior class of the University of North Carolina as their choice for graduation speaker. With the approach of the Civil War, Hughes became an ardent Union supporter, ordering the American flag to be flown from New York's Catholic churches. Although he did not oppose slavery, a position that earned him further dislike from the city's Protestant abolitionists, he felt that the southern states must be considered in rebellion.

Final Years

Even though his health had been failing, Hughes undertook a government mission in 1861 at the request of his old friend Seward and President Lincoln. To gain foreign support for the Union position, Hughes traveled to France and spoke with the French cardinals as well as Louis Napoleon. After a journey to England and Ireland, he returned to the United States in 1862. Both his European church superiors and American Catholics were unhappy with this sort of open political activity. Once again, Hughes had acted on his convictions without much thought about the consequences: again, he had been left isolated and exposed.

Through the winter of 1862–1863, the bishop's health steadily worsened. Added to his physical ills was the increased racial bigotry of his flock as manifested in the *Freeman's Journal,* a New York Catholic paper. In July 1863 there were riots in New York over the recently instituted military draft. New York priests tried unsuccessfully to calm the city's Irish, and finally Hughes called their leaders together outside his home. Although he was so weak that he had to speak to them from a chair, he reasoned with them for an hour. Influenced by the bishop the crowds dispersed. The draft riots, however, had broken the elderly bishop's spirits. Over and over during the years of strife he had insisted that Catholics could be good Americans; now, he felt betrayed by the actions of his own people.

Hughes withdrew from public view during the last months of his life, and died on January 3, 1864. Though the *Freeman's Journal* and the abolitionist press of New York gave only routine notice of his death and funeral, the city council ordered all city offices closed in his memory and the flags on public buildings flown at half mast. Some one hundred thousand people gathered in and around the unfinished St. Patrick's Cathedral to attend his funeral. This outpouring of popular sentiment was a fitting final tribute for the bishop who, as the preacher at the funeral mass remarked, had "fought the good fight."

One of the ironies of Hughes's history of educational leadership is that one of his principal accomplishments was in direct opposition to what he had set out to do. In taking on the Public School Society, his intention had been to obtain state funds for Catholic schools. Instead, he helped create a school system from which religion was absent. In Hughes's eyes such secularization was no improvement; he believed that religion was a necessary component in young people's education.

To admit that Hughes was unable to accomplish his stated goals, however, is not to say that he failed as an educational leader. Indirectly, he helped establish a principle that now dominates American public education; that is, that the local community should have some measure of control over the schools attended by their children. More directly, he was instrumental in developing the extensive network of parochial schools that has become an important part of American education.

Hughes stands most of all as a kind of symbol of the needs and aspirations of the "new Americans" of the period, for he had also suffered oppression in Europe and had immigrated to find a new future. Like them, he knew the experience of social and economic discrimination in the new land. Hughes's popularity, in spite of his blunt and autocratic style, is testimony to his ability to articulate the basic human needs for respect and tolerance felt by so many of his flock. In his fights with the Public School Society and his development of Catholic education, Hughes's forthright defense of his values and beliefs helped a whole generation of fellow immigrants feel that they too had values worth defending and an important place in American life.

CONSOLIDATING GAINS

As immigration intensified in the last quarter of the nineteenth century, the number of Roman Catholics increased significantly. The gulf between their leaders and Protestant friends of education seemed to widen. In an effort to consolidate their position, the friends of education pushed for a Department of Education as an agency of government in Washington. Representative James Garfield (R-Ohio), later to be president, led a congressional effort resulting in the March 1867 creation of the U.S. Department of Education. Advocates hoped the new department would diffuse "correct ideas respecting the value of education as a quickener of intellectual activities, [and act] as a moral renovator, as a multiplier of industry, and a consequent producer of wealth; and finally, as the strength and shield of civil liberty."[35] Henry Barnard became the first head of the new office.

Opposition to state systems of education was widespread. The idea of a federal system—particularly one that implied either general tax money or national control—appealed only to the most stringent advocates of the new common school systems.[36] A move to increase funding in 1869 gave opponents a new opening, and political ineptitude on Barnard's part weakened the ability of Garfield and other friends in defending the unit. Congress changed the department to a bureau within the Department of the Interior, where it functioned with less authority than advocates of more social control wanted for it.[37]

In two other areas, Civil War conditions produced important educational developments. One of the these was the formation of the Bureau of Refugees, Freedmen and Abandoned Lands in 1865, growing out of the need to deal with four million freed slaves. The Freedmen's Bureau, as it was known, was supposed to provide land, transitional economic support, and schools. During its brief existence, it provided more schools than land or economic aid.

African Americans in the South generally welcomed the northern teachers who came either under the auspices of one of the fifty-one voluntary Freedmen's Aid Societies or of the government. By 1870, 2,560 teachers operated 2,039 schools for the Reconstruction government.[38] In addition, a strong indigenous movement from within the black community started many schools and sustained them against considerable odds after most northern teachers returned home. These included colleges and universities, many of which have come to be known as the *historic black colleges*. Some researchers suggest that many of the Freedmen's Aid Societies and Freedmen's Bureau schools contained elements of condescension and white control that were not in the best interests of the African American community.[39]

The United States purchased Alaska from Russia in 1867. At that time a number of schools were provided by the Eastern Orthodox Church and by Russian trading companies, but these closed as the Russians withdrew. The U.S. government virtually ignored the remote region except to tax the seal, whale, and fur catches. "The Russians gave them government, schools and the Greek religion," noted one missionary. "The only thing the United States has done for them has been to introduce whiskey."[40]

John Eaton, a Presbyterian and Mason, became interested in Alaska as soon as he became the second U.S. Conmmissioner of Education in 1870. In his *Annual Report* for 1872 he noted that although Alaska was "an integral part of the boasted most progressive nation in the world," it was "yet without the least possible provision to save its children from growing up in the grossest ignorance and barbarism."[41] Congress ignored his indictment until he was joined by an ambitious Presbyterian missionary in Alaska named Sheldon Jackson, who wanted government aid for schools in that vast territory. Jackson was not to be ignored. In 1884, largely because of Eaton's advocacy, the U.S. Bureau of Education took over Alaskan schools. For the next several decades, the Commissioner of Education in Washington set policy for the education of indigenous people several thousand miles away.[42]

Sheldon Jackson (1834–1909)

Born in a profoundly religious New York home, Sheldon felt consecrated to missionary service at an early age. After attending a succession of district schools and academies, he graduated from Union College, Schenectady, New York (1855), and then from Princeton Theological Seminary (1859). From Princeton the newly ordained Presbyterian minister went to teach in a Choctaw boys' school in Indian Territory, and for the next twenty years drove himself relentlessly in various missionary undertakings in the West. Always on the lookout for new fields to conquer, he traveled to Alaska in 1877 and established a beachhead for the Presbyterian Church, but he returned convinced that his denomination could not take civilization to the natives without help.[43]

Commissioner Eaton was the avenue through which the needed assistance came. For seven years Jackson and "Brother" Eaton (both were Masons) carried on a joint campaign aimed at taking law, religion, and education to Alaska.[44] In 1884, Congress directed the Secretary of the Interior to "make needful and proper provision for the education of children of school age . . . without reference to race."[45] The Secretary in turn assigned the task to Eaton, who appointed Jackson general agent for education in Alaska.

During the first five years in this post, Jackson's position was so tenuous that he spent most of his time in power struggles. The territorial governor and a district judge, both Democrats, sought to oust Jackson, whom they regarded as meddlesome, intractable, and visionary. They appealed to fellow Democrat N. H. R. Dawson, who had replaced Eaton as commissioner soon after Jackson took office. Dawson, however, dared not dismiss the popular Presbyterian Republican. When the Democrats gave up the White House in 1889 and William Torrey Harris replaced Dawson as commissioner of education, Jackson quickly consolidated virtually all the Bureau of Education's power in Alaska. In 1881 Eaton introduced Jackson as "the Napoleon of the Presbyterian Church in the West," and from 1889 to 1907 he was the Napoleon of the U.S. government in all matters cultural and educational in Alaska.[46]

The first schools the general agent established were operated by Christian missionaries in cooperation with the Bureau of Education. Because the Bureau had severely limited funds ($25,000–$50,000 annually), the most practical approach seemed to be to have the various

Christian denominations provide teachers and buildings while the government furnished supplies and paid all or part of the teachers' salaries. In the mid-1890s, after a few years of interdenominational bickering, as well as fear of merging church and state, the government discontinued this practice.

The underlying rationale of the Bureau's activities in Alaska was that of Kipling's "White Man's Burden." Jackson described it as "the gradual uplifting of the whole man," and of course this included Christianizing everyone.[47] For Commissioner of Education Harris, it was civilizing the barbarous. "We have no higher calling in the world," he told Julia Ward Howe, "than to be missionaries of our idea to those people who have not yet reached the Anglo-Saxon frame of mind."[48]

Both Jackson and Harris believed that the best way to elevate the natives of Alaska was to make them economically indispensable:

> If the natives of Alaska could be taught the English language, be brought under Christian influences by the missionaries and trained into forms of industry suitable for the territory, it seems to follow as a necessary result that the white population of Alaska, composed of immigrants from the States, would be able to employ them in their pursuits, using their labor to assist in mining, transportation, and the producing of food.[49]

"When the native has thus become useful to the white man, . . . he has become a permanent stay and prop to civilization, and his future is provided for."[50]

Always short of funds, the Bureau could rarely afford to do more than offer rudimentary instruction in any subject. During the early years, English language instruction took precedence over everything else because this was deemed basic. Teaching English was difficult because teachers and pupils could not understand each other and there were no suitable textbooks. Commissioner Harris ordered all teachers to "take with them such books of literature as portrayed in the most powerful form and ideas and convictions of the people of England and the United States." The works of Shakespeare, Dickens, Walter Scott, and their like, he added, "furnish exactly the material to inspire the teacher and to arouse and kindle the sluggish minds of the natives of Alaska with sentiments and motives of action which lead our civilization."[51] Throughout the period when the Bureau of Education operated the schools in Alaska, many of the texts were either borrowed from normal American schools or from Indian reservation schools. Neither variety bore much resemblance to life or experience in Alaska. Though teachers complained repeatedly, the Bureau never solved the textbook problem.[52]

The problem of securing and keeping teachers was a continuing one. Most early teachers were missionaries with the virtues and limitations of their calling. Nearly all the early missionary-teachers worked conscientiously for the good of the natives within their understanding of that good. Just as Bernadino de Sahagún had done three centuries earlier, several developed profound respect for the native culture.[53] Some even exchanged their church sponsorship for Bureau of Education employment and formed the backbone of the field force. But finding teachers for the growing number of schools remained a problem. Some applicants for jobs in Alaska were leaving troublesome situations in the states and were pursuing the illusion that they would be more successful elsewhere. Others, who were adequate teachers, lacked the needed characteristics to be able to live in isolated villages and act as sanitation officers, physicians, judges, counselors, and social workers, as well as teachers. Turnover was high, salaries were low, and the risks, both physical and psychological, were great. Several teachers died in Alaska of accident or disease, or at the hands of irate natives; others returned emotionally broken. "Every year individuals come back from the Arctic regions insane who went there sane," lamented William Torrey Harris.[54] Despite problems, most of the Bureau of Education teachers in Alaska rendered conscientious service.

In the 1890s, whites from the states came pouring into Alaska in a mad scramble for gold. Rapid population growth increased the demands for schools more quickly than Congress increased appropriations. Many whites blamed the lack of schooling on Jackson. They wanted for education the money that Jackson was using to promote reindeer (in a program begun in 1892). Around the turn of the century, the territorial government acquired control over schools for most of the white population. The Bureau of Education was left with educating the native population only.[55]

In 1906, Jackson resigned from the Alaska Division, which then underwent a thorough reorganization. Jackson had made enemies, and even his friends said the change was overdue. The aging missionary was not keeping pace with the rapid changes in Alaska and he was a better promoter than administrator.

While there were many changes in administrative procedures, the aim of the Bureau remained what it had been under Jackson, and Bureau personnel became more openly protective (critics said paternalistic) toward the natives. They had ended up presiding over the collision of two cultures, trying to keep the natives from being completely crushed in the process. It was not an easy job, and there were many failures.

One of the problems of cultural conflict occurred in the field of public health. Natives had contracted white people's diseases—especially venereal diseases and tuberculosis—and had no immunity to them. The Bureau gradually extended medical aid. At first, teachers were the only agents available for imparting medical attention, and they usually knew little more than what they read in their handbooks. Later, physicians and nurses took over the medical practice, but teachers still attended to many emergency situations.[56]

Of all the difficulties faced by the Bureau in Alaska, that of making the natives immune to the economic depredations of advancing white civilization seemed the hardest to solve. Jackson's reindeer scheme was aimed at this, but it provided relief only to a small part of the Eskimo population. A partial solution was finally found. In the larger villages, the Bureau started cooperative stores so the natives could buy supplies wholesale instead of at the enormously inflated prices of traders. This worked well in some areas, but many of the stores had to be supervised closely by the local teacher. For more remote villages, the Bureau operated a boat, the *Boxer,* which took supplies to the villages and also transported furs and other salable items to Seattle, Washington, where the proceeds were put in a special fund for the use of the natives. This reached only a small part of the population.[57]

In all of their operations, officials of the Bureau admitted frankly that they were acting *in loco parentis* for the natives. This meant that the Bureau often found itself in opposition both to the whites in Alaska who wished to exploit the natives and to some of the natives. "Thus on the one side have been the white men with practically little restraint upon their actions, and upon the other the ignorant child-like natives," said a government document in 1906. "The missionaries and the school teachers have done nobly in a personal way, but the result has necessarily been a bitter disappointment to all persons of . . . humanitarian instincts."

In 1929 the Reindeer Service was transferred to the territorial governor's office. Two years later, the Bureau turned over the rest of its Alaska work to the Bureau of Indian Affairs.

Whether the natives of Alaska were better or worse off because of the change is not easy to say. Daily life went on as before. The natives were still caught in a vise not of their own making and from which escape was difficult. Many years later, in the mid-1950s, a visiting author met an old Eskimo named Segevan at Point Barrow. Segevan had been the first native to enter school at Barrow and had once owned an extensive reindeer herd. The writer asked what had been the most valuable things white men had brought to the North. The native looked at his questioner a long time, and finally replied, "The best things are coffee and cigarettes. There are sorrows too great for consolation, but the small pleasures help us to bear them."[58]

SUMMARY

Schooling is never neutral. It can occur only within a cultural framework. In nineteenth-century America, Horace Mann, Sheldon Jackson, and other friends of education shared a set of cultural assumptions and beliefs that typified mainstream educational attitudes throughout much of the nineteenth and twentieth centuries. Robert Owen's New Harmony experiment appeared radical, but his educational ideas were either the same as or quite compatible with Mann's. These views assured the superiority of bureaucratic over community control, English over other languages, European Protestant ancestry over other backgrounds, men over women, and the East (especially Northeast) over other geographic regions. These beliefs, while evident when we look back from our perspective, were not so noticeable then because they were fundamental (ontological) assumptions so basic as to be largely unconscious tenets. They constituted what historian Thomas Kuhn has labeled a *paradigm,* or an interrelated set of assumptions about how things are and must be.[59]

Bishop Hughes and several other leaders of the American Roman Catholic Church shared several of the assumptions. Of course, they rejected Protestant bias and, because Catholic immigrants were native speakers of a variety of languages, the sizable parochial school system that developed in the last quarter of the nineteenth century usually reinforced the dominant language of each local parish. Most friends of education took strong exception to this feature of parochial schooling.

At issue were two fundamentally different concepts of how the United States should develop. Most Americans assumed that some civic values needed to permeate the social fabric. The friends of education thought *cultural monism* essential: one language (with a single standard of usage) and a common set of political, social, economic religious doctrines. Others believed that the emerging country could thrive with considerable diversity in language, religion, music, dress, politics, and other aspects of culture.

In 1925, the U.S. Supreme Court blocked a move by Nebraska to strike down parochial schools by declaring that enrollment in them did not meet the state's compulsory attendance laws.[60] A debate about bilingualism has smoldered in American society with vocal advocates and opponents. The late 1980s saw a move to make English the official language of the United States, as some people feared that non-English-speaking immigrants were endangering the country. Social theorist E. D. Hirsch claimed that large numbers of Americans were "culturally illiterate" and set forth a list of standard authors, concepts, and knowledge that everyone should know. Journalist Ben Wattenburg countered with an optimistic assessment.[61]

The friends of education—committed to enforcing on everyone a single educational standard, process, and content—advocated city, state, and federal control of schools instead of community-based schooling. Their arguments became orthodox among educators trained in schools and colleges of education. As the nineteenth century drew to a close, large school bureaucracies in cities like New York, Chicago, Los Angeles, Dallas, Atlanta, and Boston became the norm. Even small-town schools became bureaucratized as educators pushed for consolidation of rural and community schools into county or town systems. Grouping by age into grades became a sign of modernity.[62]

The official adoption of centralized control as best practice in education resulted in a paradox. Horace Mann, whose adult career was devoted to replacing the common school that Americans had prized for two centuries with something quite different, became known as the father of the common school. Practical features of the one-room, multi-age school—such as family-like size, cooperative learning, flexible scheduling, individual pacing, and a natural accommodation to each child's interests—gave way to large factory-type units with rigid schedules, assembly-line procedures, and loss of personal identity. No sooner had the friends of education established their paradigm as the dominant one than they confronted problems growing out of bureaucracy. The response is detailed in Chapter 9.

NOTES

1. Lawrence A. Cremin, *American Education: The National Experience, 1783–1876* (New York: Harper & Row, 1980), 52.

2. Frederick Merk, *History of the Westward Movement* (New York: Alfred A. Knopf, 1978), 102–111.

3. E. E. Brown, *The Making of Our Middle Schools: An Account of the Development of Secondary Education in the United States* (New York: Longman's, Green, 1903), 155–203.

4. Nathan O. Hatch, "The Christian Movement and the Demand for a Theology of the People," *Journal of American History* 67 (December 1980): 561–562.

5. The ongoing interpretive controversy about the influence of the frontier in American development is ably discussed by Paula M. Nelson, "The Significance of the Frontier in American Historiography: A Review Essay," *Annals of Iowa* 50 (Summer 1990): 531–540.

6. John Waters Proctor, Diary, December 31, 1818, Houghton Library, Harvard University.

7. Proctor, Diary, January 1, 1919.

8. Merk, *History of the Westward Movement*, 119.

9. Erwin V. Johanningmeier, "Enlightenment and Education in America in the Eighteenth Century," in *Educational Thinkers of the Enlightenment and their Influences in Different Countries*, ed. D. Jedan and F.-P. Hager (Murray, KY: Murray State University Press, 1987), 94–112.

10. Noah Webster to Joel Barlow, October 19, 1807, bMS Am 1448; James G. Carter to Henry W. Longfellow, March 2, 1825, bMS Am 1340.2, Houghton Library, Harvard University; Horace Mann to *Providence Patriot*, August 25, 1821, Horace Mann Papers, Massachusetts Historical Society, Boston.

11. E. Hill to Nancy Swift, December 20, 1862, National Public Education Board Papers, Connecticut State Historical Society, Hartford.

12. Polly Welts Kaufman, *Women Teachers on the Frontier* (New Haven: Yale University Press, 1984).

13. F. Michael Perko, *A Time to Favor Zion: The Ecology of Religion and School Development on the Urban Frontier, Cincinnati, 1830–1870* (Chicago: Educational Studies Press, 1988), 145.

14. Carl E. Kaestle, "The Development of Common School Systems in the States of the Old Northwest," in *Schools and the Means of Education Shall Forever Be Encouraged: A History of Education in the Old Northwest, 1787–1880,* ed. Paul H. Mattingly and Edward W. Stevens, Jr. (Athens, OH: Ohio University Libraries, 1987), 31–43.

15. Glenn Smith, "The Gillespie/Huftalen Diaries—A Window on American Education," *Vitae Scholasticae* 2 (Spring 1983): 243–266.

16. Jonathan Messerli, *Horace Mann, A Biography* (New York: Alfred A. Knopf, 1972). Unless otherwise noted all biographical information about Mann is from this source.

17. Messerli, *Horace Mann,* 246.

18. Denison Olmstead, "On the Democratic Tendencies of Science," *Journal of American Education* 1 (January 1856): 164–171.

19. Barnard to Mann, February 13, 1843, Mann Papers, Massachusetts Historical Society, Boston.

20. Ellwood P. Cubberley, *Public Education in the United States* (Boston: Riverside Press, 1947) made this mistake, which has been replicated in many texts. Lawrence A. Cremin, *The Wonderful World of Ellwood Patterson Cubberley: An Essay in the Historiography of American Education* (New York: Teachers College Press, 1965).

21. Robert Owen, *The Life of Robert Owen* (New York: Augustus M. Kelley, [1857] 1967).

22. Robert Owen, "A New View of Society," in John F. C. Harrison, *Utopianism and Education* (New York: Teachers College Press, 1968), 44.

23. A complete account of Owen's educational program at New Lanark was recorded by his eldest son, Robert Dale Owen, in *An Outline of the System of Education at New Lanark* (Cincinnati: Deming and Wood, 1825).

24. John Fletcher Clews Harrison, *Quest for the New Moral World* (New York: Charles Scribner's Sons, 1969), 81.

25. Robert Owen, "The Social System," *New Harmony Gazette* 2 (10 January 1827): 113.

26. Owen, "The Social System," 105–108.

27. George B. Lockwood, *The New Harmony Movement* (New York: D. Appleton, 1905), 84.

28. Cited in Richard Shaw, *Daggar John* (New York: Paulist Press, 1977), 14.

29. Shaw, *Daggar John,* 21–22.

30. Shaw, *Daggar John,* 91.

31. Diane Ravitch, *The Great School Wars* (New York: Basic Books, 1974), 27.

32. Vincent Lannie, *Public Money and Parochial Education* (Cleveland: Case Western Reserve University Press, 1968), 78.

33. Ravitch, *The Great School Wars,* 76.

34. Lannie, *Public Money and Parochial Education,* 256.

35. U.S. House of Representatives, 39th Congress, 1st Sess., 1865–1866, *Miscellaneous Documents No. 5* (Washington, DC: Government Printing Office, 1966), 1–5.

36. Donald Scott McPherson, "The Fight Against Free Schools in Pennsylvania: Popular Opposition to the Common School System, 1834–1874" (Ph.D. diss., University of Pittsburgh, 1977).

37. Glenn Smith, "Founding the U.S. Office of Education," *Educational Forum* 21 (March 1967): 307–322; Donald R. Warren, *To Enforce Education: A History of the Founding Years of the United States Office of Education* (Detroit: Wayne State University Press, 1974).

38. Ronald E. Butchart, *Northern Schools, Southern Schools, and Reconstruction: Freedmen's Education, 1862–1875* (Westport, CT: Greenwood Press, 1979), 4.

39. Butchart, *Northern Schools, Southern Schools,* 4; Vincent Harding, *There Is a River: The Black Struggle for Freedom in America* (New York: Harcourt Brace Jovanovich, 1981).

40. Charles P. Poole, "Two Centuries of Education in Alaska" (Ph.D. diss., University of Washington, 1947), 29.

41. *Report of the Commissioner of Education for the Year 1872* (Washington: Government Printing Office, 1873), 134.

42. Glenn Smith, "Education for the Natives of Alaska," *Journal of the West* 6 (July 1967): 440–450.

43. Robert Laird Stewart, *Sheldon Jackson: Pathfinder and Prospector of the Missionary Vanguard in the Rocky Mountains and Alaska* (New York: Fleming H. Revell, 1908); Robert Joseph Diven, "Jackson, Sheldon," *Dictionary of American Biography,* 9: 555.

44. Theodore Charles Hinckley, Jr., "The Alaska Labors of Sheldon Jackson, 1877–1890" (Ph.D. diss., University of Indiana, 1961), 103–104, 110, 114–115.

45. U.S., *Statutes at Large,* 23: Chap. 53, 27.

46. Stewart, *Sheldon Jackson,* 354–362; Hinckley, "Alaska Labors," 204–206. Many letters between Jackson and Eaton and between Jackson and Dawson in the "Outgoing Correspondence of the Commissioner of Education," Record Group 12, National Archives, Washington, DC, also document this controversy.

47. Poole, "Two Centuries of Education," 29.

48. William Torrey Harris to Julia Ward Howe (Confidential), January 22, 1901, "Outgoing Correspondence of the Commissioner of Education," Record Group 12.

49. *Report of the Commissioner of Education for the Year 1896–1897,* 2 vols. (Washington: Government Printing Office, 1898), 1: xliv.

50. *Annual Reports of the Department of the Interior for the Fiscal Year Ended June 30, 1903: Report of the Commissioner of Education* (Washington: Government Printing Office, 1904), lxvii.

51. William Torrey Harris, "Memorandum on Alaskan Text Books," Typescript in a folder marked "Commissioner Harris, 1889–June, 1906," Record Group 12.

52. H. Dewey Anderson and Walter Crosby Eells, *Alaska Natives: A Survey of Their Sociological and Educational Status* (Stanford: Stanford University Press, 1935), 440; Jessie Ash Arndt, "Alaskan Help Melt the Igloo Image," *Christian Science Monitor,* January 7, 1967, 9: "Their elementary-school books show a horse and a chicken the same size."

53. Ted C. Hinckley, "Sheldon Jackson as Preserver of Alaska's Native Culture," *Pacific Historical Review* 33 (November 1964): 411–424.

54. Harris, "Memorandum on Alaska Text Books," Record Group 12.

55. Lester Dale Henderson, "The Development of Education in Alaska, 1867 to 1931" (Ph.D. diss., Stanford University, 1935), 140–150.

56. Henderson, "The Development of Education in Alaska," 211–222.

57. *Report on the Work of the Bureau of Education for the Natives of Alaska, 1911–1912,* Bulletin, 1913, Number 36 (Washington: Government Printing Office, 1936), 31–32. See also Tray 475, "William Hamilton Reference File," Record Group 75, National Archives, Washington, DC.

58. Sally Carrighar, *Moonlight at Midday* (New York: Alfred A. Knopf, 1958), 222.

59. Thomas Kuhn, *The Structure of Scientific Revolutions,* 2d ed. (Chicago: University of Chicago Press, 1970).

60. *Pierce v. Society of Sisters of the Holy Names of Jesus and Mary,* 268 U.S. 510, 45 S.Ct. 571, 69 L. Ed. 1070 (1925).

61. E.D. Hirsch, Jr., *Cultural Literacy: What Every American Needs to Know* (New York: Vintage Books, 1987); Ben J. Wattenburg, *The First Universal Nation Leading Indicators and Ideas About the Surge of America in the 1990s* (New York: The Free Press, 1991).

62. For example, a frontier Texas newspaper editor proclaimed (bragged) about his fledgling town in the 1880s: "We have a graded school."

The Progressives

CHAPTER NINE

The last quarter of the nineteenth century saw a sweeping victory for the educational ideas associated with Horace Mann and the friends of education. Many normal schools started to train elementary teachers. Colleges and universities added education departments with graduate programs aimed at producing leaders for school systems. As early as 1874, a Michigan supreme court judge indicated the widespread adoption as one which was part of a tax-funded, compulsory, graded entity belonging to a bureaucratic system.[1]

While these developments were taking place, Americans found themselves in a social crisis centered on several problems: (1) the growth of big business and urbanization versus agrarianism and rugged individualism; (2) inequalities in the distribution of wealth resulting in distinct class divisions; (3) political corruption and the apparent breakdown of moral and ethical codes—especially in the upper levels of society; and (4) the denial of political and economic rights to blacks, women, and other minority groups.[2]

Slavery was legally ended, but severe racial and ethnic prejudice remained. Industrialism had brought financial rewards to a small proportion of second-generation immigrants, such as Chicago's Phillip Armour, George Pullman, and Cyrus McCormick, but overcrowded conditions in the cities were intensified by the steady flow of immigrants. In Chicago the number of immigrants skyrocketed to 200,000 a year, and by 1890, 80 percent of Chicago's population was foreign-born. The Haymarket Riot of 1886 signaled serious tensions between the capitalists and immigrant workers. The number of farms tripled between 1860 and 1910, but by 1900 farmers had a smaller share of the nation's wealth than they did in 1860.

Journalists who publicized these problems came to be known as *muck-rakers*. Unmasking corporate malpractice and exposing political dishonesty became the most common form of muckraking, but there was an educational dimension as well. In 1892, Joseph Mayer Rice visited schools all over America and wrote a series of articles for the *Forum* detailing a generally grim picture of grinding boredom, uninspired teachers, lockstep memorization, and impersonal treatment. Good schools in all large cities could be found, he said; however, they "have been developed, not as a result of the system, but in spite of it." The remedy Rice proposed was to make education "scientific."[3]

The call for scientifically trained experts to reform urban schools was part of a larger set of activities and ideas that is now called the progressive movement. Uniting diverse elements in American society, it transcended the agrarianism and the sectionalism of the Populists and the humanitarianism of such urban reformers as Jacob Riis and Jane Addams, according to historian Ralph Henry Gabriel. "It was a crusade in which farmers, wage earners, and small business men all marched shoulder to shoulder. . . . They put their faith in science. . . . Pragmatism and science worship of the Progressive Faith were veneers laid on ethical beliefs which in American history were as old as puritanism."[4]

What did it mean to be scientific and progressive in education? The careers of the five people discussed in this chapter illustrate several aspects of the issue. The first biographee pioneered the development of psychology as a social science and was among the first to apply the tenets of the "new science" to education.

G. Stanley Hall (1844–1924)

Granville Stanley Hall was born to Abigail Beal and Granville Bascom Hall on February 1, 1844 in Ashfield, Massachusetts. His mother, a pious and gentle woman, frequently read to Stanley and his younger siblings Robert and Julina from the Bible, *Pilgrim's Progress, Uncle Tom's Cabin,* and the works of Shakespeare, Scott, and Dickens. She hoped Stanley would enter the ministry. His father was a stern man of Calvinistic leanings with a quick and violent temper, who demanded obedience from his children. An advocate of practical scientific farming, he seemed dissatisfied with his lot as a farmer. In 1855, he went to the state legislature on the Know-Nothing (anti-Catholic, anti-foreign) ticket.

Education

At sixteen, following his schooling at Ashfield Academy, Stanley obtained a teaching job in a nearby hamlet. In 1862, he went to Easthampton, Massachusetts to attend Williston Academy. From Williston, he entered Williams College, where his introduction to science and philosophy seemed to fuel the fire of separation not only from his father's authority, but from established religion.

Stanley found the classical studies of his first two years at Williams "fearfully hard." In his junior year, he took work in history, natural science, and modern languages, and thought the courses exciting and easy. He found time to join a scientific club and to explore and write about his natural surroundings. He drew inspiration from the romantic literature and the lectures of Ralph Waldo Emerson, who twice visited the Williams campus. In the senior philosophy course, Mark Hopkins, president of the college, presented a religious hierarchy of existence and some notions from faculty psychology. The theory that the mind consists of faculties piqued Stanley's interest in natural science, but Hopkins's moralism repelled him. In contrast, his rhetoric professor, John Bascom, supported his romantic leanings and enhanced his independence by stressing John Stuart Mill's ideas on the central role of feelings.

Following his graduation from Williams in 1867, Stanley Hall attended Union Theological Seminary in New York City. He followed the regular course of theological studies, but spent his free time reading the works of Ernest Renan and David Friedrich Strauss, both of whom portrayed Jesus as a moral man wrapped in biblical legend. Other influences at this time included George Sylvester Morris, Henry B. Smith, and Henry Ward Beecher.

Beginning in June 1869, Hall spent fifteen months studying in Germany. When he returned, he brought with him some unorthodox ideas, such as positivistic philosophy (based on the assumption of a material reality existing independently of human perception) and historical criticism, which he had studied with Adolf Trandelenburg, Morris's teacher. And he had learned a scientific version of the historical process from Johann Droysen. The clearest evidence of the influence of these ideas on his thinking came from his advisor's response to his trial sermon. All Henry B. Smith could do was pray for Hall's soul.

Early Career

Hall had stayed just orthodox enough to receive his degree, but rejected a clerical career. He wanted to teach philosophy in a college or university; however, no position was immediately available. For two years he tutored the children of a wealthy banker and finally, in late summer 1872, Hall secured a position as professor of rhetoric and English at Antioch College, over which Horace Mann had briefly presided a little more than a decade earlier.

After four years at Antioch, Hall became dissatisfied and took a leave of absence. Intending to return to Germany, he stopped in Cambridge, Massachusetts to study the "new psychology" with William James, a young Harvard assistant professor. He conducted experiments with James's equipment and in Henry Bowditch's physiology laboratory. In

1878 Hall passed his final oral examination and was awarded a Ph.D. in psychology, the first doctorate given by the Harvard philosophy department and the first in the field of psychology anywhere in the country.

The following summer Hall returned to Germany. In Berlin he attended lectures on physical science given by Herman von Helmholtz and worked with Hugo Kronecker in the new physiology institute. In 1879 he moved to Leipzig and became the first American to work in Wilhelm Wundt's experimental psychology laboratory. He continued his study of physiology with Johannes von Kries. This second foray into the natural sciences in Germany resulted in Hall's rejection of metaphysics and adoption of psychology as a natural science. Just prior to leaving for Leipzig, in September 1879, Hall married Cornelia Fisher, an acquaintance from Yellow Springs, Ohio who had come to Germany to study art.

During the next decade, Hall capitalized on the growing interest in natural science in America. He first became popular as a lecturer in pedagogy at Harvard while awaiting a permanent academic appointment. Hall brought the authority of science to the educational reform movement based on interpretations of Rousseau, Pestalozzi, Froebel, and Herbart. Although he held to traditional notions of discipline, he captivated the educational community with his theories of child development based on evolution. He believed that humans repeated or "recapitulated" the evolution of the race as they grew from childhood into adulthood, and that education should follow the natural impulses of the child under adult guidance. Hall was probably the first American academic to make a sustained argument for the scientific study of children. He thought such investigations would provide an empirical foundation for what he regarded as an overly romantic inclination to follow the child's impulses. He reported some of his findings in an article entitled "The Contents of Children's Minds," which was based on data gathered via questionnaire, one of the first of its kind in psychology.

In March 1882, Johns Hopkins University President Daniel Coit Gilman appointed Hall part-time lecturer in psychology and pedagogy, and he soon became full time. Hall opened an experimental laboratory in spring 1883, usually recognized as the first of its kind in America, and he found four graduate students who were interested in psychological observation and experimentation: James McKeen Cattell, Joseph Jastrow, Edward M. Hartwell, and John Dewey. Of the four, only Cattell and Jastrow became experimental psychologists. Hartwell became a physician and Dewey a philosopher and educator, but both retained an abiding interest in psychology.

During the 1880s Hall concentrated on laboratory studies and criticized any work in psychology that was not experimental. When he founded the *American Journal of Psychology* in 1887, to provide a means of expression for his colleagues and to define the field of psychology, he was determined that it would be a periodical devoted exclusively to experimental work. It was this aspect of the Hopkins program that was most influential in the growth of American psychology, as one university after another opened experimental laboratories.

In addition to his editorial and laboratory work, Hall began a serious attempt to devise a theoretical foundation for the new psychology. He wanted a theory that included the evolutionary ideas of Herbert Spencer and Ernest Haeckel as well as the experimental theories of Wundt and his German colleagues. He wrestled with the problem for more than twenty years, never completely achieving his goal. Two things hampered his efforts. First, he was not able to free himself of the emotional hold of German idealism. Second, he chose to give up the relative freedom of a professorial position in favor of the demanding job of university president.

University President

The board of trustees of the newly founded Clark University in Worcester, Massachusetts invited him to become president, and Hall accepted and resigned from Johns Hopkins in April 1888. The result of his work was a graduate institution with a scientific orientation. The school had five departments—psychology, biology, chemistry, physics, and mathematics—and a faculty of established and promising scholars. Like Spencer, Hall believed that scientific knowledge was the most valuable of all knowledge.[5]

Of course, Hall's own department of psychology concentrated on experimental investigations and drew on the strength of the disciplines related to the new psychology such as biology and the emerging field of anthropology. Clark's distinction in psychology, moreover, encouraged the growth of the experimental program at Harvard. The competition between these two departments was in part a product of the rivalry between two of the acknowledged leaders in psychology, Hall and William James.

Just as he reached the pinnacle of his career, certain events—some of his own doing, others beyond his control—brought Hall down. The first was the accidental death of his wife and daughter on May 15, 1890, which caused Hall to go into a deep depression that resulted in his nearly complete withdrawal from Clark. He found solace in a renewed faith in God, thus marking the end of his struggle with questions of religion. The second was a crisis over Hall's administration of Clark. In 1891 Jonas Clark became disenchanted with his school, and began to reduce his monetary support. Hall tried unsuccessfully to keep the problem from the faculty. A series of confrontations between Hall and the faculty led to the departure of more than half of the faculty and nearly three-fourths of the students. It took years for Hall and the university to recover from the devastation.

Despite the crisis at Clark, Hall remained a leader in psychology. He was instrumental in founding the American Psychological Association in 1892, and served as its first president. He also continued to edit the

American Journal of Psychology. His criticism of unscientific psychology permeated the journal, and he issued scathing reviews of textbooks written by James and George T. Ladd, the other two elders in the field. His editorial policy for the journal alienated some younger colleagues, and brought about the founding of the *Psychological Review* by Cattell and James Mark Baldwin in 1894. In an editorial in 1895, Hall claimed that he himself was the most influential leader in the establishment of experimental psychology in America. Shock waves rolled through the psychological community, contributing to Hall's fall from power and to a personal break with James.

Child Study Movement

In 1891, after an absence of six years, Hall returned to child study. Over the next three years, he increased his involvement in education through informal meetings at National Education Association (NEA) conventions, the *Pedagogical Seminary* (a journal he founded in 1891), and the summer session for educators held at Clark. By 1894 he was a prominent spokesperson for child study, addressing audiences throughout the nation, and in that same year, he enunciated the gospel of the movement before the newly founded Child Study Department of the NEA. He saw the endeavor as a moral commitment for educators: "The little child standing in our midst is, I believe again to be the regeneration of education, to moralize it, to make it religious, to bring the child (because it brings the school) home to the hearts of the men and women, where children should always find a warm place."[6] He followed this declaration with an outline of the goals for child-centered education: children should learn of the joy of good health, become sensitive to nature, and recognize that "life is for service."

For more than a decade Hall, some of his students, and numerous educators involved in the movement gathered data about children through surveys. These investigations were founded on two principal themes: physical development and psychological aspects of child development and education. Hall's studies produced a picture of childhood whose dominant characteristic was imagination. He concluded that, moved by strong feelings and impulses, the child's world was separate from that of adults but represented a true and necessary line of development. Like Rousseau, however, Hall saw a need for adult guidance as education supported natural growth.

A second and perhaps more personally satisfying result of Hall's investigations into childhood was the publication of *Adolescence* in 1904. In this massive study, he described what he thought to be the most critical step toward adulthood. Adolescence was a period characterized by rapid mental, physical, and emotional growth driven by a new burst of energy. Hall argued that adolescence should be prolonged to enable the individual to develop fully and to learn self-control. And the heart of adolescent growth lay in the treatment of sexuality, for sublimation of sexual energy through chastity and religious endeavor would enable the adolescent to accomplish the shift from selfishness to altruism. But adolescence was not solely to be focused on emotional stability, for proper adolescent development, according to Hall, should result in a "mental unity" of desires, beliefs, and volitions. Normal human growth depended on the suppression of primitive impulses by more civilized faculties and the sublimation of impulses into socially acceptable behavior.

Hall's genetic psychology also contained elements of Freudian theory. In 1909, Hall introduced Sigmund Freud directly to the American psychological community by bringing him to the second decennial celebration of Clark University. The conference was attended by a group that included the most eminent psychologists in the country, and marked the beginning of a long period of interest in Freudian psychology among Americans. This conference was Hall's most visible professional triumph.

The years following the Clark meeting, however, brought some adjustments in his acceptance of psychoanalytic theory. Many of Hall's academic and child study colleagues strongly criticized the emphasis on sexuality in *Adolescence* and in *Educational Problems,* which Hall published in 1911. As a consequence, Hall began to change his position. He became critical of the breadth of sexual symbolism in Freud's writings, and later added some of Jung's and Adler's ideas to his viewpoint. In the meantime, his frank discussions of sex had become an embarrassment to the child study group and had contributed both to its reorientation toward social development of children and to Hall's departure from the movement.

Final Years

During this period, Hall renewed his interest in social issues and religion. He remained concerned about the importance of education and science to social, cultural, and even racial progress. He also took an interest in racial minorities in America. On the subject of women's rights, however, he urged women to retain their femininity. Finally, Hall devoted much attention to religion. In 1904, he started a third journal, *The American Journal of Religious Psychology and Education,* and in 1917 presented his religious speculations in *Jesus the Christ in the Light of Psychology.* He retired in 1920 after thirty-one years as president of Clark University. In the remaining years of his life, he continued to engage in intellectual activities, producing a description of a utopian society called *The Fall of Atlantis* in 1920 and his memoirs, *The Life and Confessions of a Psychologist,* in 1923. On April 24, 1924, Hall died following a series of illnesses.

Hall was one of the most significant figures in the founding of the new psychology in America. He was largely responsible for setting psychology in the direction of rigorous experimental research. His legacy has been apparent throughout most of the twentieth century in the positivistic paradigm that has dominated psychology and education.

While Hall was hailing a new dawn for psychology and child study, Francis W. Parker was developing aspects of a new brand of education that would bring him the title of "father of progressive education." Of him, Joseph Mayer Rice said he had "done as much if not more than any other single individual to spread the doctrine of the new education throughout the country."[7]

Francis W. Parker (1837–1902)

Francis Parker's life began on October 9, 1837 in Piscatauquog, New Hampshire, a little town near Manchester that had been founded by his grandfather. His mother was a schoolteacher until she married widower Robert Parker. They raised three daughters in addition to Francis. Francis remembered his father only as an invalid, for he died when Francis was seven. The impoverished widow apprenticed her son to a farmer, and Francis grew to adolescence plowing and snatching a few weeks of schooling between harvests. When he was thirteen, he broke his bond to study in a local academy. He never quite finished his formal education, but began teaching in various country schools, "boarding around," and farming in the summers.[8]

In 1859 Parker left for Carrollton, Illinois to take charge of a district school. Carrollton, lying close to the Mississippi River and the slave culture downstream, was divided on the secession question, and Parker lost the support of his pro-Southern school directors when he voted for Lincoln. He returned to New Hampshire in the summer of 1861 and helped raise a company of Manchester youths for the Fourth Regiment. He was elected lieutenant and advanced in rank as the war progressed. The problems of a divided people would haunt him the rest of his life and quicken his resolve for social unity. He helped to liberate some of the first slaves at Hilton Head Island, and was at Port Royal when he heard black volunteers raise hosannas at Lincoln's Emancipation Proclamation in 1863. He fought with black regiments in the capture of Fort Wagner, and again during the siege of Petersburg.

Rallying his troops during an engagement, he was shot in the neck. He regained his health, but would always have a husky voice and be subject to wheezing spells. During his convalescence, Parker participated in Lincoln's New Hampshire reelection campaign. Appointed lieutenant colonel of his regiment by the Republican governor of New Hampshire, he rejoined his men as their commanding officer. Just as the last campaign of the war was ending, Confederate cavalry captured him. Released at the end of the war, he returned to teaching in his hometown.

Parker saw education, rather than military force, as the great unifier of the people, though he would retain the tile of colonel as he began to rally forces against traditional education. Known as the "Doughty Colonel" by his enemies, he was a hard campaigner. In 1868 Parker left Manchester for Dayton, Ohio, and soon became supervising principal of the Dayton system.

Theory into Practice

Dayton had a large German community which used object lessons and had kindergartens. Both appealed to Parker, who longed for a theoretical base for child-centered practices that were assuming an increasingly prominent place in his educational practice. When his wife died in 1872, he left Dayton to study pedagogy at the University of Berlin. After two-and-a-half years in Germany, where his massive person was often mistaken for that of Bismark, he brought back the German enthusiasm for national unity as well as their scientific approach to child development and lesson planning.

Parker's practices and new theories quickly came into focus in Quincy, Massachusetts, where he was hired as superintendent of schools in 1875. Under the powerful sponsorship and national eminence of Charles Francis Adams, Jr., and John Quincy Adams II, his so-called "Quincy system" attracted widespread attention. After five years in Quincy, Parker remarried and moved to Boston. Encountering opposition there, he left in 1883 for the burgeoning industrial city of Chicago. As principal of the Cook County Normal School, he began training lieutenants who would carry his battle to every corner of the nation. The new education, or what Parker sometimes called progressive education, was on the march, and in many quarters the new school movement was simply labeled *Parkerism*.

Parkerism proposed formal education as the central means of making idealized social progress. Educating children for the needs of a social democracy, Parker patterned citizenship on Christian as well as democratic and egalitarian principles. He believed there was self-evident proof for these principles in the secrets Darwin had forced out of nature. Parker saw democratic progress as God's design gradually revealed in natural evolution, and he believed the ultimate law had already been discovered in the Golden Rule. Most human beings, he said, were specimens of arrested development. Humankind could hasten evolutionary progress if the laws of natural development were found and exercised in the classroom. This meant treating the transmission of knowledge as the means and not the end of education. The development of human beings—of their full physical, mental, and moral powers—was the ultimate aim of education.

Writings

More than twenty years before Dewey's *Democracy and Education,* Parker chose the same title for the final chapter of his best-selling *Talks on Pedagogics.* He described the public school movement sponsored by the friends of education as the expressed demand of the lower classes, wrested from the private educational establishment through the rise of popular government. Curriculum and teaching methodologies, however, continued to reflect too many old world practices geared to the machinery of oppression. The old methods of pedantry prevented free action of the mind, as they limited "the mental horizon" and prevented the mind from looking outside a well-defined circle of thought. "It was the last ditch," he said, "of the rule of the few—forced by necessity to give the people education, but still acting to keep the people from the highway of freedom." Such education not only drove out the children of the lower classes but made "pauper" minds of those who remained.

Parker believed education, not economics, divided the classes and caused exploitation and alienation. He said history reflected two conflicting ideals: (1) limitation, or rule of the few; and (2) freedom, or rule of the many. Education was the source of knowledge, and knowledge was power. The ideal of limitation was to keep knowledge and power in the hands of the few and make the many dependent, and traditional education was its method. It used what he called "quantity" methods, which counted words and syllables, broke subjects into parts, and prevented an understanding of relations between parts and wholes. It divided life from school, thought from action, and mind from body. In short, it prevented what Parker called "quality" education, and thereby precluded the ideal of freedom. "Real progress," he said, "has been along the lines of the lowest state of society. The real history of a people is the history of its humblest homes." Unconsciously, perhaps, Parker sought to do away with class education by educating all in the manner of the working class. As he often said, the school was to train children into a love of work.

The Parker system was patterned after home and shop and tried to avoid passive intellectualizing. Instead it stressed doing more with things than ideas. Only a leisured class could afford knowledge for its ornamental value, so Parker favored utility and vocation. The lower classes, on the margin of survival, demanded immediate relevance and reward. *Now* was the great word of the new education, according to Parker. He opposed having facts learned by rote and "salted down like herring" for some possible future use. All children began instinctively the study of every subject, he said, and all could be instructed in these subjects at every stage of their development. Subject matter should be "spiraled" to follow human development in its evolution from the simple to the complex.

Parker used the word *integratism* as the process for bringing people together into a community of common interest and purpose. He would bring together old and young as well as the social classes in a common inquiry, in a partnership of learning. He would bring the sexes together in a nonsexist curriculum, which he and his second wife, an ardent feminist, worked to achieve. He would bring the races together. He would not impose racial integration or anything else. The teacher would supply the conditions so children would discover Christian fellowship for themselves.

Expanding Influence

In 1894 Parker addressed the Department of Superintendence of the NEA with a plea for his ideal of freedom. "In the North," he said, "we have the great problem of capital and labor; in the South, the question of what shall be done with the millions of people given liberty through the war, but not given freedom. The only means of freedom is education, and the highest problem on the solution of which we all unite is: How can we take these people and make them useful, important factors in society?" He answered himself with "education into work." He said, "I would have a shop for handwork in every schoolhouse. I would have a small farm or garden surrounding every schoolhouse. I should train these children into a love of work, ability to work, and into the honesty which is developed by honest labor." Booker T. Washington would echo these sentiments the following year at the Atlanta Exposition. Both Parker and Washington stressed that progress toward social equality required educational rather than political reform.

Parker's "integratism" included immigrant children, who had to be "fused, blended, melted into the great army of human progress under the dominance of the new civilization with the Common School for its right hand." The common school, he said, was the "Infant Republic," where children of "all castes, classes, shades of belief meet and learn to love and live for each other." He berated segregated schools at the NEA meeting in 1891 because "the Common School had for its ideal the common education of all races, classes, sexes and sects in one school." Parker believed there was not much that could be done to improve the present, but the future could be directed toward the ideal of freedom. America could be made more democratic through a revolution from below arising in one common school.

The problem of reconciling the child to the needs of a greatly expanding body of knowledge was as important to Parker as reconciling the child to the social needs of democracy. While Parker supported the claims of experimental science in the curriculum, he deplored the schism developing between old and new subjects. He believed science had to be integrated into the prevailing curricular structures without diminishing the value and moral heritage of the humanities, for self-contained subjects prevented children from seeing beyond a limited mental horizon. He further argued that there was a lack of economy in stringing separate subjects and skill courses together.

Theory of Concentration

Parker's solution to this problem was a "theory of concentration," in which the curriculum would concentrate on the child. The curriculum, like the world, should be of one piece, with all subjects taught as an "organic, inseparable, interdependent unity." Children bring to school a great curiosity about their natural and social environments. "Nature" and "man in nature" were the unifying themes. All disciplines fit into these categories, which he called "integers of life," or "central subjects." All aspects of the child's environment could be used to reveal the interrelatedness of the inorganic and organic sciences upon which the social sciences and the humanities were built. The natural sciences, less complex and less culturally controversial than the social sciences, were to be given more emphasis in the early years. "Modes of attention," such as reading and observing, "modes of expression," such as writing, speaking, drawing, modeling, and "modes of judgment" and "modes of form and number" were all to be developed as children needed them to discover the nature of the world.

Parker's enemies attacked him as a materialist because he stressed science as the foundation of the curriculum and kept defining education as the science of the economy of human effort in the direction of "all-sided human development." They alleged that his theories contained only a few islands of thought rising out of a sea of sentimentality. Some academicians demeaned his theories because he held no earned degree, and Parker was constantly fighting them as well as the political bosses who controlled the schools. Someone said that the Colonel had to "feel for his scalp" each morning at the Cook County Normal School where these bosses and their "hatchet men" were always on the warpath against him.

While Parker attacked political corruption and academic snobbishness, he gathered supporters—feminists, women's clubs, and some of the new psychologists. His emphasis on manual training gained the interest of industrialists seeking skilled labor. He formed "mothers' clubs" to reach parents. Hailed as a "lecturer for the masses," he carried his reforms to the common people. He drew crowds on the Chautauqua lecture circuit, where his appearance was often reported as the event of the year. When he was not working himself into a rage, he joked and exaggerated the position of his opponents until audiences doubled over with laughter. Like the ubiquitous peddler of patent medicine, to which he was often compared, he went everywhere to sell his brand of cure-all education.

Politicians and traditional educators found it difficult to oppose Parker. He was invulnerable to logic. He held both absolute and relative values, advocating social education on one hand and individual education on the other. He opposed utopian socialism, such as that of Edward Bellamy, because he equated it with charity; even teachers should not show charity because it might help children too much. Children should help themselves. He opposed the collective action of teacher unions, preferring that teachers make themselves individually indispensable through merit. He argued for the freedom of teachers and children; this was always couched in God-given as well as scientific principles.

Parker imputed no sinister motives to traditional educators; they were only what he called "old fogies." "Fogyism," he said, meant being stranded in a rut, accepting the "reigning method without question." Fogies, were "artisan" teachers, producing exact patterns like good workers. The "artist" teacher, which his normal school was tailoring, made new combinations out of old thoughts.

Preeminently a teacher of teachers, Parker's normal education was built around a practice school containing a kindergarten and eight grades. Each grade had its "critic" or regular teacher. The children were divided into about thirty groups, each assigned to a student teacher. Student teachers rotated from group to group and grade to grade, all the while being impressed with the importance of careful planning in accordance with ideals or principles. Such plans, and their results, were published monthly to keep everyone briefed on their progress. Practice and experiment were buttressed with a thorough study of the history and philosophy of education so students would understand the principles that must motivate methods. Instruction was also provided in the psychological order of learning and the logical order of subject matter.

The public press and many professional journals headlined Parker's struggles and practices, especially after *The Forum* published the Joseph Mayer Rice survey of schools in 1892. By the late 1890s it was recalled that Parker once made "many dry bones to rattle and aroused much indignation while his ideas were denounced as visionary and insane," but it was now difficult to find, the newspapers reported, "anyone in the commonwealth who did not acknowledge the greatness of the service he rendered in attacking the old regime." When Parker attended the annual meetings of the NEA, everyone wanted to hear and meet him. People stood and stared when he entered the room.

Some of the old fogies started coming over to Parker's side, but Parker feared they were not of the true faith. He once told an audience, "There are men who feel the new breath that is blowing among the schoolrooms of the country. They ask for a few words to label this evident movement; they are told it is the new education, and they hasten to declare they are on that side." He added, with probably a spank on his backside, that they were "old educators with a new education 'lean-to' tacked on, sometimes right in front, sometimes in the extreme *rear*. They are old educators with a 'new education attachment.' "

Final Years

Parker's new education found its greatest support in the leisured class. The Adamses sparked his movement in Quincy. Marshall Field and George Pullman, symbols of wealth and power in Chicago, advanced the private support he needed to promote manual training. Mrs. Bertha Honoré Potter Palmer, acknowledged arbiter of "society" in Chicago, was so much in the Parker camp that her husband, the mayor of Chi-

cago, once complained that his social life was ruined whenever he sided
with politicians against Parker. In 1899 Parker reluctantly changed
headquarters from his public normal school to the Chicago Institute,
especially endowed for him by Anita McCormick Blaine, reaper heiress
of Chicago.

Now removed from the political arena, he was nevertheless surrounded with problems. His dream of a free slum school in connection
with Jane Addams faltered, partly because of disagreement over a suitable site. Other dreams awakened his patrons to the high cost of progressive education; the architectural demands alone were prohibitive.
Parker's board of trustees entered an alliance with University of Chicago President William Rainey Harper, who already had Dewey on his
faculty. Harper had been interested in Parker since Blaine announced
her endowment. The move was against Dewey's preferences and Parker's better judgment. Dewey would retain his former title as head of
the department of philosophy, psychology, and pedagogy, and keep his
faltering Laboratory School. Parker became director of the university's
newly formed School of Education.

Ill and depressed over the recent death of his wife, Parker found little
to encourage him in the new arrangements at Chicago. Dewey dared not
attack the Colonel openly, but he did harass Wilbur Jackman, Parker's
chief assistant. When Parker suddenly died in 1902, Dewey succeeded
him as director of the School of Education, and a full-scale war developed between Dewey and some of his supporters and the Parker faculty.
Unable to force the Parker staff out, Dewey departed for Columbia University in 1904 to become titular head of the new education.[9]

Dewey had acknowledged Parker as the father of progressive education, but Parker was buried as its practitioner, while Dewey went on to
be proclaimed as the movement's major theorist. Parker's published
works were neglected after his living force was gone.

John Dewey (1859–1952)

The first John Dewey died in a scalding accident when he was less than
three years old. His guilt-stricken mother conceived again and gave the
same name to the son she bore on October 20, 1859 in Burlington, Vermont.[10] John was descended from English and Flemish origins and four
generations of pious Yankee pioneers who had cleared a settlement in the
New England wilderness. Family tradition held that there was royal
blood on his mother's side. Daughter of "Squire" Rich, John's mother
Lucina married working class Archibald Dewey, who was twenty years
her senior. She had college-educated brothers and brought high social
expectations to her offspring. Her liberal Universalist religious views,
turned Congregational, were strictly passed on, with perhaps an ulti-

mately negative effect on John. Archibald, from a line of farmers, had broken with the land to become a grocer in Burlington.

Impressions of poverty and human suffering sprang from John's early experience when his abolitionist mother carried him and his younger brother to northern Virginia as she followed her husband's cavalry regiment. John soon returned to his native town on the placid shores of Lake Champlain to begin school and help his father at the expanding store. He sometimes summered and worked on relatives' farms. Graduating from high school at what was then the routine age of fifteen, he entered the nearby University of Vermont.

Shy and introspective, he was an average student, and at one time was on the demerit list for contributing to a disturbance. His grades ranged from 69 in Herodotus (history) and 70 in algebra to 88 in botany and 92 in physiology. The nonelective course of study at the university passed on the general heritage without much connection to the present. In his senior year, he enjoyed a flexible course designed to introduce students to "the world of ideas." That course, he claimed, stimulated in him a "sense of interdependence and interrelated unity that gave form to intellectual stirrings that had been previously inchoate."

He did not know what to do with his life. He inquired for local teaching jobs during the summer of 1879, but he looked young and was inexperienced. A cousin who was principal of the high school in Oil City, Pennsylvania, wired the unemployed college graduate that he could teach for her at forty dollars a month. This was a relatively high salary, so he accepted and set off for the booming Standard Oil Company town.

He taught Latin, algebra, and the natural sciences. His school listed only six graduates in 1880 and thirteen the following year. The young man, under the constant scrutiny of his cousin, apparently had no trouble with the subject matter or the students. He found time to read in philosophy and write "The Metaphysical Assumptions of Materialism," which was published by W. T. Harris's *Journal of Speculative Philosophy*. The encouragement of the *Journal*'s editor led Dewey to consider devoting his life to teaching philosophy.

After two years in Oil City, Dewey returned to Vermont and taught in a local academy while taking private tutoring in philosophy with H. A. P. Torrey. He sought a fellowship at Johns Hopkins University, the new and pioneering graduate school in America. Yet even with the recommendation of Torrey, the penniless schoolteacher failed to get a fellowship or scholarship, so an aunt helped him finance his graduate studies in 1882. There he found the logic courses of Charles S. Peirce frustrating because they were mathematically oriented. (Later, Dewey would nurture and apply to education the philosophy of pragmatism that Peirce was then articulating.) More to Dewey's liking were the psychology offerings of G. Stanley Hall and the idealistic metaphysics of George Sylvester Morris, the mentor for whom he would later name a son. He completed his doctorate in 1884 with a dissertation on Kant's psychology.

Educational Philosopher

Though a degree from Germany would have been more prestigious, his Ph.D. from Hopkins got him a job teaching philosophy at the University of Michigan. Two years later he married a graduate of that university, Alice Chipman, and settled into domestic as well as academic life. He left Michigan in 1888 for one year at the University of Minnesota before returning to Michigan as chair of the philosophy department. During these years the colleague and friend influencing him most was George Herbert Mead. In 1894, Mead secured for Dewey a position at the new University of Chicago chairing the departments of philosophy, psychology, and pedagogy after President Harper failed to attract any more famous professors for $5,000 a year. He spent several months traveling in Europe before arriving in Chicago.

Chicago brought Dewey under the influence of the social settlement work of Jane Addams and the progressive education of Francis Parker, then principal of the Cook County Normal. Dewey sent his children to the controversial but socially prestigious Parker school. Two years after his arrival in Chicago, Dewey established his own "Laboratory School," merging psychology, philosophy, and pedagogy into a single academic department.

Dewey came to see philosophy and education as common endeavors and attempted to implement Harper's dream of making education an important field of study. Dewey believed that every social experience was essentially educative:"What nutrition and reproduction are to physiological life, education is to social life." He described education as the process of forming fundamental intellectual and emotional dispositions. Education was philosophy in action, and people must make themselves instruments of continuous learning. In his "Pedagogic Creed," he recapitulated Hall by saying that "all education proceeds by the participation of the individual in the social consciousness of the race." He differentiated school from education. School was a special social institution that should concentrate on the most effective way of "bringing the child to share in the inherited resources of the race, and to use his own powers for social ends." Dewey also believed that philosophy could not be separated from culture. Culture was a relative and changing human phenomenon, and education was a transmission and transformation of culture. He believed philosophy could best serve its culture by clarifying and criticizing it, by holding up the mirror to ways of behaving that had become second nature.

Dewey's quarrel with traditional education was similar to that of, and to some extent borrowed from, Parker. Traditional education separated the social classes with its academic elitism. It separated leisure and labor, people and nature, mind and body, thought and action, and was itself isolated from society. The separate subjects of its curricula were so isolated from one another that an understanding of the whole of knowledge was precluded. Such subject matter was also oriented to the past and did not connect with the present or lead to the future. Traditional education was "scholiocentric" and tried to fit the child to the school instead of being "pedocentric," or fitting the school to the child. Traditional education was a one-way channel of communication—from teacher to student through drill and memorization, fear and competition, with direct and didactic methods and indirect and abstract media.

Quoting Rousseau at length, Dewey advocated reversing the usual methods. He believed children had intrinsic interest in language, in finding out or inquiring, in making and constructing things, and in artistic expression. While the traditional school taught language for its own sake, with rules preceding use, he would have language follow interest and have its use and practice precede its rules. While the traditional school limited inquiry to what others had found out in the past, he would help children find out for themselves. Traditional schools neglected the making and construction of things and artistic expression. Dewey stressed manual training, industrial and domestic arts, and free artistic expression. As children followed their interests in making things, they learned language, arithmetic, and even history. Capitalizing on these human impulses, he conceptualized school as a place of "occupations" rather than a place of formal study.

Dewey borrowed extensively from the practices and ideas of Parker, but it was to Ella Flagg Young that he attributed the greatest influence as she implemented progressive practices in the Laboratory School. Through long discussions with her, he was able to formulate theories to capture workable practices. It was in the underlying philosophic foundations of the new and progressive educational methods that he made the greatest contribution.

One could not engineer an educational curriculum and prepare youth for participation in society unless one knew the ends toward which the children were to be directed. What was the aim of life? What was the good human being and the good society? If one assumed the absolute philosophies of Platonic idealism or religious sectarianism, the content of education could be specified precisely. The aim of life, the good life, and the good society would be knowable (and unchanging). Morals were universal and eternal truths, and teachers could mold children in accordance with an ideal blueprint. But if the aim of life was growth, as in Dewey's view, there was no absolute and predetermined end for which youth could be prepared. If life was mutable, as Darwin hypothesized, and always changing in terms of its environment, then educators could have no ultimate model of humanity for which to strive. Schooling, under these conditions, should provide for natural growth and adjustment, not preparation for a certain future. Children were to be taught how to negotiate continually with the changing world of experience about them.

The experimental nature of education was thus based on Dewey's metaphysics of an unfinished and experimental world. In the discovery method of teaching (practiced on the American agricultural frontier for two centuries), Dewey saw a reflection of the problem-solving methods of science. Science was also the model for the good, democratic society. Democracy was a continual experiment with laws whose workability needed constant testing. It was an experimental, shared way of living and working together for common interests. As community is based on communication, the good community must be based on a shared communion between people, a two-way communication between representative rulers and the ruled. So the good school, which he thought should be designed as an "embryonic democracy," must be shared inquiry between teacher and student.

Dewey repeated and amplified the criticisms of Parker and Rice. Education, as he found it, was a dead experience. Philosophy, as he had found it as a student, was a dead exercise, remote from life, suspended in a precarious balance of dualisms from which no action could come. He would struggle to turn it into an instrument for probing the meaning of life, for solving life's problems, for reconstructing society and culture in a scientific, ongoing, self-correcting process.

As he would teach educators to make use of the child's experience, Dewey taught philosophers and psychologists that the primary unit of life was the relative experience of each person as he or she was in transaction with the environment. Individual organisms would not all experience the environment in the same way. Individuals would have to think through the problematic situations of life for themselves by intelligent reconstruction of situations as they perceived them. Thinking started with a "felt difficulty," or a "forked road" that required a decision. The process of clarifying the problem was refined through stages of hypothesizing, bringing imaginative future possibilities and past experience to bear on the problem. The indeterminate situation could be resolved by a tentative but warranted assertion, tested in the reality of the concrete world, and evaluated by consequences. This method, used by scientists, was the same method of discovery Dewey advocated for teaching children to think. Only a democracy could tolerate such thinking, and only a democracy could survive in a world that demanded continual adaptation.

Columbia Years

Dewey himself was in the process of adaptation and readjustment. In 1904 he found his position at the University of Chicago untenable. He moved to New York, where President Nicholas Murray Butler of Columbia University offered him a professorship. From this base, he found large numbers of future educators—including many from other countries— available for his lectures in Columbia's enormously popular Teachers College division. He was also living in the country's intellectual center and the heart of its publishing industry.

At Columbia, Dewey interacted with professors William Heard Kilpatrick and Edward L. Thorndike. Thorndike's work in testing and conditioning through behaviorist theories of stimulus/response/reinforcement was not completely in accord with the problem-solving techniques of Dewey or of Kilpatrick, and this would become an unresolved problem in the development of what was then being called progressive education. Conditioning smacked of authoritarianism and teacher-directed learning, and might preclude the development of individual thinking and self-growth. It could imply there was no transfer of learning, only a transfer of specific responses.

Furthermore, Dewey, was not completely sold on the rage for student testing. According to his friend and colleague Professor Horace M. Kallen, "Dewey had no use for measurement. He thought that it was usually a way of stopping growth rather than of facilitating growth." And Herbert W. Schneider reminisced:

> Dewey really had a very deep resentment against standardization of all sorts; and I think many people thought that for that reason he was against standards, and every once in a while he spoke that way. I remember once when he was presiding at an educational evening in Teachers College, there was a series of papers on mental testing. And it was all on norms and so on. At the end of the meeting . . . he said, "Listening to these papers I was reminded of the way we used to weigh hogs on the farm. We would put a plank in between the rails of the fence, put the hog on one end of the plank and then pile the other end of the plank with rocks until the rocks balanced the hog. Then we took the hog off; and then we guessed the weight of the rocks!"

Nevertheless, Thorndike and Dewey were on the same side of the plank when it came to the use of scientific methods.

In keeping with his philosophy of action, Dewey moved into liberal political circles in New York and worked for social as well as educational reform. He and his wife had long struggled for women's rights, and during one demonstration he drew laughter as he marched down Fifth Avenue with a banner he apparently hadn't read. It bore the slogan: "Men can vote! Why can't I?"

Dewey worked for racial equality, and was one of the original signers of the call to action that resulted in the National Association for the Advancement of Colored People. He supported the American Civil Liberties Union in its early stages. He became a charter member of the New York Teachers Union when it joined the American Federation of Labor. Disenchanted with the two-party system, he helped organize a new political party of liberals—the League for Independent Political Action— and served as its first president. He helped organize the American Association of University Professors, which provided a national forum for protecting professors and students in their efforts to teach and learn freely, to pursue what they believed to be truth wherever it might lead. As the initial president, he gave the group the power of his name and reputation, thus assuring its subsequent growth. The association set national standards to prevent professors from being willfully dismissed for unpopular academic pursuits.

During his adult life, Dewey moved from what he called "absolutism" to "experimentalism." But in one of his rare reminiscences for *Contemporary American Philosophers* in 1930, about the time of his retirement from active teaching at Columbia, he admitted that he had always had absolutist inclinations. He recalled the conflict in his early student days between theological intuitionism, rationalism, German idealism, "sensational empiricism," and Scottish common sense. He said he was molded at home and at the University of Vermont in the absolutism of religion and the romantic philosophies that divided reality into the phenomena that could be known by science and the high world of a transcendent God that could be known only by intuition: "I learned the terminology of an intuitional philosophy, but it did not go deep, and in no way did it satisfy what I was dimly reaching for."

He conceded that his later reaction against this unscientific bent in his intellectual formation was probably a reaction against his "natural tendencies." He confessed that the educational and philosophical controversies for which he had become known were really battles going on inside himself. The "emphasis upon the concrete, empirical, and 'practical' in my later writings," he wrote, "served as a protest and protection against something in myself which, in the pressure of the weight of actual experiences, I knew to be a weakness." It was in his poems, that he let no one read, that the religion of his youth, the intuition and absolutism of his early training, showed throughout his life.

His early writings were what he called "schematic," or modeled on classical dialectics (contradictory opposites or dualisms), such as materialism versus immaterialism, body versus soul. At that time he said he was unaware of the Hegelian dialectic, which synthesized opposites. He discovered this escape from dualisms from his neo-Hegelian professor of philosophy at Johns Hopkins, and he began to break with the intuition and subjectivity of Kant. Hegel's thought "supplied a demand for unification that was doubtless an intense emotional craving." It gave him an "immediate release." (His later books, such as *School and Society, The Child and the Curriculum, Democracy and Education, Experience and Education,* opposed dualisms, expressing his view of interaction between entities as part of a continuum, not opposite or unrelated poles.)

Although Dewey believed Hegel had left a "permanent deposit" on his thinking, he "drifted away from Hegelianism." Hegel was ultimately too much of an absolutist for the maturing Dewey, who would reject the cosmic generalizations that the Hegelians made out of particulars. Dewey credited *Psychology* by James for much of his development. It helped his slow drift from Hegel and brought his philosophy into the mainstream of psychology, with its emphasis on behavior rather than consciousness. James—who once described Dewey as "laboring with a great freight toward the light"—gave Dewey the final push away from Hegel.[11]

In the end, Dewey believed his "intellectual biography" lacked a "unified pattern." He said, "I seem to be unstable, chameleon-like, yielding one after another to many diverse and even incompatible influences; struggling to assimilate something from each and yet striving to carry it forward in a way that is logically consistent with what has been learned from its predecessors." Thus his philosophy and life were a continual struggle, a continual searching. While it was said that he had an aversion for great systems of thought, or any *isms,* he believed otherwise. He longed for an integration of all thought.

His retirement from teaching in 1930 was not the end of his intellectual travels or philosophical quests. His wife had died in 1927, shortly before his visits to the Soviet Union, but he continued to lecture and write and go on growing. He married Roberta (Lowitz) Grant in 1946 and they adopted two children. He carried on an extensive philosophical correspondence with Arthur F. Bentley until December 6, 1951, when the aging Bentley wrote, "I haven't heard from you for some time. In much the same figure of speech, however, I might say that I have not heard even from myself." Dewey kept up with philosophical and psychological developments. On November 17, 1950 he wrote Adelbert Ames, Jr., that "I think your work is by far the most important work done in the psychological-philosophical field during this century—I am tempted to say the *only* really important work." He died in New York City on June 1, 1952, and accounts of his death were spread in newspapers throughout the world. His funeral services were held in the Community Church in New York City. This church had for its purpose a faith in life and the realization on earth of "the beloved community."[12]

Dewey's Thought Evaluated

After a flood of eulogies came a wave of criticisms. There were those who claimed he was a weak teacher and writer, and that progressive education for which he stood was all but discredited. (The Progressive Education Association survived him by only a few years.) His teachings were crucified as antiintellectual, antireligious, radical, and even subversive.

Even his friends and apologists found his pedagogic style less than dynamic. Of course, he never had any formal training in teaching, and he was shy by nature. One of his former students recalled that he never looked at his class during the whole semester, but that one had the feeling of "actually watching thought going on; it seemed quite laborious." Students found him a difficult lecturer; in fact, Dewey often disregarded his own notes when speaking. Horace Kallan observed that Dewey was much more at ease in "communicating with his typewriter than he was face to face, person to person." He said, "There was a kind of withdrawn quality in all his communication, I found." Dewey was said to be somewhat more effective in public speeches, especially when he was carried away by an emotional issue, although he often forgot to bring his speech. Friends would try to get a carbon copy beforehand and thus save the absentminded professor from embarrassment.

Some critics of his writing had probably not read much of his work, though William James had. He called Dewey's style "damnable," and added, "you might say goddamnable." Dewey's style, like his problem-solving techniques of teaching, left much for the reader to discover. He was often indirect in statement, writing long sentences with elaborate modifying phrases. But, as in his theory of aesthetics, beauty is in the eye or mind of the beholder, and many readers found his work attractive. Whatever the flaws may have been in his teaching and writing, he seems to have come to both activities with humility and a sense of humor about himself.

While he was associated with progressive education, reaping its praise and blame, he closed his study of *Experience and Education* in 1938 with a "firm belief" that

> the fundamental issue is not of new versus old education nor of progressive against traditional education but a question of what anything whatever must be to be worthy of the name education. I am not, I hope and believe, in favor of any ends or any methods simply because the name progressive may be applied to them. . . . What we want and need is education pure and simple, and we shall make surer and faster progress when we devote ourselves to finding out just what education is and what conditions have to be satisfied in order that education may be a reality and not a name or a slogan.

He also warned his progressive disciples that "it is not too much to say that an educational philosophy which professes to be based on the idea of freedom may become as dogmatic as ever was the traditional education which it reacted against. For any theory and set of practices are dogmatic which are not based upon critical examination of its own underlying principles."

That progressive education was antiintellectual from the standpoint of subject matter was a criticism that even Dewey raised in *Experience and Education* some years after his retirement. He believed the weakest point in progressive schools was the selection and organization of "intellectual subject matter." He said this was inevitable, because progressive schools had scarcely a generation to "break loose from the cut and dried material which formed the staple of the old education." But he insisted that "the underlying ideal is that of progressive organization of knowledge." He argued, "When education is based in theory and practice upon experience, it goes without saying that the organized subject-matter of the adult and specialist cannot provide the starting point. Nevertheless, it represents the goal toward which education should continuously move."

Dewey liked Roosevelt's New Deal and even favored a form of socialism, but the socialization of youth in school was not meant to include
any partisan economic or political indoctrination, which he hated. He
was president of the League for Industrial Democracy, and he remained
its honorary president until his death. Harry W. Laidler, director of that
organization, said, "Dewey thought in terms of democratic socialism,
but he was experimental all the way and would have liked to see, say,
public ownership of one industry and if that succeeded, go on to other
industries. He was pretty near in his thinking to some sort of mixed
system, with the retention of a private sector in our economy. With
democratic socialists, he insisted upon the strengthening of civil liberties, and contended that public and co-operative ownership was not an
end in itself, but a means to enriching the lives of all the people." While
Dewey had approved of the education he had found in the Soviet Union
in the days before Stalin's purges, he did not approve of communism,
and he once remarked while in Mexico for the Trotsky trials that it was
tragic to see such a brilliant man "locked up in absolutes." (This may
explain why Dewey was not read in the Soviet Union until the late
1980s.)

Though his books are no longer read as a catechism by all educationists in the United States, Dewey remains the best-known North
American educational theorist of the twentieth century. His writing on
the interrelationships between education, philosophy, experience, and
politics are known around the world, but much of the basis for his mature thought came out of his experiences in Chicago from 1895 to 1904.
In addition to Parker, two of the most important people in the development of his thought were Margaret Haley and Ella Flagg Young. Both
women were in turn influenced by Dewey and by each other. Their
careers intertwined significantly for more than a decade and neither can
be understood without reference to the other.

Margaret A. Haley (1861–1939)

One important aspect of education with which "progressive" educators had to deal was the working conditions of teachers, especially in
large urban systems. Early progressives such as Parker disapproved of
teacher unionization, but after 1900 unions developed anyway. Chicago's Margaret Haley was instrumental in their early formation.

Born in Chanahan near Joliet, Illinois on November 15, 1861, "Maggie" was the second oldest of eight children. Her parents, Elizabeth and
Michael, were Irish Catholics whose families had emigrated for better
working conditions and educational opportunities. From her father, Maggie received a strong sense of justice and social reform. He was largely a
self-taught man whose early jobs included bridge building and canal
dredging. By the time he married, he owned two stone quarries; he had

also become something of a self-taught expert in geography, economics, and labor politics. Maggie's mother taught her to read, and she did well in school. As her father's quarry prospered, she entered St. Angela's Academy in Morris, and the possibility of college loomed brightly. But by the time she graduated from St. Angela's, the hope of college had died with the collapse of her father's quarry. Haley owned the quarry in partnership with three other men who wanted to bribe a contractor in order to get work. Haley refused, and his partners forced the quarry to close temporarily. Haley could not sustain the financial losses as his wealthier partners could, so he was forced out. Maggie found out that the quarry had closed during her graduation exercises. She said: "If I live a hundred years, I'll never forget my father's face and all it conveyed of defeat and the consequences. It meant for me the end of school and I had to prepare to do something else."[13]

Early Career

The "something else" was teaching, and that summer she began a normal school course of study. By fall she had her first teaching job—a one-room school near Dresden Heights. At sixteen, she was only five feet tall and weighed less than one hundred pounds, and the children at first mistook her for a student. She taught in country schools for several years, keeping up with the latest educational methods through normal courses. She taught briefly in Joliet before moving to the South Side of Chicago, where she substituted while waiting for a position. During this time she came into contact with Parker. He was just making a name for himself, and Haley recalled him during his first years there:

> Colonel Parker was by no means pacific in his quest for sweetness and light. He roared, he growled, he stormed, he banged. . . . He scared the wits out of students, and he terrified teachers. He sent for parents and shamed them into aiding their children. He was Reform Rampant— and I watched him with unterrified glee. . . . In him I somehow sensed the fundamental justice of his attitude and saw the need of his method. More surely than anyone else, he taught me that a straight line was the shortest distance between two points. I was to remember that twenty years later.[14]

Haley accepted a sixth grade teaching position at the Hendricks School in 1884. The pay was meager and the principal there was, by Haley's standards, incompetent. These conditions compelled her to join a group of teachers who were organizing on a citywide basis for better working conditions. The notion that these teachers (mostly women) could have a democratic voice in their professional careers was a new one that had been supported by one of Chicago's district superintendents (and future city superintendent), Ella Flagg Young. The teachers' group brought a pension plan to passage in 1895, and were working on a salary schedule. By 1897, however, the pension was in jeopardy. Haley met the author of the pension bill, Catharine Goggin, and at a meeting to address pension and salary issues the Chicago Teachers' Federation (CTF) was born.

CTF Officer

By the spring of 1899, Goggin and Haley were the CTF's president and vice president, respectively. Because of their prodding, the school board had approved a modest salary scale. By the fall of 1899, however, the board said they could not afford all of the 1899 increases or any of those for 1900.

During Christmas break, while sitting in the reception room of her dentist's office, Haley overheard that certain large corporations had escaped paying taxes on property valued at over $100 million. She realized that if the CTF could force these corporations to pay their taxes, the city's treasury would have the necessary money to pay the increases. Haley went to see former Governor John P. Altgeld. Altgeld told Haley that she was right, but that she would never win against the powerful corporations, as he himself had tried unsuccessfully as governor. Haley's response to the ex-governor revealed one of the key motivating forces of her personality—a sort of naive determination: "I [do] not see why we should not win if we [are] right." Catharine Goggin's response was equally revealing: "I don't care whether we win or lose if we are right."

The Tax Fight

In January 1900 the CTF voted to pay the salaries of Goggin and Haley so that they could leave their classrooms to devote full time to their tax pursuits.[15] For the next two and one-half years, lawyers for both sides were in and out of court. Finally, in 1902, $600,000 in back taxes was awarded to the board of education, which voted to use the money for building and maintenance. The board also weakened the pension plan by making contributions voluntary, and at the direction of Superintendent Edwin G. Cooley, had instituted a complex marking system to evaluate teachers for pay increases. Under this system, in order to advance to the top pay levels, teachers had to be (1) reexamined with a certification test, and (2) evaluated by their principals for teaching effectiveness, with the average of both ratings having to equal at least 80 percent. Because all the results of the test and the evaluation were secret, teachers could not tell who was eligible for which pay levels. It turned out that 2,600 teachers were eligible for the top pay level, but only 61 were receiving it. Most of the teachers had not received a raise for twenty years.

At the next meeting of the CTF, discouraged teachers listened as a representative from the Chicago Federation of Labor (CFL) invited them to tell their story to 200,000 voting men. Social reformer Jane Addams spoke, encouraging them to affiliate with the CFL and later found herself at a White House luncheon trying to explain to the disapproving

President Roosevelt why she had done this.[16] The federation voted to affiliate with the labor union, thereby becoming the first teaching group to do so. The predominantly female CTF was becoming more powerful than anyone had expected a women's group to be—especially when women could not vote. The CTF's lawyers, Isaiah T. Greenacre and his neophyte partner Clarence Darrow, secured an injunction preventing the board from spending the new tax money, and the school board and the teachers went back to court.

In 1904 the courts ruled that the money should be used for back salaries, but when the board's attorneys secured an injunction against this, Haley took the CTF directly into politics. Along with representatives from the CFL, the CTF campaigned for a reform mayoral candidate because mayors appointed school board members. In 1905 their efforts were rewarded with the election of Edward Dunne, and by 1906, two-thirds of the board were Dunne appointees who voted to pay the back salaries. Thus, in June 1906, after six and a half years of fighting, each of 1,653 teachers got forty-five dollars.

From 1906 to 1909 the CTF and the board continued their tug-of-war. Superintendent Cooley tried to keep the schools moving, but factionalism continued throughout the system. At times Haley wondered if the CTF would survive. Finally, in March 1909, Cooley resigned. It took the school board five months to settle on a new superintendent, and to the delight of the teachers, the choice was Ella Flagg Young, whose *Isolation in the Schools* had become the manual for giving teachers a voice in their professional lives. From 1909 until she retired in 1915, the school system ran relatively smoothly, and she removed many of Cooley's unpopular practices.

Other Fights

Young had barely started her superintendency when Haley became convinced that the NEA could benefit from Young's pragmatic leadership. For several years Haley had been trying to help teachers gain a voice in the policy-making end of the NEA. Since its inception in 1857, this organization had been run by men. After the early 1890s it had been more and more tightly controlled by a small group of college presidents and city superintendents. Their policies had resulted in nonvoting membership status for teachers in general.

Haley's crusade started at the 1901 annual meeting when she challenged Commissioner of Education Harris. As Haley remembered it, on a hot June day he had been describing to a tired audience how the educational horizon was without a cloud and how big business was education's friend. When floor discussion opened, Haley disagreed with Harris's claims of corporate friendship for schools and described certain general revenue facts she had learned from her tax fight. Harris jumped up and said, "Pay no attention to what that teacher has said, for I take it she is a grade school teacher just out of her school room at the end of

[the] school year, worn out, tired out and hysterical." Then he continued, "Chicago is no criterion for other parts of the country, but it is morbid, cyclonic and hysterical and you can never tell what is going to happen in Chicago." But Harris fell silent when it became clear that Haley was describing the famous tax fight.[17]

Out of this experience, Haley became one of a group of insurgents fighting to democratize the NEA. Throughout the 1909–1910 school year, she ran Young's campaign for president of the organization. Amidst the old guard's empty charges of fraud, Young became the NEA's first female president. In the following years teachers began voting, and by 1914 the Department of Classroom Teachers held their first meetings and programs.

As soon as one battle was over, Haley was embroiled in another, this time with the CTF back in Chicago. During the spring of 1915, board president Jacob Loeb announced a 7.5 percent salary cut for the remainder of the year. Superintendent Young had planned to retire that summer, but because of this budget problem decided to continue to the end of the fall term. She reworked the budget while Haley lobbied successfully in the state legislature for a larger portion of the tax levy. The pay cut was killed.

Loeb was not happy. He had never liked the CTF or the two high school teacher organizations which had sprung up after 1902. That summer he convinced the school board to pass the "Loeb rule," which forbade teachers to belong to any labor-connected group and any organization whose leaders were not currently teaching. The CTF lawyers secured an injunction against the rule, and the courts eventually declared it illegal. This made Loeb furious, and the board failed to issue teaching contracts for 1916–1917 to sixty-eight teachers, thirty-eight of whom were CTF members. The CTF supported their ousted members, and Goggin and Haley went to work on a tenure bill. By the time this bill became law in spring, however, Haley was alone. An electric truck struck and killed Goggin while she was crossing a street on January 4, 1916.

In fall 1917 the ousted teachers were reinstated, but the battle had other consequences. One was that the CFL recommended that the CTF withdraw from their ranks in 1917. As a result, Haley joined with other national education figures to found the American Federation of Teachers (AFT) that same year. She also incurred Loeb's wrath on a more personal level. During the Loeb rule fight, he had given a story to the *Chicago Tribune* stating that Haley had been receiving two salaries from 1901 to 1907: one from the board and the other from the CTF. Although the *Tribune* promised to retract the story, they never seemed to get around to it, so Haley sued the paper for $50,000. *Tribune* representatives offered a $10,500 out-of-court settlement, but the Irish union leader refused. "What I wanted," she stated, "was not money, but a verdict proving I had been libeled." She won the case, but received only $500 in retribution from the newspaper.[18]

Later Efforts

During the 1920s Haley renewed her efforts for a single salary scale for Chicago teachers. During the decade after World War I, teachers saw no salary rises. The CTF leader lobbied for larger tax levies, but these never seemed to be enough. She continued to crusade against corporate control of public utilities, poor financial use of school lands by the school board, and what she regarded as corporate abuse of the tax system. Toward the end of the 1920s she managed to have the city reassessed on a more equitable basis. But tax machinery was slow and litigation held up the tax assessment. Amid efforts to get these problems resolved and tax revenue flowing again, the Great Depression hit, producing a terrible financial crisis for teachers. In 1934, Haley helped secure a national loan to bail out the city's schools, but by then teachers had gone through many payless paydays with their salaries in scrip (paper stamped "insufficient funds"), which some businesses redeemed far below face value.

Retirement

In 1935 Haley retired to California where she renewed earlier efforts to complete and publish her autobiography. She died there in 1939 of a heart attack, and her autobiography was not published until 1982. Her tireless and determined efforts to create and re-create a workable democracy consisting of enlightened men and women from all levels of society have rarely been paralleled. She firmly believed that the public must control utilities and natural resources as well as schools, although her biggest endeavors were directed at the institution in which she began her career. About her work she said:

> The teachers' fight has been a fight in the general cause of liberty. It was a fight for a time-honored American institution, the free public schools, . . . for its integrity and as a means of maintaining democracy in America. The whole idea of the public schools was that democracy had to be based on intelligence of the masses. . . . [It was the] institution through which to obtain and secure and improve in every decade this intelligence. . . . [Unfortunately] it began to run amuck whenever it disturbed a pampered interest.[19]

John Dewey wrote about the philosophical bases of industrial democracy. Margaret Haley—who liked Dewey's work—fought to make democracy real, as did her friend and colleague Ella Flagg Young.

Ella Flagg Young (1845–1918)

Journalist Joseph Mayer Rice had called attention to Chicago when in 1892 he singled out the educational work of Colonel Parker at the Cook County Normal. Rice was positively exuberant in his praise of Parker's progressive teaching methods. Cook County was an island in a sea of poorly taught, badly managed, overcrowded, and unhealthy schools throughout the nation. However, he placed the city schools of Chicago in the poor category, so the growing metropolis was both praised and condemned for its educational practices. The city schools were thirteen years away from feeling the effects of progressive reform at the hands of their first female superintendent, Ella Flagg Young.[20]

Early Life

Ella's parents were of Scottish ancestry, and were living in Buffalo when Ella, the youngest of their three children, was born. Her father, Theodore, had little formal education, having been apprenticed to the sheet metal trade at the age of ten. Her mother, Jane, had married at sixteen or seventeen.

Although her sister and brother went to school at the appropriate ages, Ella stayed home until ten. Her mother thought her sickly, delicate, and in need of a mother's protection and lots of sunshine.

By eight or nine, Ella had still not learned to read or write. One morning at the breakfast table her parents were reading an account of a school fire in which young children had to jump from upper story windows. Ella asked her mother to read the story to her. Then, crying for the fate of children her age, the little girl took the newspaper into another room. She remembered how her mother had started the story and matched that up with the words in print. When she got stuck, she asked the maid, until finally, she had worked her way through the whole article. Then she began reading other books in the house. Most of these were related to Presbyterian doctrines. One day she expounded on some of her religious knowledge when an aunt and some other women were visiting. Her aunt asked her what she had been reading; it was Baxter's *Call to the Unconverted*. While her aunt was amused, her mother was not; Mrs. Flagg calmly but sternly told her daughter to remove herself to the backyard to garden. In a couple of days, Mother Goose stories replaced Baxter.

By the time she was ten, Ella had taught herself how to write, and by eleven her mother finally allowed her to enter the grammar department of the nearby school her brother and sister attended. She found school intriguing. She had an aptitude for math, and the teacher made her a monitor (helper) in that subject, so her desk was moved up next to the teacher's. Mr. Flagg thought he noticed a rather "priggish" attitude on the part of his youngest daughter, and he blamed it on the new location of her desk. He told Ella that she could continue to help the teacher if she moved her desk back with the rest of the class.

When Ella was thirteen, the Flaggs moved to Chicago. Ella had finished grammar school in Buffalo and was ready for high school. Before she could take the entrance exams for Chicago's high school, however, she had to complete one year in a Chicago grammar school. The course of study at the Brown school was one Ella had already completed in Buffalo, so she found little challenge. Her parents had never really encouraged her to go to school, and it was not particularly common for girls to attend high school anyway. After a few months, she dropped out.

In 1860 when she was fifteen, Ella found a chance to further her education. A friend was going to take a teacher certification test and asked Ella to go along. She took the exam too, and passed it, but was told that she was too young to teach. With the encouragement of the superintendent of the city's schools, William H. Wells, she enrolled in the normal department of the Chicago high school.

Ella was entering her second year of training when her mother told her that she would not make a good teacher, because she was not accustomed to young children and knew nothing of their nature and capabilities. Ella was too hard on herself and would be the same way with children, her mother explained. Determined to test herself under teaching circumstances, Ella found a classroom where the children were friendly and the teacher was good. She arranged to help the teacher on a weekly basis, thus setting up her own student teaching situation.

Early Career

After a year of practice teaching, Ella's mother admitted that her daughter seemed to thrive on the experience. In spring of 1862 Ella graduated from the normal department of the Chicago high school; she was seventeen. The following fall, she began her long teaching career in the primary department of a Chicago ghetto school. Two weeks to the day after Ella started teaching, her mother died.

By 1863 Miss Flagg, as her students and professional colleagues called her, was an assistant to the principal of the old Brown school where she had felt bored five years earlier. From there she went to another grammar school as head of the two practice teaching rooms. In the next seventeen years, Ella Flagg experienced other aspects of public education: she taught math at the high school level; devised an object curriculum based on Pestalozzi's methods; and became principal, first of the Scammon School and next of Skinner, the largest school in Chicago. She remained at Skinner as principal until 1887, when she was called to a newly created assistant superintendent's position.

Increased Responsibility

Personally, the years paralleling her climb to the assistant superintendency were mixed with happiness and pain. In 1868 her brother Charles was killed in a freak train accident. That same year Ella Flagg married a much older friend of the family, William Young. Little is known of the circumstances surrounding her marriage. Her father may have encouraged the marriage, as he was getting older and with Charles gone, there would be no male to look after his youngest daughter. At any rate, she married Young in December 1868, but his health failed; he went West to recuperate but died there in 1873. That same year her sister and father succumbed to pneumonia. At the age of twenty-eight, Ella Flagg Young was widowed and had no living members of her immediate family. So she turned her familial affections to the teachers and children of the Chicago schools.

From 1887 to 1899 Young worked as an assistant or district superintendent, at a time when Chicago schools experienced one of their most rapid growth periods. Even with 271 new school buildings between 1884 and 1893, temporary arrangements were still necessary. Total enrollment grew from 630,000 in 1886 to about 1.5 million in 1893, and pupils attending half-day sessions rose from 6,000 to 14,000 over that same period.

Curricular changes accompanied this growth, as many of the progressive reforms were starting to gain attention. Manual arts, domestic science, music, art, and kindergarten were some of the innovations that critics derogatorily called "fads and frills." And many elementary school teachers—predominantly women—were holding meetings in order to protest their working conditions. For example, women teachers were not supposed to be married, yet they had no pension to safeguard their retirements. Whenever the city's treasury was found to be lacking, the elementary teachers were the first to receive salary cuts. The teachers also wanted to have some voice in the curriculum—which Assistant Superintendent Young allowed in her district. The outgrowth of these meetings was the CTF. Their two powerful leaders, Catharine Goggin and Margaret Haley, had been influenced by Young's democratic policies as district superintendent.

In 1895 Young was feeling the need for more academic preparation and decided to enroll in a course at the University of Chicago's newly opened Department of Philosophy, Psychology, and Pedagogy under John Dewey, and by 1898 Young was contemplating giving up the district superintendency to pursue a doctorate. She had several reasons: a new superintendent with much more autocratic and conservative policies had been hired; even though she was fifty-four, she was not ready to retire and she had gone about as far as she could without an advanced degree; and Dewey was anxious to have her come to the university and help him run an experimental school that was in trouble.

Student, Professor, Principal

In June 1899 Young submitted her resignation, and the CTF planned a protest only to discover that Young did not want it. She told them that she could not work in such a harness as the new superintendent had imposed, and she tried to squelch the rumor that she was going on the faculty at the University of Chicago. (No professorship had been offered her yet, but many rumors circulated to the effect that she had resigned for such a reason.) In pursuing a Ph.D., she was sticking to an old motto of hers: "Those who live on the mountain have a longer day than those who live in the valley. Sometimes all we need to brighten our day is to climb a little higher." Young would climb much higher before she was finished with her career.

On a blistering August day in 1900, Mrs. Young became Dr. Young as she successfully defended her dissertation entitled "Isolation in School Systems." Her dissertation embodied a philosophy of learning by experience and of social freedoms for a school community through a democratically run administration from superintendent down to student. Obviously pragmatic in her views, Dewey was later to say that she "was a practicing pragmatist long before the doctrine was ever in print," and that he got more ideas from her than anyone else when it came to education.

For the next four years Young served as professor of education at the University of Chicago. Her mission was to bring Chicago teachers to the university and to expand Dewey's scope as a leading professor in preparing elementary teachers—something like Parker had been doing. The University of Chicago had just acquired the renowned Colonel Parker and his faculty, and Dewey and his lab school were in eclipse. Even after Parker died in 1902, the fighting continued. Dewey tried to rid himself of the Colonel's faculty, but had to resign. In 1904, Dr. Young, who was tired of the petty politics, left for Europe with her friend and roommate, Laura Brayton. While she was there the principalship of the Chicago Normal School (the old Cook County Normal where Parker had been) came open. Friends suggested her name and in the fall of 1905 she entered this position.

During the four years that she was its head, the normal school became a model of pragmatic and progressive doctrines. Young screened applicants to determine their dedication to teaching and their understanding of children. She encouraged the faculty to interweave the new manual arts and domestic sciences with traditional subjects. She chose practice teaching schools for their ethnic and cultural diversity because the city's population was predominantly foreign-born. But if the normal was running efficiently and effectively, it was one of the few educational institutions in the city that was. By 1909 internal strife and factionalism were tearing the city schools apart.

Superintendency

The series of events leading to such divisiveness had built up over ten years. The biggest single element that made board of education members anxious and hostile was the growth of the teachers' organizations. The CTF, especially, had gained power, independence, and publicity because of the tax fight. The school board and Superintendent Cooley attempted to squelch the increasingly powerful teachers' organization. The result was tension and hostility throughout the system. The teachers discovered that their friend on the board, Jane Addams—while a great social reformer—had little stamina for confronting authority. Several times her sentiment lay with the teachers but she cast her vote with the board, as in the cases of the secret marking system and the voluntary pension bill.

After Cooley resigned in 1909, the board took five months to interview six candidates. Finally, on July 29, they unanimously elected Young. Apparently, the board put its trust in her because they felt that she could best handle the CTF, which had managed to reinstate compulsory pension contributions along with a pension board that was predominantly teachers and a few school board members. (There was also a clause that made the board match pension interest money.) Young had told the school board that she thought the CTF could be made to equalize representation on the pension board if it meant that the school board would match the teachers dollar for dollar.

The teachers trusted her because most of them had had some personal encounters with her; it was said that she knew all six thousand teachers in the system by name. She removed the secret marking system and began to involve the teachers in decisions that affected their professional lives. From the first she announced that her administration would be characterized by "democratic efficiency. . . . There is to be but one head," she said, "and I am it. Whenever I find that I cannot have complete charge of the educational end of the school system, I will quit. I cannot carry out my ideas unless I am given control of affairs."

The first two and a half years of her superintendency were harmonious. Courses of study reflected individual differences. Grammar schools offered domestic science and manual arts organized along the lines she had used at the normal school. The regular high schools offered more vocational work instead of placing it in separate technical high schools. Sex hygiene—called *personal purity*—was introduced, although many parents were concerned with such a topic. Young got salary increases for the elementary teachers as well as the high school teachers in two of her first three years in office.

The various parts of the school system were united enough by 1910 to successfully "boom" her to the NEA presidency. She was the first female to ever head any large school system and her picture had made the front pages of most city newspapers, including the *New York Times*. Now she was adding another first, for no female had ever been elected president of the NEA. The presidency was not without its problems, however, because the old guard was frightened by Young's announced intention of having the organization's permanent fund investigated. Rumors had circulated suggesting that all was not well when one of the fund's trustees—the superintendent of schools in Peoria, Illinois—went to prison for fraud and embezzlement after a bank which he owned failed. It was discovered that the fund had not been tampered with, but some of the money was badly invested. The permanent fund's directors instituted a campaign of threats and mudslinging. In the end Young emerged, if not completely victorious, at least as a courageous leader in the eyes of many teachers who appreciated her efforts to make the NEA more democratic.

Board Wars

In 1912, with the NEA fight behind, trouble began to loom in Chicago. A new mayor, Carter Henry Harrison, Jr., had appointed a new board under different leadership, and it was changing its relationship to the superintendent, even though it reelected her and her assistant, John D. Shoop. By early summer 1912, rumors were developing that Mayor Harrison no longer supported Young. The mayor assured her of his support and asked her to ignore the empty rumors. She acknowledged her appreciation of his support, told him that she had ignored the rumors, and wished his administration well. But her troubles were just beginning.

The next three and a half years demonstrated some of the problems of large school bureaucracies. Mayor Harrison appointed board members who reflected important political interests. Some of these members understood and agreed with what Young wanted to do, but others either did not understand or had different (often personal) agendas. For example, some board members disagreed with manual training and blocked Young's curriculum plans. One wanted to choose the texts, and others wanted control of the teachers' pension fund. After extensive behind-the-scenes conversations, the CTF called an open meeting to allow interested parties to state positions and answer questions. At stake were two basic matters. The teachers wanted mandatory contributions to the pension fund, with the board matching each dollar. A majority of the board members, for different individual reasons, were willing to agree to the match only if teachers did not constitute a majority of the proposed oversight board. The "Urion Bill" containing these two major provisions was the focus of the CTF's open meeting, called for a Thursday after school.

A few hours before the mass meeting, Haley learned that William Rothmann, chair of the school board's finance committee and the man who wanted to oversee the teacher's pension fund, had a few years earlier absconded with the interest generated by the police retirement fund. She quickly printed an alert to this effect and circulated a copy to all teachers.

The meeting, attended by a throng of teachers, opened in chaos. The acting chairman—William B. Owen, Young's successor at the normal—could hardly get the meeting called to order. Both Haley and Young asked for the floor at the same time. Owen did not know whom to recognize, so he asked the pleasure of the convention. "Amidst the cries of 'let her speak', and 'no, no, no,' [the superintendent] left the [room] because she thought she had been denied the floor." Owen sent a messenger after her. Upon her return, Young explained that Rothmann would not be able to do anything underhanded with the interest from the pension fund because he would be too closely watched, and also because the laws had been changed to forbid it. When the teachers voted, their preference was against the Urion Bill. Young lost; what was worse, she appeared to have been pitted against the teachers.

The flap over the Urion Bill had no long-term effect on Young's relationship with Haley. Young was a master pragmatic strategist in the full philosophic meaning of pragmatism. Haley was a fearless idealistic crusader who shared most of Young's educational and political values. They remained effectively allied in a number of causes throughout Young's life, and Young ended her superintendency solidly on the side of the teachers.

Resignations

Up until this time, Young's open door policy had seemed to keep her apprised of the teachers' sentiments, but now she felt more isolated. She lamented this in her 1913 annual report and called for the adoption of teachers' councils to meet monthly during school hours so teachers could express their views and make suggestions. They were to start in fall 1913, but that spring and summer it looked like they would be starting without her. In June, board members began openly expressing hostility toward her. Rothmann pestered her seeking favors, including the demotion of certain CTF teachers, but she refused. Another board member, John C. Harding, was upset because she ignored his choice of spellers. In June, Mayor Harrison wrote her another letter of support. It helped, and so did the fact that the new board president, Peter Reinberg, supported her; but hostility from other board members persisted.

On June 27, under Governor Dunne, a former Chicago mayor, Illinois women were enfranchised. An article in the *Chicago Record Herald* pictured Young with Addams and Julia Lathrop, a social reformer. The caption read "Three Reasons Why Illinois Women Won the Vote First," but it was little comfort to Young. At the end of July, she submitted her resignation, telling reporters that she "was the victim of political intrigue among board members." The interview quoted her as saying "that her retention of the superintendency would impair the efficiency of the schools." Former member of the board Dr. Cornelia DeBey told reporters that it was due to actions "of a lot of cheap politicians and the board. We women won't stand for it." But two other board members said they were sure that the board would accept her resignation. President Reinberg said he would resign if the action was approved. Another board member, William Vincent, alluded to some of her difficulties with three of the board members. "It's too bad," said Vincent, "but it's the only thing she can do to save her self-respect."

Events of the next few days, however, changed things. A delegation of women arrived at the mayor's office; the mayor wrote to the superintendent urging her to reconsider and stay as head of schools; and he apprised her of three new board appointments—Gertrude Britton, Florence Vosbrink, and Dr. Peter Clemenson. On July 30 the board voted fourteen to one to retain her. (Harding voted no.) She was encouraged. "I shall abide by the action of the board of education," she told newspapers. "It will still be my aim to make the Chicago public schools the embodiment of the thought and endeavor of the board and of Chicago herself for the children. The kind words of parents and teachers have touched me deeply." Mayor Harrison announced "her rule should be unopposed in all matters pertaining to the schools."

The fall term went smoothly, but her antagonizers had just gone underground. On December 10 the board convened to take up the reelection of superintendent and assistant. In a sudden move, Young's enemies nominated and elected her subordinate, John Shoop, as superintendent. Citywide protests by numerous groups pressured the mayor into making enough new board appointments to bring about Young's reelection, and Rothmann was ousted from the board in this process.

Final Years

Both Young and Shoop accepted their old posts, and the school administration began functioning just in time to see the schools open after the holiday break. Through a series of legal appeals, the ousted board members were reinstated by May 1914. Their original terms, however, expired shortly after they were reseated.

The time from January 1914 to December 1915 moved along without the personal struggles of the previous year, but also without the triumphs and unity of the early years. In December 1914 Young was reappointed by a fourteen-vote majority. She was able to continue her policies, and even managed to get a 5 percent salary increase for the teachers. The board members who had refused to vote for her return smoldered. Her opponents on the board resented the restraint placed upon them by the mayor, and they blamed his long arm of control and the CTF for her reelection. Real estate magnate Jacob Loeb—by now a dominant force on the board—voted for Young and publicly supported her, but he resented the CTF's power. As long as Young remained in office, he was somewhat careful in his overt activities, but when the approach of her retirement became obvious, so did his motives.

Young planned to retire on July 1, 1915. She decided, however, to remain to face a new budget deficit and threat of salary decreases. She trimmed the budget so that Loeb's threatened salary cut did not go into effect. Toward the end of August 1915, she went on vacation, and while she was gone, the board met and Loeb presented a ruling to be voted on immediately. The board approved the Loeb rule, some because of Loeb's autocratic control and others because of business interests. When Young returned there was little she could do, as her imminent December retirement made her a lame duck. All teachers had received contracts with clauses containing the new rulings. They had to sign these before they could get a paycheck. Young tried to get some recommendations for promotions approved by Loeb and the board refused approval until the contracts were signed. CTF Attorney Greenacre secured an injunction against the board, and Haley went to work for a tenure protection bill. So CTF opposition was held at bay until Young retired in December.

Before she left town, she warned the teachers that the opposition was not over, but was just lying dormant. In spring 1916, under Superintendent Shoop, Board President Loeb refused to issue contracts to sixty-eight teachers for the following year.

Even in retirement Young kept faith with the teachers. She prepared a paper for the NEA meeting in July 1916, but when Loeb preceded her and defended his stand against teachers' unions, she discarded her prepared speech and answered his criticisms. She said "no person should ever be on the board of education who does not send his own children, or did not send them while they were of school age, to the public schools." Loeb's children attended private schools.

By the fall of 1917 the United States was involved in World War I. Young and some friends went to work for the second Liberty Loan Committee. This loan was one of five huge bond issues floated to finance the war and sold to citizens in small denominations. She continued to attend NEA conventions. At Pittsburgh, in July 1918, when she walked into the meeting hall, everyone spontaneously stood in silent ovation. She stepped to the lectern, and as she began to speak glanced down at her well-worn dress and said, "Why, since the war began I haven't even thought of clothes."

In the fall, Young went on another speaking tour for the fourth Liberty Loan. In Wyoming she contracted the flu but refused to go to bed. She finished the trip and was able to get to Washington to turn her money in to Secretary of State William McAdoo, but by now she had pneumonia. She died on October 26, and her body was brought back to Chicago accompanied by a military regiment. The flags in Chicago were flown at half mast and the board of education offices were draped in black. McAdoo said that she "died in the service of her country, working like a soldier." It was a fitting homage for a leader of whom Jane Addams had said, "She had more general intelligence and character than any other woman I knew."

Ella Flagg Young had been the archetypical progressive: intelligently altruistic, open to change, always learning, democratic and humane. Even her death typified the progressive notion that everyone should work for the good of the group. However, not all educators agreed with the tenets of progressivism, as the next chapter will show.

SUMMARY

"Progressive education" or the "new education" was part of a larger movement in the United States and other countries. Much of the theoretical formulation rested on selected portions of Locke, Rousseau, Pestalozzi, and Herbart—all of whose work had in turn been affected by developments in the New World.

A substantial amount of variation permeated progressivism, but experimental and scientific approaches ran prominently through the movement. Progressivism presupposed the desirability of the cultural assumptions and organizational model advocated by Horace Mann and the friends of education. One advantage of his model was that it provided clearly articulated career paths for people who wanted to work in school systems. Another advantage was that uniform goals and curricula were possible.

Progressivism had a strong reform component because the professional/bureaucratic model also presented difficulties. One of these was alienation between what students experienced in school and in the cultures of their homes and communities. Progressive educators called for expanding the curriculum, especially as changes in the economy eliminated jobs that preteens and teenagers had traditionally held. The economic phenomenon alone produced burgeoning enrollments, especially at the secondary level. Progressives like John Dewey were not enthusiastic about standardized tests for sorting the mass of pupils, but in practice testing, "ability grouping," and tracks of differentiated curricula became standard scientific features of school systems.

Progressives tended to favor women's education and more equitable treatment of working class children and of those from minority cultural, ethnic, and racial backgrounds. Progressives did not always insist on full equality. Different curricula for working class children and those from middle class backgrounds was a de facto feature of school systems that progressives did not criticize. Different curricular emphases for males and females were also a standard feature of most progressive schools. The scientific testing movement discriminated against minority children, immigrant children, and those from working class backgrounds.

Finally, progressives were not of one mind about how to improve working conditions for teachers. Parker opposed unions, Dewey and Haley favored them, and Young accepted them. The gulf between teachers as low-paid workers in the knowledge factory and administrators as better-paid supervisors widened under progressive leadership.

NOTES

1. *Stuart v. School District No. 1 of Village of Kalamazoo*, 30 Mich. 69 (1874).

2. Samuel Eliot Morison and Henry Steele Commager, *The Growth of the American Republic*, 2 vols. (New York: Oxford University Press, 1961), 2: 443–444.

3. Joseph Mayer Rice, *The Public School System of the United States* (New York: Century, 1893), 29–30.

4. Ralph Henry Gabriel, *The Course of American Democratic Thought* (New York: Ronald Press, 1940), 331–340.

5. Clarke University, Worcester, Massachusetts: Opening Exercises, October 2, 1889, 18, 24; quoted in Dorothy Ross, G. Stanley Hall: *The Psychologist as Prophet* (Chicago: University of Chicago Press, 1972), 200.

6. G. Stanley Hall, "Child Study," *Journal of Proceedings and Addresses of the National Education Association, 1894* (St. Paul: Pioneer Press, 1895), 175.

7. Rice, *The Public School System,* 209.

8. Jack K. Campbell, *Colonel Francis W. Parker: The Children's Crusader* (New York: Teachers College Press, 1967). All biographical material and quotations are from this source.

9. Joan K. Smith, *Ella Flagg Young: Portrait of a Leader* (Ames: Iowa State University Research Foundation and Educational Studies Press, 1979), 72–100.

10. Adelbert Ames, Jr., *The Morning Notes of Adelbert Ames, Jr.* (New Brunswick, NJ: Rutgers University Press, 1966); Jane M. Dewey, "Biography of John Dewey," in *The Philosophy of John Dewey,* ed. Paul A. Schilpp (Evanston: Northwestern University, 1939); George Dykhuizen, *The Life and Mind of John Dewey* (Carbondale: Southern Illinois University Press, 1973); Sidney Hook, *John Dewey: An Intellectual Portrait* (Westport, CT: Greenwood Press, [1939] 1971); Corliss Lamont, ed., *Dialogues on John Dewey* (New York: Horizon Press, 1959); John J. McDermott, ed., *The Philosophy of John Dewey* (Chicago: University of Chicago Press, 1981); Joseph Ratner, ed., *Intelligence in the Modern World: John Dewey's Philosophy* (New York: Random House, 1939); Sidney Ratner and Jules Altman, eds., *John Dewey and Arthur F. Bentley: A Philosophical Correspondence, 1932–1951* (New Brunswick, NJ: Rutgers University Press, 1964); Robert B. Westbrook, *John Dewey and American Democracy* (Ithaca and London: Cornell University Press, 1991).

11. Quotation in Gay Wilson Allen, *William James: A Biography* (New York: Viking Press, 1967), 435–436.

12. Jo Ann Boydston, ed., *The Poems of John Dewey* (Carbondale: Southern Illinois University Press, 1977). Several love poems hint of a special relationship between Dewey and Anzia Yezierska around the time of World War I.

13. Unpublished Haley autobiography, version 4 (1934–1935), Chicago Teachers Federation Files, Chicago Historical Society, 414; Robert L. Reid, ed., *Battleground: The Autobiography of Margaret A. Haley* (Urbana: University of Illinois Press, 1982).

14. Reid, *Battleground,* 24.

15. Reid, *Battleground,* 52–53; unpublished Haley autobiography, version 1 (1910), installment 4, 2–3.

16. Unpublished Haley autobiography, version 2 (1910–1911), 114–115.

17. Joan K. Smith, "The Changing of the Guard: Margaret A. Haley and the Rise of Democracy in the NEA," *Texas Tech Journal of Education* 8 (Winter 1981): 8–9.

18. Reid, *Battleground,* 167.

19. Unpublished Haley autobiography, version 4 (1934–1935), 145.

20. Smith, *Ella Flagg Young.* All biographical information and quotations on Young are from this source.

The Outsiders

Education is never value-free. School systems reflect the most deeply held commitments of those who control them. The friends of education and their progressive offspring argued for equal schooling for all, but the educational systems they produced institutionalized many inequalities. Their curricula reflected gender role differentiation and divergent expectations for working class and middle class children. African, Asian, Hispanic, and Native American children received less or different schooling than did many males of Euro-American descent.

This chapter focuses on developments in the education of women, African, Native, and Hispanic Americans. Change was slow and often depended on economic and social status. Nevertheless, by the end of the nineteenth century, women and blacks had at least increased their access to education. True equality remained a distant goal for members of both groups, as it did for Hispanic and many Asian Americans.

WOMEN'S EDUCATION (1620–1800)

Education for girls and women in the colonial and national periods was tailored to fit their traditional future roles as wives and mothers. Because learning the three Rs was important for household recordkeeping and the early education of offspring, petty, dame, and district schools were available to women—usually in summer when the boys were in the fields. Little thought was given to educating girls for other purposes.

Although both sexes generally received rudimentary education, learning letters and basic reading skills were all girls could generally expect. In many cases, their further training in household arts and economy was conducted by their mothers or, in some cases, by apprenticeship. Because girls were not allowed to attend colleges, they were rarely admitted to the college preparatory Latin grammar schools. If their parents were financially able and willing, girls might receive further formal education from a tutor.[1]

As families of early settlers consolidated their positions, some became financially secure. Around 1700, the growth of a prospering commercial middle class triggered a new kind of secondary school. "English" schools were designed to teach subjects directly useful to their pupils. They trained boys in navigation, surveying, bookkeeping, penmanship, and accounting—skills to help them in careers. They taught girls ornamental skills: dancing, singing, music, drawing, French, and both basic and fancy needlework. These evolved into finishing schools and became popular for girls whose families could afford them. Learning such skills helped facilitate marriages with middle and upper class men; however, they did little to prepare women for any kind of life outside the home. They were a continuation of the kind of education that Sor Juana and Wollstonecraft had criticized, although the concept and the practice was as old as Sappho.

As immigration continued and European settlers pushed steadily outward from the sea coast and river mouths, carefully articulated gender role differentiation tended to break down. Well-to-do women in cities—and in Europe—could afford ornamental education. On the frontier, it was much more important to shoot straight, plant well, and trade shrewdly than to speak French. Role differences did not disappear, but they were blurred. Equality did not result, but changes in relationships between the sexes did. In fact many men, busy with wresting survival from the wilderness, were content to leave bookkeeping, shopping or trading, and culture—including abc instruction of children and keeping up with newspapers, pamphlets, and other literature—to women. The demands of a new environment and encounters with different value systems among Native Americans freed many American women from some traditional educational restraints, as had happened with Sor Juana in seventeenth-century New Spain.

During the last decades of the 1700s, special schools for girls, usually seminaries, began to be established in greater numbers. Their purposes varied: some were for polite learning, some were for the improvement of women who were or hoped to be teachers. In the latter case, the curriculum was similar to the English department of male academies with their emphasis upon study of modern languages, science, and practical subjects. Most of these were in the East. An example of a female seminary was the school of Sarah Pierce at Litchfield, Connecticut, established in 1792. The school had a long history and some distinguished students, among them Catharine and Harriet Beecher. It was located a few doors away from the Beecher house. Catharine Beecher did not speak highly of her education there, but many other people held Pierce's school in high esteem. The curriculum consisted of history, grammar, arithmetic, geography, penmanship, painting, embroidery, and music.

Some enterprising, liberal men noticed the rising demand for women's education. Joseph Emerson of Byfield, Massachusetts was a staunch advocate of women's education, and his school provided women with an extensive education. In 1820 the school enrolled about fifty or sixty students ranging in age from "gay misses of ten to sedate, grown women." Zilpah P. Grant, later famous as a teacher, was twenty-five when she attended. Emerson held devotional services both morning and evening. His course on mental philosophy (a mixture of philosophy and psychology) included logic. Emerson also taught arithmetic, reading, spelling, and vocabulary, and how best to teach these subjects. He provided English grammar, ancient history, natural philosophy (science), and astronomy. Students read some of the masterpieces of English literature, especially Milton and Shakespeare, but were steered away from sexually suggestive works. The textbook used in the second term of mental philosophy was Duguld Stewart's work, popularly referred to as "Stewart on the Mind."[2]

Emma Willard (1787–1870)

Due to the work of Emerson, Pierce, and others, the way was prepared for women to take up the task of conducting female seminaries or academies providing high-level education. Emma Willard was one who turned all of her efforts to improving the education of women. Her own educational interests began early. She was one of ten children born to Samuel Hart and Lydia Hinsdale, both of the early Connecticut families. There were also seven children from Hart's first marriage. Emma got more benefit from her father's reading to the family every evening than from the district school she attended, and she became a voracious reader. The village library supplied her with books of history, travel, and poetry.

Becoming a Teacher

Emma's own account of completing her education and becoming a teacher affords insight into the drive that made her successful:

Near the close of my fifteenth year, a new academy was opened about three-quarters of a mile from my father's house. . . . Before the opening of the academy, my mother's children had each received a small dividend from the estate of a deceased brother. My sister Nancy determined, as our parents approved, to spend this in being taught at the new school; but having at that time a special desire to make a visit among my married brothers and sisters in Kensington (whose children were of my own age), I stood one evening, candle in hand, and made to my parents, who had retired for the night, what they considered a most sensible oration, on the folly of people's seeking to be educated above their means and prescribed duties in life. So Nancy went to school, and I to Kensington. A fortnight after, one Friday evening, I returned. Nancy showed me her books and told me of her lessons. "Mother," said I, "I am going to school to-morrow." "Why, I thought you had made up your mind not to be educated, and besides, your clothes are not in order and it will appear odd for you to enter school Saturday." But Saturday morning I went, and received my lessons in Webster's Grammar and Morse's Geography.

Mr. Miner was to hear me recite by myself until I overtook the class, in which were a dozen fine girls, including my elder sister. Monday, Mr. Miner called on me to recite. He began with Webster's Grammar, went on and on, and still as he questioned received from me a ready answer, until he said, "I will hear the remainder of your lesson tomorrow." The same thing occurred with the Geography lesson. I was pleased, and thought, "you never shall get to the end of my lesson." That hard chapter on the planets, with their diameters, distances, and periodic revolutions, was among the first of Morse's Geography. The evening I wished to learn it, my sister Lydia had a party. The house was full of bustle, and above all rose the song-singing, which always fascinated me. The moon was at the full, and snow was on the ground. I wrapt my cloak around me, and out of doors of a cold winter evening, seated on a horseblock, I learned that lesson. Lessons so learnt are not easily forgotten.

The third day Mr. Miner admitted me to my sister's class. He used to require daily compositions. I never failed, the only one of my class who did not; but I also improved the opportunities which these afforded, to pay him off for any criticism by which he had (intentionally though indirectly) hit me—with some parody or rhyme, at which, though sometimes pointed enough, Mr. Miner would heartily laugh—never forgetting, however, at some time or other, to retort with interest. Thus my mind was stimulated, and my progress rapid. For two successive years, 1802–3, I enjoyed the advantages of Dr. Miner's school, and I believe that no better instruction was given to girls in any school, at that time, in our country.[3]

When Emma was fifteen she met Mrs. Peck, a woman of forty who "treated me not as a child, but an equal—confiding to me much of that secret history which every heart sacredly cherishes; and I, on my part, opened to her my whole inner life, my secret feelings, anxieties and aspirations." It was Peck who secured Emma her first teaching job just after she turned seventeen.

At nine o'clock, on that first morning, I seated myself among the children to begin a profession which I little thought was to last with slight interruption for forty years. That morning was the longest of my life. I began my work by trying to discover the several capacities and degrees of advancement of the children, so as to arrange them in classes; but they having been, under my predecessor, accustomed to the greatest license ... would ... dash out.... Talking did no good. Reasoning and pathetic appeals were alike unavailing. Thus the morning slowly wore away. At noon I explained this first great perplexity of my teacher-life to my friend Mrs. Peck, who decidedly advised sound and summary chastisement. "I cannot," I replied; "I never struck a child in my life." "It is," she said, "the only way, and you must." I left her for the afternoon school with a heavy heart, still hoping I might find some way of avoiding what I could not deliberately resolve to do.

I found the school a scene of uproar and confusion, which I vainly endeavored to quell. Just then, Jesse Peck, my friend's little son, entered with a bundle of five nice rods. As he laid them on the table before me, my courage rose; and, in the temporary silence which ensued, I laid down a few laws, the breaking of which would be followed with immediate chastisement. For a few moments the children were silent; but they had been used to threatening, and soon a boy rose from his seat, and, as he was stepping to the door, I took one of the sticks and gave him a moderate flogging; then with a grip upon his arm which made him feel that I was in earnest, put him into his seat. Hoping to make this chastisement answer for the whole school, I then told them in the most endearing manner I could command, that I was there to do them good—to make them such fine boys and girls that their parents and friends would be delighted with them, and they be growing up happy and useful; but in order to do this I must and would have their obedience. If I had occasion to punish again it would be more and more severely, until they yielded.... If my recollection serves me, I spent most of the afternoon in alternate whippings and exhortations, the former always increasing in intensity, until at last, finding the difference between capricious anger and steadfast determination, they submitted. This was the first and last of corporal punishment in that school. The next morning, and ever after, I had docile and orderly scholars.

For the next few years, Emma alternately taught and attended female seminaries in Hartford. In 1807 she became an assistant teacher in an academy at Westfield, Massachusetts, and after a year accepted the headship of a female school in Middlebury, Vermont. The school was successful at first, but Emma ran into difficulty over denominational politics. She married a physician there, Dr. John Willard, who was politically well connected. Until his death several years later, he was her companion and supporter in the cause of women's education.

In 1814 Willard opened the Middlebury Female Academy. Over time she taught less and lectured more. Ultimately, she traveled some eight thousand miles lecturing on women's education. A member of many educational associations, she contributed to women's education by this means and also through her numerous publications. Some of her more important works were *A Plan for Improving Female Education* (1819), *History of the United States* (1828), *Universal History* (1837), and *Ancient History* (1847). With William C. Woodbridge she coauthored a school geography.

Willard was convinced that public support was necessary for the orderly development of women's education and that it was in the interest of society to provide the needed money. Unlike Christine de Pisan, Sor Juana, and Wollstonecraft, she did not challenge male authority, holding that the education of men and women should differ. Women, she said, needed special training because of their role as mothers and the great influence they exerted in childrearing, and recommended boarding schools as a means of protecting and guiding young women. Women must be "good wives, good mothers, or good mistresses of families: and if they are none of these, they must be bad members of society." And they must be obedient to men. Only education could save women from frivolous, wasteful pursuits. By education, girls would be guided to intellectual goals and proper values. They, in turn, would pass these on to their children, ensuring the continuance of the republican form of government and society.

Willard's Plan

The New York state legislature invited Willard to present her *Plan for Improving Female Education* in 1819. She told the legislators:

> Studies and employments should . . . be selected from one or both of the following considerations; either because they are peculiarly fitted to improve the faculties; or, because they are such as the pupil will most probably have occasion to practice in future life. These are the principles on which systems of male education are founded, but female education has not yet been systematized. Chance and confusion reign here. . . .
>
> Not only has there been a want of system concerning female education, but much of what has been done has proceeded upon mistaken principles. One of these is, that without a regard to the different periods of life proportionate to their importance, the education of females has been too exclusively directed to fit them for displaying to advantage the charms of youth and beauty. . . . Though well to decorate the blossom, it is far better to prepare for the harvest.

While Willard acquiesced in male authority, she denied that women's education was merely to teach them how to please men.

> Reason and religion teach that we too are primary existences, that it is for us to move in the orbit of our duty around the Holy Center of perfection, the companions, not the satellites of men; else, instead of shedding around us an influence, that may help to keep them in their proper course, we must accompany them in their wildest deviations.

Yielding to male authority was a form of social contract: Whenever one class of human beings derive from another the benefits of support and protection, they must pay its equivalent obedience. Thus, while we receive these benefits from our parents, we are all, without distinction of sex, under their authority; when we receive them from the government of our country, we must obey our rulers; and when our sex take the obligations of marriage, and receive protection and support from the other, it is reasonable that we too should yield obedience.

Willard made a distinction between females seeking to make themselves "agreeable" to men and in accepting the "taste of men, whatever it might happen to be," as "a standard for the formation of the female character." Women should rather measure themselves against a standard of perfection. "A system of education which leads one class of human beings to consider the approbation of another as their highest object, teaches that the rule of their conduct should be the will of beings imperfect and erring like themselves, rather than the will of God, which is the only standard of perfection."

The legislators responded favorably, but offered no money.

Troy, New York, bought Willard a building and offered other aid. Her school at Troy opened in 1821 on a self-supporting basis and added several courses that had not been usual for women: algebra, geometry, history, geography, and natural philosophy (botany). Willard was principal of the Troy Female Seminary for seventeen years during which time the school became an important center for training teachers. Women who intended to become teachers but could not afford the tuition received loans to be repaid after they were employed. More than two hundred teachers graduated from Willard's school before there were any state-established, tax-funded normal schools. Some believed it was "the highest recommendation for a teaching position that the country offered."[4]

Willard traveled widely in Europe and America studying educational conditions. She turned the Troy seminary over to her son and his wife in 1838 and became superintendent of schools in Kensington, Connecticut, in 1840—one of the first woman to be elected to such a position. She married Christopher Yates that year, but divorced him in 1843. The Troy seminary was renamed the Emma Willard School in 1910 and is now a highly regarded college preparatory school for women.

Willard was one of a growing number of women who became active in teaching in the nineteenth century. As the country's population increased and moved West, sentiment for women's education increased. Attitudes on the frontier tended to favor useful education, and separating boys and girls in schools seemed less and less practical. In the East, more conventional (European) beliefs prevailed. The development of what we would now call women's higher education followed a parallel rather than integrated track with that for men. One of the significant people in that process was Mary Lyon.

Mary Mason Lyon (1797–1849)

Mary Mason Lyon was born in rural Massachusetts and spent much of her youth attending one-room schools and keeping house for an older brother. Her father died when she was young. At fourteen, she became a teacher. She earned seventy-five cents a week and "boarded round," a custom of having the teacher live short periods in students' homes, which let the community keep tabs on the teacher's conduct and allowed the teacher to know her pupils well. In 1817 Mary enrolled for advanced training at a nearby seminary. Over the next decade she alternated teaching with periods of dedicated study at various academies. These years increased her self-confidence and sophistication and helped her make friends who would play important roles in her future academy's development. One of these was Zilpah P. (Grant) Banister in whose Ipswich Female Academy Lyon worked as an assistant teacher from 1828 to 1834.[5]

Founding a Seminary

The years of study and teaching gave Lyon several convictions that later made her seminary unique. Wishing to ease for other women the difficulty she experienced in accumulating tuition money, she decided that her students would do domestic work around the seminary so the costs of attending school would be low. Furthermore, she expected teachers to accept modest salaries as their contribution to low-cost education. Learning that most women's schools were short-lived, usually closing because of insufficient endowment, she resolved not to establish a seminary until it could be financed soundly. She also decided that middle class women were the most appropriate students for her skill. "This middle class contains the main spring, and main wheel, which are to move the world," she wrote.[6] Lyon resolved that graduates of her school would not be parlor ornaments, but servants to humanity.

In 1834 Lyon took the first steps in making her dream of a women's school a reality. She outlined her idea in a pamphlet circulated among the many friends she had made through her teaching. A committee composed mostly of ministers sought financial backing for the school. Believing that a women's school would encounter less opposition if men obtained funds, Lyon tried somewhat unsuccessfully to stay in the background. Money trickled in—from homemakers, students, businessmen, and parents who hoped to send their daughters to the school. Lyon insisted on a New England location, and eventually chose South Hadley in western Massachusetts because it agreed to contribute $8,000 of the $20,000 needed to open the school. The community probably thought that having a well-established school would add to the town's prestige, provide better education for local women, and improve the town's economy. The school was named Mount Holyoke Female Seminary, after a nearby landmark. Ground was broken for the first building in 1836, and classes began the next year.

Life at Holyoke

Student life at Mount Holyoke was a combination of conventional educational practices and some experiments. Its first student body of eight students was chosen from twice as many applicants. In just a decade, after additional campus construction, the enrollment nearly tripled. Lyon's educational philosophy shaped and permeated the institution's growth: the school's "brightest, most decided feature will be, that it is a school for Christ."[7]

This purpose was carried out not only in the mandatory religion classes for seniors that Lyon herself taught but also in revival sessions, prayer meetings, fast days, and missionary gatherings. Each student had to classify herself as to her state of religious grace, and those "without hope" were given special attention. It is not surprising that a number of Holyoke alumnae married missionaries trained at nearby Amherst College. Others became missionaries themselves, or volunteered for teaching assignments on the frontier.

Another characteristic that Mount Holyoke shared with its contemporary collegiate institutions, male and female, was the number and extent of rules regulating student life. By 1839 there were 106 rules, and some students found them tedious. Safety rules governed the use of the Franklin stove and whale oil lamps found in every room. Other rules about running, talking, hours of rising and retiring, and tardiness were designed to develop responsible and ladylike students.

All schools functioned *in loco parentis,* which students sometimes resented. Lyon believed strongly in this concept, and preferred to think of Mount Holyoke as a large family and hoped to give the school a homelike atmosphere. Lyon herself, occasionally referred to as a "mother superior," had dynamic energy and a charismatic personality that helped soften the hard edges of the behavior code.

Only a third of the student body returned from year to year, and only 10 percent graduated from the three-year course, but this was common to most schools. Although some students were expelled and others may have left because they were unhappy, usual reasons given were impaired health, insufficient money, matrimony, and complications at home. Because any training at a school so advanced as Mount Holyoke made a woman highly educated by contemporary standards, many women probably considered one year sufficient.

Lyon sought earnest students who had proven themselves and who wanted to further their training. Women who had been teachers and who were older than sixteen received preference. Prerequisites included knowledge of grammar, geography, American history, arithmetic, and philosophy. The juniors, or first-year students, studied rhetoric, ancient geography, world history, political science, geometry, and physiology.

Second-year students, the middle class, continued grammar and added botany, algebra, natural history, and philosophy. The seniors studied chemistry (taught by Lyon herself), astronomy, geology, church history, religion, logic, and rhetoric. Greek was not offered and Latin was an elective. (Critics pointed to this lack of emphasis on classical languages as evidence that the school was not collegiate caliber.) The faculty was composed almost entirely of women educated at other seminaries; since women were excluded from degree granting colleges prior to 1836, the absence of college-educated faculty is not surprising.

Lyon's philosophy did not exclude the development of ladylike arts and behaviors, but these were secondary. Cultivating ornamental branches of knowledge like singing and drawing before mastering academics, she wrote, was "like polishing cork or sponge, instead of marble." Her desire to turn out responsible, religious women manifested itself in an emphasis on simple food and dress and the cultivation of virtues like order, punctuality, health, and economy.

One reason for Mount Holyoke's success was its domestic system, in which students and teachers cared for their own needs. Lyon believed that the system also helped develop character. Unlike Willard and Catharine Beecher, both of whom thought that teaching the domestic arts was a proper function for a woman's school, Lyon maintained that household skills were a responsibility of the family, not the school. Divided into circles with a leader, students were assigned work they had learned in their own homes, such as cooking, baking, making fires, and setting tables. They spent about an hour a day on such tasks, except on Monday, called recreation day. It began at 3:00 A.M. with fires being lighted in the laundry room, and included thorough cleaning of rooms, scrubbing floors, washing and mending clothes, and the writing of a weekly composition.

Life at Mount Holyoke was not all work. Students walked at least a mile a day and often visited nearby Amherst College, although all encounters with men were carefully chaperoned. Dancing was forbidden. Students read for self-improvement, but Lyon discouraged novel-reading as injurious. Baskets of treats often arrived from homes and provided occasions to be celebrated. Fads in the early years of Mount Holyoke included valentines, phrenology, and autograph books.

Lyon and her school were the subjects of some derogatory comments. The press called it a "rib factory" and a "Protestant nunnery," but such comments did not discourage Lyon. As one writer said, "It was called unnatural, unphilosophical, unscriptural, unpractical, and impracticable, unfeminine, and anti-Christian."[8] This catalogue of epithets is a list of all the familiar prejudices against women at that time. Critics of academic education for women said it would warp their minds and personalities, make them unfeminine, and was against religion and nature. Furthermore, it was not likely to work. The dire predictions of failure proved unfounded. Lyon, Mount Holyoke, and women's education prospered. By the time Lyon died in 1849, Mount Holyoke had gained a substantial reputation. Many other educators wishing to establish schools took Mount Holyoke as a model.

Women's Colleges

By 1850 the idea of providing women higher education did not seem so bizarre as it had when Lyon, Willard, and Beecher pioneered it in the 1820s and 1830s. Women were rapidly replacing men as teachers in elementary and sometimes secondary schools. The idea that better-educated women made more effective and morally influential wives and mothers was gaining popularity.

The effects of these new thoughts on women's education were felt first in the West and gradually drifted eastward. Oberlin College in Ohio was the first to admit women in 1837. (It had admitted African Americans at its founding four years earlier.) Antioch College, also in Ohio, began to admit women at its opening. The University of Iowa, created by the state's constitution in 1846, admitted women when it opened, and Iowa State and the University of Colorado were both coeducational when they opened. With tradition and sex stereotyping less apparent on the frontier than on the Atlantic seaboard, coeducation became the norm in the West. In the East, however, women's higher education continued its separate course.

Easterners preferred the idea of a college entirely for women. A generous endowment from Matthew Vassar in 1861 helped establish Vassar College in Poughkeepsie, New York. A decade later Wellesley College opened. In their earliest years standards were similar to Mount Holyoke's. Smith College started with fourteen students in 1875. Harvard began an "annex" for women in 1879; in 1894, it took its own name, Radcliffe College, when it received the power to grant degrees. Bryn Mawr College in Pennsylvania opened in 1885. By then it was becoming common for women's colleges to have identical entry requirements to those in male institutions.

These new schools stimulated Mount Holyoke to self-assessment. In many ways, the seminary had kept up with the times. The three-year program had been expanded to four years in 1861. With the installation of bathrooms, steam heating, and gas lighting, student living had become more comfortable. New academic buildings, several library expansions, stiffer admission and graduation requirements, and more guest lecturers had improved the academic program. Although rules were still stringent, student life included some social activism and national issues, a newspaper, and the establishment of a branch of the Women's Christian Temperance Union. The school drew students from other countries as well as from nearly every state. It had produced such well-known alumnae as the poet Emily Dickinson, Louisa M. Torrey (the mother of William Howard Taft), and the feminist Lucy Stone.

Despite these accomplishments, some unease persisted. The term *semi-*

nary had come to be applied only to women's schools, and therefore began to suggest a second-class status. Being a college graduate seemed more prestigious than being a seminary graduate. At Mount Holyoke's semicentennial in 1886, the issue of changing its name was hotly discussed. Although some wanted to rename the institution Mary Lyon College, Mount Holyoke Seminary and College was the choice. A bill making the change passed the Massachusetts legislature unanimously in 1888, and the new college was authorized to grant both bachelor of art and bachelor of science degrees. It immediately raised its entrance requirements and revamped its curriculum. The college proved so popular that the seminary was discontinued in 1893, and the name was shortened to Mount Holyoke College.

Graduate Education

Women's admission to schooling beyond the baccalaureate degree became an issue as the nineteenth century progressed. As graduate and professional schools developed, hardly anyone thought of admitting women. The 1848 women's rights conference at Seneca Falls, New York, pointed out the absence of women in medicine, law, and theology in its listing of wrongs to American women, but few steps were taken to correct this injustice until late in the century.

Two trends in the century contributed to the concern over women's post-baccalaureate education and access to the professions. A justification for excluding women that grew in popularity was the idea of women as frail creatures too pure to be sullied by the nation's seamy problems. A Harvard Medical School faculty member wrote in 1873 that women would literally endanger their lives by engaging in advanced study. It was permissible for women to teach young children and youth—a morally uplifting task—but to aspire to teach college age students, to practice law or medicine, or to preach was an outrage against female nature. In contrast, women's work as teachers, as activists in the abolitionist and other social reform movements, and as volunteers in various kinds of church and missionary activities had given them a keen sense of social ills and injustices. Heightened consciousness stimulated a desire for new avenues for service and careers.

As what we now call graduate education developed in the nineteenth century, the most prestigious institutions refused admission to women, citing several explanations. Because attending graduate school was so far removed from what was considered women's proper role, few thought that women might seek admission and fewer still thought graduate work would be appropriate for them. Another problem was women's preparation; often the academic training offered in women's colleges or the separate curriculum designed for them in coeducational schools was defined by male-dominated graduate schools as inadequate preparation for advanced work. Finally, many of the women who were qualified to do graduate work had so thoroughly internalized their dominant cultural norms that they simply chose not to try to gain admission to advanced study. Members of the middle or upper classes did not usually train for independent careers, and poor women had difficulty in obtaining the necessary skills.

Of course, there were exceptions to these generalizations. Some women developed scholarly expertise at home like Maria Mitchell, astronomer and later professor at Vassar. Other women, like Martha Carey Thomas, earned their degrees in Europe. The University of Iowa offered graduate admission to women by 1860, Iowa State University admitted women and men to graduate study from its opening in 1869, and the University of Pennsylvania offered women graduate admission in 1882. The first female graduate students helped ease the way for others. Thomas became the dean and later president of Bryn Mawr, the women's college established by Pennsylvania Quakers. Under her influence it became the first women's college to offer graduate work and fellowships. Other universities followed in the 1890s. When the University of Chicago first opened its doors in 1892, it offered graduate work to both sexes. Others followed: Columbia (1890), Brown (1891), Yale (1891), Harvard (1894), and Johns Hopkins (1907).

What could a woman do with advanced training? She was most likely to be hired by a women's college or a smaller school. Fearing that women on a faculty would lower prestige, the nation's most outstanding male or coeducational colleges were reluctant to hire them. The problems of lower salaries and rank and fewer promotions faced women as well, and have not yet completely disappeared. But growth in the nation's higher education was so rapid that some form of faculty employment in higher education was available to most women who sought it.

Professional Training

Throughout much of the nineteenth century, advanced schooling was not essential for a professional career; for example, a person was considered competently trained for a career by assisting a practicing doctor or lawyer. There had always been theological schools, but many ministers, especially in evangelical sects, were simply ordained by their congregations.

Legal Training. Women who wished to practice law had two admissions hurdles to overcome: being admitted to a law school and being admitted to the bar, the first being far easier than the second. Law schools developed somewhat more slowly than medical schools and, except for the most prestigious ones, were sometimes short of students. Being new institutions, they were not so encrusted with tradition. These factors facilitated women's admission. The law school of Washington University of St. Louis admitted both sexes when it opened in 1867 and graduated its first woman four years later. By 1900 many law schools admitted women; holdouts included Harvard, Yale, Columbia, Washington and Lee, and the University of Virginia.

After securing a legal education either through law school or an internship, a person had to get admitted to the bar before setting up practice. Women found a sizable amount of prejudice against them at this stage. It was argued that the contracts a married woman lawyer made would not be binding, that having women lawyers would conflict with common law, and that licensing women would also be to agree that they could serve as sheriffs, judges, and governors. It was even suggested that women might be an unpredictable influence on the administration of justice. Finally, there was the old saw about women being too delicate to endanger themselves with legal matters.

Because each state supreme court decided who it would license to practice law, the time of women's admission varied from state to state. Myra Bradwell of Illinois was the first to be admitted. Denied a license by the court in 1872, Bradwell was admitted the following year after the Illinois legislature passed a law that no one could be denied participation on account of sex in any occupation except the military. Women were admitted to the bar in several other states by a similar procedure. The first woman to be admitted to the bar of the U.S. Supreme Court was Belva Lockwood in 1879. Many early female lawyers worked within the legal industry rather than practicing law directly. Bradwell, for example, founded and edited the *Chicago Legal News.*

The Ministry. Establishing "firsts" in theological education and ordination is somewhat difficult because various levels of education and many denominations are involved. One name stands out, however: Antoinette Brown. Brown was the first woman to complete the undergraduate theological course at Oberlin College in 1851 and was ordained two years later as a Congregational minister. She was probably not the first American woman minister if the Quakers are considered. Believing in the equality of all people and having no paid ministry, the Quakers encouraged women's participation in all spheres of religious life, including public preaching.

Most denominations were not so egalitarian in their thinking as were the Quakers and often women were barred from ordination by the biblical injunction about women's keeping silent in the church. This prohibition also slowed women's admission to postgraduate theological seminaries; the first of these to admit women was the Hartford Theological Seminary in 1889.

Medical Education. As with other professions, both medical education and its practice presented difficulties to aspiring women. They had to struggle for admission to medical colleges and to clinical instruction, and often faced prejudice from male medical colleagues and the population they wished to serve. Opinion about the suitability of medical education for women was divided. On one hand, it was argued that medical education for women was a natural extension of their roles as moral guardians and homemakers. Who more than a mother would wish to guard a person's health? This was opposed on the other hand by the stereotype of female delicacy. Surely a physician's work was too arduous and coarse for a woman, though perhaps a woman could suitably aspire to be a nurse or other health care worker. This view prevailed throughout much of the nineteenth century.

The first medical school to admit women, Geneva College in central New York state, did so in 1847 when the faculty let the students vote whether to admit a female applicant, Elizabeth Blackwell, sister-in-law of Antoinette Brown. Thinking that her application was a joke from a rival school, they accepted it and then ostracized Blackwell when she actually registered for classes. She graduated with honors two years later. Despite Blackwell's outstanding record, Geneva College refused to admit her sister in 1851.

The reluctance of medical schools to admit women forced the development of medical schools solely for women. One was begun in Boston in 1848 and another in Philadelphia in 1850. Blackwell established another in 1868 in New York City with higher standards than the previous two. Other schools sprang up in Illinois and Ohio. Gradually major universities opened their medical schools to women, with the universities of Iowa and Michigan as early leaders. When Johns Hopkins, one of the most prestigious medical schools in the country, admitted women in 1893, others soon followed. However, many schools screened women's applications far more rigorously than men's.

A significant part of medical training involved clinical experiences, and hospitals were reluctant to allow women to train. Part of this unwillingness stemmed from a fear of patients' reactions to female doctors; another element was the hostility of the medical staff and other residents. Tension was so intense at first that several of the women's medical colleges had to open their own hospitals or dispensaries to give their students clinical experience, and some early female doctors went to Europe for further training. As major medical schools admitted women, however, access to hospital experience grew easier.

Women's success in being admitted to medical societies was similar. As late as 1859 prejudice against women was so strong that the Philadelphia County Medical Society resolved that any member who consulted a female doctor would lose his membership. But as the number of women doctors increased and no calamities resulted from their work, barriers to membership in professional societies fell.

Elizabeth Blackwell (1821–1910) and Emily Blackwell (1826–1910)

Despite the hostility of many male professionals to sharing their occupations with female colleagues, there were some men who encouraged women's achievements. Examples of those can be seen in the biographies of two extraordinary women, Elizabeth and Emily Blackwell. First within their family and later within their circle of friends and the medical establishment, men encouraged them to use their potential and develop medical careers.

Elizabeth and Emily were among twelve children born to Samuel and Hannah Blackwell of Bristol, England. Their father, a sugar refiner, was a dissenter from the Church of England and an activist in reform movements like abolition, temperance, and women's rights. His religion barred his children from English public schools, so they were all educated by private tutors who taught the same curriculum to both sexes. Their mother was supportive of her husband's reforms and her children's careers. In 1832 the family moved to New York and later to Ohio. Among their new American friends were Quakers who helped Blackwell get established in business—the abolitionist William Lloyd Garrison and minister Henry Ward Beecher and his sister Harriet Beecher Stowe. This familial and social environment produced remarkable children. Besides Elizabeth and Emily, one sister became a newspaper correspondent and another an author and artist. Brothers Samuel and Henry, also reformers, married respectively Antoinette Brown, the first American woman minister, and Lucy Stone, a crusader for abolition and women's rights.[9]

The Blackwell sisters were well educated and progressive thinkers. After their father's death in 1836, both of them taught school to help support the family and to earn money for their medical education. Elizabeth's motivations to be a physician apparently stemmed from her desire to promote moral reform and to diminish the likelihood of marriage. Emily, however, had a natural inclination toward science and nature since childhood and found medicine an obvious outlet for her interests. She was also influenced by Elizabeth's example.

Medical Education

Elizabeth first studied medicine with two physicians in the Carolinas while teaching school. She continued her studies with two Quaker physicians in Philadelphia as she began applying to medical schools. She was rejected by every medical school in Philadelphia and New York City as well as by Bowdoin, Harvard, and Yale before she was accepted by Geneva in 1847. During the summer of 1848 she was unexpectedly admitted to clinical work at Philadelphia Hospital and gained knowledge that helped her write a dissertation on typhus among Irish immigrants. Her experience helped her realize the importance of hygiene and sanitation, which remained a major part of her medical philosophy throughout her career. After graduating from Geneva in 1849, Elizabeth continued her clinical training in France and England. She returned to New York City two years later.

Emily also faced difficulty gaining admission to medical school, and was finally accepted by Rush Medical College in Chicago in 1852 only to be forced out a year later when the Illinois Medical Society censured Rush for admitting a woman. She completed her medical studies at Western Reserve in Cleveland in 1854, and then studied in Scotland and later as a physician's aide was admitted to clinical work in Germany.

Elizabeth had great difficulty setting up practice when New York City's physicians barred her from established clinics and hospitals. She gave a few lectures on hygiene and attracted the attention of some Quaker women who brought her patients. By 1853 she was able to open a part-time clinic in a tenement district and four years later expanded it into the New York Infirmary for Women and Children, which still exists. By the mid-1850s Elizabeth was not so terribly alone as she had been a few years earlier. She had adopted a daughter in 1854, and Emily and another woman physician joined her practice. Emily became the infirmary's chief administrator and surgeon and also helped win for it a small amount of state funding. The infirmary soon gained the support of some of the city's male physicians, and both the *New York Tribune* and the *New York Times* encouraged its growth in their columns.

Elizabeth took on new responsibilities in the 1860s. She helped select and train nurses for the Union army during the Civil War. In 1868 she established a Woman's Medical College associated with the infirmary. Among its innovations were entrance examinations, a three-year course (instead of the customary one or two years), and longer academic terms. The college continued until the Cornell Medical School began to admit women in 1899.

Although she had become a naturalized American citizen in 1849, Elizabeth had remained attached to England. She returned there in 1870, setting up practice in London and serving briefly as a professor of gynecology at the London School of Medicine for Women. Although poor health forced her early retirement, Elizabeth continued to write essays and to lecture occasionally. She died in 1910.

Emily remained in the United States and continued the expansion of the New York Infirmary. She began courses for nurses in 1858 and increased the program over the years. In 1866 she began a home social service, the first medical social service in the country. In 1871, fifteen years after she had begun her practice, she was invited to join the New York County Medical Society. She served as dean of the infirmary's medical school and as professor of obstetrics and gynecology for thirty years. Retiring in 1900, she died in 1910 just a few months after her sister.

Women like Emily and Elizabeth Blackwell were the exceptions as far as women's higher education was concerned. Women of northwestern European stock who had sufficient funds to attend college found that schools such as Mount Holyoke provided opportunities unavailable to their predecessors. However, not everyone had those advantages. Most

Native Americans, for example, had a far less happy and successful history of education in the nineteenth century.

NATIVE AMERICAN EDUCATION

Educators like to think of their profession as one that increases people's opportunities to live a better life. When nineteenth-century American Indian education as administered by whites is examined, this assumption is questionable. The history of the schooling of Native Americans is a sorry tale. Cultural ignorance and arrogance, political machinations, and greed skewed good intentions.

When Europeans began coming to America, there were several hundred different Indian tribes and many languages. Native Americans had obviously educated their children successfully without European-style schools. For generations, they had passed on the skills needed for survival and linguistic traditions for preserving their values and their heritage— skills and traditions so complex that Europeans could not master them even after years of practice. Although with so many tribes it is hard to generalize, methods commonly used for this education included the emulation of adults, public praise and recognition, oral recitation, and occasionally ridicule. Native American values included cooperation and loyalty to family and tribe; these clashed with nineteenth-century American ideals of rugged individualism and competition.

England and later the United States considered each tribe as a sovereign nation and negotiated treaties with them as settlers moved westward. Usually such documents contained provisions for schooling and health services, but they also contained clauses nullifying these provisions if there were tribal opposition. This often justified the government's failure to provide such services.

What the U.S. government did provide was support for efforts to educate a limited number of Indians in European ways. As noted in Chapter 8, these efforts were often jointly made by religious groups and the government. The Indian Civilization Act of 1819 appropriated a total of $10,000 and federal contracts were let with missionary societies to operate Indian schools. These contractual arrangements lasted until 1873. The goal was to Christianize and "civilize" the Indians; just as in Alaska, few attempts were made to recognize the value of native culture.

With the increasing numbers of settlers moving West after the Civil War, the "Indian problem" became more acute. Native Americans were increasingly pushed onto reservations, and traditionally nomadic tribes were given barren land for farming. Supplies and equipment for reservations were scarce, and schooling was available only to a few. Some federal legislators, fearful that education would allow Native Americans to compete more successfully with whites, were reluctant to appropriate more funds. In 1887 the

Dawes Severalty Act stripped 41 million acres from the Native Americans by converting many reservations into individually owned plots of 40, 80, or 160 acres. The Indians could not sell these allotments for twenty-five years, and the "surplus" land on these reservations was then sold to settlers and the funds used for Indian education and civilization.

The kind of schooling offered to Native Americans was obviously diverse. Some schools were run by missionaries for sectarian purposes. Many were on reservations. As frontier areas were designated as safe, old army forts were transformed into schools and run by the Bureau of Indian Affairs (BIA). Often short of supplies, they were run by teachers, usually white, appointed by the BIA, and the general goal was assimilation into the dominant culture. A sizable number of educators believed that this was more likely to happen if Native Americans were educated in boarding schools away from the cultures of their families and tribes. Here they could be forced to speak English (sometimes under the threat of corporal punishment), forbidden to practice their native religion, and boarded with white families during vacations. There were numerous instances of Native American children being forcibly removed or tricked from their homes without their parents' consent. After such an education, these children did not fit well into tribal life and were often also barred from white society by prejudice.

The most famous of the boarding establishments was the Carlisle Indian School in Pennsylvania. Founded by Richard Henry Pratt in 1879, it was closed in 1918. Subjects covered in Native American schools were typical of the day; few attempts were ever made to integrate Native American culture or language into the curriculum. In addition to religion and cultural assimilation, emphasis was increasingly placed on developing Indians' occupational skills, with agriculture and homemaking being the most common.[10] Education commissioner William T. Harris's explanation of education for Alaska natives was equally appropriate for other Native Americans: "When the native has become useful to the white man, . . . his future is provided for" (Chapter 8).[11]

Despite prejudice, there were a number of mixed marriages on the frontier. Children of these marriages were sometimes educated in the traditions of both parents. Some attended colleges and became bicultural, as did a number of full-blooded Native Americans.

Sarah Winnemucca (1844–1891)

One Native American who bridged the gap between the worlds was Sarah Winnemucca. Daughter of a Paiute chief and granddaughter of the Native American who accompanied Frémont into California, Sarah learned English by working in the home of an Army officer. At sixteen she and her sister enrolled in a California convent school but withdrew after white parents objected to their presence. They returned to their home in Nevada, and Sarah worked as a domestic while trying to continue her education alone. Although she spent part of her small earnings on books, she never read at a level that satisfied her.[12]

Winnemucca spent a large portion of her adult life working as a translator and spokesperson for the Paiutes. Her dealings with both the military and BIA agents convinced her that the former were more dependable and trustworthy than the latter. By speaking out on numerous occasions against fraud, political appointments of unqualified agents, and misuse of Indian land and labor, she became the object of a BIA investigation that sought to discredit her. However, her experience with the military and her public speaking tours first in California and later in the East made her friends who staunchly defended her against attack. She met twice with President Rutherford B. Hayes to plead for better treatment for the Paiutes.

Winnemucca had worked briefly as a teacher's aide in 1875, and an 1883 speaking tour in the East renewed her early interest in education. In Boston, she became good friends with Mary Tyler Mann, widow of Horace Mann, and Elizabeth Palmer Peabody, a pioneer in American kindergarten education. She completed a book, *Life Among the Paiutes: Their Wrongs and Claims,* which Mann edited. With proceeds from its sale and additional funds collected by Peabody, Winnemucca tried to start a school for Paiute children. At the site she originally chose, however, the teaching position was given to the local BIA agent's wife. She finally founded her own school in 1886 on her brother's farm. In addition to teaching academics, Winnemucca advocated Indian-controlled education and Indians' right to run their own lives. A visitor to the school wrote Peabody that the school was well run despite extraordinary obstacles that settlers had placed in Winnemucca's way. Neither Peabody nor Winnemucca was able to raise enough money to keep the school running after 1887. In poor health, Winnemucca worked again as a domestic and died worn out in 1891.

It would be satisfying to end this brief survey by reporting that Native American education was transformed in the current century, but that did not happen. Although most Native American children today attend nearby schools, some are still in boarding schools. The most recent decades have witnessed greater attention to Native American language and culture. A chronic problem, still not completely resolved, is who shall pay for the education of Native American children—the reservations, the state, or the federal government.

"Five hundred years after the arrival of Christopher Columbus in the New World, the Indians are everywhere in America the poorest of the poor and the least powerful of all groups," according to anthropologist Jack Weatherford:

> Future generations, however, may look back on the twentieth century
> as the turning point in the struggle for Indian autonomy and power in

the Americas. After four centuries of nearly constant losses, the Indians scored their first tentative victories. In the United States after centuries of losing on the battlefield and being shunned by the courts and government, the Indians started to win their cases in the court and found a legal base upon which to protect some of their rights. In countries such as Mexico and Bolivia they won on the battlefield even though they lacked the power to translate the victory into a permanent improvement for them. Who knows what the next half millennium may bring for Indian rights?[13]

AFRICAN AMERICAN EDUCATION

As was true for white Americans, the quality of African Americans' education in the nineteenth century was partly dependent on geographical location and economic status. Wherever African Americans lived, however, whether slave or free, racial prejudice limited educational opportunities. At the beginning of the nineteenth century, few white Americans believed in racial equality. The South relied on slavery, and in the North, African Americans had lower status. The result was disenfranchisement, job discrimination, and limited access to schooling.[14]

Until a few decades before the Civil War, many southerners taught, or allowed others to teach, their slaves. This allowed slaves to serve their owners better and made them more valuable if resold. Education, whether academic or craft-oriented, made slaves more able to serve the needs of a self-sufficient plantation, small farm, or in some cases an urban business. As abolitionist sentiment grew and slave revolts, led by literate blacks such as Nat Turner or Denmark Vesey, occurred in the 1830s, white southerners became frightened. Laws were passed prohibiting the teaching of slaves, and even schools for the region's few free blacks were closed. The only kind of education left to southern blacks had an oral tradition. White southerners sent ministers to preach the importance of Christian submission, while many black slave communities had clandestine religious services of their own and passed on their heritage in stories and songs. Slave children learned attitudes, values, and skills from the adults in their community. Occasionally they learned the rudiments of academics by playing school with white children.

The North certainly offered blacks a freer life than the South did, but racism still abounded. Horace Mann's so-called common school movement did not stimulate the North to integrate its schools. Some northern states excluded blacks from school by law, while others insisted on segregated schools. In the face of such white apathy and racism, blacks in many communities formed their own schools under the auspices of religious, philanthropic, or community improvement groups.

A major controversy in nineteenth-century black education involved deciding what kind of curriculum was most appropriate. In many instances this topic was also related to debates over intelligence. In most of the country, whites favored vocational training—so that its recipients could be self-sufficient, as in the case of free blacks, or a source of income, as in the case of slaves. In the North, racial prejudice sometimes kept workers from being hired. Also, vocational training was expensive, and many communities were simply unwilling to spend money for vocational training for blacks. In the South before the Civil War, the problems of hiring, modernity of facilities, and expense were minimal because skilled slaves generally learned their trades from local craftspeople and were employed by their owners or rented out. After the war, however, the South had little money to spend on anyone's education. The famous black vocational schools established in the South after the war, Hampton and Tuskegee, depended heavily on philanthropy.

The emphasis in white communities on vocational rather than classical academic education for African Americans fit with dominant culture prejudices about the relative distribution of academic talent among blacks and whites. It was not because they believed that people of African American descent lacked academic aptitude, however, that caused some black leaders to favor vocational over academic curricula. One of these was Fanny Coppin. She helped change the orientation of Philadelphia's black school from totally academic to vocational.

Fanny Marion Jackson Coppin (1837–1913)

Unlike many well-educated blacks of the nineteenth century, Fanny Jackson did not have the initial advantages of freedom or wealth. She was born a slave in 1837 in the District of Columbia. Fanny's Aunt Sarah, earning $6 a month, saved $125 to buy her niece's freedom. She then lived and worked with another aunt in Massachusetts and at fourteen moved to Rhode Island. There she worked in the household of a literary and cultured family who allowed her one hour every other afternoon to study. She attended a local black public school and took private music lessons. Later she graduated from the Rhode Island State Normal School, a teacher training institution that offered an education on a level similar to today's high schools. In 1860, again with help from Aunt Sarah, she entered Oberlin College in Ohio, one of the few colleges in the nation then open to blacks or women. She received her bachelor of arts degree in 1865, one of the first black women to do so.[15]

Institute for Colored Youth

College educated women of any race had limited career choices, and like the majority of them Fanny Jackson entered teaching. The Institute for Colored Youth in Philadelphia hired her to teach advanced mathematics, Latin, and Greek, and to be the principal of the girls' high school division. In 1869 she became the head principal, the first woman to hold that position.

The Institute had been established in 1837 at the behest of Richard Humphreys, a Quaker, who wanted to test blacks' capability for higher learning, and its curriculum had been academic. However, Jackson wished to expand its mission to include vocational preparation. In 1871 she persuaded its board of trustees to add a normal training program. The Philadelphia Centennial Exposition of 1876 stimulated her to expand the Institute even further. Impressed by the exhibits of industrial and manual training in other nations, she sought similar training for young black men and women. She argued that the only place in Philadelphia a black child could receive any industrial education was in a poorhouse or prison. More than a decade passed before Jackson raised enough money to open a vocational center.

Jackson married Levi Coppin in 1881 and, unlike most women of her day, continued her work outside the home. Levi was a minister and later a bishop in the African Methodist Episcopal Church. Gradually Fanny Jackson Coppin found new ways to use her educational talents through church work. She spoke on behalf of black women at conferences as far away as California and London.

In 1889 Coppin inaugurated classes in plastering, bricklaying, carpentry, shoemaking, printing, and tutoring for boys; dressmaking and millinery for girls; and stenography, typing, and cooking for both sexes. She also led the school in other educational innovations. She began sending regular reports on students' progress and conduct to parents, and introduced practice teaching into the normal program. She briefly added German to the curriculum until the board canceled it. The board also refused to allow her to open a kindergarten. In 1902, Coppin resigned from the Institute to accompany her husband to a bishopric in South Africa, where she helped with missionary work. In 1913, a few years after the Coppins' return, she died in Philadelphia.

The Institute with which most of Coppin's career was associated continued. After her resignation, it became even more vocationally oriented under a principal whose philosophy was similar to Booker T. Washington's. In 1904 the Institute moved to Cheney, Pennsylvania, becoming a state normal school in 1920 and Cheney State College in 1951.

Booker T. Washington (c. 1856–1915)

Better known than Coppin as an advocate of vocational education was another African American born in slavery. He was born sometime between 1856 and 1859 in a log cabin that measured about 14 by 16 feet. Washington's mother was the cook for both the slaves and the white owners of the plantation. His father was a white man whom he never knew. Booker's stepfather, also a slave, lived on another plantation and saw his wife and stepchildren infrequently. The Washington family's owner had ten slaves, and the "white folks' house" was a two-story log cabin. Both blacks and whites were vital parts of the plantation's economy, and even as a small child, Booker was put to work holding horses for the white women when they went riding.[16]

Early Life

As the Civil War progressed, its effects were felt on the plantation. Certain foods like sugar became scarce. Two of the white sons were wounded in the Confederate army, and one, much loved by the slaves, was killed. As the Union army moved farther south, blacks began to talk more openly of freedom. One day, a Union officer appeared on the owner's porch and read the Emancipation Proclamation. Washington was now free—at least legally.

While many freed slaves stayed on to work for their former owners, exchanging a share of their crops (hence, *sharecroppers*) for land and seed, the Washington family moved on. Washington's stepfather had left his plantation during the war, and was now working in a salt mine in Malden, West Virginia. He sent for his wife and stepchildren (two of her own and one whom she'd adopted). In many respects, Malden was worse than the plantation. Free blacks replaced slaves working in the salt mines, which were outdated and dangerous. The family's living quarters were dirty and jammed in with those of other miners. Young Booker spent life in this setting until 1871, working in salt and then coal mines, filthy and dangerous labor that he came to hate.

During this time, Booker's first attempts at schooling began. A bright child, he soon learned to distinguish numbers by looking at those used to indicate which worker had packed a particular salt barrel. In addition, his mother managed to get a copy of Webster's speller, and he taught himself the alphabet. In order to get some formal schooling, he worked early in the mornings, went to school, and immediately went back to work until evening. His stepfather, however, soon insisted that he needed the boy's income, and Booker's formal education came temporarily to a halt.

Education

To escape the mines, Booker worked as a houseboy for the mine-owner's wife. A demanding boss, she insisted that things be cleaned to perfection. For all her exactitude, however, she was kind and encouraged Booker to learn to read. Some of the men who worked in the mine had begun to talk about a school in Hampton, Virginia which had been founded to educate black teachers. In the fall of 1872, Washington set out, determined to achieve an education.

The Hampton Normal and Agricultural Institute was the product of an extraordinary man, General Samuel Chapman Armstrong. The American Missionary Association had asked Armstrong to found a black teacher training and industrial school in the Virginia area, where he had been working for the Freedmen's Bureau. It was a wise choice. The son of parents who were missionaries in Hawaii, Armstrong had commanded black troops in the Civil War and emerged as one of the Union's youngest generals. His parents' experience with industrial schools for Hawaiians, coupled with his own natural conservatism, convinced him that education in the trades was the ideal for blacks. Hampton became the theory's proving ground.

Washington arrived at the school with only the clothes on his back. His entrance exam was unique: the principal asked him to clean a room. Realizing that his future hung in the balance, Booker swept and dusted several times, and the principal pronounced herself satisfied. Washington's student days had begun.

Washington's career at Hampton lasted three years. During this time, he learned a good deal about discipline and reconfirmed the value of hard work, serving as a janitor to pay his tuition and wearing second-hand clothing sent from the North. Nevertheless, he thrived. A summer visit to Malden with its sense of aimlessness contrasted sharply with the orderly life at Hampton. In General Armstrong, Washington found a father. He absorbed Armstrong's philosophy of vocational education to produce black self-reliance, which would later direct his life.

Washington was one of the 20 percent of his entering class who graduated from Hampton in 1875. He went back to Malden, quickly becoming involved in day, evening, and Sunday schools and soon teaching more than 180 students. In 1878, he left Malden to study at Wayland Seminary, a small Baptist theological school in Washington, D.C. Wayland, unlike Hampton, emphasized the liberal arts. It reinforced Washington's conviction that liberal education was not practical for most blacks, because it gave them no skills with which to earn a living. After an 1879 invitation to return to Hampton to give a commencement speech, Washington was invited by Armstrong to accept a teaching position there.

Political Climate

Southern political life was in a state of flux during these years. Under the "home rule" policy of Andrew Johnson, Lincoln's successor, southern states passed laws to keep blacks in their place. A radical Republican Congress retaliated by passing legislation to promote civil rights and punish the South. The 1867 Reconstruction Act divided the southern states into military districts policed by Union troops, and ordered new state constitutions that allowed blacks to vote. In reaction, whites founded the Ku Klux Klan and the Knights of the White Camellia, terrorizing the black community and promoting racial hatred.

As time went on, southern whites gradually gained control of state governments. By the middle 1870s, all of the former states of the Confederacy except South Carolina, Louisiana, and Florida had "redeemer" white governments. Tennessee passed a law forbidding intermarriage in 1870, and the first laws mandating segregation in schools, on trains, and in public places had appeared by 1875. More conservative Republicans gained control of the party in 1876, spelling the end of its support for black rights. A southern Senator described the situation in the South after the 1876 departure of federal troops: "Whites rose in righteousness and right. We took the government; we stuffed the ballot box; we bulldozed the niggers and we shot them. And we are not ashamed of it."[17]

It was in this context that Washington began the work for which he would become famous, the founding of Tuskegee Institute. In 1881, Colonel W. F. Foster, an ambitious Alabama politician seeking the black vote, went to a former slave turned hardware store owner and struck a bargain. In return for swinging the black vote in his favor, Foster would sponsor a bill in the Alabama legislature for a state-supported black teacher training school. The result was an appropriation of $2,000 a year for a school at Tuskegee.[18]

Tuskegee Institute

Although the citizens had wanted a white teacher, Washington was what they got. In this town of two thousand people, he began the school with thirty students in an old church and an abandoned shack. Soon after his arrival, he spotted a plantation on the edge of town for sale at $500. Between money raised by local citizens and a large personal loan from the Hampton treasurer, Washington was able to purchase the property. The plantation was a bargain because the main house had burned down and the fields were overgrown. That first winter the students lived in shacks, and frostbite was common in the schoolrooms.

With little cash, the Tuskegee Normal and Industrial Institute had to depend on student labor to provide its necessities. Washington's biggest job was persuading the students, whose educational model was white liberal arts schools, that manual labor was not a disgrace. By diplomacy and example, Washington got them to work. Students began to repair buildings and plant crops. In 1883, he started his most famous self-help project. Noticing that the local soil was mostly clay, he became convinced that the students could make their own bricks, but no one at Tuskegee knew how bricks were made. Three times they tried and failed. Washington pawned his watch to finance another try, and the experiment worked. Soon the bricks were going not only into Tuskegee buildings but into new construction in the town. The brickmaking venture became a symbol of how young blacks with industrial training could achieve economic independence and, in the process, contribute to the prosperity of the local community.

Starting with those skills most necessary to the school's survival, Washington moved on to found a variety of industrial departments. Between 1883 and 1892, Tuskegee got into the business of carpentry, printing, cabinet and mattress making, wheel making and wagon building, tinsmithing, harness and shoe making, home economics, and nursing. The agricultural department, which had started with a blind horse as its only livestock, had branched out into scientific farming; poultry, cattle, and pig raising; and beekeeping. The original 30 students had become 169 by 1884 and had grown to 712 in 1894, with 54 teachers and administrators.[19] Students' days began at 5:00 A.M. and ended at 9:30 P.M. Almost all time was programmed in detail. Students were required to work, and not allowed to smoke, drink, or gamble. In many respects Tuskegee looked like a military school. Only officers were allowed to go to dances which the girls on campus sponsored.

Expansion required money, and Washington's role soon moved from that of principal to professional fund-raiser. These efforts eventually projected him into the national spotlight, but in the early days, Washington often returned from trips depressed with the results. However, he gradually perfected his skills. Individuals who initially gave small gifts found themselves courted, and frequently became major benefactors. The railroad magnate Huntington, steel tycoon Carnegie, and the Alabama legislature all made sizable contributions. Endowments by the Peabody and Slater funds provided regular help. Washington's combination of homespun eloquence and apparent support of the status quo struck exactly the right note. By 1915, Tuskegee's endowment totaled $2 million, the largest of any black or white college in the South.[20]

Educational Politician

Washington gave his first speech in 1893, a five-minute presentation to a Christian conference in Boston. Much to his surprise, he was received enthusiastically. An articulate black who preached a gospel of self-help appealed to northern industrialists and southern whites alike. These fund-raising trips gave Washington wide exposure. A variety of other opportunities came his way, until he received an invitation to speak at the opening of the Atlanta Exposition in 1895.

The Atlanta speech (also called the "Atlanta Compromise") marked Washington's entry onto the national scene. For the first time, an African American appeared in the South on the same program as white dignitaries, and Washington was determined to make the most of it. His speech stressed the solidarity of interest between southern whites and blacks, and emphasized his evolutionary (rather than revolutionary) approach to civil rights. Admitting that serious errors had been committed in the Reconstruction Era, he went on to assure his audience that "the wisest among my race understand that the agitation of questions of social equality is the extremist folly, and that progress in the enjoyment of all the privileges that will come to us must be the result of severe and constant struggle, rather than of artificial forcing." Washington ended with a plea for economic cooperation between blacks and whites, predicting that "this, coupled with our material prosperity, will bring into our beloved South a new heaven and a new earth."[21]

The speech was a thundering success. "The fairest women in Georgia stood up and cheered," one observer commented. "It was as if the orator had bewitched them."[22] The governor rushed across the stage to shake his hand. With difficulty, Washington got through the crowd. Well-wishers stopped him on every street corner. Newspapers across the country hailed him as spokesman for the black race. Washington was the man of the hour. (Ironically, many blacks boycotted the exposition because of its segregated facilities.)

The next several years brought a flood of speaking engagements and civic honors. Harvard gave him an honorary degree in 1896, and the *Washington Post* proposed him for Secretary of Agriculture. In 1897, he took Boston by storm, speaking at the unveiling of a statue commemorating a white soldier who led black troops in the Civil War. In 1898, the Slater Fund sent Washington on a speaking tour of the South. Whites were impressed with his rags-to-riches story and relieved that the most prominent black American held little hatred for past injustices. His philosophy of gradual change in race relations was reassuring. In 1897 the Secretary of Agriculture toured Tuskegee, followed by President McKinley in 1898. When Theodore Roosevelt became president after McKinley's assassination, Washington became black America's principal advocate. On most matters concerning blacks, including political appointments, Roosevelt depended heavily on him.[23] Their relationship led to a national furor in 1901 when Roosevelt invited Washington to dinner at the White House. Southern newspapers were outraged, although the controversy soon blew over. Washington had become a major figure in American civic life.

Tuskegee was still the primary focus of Washington's attention. Even on the road, he received daily reports about the most minute happenings at the school and continued to rule it with an iron hand. Unlike Hampton, which had a largely white faculty, Tuskegee's permanent faculty (at Washington's insistence) were all black. In 1896, he hired the noted agricultural chemist, George Washington Carver, and continued to recruit talented black teachers. He also broadened Tuskegee's scope. The first Tuskegee Negro Conference was held in 1892 to provide a forum for blacks to discuss the future progress of the race. In 1900 he founded the National Negro Business League to provide the same opportunity for exchange by black business leaders. Washington's flair for taking his message to the people showed in the Movable Farm Demonstration, a traveling exhibit that included animals, growing plots of vegetables, and modern farm machinery, aimed at introducing rural farmers to the wonders of scientific agriculture.

Another major concern for Washington was his family. His first marriage to childhood sweetheart Fannie Smith ended when she died in 1894. The following year, he married Tuskegee's first teacher, Olivia

Davidson. These marriages left him with three children when Olivia died in 1889. His marriage in 1893 to another teacher, Margaret Murray, brought the family together once again. While Washington's love for Olivia seems to have prevented a close relationship with Margaret, he remained a concerned father and educational guide for the children.

Under Fire

In spite of all his achievements, Washington was not universally praised. Some blacks, especially among the college-educated, saw his gradualism as a sellout, and believed that industrial education condemned future generations to second-class citizenship. The Harvard- and German-educated social philosopher W. E. B. DuBois criticized Washington's vocational philosophy, preferring to stake the future of black America on the "talented tenth" of college-educated black youth. Writers like Kelly Miller challenged Washington's right to speak for the black community: "Mr. Washington is not a leader of the people's own choosing. He does not command an enthusiasm and spontaneous following. . . . His method is rather that of a missionary seeking the material and moral betterment of an unfortunate people, than a spontaneous leader voicing their highest self-expression."[24] Articulate northern blacks like Monroe Trotter and George Forbes attacked him continuously in print.

People disenchanted with Washington's policies came together in 1905 in the Niagara Movement. By 1910, this organization had become the National Association for the Advancement of Colored People (NAACP). Washington's stubborn insistence that his was the only approach led him to rehabilitate the defunct Afro-American Council and support the more moderate Urban League (1911) in an effort to check the militants.

National events also contributed to a lessening of his political influence. The election of Taft in 1908 reduced his political clout, although he still had a voice in political appointments. The 1912 election presented him with a problem. Theodore Roosevelt, running on the Progressive ticket, had trimmed his views on race to woo southern support. Taft, the Republican, was not a black favorite, and Wilson, a southern Democrat, was seen as dangerous. Unwilling to abandon the Republican party, Washington supported Taft. When Wilson won, Washington lost his place in the corridors of power.

In spite of these problems, Tuskegee's president was still involved with a variety of projects. In 1911, at the insistence of the school's directors, he took a three-month educational and social trip to Europe, which he turned into a study of social conditions published as *The Man Farthest Down* (1912). His earlier *The Story of My Life* (1900) and the more refined *Up from Slavery* (1900–1901) had long since been translated into many languages, making him an international celebrity. Programs ranging from John D. Rockefeller's General Education Board and the Julius Rosenwald Fund for black schools to National Negro Health Week occupied his attention.

Washington's school also required his presence. By the twenty-fifth anniversary, 1,600 students (who had made 970,000 bricks that year) were enrolled. Younger faculty were unhappy with some policies. Washington's extensive time away from campus and lack of attention to detail almost cost him older teachers like Carver, who threatened to quit in 1914 because he had not had a raise in salary since he arrived in 1896. In 1913, the addition of a new heating plant pushed the school beyond its budget.

Washington simply pushed himself harder to make ends meet. In spring 1915, he took to the road again, touring Massachusetts, New York, Illinois, Iowa, Kansas, Nebraska, and Nova Scotia to raise money for the 1913 deficit. He collapsed in New York of nervous exhaustion and advanced arteriosclerosis. Knowing that he was near death, he asked to return home. He died on November 14, 1915, the day after he arrived at Tuskegee.

The controversy surrounding Washington has continued after his death. Critics have argued that his public statements hindered the civil rights movement. Certainly the Atlanta Exposition speech helped to establish the "separate but equal" doctrine, which the U.S. Supreme Court made the law of the land in 1896.[25] Washington, however, was more involved in promoting civil rights than was known during his lifetime. Working behind the scenes, he lobbied against efforts to restrict black voting rights, tapping even Catholic bishops to obtain support.[26] An expert fund-raiser, he frequently supplied money for court cases involving black rights and helped plan legal strategy. While his public image was one of passive acceptance, he worked to undermine the very institutions he seemed to tolerate. More than most people, the sharp separation between public and personal life makes any accurate assessment of what Washington really believed difficult.[27]

Questions have also been raised about the value for African Americans of the sort of industrial education Washington advocated. Were vocational schools aids or obstacles to success? For the critics, Washington's educational philosophy was as much a sellout as his political and economic stances. This judgment may be a bit harsh. Washington came onto the scene during a time when black attempts at political and social equality were frustrated by the South's increasingly repressive laws. Economic independence seemed to offer the only realistic vehicle for black improvement, so industrial education emerged as the most logical strategy for him. Washington's concern for agricultural education for rural blacks was part of a general concern of both black and white industrial educators to keep America's rural population on the farms.

Washington may have been wrong in believing that economic success would produce respect for African Americans—the question of racial tension involved far more than economics—but economic power was surely part of the equation. In the final analysis, Washington deeply influenced American educational development. Tuskegee shaped the lives of countless black schoolteachers and professionals who made significant contributions to American life. Its programs served as stepping stones for many to the kind of university education DuBois favored. Indeed, by Washington's death, Tuskegee was already beginning to look more like a college than the elementary and high school he had begun. Washington's greatest contribution, however, had more to do with personality than institution building. He helped to create a national climate that supported education for blacks even in the face of southern resistance. His success in fund-raising generated income not only for Tuskegee but for a host of other educational projects as well. Most of all, he offered in his person a success story with which black and white alike could identify. His own desire for education and a better life inspired many to sacrifice for the same ends.

Future generations would rightly insist that the doctrine of "racial merit," which based human rights on ability to perform, had no place in American society. However, Washington's larger belief that schooling could be used to improve the social, political, and economic lives of people continues in the present with the development of special and bilingual education, academic enrichment, and affirmative action programs to meet a wide variety of needs. While American education may never justify the high hopes Washington had for it, the challenge he offered and the bridges he built have helped schooling in the United States to become more sensitive to the great diversity of people it must serve. "Washington's journey," according to a recent assessment, "was unparalleled, bringing momentous social change to the masses through adult education."[28]

HISPANIC AMERICAN EDUCATION

The earliest European-style schools in what is now the United States were started by Spanish missionaries. In the nineteenth century, when common school still meant a community-controlled enterprise, schools in California, Colorado, New Mexico, and Arizona were sometimes taught in Spanish or in Spanish and English. As statewide systems replaced local schools, this practice ceased. By the end of the nineteenth century, school opportunities for Spanish-speaking Americans were seriously restricted.

When the United States conquered Puerto Rico in 1898, John Eaton, Jr., a friend of education who had been second U.S. Commissioner of Education, visited to inspect the schools and reported that education on the Catholic island needed a total revamping. English was the greatest need in his proposed curriculum. Yet Puerto Rico had some educational strengths. One of these was a quiet cigarmaker who offered instruction to many Puerto Ricans during his long life. His name was Rafael Cordero y Molina.

Rafael Cordero y Molina (1790–1868)

A black educator who contributed to the development of elementary education in Puerto Rico occupies a heretofore unacknowledged place in the history of American education. Rafael Cordero was born in San Juan in October 1790.[29] His mother, Rita Molina, and his father, Lucas Cordero, both free blacks, taught him how to read. He did not receive any formal schooling, for the school in his area at that time admitted only white children.

As soon as he learned how to read he continued his studies autodidactically. He was an avid reader, and developed enough skills to begin his lifelong career as an elementary school teacher. He dedicated fifty-eight years of his life to educating black children.[30] He made cigars to support himself, and he is said never to have charged his students for their lessons.

In 1810, thirty-five years before the Puerto Rican government had officially organized elementary school systems, Maestro Cordero opened a small school in San German. He realized the need to teach black children who were denied an education due to their color. Years later, Cordero moved his school to Luna Street in San Juan, where he continued teaching until his death.[31]

His curriculum consisted of reading, calligraphy, math, and catechism. He taught black children as well as poor white children, and his methods attracted rich white children also. It is said that all his students loved him and appreciated his teaching efforts. They learned to read quickly under his tutelage. He was a kind and dedicated teacher.[32]

After many years, the Sociedad Economica de Amigos del Pais (a civic organization) wanted to reward him with one hundred pesos. He refused, saying that what he was doing was his vocation (out of dedication). When he was pressed to accept the award, he divided the money among his most needy pupils.[33]

After he had taught without monetary compensation for more than fifty years, the government of Puerto Rico named him Maestro Incompleto (incomplete teacher). This title had a monthly salary of fifteen pesos. Initially he refused, but finally accepted on the insistence of his friends.

On July 5, 1868, Cordero died in San Juan at seventy-eight, five years before slavery was abolished in Puerto Rico. He is remembered as the pioneer of instruction for the most humble classes of Puerto Rico.[34]

Mexican Americans

While Puerto Ricans became the largest Spanish-speaking group of American citizens overnight in 1898, years of steady immigration created a growing population of citizens of Mexican descent in the United States.

During the first thirty years of the twentieth century, Mexican Americans were discouraged from participating in the educational process. Very few "attended school past the primary grades," according to historian Thomas Carter, even though approximately 700,000 legal immigrants entered the United States between 1900 and 1930. During the period from 1921 to 1930, when Mexican immigrants to the United States accounted for almost 3 percent of Mexico's total population, immigration had a strong impact on the schools.[35] Like so many others during the depression years of the 1930s, Mexican Americans migrated to cities in increasing numbers. As public school districts felt the impact of their numbers, school authorities responded by encouraging these students, who were mainly of low socioeconomic status, to pursue "vocational and manual arts training, the learning of English, health and cleanliness, and the adoption of such American 'core values' as thrift and punctuality."[36]

Educators began to define the "problem" of their education as one caused by bilingualism and lack of motivation. Bilingualism was "detrimental to intellect and thus to the child's teachability." The general attitude about motivation was exemplified in a 1938 Los Angeles high school study: "The Mexicans, as a group, lack ambition. The peon of Mexico has spent so many generations in a condition of servitude that a lazy acceptance of his lot has become a racial characteristic."[37]

Many school districts created separate schools where the children would learn English (even if they were already fluent in English) and become Americanized. In some towns, such as Del Rio, Texas, there were actually two school districts, one for Mexican Americans and one for Anglo Americans, but the facilities, teacher preparation, class size, and enforcement of attendance in the Mexican American schools did not compare favorably with the Anglo schools. Where separate schools or school districts did not exist, Mexican American children frequently were put in separate classrooms throughout the elementary grades, and the few who went on to high school were usually assigned to the vocational track. An especially distressing practice was the placement of disproportionate numbers of Mexican American children in special education classes. As recently as 1967 it was reported that "while mental retardation is certainly higher among Mexican Americans than among the Anglo population, . . . the overrepresentation is entirely among those with I.Q. scores of over 50. The higher level mental retardates are those most likely to be retarded because of cultural and familial factors rather than genetic factors and, most important, to be reported retarded because of problems in test instruments."[38]

Discrimination also occurred in Americanization programs and in extracurricular activities. During the 1930s and 1940s assimilation programs were popular with educators who hoped that they could "modify . . . Mexican American children from half-hearted Americans into law abiding and useful American citizens." English was rewarded; Spanish was punished. Ironically, most Mexican Americans were isolated from Anglo children, so

Americanization was to be accomplished by the negative method of denigrating the children's culture while teaching them a new one. Spankings were given to children who spoke Spanish on the playground, and educators modified the dress and even the names of Mexican American students.[39] But at the same time that school personnel were working diligently to Americanize Mexican American children, these children were not invited to join school clubs. In many towns their social isolation was complete: public parks and swimming pools were closed to them, and when they attended movies, they had to sit in "Mexican" sections. In Mission, Texas in the 1930s and 1940s, the only swimming pool was privately owned but "open to the public." Eligio "Kika" de la Garza, who later chaired the powerful Agriculture Committee in the U.S. House of Representatives, was not a part of that "public" when he was growing up in Mission.[40]

Migrant students presented a different problem. Because they came to school late and left early, they did not fit regular school schedules and their attendance was not encouraged. Migrant schools or classes only went through the eighth or ninth grade, usually for an extended day from October through April. After that the students had to enroll in regular high school classes. Unfortunately, in high school the students still had to enroll late and leave before the school year ended. This disruption of routine so concerned one principal of a large high school in the Rio Grande Valley that in 1969 he directed all of his teachers to give such pupils a zero for each day missed. This meant that a migrant student starting in October could not pass any subject even if he or she made straight As after entering.[41] Eventually such practices and attitudes fell into disfavor as the numbers and political power of Mexican Americans began to be felt. While many discriminatory practices have ceased or diminished, the quality of the educational experience for Hispanic American children continues to be questioned as test scores and enrollment in higher education fall below the national averages.

George I. Sanchez (1906–1972)

George I. Sanchez was born on October 4, 1906. His own school years were pleasant; he later spoke of the schools that he attended in Jerome, Arizona (1913–1921) and Albuquerque, New Mexico as being "A-1." Upon graduation from high school in Albuquerque in 1923, not yet seventeen years of age, he moved to the other side of the desk as a teacher at Yrrisarri, a rancheria about forty-five miles east of Albuquerque, across the Sandia Mountains, where he taught in a small one-room school. "Though I owned a stripped down Model T, much of the time I had to get there on horseback—across the mesa to Tijeras Canyon, up that canyon to Cedro Canyon, and up that one to the divide called Tiroteo ('Shootout'), then down to my one-room bachelo[r] abode," he later recalled. "I made the round-trip once a week. On very cold days (nights, really, for I had to start out from Albuquerque around midnight), I would have to stop now and then to build a tumbleweed or pine needle fire to thaw the icicles on my horse's nostrils." The following year he was "assigned about the same distance across the county, to the one-room school at San Ignacio (better known as 'El Ojo Hediondo' ['Stinking Springs'] [sic]). The traveling hazards there were sand, desert mexas [sic], sand, the Rio Puerco (which my horse waded or swam across, depending on rains in the river's upper reaches), and more sand."[42]

He enjoyed telling his students about commuting in that old Model T. One day as he was driving "in the middle of nowhere" the engine of his car fell out. No towns were near. He finally chained the engine back into the car, and drove on.[43] During these difficult circumstances, for eight long years, he pursued a degree at the University of New Mexico, graduating in 1930 with a degree in education and Spanish.

Fellowships from the General Education Board (a Rockefeller Foundation) provided opportunities for graduate study. Sanchez received an M.S. in educational psychology and Spanish from the University of Texas in 1931, where he wrote a thesis on the lack of validity of English language intelligence tests for Spanish-speaking children. In 1934, he received an Ed.D. from the University of California at Berkeley in educational administration. Upon his return from California, he served as Director of the Division of Information and Statistics for the New Mexico State Department of Education working under a General Education Board Grant. During 1934–1935 he was the president of the New Mexico Educational Association. The experiences that he had in these two positions, especially as a leader of state school finance reform during the fight for a school equalization fund, served as an initiation into the importance of knowing how to use politics and law to attain goals.[44]

In 1936 Sanchez published *Mexico—A Revolution by Education*. From 1935 to 1937 he worked for the Julius Rosenwald Fund of Chicago as a research associate surveying rural schools in Mexico as well as "rural and Negro education in the South." In 1937 the Venezuelan government invited him to be in the ministry of education and to be the president of the newly established National Teachers College for one year. Then from 1938 to 1940 he taught as a nontenured faculty member at the University of New Mexico and directed a Carnegie Foundation Survey that resulted in *Forgotten People: A Study of New Mexicans*.

In 1940 Sanchez was elected president of League of United Latin American Citizens (LULAC), and accepted the first professorship in Latin American studies in the United States. He had been promised a tenured position at the University of New Mexico, but he realized that the position was no longer available because of his writings on the "handling of the School Equalization Fund in New Mexico." Then the University of Texas offered Sanchez "a full professorship yet! In New Mexico, the best that the University had offered me was a nontenure job as 'Research Associate' (whatever that is) or as an Instructor. A bit unflattering. No? So, Texas here we come."[45]

Sanchez in Texas

In Texas Sanchez began his crusade in the courts to effect changes in the educational opportunities for Mexican American children. However, the first and greatest obstacle was funding. The amount of money that would be needed would be more than an impoverished minority group could raise. Through his work with the Julius Rosenwald Fund and Carnegie Foundation, he had come to understand the power of foundations in supporting causes involving human rights. He decided to organize such a group through the funding of a foundation. He corresponded with Roger Baldwin, chairman of the ACLU and also director of the Marshall Trust, about this idea, and soon Baldwin notified him that he had talked to the Marshall Trust and that they would donate $3,000 for an organizational meeting "to set up a national organization to concern itself with the civil liberties of Spanish-speaking people." They met in El Paso in 1951 and the articles of incorporation were drawn up by Sanchez and Gus Garcia. Representatives were selected from Texas, California, New Mexico, Arizona, and Colorado. The first year the Marshall Trust underwrote expenses of $15,000 and the American GI Forum gave $2,000. Funding continued for several years during which time Sanchez also was involved with Alianza Hispano-Americana, LULAC, and American GI Forum, all of which contributed to lawsuits for equal rights.[46]

The conditions that Sanchez found to be intolerable for Mexican American schoolchildren improved but did not disappear during his lifetime. Sanchez's papers include a news article from the *Austin American Statesman* (January 26, 1947), which describes conditions of the Colorado School District at Montopolis near Austin. The "Latin American" youngsters were packed into a small one-room school with ninety-six students and one teacher who was responsible for teaching all seven grades. Even when the students were split, the strain proved to be too great for the new teacher, and she left. The physical facilities were abysmal, with a faulty bridge in front of the school, no drainage in the schoolyard, and drinking water supplied by a hydrant outside the school building. In the same school district the Anglo-American school was a "modern, brick structure. State school funds [were] the same per capita for both groups." The article said, "Persons interested in the problem would like to see a workshop included in the [Latin American] school to teach the boys to work with their hands."[47]

As late as 1962, Sanchez was protesting the treatment of Mexican American schoolchildren by Austin police. In a letter to the mayor of Austin, Sanchez said he had been told that:

It is not uncommon for persons representing themselves as police officials to be permitted to interrogate little children in the public schools, without the knowledge (or consent, of course) of their parents or guardians. I am told further, that little children have been taken away from public schools, by persons representing themselves as officers of the law, for temporary detention and further interrogation elsewhere. . . . Those same informants tell me that persons representing themselves as police officers have pushed their way into the homes of "Latin Americans" in the middle of the night to lif[t] the covers off sleeping children in purported attempts to apprehend fugitives without warrants, without identification, and without arrest.[48]

With segregation and injustices firmly entrenched, Sanchez faced an almost overwhelming challenge in trying to right past wrongs. He decided, wherever other means did not work, to use the law to enforce a greater law: equality for all. He served as a fundraiser, strategist for the lawyers trying the cases, and expert witness in numerous cases. He consistently advised the attorneys to use the "class apart" theory which he, Carlos Cadena, and Gus Garcia established in a 1954 Supreme Court case (*Hernandez v. Texas*) concerning biased jury selection, to try cases only in federal courts, and to discredit the use of culturally biased standardized testing.[49]

Court Cases

In *Delgado v. Gracy et al.* (1948), Sanchez found the necessary $10,000 to try the case through LULAC and other organizations as well as his own contributions. According to Sanchez:

[In this case] certain public school districts in Texas were enjoined from segregating children of Mexican descent. At the same time the State School Superintendent, as a co-defendant, was enjoined "from in any manner, directly or indirectly, participating in the custom, usage or practice of segregating pupils of Mexican descent . . . in separate schools and classes."[50]

Years later he counseled the following strategies:

[To Pete Tijerina]: Amend to ask for damages. We did in the Delgado case and scared the stuffing out of the defendants. We traded on it. . . . School district lines are arbitrary and capricious, per se. The S[an] A[ntonio] school district is a creation of the State. . . . Sue the State Board of Education, the State Commissioner of Education.[51]

[To Mario Obledo]: If you sue New Braunfels and others, include the State Board of Education and the State Commissioner of Education as defendants. After all, the schools are State schools.

We did this in the Delgado case, to good advantage. Price Daniel, then Attorney General, was forced to make a "deal" with us—for he saw he couldn't win. . . . If you put the Attorney General on the spot, he will back down (politics) if it will make him look bad. And, you know, the AG can't appear to be anti-Mexican. The Delgado case took 15 minutes in

Rice's court! . . . P.S. Ask for $1.00 damage against each defendant. Good trading point. Scares hell out of them. If you can get $1.00, you can amend, if they appeal, and ask for $100,000 or any figure. This worked in the Delgado case. Sue individually and collectively.

P.P.S. . . . If your outfit wants to go whole hog, we have the guns and the ammunition—nearly all free.[52]

Sanchez would use the principles of *Delgado* to build a legal barrier against discrimination with one case frequently serving as precedent for the next in a carefully planned attack. Three of the cases with which Sanchez was involved and to which he frequently referred were *Herminio Hernandez, et al. v. Driscoll Consolidated Independent School District, Trinidad Villareal, et al. v. Mathis Independent School District,* and *Diego Chapa, a minor, et al. v. Odem Independent School District.* Sanchez selected James de Anda and Gus Garcia as attorneys for the Driscoll case, and they "negotiate[d] an out of court settlement that gave plaintiffs all they had asked for in the complaint."[53]

Both Sanchez and de Anda visited the Driscoll and Mathis school districts. In Driscoll they found that all "Latin" children had to spend at least two years in the first grade and were placed there solely on the basis of their inability to understand English. Also, "all children of Latin American or Mexican descent [were segregated] in the first and second grades and for a period of three or four years for alleged language deficiency." Tempers evidently were high. A story in the *Austin American* reported that the school district responded to the suit by filing "a counter suit for an injunction requiring the plaintiff parents to speak only English in the presence of their children."[54]

In the Mathis case Sanchez found that there were in the district two schools referred to as the "New Elementary" and the "Old Elementary" schools. In the New Elementary, all first grades were 100 percent Anglo, and there were 100 percent "Latin" sections of all other grades except eighth. The Old Elementary was 100 percent Latin. The New Elementary had a full-day session while the Old Elementary had a half-day session for all except the third grade. The practice of segregation was especially blatant because the two schools shared the same campus and the same geographical attendance area. The Mathis suit was risky because the school board based its separation of children on test scores, and Sanchez was afraid that "a court might side with the school board in the exercise of its discretion in the assignment of children on the basis of tests." The negotiated settlement included a resolution by the school board affirming its commitment to serving all students regardless of national origin or native language. There would be no more separate schools for "children of Mexican or Latin descent," home language would not serve as a criterion for first year school placement, there would be no more segregated sections within schools, a normal first grade curriculum would be provided for first graders of Mexican or Latin descent, placement would be on a first come, first served basis for all children, and those enrolling late would be placed in various sections, not segregated in one.[55]

In 1967, James de Anda requested that Sanchez review the pretrial brief in *Diego Chapa, et al. v. Odem ISD*. Sanchez's reply is illustrative of the types of arguments he used in testifying as an expert witness and advising lawyers.

> In Defendant's motion . . . a most damaging admission is made, that 35 out of 105 children who will be in the First Grade in the Fall are repeating that grade (presumably some for more than the first time). . . . This would suggest that the school makes virtually no effort . . . at remedial teaching for children—or that these efforts are highly misguided and indefensible. It would suggest, further, that the criteria used in determining promotions are unrealistic and inapplicable.
>
> The proposed testing and classification program is, as you have pointed out, just another way of arriving at . . . "genteel segregation." . . . To apply the Gates Reading Test to children who are not proficient in English, and who do not know and *are not expected to know* how to read, is a brutal perversion of pedagogy. This travesty is compounded by giving the children a test in oral English. As the saying goes, these poor kids can't win for losing! . . . Further, these tests were standardized on children who are not representative of the Spanish-speaking children of Odem. Therefore, the norms of these tests do not apply for the children of Odem. Sectionalizing children in the elementary school is hazardous at best, and easily challenged—unless the groupings are heterogeneous (random) ones. It is only intraclass that we are justified in "homogeneous" groupings in the elementary school.
>
> The stress placed on tests, and the percentages of children to be assigned to grade sections is a pseudo-scientific way of assigning children arbitrarily and capriciously. . . . These people in Odem are clinging desperately to the idea that English and education are synonymous, and are overlooking the obvious fact that these Spanish-speaking children are normal children and that their knowledge of Spanish is a natural cultural resource that should be cultivated. It is not a handicap.[56]

The court order came quickly (July 1967), for previous court cases had paved the way for the speedy execution of justice in this situation. The court found that segregation existed and ruled that the school district was "permanently enjoined from maintaining separate classes and/or sections of classes on the basis of ethnic or national origin, and from discrimination . . . against students of Mexican extraction."[57]

For over four decades Sanchez devoted himself, frequently at great personal sacrifice, to ensuring that all Americans, especially those of Mexican heritage, would have equal rights. Even in ill health he kept up the fight. He wrote letters right up until his death on April 5, 1972, instructing, advising, outlining his philosophy and strategies. He was always looking ahead, always planning the next battle, and always believing that right would prevail—with a little help.

Sanchez's contributions were extensive. In 1984, the University of California at Berkeley School of Law honored him with a retrospective of his contributions to laws affecting Mexican Americans. In 1978 the U.S. Office of Education named a "Work Section" in the Horace Mann Learning Center for him and in 1985 named a room in the new U.S. Office of Education Building in his honor. Peter Flawn, president of the University of Texas at the time of Sanchez's death, said, "There is no question but that he was the intellectual leader of the Mexican-American movement in Texas and the Southwest. He was speaking out in the Mexican-American cause long before anyone else was, and is really the father of Mexican-American studies." In a letter to Thurgood Marshall in 1955 Roger Baldwin, chairman of the American Civil Liberties Union, called him the ablest man in the United States on the problem of segregation as applied to Mexican-Americans."[58]

SUMMARY

The official ideology of the friends of education and their offspring, the progressives, was equal schooling for all. In practice, however, women got less than men; Asian, Hispanic, African, and Native Americans less than whites of European descent; recent immigrants less than those who had arrived earlier; the working class and poor less than their affluent neighbors. Several aspects of scientific school management reinforced inequality: standardized testing and tracking, differentiated curricula, and institutionalized stereotyping.

Thousands of unsung heroes swam against the current to change the prevailing climate in American society. In doing so, they helped diminish the intensity of inequality pervading school systems.

Equity is far from complete in American education. Because of the rich diversity of backgrounds, America has become what one social commentator calls "the first universal nation." Educational achievement in the face of considerable difficulty is one reason. "It is very much in the American interest—commercial, geopolitical, demographic, and ideological—to encourage this tendency toward diversity," writes Ben J. Wattenberg. "We ought to encourage it, even if it itches a little. It's the one big reason America is, and will be, the omni-power."[59]

NOTES

1. Thomas Woody, *A History of Women's Education in the United States*, 2 vols. (New York: Science Press, 1929); Eleanor Flexner, *Century of Struggle: The Woman's Rights Movement in the United States* (Cambridge, MA: Harvard Uni-

versity Press, 1959); Phyllis Stock, *Better Than Rubies: A History of Women's Education* (New York: G. P. Putnam's Sons, 1978).

2. L. T. Guilford, *The Uses of a Life* (New York: American Tract Society, 1885), 32.

3. Henry Fowler, "Educational Services of Mrs. Emma Willard," *American Journal of Education* 6 (1859): 125–168. All Willard quotations are from this source unless noted otherwise.

4. Willystine Goodsell, *Pioneers of Women's Education in the United States* (New York: McGraw Hill, 1931), 20–62.

5. Arthur C. Cole, *A Hundred Years of Mount Holyoke College: The Evolution of an Educational Ideal* (New Haven: Yale University Press, 1940); Elizabeth Alden Green, *Mary Lyon and Mount Holyoke: Opening the Gates* (Hanover, NH: University Press of New England, [1979] 1983).

6. Mary Lyon, *Mount Holyoke Seminary* (Boston: Old South Work Leaflet No. 145, n.d.).

7. Lyon, *Mount Holyoke Seminary*.

8. *Cyclopedia of Education*, s.v. "Lyon, Mary."

9. Elizabeth Blackwell, *Pioneer Work in Opening the Medical Profession to Women: Autobiographical Sketches* (New York: Source Book Press, [1895] 1970); Dorothy Clarke Wilson, *Lone Woman: The Story of Elizabeth Blackwell, The First Woman Doctor* (Boston: Little, Brown, 1970).

10. Estelle Fuchs and Robert J. Havighurst, *To Live on This Earth: American Indian Education* (Garden City, NY: Doubleday, 1970).

11. Annual *Reports of the Department of the Interior for the Fiscal Year Ended June 30, 1903: Report of the Commissioner of Education* (Washington: Government Printing Office, 1904), lxvii.

12. Catherine S. Fowler, "Sarah Winnemucca, Northern Paiute, 1844–1891," in *American Indian Intellectuals: 1976 Proceedings of the American Ethnological Society,* ed. Margot Liberty (St. Paul, MN: West, 1978); Katherine C. Turner, *Red Men Calling on the Great White Father* (Norman: University of Oklahoma Press, 1951); Gae Whitney Caufield, *Sarah Winnemucca of the Northern Paiutes* (Norman: University of Oklahoma Press, 1983).

13. Jack Weatherford, *Indian Givers: How the Indians of the Americas Transformed the World* (New York: Fawcett Columbine, 1988), 172–173.

14. Meyer Weinberg, *A Chance to Learn: A History of Race and Education in the United States* (Cambridge: Cambridge University Press, 1977).

15. Benjamin Brawley, *Negro Builders and Heroes* (Chapel Hill: University of North Carolina Press, 1937); L. J. Coppin, *Unwritten History* (New York: Negro Universities Press, [1919] 1968).

16. Most biographical material is from Washington's two autobiographies: *The Story of My Life and Work* (1900) and *Up from Slavery* (1901).

17. U.S. Senator "Pitchfork Ben" Tillman cited in Samuel R. Spencer, Jr., *Booker T. Washington and the Negro's Place in American Life* (Boston: Little, Brown, 1955), 125–126.

18. Louis R. Harlan, *Booker T. Washington* (New York: Oxford University Press, 1972), 113–115.

19. Washington, *The Story of My Life and Work* in *The Booker T. Washington Papers,* ed. Louis R. Harlan (Urbana: University of Illinois Press, 1972), 1: 47.

20. Spencer, *Booker T. Washington,* 116.

21. Booker T. Washington, "Address to the Atlanta Exposition," in *The Ne-*

gro in American Life, ed. Murray Eisenstadt (New York: Oxford Books, 1968), 152–153.

22. New York *World,* cited in Spencer, *Booker T. Washington,* 99–100.

23. August Meier, "Toward a Reinterpretation of Booker T. Washington," in *The Making of Black America,* ed. August Meier and Elliot Rudwick (New York: Atheneum, 1969), 126–127.

24. Kelly Miller, "Washington's Policy," in Meier and Rudwick, *The Making of Black America,* 123, originally in the Boston *Evening Transcript,* September 19, 1903, 18.

25. Spencer, *Booker T. Washington,* 105.

26. Meier, "Toward a Reinterpretation of Booker T. Washington," 126–127.

27. Harlan, *Booker T. Washington,* 157–158.

28. Virginia Lantz Denton, *Booker T. Washington and the Adult Education Movement* (Gainesville: University of Florida Press, 1993), xiii.

29. Rafael L. Cortada and Jean Challman, "Cordero y Molina, Rafael" *Biographical Dictionary of American Educators* (Westport, CT: Greenwood, 1978), 312.

30. Federico Ribes Tovar, *100 Biografías de Puertorriqueños Ilustres* (New York: Plus Ultra Educational, 1973), 83.

31. Tovar, *100 Biografías,* 82.

32. Tovar, *100 Biografías,* 82.

33. Tovar, *100 Biografías,* 83.

34. Tovar, *100 Biografías,* 84.

35. Thomas Carter, *Mexican Americans in School: A History of Educational Neglect* (New York: College Entrance Examination Board, 1970), 10; Leo Grebler, et al., *The Mexican American People; The Nation's Second Largest Minority* (New York: Free Press, 1970), 44, 65.

36. Carter, *A History of Educational Neglect,* 10–11.

37. Joan Moore with Alfredo Cuellar, *Mexican Americans* (Englewood Cliffs, NJ: Prentice Hall, 1970), 77.

38. Moore and Cuellar, *Mexican Americans,* 74.

39. Carter, *A Decade of Change,* 17, 100–101.

40. Rep. Eligio de la Garza; Robert de la Garza.

41. School principal in South Texas, statement to author and directive given to author, 1969.

42. Sanchez to Harold J. Alford, December 30, 1971; Sanchez, "Inter-American Relations—A Memoir," Sanchez Papers, Bensen Latin American Collection, University of Texas at Austin Library.

43. John Pulliam, Dean Emeritus, University of Montana, interview by author, Austin, TX, November, 1986.

44. Sanchez, "Inter-American Relations—A Memoir"; Sanchez to Gerald R. Lopez, November 19, 1968; *Biographical Data* (to December 31, 1960), Sanchez Papers; Frank Angel, Professor Emeritus, University of New Mexico, Interview by Author, Albuquerque, New Mexico, November 8, 1989; Sanchez, "Southwest . . . ," 22.

45. *Biographical Data* (to December 1960), 5–7, Sanchez Papers; Sanchez, "Southwest . . . ," 23.

46. A. L. Wirin to Ralph C. Estrada, July 18, 1951; Sanchez to Lyle Saunders, April 4, 1951; Sanchez to Roger Baldwin, September 7, 1951, July 8, 1952; Sanchez to Dennis Chavez, June 9, 1952, Sanchez Papers.

47. Virginia Forbes, "Double-Up: Crowded Rural Schools Lack Pioneer Facilities," *Austin American Statesman,* January 26, 1947.

48. Sanchez to Lester Palmer, February 18, 1962, Sanchez Papers.

49. Sanchez to Alford, 3–4; Sanchez to Baldwin, June 2, 1955; Sanchez to Lopez, November 19, 1968, Sanchez Papers.

50. Civil Action No. 3888, U.S. District Court, Western District of Texas, Austin, Texas, June 15, 1948; Sanchez to U.S. Commission on Civil Rights, July 12, 1967, Sanchez Papers.

51. Sanchez to Tijerina, November 12, 1969, Sanchez Papers.

52. Sanchez to Obledo, October 15, 1968, Sanchez Papers.

53. All three cases were filed in the District Court of the United States for the Southern District of Texas, Corpus Christi Division; Sanchez to Simon Gross, August 19, 1957, Sanchez Papers.

54. Plaintiff's Pretrial Memorandum: *Herminio Hernandez, et al. v. Driscoll CISD* (Civil Action N. 1384) and *Trinidad Villareal, et al. v. Mathis ISD* (Civil Action N. 1385), District Court of the United States for the Southern District of Texas, Corpus Christi Division, [no date]; Sanchez to James De Anda, October 28, 1955; *Herminio Hernandez, et al. v. Driscoll Consolidated Independent School District, et al.* (Civil Action File N. 1384), Plaintiff's Reply to Defendant's Brief, United States District Court for the Southern District of Texas, Corpus Christi Division, [no date]; "UT Professor Testifies on Segregation Changes," *Austin American Statesman,* November 1, 1956, photocopy in Sanchez Papers.

55. Sanchez to de Anda, October 28, 1955; Complaint to Enjoin Violation of Federal Civil Rights and for Damages, *Trinidad Villarreal, et al. v. Mathis Independent School District, et al.* (Civil Action N. 1385), District Court of the United States for the Southern District of Texas, Corpus Christi Division, [no date]; Sanchez to de Anda, 28 October 1955; Sanchez to Roger Baldwin, 7 May 1957; Resolution Adopting Policies and Administrative Procedures Concerning Students of the Mathis Independent School District," October 1956, Sanchez Papers.

56. Sanchez to de Anda, 7 July 1967, Sanchez Papers.

57. *Diego Chapa, a minor, et al. v. Odem Independent School District,* ORDER Civil Action N. 66-C-92, District Court of the United States for the Southern District of Texas, Corpus Christi Division, July 28, 1967.

58. Roger Baldwin to Thurgood Marshall, June 3, 1955, Sanchez Papers. This section on Mexican American education and Sanchez has been revised and expanded from a paper delivered by Martha Tevis to the Texas State Historical Association, March 8, 1991.

59. Ben Wattenberg, *The First Universal Nation: Leading Indicators and Ideas about the Surge of America in the 1990s* (New York: Free Press, 1991), 46.

The Critics

The progressives were in the mainstream of educational thought and practice in America until well into the twentieth century, but they were not the only ones concerned about schools. Conscientious educators all over the world struggled to adapt educational curricula and teaching methodologies to conflicting demands. From the 1890s through the 1930s, changes took place at all levels of schooling. Some educators saw this as the realization of Plato's desire to sift out the born leaders of society—the philosopher-kings. Psychologists like Carl Brigham of Princeton, H. H. Goddard of the training school at Vineland, New Jersey, and Lewis Terman of Stanford concluded that intelligence was basically hereditary and argued for federal immigration policies to turn away the intellectually inferior. Social reformers like Jane Addams favored separate schools for "special students"; that is, the morally defective, mentally subnormal, and behaviorally deviant. Parents would be told that this procedure was of enormous benefit to their children. In the 1890s, the NEA's Committee of Ten recommended that collegiate education be composed of courses of study that would include choices ranging from the classical liberal arts to modern languages and science.

In 1918, after three years of meeting, the Commission on the Reorganization of Secondary Education (CRSE) advocated a comprehensive high school composed of three tracks: the traditional college prep or general track; a business or commercial track; and a new technical (industrial) track. In addition, the CRSE enunciated "seven cardinal principles" that should be stressed by comprehensive high schools: (1) health, (2) command of fundamental processes, (3) worthy home membership, (4) vocational training, (5) citizenship, (6) good use of leisure time, and (7) character building. Also, sports and extracurricular activities for all students would allow parttime, working class students to become acquainted with fulltime, college-bound people. The report advocated social solidarity among students whose families came from all social classes and represented all ethnic groups. Elementary reading books like the Sally, Dick, and Jane series sent messages about the standards of American life to newly arrived school-age children.

Many critics offered alternative visions of education. Some developed strains from earlier themes; others offered novel solutions and ideas. To include all critical contributors would necessitate another volume. Instead, we have chosen seven: (1) Maria Montessori for her highly successful application of sensory learning principles, (2) John B. Watson for his advocacy of behaviorism and conditioning,(3) Margaret Naumburg for her insights into the value of psychoanalysis for educational settings, (4) Jacques Maritain for his reassertion of the values of Thomism in modern life and education, (5) W. E. B. DuBois for his critique of the vocational education movement for blacks championed by Coppin and Washington, (6) George S. Counts for his insistence that progressive educators be political and social reform leaders in order to bring about a better world, and (7) Miles E. Cary for advocating grass-roots educational democracy and multicultural respect. These people did not disagree with each other or with the progressives about everything. Their lives and thoughts illustrate the rich and complex background of the contemporary issues around which debate still swirls in education circles.

Maria Montessori (1870–1952)

In 1914 Professor William Boyd of the University of Glasgow explained the great interest in Maria Montessori's educational views as "no doubt due to the fact that they come before the world at a time when there is widespread discontent with the traditional methods of the schools and an eager desire for some kind of reform that will make popular education more effective than it is at present."[1] Montessori's ideas and methods remain popular nearly a century after she publicized them.

Education

Born at Chiaraville, Italy in 1870 to parents of comfortable social standing, Maria learned early in life to help with the daily practical chores of the household and to work for those less fortunate than herself. She attended a state day school until, at the age of twelve, her parents moved to Rome. There they discovered that Maria had an interest in and aptitude for math. Her parents hoped she would become a teacher, but she refused to consider the idea, and instead took up engineering. She was one of the few girls of her era to enter the technical curriculum. By the time she was ready to graduate from the technical institute, she had developed an interest in biology and decided to undertake medicine instead of engineering.

Her mother approved of the change; her father resisted it, for nineteenth-century Italy stigmatized both the female student and her family. Despite serious odds, Maria entered the University of Rome in 1890, and two years later began the four-year medical program. Her father accompanied her to lectures to discourage other medical students from heckling or molesting her. She had to work alone at night in human anatomy laboratories because it was unthinkable for a woman to dissect a body in the presence of men. In 1896, after exhibiting great stamina, she graduated with a double honors degree in medicine and surgery—the first woman in Italy to do so.

Early Career

Shortly after graduation, Dr. Montessori accepted the chair of hygiene at one of the two female colleges in Rome. She also became an assistant physician at the University of Rome psychiatric clinic. As part of her duties, she visited insane asylums in the city looking for suitable subjects for the clinic. It was a practice of the time to house mentally deficient children in these adult asylums. What she saw increased her compassion for the plight of such children. She concluded that mental deficiency was more an educational than a medical problem. This premise put her in contact with the works of two French scientists—Dr. Jean Itard and his student Dr. Edouard Seguin. Itard had gained recognition for his work with the wild boy of Averyon (Chapter 6), and Seguin had been labeled as "the apostle of the idiot" for his success in freeing the "deficient mind" from the "bondage of its imperfect organs by a physiological education." Montessori translated Itard's book and Seguin's six-hundred-page volume, writing them out by hand in order to gain "the sense of each word and read in truth the spirit of the authors."[2]

After Montessori gave a series of lectures on the education of the feeble-minded, the minister of education asked her to direct a newly established state "orthophrenic school" for "deficient children." From 1899 to 1901, she spent long days with the children and then stayed up half the night assessing her day's work. Ultimately, her endeavors bore fruit. Some of her "mental defectives" passed the public reading and writing examinations taken by normal children. While a chorus of applause greeted their performances, Montessori was pondering its meaning: "Whilst everyone was admiring my idiots, I was searching for the reasons which could keep back the healthy and happy children of the ordinary schools on so low a plane that they could be equaled in tests of intelligence by my unfortunate pupils."[3]

She resigned her directorship to look for answers in the study of philosophy. In 1904 she was appointed to the chair of anthropology,

University of Rome, a position she held until 1908. Throughout these years she also managed to make a special study of the nervous diseases of children and publish her results, visit and observe children in other European countries, practice medicine in private as well as in the clinics and hospitals of Rome, deliver an address as the Italian representative to a feminist congress at Berlin with such success that her picture appeared in many European newspapers (1896), address a pedagogical congress on moral education at Turin (1899), and write her first major volume, *Pedagogical Anthropology* (English version, 1910). Her manner and style as a lecturer during these years were described by a formal pupil and future close associate, Anna Maccheroni:

> The hall was large, and over the lecturer's chair was a canopy. Having taken a place on one of the two benches at the right side of the platform, I could see the hall crowded with young people of both sexes. The lecturer herself stood, looking eagerly at them, with her searching look—so penetrating but never disturbing, never making uncomfortable the person at whom she looked. As I found afterward, she could take in each one, individually, in what was a kind of spiritual contact.
>
> Of course I noticed at once that she was a very good looking woman, but what impressed me even more was that she was not following the general custom of the learned women of her time. They were few, and chose to dress in a rather masculine style. Not she! In her attire, however simple it was, she retained a feminine and elegant touch. And she was smiling. She spoke—not about anthropology, but about schools. She told us what a school should be like.[4]

School Administrator

In 1907, the thirty-seven-year-old physician-turned-educator got the chance to try out her approaches on normal children. In that year a building society in Rome decided to clean up the poverty- and crime-ridden San Lorenzo quarter, one of the worst slums in the city. The society resurrected two blocks of tenement housing, which were immediately inhabited by more than one thousand families who promised to observe the rules of "decency and hygiene." Most adult members of these households had to work. A member of the building society who was familiar with Montessori's work asked her to take charge of the children left unattended. She consented, and her first *Casa dei Bambini* (Children's Home) was founded—a barren room in a tenement house filled with sixty tearful, shy, and frightened children. In Montessori's words:

> I set to work like a peasant woman who, having set aside a good store of seed corn, has found a fertile field in which she may freely sow it. But I was wrong. I had hardly turned over the clods of my field, when I found gold instead of wheat: the clods concealed a precious treasure. I was not the peasant I had thought myself. Rather I was

foolish Aladdin, who, without knowing it, had in his hand a key that would open hidden treasures.

Former pupil and colleague E. M. Standing described these treasures as the "normal characteristics of childhood hitherto concealed under a mask of deviations. Montessori discovered that children possess different and higher qualities than those often attributed to them. It was as if a higher form of personality had been liberated, and a new child had come into being."[5] More specifically, she found that children had amazing powers of mental concentration regardless of noise or commotion; they *preferred* working in silence to working in commotion; they loved to repeat those tasks which held their attention; when they could understand and grow accustomed to order, they reveled in maintaining it; when given choices they would pick certain activities over others; they preferred working with didactic materials to playing with toys; they could exhibit great motor coordination and control when they themselves were allowed to discover and deal with their own clumsiness; and they needed no reward or punishment.

Montessori observed these traits in the children; she did not impose them. She concluded that teachers needed genuine love and respect for the individual child and an ability to observe. Indeed, Montessori's motto was "to wait and to observe while waiting."[6] A prepared environment allowing for the exhibition of the above traits produced a spontaneous degree of self-discipline that amazed Montessori.

Montessori's *Casa* was both similar to and different from Froebel's kindergarten (Chapter 6). Both featured developmental growth through self-activity; Froebel called it play and Montessori called it work. While both developed special didactic materials, Froebel's "gifts" were creations from his own imagination whereas Montessori's methods came from observation of children. And finally, while Froebel took a more central and active teaching role, Montessori called herself a directress. She was there to encourage and help when necessary, but mostly stayed in the background letting the children learn from the materials.

Other *Casas* opened under Montessori's direction, and eventually she was devoting full time to advocating this type of education. Students from all over the world came to study with her. Returning to their native countries to open schools, they usually had results similar to those achieved in the original *Casa*. Soon she was invited to other countries to lecture and conduct teacher training classes. She visited the United States twice, briefly in 1913 and again in 1915 for a longer stay.

A teenage boy, Mario, whose biological identity is still shrouded in mystery, began accompanying Montessori on her trips. In 1913, after he had come to live with her, she identified him as her fifteen-year-old nephew. By the 1920s he was officially her son. Mario's own account was that Montessori had a love affair with a certain Dr. Montesano and then gave birth to Mario out of wedlock. He then spent his early years in the country with a wet nurse and her family. At some point a stranger (Montessori) began visiting him. The little boy was convinced that she was his real mother. One day, as a teenager, he asked to go with her to live, and she agreed.

Given Montessori's high visibility addressing conventions and working in her orthophrenic school in spring 1898 when she would have had to give birth, it is unlikely that she was his biological mother. More likely was that Montessori knew of his existence because she knew of her colleague Montesano's affair with someone else. She decided, like many single career women in the late nineteenth and early twentieth centuries, to adopt a child, and she allowed the orphaned child to keep his fantasy. In any case, Mario became her closest companion and to him she passed her educational legacy.[7]

In the two years between her visits to the United States, many American educators (such as Dewey and Young) praised her efforts. Such notables as Mr. and Mrs. Alexander Graham Bell, Woodrow Wilson's daughter, and S. S. McClure of *McClure's Magazine* became staunch supporters. McClure offered to set her up in her own school with whatever equipment and facilities she desired, but she turned down the offer. By World War I, although Montessori associations sprang up, she was largely forgotten in the United States, and interest in her practices was not rekindled until the late 1950s.

During her lifetime, Montessori saw her methods and beliefs spread over Europe, India, Ceylon, and Indochina. She was preparing for a trip to Africa in 1952 when she died in Holland with her devoted Mario at her side. She was paid many tributes. In gratefully acknowledging one of her last, she expressed her lifelong concern that people should turn their attention from her to what she had been talking about—the child.[8] She left the future of her work in the hands of Mario and his family.

The Epochs

What was her legacy? What were these ideas and methods that even today seem so controversial, yet popular? The following description (from 1915) of a *Casa* in California will serve as an introduction to her theories. Because Montessori did not speak English, this *Casa* was conducted by her good friend Helen Parkhurst:

> We see some thirty to forty children, aged four to seven, scattered over a large room, all doing different things. Most are working at little tables, but some are on rugs spread out on the floor. It is not in the least like a school such as we knew it. . . . Gone are the rows of desks with benches; gone is the teacher's high desk and stool; and—most remarkable of all—it seems at first glance as if the teacher herself has vanished too. We do discover her, eventually, down on her knees at the far end of the room, explaining something to a couple of children who are working with number materials spread out on a rug. The rest of

the children in the room (except for two or three who are waiting to speak to her) are all carrying on their own business without taking any notice of the directress whatever. It all fits in with our general impression. This is obviously a kind of school in which the adult has retired into the background, whilst the children are correspondingly more active; one might almost say have taken over the initiative. Even the teacher's blackboard has been transmuted into a long low blackboard built into the wall, at which children are writing, not the teacher.

Gone too—completely—is the stillness of the old-fashioned school (so often a stillness of suppression), and with it that immobility which was the immediate cause of it. Instead we are aware of a bustle of activity. In fact the scene before us resembles more the busy stir that goes on in a bank or store than in a schoolroom as we knew it. We see people coming and going, opening and shutting drawers, moving objects here and there, conferring together in low tones, working singly or in groups—in fact anything except all sitting together listening to one person talking.

The most astonishing part about it all is that these persons who are doing all this are not grown-ups at all, but children—and quite small children at that, the eldest being not more than seven or eight. Yet what absorption in their tasks, what seriousness in their expression, what quiet purposefulness in their manner, what precision of movement, and what astonishing self-discipline! They remind us of "little men and women"; yet at the same time they have all the spontaneous charm of childhood.[9]

Montessori observed that from birth to around the age of eighteen children went through a mental metamorphosis that could be divided into three epochs. The first epoch spans the ages of birth to six when the mind is like a sponge absorbing impressions from the environment. This epoch can be subdivided into two stages: birth to three, and three to six. In the first three years the child's mind operates unconsciously, and in those first months before extensive physical movement, the child takes in the whole of the environment with this absorbent but unconscious power. In explaining this mind, Montessori made an analogy between the work of a camera (the child's mind) and the drawing of an artist. The directress had her readers suppose that there was a picture of ten men, or even one hundred. The artist would draw each separately, and it would take much time for ten and longer for one hundred. The photographer could record ten or a hundred instantaneously. "It is similar to the absorbent mind," said Montessori. "It works rapidly taking in everything without effort and without will."[10] Continuing with this analogy, she went on to explain that just as a photo is taken and developed in darkness before being fixed and then brought to light, so are the impressions in an absorbent mind. They are taken during the unconscious period, developed, fixed, and then finally emerge into consciousness where they remain permanently set.

This brings us to the conscious stage (ages three to six) of the first epoch. The "faculties" (such as memory) and "processes" (such as thinking and writing) are now created to be expanded upon and further developed. As her colleague E. M. Standing said, the child

> has forgotten the events and experiences of the preceding [stage] (0–3 years); but, using the faculties he created then, he can now will, think, and remember. For memory itself is one of the faculties which has been created. Therefore, *now,* when the things . . . acquired unconsciously in the first stage are brought to the surface (through the work of his hands) they are remembered; for memory is now there to receive them. So too is it with the will. . . . For that, too, has come into being. Before, it was as if a force outside . . . moved [the child]; now it is the child's own ego which guides and directs. . . . Whereas in the first [stage] the child absorbed the world through . . . unconscious intelligence, merely by being moved about in it, now he takes in consciously, using his hands. The hand has now become the instrument of the brain; and it is through the activity of [the] hands that he enriches his experience, and develops [the self] at the same time.[11]

In general the first epoch can be seen as the construction of the human individual through the acquisition and perfection of new faculties. Children do not, according to Montessori, need direct adult help or intervention; instead, they need to be able to act under their own initiative. That is why she found it best to place them in environments prepared especially to facilitate these new psychic, but not yet social, developments so there would be no insurmountable frustrations or obstacles that they could not control. Under such conditions children learn writing, reading, and fundamental arithmetic concepts, which Montessori called the work of the child. She thought it happened spontaneously and exhilaratingly without fatigue. By age six, children will have been transformed from rather unconscious, immobile creatures into new psychic individuals. Montessorians described this process as the "revelation of the child."[12]

Compared to the first and last epochs, little metamorphosis happens during the second. During this epoch (six to twelve years), children show stability as physical and psychic growth continue. Under the correct conditions, Montessori believed children could accomplish much mental work and store a great deal of cultural information. She thought there was a considerable development of the reasoning abilities at this point. Socially, children develop not only individual ego strengths but also group consciousness—the "gang stage" or the "herd instinct"—with a growing interest in fairness and right and wrong.

Finally, the third epoch (ages twelve to eighteen) is another period of transformation that can be subdivided into the stages of puberty (twelve to fifteen) and adolescence (fifteen to eighteen). After the third epoch, Montessori thought growth ceases and the individual simply becomes older. New psychological characteristics may emerge. Montessori listed some of these as "doubts, hesitations, violent emotions, discouragement, and an unexpected decrease in intellectual capacity," plus "a tendency toward creative work and a need for the strengthening of self-confidence."[13] Whereas during the second epoch the children were extroverted, participating in gangs, now they become more introverted. At the end of this introversion, the adolescent emerges as a socially conscious adult, not just an individual or a group member but a separate member of human society. Again, a specially prepared environment is needed so that feelings of dependence, inadequacy, and inferiority do not develop and endure for years.

Sensitive Periods

Another key in Montessori's theory was the notion of "sensitive periods" in child development. She described a sensitive period as a predisposition "related to certain elements in the environment toward which the organism is directed with an irresistible impulse and a well-defined activity." The periods are transitory, and "serve the purpose of helping the organism to acquire certain functions, or determined characteristics," said Standing. "This aim accomplished, the special sensibility dies away, often to be replaced by another and quite different one. . . . When a sensitive period is at its height we may compare it to a searchlight— coming from within the mind—illuminating certain parts of the environment, leaving the rest in comparative obscurity."[14]

There are sensitive periods for learning to walk, talk, write, and read; and there are also sensitive periods for such needs as good manners, social developments, and order. The order sensitivity usually develops in the first epoch, and small violations can produce extreme protests, even tantrums, from the child. In her *Secrets of Childhood,* Montessori gave an account of a young mother with her one-and-a-half-year-old son in a group visiting Nero's grotto in Naples:

> After a time the child grew tired and his mother picked him up, but she had overestimated her strength. She was hot and stopped to take off her coat to carry it on her arm, and with this impediment once more picked up the child, who began to cry, his screams growing louder and louder.
>
> His mother strove in vain to quiet him; she was plainly tired out and began to grow cross. Indeed the noise was getting on the nerves of all, and naturally others offered to carry him. He passed from arm to arm, struggling and screaming, and everyone talked to him and scolded, but he only grew worse.

I thought of the enigma of infancy, of how reactions must always have a cause: and going up to the mother I said, "Will you allow me to help put on your coat?" She looked at me in amazement, for she was still hot; but in her confusion she consented and allowed me to help her on with it.

At once the baby quieted down, his tears and struggles stopped, and he said, "Mamma, coat on." It was as if he wanted to say, "Yes, Mamma, a coat is meant to be worn"; as though he thought, "At last you have understood me," and stretching out his arms to his mother he came back to her all smiles. The expedition ended in complete tranquility. A coat is meant to be worn, and not to hang like a rag over one arm; and this disorder in his mother's person had affected the child as a jarring disturbance.

Montessori thought the need for order more intense in young children than in adults who might want it but really don't need it. She believed that children, who are "constructing" themselves "out of the elements of the environment" can become ill without it.[15]

What we have described so far are developments that take place in the normal child. But what about the abnormal? Montessori believed that all psychological deviations could be cured—that is, returned to normality— if the directress knew what she was doing. This meant treating abnormal children with firmness and respect, while being certain to protect the other children from deviates' distorted behaviors. It also meant continuing to present new occupations while allowing children to roam freely. Then, "one day will come the great event. One day—Heaven knows why—[a deviated child] will choose some occupation . . . and settle down seriously to work at it *with the first spontaneous spell of concentration that he has ever shown*." The directress would then know that the child is on the road to normality—ready to develop the characteristics listed previously. Now the child is set free from adult intervention in a prepared environment where the child "can live its life according to [these] laws of development."[16] This last quotation is a summation of Montessori's beliefs, and it was also her definition of school.

Toy manufacturers discovered the importance and popularity of Montessori materials and produced such items as stacking toys, wooden puzzles, and post offices with geometric shapes to fit corresponding slots. Her influence also shows in the work of psychologists Jean Piaget and Jerome Bruner. Genetic psychologists such as Arthur Jensen dissociate mental functions from environmental factors, but many parents believe that Montessori's didactic materials help children do well on the major or general factor part of I.Q. tests—spatial relations. On the other hand, environmental psychologists like John B. Watson affirmed the stress on prepared environments, while rejecting any notions of consciousness.

John B. Watson (1878–1958)

In the early years of the twentieth century, the work of G. Stanley Hall and others made the study of psychology increasingly experimental and less philosophical. This was true despite the fact that some important writers who had specialized in the study of behavior—notably William James and John Dewey—called themselves philosophical psychologists. Within the growing experimental group, some, like John B. Watson, were becoming annoyed at the fact that psychology was still seen as the study of human consciousness. They were beginning to believe that terms such as *consciousness, will, image, perception,* and *sensation* referred to unscientific conceptions that hindered empirical investigations of human behavior, the true subject of psychology. But it took someone like Watson to declare psychology's independence from both philosophy and those psychological theories that assumed the existence of consciousness.

Early Life

This brash young man was born on January 9, 1878 near Greenville, South Carolina. Named for a popular local evangelist, John Broadus Watson was the second of Pickens Butler and Emma Kezia Watson's five children.

Both Emma and Watson's older brother, Edward, were fanatically devoted to a harsh, literal Baptist doctrine. John came to despise this religious fundamentalism, although he did his best to hide his feelings from his mother. He regretted having permitted himself to be baptized, and as an adult reacted against his narrow upbringing by swearing and drinking. On the other hand, he was proud of childhood accomplishments. "At nine years of age," he remarked, "I was handling tools, half-soling shoes, and milking cows. At twelve I was a pretty fair carpenter."[17]

In 1894, at the age of sixteen, Watson entered Furman University. His family paid the bulk of his school expenses while he earned some money in the first two years working as an assistant in the chemistry laboratory. Though he studied Greek and Latin with some success, he retained little. He passed his senior Greek examination only by cramming all the afternoon and night before the test. In mathematics he did no better. On the other hand, philosophy and psychology aroused his serious interest.[18]

Watson took George B. Moore's ethics course in his senior year. He was an honor student that year and enjoyed these subjects, yet he recalled failing Moore's course, for Moore had decided that any student who dared hand in the final examination with the order of pages reversed would fail the course. Watson took the dare and paid the consequences. At that point he vowed to get even someday by having Moore come to him for research. To his "surprise and real sorrow," Moore did just that when Watson was at Johns Hopkins. He wanted to be Watson's research student, but his eyesight failed before arrangements could be made.

Although his transcript does not indicate that he failed Moore's course, Watson remained at Furman for a fifth year and in 1900 received a master's degree instead of a bachelor's degree. He also spent the year as teacher and principal of Batesburg Institute in South Carolina. During this year his mother died, thus removing most of the pressure for him to attend seminary. This event and his genuine interest in philosophy and psychology contributed to Watson's decision to pursue a doctorate. At first he was undecided whether to go to Princeton or the University of Chicago, but when he found that a reading knowledge of Greek and Latin was necessary at Princeton, he chose Chicago. Moore may have had some influence on that decision, for having studied psychology at Chicago during his sabbatical year of 1897–1898, he told Watson about the faculty in John Dewey's department, which perhaps further aroused his interest in philosophy.

University of Chicago

In the fall of 1900, Watson left for Chicago with fifty dollars in his pocket. When he arrived, he met a relative, John Manly, along with Dewey and psychologist James R. Angell.

Angell guided Watson into experimental psychology as his major field; philosophy with Dewey, Addison W. Moore, and James Haydn Tufts as a first minor; and neurology with Donaldson as his second minor. He also took work in biology and physiology with Jacques Loeb. Loeb wanted him to study the physiology of a dog's brain, but Donaldson and Angell discouraged his working under Loeb, whom they regarded as excessively mechanistic. They convinced Watson to conduct an experiment to measure the relationship between the increasing complexity in the behavior of young rats and the growth of the myelin sheaths surrounding the nerve fibers in their central nervous systems. In the process of conducting the research, Watson incurred the ire of local antivivisectionists, but his combative nature spurred him on. In 1903 he published his dissertation (*Animal Education: The Psychical Development of the White Rat*) with the aid of $350 lent by Donaldson.

In his graduate work, Watson studied a branch of the new psychology called functionalism, seeds of which were planted by William James and flourished in the work of Dewey and Angell at Chicago and James McKeen Cattell at Columbia. Functionalism differed from the older structuralism of Edward Titchner: The former was concerned with *why* the individual behaved in a certain way, while the latter focused on *what* happened and *how* it occurred. The rule of functionalism at the time was that you observed the behavior of the animal, used the data to infer the nature of its consciousness, and then inferred how conscious processes functioned in its behavior. Watson eventually objected to the whole notion of consciousness after he graduated.

Compared to his work in psychology, Watson's study of philosophy proved disappointing. He took courses with Dewey, Tufts, Moore, George Herbert Mead, and Edward Scribner Ames on topics ranging from Greek philosophy to Dewey's instrumentalism, and including Hume, Locke, Hartley, and Kant. He even studied Wilhelm Wundt with Tufts. Out of these, Dewey became Watson's nemesis. "I got . . . least of all out of Dewey. I never knew what he was talking about then, and, unfortunately for me, I still don't know."[19]

As a graduate student Watson pushed himself hard, working day and night to complete his degree in a little more than three years. As a consequence he suffered from severe insomnia in the fall of 1902, awakening at three in the morning and walking eight to ten miles. He finally recovered after a month's vacation, three weeks of which he slept with a light on. The experience taught him to be more careful with his physical condition and, according to his own account, prepared him to accept a large part of Sigmund Freud's theories.

Watson had a deep need to succeed and to feel affirmed. He graduated in 1903 magna cum laude, but was he was deeply disappointed when Dewey and Tufts told him that his examination was much inferior to that of Helen Thompson (Woolley), who had graduated summa cum laude two years earlier. Watson married Mary Ickes in 1903, and they later had two children, Polly and John.

Watson remained at the University of Chicago until 1907. He had received several job offers, including an assistantship in neurology from Donaldson and an assistantship in psychology from Dewey. Although he was quite proud of the former proposal, he accepted the latter in order to work with Angell. He served in that position until 1905, when he was promoted to the rank of instructor.

An energetic young man, Watson pursued his work with vigor and enthusiasm. He praised Angell both for teaching him psychology and for sharpening his rhetorical skills. He could not say enough about the scientific research techniques he had learned from Donaldson and Loeb. Watson wanted to study medicine following his Ph.D., but could not afford medical school tuition. He spent the summer following his first year on the Chicago faculty studying surgical techniques with William Howells at the Johns Hopkins Hospital. While he was in Baltimore he renewed his acquaintance with James Mark Baldwin, an event which began a long friendship and later proved professionally beneficial.

Within a short time after entering the psychological profession, Watson's effort to make a name for himself began to bear fruit. In 1906 he accepted an invitation to prepare the annual summary of comparative psychological literature for the *Psychological Review*. Two years later he became the journal's editor, a position he held until 1915. Also, in 1911 he became editor of the *Journal of Animal Behavior*.

Amid this flurry of activity, Watson's career received a tremendous boost. In 1907 G. M. Stration left Johns Hopkins University and Baldwin offered Watson an associate professorship at the substantial salary of $2,500. Watson hesitated, hoping to receive a better offer from Chicago. Baldwin increased the offer to $3,500 and the rank of professor. At the same time Chicago proposed to make him an "assistant professor elect." Although he thought he would be happier remaining at the University of Chicago, he decided that it would be foolish to refuse the Hopkins position.

The Young Professor

Watson regretted leaving Chicago, but found an environment conducive to his professional interests and growth at Johns Hopkins. In 1909 the chair of the psychology department resigned, and he inherited the job. At thirty-one, he found himself able to shape the future of the psychology department at one of America's leading institutions of higher education. He immediately set about convincing the university's president to sever the department's connections with philosophy and strengthen those with biology. As editor of the *Psychological Review,* he was also in a position to present his developing theories to a wide audience.

For some time Watson had been struggling with the idea of building a theory of animal psychology strictly from observed behavior without any inferences about consciousness. Something that Cattell had said in a 1904 paper further stimulated Watson's thinking. Cattell had argued that the goal of psychology was the study of human beings and that psychologists should reject introspective techniques of investigating mental functioning. When he broached this subject with his Chicago colleagues, Watson had found none of them sympathetic to the idea, except perhaps Jacques Loeb. At Hopkins he continued this line of research while he taught general psychology along the lines of James's viewpoint and experimental courses using Tichner's manuals.

By 1908 his ideas had begun to jell. In that year he lectured on comparative psychology at three different professional meetings. Having concluded that animal psychology could serve as a basis for human psychology, he attempted to make the point that scientists should not atttribute mental content to animals but should stick to objective observations of their behavior. During the next four years, he focused his efforts on producing a more thorough and systematic statement of his position.

The Behaviorist

Watson achieved that significant milestone in a lecture given at Columbia University in 1912 and published in the *Psychological Review* in 1913. He boldly declared his independence from traditional psychology in what might be called the behaviorist manifesto, entitled "Psychology as the Behaviorist Views It." He argued that psychology was a natural science relying for its data on objective observations instead of introspection; unlike traditional psychology, which sought to describe and explain consciousness, the goals of psychology were to predict and control behavior; and the behaviorist does not recognize any dividing line between humans and animals. The obvious implication was that studies of various laboratory animals were important sources of information for achieving the goals of this brand of psychology.

Watson reiterated and expanded these ideas in *Behavior: An Introduction to Comparative Psychology*. This textbook met with a receptive audience, particularly among American psychologists. In 1915 Watson was elected president of the American Psychological Association. His presidential address dealt with Pavlov's theory of conditioned reflex and suggested that this reaction could become the basis of a theory of human psychology ranging from habit formation to emotional disorders. Even though his behaviorism began as little more than a point of view, it held enormous potential for becoming a serious research program and a systematic theory of human behavior.

World War I interrupted Watson's work in 1917. He served as a staff officer with the Committee on Personnel in the Army. In that capacity, he was responsible for organizing and conducting the aviation examination boards. He spent his tour in the United States except for'three months with the American Expeditionary Force where he attempted to gather data to aid in the selection of aviators. Watson viewed his military service as a nightmare and thought many of the career army officers that he encountered were incompetent. He gladly returned to his work at Hopkins in November 1918.

Beginning where he left off, Watson undertook to develop his behavioristic principles into a human psychology. Clear evidence of the extent of his thinking appeared in 1919 when he published *Psychology from the Standpoint of a Behaviorist*. His first book had been limited to comparative psychology, but this one purported to be a general psychology text. In addition to a description of the field of psychology and its methods, Watson dealt with stimulus and response, emotions, instincts, language, and personality development and disturbances. Of particular note in this book was his application of Pavlov's conditioned reflex theory to the discussion of human emotions.

From observation, Watson postulated that humans had only three kinds of unconditioned reflexes: fear, rage, and love. He also determined that these reflexes were elicited by a narrow range of stimuli. Therefore, he concluded that all other human emotions were the result of conditioning, but he had little experimental evidence to support his conclusions. He conducted a controversial experiment aimed at producing a conditioned fear response in an eleven-month-old child. Though the experiment was successful, today it would raise serious ethical questions.

Business Career

In the fall of 1920, Watson's academic career ended. He had become romantically involved with his graduate student, Rosalie Rayner, and this affair, along with his divorce from his first wife, and subsequent marriage to Rayner became a front-page scandal that was too much for Baltimore in 1920. Consequently, Johns Hopkins asked Watson to resign.

Finding his academic career destroyed, the resourceful Watson wasted no time in obtaining an opening in the business world. He went to New York and with the help of a friend secured a position with the J. Walter Thompson advertising agency. Following a successful trial assignment to determine the market for rubber boots in the Mississippi River region south of Cairo, Illinois, he sold a well-known brand of coffee to wholesale and retail stores in Pittsburgh, Cleveland, and Erie. With characteristic vigor and enthusiasm, he devoted the next year to learning the advertising business from top to bottom. He later remarked, "I began to learn that it can be just as thrilling to watch the growth of a sales curve of a new product as to watch the learning curve of animals or men."[20] By 1924 he had become a vice president of the company.

Watson had not severed all ties to the academic world. Soon after he came to New York, he accepted invitations to lecture at the New School for Social Research and the Cooper Institute, and in 1924 published these lectures under the title *Behaviorism*. This widely acclaimed and successful book contained discussions of his favorite topics, many of which had appeared in his 1919 textbook but were now expanded and revised.

Watson began his lively discussion by defining behaviorism as a natural science concerned with the entire scope of human adjustment. Like the physical scientist who wanted to control and manipulate natural phenomena, the behaviorist aimed at predicting and controlling human activity. He then presented his most mature theories of human instinct, emotion, and thought. He extended his previous description of thinking to include the psychoanalysts' conception of unconscious thought. Conscious thought was a series of vocal or subvocal responses in a chain where one response served as a stimulus to the next response. But not all responses in the chain had to be verbal; some could be visceral or emotional reactions that he believed were unconscious thoughts.

The most striking feature of this book was Watson's radically environmentalist theory of instinct and emotion. In 1914 he had noted the importance of instinct and habit and the difficulty of finding instincts unaltered by the environment. By 1919 he added that there were only three innate human emotions. Now he carried this line of thinking to its logical conclusion by arguing that virtually all innate factors were obscured by learned responses and could therefore be ignored. In addition he accounted for individual differences by suggesting that they were the products of early experiences. He went so far as to argue in a later edition of *Behaviorism* that, given the proper environment and control, he could completely mold an individual's character. Since that time, critics of behavioristic theories have asked, "But who will control the controllers?"

Final Years

In the years following the publication of *Behaviorism,* Watson's work in psychology reflected the shift in his thinking away from scholarly discourse and toward topics of interest to the general public. He wrote several articles for popular magazines. In 1928 Watson and his wife published a book on child-rearing entitled *Psychological Care of Infant and Child.* The thrust of their discussion centered around the notion that infants should not be cuddled or spoiled but conditioned to lead independent lives. This enormously successful book became the first in a series of child-rearing guides to be published in America.

Following the death of his wife in 1935, Watson made fewer public appearances. He left the Thompson agency to become vice president of another advertising firm, William Esty and Company, remaining there until his retirement in 1945. Watson spent the last years of his life farming and working on building projects, and he died on September 25, 1958.

Watson was one of the most important and controversial figures in the history of modern psychology. His bold efforts accelerated the growth of the environmentalist viewpoint, and he also aided the development of animal studies by emphasizing the analogy between animal and human behavior. Although he had few immediate followers, his extreme positions fostered the work of two generations of behavioristic psychologists. His legacy is apparent in some current theories of educational psychology and classroom management. However, Watson's behaviorism was not without competition in psychology and education. Psychoanalytic theory also spilled over into the child-centered pedagogy of the postwar years. Freudianism, along with a Rousseauian view of children, put pupils in the center of the educational experience. Child-centered educators believed that the child was potentially creative and that a school which promoted the free development of those unique abilities was the best assurance of a society truly concerned with the value and achievements of humanity. To this end they promoted psychoanalytic doctrines to develop the creative potentialities of their students. Most prominent among the educators who combined psychoanalysis with the credo of self-expression was Margaret Naumburg, founder of the Children's School, later named the Walden School.

Margaret Naumburg (1890–1983)

Born on May 14, 1890 in New York City, Margaret was the daughter of Max Naumburg, who had come to the United States from Bavaria as a young child, and Theresa Kahnweiler of North Carolina. Margaret attended New York Public School 87, the Horace Mann School, and the Sachs School. In 1908 she entered Vassar for the first year of her undergraduate education. Upon transferring to Barnard, she took work in economics and in philosophy with John Dewey. In addition to her studies, she served as president of the Socialist Club at Barnard.

Searching for a Method

Margaret Naumburg was convinced that society could be improved, but was at first unsure about the most effective means of achieving that. Upon graduating from college in 1912, she set out for England to continue her study of the "dismal science" at the London School of Economics. There, under the tutelage of the Fabian Socialists Sidney and Beatrice Webb, she observed firsthand the social conditions and labor problems of the British film industry. Within six months she lost her enthusiasm for socialism, concluding that social reform began not with groups and institutions but with individuals.

On her way to London, Naumburg had read *The Montessori Method*. In place of the common method of "stuffing" children with information, she saw that education could become a means of grasping "the fundamental realities of life" by focusing on curiosity, interest, and imagination. In January 1913 she departed London for Rome to study with Montessori. The two women did not get along well, and Naumburg returned to New York the following fall. Despite their personal differences, however, Naumburg saw sufficient value in Montessori's educational method to accept a position as teacher in Lillian Wald's Henry Street Settlement kindergarten, which was organized on Montessorian principles.

Convinced that education was the best means for improving individuals and society, Naumburg was still dissatisfied with the methods she was using to achieve that goal. But the events of 1914 in her professional and personal life would significantly alter her attitude. She had already concluded that early introduction of the basic skills was attractive to American parents, but she thought that Montessori's didactic materials did not lend themselves to creativity. In an attempt to find a more satisfactory method, she spent the summer of 1914 with Marietta Pierce Johnson at her Organic School in Fairhope, Alabama. Much to her delight, Naumburg found an educational program that viewed children as organisms and aimed at developing them physically, intellectually, and emotionally. Returning to New York in the fall, she rented two rooms in the Leet Street schoolhouse where she taught a small group of three- to five-year-old children. At the same time, Naumburg became associated with a group of people who were intensely interested in psychoanalysis.

Freud's visit to Clark University in 1909 generated serious interest in his theories. Beginning in 1910, English translations of his works were prepared by psychiatrist A. A. Brill, and some psychiatrists gradually began to see psychotherapy as an effective method for treating neuroses. They recognized, said John Burnham, "the medical value of a constructive intellectual and emotional environment."[21] This led to a concern for their patients' families and the society, and generated particular interest in the influence of childhood experiences on later life. As a consequence, these psychiatrists soon found themselves committed to social improvement.

The excitement over Freudianism was not confined to the medical community, and especially in New York, a number of people quickly became familiar with psychoanalysis. Some read the works of Freud, Carl Jung, and Alfred Adler. Others heard interpretations of the doctrines at gatherings in places such as Mabel Dodge's salon in Greenwich Village. Still others encountered psychotherapy on the couches in their analysts' offices. Naumburg learned about psychoanalysis in all three ways. In 1914, while studying psychoanalytic theory, she began a three-year analysis with Jungian psychiatrist Beatrice Hinkle. Finally, as an active participant in the intellectual life of Greenwich Village, Naumburg absorbed the popular forms of Freudianism. Combined with her knowledge of psychoanalytic theory, this became a fundamental element of her educational ideas.

An equally important thread in the cloth of her educational thought was artistic self-expression. As a proponent of child-centered education, Naumburg was already interested in finding ways of releasing the creative impulses that she believed were within each child. This interest must have been heightened as she moved among people in the Village who depended on their ability to express themselves creatively in a variety of art forms. One such artist was Waldo Frank, writer and editor of *The Seven Arts* magazine, whom she married on December 20, 1916. As Frank's wife, she came to know post-Impressionist art and associated with experimenters in writing, painting, and sculpture. Her friends came increasingly from the arts, and she lived in a world pervaded by new forms of expression and technique. The influence of art on her life was apparently sufficient that she later came to see it as a particularly effective medium for psychotherapy.

Naumburg's Views

The war years were a time of intellectual and professional growth for Naumburg. While she wove the threads of organic education, psychoanalysis, and creative self-expression together, she expanded the program of what was at first called the Children's School. In 1915, she added to the school a second group of children and three teachers, including her sister, Florence Cane. Two years later, she moved the school to 34 West 68th Street and changed the name to the Walden School.

The school's curriculum emphasized the arts, which Naumburg saw as a means of creating socially and emotionally mature children. By building the program on a foundation of psychoanalytic doctrine, she aimed at producing children with integrated personalities. Furthermore, she wanted teachers who were fully prepared to help students achieve this goal; thus, she recommended that teachers undergo analysis. An example of what she intended could be found in the work of Cane. Influenced by Jung and by her analysis under Beatrice Hinkle, Cane focused on painting as a medium of expression. She encouraged the children to paint whatever they felt impelled to as a means of expressing their feelings toward the environment. At other times paintings were to represent dreams or moods. Gradually, art forms that enhanced individuality and self-expression began to replace those of social value in the Walden program. In Naumburg's words, "from our point of view there must be a recognition of the subjective inner life, of feeling as coexistent with and coessential to our life action."[22]

Rousseauian ideas were much in the air in the early twentieth century, and Naumburg's work reflected these interests in addition to psychoanalysis. From her earliest essay in 1915 to her detailed description of the Walden School (*The Child and the World,* 1928), Naumburg's work often included Rousseau's ideal of natural development. As she became convinced of the efficacy of psychoanalysis for promoting self-expression, her writings showed the intensity of her belief. It was not, however, the doctrines of Freud that influenced her most. Rather, from the time of her analysis with Hinkle, Naumburg became convinced that Jung's analytic psychology was more compatible with her ideas.

Naumburg's first published statements about education appeared in *Outlook* the summer following the founding of her school at Leet Street. After describing a parade of children from William Wirt's Bronx Public School 45, she indicated her obvious preference for a child-centered school.

> To catch the spirit of a Wirt school one ought to be familiar with the atmosphere of the typical public school, with its long hushed corridors, its wriggling classes, and its hordes of silent children shuffling into overcrowded playgrounds. And then step into a Wirt school and see the corridors filled with spontaneous, animated children going and coming about their particular tasks. Everywhere small groups [are] eagerly active in their chosen work in the shops, the studios, the playgrounds, and other special activities.[23]

Naumburg noted with approval that Wirt allowed older children to serve as teaching assistants and younger ones to act as shop helpers. Teachers were in the background—that is, "in their rightful place as sharers and helpers in the children's activities."[24] She was pleased that Wirt had worked against the "intellectualized elementary school" with its prevailing notion that the program was more important than the facilities for the children and the assumption that everyone did the same work at the same time and in the same way.

A more significant piece was an essay about the Walden School that Naumburg wrote in 1926 for a yearbook of the National Society for the Study of Education, wherein she revealed her maturing educational ideas. Without naming other progressive schools, she noted that the

Walden School occupied a position between the extreme laissez-faire school and the school that emphasized socialization. Walden, she asserted, "believes in the social function of the school toward the creation of a more harmonious and equitable future society, and it believes in the development of individual potentials as the swiftest means of insuring just such a socialization."[25] This statement typified the lack of concern about social reform among many educators and former progressives in the 1920s. It further indicated that Naumburg continued to believe that improving society depended on the proper education of individuals.

Naumburg saw little good in traditional education, and was outraged at the thought of the "terrible injuries" that occurred to children daily in the name of orthodox education. In a statement that seemed to blend Rousseau's view of children with Jung's notion of libido as psychic energy, she condemned traditional schools: "The constriction, repression, and misdirection of the original power and spontaneous energy of thousands of school children is something I am prepared to denounce as a menacing evil of orthodox education."[26]

To avoid such danger, she opposed the continued use of outworn methods and advocated the search for new means of preserving the vitality with which each new group of children entered school. Of course, this was precisely the kind of education Walden tried to provide by combining regular school subjects with life activities and by regarding reading, writing, and arithmetic as necessary means to complete living, not as ends of life. All of this was accomplished in an atmosphere that had the warmth and intimacy of home. She believed, as did Rousseau, that the products of nature were good and that people and society corrupted them. She objected to the common belief that equality of opportunity meant giving equal value to all levels of ability because it resulted in an education that ignored the gifted and talented. As she put it: "Nature has always had the sense to cultivate variation in every one of her species. Only man is fool enough to try to improve on nature by a system of education that makes every child as indistinguishable as possible from any other."[27]

At another point, Naumburg described how children learned to distrust adults when they received evasive answers to questions about the sanctity of human values such as private property, social distinctions, or control of human life. The tragic drama that ensued in these instances, she remarked, affected both child and adult. By attempting to affirm their innate values with such queries, children brought adults face-to-face with values that either lay dormant or were denied. When the answers avoided the real questions, the relationship between adults and children was often degraded. A similar result occurred when parents failed to deal with the contradictions between theory and practice on such moral issues as killing; children were shocked, said Naumburg, when they discovered that adults said one thing and did another. Finally, she complained that society's imposition of time standards on the realities of "joy, sorrow, love, work, and play" in the lives of children made them suspicious of adults. She grudgingly admitted, nevertheless, that a certain amount of routine in the form of habits of order and organization were necessary for adjustment. Then she quickly added that art—which was natural to life and not a specialized function— might help to return values to their proper order. To put it another way, allowing the child's natural creative tendency to develop would ameliorate the harsh effects of society.

Theoretical Underpinnings

Naumburg needed a modern psychological theory to give credibility to her Rousseauian philosophical views. Dewey's functionalism was too concerned with the social aspect of psychology for her—it lacked sufficient concern for the individual in general and human emotion in particular—so she turned instead to psychoanalysis. But Freud's interest in the neurotic individual and his theory that the source of neurosis lay in human sexuality failed to meet her needs. In contrast, Jung's interpretation of the unconscious, the libido, and psychological types supported her beliefs about human nature. Although Naumburg never took the time to define the term *unconscious*, except to suggest that it contained the major portion of the emotional life, there was a vague connection to Jung's conception that the unconscious held all psychic processes that were not perceptibly related to the ego. Her use of the term *libido*, however, was much closer to his idea of psychic energy.

For Naumburg, psychoanalysis explained the natural essence of the human being that Rousseau had held would unfold from within if given the right environment. It gave the emotional life greater importance. At one point, she noted that modern medicine had found that one of its important duties was curing sick souls. By analogy, modern education ought to pay attention to the spiritual health of the child. In order to accomplish this, teachers had to be aware of their own unconscious life and that of their pupils. Parents, she continued, should also be more concerned about the inward life of their children.

Walden School

At first, because of prejudice against psychoanalysis among physicians and a lack of knowledge about it among educators, Naumburg avoided theoretical jargon. She endeavored to create a correct environment for releasing the unconscious emotional life of children into positive and personal expression. By 1928 Walden had a group of teachers and parents who had overtly turned to analysis as a means of understanding their own lives and those of the children. At least half of the faculty, she claimed, had been psychoanalyzed, and the other half were interested in applying analytic principles to education.

Naumburg believed that the deepest wish in a human being was some form of power and control that manifested itself in various ways depending on psychological type, temperament, and early environment. This power was the motive force of our actions, which psychoanalysis sought to explain. This psychic energy, she contended, may or may not be in harmony with nature; thus, Walden was intent on mastering this power for its own purposes. It planned to go beyond intellectual training because external responses were all too often directed by unconscious feelings. Naumburg firmly believed that education provided both the civilization and the individual with a practical means for conveying psychic energy and positive social and personal activities.

Another important Jungian conception that Naumburg used was that of psychological types—the extrovert and the introvert. She was concerned that educators knew too little about these concepts. "Until we truly comprehend the fundamental difference in psychic mechanisms between the jolly, outgoing, sociable child [extrovert] and the acutely reticent, over-moody one [introvert], we can't help educationally to fulfill their own potentialities or to overcome their psychic difficulties."[28] She and her staff attempted to connect the school's activities with the child's psychological temperament. They also avoided gender roles, refusing to educate children according to sexual stereotypes and treating them as individuals.

Later Years

Naumburg served as director of Walden until 1922, when she relinquished that position to become advisory director. She turned over the responsibility for the daily activities of the school to her longtime associates, Margaret Pollitzer and Elizabeth Goldsmith, who functioned as executive directors. One immediate reason for limiting her professional work was the birth of her son, Thomas, on May 12, 1922, and the arrangement also enabled her to maintain contact with the activities of the school while at the same time having an opportunity to reflect upon its work. In 1926 she ended her official connection with Walden. Two years later, she published *The Child and the World,* which contained a record of the school's aims and activities and an exposition of her educational thought.

From her early years as a teacher and school director, she was committed to the idea of educating children intellectually, physically, and emotionally. But because she thought too much emphasis was being given to the first two capacities, especially the first, she tried to shift the weight of educational activities toward emotional growth. As a consequence, Naumburg's critics accused her and Walden of being fundamentally anti-intellectual and somewhat opposed to social reform. With regard to the latter criticism, she consistently argued that individual growth had to occur before society would change. This attitude brought her into direct conflict with Dewey in 1928, when she criticized his emphasis on shared concerns, and in 1930, when she used Jung's doctrine of human types to argue against Dewey's "new individualism."

In the early 1930s, Naumburg began to conduct research with children at the New York Psychiatric Institute. Using the techniques she had perfected at Walden, she attempted to get the children to express themselves freely in their artwork. At about the same time, she accepted an appointment as lecturer at the New School for Social Research. This post, which she held from 1932 to 1952, provided her with a forum in which she could discuss her evolving ideas about art and psychotherapy.

After years of study and research, Naumburg attempted to spread her theories and techniques beyond the confines of the New School. In 1947 she began conducting courses and seminars at leading medical schools and psychiatric clinics in the United States and Europe. She published her ideas in several professional periodicals, including the *Psychiatric Quarterly,* the *Journal of Nervous and Mental Diseases, The Nervous Child,* and the *Journal of Aesthetics and Art Criticism.* She also found time to write four books on the subject of art therapy: *Studies of the Free Art Expression of Behavior Problem Children and Adolescents* (1947), *Schizophrenic Art: Its Meaning in Psychotherapy* (1950), *Psychoneurotic Art: Its Use in Psychotherapy* (1953), and *Dynamically Oriented Art Therapy: Its Principles and Practices, Illustrated with Three Case Studies* (1966).

Naumburg completed her academic career at New York University, where she held two lectureships, beginning in 1959 in the department of art education and a year later in the department of psychology. She remained in New York City until 1975, when she moved to Needham, Massachusetts. There she lived out the last years of her life near her son, Dr. Thomas Frank of Cambridge, and her five grandchildren. She died at her home on February 26, 1983 at ninety-two.

By the 1920s science had become the principal source of authority for American education. This phenomenon was a result of the radical alteration of American society by science and technology and of the concomitant reorientation of the American mind toward scientific thinking. It was also an outgrowth of the work of educational reformers of the late nineteenth and early twentieth centuries: the Herbartians, the new psychologists, and the progressives. Science had become so important to education that it was surprising to find someone who had the audacity to question its validity.

In the 1930s, a political and intellectual movement of substantial proportions developed in Europe. It centered around the revival of Thomas Aquinas's philosophy and theology, and it fostered numerous movements on behalf of political liberty. It spread through Europe and Latin America and found a sizable audience in the United States. Its central author was the philosopher Jacques Maritain. Not only did he join a growing chorus of voices that were criticizing progressive education, he also harmonized with an ensemble that refused to accept the scientific outlook as the basis of educational theory. Maritain's belief that education could only proceed from a theological and philosophical perspective had its origin in his own intellectual struggle with science and philosophy, and was deeply rooted in the theology of Aquinas.

Jacques Maritain (1882–1973)

Born in Paris on November 18, 1882, Jacques was the son of Paul Maritain, a Burgundian lawyer, and Geneviève Favre, a vibrant and thoughtful woman. His father had little influence on him: a quiet, philosophical man, Paul Maritain spent his leisure hours reading poetry. Although he lived to see Jacques enter the Sorbonne, he was said to have been speechless at the thought of his son as a philosopher. Since he was not a practicing Catholic, he was not concerned about the religious education of his children, and following his divorce from Geneviève, he apparently had little contact with them.

Geneviève Favre Maritain, on the other hand, affected her son's thoughts profoundly. The daughter of Jules Favre, an architect of the Third Republic, she passionately believed in republicanism and an intellectual elite as the salvation of France. Ostensibly a liberal Protestant, she paid little attention to the religious upbringing of her children, being more concerned with gathering a small coterie in her home every Thursday for lunch and conversation about current political and social issues. Undoubtedly young Jacques cut his intellectual teeth amid discussions with such notables as the socialist writer and bookseller Charles Péguy, who later played an important role in his life.

These meetings took place at a time when the French intelligentsia were interested in the ideas of August Comte, Ernest Renan, and Hippolyte Taine, who argued that human progress was inevitable and that empirical science was the only truly positive form of knowledge attainable by the human mind. Many intellectuals held that without science, progress was impossible. This positivism had permeated French secondary and higher education. When Maritain entered the Lycée Henri IV, and later the Sorbonne, he found positivism at every turn, a condition which proved both satisfying and frustrating. At first, he vigorously studied science and positivism, sharing these interests with Ernest Psichari, the grandson of Ernest Renan. Theirs was a deep and abiding friendship that lasted in spirit beyond Psichari's untimely death in World War I. Even their families became close.

Despite his interest in science, Maritain became increasingly dissatisfied with his teachers' answers to questions about why things were as they described. When he entered the Sorbonne in 1901, he found no more acceptable answers when he questioned the faculty of philosophy, because that ancient discipline was also dominated by positivism. To no avail, he continued to ask "Why?" as he took advanced work in science. His dissatisfaction soon turned to despair, and he began to share his doubts with Raïssa Oumansoff, a science student and the daughter of

Russian Jewish immigrants, whom he had met while organizing a protest over the treatment of Russian socialist students.

In time, Raïssa and Jacques became inseparable. Their mutual search
for answers to the ultimate questions about life led them to vow in 1902
that, unless they found a suitable explanation within one year, they
would commit suicide. They took this quest seriously, whether or not
they would have actually gone through with their plan. Fortunately,
their friend Péguy introduced them to the philosophy of Henri Bergson.
Péguy, George Sorel, Psichari, Jacques, and Raïssa joined a growing
group attending the Bergson's lectures at the Collège de France. Bergson had defied the positivists and developed an intuitionist philosophy
grounded in the absolute. He introduced these young pilgrims to metaphysics and to the works of Plotinus and Plato, which seemed to nourish
their intellectual appetites. Gradually, as they saw answers to their
questions, they rose from the depths of despair. Yet Bergson's philosophy
had its limits, and served principally as the first crucial step of their
journey into the world of metaphysics. In the meantime, Jacques and
Raïssa decided to marry before he finished his *aggregation,* which would
entitle him to teach in a state university. Following a delay of some
months due to Raïssa's serious illness, they were wed on November 26,
1904, and together they continued their search for philosophic answers.

A Religious Quest

During the next year, they rediscovered the religious perspective. The
Maritains began reading the works of Léon Bloy, the "thankless beggar,"
who impressed them with the strength of Christian belief conveyed in
his novels. When they finally met Bloy at his home, their lives were
permanently altered. A true witness of sainthood, Bloy lived an ascetic
life and devoted himself entirely to religious work. In their conversations with him, Jacques and Raïssa came face-to-face with the question
of God. After several months of discussion and serious thought, they
decided to join the Catholic church. On June 11, 1906 the Maritains and
Vera Oumansoff, Raïssa's sister, accepted the Roman Catholic faith at
the Church of Saint John the Evangelist in Montmartre. Neither the
Oumansoffs nor Geneviève Maritain knew of this event at the time, but
when they found out what had transpired, their reactions were not unexpected. The Oumansoffs took it that their daughters had betrayed their
faith and heritage, but in time they forgave their children and converted
to Catholicism themselves. Madame Maritain, however, was outraged.
She did everything possible to get her son to change his mind, including
enlisting the aid of Péguy, but to no avail. Madame Maritain apparently
never forgave her son.

After completing his work at the Sorbonne, Maritain accepted a fellowship from the Michions Fund to study at the University of Heidelberg. There he met the biologist Hans Driesch, who was working on a
theory of dynamic vitalism—that is, explaining life chemically or me-

chanically. In the many hours spent with Driesch, their conversations often turned to Bergson's recent book *Creative Evolution,* and these discussions revived Maritain's desire for a philosophical career.

From 1906 to 1908 the Maritains enjoyed the peace and quiet of Heidelberg. Raïssa was frequently ill, which complicated the routine tasks of living. As a consequence, Vera Oumansoff became a permanent member of the Maritain household, helping to maintain the house and serving as Jacques's secretary. When his fellowship ran out, Maritain began looking for work. He could have taken a position in a French state university, but because of the French government's strong anticlerical attitude, he knew that there was no guarantee that he could teach according to his own principles, and chose not to apply for a teaching position. Instead, he accepted an offer from Hachette Publishing Company to compile an orthographic lexicon and a dictionary of practical life. Thus the trio was able to move back to Paris in 1908, where Jacques could work on the books and continue his scientific and philosophical studies.

During the next four years, Maritain worked diligently on the dictionaries. He and Raïssa also spent many hours studying the Catholic faith and the works of the great theologians. Their mentor was Father Humbert Clérissac, a Dominican priest who firmly adhered to the intellectual traditions of his order. He was responsible for introducing the Maritains to the writings of Aquinas. Raïssa found great comfort in *Summa Theologica,* Thomas's great work, and was anxious for Jacques to read it. But it was not until 1910 that he opened the book and found the answers to his questions about life. This proved to be a watershed in his life, from which he emerged as a Thomist. He later described his thoughts about his first encounter with St. Thomas's theology:

> My philosophical reflection leaned upon the indestructible truth of objects presented by faith in order to restore the natural order of the intelligence to being, and to recognize the ontological bearing of the work of the reason. Thenceforth, in affirming to myself, without chicanery or diminution, the authentic value of reality of our human instruments of knowledge, I was already a Thomist without knowing it. When several months later, I was to come to the *Summa Theologica,* I would erect no obstacle to its luminous flood.[29]

For Maritain, Thomism was more than an illuminating theology. He saw it as the foundation of his philosophical vocation when he said, "Woe unto me, should I not Thomize."[30]

He began his work by studying the entire range of writings associated with Aquinas's thought, from its origins in the works of Aristotle to the books of the modern neo-Scholastics. In 1910 he made his first contribution to the subject in the article "Reason and Modern Science," which appeared in the *Revue de Philosophie.* With fire and passion, he tried to show the errors and limitations of modern science, not to turn back the clock but to put science in perspective. A year later, he published a critique of his philosophical master's ideas in "L'évolutionnisme de M. Bergson."

These articles brought him the respect of Father Peillaube, editor of the *Revue de Philosophie,* who recommended him for a teaching post at the Collège Stanislas. When the position of instructor was offered in 1912, Maritain did not hesitate to accept it, thinking that he could teach philosophy from a Thomistic standpoint, but much to his dismay, he found many of his colleagues skeptical of Thomism. Determined to stand his ground, Maritain persisted and eventually won their approval, and the high academic standing achieved by his students reinforced his position.

The next year Maritain gave a series of lectures entitled "The Philosophy of Bergson and Christian Philosophy" at the Institut Catholique de Paris. These talks were a part of his continuing critique of Bergson's philosophical system, and marked the beginning of the Catholic renaissance of this century. His provocative and exciting ideas, furthermore, brought him an enthusiastic following, particularly among science students who were now reading the works of Paul Claudel, Péguy, Francis Jammes, and Bloy. Maritain rapidly became a leading spokesperson for neo-Thomism, a title he did not like since he saw himself as a pure Thomist bringing Aquinas's principles to bear on modern problems. In 1914 he became professor of philosophy at the Institut Catholique, and in the same year published several articles and the 1913 lectures in his book *La Philosophie Bergsonienne: Études Critiques.*

Maritain continued his work at the Institut during World War I. He also taught at the Collège Stanislas from 1915 to 1916 and at the preparatory seminary in Versailles from 1917 to 1918. Throughout the war he tried in vain to serve in the French army but was rejected for health reasons until August 1918, when he was assigned to an artillery regiment at Versailles. In the meantime, at the request of the French bishops, he began writing a series of seminary textbooks on the various branches of philosophy; only *An Introduction to Philosophy* and *Formal Logic* were ever completed. The war years brought grief to the Maritains. They lost four of their closest friends: Psichari, Péguy, Clérissac, and Bloy. Toward the end of the war, Maritain became acquainted with Pierre Villard, a French army officer who was experiencing a spiritual crisis. He had developed an interest in Maritain's ideas as well as those of Blaise Pascal and Charles Maurras, the leader of Action Française, a strongly nationalistic organization whose chief goal was the restoration of the French monarchy, and he apparently found comfort in his correspondence and conversations with Maritain. Two months after Villard died in battle on June 28, 1918, Maritain received the shocking news that Villard had willed a substantial portion of his family's fortune to him and Charles Maurras. The bequest was enough to enable him to give up his salary at the Institut (although he occasionally lectured at the school) and to devote his time to writing.

The interwar period was a time of important intellectual activity for Maritain. In the fall of 1919, Jacques, Raïssa, and Vera began holding monthly meetings with friends and acquaintances to discuss Thomistic theology and philosophy. By 1923 these gatherings had grown to the point that larger accommodations were needed. They found a house that suited their needs in Meudon, a town between Paris and Versailles. For the next sixteen years a steady stream of visitors came to the meetings at Meudon: old and young, students and teachers; philosophers, scientists, writers, musicians; members of the clergy including Roman Catholics, Orthodox Christians, Protestants, and Jews; and even atheists. There also were annual retreats, at first in Meudon and later in Thomistic centers in England, Switzerland, and Belgium. Among the many participants in these meetings was the Russian author Nicolas Berdyaev with whom Maritain worked to end the rift between the Roman Catholic and Orthodox churches.

The Philosopher

Until 1926 Maritain wrote almost exclusively on metaphysics, epistemology, and the philosophy of nature. The thought of writing on political or social issues apparently did not cross his mind. But he soon changed his thinking when he unintentionally became embroiled in a controversy involving Action Française. By the mid-1920s a sufficiently large number of Catholics had joined this group so that it appeared to be a semiofficial arm of the Church. Although he was not a member, Maritain had occasionally written articles for *La Revue Universelle,* a magazine published by the organization. When the influence of Action Française began to interfere with the educational authority of the Church, Pope Pius XI condemned it.[31] Threatened with the loss of the sacrament of absolution, most Catholics left the organization. But some believed the pope had overstepped his bounds and refused to resign.

Maritain recognized the seriousness of this affair and the awkwardness of his own implied association with the group. He thus issued a statement in 1927, entitled *The Things That Are not Caesar's,* in which he argued that spiritual matters were prior to secular ones. The book won him numerous supporters and secured his position with Catholic officials, but it also cost him several friends and brought a vehement condemnation from Action Française.

This affair marked the beginning of Maritain's career as a political and social philosopher. It did not, however, completely divert his attention from speculative philosophy. He wrote his most important epistemological studies during this time. *The Degrees of Knowledge* came out in 1932, and its sequel, *Science and Wisdom,* appeared in 1935. During the preceding year he had finished his most complete metaphysical work, *A Preface to Metaphysics: Seven Lectures on Being.* In the years not devoted to speculative matters, he turned to the realm of practical philosophy. Beginning in 1933 with the issue of freedom, he published *Freedom in the Modern World,* which was followed in 1936 by a masterpiece of Thomistic philosophy, *True Humanism.* He helped to found the Catholic review *Esprit* and served as an advisor for that periodical and for the Catholic weekly *Sept.* In response to the political extremism of the 1930s, Maritain joined Étienne Gilson, Gabriel Marcel, and others in a call for the application of moral principles to all political systems expressed in a pamphlet entitled *For the Common Good.* From this time forward, Maritain focused his attention on political, social, and ethical concerns.

In addition to writing on practical philosophy, Maritain spent much of his time lecturing in Europe and North America. His European tour took him to Geneva, Salzburg, Louvain, Milan, and Rome. His first trip to North America came in 1931, when he received an invitation to lecture at the Pontifical Institute of Medieval Studies, St. Michael's College, an affiliate of the University of Toronto. The following summer he spoke at the University of Chicago, where he met President Robert M. Hutchins and Professor Mortimer Adler, both of whom would later join him as critics of progressive education. In 1938 he lectured at the University of Notre Dame and the Catholic University of America.

Educational Views

The Maritain family sailed from Marsailles in January 1940 bound once again for North America, unaware that they would not be able to return home for nearly five years. When they heard the news in June that France had fallen to the Nazis, their distress was tempered by the realization that Jacques could not return home because of his opposition to fascism. The Maritains took up residence in New York, while Jacques continued to lecture at the Pontifical Institute and at Columbia University. In 1942, with the aid of Alvin Johnson, president of the New School, Maritain established the École Libre des Hautes Études, a French university in exile. He was a frequent contributor to *Commonweal* and condemned antisemitism in *A Christian Looks at the Jewish Question.* He also worked with Professor Carlton J. H. Hayes on the National Conference of Christians and Jews.

In 1943 officials at Yale University invited Maritain to give the Terry Lectures for that year. He took this opportunity to offer the world his thoughts concerning education, which were later published under the title *Education at the Crossroads.* As might be expected, Maritain reiterated his fundamental thesis that science, although useful for understanding the physical environment, was insufficient as a source of knowledge about ultimate truth. He began by asserting that the principal task of education was "to shape man, or to guide the evolving dynamism through which man forms himself as man."[32] The bulk of his discussion combined criticisms of American education with suggestions for improving it.

Maritain thought that education was hindered by certain misconceptions held by American, and in particular progressive, educators. First, there was a disregard for ends: too much emphasis on means or methods for their own sake caused educators to lose sight of the purposes of education. Second, education was too concerned with creating the scientific person. Third, the pragmatic theory of knowledge could do nothing but produce skeptics who distrusted truth. Fourth, education began wrongly by trying to adapt people to society, instead of first making the individual. Fifth, he criticized the demand for specialization then being promoted by traditionalists who believed that essential knowledge was contained in the disciplines. Sixth, he chided those whom he believed wrongly opposed proper intellectual development and tried in the tradition of Rousseau to free natural potentialities, thought to be good, in order to develop the human will. And finally, he pointed out that many educators mistakenly believed everything could be learned, resulting in a course to cover every conceivable subject. Maritain thought that as long as educators held to these misconceptions, schools could not produce humane, thoughtful people who could stop the spread of totalitarianism and avoid the tyranny of uncontrolled technology.

A proper education, he argued, began with the Christian conception of humans as animals endowed with reason and intellect who were free in personal relations with God, but who were sinful creatures called to grace through love. With this notion in mind, education was to shape humans by arming them with knowledge, strength of judgment, and moral virtues, and to convey the heritage of the nation and civilization. It was also to show the utilitarian purpose in these things without allowing that end to supersede the essential aim of molding the child as a human being. Maritain held that education should endeavor to help humans become intellectually free through the progressive understanding of new truths and socially free through the recognition of their obligations to society.

Like St. Thomas, Maritain saw the art of teaching as analogous to the art of medicine: both aided nature in their respective work. The teacher's intellectual guidance and the student's mental capacity were the active elements in education, but the motive force came from the student's mind. The teacher was to help the student aim at self-perfection by fostering a love of goodness and justice, an acceptance of one's natural limitations, a sense of a job well done, and a sense of cooperation. He also believed that the dynamics of the educational process demanded that certain rules had to be followed in addition to promoting the above dispositions: education must awaken the human spirit, unify experience and reason in the mind, and liberate intelligence.

Following these rules, according to Maritain, required a curriculum built of knowledge that would enable the mind to grasp the truth. At the elementary level the child's imagination must be developed by focusing on stories and fables. Adolescent curiosity could only be satisfied if the youth had the intellectual instruments to develop natural reason and to answer those important questions—such tools as languages, grammar, history, natural history, and the art of expression. Finally, the undergraduate curriculum should include a year each of mathematics and poetry, natural sciences and fine arts, philosophy, ethics, and political philosophy. Maritain fervently hoped that education could foster an integral humanism that would save the world from destruction.

Final Years

He continued his scholarly activities for most of the next three decades, except from 1945 to 1948 when he served as the French ambassador to the Vatican.[33] When his work in Rome was completed, Maritain returned to the United States to teach philosophy at Princeton University until his retirement in 1953. Although he suffered a heart attack in 1954, he spent most of the next six years writing and lecturing. In 1958 he spoke at the University of Chicago and later published his comments in one of his most popular books, *Reflections on America*. On December 31, 1959 Vera Oumansoff died, and less than a year later Raïssa passed away. For the first time in more than fifty years, Maritain found himself alone.

Soon after Raïssa was buried, he made arrangements to settle in Toulouse, France with a religious order, the Little Brothers of Jesus. In the remaining years of his life he served as a seminar guide for the fraternity, and later took its vows. At the closing session of the Second Vatican Council in 1965, Maritain witnessed the act of reconciliation between the Orthodox and Roman Catholic churches, and heard Pope Paul VI pay tribute to him as a great Christian philosopher. The next year he published what was to have been his final statement, *The Peasant of the Garonne*. But the book caused a storm of controversy when his readers discovered that he did not support many of the recent reforms of the Catholic Church. They failed to understand that he had always combined political and social liberalism with religious conservatism. As a consequence he attempted to clarify his position in two more books: *On the Grace and Humanity of Jesus* in 1967 and *On the Church of Christ* in 1970. Maritain died on April 28, 1973 and was buried at Kolbsheim beside his beloved Raïssa.

Jacques Maritain was one of the most important philosophers of the twentieth century. He was instrumental in both the revival of Thomistic thought in philosophy and theology and the Catholic renaissance in France. He joined his countrymen Henri Bergson, Étienne Gilson, Gabriel Marcel, and Jean Paul Sartre in presenting alternative philosophical viewpoints to the positivism and scientism that dominated Western thought at the beginning of this century. His fundamentally liberal political and social philosophy generated some opposition among conservative Catholics in the 1920s, but for the most part won him the admiration of his coreligionists. However, many failed to understand the paradox of his liberal social and political philosophy combined with traditional and conservative theology. Liberal Catholics were upset at his refusal to endorse all of the positions taken by the Second Vatican Council.

Finally, Maritain was an effective and highly respected teacher of philosophy. As a philosopher of education, he strongly criticized progressive education for its overemphasis on means, on society, and, most importantly, on science. Some have viewed this as reactionary; others have said he was dogmatic in his opposition to naturalism. The former criticism ignores Maritain's philosophy as a whole. The latter comment seems more appropriate, but must be qualified. Having found early in his adulthood that science could not answer the ultimate questions of life and that the theology of St. Thomas Aquinas could, Maritain endeavored to apply the Thomistic standard to a world where scientific truth was necessary, but for him, certainly not sufficient for understanding life.

His religious conservatism was a philosophical element that would have found little support in the views of our next subject, educator W. E. B. DuBois. On the other hand, Maritain's social and political liberalism might have appealed to DuBois—perhaps as much as the neo-Thomist's native country of France did.

W. E. B. DuBois (1868–1963)

The various biographers of DuBois (pronounced DuBoyce) have been struck by the complex, paradoxical nature of his personality. August Meier noted that he skillfully played the roles of "scholar and prophet; mystic and materialist" as well as a "Marxist who was fundamentally a middle class intellectual." Jack Moore said that because DuBois's "own being was so paradoxical he could maintain in suspension, like a juggler . . . many sympathies and longings, even while containing intense hostilities and emotional twists."[34] He was shaped by the extreme social conditions of the times. Born three years after the Civil War, he grew up chafing under the harness of Booker T. Washington's cautious leadership—which to DuBois could only result in a postponement of civil, political, educational, and social equality for African Americans. Picking up Washington's scepter after his death in 1915, DuBois spent the next fifty-five years prodding black Americans to stand up and be counted. He died in Ghana in 1963, on the hundredth anniversary of the Emancipation Proclamation, without knowing how well his voice had been heard by his African American brothers and sisters.

Youth and Schooling

In his autobiography Will DuBois stated that he was born in Great Barrington, Massachusetts, on February 23, 1868, "the day after the birth of George Washington was celebrated, . . . the year that the freedmen of the South were enfranchised," and a week after "Thaddeus Stevens . . . made his last speech, impeaching Andrew Johnson." He was the product of French Huguenot, Dutch, and African strains. His mother's family, the Burghardts, had been in Great Barrington since the American Revolution. Great-grandfather Burghardt was a slave who was emancipated after fighting in the Revolutionary War.[35]

His paternal great-grandfather, Dr. James DuBois of Poughkeepsie, New York, had moved to the Bahamas after having been given several plantations by the governor of New York. In the Bahamas he had two sons—Alexander (DuBois's grandfather) and John—with a black woman who was probably his common law wife. DuBois brought his sons to Connecticut and to a private school where they stayed until he died in 1820. After his death the seventeen-year-old Alexander left for Haiti, married a Haitian woman, and had a son, Will's father Alfred. Eventually he moved the family to New Haven, where Alfred grew up and then fled his own father's strict authoritarianism.[36]

Alfred was known as a barber when he made his way to Great Barrington at the age of forty-two. He met the sad and complacent Mary Burghardt and married her against her family's wishes. Alfred left Great Barrington shortly after his son Will was born. For unknown reasons Mary did not go with her husband—perhaps because of her parents' objections. She suffered a stroke that left her lame in one leg, and moved back to her parents' country home with her young son Will.[37]

When Will reached school age Mary moved back to town so that her son could have the best schooling available. Great Barrington was a town of five thousand people, fifty of whom were free blacks, and the color line was not evident to Will as a young boy. He was a good student in an integrated school, and his white schoolmates seemed to include him happily in their social activities. However, he never dated while in school and left Great Barrington shortly after graduating at the top of his twelve-member high school class of 1884. He gave the valedictory address, and encouraged by his principal, who even raised money for him, made plans to attend college along with two or three other graduates in his class. (He was the only African American in his class.)

He worked at odd jobs for a year to raise money for college, and entered Fisk University in the fall of 1885 shortly after his mother's death. (In later years he would credit his mother and his Harvard professor, William James, with forming the crucial attitudes essential to his successful career.) He was seventeen, slight in build, blue-eyed, light-skinned, wavy-haired, and on his own for the first time in the color-conscious state of Tennessee.

At Fisk, DuBois was exposed to students who were five to ten years older than he was and who had experienced lives as southern blacks. They were more worldly and more sophisticated, having survived the worst tortures of racial bias. To Will this group of thirty-five students represented the beauty and intellectual power of the race. Although younger than his colleagues, he was not modest about his own accomplishments and capabilities, and he began to envision himself as their leader. He became editor of the *Fisk Herald* and spent three enriching years at the university. During his two summer vacations he worked as a rural schoolteacher in Wilson County, where he learned of the poverty and hardships of the rural black southerner. In the house where he rented a room, he lost his virginity, or as he put it, "I was literally raped by the unhappy wife who was my landlady."[38]

He graduated from Fisk in 1888 after giving the commencement speech. His ambitious future had been fueled by the praise of his teachers, and he looked forward to graduate study at Harvard. Through letters of recommendation his Fisk professors painted a picture of him that included traits such as ambition, manliness, earnestness in study, excellence in scholarship, and a possible conceitedness that would not "prevent faithful work."[39]

He entered Harvard as a junior and took another bachelor of arts degree (this time cum laude in philosophy) in 1890. He kept his own company at Harvard, never mingling with white counterparts. As one biographer put it, "He never developed any affection for the university. Glorying in his isolation and eschewing Harvard life . . . he came to think of Harvard as a library and a faculty, nothing more." Through faculty support from George Santayana and James, DuBois took a master's degree in history in 1891. His thesis became the first volume of the Harvard Historical Studies and was entitled *The Suppression of African Slave-Trade to the United States of America, 1638–1870.*[40]

It was common in the late nineteenth century for young scholars to look to German universities to further their intellectual prowess, and DuBois was no exception. In 1892 he applied to the Slater Fund and received a grant (half gift, half loan) to study at the University of Berlin. Originally for one year, the grant was extended to two. He planned to take a Ph.D. there but never did. He spent the time studying at the feet of great German masters, changing his academic thrust from history to political economy and sociology. He traveled in England, France, Italy, Austria, Germany, Poland, and Hungary. These years gave him the chance to think in broader terms about color barriers. He was amazed to find himself being accepted on equal social grounds. He lived with a German family who treated him like a member and he fell in love with their daughter. Although he felt no color barriers, he seemed to become a little antisemitic. Returning in steerage class to America in the summer of 1894, he wrote in his diary: "There is in [the Jews] all that slyness that lack of straightforward open-heartedness which goes straight against me."[41]

University Professor

Filled with a messianic commitment to black liberation—what he later would call his real life work—DuBois started his scholarly career in Xenia, Ohio at Wilberforce University as the chair of the classics department. Later that summer offers came from Tuskegee and from Lincoln Institute in Missouri, but DuBois stuck with Wilberforce. By

1895 he had his Ph.D. from Harvard and was congratulating Booker T. Washington for his exposition speech at Atlanta. But all was not rosy in Xenia. DuBois found the Afro-Episcopalian dogma stifling. He resented the stress on Sunday school attendance over academic classes and, although he added German to the chair he held in classics, the college authorities refused to allow him to offer sociology. The one bright spot was his association with a pretty student from Cedar Rapids, Iowa, Nina Gomer, whom he married in 1896. That same year the University of Pennsylvania offered him a fifteen-month appointment as assistant instructor to do research on the black community in Philadelphia's Seventh Ward.

When his work on *The Philadelphia Negro: A Social Study* was completed, DuBois accepted a position as sociologist at Atlanta University, where he spent the next thirteen years directing black studies and gathering data on the black condition in an effort to affect social policies. Through lectures and publications he tried to present the black plight to the public at large. He taught and trained his students to become cultured intellectuals—the "talented tenth" of the race—capable of leading the masses. When he was not in his office, he was on the road lecturing and delivering speeches. In July 1900 he attended the first Pan African Congress in London and was elected as its secretary. He refused to be humiliated, never entering a streetcar, theater, or concert hall. The little social life he had was with a small group of black friends including John Hope and James Weldon Johnson, to whom he showed a side other than the austere, driven, missionary sociologist. Johnson said in 1904 that he was "astonished . . . to find that DuBois's brooding, intransigent, public demeanor could dissolve into joviality, even frivolity." DuBois wrote the *Souls of Black Folk* almost as a eulogy on the death of his infant son, Burghardt, who was denied medical care because he was black. In the book he turned his sense of loss into victory for his son: "Well sped, my boy, before the world has dubbed your ambition insolence, has held your ideals unattainable, and taught you to cringe and bow."[42]

As racial riots broke out in Boston and Atlanta, DuBois began to break with Booker T. Washington's conservative message to blacks. He organized the Niagara Movement, which held its first conference in 1905. The movement held annual conferences until 1910, when it merged into the National Association for the Advancement of Colored People (NAACP).

NAACP Work

In 1910 he severed his connections with Atlanta and moved his wife and young daughter Yolande to New York where he was to be the director of publications and research for the NAACP. His first issue of *The Crisis* appeared that November. By 1919, the magazine's subscribers grew to 104,000. This growth seemed to reflect DuBois's claim as the liberal leader of the black cause. DuBois grew farther away from Washington as he became convinced that the latter was "betraying the Negro into permanent servility." He spoke out against the peaceful picture of black conditions that Washington painted to Europe. *The Crisis* became his mouthpiece and, even as the association was becoming more liberal, DuBois, their editor, was becoming radical. His "talented tenth" concept seemed exclusive and aristocratic, and Washington maintained his popularity and leadership position with blacks until his death in 1915.[43]

In the prewar years DuBois grew more aggressive and outspoken, and friction between him and the association grew. He found no friend in any political program, including Wilson's brand of progressive democracy, but he did support female suffrage: a vote for white women meant a vote for black women. After a 1916 lynching, *The Crisis* editor counseled resistance by force: "In God's name let us perish like men and not like bales of hay." The period from 1910 to 1920 has been described by one historian as DuBois's great years, and he moved with ease into the leadership position vacated by Washington's death. His influence was felt more in the North than the South, although through his lecture tours he managed to reach most states, and he found particular hope in urban blacks.[44]

During World War I DuBois began to hope again because Wilsonian policies had produced wartime job opportunities for blacks, and black soldiers had helped to win the war. This hope was short-lived, however, when in the "Red summer" of 1919 black blood was shed in numerous urban race riots. Also, a study of black soldiers during the war revealed many discriminatory practices by the army. Hurt, shocked, and angered by this, DuBois returned to his earlier threats of violence. His editorials struck some as arrogant, self-righteous, and pedantic. These attitudes hardly set well with white liberals, nor did they ease the tensions between him and the NAACP. Even James Weldon Johnson's appointment as executive secretary of the NAACP could not bridge the gap.

Throughout the 1920s and early 1930s, DuBois became preoccupied with Africa. He developed three goals that the association endorsed: (1) the formation of an African state from German possessions; (2) a program for these former colonies to be led by educated, African, American, West Indian, and South American blacks; and (3) the spread of science and other modern cultural advantages to existing African institutions. To promote these goals Pan African conferences were organized, in Paris in 1919, in London in 1920, and in Brussels in 1921. Although Europe met these conferences with indifference, DuBois seemed to gain encouragement from them, and he continued to organize them through the 1920s. The NAACP withdrew their support after the second one, and his final effort met with collapse in 1929.

In 1926 he took his first trip to Russia and found new hope for his cause in what freedom from color lines and working class psychology he saw there: the latter promised to replace the millionaire with the worker as the center of power and culture. For DuBois socialism and Russian communism were becoming the voices of the oppressed peoples, both white and black. He was less than enthusiastic about the American Communist party, however, and after the Scottsboro case he had only contempt for the group. (In 1931 nine black youths were arrested in Scottsboro, Alabama and charged with raping two white girls. The nine turned their case over to a communist labor defense group who, through bribery and sensationalist tactics, lost the case. The NAACP took charge and won, and DuBois denounced the communist tactics in a *Crisis* editorial.)[45]

The depression of the 1930s convinced DuBois that a new direction must be taken in the black cause. By 1934 he believed that full equality would never be gained, and he began calling for nondiscriminatory segregation, or the development of an independent black culture. However, this hit the NAACP executives right between the eyes, because fighting legal and administrative segregation had been the primary reason for the association's existence. The chairperson of the board, Joel Springarn, said that no organ of the NAACP could be allowed to criticize its policies. DuBois countered that the *Crisis* was never intended to be an organ of the association, and resigned to accept the chair of sociology at Atlanta University under the presidency of his old friend John Hope. (Nina DuBois remained in Baltimore due to her hatred of the South.)

DuBois's Leadership

From 1934 to 1944 DuBois was regarded as the stately spokesperson for black politics. Atlanta, Fisk, and Wilberforce bestowed honorary degrees upon him, and he gained membership in the National Institute of Arts and Letters. He wrote two more books, started work on a Negro encyclopedia, and was founding editor of *Phylon*. During these years he resumed his efforts to create an intellectually talented elite by transforming black universities into the finest centers for higher learning in the country. Trouble did not really surface until a new president, Rufus Clement, with unknown ideas, was elected at Atlanta. Then in 1944, without warning, Atlanta's board of trustees voted to retire DuBois with no pension. Fortunately for DuBois, NAACP Executive Secretary Walter White hired him as director of special research. However, it did not take long for old tensions to surface. DuBois was still out of step with the officers of the association, and when he openly criticized White's appointment as consultant to the UN's American delegation in Paris as a political sellout, he was fired, although a pension was included this time.

DuBois was not destined to live his final years in peace. After travel to France and Russia in 1949, the eighty-two-year-old settled down to head up the Peace Information Center, which had been organized to spread sentiment for international peace. He also ran unsuccessfully for the U.S. Senate on the American Labor party ticket. His wife died in 1950, and in 1951 he was planning a Valentine's Day wedding to Shirley Graham (the daughter of an old friend) when he was indicted for failing to register the Center as an agent of a foreign principal—the World

Congress of the Defenders of Peace. Two days after his marriage he was arraigned, and the trial was set for April 2. These charges stunned DuBois. As required by the Foreign Agents Registration Act, DuBois and four others were indicted for "failing to cause the organization" to register. DuBois knew that the Justice Department wanted the Center to register, but he had not done so because he had conceived it as an American group operated by American citizens. The trial was postponed until November, when the case was thrown out by federal judge Matthew F. McGuire. However, this did little to restore DuBois's faith in American policies, nor did the government's refusal over the next six years to issue him a passport.[46]

Finally, in 1958 he was allowed to travel to China, France, England, Sweden, eastern Europe, and the USSR—where he won the Lenin Peace Prize. He left the United States again in 1961, this time for good, to live in Ghana. It was a hurried departure, because he anticipated that new restrictions would be placed on him since he had become a communist. President Nkrumah of Ghana had invited him there to do work on an African encyclopedia, and in 1963 he gave up his American citizenship to become a citizen of Ghana. He died in his adopted country on August 27, 1963.

Poet, novelist, essayist, scholar, teacher, agitator, W. E. B. DuBois became the loudest voice demanding equal rights for African Americans and in so doing he bolstered the morale of his people. In 1941 when DuBois was attacked as a racial chauvinist, the seventy-three-year-old responded caustically that "if you want to lose friends and jobs, then oppose wars, defend strikes, and say that even communists have rights." Perhaps Roy Wilkins captured his influence best when on August 28, 1963—the day after DuBois's death—he told a crowd of thousands gathered in front of the Lincoln Memorial that DuBois's voice from the beginning of the century has been "calling you here today."[47]

DuBois championed a new social order led by a talented black elite, but he failed to see this cause realized. After the Great Depression there were other voices added to the call for a new American social order to be led by the teachers and educators of the country. They too were unsuccessful in having their views materialize. Nevertheless, they left a legacy of social reconstructionist thought. Such an advocate was educator and philosopher George S. Counts.

George S. Counts (1889–1974)

For nearly five decades, George Counts was a leading figure in American education. Through his study of American and Russian civilization, he developed insights into the relationships among social, economic, political, and educational forces. While he enjoyed studying the past, Counts, like his friend Charles A. Beard, saw history as an instrument to shape a plan for a new society. For him education was an important means by which human beings could create a new social order. To some people, Counts, like DuBois, was a dangerous radical bent on bringing collectivist ideology into American schools. Others saw him as an educator who had a prophetic insight into the course of human events. Friends and foes alike remembered him as the man who posed the question, "Dare the school build a new social order?" in the depths of the Great Depression.

The Making of an Educator

The son of a Kansas farmer, George Sylvester Counts was a true child of America's middle border. Although he was to teach in leading universities and travel throughout the Orient, South America, and the Soviet Union, he never lost the down-to-earth plainness that came from growing up in America's heartland. Born in Baldwin, Kansas in 1889, George attended local schools. He earned his bachelor's degree from Baker University in 1911 and his doctorate from the University of Chicago in 1916. As a graduate student at Chicago, he learned the research techniques of scientific education from his mentor, Charles Judd. His work there with Albion W. Small, the pioneer sociologist, gave him skills for the social analysis of education. He taught at the universities of Washington, Chicago, Yale, and Columbia Teachers College, and was also director of research for the Commission of the American Historical Association on the Social Studies from 1931 to 1933 and editor of the *Social Frontier* from 1934 to 1937.

In the decade before the Great Depression, Counts examined education's broader historical, sociological, and philosophical themes. In *The Selective Character of American Secondary Education* (1922), he charged that American high schools served the interests of upper socioeconomic classes: children of native (European) stock were more likely to attend high school than the offspring of recent immigrants. Also, the enrollment of black children in high school was much less than the total proportion of blacks in the population. In *The Senior High School Curriculum* (1926), Counts criticized educators for failing to create a curriculum relevant to a technological society. In *The Social Composition of Boards of Education* (1927), he depicted public education dominated by a powerful socioeconomic elite with boards of education composed primarily of members from the favored occupations of merchant, lawyer, manufacturer, banker, and physician. Because of their backgrounds, he said, board members were often unresponsive to social change and the needs of lower socioeconomic groups. Increasingly, Counts realized that schools could not function successfully if they remained in isolation from social and economic forces. In *Secondary Education and Industrialism* (1929), he noted that the rapid rise of the public high school was a product of America's modernization, industrialization, and urbanization.[48]

Counts could shift easily from the role of sociologist to that of historian. While he proclaimed the public school to be a major American cultural force, he also chided Americans for their immature faith that schools could be effective social agencies if they remained isolated from social, political, and economic change and controversy.[49] He also enjoyed a reputation as a noted scholar on Soviet culture and education. For him the absence of social planning was a major cause of social and economic crisis. Like many other liberal intellectuals, he saw social planning as a means of solving the economic crisis:

> The economic depression which . . . continues to hold the entire Western world in its grip, depriving millions . . . of employment and bringing misery to vast populations, has revealed weaknesses in the contemporary industrial order and has turned the minds of economists and statesmen everywhere to the question of social planning. Although we in America at least possess a mastery over the forces of production which should enable us to satisfy all of our material wants with ease, multitudes go hungry and experience all the terrors and humiliations of profound physical insecurity. This is tragedy; not because men have not suffered before, but because they now suffer so needlessly. The dreams of mankind through the ages now are at least capable of realization, but our present economic, educational, and political leadership has . . . failed to rise to the opportunity created by science and technology. A general condition of uncoordination paralyzes the economic system and dissipates its matchless energies.[50]

Counts argued three main points: (1) Because Americans traditionally had viewed schooling as an intrinsically good cultural instrument, they did not comprehend that the school was but one of many educational agencies. Neither did they realize that the school could be used for a variety of social, political, and economic purposes. (2) The American people were facing a catastrophic economic depression that was causing severe social, political, and educational dislocation. (3) Instead of providing strong leadership, American educators were ignoring problems of the depression. Many progressive educators, devotees of child-centered educational theory, scrupulously avoided major national issues. Either ignorant of socioeconomic realities or striving for political neutrality, American educators deliberately or unconsciously maintained the status quo.

Dare the School

In his best known work, *Dare the School Build a New Social Order?*, Counts recognized the crisis of the Great Depression. As the nation struggled against massive economic and social dislocation, he argued that educators needed to combat retrenchment and restore faith in schooling. Although these were the immediate problems facing the nation and its schools, they were but symptomatic of a larger crisis precipitated by America's feeble attempt to come to grips with the great social transformation of the technological revolution. Science and technology had already created an industrialized, urban, interdependent society, and human material inventiveness, stimulated by the instruments of science and technology, had outdistanced social imagination. Patterned in an age of agricultural and industrial individualism, American political, social, and educational institutions had failed to meet the challenges of human interdependency. In clinging to an obsolete individualism, American society and schools had failed to provide the needed planning and social and educational engineering for the new technological civilization.[51]

Dare the School Build a New Social Order? was a dramatic event in the history of American education as well as a daring proposal to educators. While critics condemned his proposal as a dangerous radicalism pernicious to individual and educational freedom, his supporters saw Counts's challenge as a call to revitalize the commitment to democratic and egalitarian education. In retrospect, Counts was responding to the problems of a particular decade and also addressing larger issues that would require answers from future generations of educators.

Civilizational Philosophy

Counts called upon American educators to create an educational philosophy that would sustain and equip them to meet the challenge of a technological society. He sought to formulate a "civilizational philosophy" by turning to the "new history" of Charles Beard and Carl Becker. Counts found that the American cultural heritage had replaced European medieval residues such as feudalism, landed aristocracies, established churches, and social hierarchies with two conflicting historical traditions: Hamiltonianism and Jeffersonianism. Hamiltonianism advocated rule by a privileged elite pursuing special interests: economic individualism, ruthless environmental exploitation, maximization of profits, and wasteful competition. Jeffersonianism was a preferable alternative, originating with the independent farmer who lived in basic equality with neighbors. For Counts the egalitarian, democratic ethic was a viable element in the American heritage that needed to be preserved for the oncoming generations by the nation's schools.

Having identified egalitarian democracy as the ethical component to be transmitted in the schools, Counts developed a theory of social change that predicted the direction of American civilization. Essentially, the United States was experiencing a cultural crisis as it was transformed from an agrarian society into a technological, industrialized, urbanized, and modernized social order. The emergence of an industrialized and technological society not only affected the economic realm but also had social and cultural repercussions. Science, technology, and invention had advanced far beyond society's reconstruction of ethical, legal, and political systems. The obsolescence of inherited conceptions of human nature, the rejection of traditional theological, philosophical, and political doctrines, and the rise of totalitarianism reflected the anxiety of people caught in profound social crises. Counts continually referred to this "great transition," and believed that it was neither possible nor desirable to "turn back the clock."

Periods of profound social transformation brought not only social turmoil and anxiety but also promises of greater control over nature, of increased material abundance, and of liberation from the scarcity of a subsistence economy, said Counts. He thought the immense social, economic, political, and educational problems of the twentieth century could be solved in a way that would achieve the promise of American life. The time had come, he argued, to replace competitiveness, maldistribution, and exploitation with cooperation, planning, humaneness, and democracy in a technological society. Such a new social order would preserve the democratic ethic by reconstructing it to meet the requirements of the new technology.

Theory into Practice?

Counts developed a "program of action" that called for affirmation of democratic values and processes, dissemination of the knowledge needed by free people, maintenance of military and police power by legally constituted authorities, guarantee of civil liberties, systematic exposure of major campaigns of political propaganda, conservation of the democratic temper, and avoidance of war.[52] Some who were sympathetic to Counts's *Dare the School* challenge claimed that they were inspired by his call but did not know how to implement it. He never developed a specific program for social and educational reconstruction nor formed an organization to lead the creation of a new society. Nor did Counts associate in any formal sense with those who styled themselves "social reconstructionist" educational philosophers.

Although a scholar, Counts was also a political activist. He won the presidency of the AFT in 1939, and was the Liberal party candidate for the U.S. Senate from New York in 1952. His programmatic efforts, however, were of limited dimension when compared to the magnitude of his challenge to educators to use schools to improve society.

In education, Counts was operationally and theoretically a cultural relativist. When the national priority moved from the problems of economic depression to the defense of democracy against totalitarianism during World War II, Counts's attention also moved in that direction. In the Cold War era, his expert knowledge of Soviet society and education took on new relevance as he explained Soviet political and educational policies to U.S. audiences.

Counts clearly pointed out that education was related to a given civilization and its problems at a particular time in history. He argued forcefully that schooling could be an instrument of broad and significant national policy. He challenged educators to go beyond daily concerns and formulate policy rather than having the dictates of others imposed on them, and anticipated much of the current research on modernization and its educational consequences. He reasserted that educational philosophy was not a completed product, but rather an instrument for dealing with changing issues in a changing world.

Miles Elwood Cary (1894–1959)

Not all experimentalists agreed with the direct reconstructionism of George Counts, for some were convinced that no one should predetermine a new social order. Among those advocating an *indirect* democratic approach was Miles E. Cary. He thought schools should furnish an environment in which youth could criticize society's wrongdoings and develop corrective social actions. Advocates of indirect action rejected the idea of class struggle as an enduring feature of the social order. They saw schools as places to discover conflicts in one's cultural heritage, reinterpret the meaning of democracy, and "become an energizing center for study and activity for the entire community."[53] Democracy provided the means and the base from which to develop future culture.

Background

Miles Elwood Cary was born on November 1, 1894 in the small town of Orting, Washington. His father died when Miles was seven, and Anna Cary made a new home in Edmonds, Washington with her children. Anna was widowed twice and had to work hard to raise her family. With her sons (Miles, Gordon Cary, and their half-brother Roy Venn) she bought and operated a fruit grower's company. Miles also had a sister Bertha ("Bea") and half-sister Essie.

Miles and his neighbor and wife-to-be Edith Brackett were among the twelve graduates from Edmonds High School in 1912. History and math were Miles's favorite subjects. He was an athlete and a bookworm, having a particular interest in historical novels. Despite high school aspirations to be a lawyer or an engineer, he studied education at the University of Washington. "I'll never regret it," he later said. "Education is the most thrilling work a person can be engaged in today."[54] During World War I, Miles left college for six months in the army, but still managed to graduate in 1917. He became principal and teacher in Morton, near Seattle. After his marriage to Edith, the couple took positions in the town of Ferndale, Washington: Miles was high school principal, Edith was an elementary teacher. The influence of progressive educational ideals, then widespread in the state of Washington, would have a lasting impact.

Move to Hawaii

Teacher placement agencies heavily recruited in the Pacific Northwest for teachers needed in the Territory of Hawaii. Miles and Edith visited the islands in 1921. Intrigued by a progressive movement in the islands and undeterred by growing problems with the educational system there, the Carys accepted the challenge of a new culture. It immediately became their new home. Hawaii provided them the opportunity to implement progressive principles gaining momentum on the mainland into a school system ready for educational change.

Cary went to Hawaii at a time when its teaching force was characterized as unstable, for teachers often left after satisfying their sense of adventure and sightseeing. Thus, the islands had many inexperienced teachers. Low salaries, high travel costs, and inadequate housing were additional drawbacks in teacher recruitment. Distance increased the problems of interviewing, as well as the uncertainty of whether mainland interviewees would show up if offered jobs. On the positive side, mainland educators brought new ideas to the island community. In fact, the teachers of the 1920s and 1930s were considered "the godparents of modern Hawaii."[55]

In September 1921, Cary made his debut at McKinley High School as a history teacher and coach of the junior football, track, and basketball teams. In 1922, he served as advisor for the newly formed school newspaper, *The Daily Pinion*. The next year, he became the principal of Maui High School, but returned to McKinley in 1924 as principal—a position he held for twenty-four years. "McKinley High Starts Year as One of the Best Equipped in the World," proclaimed the *Honolulu Advertiser*. "Other vital changes will be found in the high school too. Most important is the new principal."[56]

Curriculum Revision

Cary realized that a significant factor complicating the Hawaiian educational system was the emphasis by community leaders on traditional aims and objectives. Three distinct attitudes toward education had crystallized. The first was that expanding educational opportunities should be compatible with Hawaii's basic industries, and education for *nonhaoles* (nonwhites) should serve citizenship and contribute to the economy. A second group felt that education would destroy "an economy based on the utilization of masses of ignorant workers." The third position "urged education to liberate talent and creativity, with the hope of someday transforming the social structure of Hawaii."[57] Cary, the principal advocate of the third group, quoted George Counts: "The traditional program, in so far as it was ever adapted to the achievement of any genuine educational purpose, was designed to provide a narrow academic education for the children of a small, privileged social class or for the exceptional children of less favored parentage."[58]

Cary wrote a master's thesis at the University of Hawaii in 1930, laying out a plan to vitalize the curriculum of McKinley High School. He criticized both the NEA's Cardinal Principles of Secondary Education and its research bulletin *Vitalizing the Curriculum* for their lack of "suggestions looking toward a broader concept of method, or possible regroupings, or integrations of subject matter."[59] Cary cited the writings of Dewey, William H. Kilpatrick, Boyd H. Bode, and Harold Rugg for their advocacy of experience-based, child-centered, experimental learning. He urged that the curriculum make full provisions for the improvement of society.[60]

Cary's democratic movement involved McKinley students in community problems. By studying conflict from a student perspective—focusing on the contradictions between democracy and authoritarianism in Hawaii—and studying the impact of education on the economy, McKinley played a key role in transforming the vision of Hawaii's labor force. The student body largely descended from the plantation workforce, and they drank deeply of the educational and democratic idealism offered by dedicated teachers who provided an opportunity for students to criticize the social system and make decisions about the conditions under which they lived. The worst nightmare of powerful plantation managers was coming true: "Public education beyond the fourth grade is not only a waste, it is a menace. We spend to educate them and they will destroy us."[61]

Cary's strength was in process, not in theory. Concerned about participatory democracy, he saw communication as a device for human empowerment.[62] "Traditional schools directed young people into the community's preferred jobs. The new high school will help young people to discover the wider social meanings and values that may be experienced by those who engage in the common occupations of the community," he said.[63] Education's aim lay in its method—not the devices by which prescribed subject matter is covered, but "the way in which young people live and work together."[64] According to Cary, such method was "purposeful, constructive activity carried on with thoughtfulness and in an atmosphere of democracy."[65]

Cary's concern for a vitalized education evolved into a new, reorganized core curriculum. School policy under democratic conditions empowered students to develop a meaningful curriculum:

> The central purpose of the public schools in an American community—and Hawaii is American—is that of preparing its children and youth for intelligent, effective participation in the affairs of the community. . . . This means helping children to improve their communication skills, to think critically concerning the problems of the day, to develop social sensitivity, to choose wisely and prepare themselves for a vocation, to grow in sensitivity to beauty, to develop wholesome personalities, and to learn how to cooperate to promote common interests.[66]

In 1931 the school commissioners gave Cary approval for a trial of the core studies program at McKinley. Developed through the assistance of parents, neighbors, teachers, and students, the core curriculum helped identify critical problems of local, national, and international significance. McKinley's young people were given the opportunity to sense the deeper meanings of democracy through participation in managing the school.[67] Students assumed responsibility for classroom organization and management. They cared for books, took attendance, kept certain types of records, and maintained and improved the classroom environment. Instead of academic problems and subject matter, the core studies were based upon the out-of-school activities and pupil needs that encouraged the study of vital problems faced in the world beyond school. The school was open from 7:30 A.M. until 9:00 P.M., teachers worked in shifts, and pupils attended school at hours that did not conflict with their outside work.[68] The procedure for problem solving was largely a directed study plan: core studies rooms had tables around which groups developed working plans, with students working singly or in groups with teachers actively assisting. Reports, questions, and general discussion brought each problem to a close.

Two years after the implementation of core studies, McKinley received national attention as a laboratory school for citizenship. Cary's belief that "the real test of education is what people are encouraged to do in their own community to improve the quality of living" was leaving its mark.[69] Cary thought the real test of success was students' ability to thoughtfully analyze the results of the work before them, rather than the results of standardized test scores. Human development and learning, which integrate thought and action, furnish the best basis for educating the whole person by prizing independent thinking and encouraging pupils to work out their own philosophy of life.[70] McKinley empowered students and teachers to evaluate the quality of their own work.

Student Government

The first step toward McKinley's laboratory school operation was a change from the traditional student council to the formation of a more far-reaching student government organization that included the entire student body. An executive council consisted of three elected student officers, the class presidents and their respective faculty advisers, the principal, the student government adviser, the treasurer appointed by the principal, and the editor of *The Daily Pinion*. The representative assembly was comprised of sixty-seven homeroom delegates and a representative from each of over seventy clubs and organizations. Student government activities were incorporated into the regular school program as a laboratory for deliberate training for citizenship. Each homeroom was a local unit of the student government. Students could volunteer, be elected, or be "drafted" into school government, but participation was a necessary component of McKinley's democratic process. In addition, the establishment of a school deputy and court system allowed for increased student responsibility in controlling the school. Cary believed that students should be addressed as "citizens" whenever possible to form the connection between their responsibilities in the school to those in the community. "We learn to do a thing by actually doing it, just so we learn to be worthy citizens by carrying out activities in citizenship," Cary wrote.[71]

Communication

The student forum and the school newspaper were key devices for developing democratic thinking skills. Both vehicles helped students build awareness of real life issues. The student forum provided open discussion of problems of the school, community, and territory. Students developed clear written solutions for each problem. Limited oral presentations included presentations of minority group opinions. Following remarks from the audience, a guest speaker from the community commented on the opinions expressed. By 1933, the forum developed into citywide debate. Such themes as Pacific affairs evolved.

The student newspaper became a daily publication in 1925. As the official organ of an active student government, *The Daily Pinion* became a vital link between community and school. The unique place of the school newspaper at McKinley was described as a model: "While it naturally plays up athletics and other adolescent activities and has occasional youthful jokes, the tone is distinctly serious and evidences a highly commendable spirit of fine citizenry."[72] Cary wrote almost daily to students regarding a variety of issues, and *The Daily Pinion* reflected both the life and philosophy of Cary and the pulse of the high school—student body, teachers, community members: the history of people being transformed.

Education in a Relocation Center

The December 1941 attack on Pearl Harbor brought new concerns to Cary and his students. Schools closed for two months. Mainland principals, eager to know how Hawaii was carrying on, asked Cary to serve as the Coordinator of the National Discussion Group of the National Association of Secondary-School Principals.

In February 1942, President Roosevelt signed Executive Order 9066 authorizing the U.S. Army to exclude populations from designated zones for security reasons. Magnified concern about the war in the Pacific resulted in Executive Order 9102, which set up the War Relocation Authority (WRA), a federal agency whose purpose was to relocate and supervise the excluded population brought into assembly and reception centers by the army. During spring 1942 more than 110,000 Japanese Americans were incarcerated in ten camps surrounded by barbed wire and guard towers. Two-thirds of them were American citizens, and approximately thirty thousand were school-age children.[73] These temporary housing projects were designated for people whose crimes were that they, their parents, or their grandparents were from a country at war with the United States.

Cary believed the relocation of Japanese Americans was immoral. He took a leave from McKinley in the summer of 1942 to organize the educational program at one camp in Poston, Arizona, a dusty desert filled with mesquite and cactus and surrounded by mountain ranges. California was displacing thousands of American-born Japanese into relocation centers as the Carys left for California in the summer of 1942.

Relocation was just one step in a series of actions taken by the U.S. government that limited opportunity for Japanese immigrants, individuals who had come to the United States with a commitment to schooling due to the expansion of education in Japan during the Meiji Era (1868–1912). In 1911 the Dillingham Commission reported to Congress that it was struck by the eagerness of the Japanese to assimilate: No immigrant group except the Jews had shown such "great desire to learn the English language."[74] In 1894 a U.S. District Court held that immigrants born in Japan were members of a race not eligible for citizenship, a decision that was upheld by the Supreme Court in 1922, but their children born within United States territorial borders, were secure under the Fourteenth Amendment. Thus, within families, children who were natural-born citizens with guaranteed rights to education were living side by side with alien parents who were ineligible for citizenship. California and other western states passed alien land laws in 1913 and 1920 to prevent Japanese farmers from buying property.

Some Americans pressed for greater exclusion of rights for American-born Japanese as well, feeling that the children held dual citizenship and were not loyal to the United States. In 1921 California passed a law to segregate Japanese Americans in separate schools, but because most children were well-integrated into the public schools, only a few rural areas enforced the law. Many Japanese American families remained separate from the general population who discriminated against them. The anti-Japanese movement culminated in the Immigration Act of 1924, which closed further immigration of the Japanese to the United States. As first-generation Japanese immigrants (Issei) died, the American-born second generation (Nisei) became more aware of the restrictions that distinguished their adult lives from their childhood. Their educational accomplishments compared favorably to white classmates', but they lived isolated lives. This condition increased as political tensions grew between Japan and the United States. Discrimination against them increased, but nothing could prepare these American citizens for the new lessons in democracy that awaited them. Families were taken from their communities and moved into racetracks, public facilities, and fairgrounds. Military police "protected" them from watchtowers with machine guns, searchlights, and rifles with bayonets. The elders ridiculed the "worthless" citizenship of their children and grandchildren, a younger generation of more than 70,000.

Ten camps employed about 600 white teachers, 50 certified Japanese American teachers, and 400 Japanese American assistant teachers. (The Japanese Americans were residents of the camp who received stipends for their work, as did other individuals who were employed in various capacities. Some received FBI clearance to work outside the camps.) The class size inside the camps was forty-eight for elementary and thirty-five for secondary, whereas the national norm was twenty-eight.[75]

Poston Center was on Indian land in the Arizona desert, 165 miles east of Phoenix and close to a mountain range separating Arizona and California. The intense summer heat averaged 10 degrees hotter than the Libyan Desert, and in winter the temperature dropped to almost zero. A powdery alkali dust rose with every step and hung suspended in the still desert air—a condition known as Poston Fog. One child wrote as she first arrived, "I thought it was a place where no man should live."[76]

Poston was an unfinished camp of tarpaper huts, and teacher anxiety was high. "They found nothing resembling a school. Several classes were to take place simultaneously in a 20 × 120 foot room lacking partitions. In some instances when no classrooms were available, teachers assembled their students in mess halls, amidst the clatter of setting up tables and cleaning up, until more facilities could be constructed."[77] These difficulties tempered enthusiasm astonishingly. One teacher wrote:

> To see the word "pioneer," to speak it, to hear it, all are different—indeed, how well I know it—from actually being in a place where everything is new and just beginning. If, on top of the confusion of the difficulties of communication, transportation, housing, and administration in the middle of the desert, you pile the problems of the great emotional upheaval brought about by the evacuation of thousands of people of enemy ancestry, you have some conception of what I found on arriving at Poston.[78]

Cary brought his progressive philosophy and belief in community-based curriculum to Poston. He often traveled at his own expense throughout the West to find teachers, and was more successful than superintendents in other camps. He tried to find teachers who had taught Japanese Americans before the war. Although he signed up more than enough teachers for the 101 authorized positions, only seventy-two teachers came and two of these left as soon as they saw the place.[79] Most teachers only stayed four to eight months.

Despite the harsh environment, lack of facilities, scarce materials, and inadequate teaching and administrative staffs, the most difficult situation the Japanese Americans faced was the uprooting of thousands of peaceful families, the loss and damage of valuable property, and the despondency of innocent and loyal citizens who were placed in isolated, congested living quarters where the strong family unit and parental authority began to deteriorate. Although it was impossible to make a normal American community out of a relocation center, it was possible through schools, libraries, poetry clubs, novel huts, newspapers, and community education to keep alive the recollection of former life. The intent of the WRA was to provide an American education for the children of evacuees, for "it was not the democratic tradition to make war on children."[80] One teacher recalled:

> Having behind me nine years of teaching experience in the public schools of Hawaii, I knew that young Japanese Americans were not to be listed among my problems simply because of their ancestry. The psychological and emotional difficulties of these people I found to be those of any human beings who find themselves ostracized from society. Their problem and mine . . . was to become adjusted to the new environment and to understand why relocation was necessary and to prepare themselves for "relocation" into inland parts of our nation as constructive, loyal citizens.[81]

The effects of relocation on education may never be fully understood. Japanese Americans, already committed to education, family, and community, had to rise from oppression. The relocation centers provided contrasts in American public policy. "As social institutions the camps for Japanese Americans brought together incongruous elements of coercion and idealism; they combined barbed wire and military police with government services, a subsidized economy, community councils under administrative control, public education, and conditional opportunities for resettlement into communities on the outside."[82] Loyalty oaths and denial of civil liberties created "an education [for children of war] that was broader than schooling itself, for the incarcerated population had its own form of social organization and cultural expression, its own way of preserving meaning and coping with adversity."[83]

The educational program at Poston, in spite of government control, had the personal monogram of Miles Cary. The community built the schools—teachers and students making the adobe bricks together, fathers building chairs for their children to sit on. Like McKinley in Hawaii, Poston was a center for the unempowered in society. Democracy took on meaning as individuals took charge of the limited freedoms they were given.

Poston named its high school Miles Cary High School.[84] Students from McKinley in Hawaii collected over $500 for recreational supplies for Poston's schools. Poston students wrote:

> Words can hardly express the gratitude that we feel for the gift you kindly sent us. We realize now that it is wartime, you have made great sacrifices to send us this huge sum of money. With a lack of funds we were unable to get athletic equipment. In many cases when we wanted to play, there was a bat but no ball or vice versa. The $500 you have sent will enable us to buy many of the things we need. We can assure you that our lives will be made more pleasant by this.
>
> It certainly makes us happy to think that we do have friends so far away in Hawaii. Knowing this, we believe that we are much closer to you. May it stay this way for we are both Americans and stand for the same cause and purpose.[85]

In 1945 the final edition of the *Poston Poetry Club* was published, an illustrated book written entirely in Japanese until the last edition, when reflections of some administrators were included. The editor wrote, "the only absolute thing is the constant struggle for survival." The chief nurse at Poston said: "As there cannot be freedom, so in turn there cannot be well-rounded life based on the individual's own efforts to sustain himself as he chooses and there cannot be completely healthy existence under such circumstances."[86]

Cary stayed at Poston only one year. He returned to McKinley briefly, and by 1947 left to teach at the University of Minnesota. (He had earned a Ph.D. at Ohio State under Boyd Bode in the late 1930s.)

The last years of Cary's life were a dim reflection of what had been an outstanding career in Hawaii. He left Minnesota in 1951 to direct the Ethical Culture School in New York, but after a nationwide search resulting in his employment, the Ethical Culture School failed to renew his contract. What appears to have been a mutual disappointment for both parties left Cary bitter.

After two years at the University of Tennessee, Cary spent his final years in the Education Department at the University of Virginia. To be able to share the land that Thomas Jefferson had walked before him, and to be part of an institution founded on democratic principles was an appropriate closing for the life of Miles Cary, whose commitment to democracy was demonstrated in the school culture of McKinley High School. He had developed a community at McKinley that, in some respects at least, might serve as a model for the reform and restructuring of school systems today. His nonauthoritarian leadership empowered the entire school community.

From October 1948 to May 1949, Cary wrote a monthly editorial in *Educational Leadership*. The democratic theory surrounding his educational ideals began to surface into a philosophy aimed toward a world culture—a culture that began with the school and, more specifically, with the role of the teacher. Cary developed a cultural democracy—not a plea for separating groups of people, but a legal right of each individual to be different while at the same time a responsible member of a larger, dominant society. This was achieved by a process of building habits that made students productive community members. Cultural democracy provided completely different, yet equally legitimate, ways of choosing, making judgments, and prizing things. In an expanding global society, different cultures and ethnic groups lived beside one another with respect and understanding of differences. Cary successfully contributed to cultural democracy at McKinley, and saw education playing a key role in contributing to the world culture.

The Poston senior class of 1944 dedicated their yearbook to him:

> We, the senior class of 1944, pay homage to a great man, great not in the sense of riches nor of power, but great in his understanding of the need of humanity for people like himself in times of strife like these.

An unselfish, self-sacrificing person, he left his beautiful island of paradise, Hawaii, to come to Poston in the hope that he might help us, lead us, encourage us, in building a school of which we might be truly proud.

And so today because of his overflowing kindness as well as because of his guidance, we have an oasis of good fellowship which will live in our hearts forever.

SUMMARY

There have been many critics of education: we have discussed only a few. Each added to the emerging knowledge base of educational theory and practice, and each had at least a partial antidote to the ills of large, urban, bureaucratized systems of education.

Maria Montessori understood the value of removing the teacher from the place of central focus to allow greater autonomy for children as self-directing learners. Margaret Naumburg understood that teachers can unconsciously project their own unresolved inner struggles into their classrooms, that group pressure can hinder individual development, and that overemphasis on intellectual and vocational skills can abridge emotional growth. John B. Watson joined Montessori in stressing the need for schools to pay careful attention to the learning environment. Jacques Maritain offered a corrective for the overemphasis on positivistic sciences prevalent in twentieth-century mainstream schooling. He also reminded educators that education has a spiritual dimension often ignored in schools. W. E. B. DuBois brought the racism in American society into plain view and challenged all Americans—and especially those of African descent—to find solutions. George S. Counts reminded everyone that schooling is not neutral and that it can either make social problems worse or help solve them. Miles Cary saw the need for multicultural tolerance and cultural pluralism.

Many other critics could be cited. Education in most countries, including the United States, has come under scrutiny in recent years. Issues of gender, social class, and ethnic equity are worldwide. Curricular, methodological, organizational, and economic questions engage the attention of citizens, educators, and politicians in many countries. As George Counts noted, education and society are in constant evolution, so the job of sorting out educational issues is never finished: today's solutions are the basis of tomorrow's problems. There will always be a need for educational critics.

NOTES

1. William Boyd, *From Locke to Montessori* (London: George G. Harrap, 1914), 8.

2. Boyd, *From Locke to Montessori*, 88, 91; E. M. Standing, *Maria Montessori: Her Life and Work* (New York: New American Library, 1962), 32.

3. Standing, *Maria Montessori*, 30.

4. Anna M. Maccheroni, *A True Romance: Maria Montessori as I Knew Her* (Edinburgh, Scotland: Darien Press, 1947), 1.

5. Standing, *Maria Montessori*, 39.

6. Maccheroni, *A True Romance*, 42.

7. Rita Kramer, *Maria Montessori: A Biography* (New York: G. P. Putnam's Sons, 1976), citing an interview with Mario, accepts his version although she provides more conflicting than corroborating evidence. See, for example, pages 92–94, 184–185, and 368–389.

8. Paula Polk Lilliard, *Montessori: A Modern Approach* (New York: Schocken Books, 1972), xiii.

9. Standing, *Maria Montessori*, 184. Parkhurst went on to Columbia University where she developed her own "Dalton Plan" for secondary education.

10. Standing, *Maria Montessori*, 110.

11. Standing, *Maria Montessori*, 112.

12. Standing, *Maria Montessori*, 113.

13. Standing, *Maria Montessori*, 114.

14. Standing, *Maria Montessori*, 119–120.

15. Standing, *Maria Montessori*, 123–124, 126.

16. Standing, *Maria Montessori*, 173, 118.

17. John Broadus Watson, "Autobiography," in *A History of Psychology in Autobiography*, ed. Carl Murchison (New York: Russell and Russell, [1936] 1961) 3: 271.

18. Watson, "Autobiography," 271–272. For more details on Watson's education, see Kerry Buckley, *Mechanical Man: John Broadus Watson and the Beginning of Behaviorism* (New York: The Guilford Press, 1989).

19. Watson, "Autobiography," 274.

20. Watson, "Autobiography," 280.

21. John Chynoweth Burnham, "Psychiatry, Psychology and the Progressive Movement," *American Quarterly* 12 (Winter 1960): 459–463.

22. Naumburg, *The Child and the World: Dialogues in Modern Education* (New York: Harcourt, Brace, 1928), 115. For a more detailed treatment of Naumburg, see Dalton B. Curtis, Jr., "Psychoanalysis and Progressive Education: Margaret Naumburg at the Walden School," *Vitae Scholasticae* 2 (Fall 1983): 339–361.

23. Margaret Naumburg, "A Pageant with a Purpose," *Outlook,* 23 June 1915, 421–422.

24. Naumburg, "A Pageant," 422.

25. Margaret Naumburg, "The Walden School," *The Foundations and Technique of Curriculum-Construction,* the *Twenty-Sixth Yearbook of the National Society for the Study of Education,* part 1 (Bloomington, IL: Public School Publishing, 1926), 333.

26. Naumburg, *The Child and the World,* 4.

27. Naumburg, *The Child and the World,* 17–18.

28. Naumburg, *The Child and the World,* 118.

29. Quoted in Charles A. Fecher, *The Philosophy of Jacques Maritain* (Westminster, MD: Newman Press, 1953), 32–33.

30. Quoted in John M. Dunway, *Jacques Maritain* (Boston: Twayne, 1978), 18.

31. The two previous popes, Pius X and Benedict XV, had been concerned about Action Française. Benedict wrote an unpublished critique of Charles

Maurras's works, but neither pontiff acted to separate the Church from the organization. See Julie Kernan, *Our Friend, Jacques Maritain: A Personal Memoir* (Garden City, NY: Doubleday, 1975), 70–77.

32. Jacques Maritain, *Education at the Crossroads* (New Haven: Yale University Press, 1943), 1.

33. Maritain's counterpart in Paris was Archbishop Angelo Roncalli, the future Pope John XXIII. An associate in Rome was the Vatican Secretary of State, Monsignor Giovanni Battista Montini, the future Pope Paul VI, who later referred to Maritain as his teacher. Kernan, *Our Friend, Jacques Maritain,* 138–146.

34. For accounts of DuBois's character and personality, see August Meier, *Negro Thought in America, 1880–1915: Racial Ideologies in the Age of Booker T. Washington* (Ann Arbor: University of Michigan Press, 1963), and August Meier, "The Paradox of W. E. B. DuBois," in *W. E. B. DuBois, A Profile,* ed. Rayford W. Logan (New York: Hill and Wang, 1971), 64–85. For biographical accounts, see Jack B. Moore, *W. E. B. DuBois* (Boston: Twayne, 1981), quoted from 11; Francis L. Broderick, *W. E. B. DuBois: Negro Leader in a Time of Crisis* (Stanford: Stanford University Press, 1959); and W. E. B. DuBois, *The Autobiography of W. E. B. DuBois* (International Publishers, 1968).

35. DuBois, *The Autobiography,* 61.

36. DuBois, *The Autobiography,* 65. James either "took a slave as a concubine, or married a free Negro woman."

37. DuBois, *The Autobiography,* 72–75. Will was Mary's second son. The first was fathered by a cousin out of wedlock. There are discrepancies about how and when Alfred left. DuBois said it was shortly after his birth that Alfred settled in Connecticut near Great Barrington. See also Moore, *W. E. B. DuBois,* chap. 1.

38. DuBois, *The Autobiography,* 280.

39. Broderick, *W. E. B. DuBois,* 10.

40. Broderick, *W. E. B. DuBois,* 13, 17. As an undergraduate at Harvard, he got nine A's, three B's, and one C (in English composition). His thesis was published in 1896.

41. DuBois, *Autobiography,* 161. Will said that Dora wanted to marry him, but that he did not think it would be fair to her to do so. See also Broderick, *W. E. B. DuBois,* 26.

42. DuBois, *Autobiography,* 54, 46.

43. DuBois, *Autobiography,* 55.

44. DuBois, *Autobiography,* chaps. 3, 4.

45. DuBois, *Autobiography,* 45.

46. DuBois, *Autobiography,* 216.

47. DuBois, *Autobiography,* 190; Moore, *W. E. B. DuBois,* 17.

48. George Counts, *The Selective Character of American Secondary Education* (Chicago: University of Chicago Press, 1922), 140–143; George Counts, *The Senior High School Curriculum* (Chicago: University of Chicago Press, 1926); George Counts, *The Social Composition of Boards of Education* (Chicago: University of Chicago Press, 1927), 83; George Counts, *Secondary Education and Industrialism* (Cambridge: Harvard University Press, 1929).

49. George Counts, *The American Road to Culture: A Social Interpretation of Education in the United States* (New York: John Day, 1930), 184.

50. George Counts, *The Soviet Challenge to America* (New York: John Day, 1931), ix.

51. George Counts, *Dare the School Build a New Social Order?* (Carbondale: Southern Illinois University Press, 1978).

52. George Counts, *The Prospects of American Democracy* (New York: John Day, 1938), 37–38.

53. Miles E. Cary, "Integration and High School Curriculum," Ph.D. diss., Ohio State University, 1937), 230.

54. *Daily Pinion,* October 17, 1940, 1.

55. Mary E. Morris, "Development of Secondary Education in Hawaii," (Master's thesis, University of Hawaii, 1929), 23; Lawrence H. Fuchs, *Hawaii Pono* (New York: Harcourt, Brace & World, 1961), 282.

56. "McKinley High Starts Year as One of the Best Equipped in the World," *Honolulu Advertiser,* September 2, 1924, 1.

57. Fuchs, *Hawaii Pono,* 279.

58. Counts, *The Senior High School Curriculum,* as quoted in Cary "A Vitalized Curriculum for McKinley High School" (Master's thesis, University of Hawaii, 1930), 31.

59. Cary, "A Vitalized Curriculum," 162.

60. Cary, "A Vitalized Curriculum," 129.

61. Fuchs, *Hawaii Pono,* 263.

62. Statement by Robert H. Beck in interview with Shirley Williams, October 26, 1989. Beck and Cary were colleagues in the Education Department at the University of Minnesota from 1948 to 1951.

63. Frederick E. Bolton and Miles E. Cary, "Going to School in Hawaii," *Nations Schools* 8 (October 1931): 48.

64. E. V. Sayers, "Some Beliefs Underlying the Activity Program," *Hawaii Educational Review* 18, 5 (1930): 115 quoted in Cary, "A Vitalized Curriculum," 155.

65. Sayers, "Some Beliefs," quoted in Cary, "A Vitalized Curriculum."

66. Miles E. Cary, "Education in Hawaii," *Progressive Education* 24 (April 1947): 218.

67. Miles E. Cary, "Intergroup and Interracial Education," *Bulletin of the National Association of Secondary-School Principals* 32 (March 1948): 43.

68. Bolton and Cary, "Going to School," 47–48.

69. Miles E. Cary, "The Ethical Culture Schools: A Unique Type of Independent School," Unpublished manuscript, December 19, 1952, 2. Archives, New York Ethical Culture/Fieldston Schools, New York City, 1.

70. Cary, "Educating for Democratic Living," *Hawaii Educational Review* 26, 10 (June 1938): 293–295, 313–315.

71. Bolton and Cary, "Going to School," 44.

72. Bolton and Cary, "Going to School," 46.

73. Thomas James, *Exile Within* (Massachusetts: Harvard University Press, 1987), 3.

74. Immigrant Commission, *The Children of Immigrants in Schools,* vol. 5, 61st Congress, 3rd Session, Senate Document No. 749 (Washington, U.S. Government Printing Office, 1911), 153, in James, *Exile Within,* 10.

75. James, *Exile Within,* 43.

76. Manning, 372.

77. James, *Exile Within,* 44.

78. Gertrude Silva, "A School Teacher Observes the Nisei," *California Journal of Secondary Education* 18 (December 1943): 487.

79. Thomas James, *Exile Within,* 50.

80. Manning, 373.

81. Silva, "A School Teacher Observes," 487.

82. James, *Exile Within,* 168.

83. James, *Exile Within,* 168.

84. Edith Derrick, "Effects of Evacuation on Japanese-American Youth," *School Review* 55 (January-December 1947): 357.

85. *Daily Pinion,* March 16, 1943, 2.

86. The Poston Poetry Club publication, Poston Relocation Center, 1945 Japanese American Research Project (JARP) Collection, University Research Library, University of California at Los Angeles, Box 342, Folder 7.

The Paradigm Shifters

European and American educators have generally interpreted their occupational past as an outgrowth of the Enlightenment. From this perspective,
the history of education is a story of moving from ignorance toward rational
and humane practice. Comenius, Rousseau, Locke, Pestalozzi, Mann,
Dewey, and Montessori are noteworthy because they "advanced" the
cause of education. The task of contemporary educators is to build on their
legacy—to nudge educational practice ever closer to perfection. Using this
way of thinking, the social sciences, including education, are moving like
the "hard" sciences, only more falteringly, toward accurate knowledge of
how things really are. Progress is the expected norm: just as next year's
refrigerators, automobiles, and computers are expected to be better than
last year's, so should educational arrangements improve as well.

Not everyone agrees with this optimistic world view. In the nineteenth
century, German philosopher Friedrich Nietzsche (1844–1900) rejected
both human rationality and "progress." And as the twentieth century
wanes, historians, social scientists, philosophers, and other analysts have
questioned both the idea of epistemological (knowledge) progress and of
social/historical improvement. They have rejected "the belief that science
progresses, that knowledge grows in a cumulative fashion and, in short,
that we know better than our predecessors did, even to the point of
understanding them better than they understood themselves. Whereas
[Immanuel] Kant sees his Copernican Revolution as being of a piece with
the cumulative growth of knowledge, the new historicists see philosophical
revolutions as producing not necessarily better forms of knowledge, only
different ones."[1]

No single label covers all those who dissent from a progressive view of historical development. "Post-modernists," "deconstructionists," and "post-structuralists" are among the terms for important segments of this multifaceted tradition. This chapter discusses only a few of these ways of viewing the world. All have profound implications for education generally and schooling specifically.

Thomas S. Kuhn (b. 1922)

One of the English documents currently influencing the way people view their past and present appeared in 1962. With the unlikely title *The Structure of Scientific Revolutions,* this book is now a classic. It popularized the use of *paradigm,* a word that has become part of every-day language for many college-educated people. The author was a forty-year-old professor whose interests had shifted from physics to the history and philosophy of science. His insights into the patterns of scientific discovery have implications for how everyone learns, as well as for how we do research in education.

Thomas was born in Cincinnati on July 18, 1922. At Harvard University, he specialized in physics, receiving a bachelor's degree in 1943, a master's in 1946, and a doctorate in 1949. His education prepared him for a traditional career as a physicist. But during his doctoral studies, Kuhn had an experience that took his reflection and research in a different direction. He was teaching science to undergraduate humanities majors. While searching for a case history to illustrate the bases of Newton's mechanics, he looked at Aristotle's *Physics.* He began to wonder how such a brilliant observer and analyst could have created a physics that was so completely wrong.

Staring out the window of his dormitory room, Kuhn realized that Aristotle's views of such basic ideas as matter and motion were utterly unlike those of Newton. For Aristotle, *motion* meant any sort of physical change (change in the sun's color, for example) as well as change in position. Newton and those who followed him defined motion only as change in position. As a result, Kuhn saw that Aristotle wasn't wrong; he had simply had a different conceptualization of the natural happenings of the universe. Aristotle had viewed the physical world through a different set of glasses than those worn by Newton. This insight allowed Kuhn to fully understand Aristotle for the first time and suggested to him that each person's life, thought, and work must be understood within the context of the fundamental assumptions from which she or he operates.

Kuhn finished his doctorate in physics, but his interest had already shifted to the history and philosophy of science. He remained at Harvard teaching history of science until 1956. During this time, he wrote *The Copernican Revolution: Planetary Astronomy in the Development of West-*

ern Thought (1957). From Harvard, he moved to the University of California at Berkeley, where he remained until 1964. There he finished writing the work for which he has become most famous.

Kuhn's subsequent career has been that of a distinguished academic. From 1964 to 1979, he was professor of history of science at Princeton University. He also served as a fellow of the Institute for Advanced Study at Princeton (1972–1979). During this time, he published *Black Body Theory and the Quantum Discontinuity, 1894–1912* (1974) and *The Essential Tension* (1977). In the early 1980s, he was a member of the National Science Academy and the National Research Council. He received many awards and two honorary doctorates. In 1993, he was Laurance S. Rockefeller Professor of Philosophy at the Massachusetts Institute of Technology.

Kuhn's major intellectual insight has had to do with the notion of paradigm. Kuhn uses the term in two related ways: "On the one hand, it stands for the entire constellation of beliefs, values, techniques and so on shared by members of a given community. On the other hand, it denotes one sort of element in that constellation, the concrete puzzle-solutions which, employed as models or examples, can replace explicit rules as a basis for the solution of remaining puzzles of normal science."[2] An example of the first use is all the attitudes, values, and beliefs that scientists hold in common. An example of the second is the particular construct(s) that lead physicists to believe in a partial law.

Kuhn's insight about Aristotle and Newton was that the two thinkers were not operating in a common paradigm. It was not that one was more astute or more logical than the other. Further, Kuhn's analysis of the history of science convinced him that no universal criteria exist by which paradigms can be compared. Each must be understood in its own context.

According to Kuhn, all knowledge is ultimately social and is paradigm-dependent; it is based on concepts and cast in language made possible by the paradigm, and much of the paradigm is inherited. A main job of formal education—whether kindergarten or doctoral seminar—is to enculturate members into those aspects of the paradigm appropriate to their level and type of schooling. The paradigm not only shapes the language and logic of explanation, it also determines which phenomena or potential experiences become part of the knowledge base.

Far from Locke's notion that experience with the physical world translates directly into ideas, Kuhn believes that sense perception is not an experience until it is filtered through our paradigms. It is difficult to experience something meaningfully for which one has no category of existence.

Every paradigm asks some questions but not others. Some issues are not interesting within a given paradigm; some are not possible. And of those questions that are askable, a particular paradigm answers some better than others. The failure of a paradigm to satisfactorily deal with one or even many issues, however, does not automatically lead to its abandonment. But when a sense of crisis strikes a significant number of those directly concerned over a paradigm's failure to provide appealing solutions, competing alternatives surface. After a period of struggle between interested factions, a new paradigm emerges and relegates its predecessor to the history books as a quaint notion that people once mistakenly believed.

In the early stages of a new paradigm, exciting discoveries often appear. "Led by a new paradigm, scientists adopt new instruments and look in new places. Even more important, during revolutions scientists see new and different things when looking with familiar instruments in places they have looked before."[3]

Kuhn's assertion that propositions are true or false only with a given paradigm challenged the Enlightenment claim of the accumulation of knowledge through individual reason and experience. "We are now on our way to discarding this intolerably narrow view," wrote Barry Barnes in a commentary on Kuhn. "We need to understand ourselves not simply as organisms but as communities," he continued. "This is because knowledge is . . . a collective creation, founded not upon isolated individual judgments, but upon the evaluations we make together in social situations. . . . Even scientific influences must be seen as instances of customary behavior, and not treated purely as manifestations of the universal reason of the individual."[4]

Howard E. Gardner (b. 1943)

Many physicists, biologists, and chemists rejected Kuhn's analysis. Educators and other social scientists have accepted his insight more readily than have natural scientists. A social scientist who questioned customary beliefs was Harvard cognitive scientist Howard Earl Gardner. In 1983, at age forty, he published *Frames of Mind,* espousing a theory of human intellect that directly challenged the traditional view of intelligence. He postulated that *intellect* consists of several relatively independent intelligences, not one general ability. Educators, under criticism for press reports of school failure, found in his work the possibilities for a new, more inclusive paradigm about what constitutes "intelligent" behavior. The path that brought Gardner to his theory had several turns and twists.

Gardner's parents emigrated from Nürnberg, Germany in 1938, narrowly escaping the Holocaust. They settled in Scranton, Pennsylvania with relatives who had also fled Nazi Germany and with their three-year-old son Eric. Eric adapted quickly to American culture, skipping first grade. A freak sleighing accident claimed his life at age eight when his mother was pregnant with Howard. Although they kept pictures of Eric in the house, Howard's parents said nothing about Eric. Howie, as he was called, was ten when he began to learn about his brother and in his teens when he read newspaper accounts of the tragedy.[5]

As his own identity formed, Howard became preoccupied with his family's secret background, especially the escape from Germany and his brother's death. Uncovering his family's Jewish identity was a shock. He was aware of being "different," both from parents who had been socially prominent under the Weimar Republic and from peers who seemed entrenched in American culture. He wondered what life might have been like for him as part of a European culture that honored and produced German/Jewish luminaries such as Freud, Marx, Einstein, and Mahler. Even in the impoverished Pennsylvania valley where he grew up, he was aware that, as the eldest son of this extended family, he was expected to attain success in their adopted country.

As a boy Howard's successes centered around his piano-playing ability. When he was twelve, his teacher told him that he should increase his daily practicing from one hour to three. Had there been more creativity and less drill in his piano study, musical composition might have been his forte. But that was not the case, and he renounced the piano as the way to bring himself and his family honor.

Young Howie had taught himself to read before he started school, and he became an avid reader of anything he could find. He also began producing his own newspaper—an activity that he loved, but that went unnoticed by even his parents. He decided that he liked language even more than music. In addition, Howard became an Eagle Scout, a local radio performer judging weekly record releases, and a regular attendee of Sunday and Hebrew schools, "being both 'bar mitzvah-ed' and confirmed."[6] He was color-blind, had such poor eyesight that he could hardly see people's faces well enough to remember them, and was not large or especially agile.

Education and Professional Development

Young Gardner's parents wanted him to attend Phillips Academy, a famous prep school in Andover, Massachusetts, but he refused. They settled on Wyoming Seminary, a small prep school located in the nearby town of Kingston, Pennsylvania. Howard excelled at "Sem." He also developed socially and professionally, becoming a clique leader and coediting the school newspaper/magazine. He read a story about the cultural pluralism that existed at Harvard in the 1940s and decided that he would be at home there, matriculating in the fall of 1961.

His tutor was Eric Erikson, a famous psychologist. Although he did not take a formal course from Erikson until his junior year, Howard soon discovered that he was interested in the psychological facets of history and biography. He turned away from law and medicine toward the social sciences with a senior thesis on a new California retirement community. He graduated *summa cum laude* in 1965.

After graduation, Gardner worked briefly with Jerome Bruner on his

"Man: A Course of Study" (MACOS) project before accepting a Knox Fellowship to study abroad. He read the works of the French anthropologist Claude Levi-Strauss and the Swiss cognitive psychologist Jean Piaget and met both of them during his year in Europe. In fall 1966, Gardner entered Harvard's doctoral program in developmental psychology, and the following year became part of the Project Zero research team on arts education, headed by philosopher Nelson Goodman. He served as unpaid assistant, then paid graduate assistant, doctoral research associate, and from 1972 to the present, codirector with David Perkins. Project Zero has been the incubator for many of his ideas on intelligence.

Gardner finished his Ph.D. in 1971 with a dissertation on style sensitivity in children. At Harvard, in addition to Project Zero, he has been lecturer (1971–1986) and professor (since 1986) in education and affiliated professor of psychology (since 1987). He also served as professor (1984–1987) and adjunct professor (since 1987) of neurology at Boston University's School of Medicine.

Gardner's first book, *The Shattered Mind,* appeared in 1975, followed by *Art, Mind and Brain* in 1982, *Frames of Mind* in 1983, *The Mind's New Science* in 1985, *To Open Minds* in 1989, *The Unschooled Mind* in 1991, and *Multiple Intelligences: The Theory in Practice* in 1993. During this period, he was married twice. He has three children from the first marriage and an adopted Chinese son from the second.

The Theory of Multiple Intelligences

Gardner's work challenges two central principles in psychology. First, it contradicts the cognitive developmental work of Piaget, who described a series of cognitive stages that characterize changes in intellectual growth as a person matures into adolescence. Gardner assembled data that countered the Piagetian view that "all knowledge at a certain stage of development hangs together in a 'structured whole.'" He discovered that a child can be at different developmental stages in number development and spatial/visual maturation. (His own language/verbal skills had been more advanced than his spatial growth, which progressed poorly and continued to cause him difficulty remembering people's faces.) Piaget described children developing into empirical scientists; Gardner began to see them as miniature artists "who may someday participate in the artistic process."[7]

The second dominant belief in psychology that Gardner's research calls into question is that intelligence is the result of a single general factor (*g* in psychological literature) reflected by IQ (intelligence quotient) tests. This insight came through his work with right-hemisphere-damaged patients, who had difficulty telling jokes and stories and appreciating music and drawings even though their language and reasoning powers were unimpaired. He tentatively concluded that multiple intelligence "faculties" or "kinds of minds" might exist and that these varied capacities were not particularly related to one another. He also looked for evidence in

other places. He read descriptions of the intellectual capacities of autis-
tics, idiot savants, and learning-disabled persons. He studied anthropo-
logical reports of people and practices in other cultures. If a particular
ability appeared in several types of data, Gardner defined it as a type of
intelligence. To date Gardner has described seven types of intelligences or
"frames of mind": linguistic, musical, logical/mathematical, spatial,
bodily/kinesthetic, intrapersonal, and interpersonal.

   Linguistic intelligence (commonly called *verbal ability*) consists of the
capacity to speak skillfully, to comprehend oral material, and to understand metaphoric language. Poets and other literary figures are the
geniuses of this intelligence. *Musical* intelligence, often one of the earliest to emerge, depends on ability to decode tonal patterns. Children with
this special ability may be able to play Bach with feeling and technical
skill; they may have composed and played a simple piece, or they may
have the artistic talent to perform an operatic aria after hearing it once.
Logical/mathematical intelligence (or lack thereof) can be seen as children learn arithmetic, algebra, and symbolic logic. Theoretical mathematicians and high energy physicists are among those deserving the
label of genius. *Spatial* intelligence includes finding hidden figures in
diagrams or pictures or mentally rotating figures in space to identify or
describe them. Architects have talent in spatial relations. *Bodily/
kinesthetic* intelligence is characterized by a good sense of timing, balance, direction, and pattern sequence. Dancers and athletes are the
geniuses. *Intrapersonal* intelligence involves knowledge of one's own
feelings and other personal internal realities. Indian fakirs with unusual control of their bodily functions are exemplars. *Interpersonal* intelligence (also known as social intelligence) can be seen in one's ability to
understand and operate effectively in complex social environments.[8]

   Gardner's work is revolutionary not because of the specific number of
intelligences he identifies or because of the particular names he assigns.
It alters the old paradigm because it turns *intelligence* into a label for
describing socially valued human behaviors and characteristics rather
than a preoccupation with finding and describing a fixed, unitary phenomenon of nature. Thus, whatever has its meaning because of social
agreement can be changed by a new agreement. To take multiple intelligences seriously is to abandon twentieth-century IQ and achievement
tests. It is to celebrate bodily/kinesthetic or musical talents as gifts of
intelligence instead of entertainment commodities to be exploited.
Schools as "instances of customary behavior," to borrow Kuhn's phrase,
will change dramatically if Gardner's formulations undergird a new paradigm of reform.[9]

   In addition to IQ as an expression of general intelligence, another
instance of "customary behavior" widely rationalized as a manifestation
of universal reason was a phenomenon that has come to be labeled in
English as "colonialism." Any time people interact with each other, the
practical question arises of whether the interchange will be on equal

terms or whether some people will overpower others. The phenomenon of domination finds classic expression in nation-states or empires ruling subject peoples: The Romans over the Greeks; the German tribes over the Romans; Europeans over Native Americans; the United States over Alaskan, Hawaiian, and Puerto Rican inhabitants; or the French over the Algerians and Vietnamese. Some commentators have suggested that the label *colonialism* is appropriate even within national groups whenever some people dominate others because they have the power to do so. In this case parents who coerce their children, teachers who overpower their pupils, or men who use inherited economic power over women can be described as colonial masters.[10]

Frantz Fanon (1925–1961)

One of the people who critiqued the paradigm of colonialism most forcefully was an Algerian psychiatrist named Frantz Fanon. He wrote not only about what domination does to the colonized, but also commented extensively on its destructive effects on the colonizer.

One biographer has described Frantz Fanon's life as "hectic, violent, and very short." The same author wrote: "He worked seventeen hours a day, had an astounding memory, a cutting sense of humor, an unusual stage presence." He was also "very attractive and an extremely good athlete. Women were attracted to him in unusual numbers."[11]

Frantz was born on the island of Martinique in a family that copied, to the extent they could afford to, the upper middle class life-style of the white governing class. The Fanons lived in a large apartment on a fashionable street of the capital of Fort-de-France. His mother worked as a shopkeeper to supplement the family income so they could have a cook and meat on weekends. Frantz had four sisters and three brothers. He described his mother as domineering but thought that she took pride in his accomplishments.[12] His father spent little time with the family because of the demands of his work as a government official.

All the Fanon children attended free elementary schools and then a local fee-charging college preparatory secondary school (lycée). From 1939 to 1943, Frantz continued his studies at the all-black lycée. He and his brothers and sisters went to movies a few times each year, an extravagance few native families could afford.

Frantz traveled to France for medical training. He then practiced general medicine in Martinique while working on his psychiatric specialty. All this time his education had led him to want to be a white Frenchman. While in Paris, he met Josie Duble, a white woman who would eventually become his wife. Together they had one child, a son named Olivier. During World War II, Fanon was twice wounded while serving in the French Army. At the same time, he began to be politicized about power and domination issues as he watched white French soldiers brutalize black Martinicans, often beating (with police indulgence) the men and raping the women.

After completing medical training, Fanon began as a psychiatrist at the French military hospital in Blida, Algeria. Algeria had been a French colony for more than a century. An underground resistance, the Front de Liberation Nationale (FLN), had developed, and French military officials routinely tortured Algerians to get information they might be able to use in combating the movement. Fanon had to deal with the personality malfunctions of both the victims and the administrators of the torture. The latter group included officers who could not sleep because of screaming hallucinations brought on by years of doling out painful torture and of killing people, many of whom had no connection with the FLN.

Fanon's experiences at Blida had a profound impact on him. He came to believe that violence inevitably produces violent reactions. Those who receive the violent treatment either subject themselves to further violence (suicide, as an extreme example), externalize their own violence to other members of the powerless group (burning and looting their own communities in extreme cases), or direct violence back against their torturers. Of these three forms of violent expression, often present simultaneously, Fanon recognized only the third as psychologically and morally productive.

Fanon's Martinican background, as well as his personal experiences as a black man, took him beyond sympathy for the colonized to complete identification with the struggle for Algerian independence. For a time, he maintained his position as a psychiatrist while covertly helping the independence movement. Finally, the internal discrepancy of restoring "disturbed patients to a rational position within a society that was itself irrational" was too much. In 1956 he turned his back on the racially integrated life he had experienced in Paris and left government employ to work full time for the FLN. Until his death five years later, he was a leading spokesman and publicist for the FLN and represented the movement at many international conferences.[13]

As a partisan in the Algerian struggle for independence, Fanon continued to write about the undesirable consequences of the colonial paradigm. In his lifetime, he wrote three plays, fifteen psychiatric research reports, and four books that analyzed the psychological and material costs of colonization—of dominant/subordinate relationships—in the world. His books were *Black Skin, White Masks, A Dying Colonialism, Toward the African Revolution,* and *The Wretched of the Earth.* The later writings were much more sharply focused analyses of colonialism than were the earlier ones.

Fanon described the colonization process as consisting of several stages and elements. The colonizers (*settlers* in Fanon's terms) view themselves as socially, economically, politically, and morally superior. They come to help the unfortunate people of an underdeveloped nation, but end up maintaining their position by military force. Not content to rule and exploit, the colonizer inevitably seeks justification and consolidates power by erasing the native's history. "The settler makes history and is conscious of making it. And because he constantly refers to the history of his mother country, he clearly indicates that he himself is the extension of that mother country. Thus the history which he writes is not the history of the country which he plunders but the history of his own nation in regard to all that she skims off, all that she violates and starves."[14] Meanwhile, the colonized people's history is relegated to myth or obliteration.

Another step in colonization is to create a small, artificial, second-level aristocracy from among the natives. They become an intermediate force between the ruling elite and the mass of colonized natives. They receive schooling in the settler's culture—perhaps, as in Fanon's case, in the settler's home country—and they represent "making it." The mass of colonized people get enough formal schooling to teach them that their native culture and language are inferior to that of the colonizer, but not enough to compete successfully for jobs in the newly anointed official culture.

Inevitably, two societies coexist uneasily in such an arrangement. The minority of settlers live genteel lives in large houses in the most desirable, brightly lighted, and well-policed areas. The mass of peasant natives barely subsist in the countryside or live on top of one another in dangerous slums. "The settler's town is a well-fed town, an easygoing town; its belly is always full of good things. The settler's town is a town of white people, of foreigners. . . . The native town is a hungry town, starved of bread, of meat, of shoes, of coal, of light, . . . a crouching village, a town on its knees, a town wallowing in the mire. It is a town of niggers and dirty Arabs,"[15] Fanon wrote.

> In developed countries, the hegemony of school, church, and aesthetic expressions of respect for the established order serve to create around the exploited person an atmosphere of submission and of inhibition which lightens the task of policing considerably. In the capitalist [developed] countries a multitude of moral teachers, counselors, and "bewilderers" separate the exploited from those in power. In colonial countries, on the contrary, the policeman and the soldier . . . maintain contact with the native and advise him by means of rifle butts and napalm not to budge.[16]

Under these circumstances, Fanon pointed out that colonized people want not only to oust the colonizers but also to take their privileged place. This means violence, because the colonizers have maintained their own privilege through violence and by example have taught violence to the colonized. Fanon saw counterviolence to that used by the settlers as an inevitable ingredient in the process of securing independence. And he thought no person could be whole without also being independent.

People who succeed in throwing off the yoke of colonial rule normally spend some time intensely reclaiming their own identities. In the process, they exhibit enormous creative energies. "Having formerly emigrated from his culture, the native today explores it with ardor," Fanon wrote in 1956 with specific reference to the Black Power movement in the United States. "It is a continual honeymoon." This was a direct reaction against assimilationism or requiring all people to adopt the culture of a diverse society's most powerful group. "Assimilationism does not suppose any kind of reciprocity. There is always a culture which has to disappear to the profit of another culture."[17]

Fanon described the reclaiming of a colonized people's culture as a phase of decolonization and called for deliberate social planning to direct it. Opposing the tendency of some recently independent African countries to spend resources on Olympic athletes as a symbol of their new strength, Fanon called instead for all energy to be focused on internal development. "The youth of Africa ought not to be sent to sports stadiums but into the fields and into the schools," he wrote. The task was not to turn out skilled athletes, but rather "fully conscious" citizens. "The stadium ought not to be a showplace erected in the towns, but a bit of open ground in the midst of the fields that the young people must reclaim, cultivate, and give to the nation."[18]

At the age of thirty-six, Fanon contracted cancer. He continued his work with the FLN and rushed to finish *The Wretched of the Earth*. He died in Washington, D.C., where he had traveled for treatment of leukemia, but not before finishing a ringing call for a new paradigm that would abandon Europe as a primary reference—"this Europe where they are never done talking of Man, yet murder men everywhere they find them." Fanon called for a new history that would include all the people whose existence had seemed unimportant from a Eurocentric perspective. And he called for inventiveness: "For Europe, for ourselves, and for humanity," he concluded, "we must turn over a new leaf, we must work out new concepts, and try to set afoot a new man."[19]

Among the new men and women seeking to claim and form their identities in the 1950s were millions of United States citizens of African descent. Fanon specifically included African Americans in his analysis as among "third world" or colonized people. His written work directly informed the thought of several leaders of the civil rights movement in the United States. Eldridge Cleaver's "*Soul on Ice* might be described as Fanon coming home to roost," wrote one of Fanon's biographers. "*The Wretched of the Earth* marks, within the black civil rights movement, the change from passive resistance to active defense; Fanon's writings are of central importance to the Black Panthers, representatives of the changed politics of black America."[20] One of the most active and controversial figures of the U.S. civil rights movement influenced by Fanon was a contemporary born Malcolm Little; the world would come to known him as Malcolm X.

Malcolm X (1925–1965)

Malcolm was born in Omaha, Nebraska, on May 19, 1925, the fourth of eight children to Early and Louise Little. Early was a Baptist minister and leader in Marcus Garvey's "back to Africa" movement. Louise was born in 1897 in Grenada, British West Indies to a black mother and white father. Early met and married Louise in Philadelphia. The Littles had a conflict-filled marriage, further strained by a climate of racism, Klan harassment, and economic hardship. In 1925, Rev. Little and his wife moved to Omaha, where he became president of the Omaha division of Garvey's Universal Negro Improvement Association (UNIA).[21]

Louise Little played an instrumental role in the movement. She served as the branch reporter for the UNIA publication, the *Negro World*. Both parents authored dissident articles and suffered harassment because of their activism.[22] Malcolm recalled being told that once, while Rev. Little traveled through the area speaking in churches and private homes, Klansmen had threatened his pregnant mother.[23]

The family left Omaha for Milwaukee. After a brief stay there, they moved to Lansing, Michigan and finally settled in a predominantly black area of East Lansing. In Michigan, the Littles continued organizing. In 1931, suspected Klansmen killed Early Little. Louise was destitute at thirty-four with eight children. She was later hospitalized for a mental breakdown, and the children were separated and placed in foster homes.

Early Education

Through the seventh grade, Malcolm attended predominantly white schools in Lansing. After his father's death, a free-ranging life-style and petty thievery marked him as being beyond his mother's control. Malcolm was the first of the Little children to become a ward of the state. During his stay with his first foster family, he attended the junior high school in Lansing. He showed academic ability, but his continual defiance of authority led to placement in a detention home in Mason, Michigan.[24]

After a term of good behavior, Malcolm attended the local junior high school, where he became popular as a basketball player, class president, and academic achiever. He recalled most vividly, however, constantly being called "nigger." A racist high school teacher discouraged him from pursuing even the limited goals of the rural children of that place, and he left school at the end of eighth grade.[25]

City Life

At fifteen Malcolm went to Boston to live with his older sister, Ella. Seeking to be "hip" instead of an unsophisticated country boy, he carefully emulated the hair styles, clothing, and mannerisms of black youth in Boston's Roxbury. His occupations included those "Negro jobs" open to the masses of black males at the time: dishwasher, shoeshine boy, soda jerk, and railroad dining car attendant. He enjoyed dancing the lindy, attracting women, and mentoring other young black newcomers to the North.

At seventeen Malcolm moved to Harlem and became immersed in the marginal life of hustling. When he was twenty-one, he began serving a seven-year prison term for burglary. In prison, his drug addictions left him recalcitrant and in despair, but a fellow inmate, Bimbi, told him about educating himself to discipline and self-respect. Through his sister's efforts, Malcolm got a transfer to Norfolk, Massachusetts, where he gained access to an excellent prison library. He read Schopenhauer, Kant, Nietzsche, Spinoza, and other writers.[26] Jakob Grimm's philology of consonants in the *Loom of Language* also helped him form and articulate new concepts.[27]

Black Muslims

Elijah Muhammad founded the Nation of Islam (Black Muslims) in 1931 after Wallace Fard revealed to him "Yacub's History," a tale that described white people as the inferior result of the scientist Yacub's experimentation in eugenics on black people. Fard saw Elijah as Allah's messenger. Elijah's preaching described the white race in demonic terms and prophesied the glorious destiny of the black race.

Malcolm discovered the Nation of Islam through his brother, Philbert, a convert who urged him to learn of this "natural" religion for the black man. Malcolm was impressed with what he learned. He abstained from drugs and began following Black Muslim dietary restrictions. After corresponding with Elijah Muhammad, he became a member.[28]

At the time of Malcolm's conversion, the Black Muslims emphasized separatism and an ascetic life-style with extreme obedience to the leadership of Elijah Muhammad. Their goal of return to Africa was later transformed to a quest for a separate black nation in North America. They proselytized in prisons, on city street corners, and through their publication, *Muhammad Speaks*.

Following Black Muslim custom, Malcolm Little rejected his "slave name" and became Malcolm X. After his release from prison in 1952, he worked in Black Muslim temples. His talent for organization and devotion to Elijah Muhammad led in 1963 to his appointment as the first national minister of the Nation of Islam. Malcolm credited Muhammad with reaching "down into the mud" to save him from a criminal life,[29] although he would later call himself a "zombie" for his overveneration of Muhammad. Malcolm atttributed the phenomenal growth of the Black Muslim movement to his own talents, saying that he had taken an organization of four hundred and increased the membership to forty thousand.[30]

In 1964, Malcolm X and the Black Muslims gained credibility in the African American community for publicly opposing Los Angeles police brutality against Muslim ministers. Malcolm's skillful use of television advanced the Black Muslim message, but he got a public reprimand and a ninety-day gag order from Elijah Muhammad for characterizing President Kennedy's assassination as "chickens coming home to roost" in a violent society. Already a public figure because of interviews in the *Village Voice,* and appearances in many places, including talk shows to explain Black Muslim beliefs, Malcolm accepted the censure, though he felt deeply humiliated.

From April 13 to May 21, 1964, Malcolm traveled in Africa and the Middle East. During this trip, he made the hajj (pilgrimage) to Mecca and Medina. The pilgrimage earned him the title el-Hajj Malik el-Shabazz. His observations of race relations outside of the United States and first-hand encounter with Islamic religion led to a revelation:

> In the past I have permitted myself to be used in making sweeping indictments of all white people, and these generalizations have caused injuries to some white people who did not deserve them. . . . The spiritual rebirth which I was blessed to undergo as a result of a pilgrimage to Mecca . . . served to convince me that perhaps American whites can be cured of the rampant racism.[31]

Experiences on the trip abroad altered Malcolm's views of racism. In an interview printed in the *Young Socialist,* he attributed racism to "a skillfully designed program of miseducation that goes right along with the American system of exploitation and oppression."[32] While in Africa, he had talked to an American ambassador who admitted that his attitude toward nonwhites changed from casual acceptance to acute awareness of skin color when he returned to the United States. Malcolm attributed the attitude to institutional racism: "What you are telling me . . . is that it is not basic in you to be a racist, but that society there in America . . . makes you a racist."[33]

Malcolm X also began to alter his views regarding American black migration to Africa: "If we migrated back to Africa culturally, philosophically, and psychologically, while remaining here physically," he said, "the spiritual bond that would develop between us and Africa would enhance our position here because we would have our contacts with them acting as roots or foundations."[34] This insight led him to espouse an international view stressing human rights rather than civil rights, thus taking the issue of race out of the arena of U.S. constitutional law and placing it within an international context. No longer would black people need to appeal to the federal government for protection and rights. Instead, the United States could be labeled the aggressor against its black citizens and prosecuted before the World Court of the United Nations.

The Organization of Afro-American Unity

To implement his new ideology, Malcolm X founded the Organization of Afro-American Unity (OAAU), patterned on the Organization for African Unity. The OAAU affirmed the need for African Americans to unify across political differences, acknowledge common African roots, and encourage peace but seek security, if necessary, in armed self-defense. OAAU purposes included political organizing, self-knowledge acquisition, direct communication with Africans (without white intercession), and a "cultural revolution" in art, music, film, writing, and history.

Educational Purposes

"Education is an important element in the struggle for human rights," Malcolm wrote in the third article of the OAAU statement. "It is the means to help our children and people rediscover their identity and thereby increase self-respect."[35] The article described black children as criminally short-changed by public schools, charging principals and teachers with failure to understand black children and the curriculum with silence about black people's contributions to the country.

New York City had an integration plan that predicted 10 percent of schools in the Harlem and Bedford-Stuyvesant areas would not be improved. Malcolm proposed that the OAAU take over these schools, appoint black principals and teachers, and purchase textbooks written by black authors. He urged boycotts if OAAU ends were not met, and stressed the importance of parents in every phase of school life. He wanted African American parents to go into schools to advocate proper education or establish schools of their own. Malcolm also noted the need for adults to be retrained for technological jobs. The OAAU was to "use the tools of education to raise our people to unprecedented levels of excellence and self-respect through their own efforts."[36]

Malcolm's ideas regarding self-knowledge, self-sufficiency, and the liberating, character-forming nature of education for black people had been previously addressed by W. E. B. DuBois, D. O. W. Holmes, and others. He saw the need to influence the power structure of the school system by making teachers and administrators responsive to the needs of black children and their communities. He advocated gaining seats on school boards and other policy bodies to help accomplish this goal. Even his ideas of separate schooling involved preparing African Americans for mainstream technological and economic development. But formation of a black cadre of specialists to provide resources for the African American community and the pan-African world community extended his educational purposes beyond the limits of American integrationist goals and encouraged blacks to seek educational relevance outside of formal schooling and the confines of "official" society.

Break with Elijah Muhammad

Malcolm X formally left Elijah Muhammad and the Black Muslims in 1964, criticizing the leadership's extravagant life-styles and sexual exploits. After the separation, he experienced threats from many quarters. When his home was firebombed on February 14, 1965, he said: "All of us believed 100 percent in the divinity of Elijah Muhammad. . . . We actually believed that God, in Detroit by the way, that God had taught him and all of that. I always believed that he believed it himself. And I was shocked when I found out that he himself didn't believe it."[37] In this speech and others, Malcolm commended Black Muslims for contributions to the changing "psychology" of African Americans, but indicted the movement for failing to implement goals. His test for the relevance of black activism was whether the strategies involved "just talk" or accomplished some end. On February 21, 1965, his wife and daughters accompanied him to the Audubon Ballroom in Harlem where he was to speak. A group of African American men "believed to be sympathetic to Black Muslims" gunned him down.[38]

Significance

Malcolm presented most of his ideas in speeches and they are preserved in recordings and transcriptions. Initially, the major themes of his speeches involved the Black Muslim principles of male responsibility and the need to avoid drugs, alcohol, illicit sex, gambling, and criminal life. He emphasized the superiority of black over white. He ridiculed integration and emphasized economic self-sufficiency.

The change in ideology evident in the later speeches, especially his attitude toward white people, remains a subject of controversy. Integrationists, socialists, separatists, militants, and moderates all claim his words support their own ideologies. "What they do is chop Malcolm up," wrote George Breitman, "keeping the parts they like, the parts it suits their purposes to remember."[39]

Initially, critics of his militant and separatist arguments argued that Malcolm's life had been unimportant in education and politics. Recently, political writers have reassessed and rejected this analysis. Now he seems a significant figure who had a realistic view of U.S. racism and who predicted a rising tide of dissatisfaction among African Americans. In common with Fanon, whose life and work were in so many ways parallel, Malcolm embodied the existential tenet that existence precedes essence. Verbal declarations mattered less than specific actions. And his life was full of action that illustrated his tireless belief in trusting his own critique, even though it obviously did not agree with the dominant paradigm. Director Spike Lee's widely acclaimed 1992 film biography starring Denzel Washington heightened public consciousness of Malcolm's contributions to the ongoing critique of contemporary society and living conditions.

Paulo Freire (b. 1921)

A contemporary of Malcolm X and Fanon whose life has embodied the latter's prescription that the job of intellectuals is to educate and awaken their peoples' consciousness is a Brazilian named Paulo Freire.

One contemporary has called him a "post-modern and radical peda-
gogist."[40] He was born in Recife on September 19, 1921. His parents,
Joaquin Temistocles Freire and Edeltrudes Neves, lived in the north
section of Recife in the district of Estrada do Encaramento. Paulo was
the youngest among three boys and a girl.[41]

The family lived a comfortable middle class life until the Great Depression, when Paulo's father lost his job as a military officer. The family
moved to a smaller house in Jabotao in 1931. This marked the beginning
of a series of painful experiences. The move represented loss of prestige
for the family; they suffered further economic hardship, and for the first
time, Paulo experienced hunger. Even more painful was the death of his
father.[42]

Education

Freire later characterized his relationship with his parents as one of
"mutual respect, dialogue, [and] free choice." They taught him the
alphabet and gave him his first reading instruction. Throughout his
early years, Freire "enjoyed dialogue with his parents." Dialogue later
characterized his literacy program in Brazil.[43] "Whoever enters into
dialogue does so with someone about something; and that something
ought to constitute the new content of our proposed education," he later
wrote.[44]

Paulo had problems in elementary school. According to Colorado
State University professor William Timpson, Freire fell behind in his
schoolwork "because of the listlessness his hunger produced."[45]

Paulo was sixteen when he entered the *ginasio* (secondary school).
The difficulty of the required *examen de madureza* (entrance test) varied
inversely with the cost of attending school in preparation for it. Paulo's
family had no tuition money, so he attended a free state school. Despite
much anxiety on his part, he scored well enough for entry. He remembered the experience as difficult and disagreeable.

After completing the *ginasio,* Paulo taught Portuguese in a similar
secondary school in Recife. While teaching, he also studied law at the
University of Recife.[46] Though he ultimately graduated with a law degree, he never had much interest in practicing law. In fact, his first job
as an attorney was to collect money from a young dentist. He felt sorry
for the man, let him go without paying, and ended his legal career.

During this time, Freire married Elza Maria Costa de Oliveira, a
local school principal. They had five children. Freire said his family life
was a source of comfort, inspiration, and learning. He described his
marriage as a happy one; it lasted until Elza's death in 1989.

While Freire was studying law, he read political philosophy, new
Catholic theology, and social criticism. He found the writing of Jacques
Maritain (Chapter 11) especially cogent. He also participated in the
University Catholic Action group, an organization devoted to eliminat-
ing poverty and hunger in Northeastern Brazil. Except for a few months

of doubt at age nineteen, Freire has remained an activist Catholic. Throughout his life he has been committed to doing something for the "wretched on the earth."[47]

Through studying Portuguese in order to teach it, Freire came to see language as an expression of power. As he investigated syntax and linguistic codes and experimented with teaching Brazilian peasants to read and write, he concluded that illiteracy was something other than a deficiency in skills. Most literacy programs had drilled people in the rules of usage. This approach enjoyed limited success, not because peasants could not learn the rules but because to become literate was to become powerful. Brazilian peasants not only knew they weren't powerful; they believed that to become powerful would be an offense against nature.

Freire saw that for illiterate peasants to read and write Portuguese meant giving themselves permission to acquire the power implicit in such an act. To facilitate this happening meant making explicit and conscious what people unconsciously felt: that becoming literate was an act of taking control, of exercising power. Freire called this *conscientizaçao,* sometimes translated "conscientization" or "consciousness raising." But much more than increased awareness is implied. "Learning to perceive social, political, and economic contradictions and to take action against the oppressive elements of reality" is how one Freireian translator has defined it.[48] At the heart of conscientization is a personal ontological shift that claims the right to know and to express. It is what Freire called going from a "culture of silence" to finding one's voice.

Through experimentation, Freire and a few colleagues developed what they referred to as "circles of culture" aimed at producing literacy. Each circle consisted of approximately thirty *participants* and one *facilitator.* At the heart of the interaction was dialogue focused on "problematizing." "Paulo Freire's central message is that one can know only to the extent that one 'problematizes' the natural cultural and historical reality in which s/he is immersed. Problematizing is the antithesis of the technocrat's 'problem-solving' stance."[49]

Before beginning a culture circle, facilitators spent time listening and observing in their future participants' environment. The purpose was to find "generative words"; that is, words that generated animated discussion because they were emotionally charged and words that contained Portuguese phonemes (consonant-vowel combinations) so that participants could build (or recognize and pronounce) other words from their phonetic knowledge. In practice, a list of sixteen to seventeen words meeting these two requirements could be generated in any location. Some (*tijolo,* "brick"; *voto,* "vote") recurred in most locations. Others (*charque,* "dried meat"; *manque,* "swamp") made the list only in a region where they were an important part of daily life.

When they had chosen their list of generative words for a particular area, facilitators convened a culture circle. These usually met every day for one hour until a total of thirty or forty hours had elapsed. This turned out to be enough time for participants to grasp and internalize the skills needed to read, spell, and write basic Portuguese or Spanish.

Before examining the first generative word, culture circles spent two to eight hours discussing a sequenced series of ten sketches produced by an artist friend of Freire's. All ten sketches included familiar objects, some of which represented human creations (culture) and some items from nature. Discussions focused on distinctions between these two categories. The tenth picture in the series showed a culture circle.

When participants first discussed the two categories of what was cultural and what was natural, they usually described their own illiteracy as in the natural group—something unalterable with the status of God's will. By the tenth picture, almost all saw literacy as a cultural phenomenon subject to their control. They not only wanted to learn to read, but more importantly they knew they could learn because reading was like cooking, making a clay pot, or sewing a garment. They were free to choose to learn to read. The next step was to address the generative words.[50]

Facilitators discovered that starting with a basic three-syllable word from the generative list worked best. They put words with $x, z, q,$ and ao toward the end. At the end of thirty or forty hours, about 75 percent of those who began the culture circle experience could "read and write simple texts, make something of the local newspapers, and discuss Brazilian problems."[51]

In the early 1960s, under the auspices of a reform-minded government, Freire hoped for twenty thousand culture circles. The United States Agency for International Development (USAID) even briefly endorsed the program. But in 1964 a reactionary government came to power in Brazil. Discussing "Brazilian problems," or personal realities for that matter, was far from politically neutral. "On one occasion, a woman in a circle of culture . . . read aloud a telegram in a newspaper. . . . [It] discussed the exploitation of salt in Rio Grande do Norte. A visitor to the circle asked the woman, 'Lady, do you know what exploitation means?' 'Perhaps you, a rich young man, don't know,' she replied. 'But I, a poor woman, I know what exploitation is.' "[52] The new government declared the literacy campaign subversive, USAID suddenly found the experiment unacceptable, and Freire spent seventy days under house arrest before leaving Brazil.

Freire moved his activities to Chile at the request of the Allende government, but when the Pinochet regime seized power there, Freire and most of the people who had worked in the program had to flee. Freire worked at Harvard and for the World Council of Churches in Geneva. He traveled, lectured, and produced several widely read books. The first was translated into English as *The Pedagogy of the Oppressed.* In it Freire cited the work of Albert Memmi and Frantz Fanon in his call for those oppressed by a dysfunctional paradigm to find their voices:

The important thing . . . is for men to come to feel like masters of their thinking by discussing the thinking and views of the world explicitly or implicitly manifest in their own suggestions and those of their comrades. Because this view of education starts with the conviction that it cannot present its own program but must search for this program dialogically with the people, it serves to introduce the pedagogy of the oppressed, in the elaboration of which the oppressed must participate.[53]

In the early 1980s, Brazilian politics again shifted. Freire returned to Brazil as a professor at the Catholic University of São Paulo. For a time, he also occupied a high position in the government of São Paulo. He remarried, and in 1991, he visited Chile. Interviews from that visit showed him to be vigorous and optimistic as he entered his seventies. He described himself as a resilient intellectual with dreams. "History is not finished," he said. "None of us can say 'the end.' . . . Dreams are not only part of political life but also of human existence. Furthermore, reactionaries dream and struggle to maintain what cannot be maintained. I continue to dream, full of faith and hope in a social transformation. What we need to do is to redefine the capacity to read history."[54]

Redefining the capacity to read history was a focus of several late-twentieth-century French critics of humanism whose writings have had substantial impact on social thought in the Americas. "Skeptical of rationalist and personalist philosophies, critical of teleological treatments of history as a story with a happy ending, they were wary of liberalism . . . and impatient with Marxism."[55] The most controversial and probably the most influential of these was Michel Foucault. He would expand even further than Freire had done the scope of what should be considered social (therefore changeable) rather than natural (therefore fixed).

Michel Foucault (1926–1984)

Paul-Michel Foucault was born on October 15, 1926 in Poitiers, France. He was the firstborn son and second of three children of Dr. Paul Foucault, a locally respected surgeon. His father forced Michel to watch an autopsy as an adolescent (perhaps as a kind of male initiation ritual), and images of the cut-up body haunted Michel, who considered his father a "bully." As an adult, Michel was distant from his older sister, his younger brother, and their father. He did apparently feel close to his mother, whom he visited regularly. His father chose for him a strict Catholic secondary school in Poitiers. Michel studied hard and was a top student, but he resisted his father's insistence on a medical career. Instead, he gained admission to one of the "great schools" in Paris, the elite and highly selective École Normale Superieure, where he studied the humanities, especially philosophy.[56]

Between 1960 and 1968, Foucault taught philosophy and French literature at the Universities of Lille, Uppsala, Warsaw, Hamburg, Clermont-Ferrand, São Paulo, and Tunis. He became a professor at the University of Paris, Vincennes in 1968, witnessing part of the dramatic worldwide student protests of that year. "For the rest of his life, he routinely commented on current affairs, signed petitions, and partici-pated in demonstrations, always ready to protest the plight of the wretched and powerless: French prisoners, Algerian immigrants, Pol-ish trade unionists, Vietnamese refugees."[57] In 1970, he was elected to the Collège de France, a symbol of having achieved the ultimate in French academic politics.

Foucault wrote prolifically: *Madness and Civilization: A History of Insanity in the Age of Reason* (1965); *Mental Illness and Psychology* (1976); *Death and Labyrinth: The World of Raymond Roussel* (1963); *The Order of Things: An Archeology of the Human Sciences* (1971); *The Archaeology of Knowledge* (1972); *I, Pierre Rivière, Having Slaughtered My Mother, My Sister, and My Brother. . . . A Case of Parricide in the 19th Century* (1975); *Discipline and Punish: The Birth of the Prison* (1977); *The History of Sexuality* (1978–1984). He was extensively translated and internationally known.

Foucault explained how some human experiences have historically been permitted or encouraged and others prohibited or discouraged. The division of experiences between death and life, rational and irrational, reasonable and mad, normal and criminal, that we accept as being scien-tifically established were different in each historical context, he said. And much that we have assumed to be biologically fixed is ultimately fluid and socially established. Take, for example, madness, which Fou-cault said "exists only in society."

> It does not exist outside of the forms of sensibility that isolate it, and the forms of repulsion that expel it or capture it. Thus one can say that from the Middle Ages up to the Renaissance, madness was present within the social horizon as an aesthetic and mundane face; then in the seven-teenth century—starting with the confinement (of the mad)—madness underwent a period of silence, of exclusion. It lost the function of mani-festation of revelation that it had in the age of Shakespeare and Cervan-tes (for example, Lady Macbeth begins to speak the truth when she becomes mad); it becomes laughable, delusory. Finally the twentieth century collars madness, reduces it to natural phenomenon, linked to the truth of the world. From this positivist exploration derive both the misguided philanthropy that all psychiatry exhibits toward the mad, and the lyrical protest that one finds in poetry from Nerval to Artaud, and which is an effort to restore to the experience of madness the profun-dity and power of revelation that was extinguished by confinement.[58]

Reminiscent of Rousseau, Foucault declared society, not the person la-beled mad, as guilty.

Foucault applied the same kind of reasoning to criminality and sexuality. The Greeks had no jails. Today most U.S. states are building additional facilities to relieve prison overcrowding. Not only sex roles but all aspects of reality referred to by male and female seemed to Foucault socially rather than biologically derived. At the heart of much of what we assert to ourselves as the way things are, argued Foucault, is power. We seek and use power on ourselves and on others to control, dominate, and punish, and we hide this fact from ourselves. "The figures haunting his [Foucault's] pages enact an allegory of endless domination, from the hangman torturing the murderer to the doctor locking up the deviant," observes James Miller. "The modern prison epitomized an unobtrusive, essentially painless type of coercion typical of the modern world generally. From schools and the professions to the army and the prison, central institutions of our society, charged Foucault, strove with sinister efficiency to supervise the individual . . . to alter his conduct by inculcating numbing codes of discipline. The inevitable result was 'docile bodies' and obedient souls, drained of creative energy."[59]

Foucault seemed to suggest, though his writing is enigmatic, that if we could be more open our need to dominate might diminish and our deepest fears might prove unfounded. " 'Everything that we today feel shaped by the limit, or by the uncanny, or by the intolerable'—from the most untamed of impulses to the wildest of fantasies—might somehow, Foucault speculated, 'be transferred to the serenity of positive things.' If that were to happen, what now seems 'exterior'—dreaming, intoxication, the uninhibited pursuit of pleasure—might 'indicate our very selves.' "[60]

Foucault made several trips to California, where he pursued "the transformative potential of cruel and unusual forms of eroticism" in gay bars specializing in sadomasochism.[61] In 1983, before the public knew much about AIDS, he became ill with AIDS-like symptoms. On June 25, 1984 he died, officially of a neurological disorder. There is now little doubt that AIDS was the cause and at least a strong probability that Foucault deliberately exposed himself repeatedly. He was at the time, according to a recent biographer, "perhaps the single most famous intellectual in the world."[62]

Whatever one's judgment of Foucault, he tried to show the hidden hypocrisy and dogmatism of modern civilization and history by questioning and examining the assumptions, divisions, and norms of social practices. He tried to tell us that "the idea of truth is itself a fiction . . . and everything that we hold as solid and certain about the world is, upon closer examination, demonstrably accidental, contingent, or false: laws, ideas, philosophers, religions, moralities, everything."[63] "To change the world required changing our selves, our bodies, our souls, and all of our old ways of 'knowing,' in addition to changing the economy and society."[64] "He is clearly one of the thinkers about whom it can be stated that whether we agree or not with all of his theories, we can never think again quite the same way about our lives and our society."[65]

While many people disagreed with and even felt repelled by Foucault's analyses, neither his apocalyptic challenges nor his bisexual/homosexual life-style diminished the recognition he received in academic and popular circles. In fact, he is even more popular now than when he was alive. This has not been the case with a Viennese contemporary who has challenged many social practices so commonplace that they have seemed beyond question. His name is Ivan Illich. His motto is *"de omnibus dubitandum—everything must be doubted."*[66]

Ivan D. Illich (b. 1926)

Ivan (accent on the second syllable) was born on September 4, 1926 in Vienna, Austria. His father, Ivan Peter, a Roman Catholic from Croatia, was a civil engineer who owned property in Vienna and on the Dalmatian coast. His mother, Ellen Regenstreif-Ortlieb, came from Heidelberg, but her family traced its roots to Spanish (Jewish) shepherds. Her grandfather was a United States citizen who had spent his youth in Texas. Ivan and his younger twin brothers, Sasch Alex and Michael, traveled extensively in Europe, spent summers on his father's coastal estate, and attended good schools. Ivan was an honors student at the Piaristengymnasium in Vienna from 1936 to 1941, when the Nazi occupation expelled him because of his mother's Jewish ancestry. He completed pre-university studies in Florence, passing with high marks the state examinations required for university admission.[67]

After a brief period at the University of Florence, Illich attended the Gregorian University in Rome while preparing for the priesthood. He wrote licentiate (roughly equivalent to a master's degree) theses in philosophy on precursors of existentialism and in theology on motives for the act of religious faith. In 1951, he completed a Ph.D. at the University of Salzburg with a dissertation on the problem of historical knowledge. He was ordained and took up work at a pastorate in the Washington Heights section of New York in the same year.

Assignment to a Puerto Rican neighborhood was Illich's idea. Given his family background, educational achievements, and interpersonal skills, Church officials would have gladly groomed him for a career in the Vatican diplomatic service. Already fluent in several languages, Illich quickly perfected Spanish while interacting with parishioners and other members of the local community. Within a short time, he began to speak out for Puerto Rican culture and against "cultural ignorance" on the part of the dominant culture. "What they need is not more help but less categorization according to previous schemes," he wrote in *Commonweal* in 1956. The same year, Illich became vice-rector (president) of the Catholic University of Puerto Rico. A year later he became monsignor.[68]

He spent only four years in Puerto Rico. In 1960 the Most Rev. James

McManus, mainland-born bishop of Ponce, where the Catholic University was located and where Illich lived and voted, forbade Catholics in his diocese to vote for Governor Luis Munoz Marin because the governor advocated state-sponsored birth control. When Illich ridiculed this censorship, McManus forced him out.

At this time, President Kennedy was launching the Peace Corps, and the Vatican was calling for 10 percent of North American priests and religious to form the Papal Volunteers for Latin America. Illich's philosophy differed from the self-conscious altruism that was a component of these programs. Still committed to the Church, but fearful of what harm missionaries might do, Illich founded the Center for Intercultural Formation. Initially, this was at Fordham University because influential Jesuits there supported him, but he thought the institution should be in Latin America. After walking and hitchhiking three thousand miles from Santiago, Chile to Caracas, Venezuela, Illich finally settled on Cuernavaca, Mexico as a site for his renamed Centro Intercultural de Documentación (CIDOC). He wanted well-intended volunteer missionaries to learn Spanish, encounter and accept the limitations of their own cultural experiences, and develop assumptions that would allow them to assume their duties as self-proclaimed adult educators with humility and respect. "By adult education I mean . . . the education of a man who has reached in some ways the frontier of that which has been known up to this moment," he wrote in 1966.[69]

For several years Illich and a small staff lived in a sparsely furnished rented villa under the shadow of the Popocatepetl volcano in the idyllic resort town of Cuernavaca. A few hundred students per year, at first almost all Catholic missionaries, learned Spanish and talked and confronted each other and themselves. Illich described CIDOC as "a free club for the search of surprise, a place where people go who want to have help in redefining their questions rather than completing the answers they have gotten." "We want to get people [at CIDOC] who are alive and have sense of humor. . . . It is the sense of humor which denotes a certain degree of distance from self, and the faculty of looking at a question from different dimensions which we most seek."[70]

CIDOC became a magnet for people who wanted to talk about change. And as the conversants explored and discussed issues, many of them moved farther away from mainstream answers. A 1967 "discussion outline" by Ceslaus Hoinacki and Illich declared:

> During the past six years, CIDOC . . . has created a milieu in which thousands of North American and European religious have had to face: A violent uprooting from their familiar surroundings; agonized questioning about the relevance of their lives; the terrifying realization that they are *poor;* the bewildering confusion consequent upon the awareness that the words and symbols of their lives can no longer "justify" their religious commitment; the possibility that the Church

and their respective institutes do not provide the theological foundation, nor the structural framework for generous life-long dedication; the black terror that they live *now* the moment of death—alone, stripped of everything, staring into the uncharted night of radical change.

Many of these persons have their first sharp insight into the confused, but common experience of *all* men in contemporary revolutionary society. They suddenly see into the predominant characteristic of our times: CHANGE. Rigid frameworks crumble. Known patterns dissolve. Meaningful symbols are ridiculed. The languages of the arts agonize and frolic in the world of the absurd. Human communication blacks out between alienated silence and belligerent outburst. The violence of massive destruction and of the corrosive lie rot the heart of man.[71]

Illich, accustomed to self-confrontation in six-week solitary retreats, found this refreshing, but not all prospective missionaries did. Some went home disillusioned. Jesuits continued to support Illich and CIDOC by offering their magazine *America* as a forum. He declared that much of the Roman Catholic missionizing effort in Latin America was colonialism reasserting itself. "Next to money and guns, the third largest North American export is the U.S. idealist," he told students headed to Mexican villages for a few months to help the poor "develop." The U.S. volunteer's good intentions "can usually be explained only by an abysmal lack of intuitive delicacy. . . . You cannot help being ultimately vacationing salesmen for the middle-class 'American way of life,' since that is really the only life you know. . . . Travel in Latin America. Come to look, come to climb our mountains, to enjoy our flowers. Come to study. But do not come to help," he entreated.[72]

New York's Cardinal Cushing publicly rebuked Illich.[73] Vatican officials used the Congregation of the Faith (successor to the Inquisition) to call him "an object of curiosity, bewilderment, and scandal" and ordered him to leave CIDOC. With the bishop of Cuernavaca's support, Illich ignored or effectively countered these efforts, but he resigned all offices and church salaries. These activities brought considerable secular press attention and spread Illich's message.[74]

In 1967, Illich's critiques had already gone beyond the bureaucracy of the institutional church and the destructive impact of most aid to Third World countries to the bureaucracy of schooling. By 1969, Illich declared schooling "a craze, a mad religion, an initiation rite to power which is inaccessible to 95 percent of humanity, but which is being preached to them as their only way to salvation."[75] That same year, CIDOC mailed a promotional flyer asking: "Can the world afford schools which exclude most of its children? Can we afford schools which make dropouts of the lower class? Are schools the straightjackets of our thinking about education? Do we need schools . . . or are there: *Alternatives in education?*"

In the *New York Review of Books,* Illich explained "Why We Must Abolish Schooling":

Many students, especially those who are poor, intuitively know what the schools do for them. They school them to confuse process and substance. Once these become blurred, a new logic is assumed: the more treatment there is the better are the results; or, escalation leads to success. The pupil is thereby "schooled" to confuse teaching with learning, grade advancement with education, a diploma with competence, and fluency with the ability to say something new. His imagination is "schooled" to accept service in place of value. Medical treatment is mistaken for health care, social work for the improvement of community life, police protection for safety, military poise for national security, the rat race for productive work. Health, learning, dignity, independence, and creative endeavor are defined as little more than the performance of the institutions which claim to serve these ends, and their improvement is made to depend on allocating more resources to the management of hospitals, schools, and other agencies in question. Not only education but social reality itself has become "schooled."[76]

Participants at CIDOC wore lapel buttons that read: "All Schooled Up" and "School You!"

Publicity about Illich made him a popular speaker. Two thousand curious people turned out for a public lecture in Ames, Iowa in December 1971. He continued to write powerfully analytical and wonderfully readable pieces collected into books: *The Celebration of Awareness, Deschooling Society, Tools for Conviviality, Energy and Equity, Medical Nemesis, Towards a History of Needs,* and *Gender* all appeared between 1970 and 1982. His trenchant insights continued as he rejected sentimentality and called for openness to surprise. "Crisis . . . can mean the instant of choice, that marvelous moment when people suddenly become aware of their self-imposed cages and of the possibility of a different life."[77] But the man who climbed stairs three at a time, evoking adjective after adjective—petulant, adventurous, imprudent, fanatical, hypnotizing, high-strung, dazzlingly brilliant, prayerful, ascetic, zealous, strange, suave, devious, admired, feared, unbalanced genius, slippery personage—was no longer interesting to educators. His name disappeared from the press. As the wave of Latin America-bound missionaries dwindled to a trickle, CIDOC faded as an institution.

Because the issues about which Illich has spoken and written continue to preoccupy educators, the question arises as to why his analyses are not part of the discussion. David Allan Gabbard, using Foucault's "archaeological method of textual analysis" to address this question, concluded that "Illich transgresses a cardinal rule that decides which discourses are acceptable." The transgression was denying what Gabbard called the "messianic principle"—that "the school as an institution . . . can deliver either the single individual or society as a whole, or both, into a state of secular salvation."[78] Perhaps educators are not ready to hear that "deschooling society means above all the denial of professional status to the second oldest profession, namely, teaching. The certification of teachers now constitutes an undue restriction on the right to free speech."[79]

If denying the "pastoral power of the school to bring about secular salvation" is too shocking for professionalized educators to consider, perhaps some of Illich's other formulations may be more acceptable. "The fear that new institutions will be imperfect, in their turn, does not justify our servile acceptance of present ones."[80] "Look here," he said in an interview, "I am not a prophet, and I do not want to become a futurologist. . . . What we should be concerned with . . . is to be humorists. That is, people who are constantly aware of the constraints and limitations of the categories with which we think, people who are continuously aware that through the development of imagination and by looking at flowers you can kind of imagine an analog to every social system that is just slightly off-key and, therefore, makes you smile."[81]

SUMMARY

Post-modern challenges to the Enlightenment faith in progress present an especially acute problem for all contemporary "professionals." Police officers, social workers, psychiatrists, nurses, and teachers struggle to keep their parts of society functioning normally. The analysts treated in this chapter would all agree that the concept "normal" is itself at the heart of why so many work so hard and daily confront a world no better than the one they left the day before. Only by shifting our fundamental (ontological) assumptions can real change occur, they argue.

Kuhn's special insight was that the history of any science (including education) is our narrative of the way particular groups conceptualize and put into language their explanation of how things work. Value judgments such as "primitive" and "advanced" have no place in this method of explanation. To understand any theoretical formulation is to make explicit the assumptions and definitions that constitute its paradigm.

All of the commentators in this chapter share Kuhn's basic attitude toward knowledge and history, and each adds a special focus that, taken seriously as part of new paradigms, would dramatically change current institutional practice. Adopting Gardner's definition of intelligence would revolutionize schools. Recognizing the self-interested power relationships (individual and collective) revealed by most transactions could lead to radical alterations in social and personal relationships. At the root of all the formulations discussed in this chapter—explicitly those of Fanon, Malcolm X, Freire, Foucault, and Illich—lies *power*: Whose knowledge? Who does what to whom and under what circumstances? To doubt power relationships in any social system is to threaten vested interests and to risk being defined as aberrant. Perhaps this is why all who question established paradigms become famous in the original Roman sense of being singled out (separated) from their group. All seven paradigm questioners treated in this chapter have received their share of this fame.

NOTES

1. David Hoy, "Jacques Derrida," in *The Return of Grand Theory in the Human Sciences,* ed. Quentin Skinner (Cambridge: Cambridge University Press, 1985), 48.

2. Thomas Kuhn, *The Structure of Scientific Revolutions,* 2nd ed. (Chicago: University of Chicago Press, 1970), 175.

3. Kuhn, *Structure,* 111.

4. Barry Barnes, "Thomas Kuhn," in *The Return of Grand Theory,* 99.

5. For accounts of his life and early career see Howard Gardner, *To Open Minds* (New York: Basic Books, 1989).

6. Gardner, *To Open Minds,* 27.

7. Gardner, *To Open Minds,* 79.

8. Howard Gardner, *Frames of Mind* (New York: Basic Books, 1983), 73–276.

9. Gardner has published a practical guide on how to use and apply multiple intelligences in a variety of educational environments from preschool to college. Theodore Sizer, chair of the Coalition of Essential Schools, has touted Gardner as the premier American schoolperson addressing educational reform. Publisher's pamphlet advertising Gardner's books (New York: Basic Books, March 1993).

10. Philip G. Altbach and Gail P. Kelly, eds., *Education and Colonialism* (New York: Longman, 1973), especially Bonnie Cook Freeman, "Female Education in Patriarchal Power Systems"; Charles H. Lyons, "The Colonial Mentality: Assessments of Intelligence of Blacks and Women in Nineteenth-Century America," 181–206; Gene Grabiner, "Education, Colonialism, and the American Working Class," 243–269.

11. Peter Geismar, *Fanon* (New York: Dial Press, 1971), 1, 3.

12. Irene L. Gendzier, *Frantz Fanon: A Critical Study,* trans. C. Farrington (New York: Pantheon Books, 1973), 11.

13. Geismar, *Fanon,* 96.

14. Frantz Fanon, *The Wretched of the Earth,* trans. Constance Farrington (New York: Grove Press, [1963] 1968), 51.

15. Fanon, *The Wretched of the Earth,* 39.

16. Fanon, *The Wretched of the Earth,* 38.

17. Geismar, *Fanon,* 85, 150.

18. Geismar, *Fanon,* 196.

19. Geismar, *Fanon,* 311–316.

20. Geismar, *Fanon,* 152, 199–200.

21. Ted Vincent, "The Garveyite Parents of Malcolm X," *Black Scholar,* 209.

22. Vincent, "The Garveyite Parents," 209.

23. Alex Haley, *The Autobiography of Malcolm X* (New York: Ballantine Books, 1964), 1.

24. Haley, *Autobiography of Malcolm X,* 17 passim.

25. Haley, *Autobiography of Malcolm X,* 18 passim.

26. Haley, *Autobiography of Malcolm X,* 180.

27. Haley, *Autobiography of Malcolm X,* 393.

28. Haley, *Autobiography of Malcolm X,* 155–168.

29. George Breitman, *The Last Year of Malcolm X: The Evolution of a Revolutionary* (New York: Schocken Books, 1967), 9.

30. Haley, *Autobiography of Malcolm X,* 410.

31. George Breitman, *Malcolm X Speaks* (New York: Grove Press, 1965), 58.

32. Breitman, *Malcolm X Speaks,* 196.

33. Breitman, *Malcolm X Speaks,* 213–214.

34. Breitman, *Malcolm X Speaks,* 210.

35. Breitman, *The Last Year of Malcolm X,* 107.

36. Breitman, *The Last Year of Malcolm X,* 107–108.

37. Breitman, *The Last Year of Malcolm X,* 157–177.

38. S.v., "Little, Malcolm," in *Black Writers,* ed. Linda Metzger et al. (Detroit: Gale Research, 1988). Cf. s.v. "Malcolm X (Al Hajj Malik Al-Shabazz)," in *Encyclopedia of Black America:* "Malcolm X was killed by a dissenting black group."

39. Raymond Rodgers and Jimmie Rogers, "The Evolution of Malcolm X's Attitude toward Whites," *Phylon* 44 (1983): 108–109.

40. Soraya Rodriguez, "Gestor de la education popular visita Chile—Paulo Freire: Como educar para la libertad," in *Diario La Epoca* (Santiago de Chile), November 23, 1991, reprinted in *Paulo Freire en Chile: Conversaciones, conferencias y entrevistas* (San Bernardo, Chile: Centro el Canelo de Nos, 1991), 14.

41. Jorge Jeria, "Vagabond of the Obvious: A Bibliography of Paulo Freire," *Vitae Scholasticae: The Bulletin of Educational Biography* 5 (Spring/Fall 1986): 4–5.

42. Jeria, "Vagabond," 7.

43. Jeria, "Vagabond," 6–7.

44. Paulo Freire, *Education for Critical Consciousness* (New York: Seabury, 1973), 46.

45. William M. Timpson, "Paulo Freire: Advocate of Literacy Through Liberation," *Educational Leadership* 45 (Fall 1988): 64.

46. Jeria, "Vagabond," 11–12.

47. Jeria, "Vagabond," 13.

48. Freire, *Pedagogy of the Oppressed,* trans. Myra Bergman Ramos (New York: Continuum, 1970), 19, trans. note 1.

49. Denis Goulet, "Introduction," Paulo Freire, *Education for Critical Consciousness,* trans. Center for the Study of Development and Change (New York: Seabury Press, 1973), ix.

50. Cynthia Brown, "Literacy in 30 Hours: Paulo Freire's Process in Northeast Brazil," in *Freire for the Classroom: A Sourcebook for Liberatory Teaching,* ed. Ira Shor (Portsmouth, NH: Boynton/Cook, 1987), 215–231.

51. Brown, "Literacy in 30 Hours," 230.

52. Brown, "Literacy in 30 Hours," 230.

53. Freire, *Pedagogy of the Oppressed,* 118.

54. Francisco Vio Grossi, "Presentación," in *Paulo Freire in Chile: Conversaciones, conferencias y entrevistas* (San Bernardo, Chile: Centro el Canelo de Nos, 1991), 8.

55. These included Louis Althusser, Jacques Lacan, Roland Barthes, Jacques Derrida, and Michel Foucault. James E. Miller, *The Passions of Michel Foucault* (New York: Simon & Schuster, 1993), 16.

56. Some information was taken from *Contemporary Authors*, New Revision Series, Volume 34; and James Miller, *Passions of Michel Foucault* (New York: Simon & Schuster, 1993), 39–40.

57. Miller, *Passions of Michel Foucault*, 15.

58. Interview in *Le Monde*, July 22, 1961, 9, quoted in Miller, *Passions of Michel Foucault*, 98.

59. Michel Foucault, *Discipline and Punish*, trans. Alan Sheridan (New York, 1977), quoted in Miller, *Passions of Michel Foucault*, 15.

60. Michel Foucault, *Histoire de la folie à l'âge classique* (Paris, 1972), 575, quoted in Miller, *Passions of Michel Foucault*, 122.

61. Isabelle de Courtivron, "The Body Was His Battleground," *New York Times*, January 10, 1993, Sect. 7, p. 1.

62. Miller, *Passions of Michel Foucault*, 13.

63. Miller, *Passions of Michel Foucault*, 218.

64. Miller, *Passions of Michel Foucault*, 234.

65. Courtivron, "The Body Was His Battleground," 10.

66. Ivan Illich, *Celebration of Awareness: A Call for Institutional Revolution* (Garden City, New York: Doubleday, 1970), 7.

67. S.v., "Illich, Ivan," *Current Biography 1969*, 217.

68. June 22, 1956, quoted in "Illich," *Current Biography 1969*, 218.

69. Illich, undated and untitled typescript (c. 1966), Illich file, CIDOC Library, Cuernavaca, Mexico.

70. Illich, Undated and untitled typescript, CIDOC, 12.

71. Ceslaus Hoinacki and Ivan Illich, "Religious Orders and Crisis: A Discussion Outline . . . for a Five-Day Seminar Held in Cuernavaca June 12–16, 1967," CIDOC, Doc. 67/21.

72. Ivan Illich, "Talk to be Delivered at the CIASP Meeting in Chicago," undated typescript in the Illich File, CIDOC.

73. "Four Join Cushing in Jesuit Rebuke; Cardinal Defends Motives of Latin Mission Aid," *New York Times*, January 28, 1967, 15.

74. Some examples are "Roman Catholics: Get Going and Don't Come Back," *Time*, February 14, 1969, 48; Edward Fiske, "Vatican Curb Aimed at Cultural Center of Reform Advocate," *New York Times*, January 23, 1969 (sec. 1), 1; "Controversial Priest, Ivan Illich," *New York Times*, January 23, 1969 (sec. 2), 3.

75. "Schooling: The Five Most Wasted Days of the Week," an interview with Ivan Illich by L. I. Steel, *Tempo*, March 15, 1969.

76. Ivan Illich, "Why We Must Abolish Schooling," *New York Review of Books*, July 2, 1970, 9–15.

77. Ivan Illich, *Towards a History of Needs* (New York: Pantheon Books, 1978), 4.

78. David Allan Gabbard, "The Second Death of Ivan Illich: A Theoretico-Active Analysis of a Discursive Practice of Exclusion," (Ed.D. diss, University of Cincinnati, 1991).

79. Illich, *Towards a History of Needs*, 85.

80. Illich, *Celebration of Awareness*, 134.

81. From page 25 of an undated typescript of an interview with Illich, Illich File, CIDOC.

Epilogue

At the close of this saga it is appropriate to remember its limitations. First, it is not the history of education; it is a history of some aspects of some parts of European and American education. Even within that limited context, we have ignored many interesting educators, partly because of available space, partly because of what is possible. We can only write, talk, or think about a past for which there is some kind of information. There is no written or other "material culture" residue for more than 99 percent of the events or people in human history. Many of our predecessors left no clay tablets, pottery, weapons, letters, memorandums, books, scrolls, photographs, sketches, or paintings. Most of what has been written, said, or done has disappeared. Only a minuscule portion of what "really happened" is available for our inferential examination. And of the material that is extant, much has not been examined. Indeed, many rich sources are not catalogued in archives but rather exist in people's attics, in church basements, in small-town newspaper offices, and in other relatively inaccessible places.

The other major factor shaping historical and biographical accounts is that what really happened is not obvious. The story does not leap unaided out of dusty records. Rather, authors choose which story to investigate, and then search available evidence on which to build and with which to document their narratives. They select language, metaphors, and images suited to themselves and to their intended audiences, within the contexts of shared value systems.

The account we've presented is an outgrowth, as history always is, of contemporary preoccupations generally and of our own beliefs particularly. "Significance" is a value judgment. Sometimes we look to the past to enlighten our present, and the present we most want to illuminate is the unresolved one. The problematic and controversial preoccupy our attention. More often, we use the past to legitimate some aspect of the present in which we feel a particular investment. If Kuhn is right, the past and the present in our field of view will be those that our paradigmatic assumptions make visible and important. There is no such thing as objective history.[1]

So while we as authors have one foot resting in the Enlightenment tradition of arguing for knowledge of the standard canon as a precursor to progress, we also acknowledge that educational practice is not growing steadily better. Given our conviction on this point, we believe the post-modern insights of the people presented in Chapter 12 deserve careful attention. While they may at first seem pessimistic when compared with the march to perfection predicated by the Enlightenment tradition, they present a different basis for optimism. They all assume, no matter how negatively they present certain aspects of the contemporary world, that most conditions are social, not natural, and that human beings have the potential to develop arrangements that work better.

This means that a great deal of work, including in educational history, remains to be done. This edition of *Lives* is only a beginning. Because it is a text, it must reflect much of the consensus as well as the boundaries of current and emerging thought. But the old consensus is dying. The calls of Diane Ravitch, Arthur Schlesinger, Jr., E. D. Hirsch, and Allan Bloom for everyone to learn a Eurocentric curriculum are not the wave of the future.[2] The history of anything can never be written with finality. No two people ever tell quite the same story. This is especially relevant in the world's diverse societies, like the United States. "The central problem in American education . . . is a result of a clash of cultures, a conflict of interests and a struggle for power," writes Afrocentric advocate Floyd Hayes.[3] This conflict, and the diversity that underlies it, is now widely recognized within the educational bureaucracy. "To endorse cultural pluralism is to endorse the principle that there is no one model American," said the American Association of Colleges for Teacher Education. It "is to understand and appreciate the differences that exist among the nation's citizens . . . as a positive force. . . . Cultural pluralism is more than a temporary accommodation to placate racial and ethnic minorities. It is a concept that aims toward a heightened sense of being and of wholeness of the entire society based on the unique strengths of each of its parts."[4] "We don't need to be afraid of our diversity," is the conclusion of Japanese American historian Ronald Takaki.[5]

In the Preface we noted that what readers bring to their task is as important as what the authors have tried to provide, and we invited each reader to examine our sources and come to a personal conclusion about our conclusions. Now we challenge each of you to go another step. Think about your own educational history. What brought you to where you are today? What influenced your thought and your praxis? What do you hold most true and valuable? Where does this fit with the family, ethnic, racial, national, religious, linguistic, and sexual groups most important in your life and identity? How did those groups develop, and what was their relationship to the larger social entity in which they exist? Do the "standard accounts" adequately account for the stories of these groups? Are there lessons from your personal history or from those of your defining groups that would change the way education operates? If your story and that of the significant groups in your life were adequately represented in the "big picture" histories of education, would that story change?

It is in this sense that we began the book by saying that whether or not you agree with our account, we hope you will be informed, strengthened, encouraged, and empowered. We all have the right to understand and explain ourselves. History is the means, not the end.

NOTES

1. Even a majority of the members of the American Historical Association appear ready to concede that there is no such thing as "objective history." Peter Novick, *That Noble Dream: The "Objectivity Question" and the American Historical Profession* (New York: Cambridge University Press, 1988).

2. Diane Ravitch, *The American Reader: Words that Moved a Nation* (New York: HarperCollins, 1990); Arthur M. Schlesinger, Jr., *The Disuniting of America* (New York: W. W. Norton, 1992); E. D. Hirsch, *Cultural Literacy: What Every American Needs to Know* (Boston: Houghton Mifflin, 1987), and *A First Dictionary of Cultural Literacy: What Our Children Need to Know* (Boston: Houghton Mifflin, 1991); Allan Bloom, *The Closing of the American Mind* (New York: Touchstone Books, 1988). Cf. Molefe Kete Asante, *Afrocentricity: The Theory of Social Change* (Trenton, NJ: Africa World Press, 1990); Martin Bernal, *Black Athena*, Vol. 1: *The Afroasiatic Roots of Classical Civilization: The Fabrication of Ancient Greece, 1785–1985*, Vol. 2: *The Archaeological and Documentary Evidence* (Rutgers: Rutgers University Press, 1987–1991).

3. Floyd W. Hayes III, "Politics and Education in America's Multicultural Society: An African-American Studies Response to Allan Bloom," *Journal of Ethnic Studies* 17 (Summer 1989): 71.

4. AACTE, "No One Model American: A Statement of Multicultural Education" (Washington DC: American Association of Colleges for Teacher Education, 1972), 9.

5. Ellen K. Coughlin, "New History of America Attempts to Make Good on the Claims of Multiculturalism," *Chronicle of Higher Education,* May 26, 1993, A9, quoting an interview with Dr. Takaki, in a review of Ronald Takaki, *A Different Mirror: A History of Multicultural America* (Boston: Little, Brown, 1993).

Contributors

Michael V. Belok is emeritus professor of education, Arizona State University. His Ph.D. is from the University of Southern California. [Erasmus, Locke, Webster, and Lyon]

Jack K. Campbell, professor emeritus, College of Education, Texas A&M University, has previously taught at Brooklyn College and high schools in New Jersey and New York. His doctorate at Columbia pursued the history of education, and his career has focused on the use of biography as a medium of research and mode of teaching. [Parker and Dewey]

Carmen Aida Cruz was born in Puerto Rico and taught in the public schools of Chicago before working on her doctorate in education at Northern Illinois University, where she is currently on the faculty. [Fanon]

Dalton B. Curtis, Jr., teaches history of education, philosophy of education, and intellectual history, and serves as director of interdisciplinary studies for the School of University Studies at Southeast Missouri State University. He holds an M.A. in history from the University of Rhode Island and a Ph.D. in historical, philosophical, and social foundations of education from the University of Oklahoma. [Maritain, Watson, Hall, and Naumberg]

Gerald L. Gutek is professor of educational leadership and policy studies and professor of history at Loyola University (Chicago). He teaches courses in the history of education and international education. He received his Ph.D. in education from the University of Illinois, Urbana. [Owen and Counts]

Ann Horton holds a doctorate in educational leadership and policy studies from Loyola University (Chicago) where she is also an instructor. She has been a school social worker for the Chicago public schools. [Malcolm X]

Kyung Hi Kim taught English in Korea before becoming an instructor in the Department of Leadership and Educational Policy Studies at Northern Illinois University, where she is also an Ed.D. candidate. [portions of Foucault]

Elizabeth L. Ihle is a professor in the Department of Secondary Education, Educational Leadership, and Library Science at James Madison University in Harrisonburg, Virginia. [Elizabeth Blackwell and Emily Blackwell, Winnemucca, and Coppin]

William Burt Lauderdale is professor of education at Auburn University. He received his B.A. and Ed.M. from the University of Illinois. After teaching middle school, he earned his Ph.D. in history and philosophy of education at Michigan State University. [Mann]

F. Michael Perko, S.J., is professor of education and history at Loyola University (Chicago). He holds a Ph.D. from Stanford University. [da Feltre, Machiavelli, Luther, Melanchthon, Loyola, Hughes, Washington, DuBois, and portions of Kuhn]

Joan K. Smith is associate dean of the graduate school and professor of education and history at Loyola University (Chicago). [Aristotle, Cicero, Quintilian, Guibert, Abelard, Heloise, Rousseau, Victor of Aveyron, Froebel, Haley, Young, Montessori, and Gardner]

Glenn Smith is professor and chair, Department of Leadership and Educational Policy Studies, Northern Illinois University. [Sappho, Protagoras, Socrates, Plato, Hypatia, Augustine, Cassiodorus, Benedict, Charlemagne, Alcuin, Euphemia of Wherwell, Christine de Pisan, Butzbach, Wycliffe, Hus, Comenius, Pestalozzi, Sahagún, Jackson, Willard, Illich, and portions of Kuhn and Foucault]

Jeffrey R. Smith is a Ph.D. candidate at the University of Illinois, Urbana, currently on a DAAD dissertation fellowship in Germany. [Dock]

Norma Salazar is assistant professor of education at Chicago State University. She holds an Ed.D. from Northern Illinois University. [Sor Juana, Cordero y Molina, and Freire]

Claudia M. Strauss is director, New York office, World Information Transfer, an international environmental organization. She holds an Ed.D. from Columbia University, Teachers College. [Wollstonecraft]

Martha Tevis is professor of foundations of education, University of Texas, Pan American. She holds a Ph.D. from the University of Texas. [Boethius, Aquinas, and Sanchez]

Shirley J. Williams is visiting professor at University of Hawaii, Hilo. [Cary, Jefferson]

Index